Modern
Money
and
Banking

Roger LeRoy Miller

Center for Policy Studies
and
Department of Economics
Clemson University

Robert W. Pulsinelli

Department of Economics
Western Kentucky University

**McGraw-Hill
Book Company**

New York
St. Louis
San Francisco
Auckland
Bogotá
Hamburg
Johannesburg
London
Madrid
Mexico
Montreal
New Delhi
Panama
Paris
São Paulo
Singapore
Sydney
Tokyo
Toronto

MODERN MONEY AND BANKING

MODERN MONEY AND BANKING

2 3 4 5 6 7 8 9 0 DOC DOC 8 9 8 7 6 5

ISBN 0-07-042163-3

This book was set in News Gothic by University Graphics, Inc.
The editors were Patricia A. Mitchell, Michael Elia, Gail Gavert, and Sheila H. Gillams;
the designer was Joseph Gillians;
the production supervisor was Phil Galea.
The drawings were done by J & R Services, Inc.
R. R. Donnelley & Sons Company was printer and binder.

Library of Congress Cataloging in Publication Data

Miller, Roger LeRoy.
   Modern money and banking.

   Bibliography: p.
   Includes indexes.
     1. Money. 2. Banks and banking. 3. Finance.
I. Pulsinelli, Robert W. II. Title.
HG221.M646 1985   332.1   84-15496
ISBN 0-07-042163-3

Contents

UNIT 4 CENTRAL BANKING

UNIT 5 MONETARY THEORY

UNIT 6 THE MONETARIST-KEYNESIAN DEBATE

UNIT 7 MONETARY POLICY

UNIT 8 INTERNATIONAL FINANCE

Preface

The 1980s have seen more changes in the world of money and banking than during the entire period of the Federal Reserve System's existence. Therefore, it is not without meaning that we have entitled this text *Modern Money and Banking.* Indeed, the only way to present money and banking materials today is to present them in the most modern, up-to-date way possible. Otherwise, the institutional information contained therein would be hopelessly dated and thus without merit.

A FLEXIBLE THEORETICAL/ INSTITUTIONAL/HISTORICAL APPROACH

This book is a blend of theoretical economics (Chapters 6, 8, 9, 13, 17 to 25, 26, 27, and 29), institutional economics (Chapters 3, 5, 7, 10, 12, and 14 to 16), and economic history (Chapters 1 to 4, 11, 12, and 28). We have made it flexible so that instructors who prefer one of these approaches over another will find enough subject matter to satisfy their needs. Of course, some of these areas overlap. For example, the theory chapters are presented in a historical perspective, and the text points out the theoretical (and actual) implications of the institutional changes.

The most significant feature of our text is its blending of the changing institutional environment and the changing theoretical framework; at the same time the text provides a historical perspective. Chapter 1 sets the stage by showing how an institutional framework crumbled when the economic environment changed, and how this led to a new institutional framework—deregulation—which has had important implications in the meaning and measurement of money. Problems in operationally defining money are then discussed in terms of the implications for monetary control. This chapter organizes the rest of the book.

Throughout the theoretical chapters the student was kept in mind at all times. Consequently, the chapters were developed patiently, and they represent the culmination of our combined 35 years of classroom experience.

PEDAGOGICAL FEATURES

This text utilizes a number of pedagogical aids to keep the student's interest level high and to provide the student with a well-organized body of thought to study and to learn.

Chapter Preview   Each chapter has five or six preview questions which serve as learning objectives.

Glossary of Key Terms   Every key term is presented in **boldface** and then defined at the end of each chapter.

Highlights   Most chapters contain one or more interesting but light readings, set off from the rest of the text. The goal of these readings, or highlights, is to maintain student interest in the subject matter and to present to the student relevant applications of money and banking theory.

Current Controversies   At the end of most chapters there is a Current Controversy. Each of these was designed to generate student and instructor interest and to help the student to understand that even the experts often disagree about appropriate policy in the money and banking area. These Current Controversies are set off from the rest of the text.

Examples   Approximately two worked examples appear in most chapters, thereby giving the student a more applications-oriented view of the theory presented.

Chapter Summaries   At the end of each chapter there is a point-by-point chapter summary that can be used as a reinforcement of what was just learned and as a checklist in studying for midterms and finals.

Selected References   At the end of each chapter there are four or five appropriate selected references that a student may consult for additional information about the chapter materials.

Biographies   A number of important persons have been selected for short biographical sketches interspersed throughout the text at the appropriate locations.

A Complete Teaching-Learning Package This text forms part of a complete teaching-learning package which includes a *Student Guide* and an *Instructor's Manual.*

The *Student Guide* If the enormous number of copies of a study guide sold is a measure of its usefulness and proof of the mastery of its author, then Robert C. Bingham is indeed a master author who provides students with academic utility. Robert C. Bingham wrote the *Student Guide* to be used with our *Modern Money and Banking.* Each chapter in the *Student Guide* is made up of: a precis of the text chapter, as well as a checklist of learning objectives and an outline of the key concepts for each chapter within the text, followed by self-test material comprising completion questions, problems to be worked out, true-false and multiple choice questions, and for those who prefer some essay work, there is a section of short answer questions. All answers (except short answer questions) are provided in the back of the *Student Guide.*

The *Instructor's Manual* The *Instructor's Manual* was written by Robert Pulsinelli. Each chapter in it includes:

1 A one- or two-paragraph introduction that places the chapter in perspective
2 Three to five suggested class discussion topics
3 Answers to the Chapter Preview questions that begin each chapter
4 At least 15 multiple choice questions with answers

Acknowledgments We wish to thank the following individuals for their numerous critical and constructive comments that we ultimately utilized through the various (and numerous) drafts of the manuscript. Robert C. Bingham, Kent State University; James Gale, Michigan Technological University; John Wassom, Western Kentucky University; Philip Wiest, George Mason University; Charles C. Fischer, Pittsburg State University (Kansas); Richard Cantrell, Western Kentucky University; and Paul Crowe, Agency for International Development.

Finally, we wish to thank Lavina Leed for her typing, editing, and proofreading services. All remaining errors are, of course, our own responsibility. We welcome all comments and criticisms from adopters and students alike.

Roger LeRoy Miller
Robert W. Pulsinelli

Introduction

Chapter 1

A Revolution in Money and Banking

CHAPTER PREVIEW

1 Why can the banking industry before 1970 be characterized as a governmentally regulated cartel?

2 What combination of changes caused a revolution in the banking industry?

3 Why did the banking industry cartel break down?

4 Why have high interest-rate levels and increased interest-rate variability harmed thrift institutions?

5 What are some recent examples of deregulation?

6 What are some current issues resulting from the revolution in money and banking?

An old Chinese curse says, "May you live during interesting times." Be it a curse or a blessing, this is an extremely "interesting time" to be studying the U.S. banking system. By the late 1960s, this system had evolved into a cartel-like structure overseen by governmental and quasi-governmental regulatory agencies. It was characterized by a large amount of market segmentation, price fixing, and entry restrictions. During the 1970s, however, a combination of changing economic conditions and changing technology made it unprofitable for some cartel members to remain in the cartel—at least under the old rules. What had previously seemed like the protective bonds of regulation now appeared to be shackles, and, as a consequence, there was growing political pressure to deregulate.

A revolution in technology had made it unfeasible to maintain the old division of banking services and the former geographic divisions of interests. Improvements in technology had created a situation in which *each* institution could cheaply provide *all* services. Indeed, the new technology may eventually prove to be so revolutionary that the distinction between financial and nonfinancial corporations—already somewhat blurred—may entirely disappear. The technological revolution has even changed the form of money itself—which makes it a revolution in money *and* banking.

It is not yet clear how the banking system will evolve in the future. A certain amount of deregulation of the banking industry has occurred already, and there is growing competition from new—and unregulated—types of financial institutions, such as money market mutual funds. If this trend continues, will it mean financial instability during the transition from the old regulatory system to the creation of a new one? And, if so, what might the consequences be? Are the services provided by the financial industry so distinct and special that stability should be assured, relative to other industries? These weighty issues will be considered later in this book. Our task in this chapter will be to provide a framework for analyzing our evolving financial structure and to provide an overview for the remainder of the text. Don't be unduly concerned with mastering this chapter on a first reading. Rather, if you "lose the forest for the trees" when reading later sections, you can return to Chapter 1 for an overall perspective.

In order to understand the current revolution in the banking and financial industry, it is important to look first at (1) the original goals of the regulatory agencies, (2) the cartel arrangement, (3) how technological changes and changes in the economic environment have upset the cartel, (4) recent deregulation changes, and (5) the problems that have been posed as a result of the banking revolution. We consider each of these factors in turn.

GOALS OF THE REGULATORY AGENCIES

Traditionally, the U.S. banking industry has been regulated by state and federal governments, and by specific agencies of these governments. Chapter 10 is devoted to a fuller discussion of the regulation of depository (banking) institutions. The main purposes of regulation, in the past, seem to have been:

1 To assure a stable financial system.

2 To contribute to the achievement of national economic goals *by controlling the money supply*. Such national goals include price stability, high employment rates, economic growth, and a payments equilibrium in our international transactions. Chapters 4, 14, 15, and 16 indicate how regulators can change the supply of money by transacting with financial intermediaries; Chapters 2, 20, 21, and 29 show that changes in the money supply can affect the price level, the rate of employment, the national output rate, and the balance of payments. Chapters 2 and 3 deal with money, and Chapters 2, 8, and 9 deal with banking.

3 To promote efficiency in the financial intermediation process. Financial institutions, such as commercial banks, savings and loan associations, mutual savings banks, and credit unions (financial institutions are discussed in Chapter 5) typically borrow money (accept deposits which become liabilities to the financial institution) and relend this money (acquire assets in the form of IOUs from borrowers, government bonds, and various other credit instruments—also discussed in Chapter 5). If the interest rate they pay to ultimate lenders (from whom they borrow these funds) is less than the rate they can charge to ultimate borrowers (who use the funds to buy consumer or investment goods), financial institutions can earn profits. The process of providing the service of connecting ultimate lenders to ultimate borrowers is referred to as "financial intermediation" and is discussed in Chapter 4. This process is of obvious importance. It (a) allows certain households to consume goods sooner than otherwise would have been possible, (b) allows those who can see a profitable investment opportunity to make an investment without having to save personally, and (c) promotes economic growth and high employment by facilitating the saving-investment process. Regulators, therefore, want the financial intermediation function played by depository institutions to be carried out efficiently.

4 To provide low-cost financing for home buyers, in the form of low interest rates on house mortgages.

THE CARTEL ARRANGEMENT

Having these purposes in mind, the regulators, with the consent of the financial institutions (the regulatees), oversaw the financial system that evolved through time. By the late 1960s the following arrangement existed:

Market Segmentation   Market segmentation existed to restrict "ruinous competition" and to encourage low-cost home financing. Specific types of depository institutions were encouraged to provide specific types of financial services and were discouraged or prohibited from providing others. For example, commercial banks were allowed to accept deposits (from households or businesses) upon which checks could be written, but the "thrift institutions" (savings and loan associations and mutual savings banks) and credit unions were not. Thrifts and credit unions were permitted to accept only saving deposits (deposits without a maturity date) and time deposits (deposits with a maturity date) *upon which checks could not be written.*[1]

Market segmentation also existed with respect to the types of *assets* that could be acquired by the different types of financial institutions. In general, the thrift institutions were encouraged to specialize in housing loans; commercial banks were expected to specialize in business and consumer loans; and credit unions were to specialize in consumer loans to their members.[2] Further market segmentation existed because thrift institutions were expected to make housing loans *locally.*

Price Fixing   The regulations also fixed "prices"—or interest rates. Commercial banks were disallowed from paying interest on checking account deposits. The rate that thrift institutions could pay on savings and time deposits was also fixed— at a rate slightly higher than commercial banks could pay, and slightly below that which credit unions could pay. Allegedly, such price fixing was instituted to assure financial stability (interest-rate competition might induce financial institutions to seek out "riskier" loans, or other credit instruments, to offset higher borrowing costs) and low-cost financing for home purchasers (thrift institutions were given a competitive advantage over commercial banks in attracting savings deposits; they were assured a regulated, relatively low cost for funds).

Also, price fixing existed with respect to the rates that financial institutions could *charge* ultimate borrowers. Interest-rate ceilings—otherwise known as usury laws—existed in most states.

Restricted Entry[3]   The territorial prerogatives of specific financial institutions were protected. One was not allowed to enter the financial institution business at will; state or federal licenses or "charters" were required, and the burden of demonstrating the "need" for another financial institution was placed on the would-be entrant. Moreover, specific financial institutions were often forced to operate under state laws that permitted each bank to have only one geographic location. Traditionally, interstate banks have been prohibited; under restricted entry, a successful bank was not allowed to expand into other states.

In short, a governmentally regulated banking cartel had emerged, complete with segmented markets, price fixing, and entry restrictions. Such an

---

[1]Commercial banks were also permitted to accept such deposits. In general, commercial banks were permitted to acquire a greater variety of both assets and liabilities than were other financial institutions.

[2]Furthermore, thrift institutions were regulated in the following ways: adjustable mortgage-payment schedules (with respect to monthly payments) were prohibited until April 1981, and ceilings were placed on the ratio of the size of the loan to the value of the house.

[3]Chapter 10 includes a more complete discussion of this topic.

arrangement worked reasonably well, and for a fairly long time. The banking system was reasonably stable, and financial institutions were rewarded with profitable, segmented markets for specialized services. Of course, market efficiency suffered—as it often does when competition is disallowed. An overinvestment in housing resulted; banking services were overpriced; the spread between the rate that depository institutions paid for deposits and the rate that they charged was certainly greater than it would have been under a competitive system; and financial innovations were stifled.

THE WINDS OF CHANGE

In the late 1960s and the 1970s technological changes[4] and changes in economic conditions[5] revolutionized the banking industry and changed the form of money.

Technological Changes   The inventions of the automatic teller machine (ATM) and computer storage and electronic transfer-of-information systems have undermined the cartel's market segmentation scheme. They have created a situation under which (1) it has become economical for *any* financial institution to provide *packages* of financial services such as checking accounts, savings accounts, check clearing, customer bill paying, purchases of life insurance, and so on; and (2) the costs of financial transactions have been driven down dramatically.

The electronic transfer-of-information systems also have helped to change the form of money (the changing definition of money is discussed in Chapter 3). Money is usually thought of as that asset which is used to make transactions. Coins and paper currency are clearly money; they are generally accepted as payment for goods and services. Checking deposit accounts, too, are money; people generally accept checks written on such accounts in exchange for goods and services. Previously, savings accounts were *not* counted as money; in order to spend savings, you had to withdraw them from your account (legally, the thrift institution is not required to honor your request immediately) and convert this asset form into coins, currency, or checking-account deposits. Electronic transfer systems, however, have made it possible for funds to be shifted into and out of savings and/or checking accounts at will. Depositors can earn interest on "savings accounts," and when they are overdrawn on their checking accounts, the electric transfer system automatically covers those checks with funds transferred from the savings account. In short, savings (and other) account deposits can *also* be

---

[4]Edward J. Kane, "Policy Implications of Structural Changes in Financial Markets," *American Economic Review,* Papers and Proceedings of the 95th Annual Meeting of the American Economic Association, vol. 73, no. 2 (May 1983), pp. 96–100.

[5]See Jan G. Loeys, "Deregulation: A New Future for Thrifts," *Business Review,* Federal Reserve Bank of Philadelphia, January–February 1983, pp. 15–26, for a very readable account.

considered as money. Changes in the cost structure of financial institutions have made it feasible also to broaden the geographic area over which existing firms may profitably operate; distances between financial transactions have become less important. The result has been that electronic technology has shifted the focus of financial institutions from the provision of specific services for local clients to the offering of a package of services for a national (and even international) clientele. Moreover, these innovations have made it feasible for previously nonfinancial institutions, such as stock-brokerage houses and retail stores, to enter the financial services arena.

Changes in the Economic Environment In the late 1960s and throughout the 1970s the rate and variability (fluctuation) of inflation have increased, and therefore the level and variability of interest rates have increased. In turn, the *combination* of certain regulated interest rates and an increased level and variability of other (free) interest rates have placed thrift institutions in a vulnerable position. The combined net worth of thrift institutions fell from $44.7 billion in December 1980 to $33.6 billion in August 1982; since the beginning of 1981, over 700 thrift institutions (of a total of 5,016) merged with or were acquired by other institutions, and many others face liquidation or merger into stronger firms.[6]

Why has the combination of regulatory ceilings on some interest rates and the changing economic environment of higher market interest-rate levels and variability created problems for thrift institutions and compromised the cartel arrangement? Recall that thrift institutions were mainly in the business of accepting savings and time deposits and of using those funds to acquire mortgages from homeowners. Because these mortgages were nonadjustable with respect to interest rates and with respect to monthly payments (until April 1981; see footnote 2), thrift institutions were locked into fixed-rate earnings. This system worked well when interest rates were low and didn't vary, and when long-term interest rates were higher than short-term rates. The spread between what thrift institutions paid to acquire short-term funds and what they charged for long-term mortgage loans was sufficiently high to assure profitability. However, after 1966 short-term interest rates occasionally exceeded long-term rates. Thrift institutions found that their costs were rising while their earnings were fixed—and profits turned to losses. Moreover, they found it difficult to acquire new funds or maintain old deposits as lenders withdrew their funds and bought credit instruments directly or placed their savings in money market mutual funds.[7] (This depositor behavior, referred to as "financial disintermediation," is discussed in Chapter 10). Thus, when higher market interest rates surpassed regulated ceiling rates, thrift institutions lost deposits. Several deregulation measures permitted the thrift institutions to offer several

---

[6]Ibid., p. 16.

[7]Discussed in Chap. 3.

HIGHLIGHT   Dealing with Failing Thrifts

Deposits up to $100,000 at most depository institutions are insured by either the Federal Deposit Insurance Corporation (FDIC) or the Federal Savings and Loan Insurance Corporation (FSLIC). Not surprisingly, these insurance corporations are the main government agencies in charge of dealing with failing thrifts. The FDIC and FSLIC can follow several alternative procedures when confronted with a troubled thrift. First, they can choose to liquidate the institution, acting as a receiver of the assets and making direct payments to insured depositors. Second, they can help the institution to survive on its own by providing subsidized loans or direct aid. Third, they can take it over, arrange for new ownership and management, or facilitate a merger, thereby protecting all depositors.

The first alternative—selling off the assets and paying off the liabilities—is a solution that the insurance corporations prefer to avoid because this option is usually the most costly. At liquidation, the tangible nonfinancial assets (such as buildings) will probably yield less than replacement cost, while the intangible assets (expertise, reputation) are destroyed in the liquidation. The liabilities will have to be paid off at face value, not at the value they have to the institution as a going concern. The benefit of marking liabilities to market is lost. By mid-1981, this difference added up to an estimated $24.7 billion for the thrift industry as a whole.*

To avoid the high costs of liquidation, the FDIC and FSLIC usually have tried to provide direct assistance or to arrange a merger. Direct aid can take the form of outright cash grants, subsidized loans, or mortgage warehousing (purchase of low-yielding mortgages at face value). To be effective, an aid program must be set up as a temporary device to help an institution bridge some transitional adverse conditions and should only be granted to thrifts that have a clear prospect of becoming profitable in the future. Compared with liquidation, direct assistance leaves insured depositors equally well off, but it provides a subsidy to uninsured depositors, to the owners, and to management; and if financial institutions expect the government to cover their losses each time things turn bad, they will be more apt to take excessive risks. To circumvent this problem, FDIC/FSLIC aid programs usually require increased stockholder participation, profit-sharing with the insuring agency, or increased supervision of management.†

A third approach that the insuring corporations are now using more frequently is the merger of failing thrifts into healthier organizations. If the market net worth of the failing institution is negative, the price that the acquirer will pay is likely to be negative also: the FDIC/FSLIC will have to subsidize the acquisition. There are reasons to believe, however, that the acquiring firm will be willing to pay a premium above the failing thrift's going-concern value. First, given that geographic constraints have created a multitude of small thrifts operating at less than optimal scale, a merger could lead to economies of scale.‡ Second, if the acquiring firm is not a thrift or operates in a different geographic area, diversification gains could be realized. Third, if the acquiring firm has superior management, the new combination could raise earnings due to increased efficiency. Fourth, nonthrifts could be attracted by the tax advantages that thrifts enjoy.§

To minimize the impact on their insurance funds, the FDIC/FSLIC must try to get the best price for the thrifts they put up for sale. This approach explains the insurers' recent efforts to attract not only healthy thrifts but also commercial banks, out-of-state institutions, and even nonfinancial firms as potential acquirers of failing thrifts.

types of deposits at competitive interest rates, but the thrifts were still locked into long-term home mortgage earnings. When unexpected inflation drove interest rates up in 1979, this led to increased costs for thrift institutions, while their earnings remained fixed.

When interest rates fell, symmetry was absent. That is, when interest rates fell, homeowners had the option to *refinance* their loans. Because homeowners could refinance when interest rates fell, but thrift institutions were not allowed to adjust interest rates upward on previous mortgages when interest rates rose, increased interest-rate variability was disadvantageous to thrift institutions.

Although higher market interest rates caused commercial banks to lose some checking-account deposits (which paid no interest), they nevertheless were not hurt as badly as the thrift institutions. Recall that commercial banks were allowed to acquire a larger variety of assets than were thrift institutions. As a consequence, commercial banks were better able to match the maturities of their assets and liabilities; commercial banks were able to acquire short-term loans and short-term credit instruments. When market interest rates rose, commercial banks were able to acquire higher-interest-rate-yielding assets when their previously acquired lower-earnings assets matured.

The result of the changing economic environment was that financial institutions (especially thrift institutions) came to see regulation as a threat rather than as a blessing. The seeds of discontent thus sown, financial institutions looked forward to the fruits of deregulation. Financial institutions mustered their considerable political power to push for *selective* deregulation. Changes in technology allowed them to bypass regulations in clever ways. The combination of deregulation and financial innovation radically upset the old cartel arrangements and the stage was set for a revolution in banking.

*Andrew S. Carron, *The Plight of the Thrift Institutions*, p. 19.

†See Paul M. Horvitz and R. Richardson Pettit, "Short-Run Financial Solutions for Troubled Thrift Institutions," *The Future of the Thrift Industry*, Federal Reserve Bank of Boston, Conference Series No. 24, 1981, pp. 44–67.

‡For some evidence on these economies of scale, see James E. McNulty, "Economies of Scale in the S&L Industry: New Evidence and Implications for Profitability," *Federal Home Loan Bank Board Journal*, February 1981, pp. 2–8. Andrew Carron calculated that on average more than 400 smaller thrifts should be able to save themselves by expanding through voluntary mergers (Carron, chap. 2).

§John T. Mingo, "Short-Run Structural Solutions to the Problems of Thrift Institutions," *The Future of the Thrift Industry*, p. 94.

Source: Reprinted from *Business Review,* Federal Reserve Bank of Philadelphia, January–February 1983, p. 25.

DEREGULATION

Regulatory agencies, not insensitive to the plight of the thrift institutions, initially concerned themselves with the inability of thrift institutions to attract deposits. Rather than removing interest-rate ceilings on previous deposit forms, regulators chose to authorize *new* types of deposits on which ceilings were not placed. The most important was the "money market deposit account" (MMDA), which allowed thrift institutions to compete directly with money market mutual funds. This account went into effect on December 14, 1982, and is discussed in Chapter 5. Regulators also allowed thrift institutions to accept deposits whose interest rate was linked to "unceilinged" market rates of interest. Additionally, a *long-term* deposit with no interest-rate ceiling was authorized in 1982.

The thrift institutions, however, were not mollified; they pointed out that such freedom merely raised their costs of acquiring funds without improving their earning capacity. Eventually, Congress attempted to increase the ability of thrift institutions to diversify their assets. The Depository Institutions Deregulation and Monetary Control Act of March 1980 (analyzed in detail in Chapter 10) allowed savings and loan associations to invest up to 20 percent of their assets in consumer loans and other credit instruments. That act also permitted mutual savings banks to make corporate, business, and household loans up to 5 percent of their assets. Also importantly, that act set in motion a gradual phase-out of interest-rate ceilings over a six-year period.

More recently, the Thrift Institutions Restructuring Act of October 1982 authorized savings and loans to broaden even further their asset investments—into such areas as consumer loans, nonresidential real estate, educational loans, and small business loans. Also, in April 1981 thrift institutions were empowered to issue adjustable mortgage loans. In effect, these mortgage loans fix interest rates for only a short period; when the period is up, the loans can be refinanced at a higher (or a lower) rate.

CURRENT PROBLEMS

The revolutionary changes in the banking industry have had sweeping consequences. The distinctions among financial institutions are becoming more apparent than real. It is even possible that the difference between financial and nonfinancial institutions will disappear in time. Exciting new financial instruments have appeared on the banking scene. The spread between what financial institutions pay for deposits and what they receive on loans has narrowed, and the costs of financial transactions have fallen. The relationship between regulators and regulatees is changing.

With all these changes have come several potential problems. At the top of the list is the issue of whether so much change and deregulation has impaired the stability of the financial structure. Has increased competition and efficiency in financial intermediation been bought at the price of decreased financial stability? Second, how are the new (previously nonfinancial), unregulated entrants to be treated? The issue of fairness exists. Will the new entrants be regulated, or will the older financial institutions be deregulated further? Third, somehow a decision must be made about banking institutions. Are they different enough, special enough, and important enough to be treated differently from nonfinancial institutions? Are the consequences of a financial-institution failure more important than the consequences of a nonfinancial-corporation bankruptcy? Indeed, consider a corporation that has only minor banking interests and is in overall financial straits. Should it be subsidized or "married" to another corporation, or otherwise prevented from going bankrupt merely because it has *banking* interests? Now that the extent and nature of regulation is changing we might even anticipate some disagreement among the various regulatory institutions as to the future of regulation. Fourth, recent financial innovation is changing the form of money; Chapter 3 points out how recent changes have changed the definition of money. Because the amount of money in circulation is an important factor in the realization of our national economic goals, we must be concerned with whether the changes in the form of money have hampered regulators' ability to *control* it. The issue of monetary control is discussed in Chapters 11 to 16; a discussion of monetary policy is found in Chapters 26 and 27.

HIGHLIGHT   The Position of the Thrift Institutions in 1983

The assets of the 25 largest savings and loan associations shown in the table above increased dramatically—from $125 billion to $153 billion during 1982—mostly because of mergers and acquisitions.

Billions of dollars in new deposits have been drawn to these institutions as people have rushed to take advantage of the "money market deposit account," which has an unceilinged interest rate, requires a minimum deposit of only $2,500, permits limited checking services, and is insured. Another source of funds for the thrifts is from public offerings. Since 1975 thrifts have been allowed to issue stock ownership to the public; some 129 thrifts "went public" and raised nearly $675 million.

Two sober notes should be added to this tale of thrift-institution revitalization. First, much of the new money is not going for expansion, but to rescue the thrifts from huge mortgage delinquencies and defaults in 1983. Second, consider the "net income column"; it indicates that only 6 of the 25 largest savings and loan associations had a positive net income in 1982—the remainder suffered losses.

Source: "1983 Annual Banking Survey," *Forbes,* Apr. 11, 1983, pp. 138–139.

The 25 Largest Savings and Loan Associations

In an effort to save or be saved, mergers were commonplace in the savings and loan industry in 1982. The 25 largest S&Ls now have assets totaling $153 billion, up from last year's $125 billion—mainly because of mergers and acquisitions. Profits are another story. Only six S&Ls were profitable.

1982 size measures ($ millions)

Rank	Total Assets	Savings Accounts	Loans Receivable	Investment Securities	Advances from FHLB	Total Revenues	Net Income	Company (State)
1	$16,864	$11,815	$10,946	$1,712	$1,830	$2,015	$ -44.5	HF Ahmanson (Cal)
2	12,675	9,561	10,174	1,920	1,855	1,387	-74.7	Great Western Financial (Cal)
3	10,415	7,635	7,809	1,126	1,154	1,153	4.8	California Federal S&L[2] (Cal)
4	9,388	6,221	8,524	507	1,144	1,009	-61.1	First Charter Financial (Cal)
5	7,869	5,952	5,710	656	1,092	779	-17.0	Glendale Federal S&L[2,3] (Cal)
6	7,270	4,454	6,016	540	1,714	859	6.9	FN Financial Corp[4] (Cal)
7	7,269	4,835	5,880	510	964	799	-19.8	Golden West Financial (Cal)
8	6,612	4,904	5,988	223	250	775	36.7	Financial Corp of America (Cal)
9	6,361	4,860	3,668	727	648	484	-107.8	Talman Home Federal S&L[2,3] (Ill)
10	6,112	4,514	4,651	660	1,172	668	-28.9	Home Federal S&L[2] (Cal)
11	5,943	4,675	3,730	918	621	481	-8.7	Empire of America[2] (NY)
12	5,271	3,811	4,379	470	951	549	-61.1	Imperial Corp of Amer (Cal)
13	5,235	3,281	3,885	1,100	1,030	484	-23.5	First Federal Svgs of Mich[2] (Mich)
14	4,847	2,937	3,957	449	1,193	546	-26.7	Gibraltar Financial (Cal)
15	4,528	3,386	3,607	331	427	554	13.2	City Federal S&L (NJ)
16	4,044	3,233	3,010	219	429	365	-94.2	First Fed S&L of Chicago[2,3] (Ill)
17	3,888	2,661	3,416	293	491	447	-32.0	AmeriFirst Federal S&L[2] (Fla)
18	3,882	2,845	3,048	259	650	418	-26.7	Great American Federal S&L[2,3] (Cal)
19	3,748	2,724	2,782	526	428	411	-22.7	Gibraltar Savings (Tex)
20	3,629	2,932	2,601	674	340	315	8.7	Carteret S&L[2] (NJ)
21	3,573	3,171	3,110	240	159	354	-46.2	Standard Federal S&L[2,3] (Mich)
22	3,541	2,516	3,022	215	672	352	-28.4	Allstate S&L[5] (Cal)
23	3,348	2,305	2,342	354	464	394	-21.4	Coast Federal S&L[2,3] (Cal)
24	3,344	2,240	1,110	466	684	308	-33.4	First Federal S&L of Rochester[2,3] (NY)
25	3,223	1,949	2,011	232	1,012	263	44.5	Benj Franklin Federal S&L[2] (Ore)

Growth measures[1]

Dec. 31, 1982

Assets		Savings		Revenues		Net income		Yield on Earning Assets	Cost of Funds	Spread
4-year Average	1982 vs. 1981	4-year Average	1982 vs. 1981	4-year Average	1982 vs. 1981	4-year Average	1982 vs. 1981			
11.4%	12.1%	9.0%	6.8%	18.4%	28.8%	P-D	D-D	11.49%	10.12%	1.37%
6.1	0.8	4.7	2.7	13.0	0.4	P-D	D-D	11.07	10.38	0.69
17.6	37.1	16.4	46.8	26.2	61.3	-44.3%	D-P	12.50	10.65	1.85
3.0	-3.7	0.1	-2.3	9.1	0.6	P-D	D-D	10.34	10.31	0.03
23.4	50.1	20.4	48.6	29.3	38.7	P-D	P-D	NA	NA	NA
30.2	3.6	21.1	-4.4	39.6	71.8	-29.9	-40.1%	10.98	10.21	0.77
21.9	31.2	19.0	60.0	31.8	28.1	P-D	D-D	12.10	10.70	1.40
68.5	76.0	71.6	78.5	80.6	99.8	50.5	106.0	13.59	11.80	1.79
32.9	72.7	31.7	77.1	33.1	47.1	P-D	D-D	NA	NA	NA
18.9	20.7	18.3	35.7	23.2	17.8	P-D	D-D	12.32	11.20	1.12
33.0	109.3	28.1	95.8	35.6	95.0	P-D	D-D	11.36	11.03	0.33
10.5	2.0	8.4	4.6	15.3	8.8	P-D	D-D	11.07	10.88	0.19
9.2	31.6	1.6	2.2	10.1	22.2	P-D	D-D	10.65	10.13	0.52
11.1	1.6	2.8	12.8	19.7	12.7	P-D	D-D	11.31	10.50	0.81
28.9	35.3	29.3	40.9	46.1	68.6	9.9	D-P	13.05	11.53	1.52
15.3	11.9	13.6	14.5	20.1	7.5	P-D	D-D	NA	NA	NA
14.7	16.1	9.0	4.8	26.6	25.5	P-D	P-D	NA	NA	NA
26.8	41.2	22.6	48.6	32.6	42.7	P-D	P-D	NA	NA	NA
14.5	11.4	12.1	8.5	24.5	14.6	P-D	P-D	11.99	12.84	-0.85
33.5	88.0	33.3	93.5	39.6	63.0	14.9	D-P	12.10	10.73	1.37
11.8	4.9	11.1	7.1	20.5	9.8	P-D	D-D	NA	NA	NA
10.3	8.6	5.9	10.9	14.8	7.7	P-D	D-D	10.99	10.26	0.73
10.1	8.3	7.3	7.6	21.3	24.7	P-D	D-D	NA	NA	NA
31.7	179.8	26.1	126.5	37.7	186.0	D-D	D-D	NA	NA	NA
31.6	183.5	24.0	129.9	31.6	160.6	41.1	D-P	13.24	11.59	1.65

[1] Four-year average is a compounded annual rate: 1978/82.

[2] Mutual savings and loan association.

[3] Based on data from the Federal Home Loan Bank; figures are derived for the period ending June.

[4] Subsidiary of National Steel.

[5] Subsidiary of Sears, Roebuck. NA: not available. P-D: profit to deficit. D-D: deficit to deficit. D-P: deficit to profit.

CHAPTER SUMMARY

1 In the United States, by the late 1960s, the banking industry had evolved into what could be described as a governmentally supervised cartel.

2 The main purposes of regulation seem to have been (a) to assure a stable financial system, (b) to contribute to the achievement of national economic goals by controlling the money supply, (c) to promote efficiency in the financial intermediation process, and (d) to provide low-cost financing for home buyers.

3 The banking industry resembled a governmentally supervised cartel in that it provided (a) market segmentation, geographically and by the type of financial services offered; (b) price fixing in the form of ceilings on interest rates (i) that financial institutions could pay for funds and (ii) on loans they could make; and (c) segmented markets which were protected from the entry of existing financial institutions and of would-be entrants.

4 In the late 1960s and the 1970s technological changes and changes in economic conditions revolutionized the banking industry and changed the form of money.

5 Technological changes in the form of (a) automatic teller machines and (b) computer storage and electronic transfer-of-information systems undermined the market-segmentation scheme of the banking cartel. Specifically, these innovations changed the cost structure of financial institutions such that now it is economically feasible for *each* institution to offer a *wide* range of financial services over *broader* geographic areas. Moreover, these innovations have made it feasible for nonfinancial corporations to enter the financial-services market.

6 Technological changes in the electronic transfer-of-information systems have also changed the form of money. It is now possible to transfer funds from savings to checking accounts rather easily. In effect, people can write checks on their savings accounts—which now becomes acceptable as a means of payment, or money.

7 Since the late 1960s the economic climate has also changed. Higher rates of inflation and increased variability of inflation have led to both higher levels and increased variability of interest rates.

8 Higher levels of market interest rates, in combination with ceilings on interest rates that thrift institutions can pay to depositors, led to financial disintermediation. Depositors removed their funds from thrift institutions (and to a lesser extent, from commercial banks) and placed them where they could earn higher returns.

9 Thrift institutions applied political pressure for deregulation, which came in the form of allowing thrifts to accept new types of deposits that paid more competitive interest rates. However, because thrift institutions were locked mostly into fixed long-term earnings on home mortgages, the new deregulation seemed to increase their costs while leaving their earnings constant. The net result was losses and decreases in the net worth of many thrift institutions and a reduction in the number of thrifts.

10 Recent deregulation allows thrift institutions to acquire assets of shorter-term duration and allows them to offer variable interest rates on home mortgages.

11 The revolution in money and banking has not yet run its course; several issues remain. It is not yet certain whether increased deregulation has made the country's entire financial structure more unstable or not. Also, it is not yet resolved

whether new entrants to the financial services industry will be regulated, or whether the traditional financial institutions will become even less regulated. It is not apparent yet whether "banking" will preserve its identity, or whether its financial security is more important to the nation than the financial security of other industries. The form of money is changing rapidly. This change leads to problems in the definition and measurement of money, which may lead to difficulty in the *control* of the money stock, and therefore to difficulty in pursuing a monetary policy that can help to achieve national economic goals.

SELECTED REFERENCES

Greenspan, Allen, "Onward the Revolution in Financial Services," *Wall Street Journal,* editorial page, Sept. 16, 1983.

Kane, Edward J., "Policy Implications of Structural Changes in Financial Markets," *American Economic Review,* Papers and Proceedings of the Ninety-Fifth Annual Meeting of the American Economic Association, vol. 73, no. 2 (May 1983), pp. 96–100.

Loeys, Jan. G., "Deregulation: A New Future for Thrifts," *Business Review,* Federal Reserve Bank of Philadelphia, January–February 1983, pp. 15–26.

Schroeder, Frederick J., "Developments in Consumer Electronic Fund Transfers," *Federal Reserve Bulletin,* June 1983, pp. 395–403.

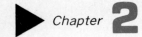
Money and Its Functions

CHAPTER PREVIEW

1   What is money and what are its functions?

2   Is money related to economic variables?

3   Different items have been used as money. How do they differ?

4   What properties are necessary to make something money?

5   Why is a money standard superior to a barter system?

The subject matter of this text is money and banking. We will use the term "money" to mean any generally accepted medium of exchange. Money is most often thought of as the paper bills and coins that you carry in your wallet or purse. But the concept of money can be more inclusive. For example, the money supply in the United States includes a variety of items in addition to paper bills and coins **(currency).** One of the most important elements of any measure of the amount of money in circulation is transaction (checking-account) balances. Transaction balances are a medium of exchange because, like currency, they can be exchanged immediately for the goods and services that people wish to buy.

MONEY AS AN ASSET

Money can be considered an asset, or something of value. As such, it is a part of your wealth (net worth, or assets minus debts). Wealth in the form of money has a unique characteristic; it can be *directly* exchanged for some other asset, good, or service. Although not the only form of wealth exchangeable for goods and services, money is the one most widely accepted. This attribute of money is called **liquidity.** An asset is liquid when it can be easily exchanged for a good or service without high transactions costs and with relative certainty as to its nominal (non-inflation-adjusted) value; there is a minimum probability of capital loss for money holding. By definition, money is the most liquid of all assets. Compare it, for example, to a stock listed on the New York Stock Exchange. To sell that stock, you must call a stockbroker to place a sell order for you. This must be done during normal business hours, and you must pay a percentage commission to the broker. Moreover, there is a distinct probability that you will receive more or less for the shares of stock than you originally paid for them. This is not the case with money. Money can be easily converted into other asset forms, and it always has the same *nominal* value. Most individuals, therefore, hold at least part of their wealth in this most liquid of assets.

THE IMPORTANCE OF STUDYING MONEY— THE RELATIONSHIP BETWEEN MONEY AND ECONOMIC ACTIVITY

There are many ways to analyze overall economic activity. One of the most common measures of overall economic activity is the **gross national product (GNP),** defined as the dollar value of all final goods and services produced in one year in the economy. Look at Figure 2-1, which shows the historic rela-

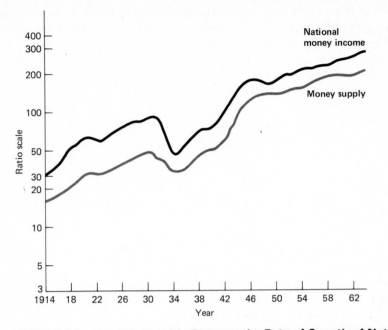

FIGURE 2-1 The Relationship Between the Rate of Growth of National Money Income and the Rate of Growth of the Money Supply. These graphs, adapted from a classic book on the role of money in the economy, indicate a very close direct relationship between money-supply growth and growth in the level of (noninflation-adjusted) national income. The growth rates rise and fall together. (*Source:* Adapted from Friedman and Schwartz, *A Monetary History of the United States, 1867–1960* (Princeton: Princeton University Press, 1963), p. 678)

tionship between money and *nominal* national income.[1] Nominal national income refers to the dollar amount of gross output expressed in the prices that prevail each year; and it is not adjusted for changes in the level of prices. An examination of Figure 2-1 reveals a loose but consistent relationship between the money supply (defined in Chapter 3 in detail) and nominal GNP. Some economists use this evidence to argue that money is an important determinant of the level of economic activity in the economy; others disagree. Whether money-supply changes affect real (inflation-adjusted) GNP and output is an issue to which we return in later chapters. Nonetheless, because of the relationship between money and overall economic activity, most economists agree that money demands serious study.

Money and Prices Another key economic variable in our economy is the price level and how it changes. **Inflation,** defined as a rise in the (weighted) average of all prices, has been linked to a variety of causes. The measurement of inflation is analyzed in Chapter 21. One theory attributes inflation to changes in the

---

[1]Adapted from Milton Friedman and Anna Schwartz, *A Monetary History of the United States, 1867–1960* (Princeton, N.J.: Princeton University Press, 1963), p. 678.

amount of money in circulation. Figure 2-2 shows the relationship between the rate of change of the money supply (its growth rate) and the inflation rate. Again, as with money and economic activity, there is a loose, albeit consistent, direct relationship between changes in the money supply and changes in the rate of inflation; increases in the growth of the money supply seem to lead to an increase in the inflation rate—after a time lag.

Money and Interest Rates Interest rates have fluctuated dramatically in the United States over the last decade, and changes in the growth rate of the money supply may be partially responsible for these fluctuations. Look, for example, at Table 2-1, which shows the relationship between the rate of change of the money supply, the inflation rate, and various measures of the interest rate. A consistent direct relationship exists among the three variables. Thus, what constitutes money and the money supply are key concepts in understanding changes in the economy's interest rates.

THE FUNCTIONS OF MONEY

Money has four basic functions.

1 Medium of exchange

2 Store of value

3 Unit of accounting (standard of value)

4 Standard of deferred payment

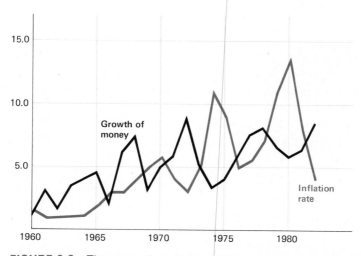

FIGURE 2-2 These graphs indicate a loose correspondence between money supply growth and the inflation rate. Actually, closer inspection reveals a direct relationship between changes in the growth rate of money and changes in the inflation rate *in a later period*. Increases in the rate of growth of money seem to lead to later-period increases in the inflation rate; decreases in the rate of money growth seem to lead to subsequent reductions in the inflation rate. (*Source:* Economic Report of the President, 1983, and various Federal Reserve Bulletins.)

Money as a Medium of Exchange   To say that money serves as a **medium of exchange** means that market participants will accept it as payment. Individuals can sell their output for money and use that money to make purchases in the future. In the process, money makes specialization possible. Specialization is essential to any efficient economy; it allows individuals to purchase most products rather than produce the products themselves. Individuals will specialize in areas where they have a **comparative advantage,** and they will receive money payments for the fruits of their labor. These money payments can then be exchanged for the fruits of other people's labor. As the volume of trade and the range of available goods and services increase, money assumes a more significant role in the economy. As a medium of exchange, then, money is critical to modern economies; however, in a self-sufficient family unit money would play a minor role.

Money as a Store of Value   To see how money is a **store of value,** consider this simple example: A fisherman comes into port after several days of fishing. At the going price of fish that day he has $1,000 worth of fish. Those fish are not a good store of value because if the fisherman keeps them too long they will rot. If he attempts to exchange them with other tradespeople, some of the fish may rot before he can exchange the entire catch for the goods and services he desires. On the other hand, if the fisherman sells the entire catch for money, he can store the value of his catch in the money that he receives. (Of

TABLE 2-1   Average Annual Growth Rates of Money and Prices and Average Levels of Interest Rates in the United States*

	Period	
	1954–66, %	**1967–82, %**
Money growth	2.47	6.37
Inflation rate	2.19	6.49
Aaa corporate bond rate	4.06	8.76
20-year Treasury yield	3.78	8.12
Commercial paper rate	3.45	8.13
90-day Treasury bill rate	2.86	7.20

*This table indicates a consistent direct relationship between annual rates of growth of the money supply, annual rates of inflation, and various interest rates for two separate periods. They all rise together.
Source: Adapted from G. S. Santoni and Courtenay C. Stone, ''The Fed and the Real Rate of Interest,'' *Review,* Federal Reserve Bank of St. Louis, vol. 64, no. 10, December 1982, table 2.

course, he can freeze the fish, but that's costly; it's also not a very precise way to store the value of *fresh* fish.)

Under certain conditions, holding money as a store of value may cause the holder to incur a cost. Particularly in the past (when bank regulators prohibited banks from paying interest on transaction accounts) holders of currency and transaction account balances paid an **opportunity cost** (what must be given up) for any benefits obtained from holding money as a store of value. The opportunity cost is the interest income that can be earned if the money is held in another form, such as a savings account. In other words, the cost of holding money—its opportunity cost—is measured by the highest alternative interest yield obtainable by holding some other asset. This analysis applies to all *currency* held as a store of value. Today, however, it has only a limited application to those transaction accounts held in various financial institutions which now pay interest on such balances. Nevertheless, often the interest rate paid is less than the interest rate that can be earned if the money is transferred to an alternative asset form. In this case the opportunity cost incurred can be measured by the interest-income *differential* that would be earned by that same amount of money stored (invested) in a higher-interest income-earning asset.

Money as a Unit of Accounting (Standard of Value)

A **unit of accounting** is a way of placing a specific value on economic goods and services. Thus, as a unit of accounting, the monetary unit is used to measure the value of goods and services relative to other goods and services. It is the common denominator or measure. The dollar, for example, is the monetary unit in the United States. It is the yardstick that allows individuals to compare easily the relative value of goods and services. Accountants at the Department of Commerce use dollar prices to measure national income and national product; a firm uses dollar prices to calculate profits and losses; a typical household budgets daily and regular expenses using dollar prices as its unit of accounting.

Another way of describing money as a unit of accounting is to say that it is a standard of value that allows economic transactors to compare the relative worth of various goods and services.

Money as a Standard of Deferred Payment

The fourth function of the monetary unit is as a **standard of deferred payment.** This function simultaneously involves the use of money as a medium of exchange and as a unit of accounting. Debts are typically stated in terms of a unit of accounting; they are paid with a monetary medium of exchange. That is to say, a debt is specified in a dollar amount and paid in currency or by check. A corporate bond, for example, has a face value (the value stamped on it, which is paid upon maturity) stated in terms of dollars. The periodic interest payments on that corporate bond are specified and paid in dollars. When the bond comes due (at maturity), the corporation pays the face value to the holder of the bond in dollars.

Not all countries nor the firms and individuals in those countries will specify debts owed to be repaid in their own national monetary unit. For example, individuals, private corporations, and governments in other countries incur debts in terms of the U.S. dollar, even though the dollar is neither the medium of exchange nor the monetary unit in those countries. Additionally, contracts for some debts specify repayment in gold rather than in a nation's currency.

HIGHLIGHT   Hyperinflation and the Functions of Money

When the rate of inflation is extremely high, *hyperinflation* is said to exist. A sign of hyperinflation is a very rapid and sustained rise in the price level. From 1920 to 1924, a classic case of hyperinflation occurred in Germany; the rate of inflation was 80 percent in 1920, 140 percent in 1921, and 4,100 percent in 1922. Then things really got interesting. From December 1922 to November 1923, the rate of inflation was 100 million percent. The greatest of all hyperinflations, however, occurred in Hungary during 1945 and 1946; there the rate of inflation averaged 20,000 percent per month; in a 13-month period prices rose by approximately 5.2×10^{27} percent.

Inflation reduces the value of a unit of money; it takes more units of money to buy the same quantities of goods and services when the price level is rising. Hyperinflation reduces the value of a unit of money by a large amount—in a short period of time. This is a way of saying that during times of hyperinflation (or even during times of inflation) money is less valuable as a store of value.

Consequently people want to hold as little of it as possible, for as short a period of time as possible. They prefer to exchange money for goods which retain their value better (hence the term "hedge against inflation"). During the German hyperinflation episode it was widely reported that at noon, family members would meet workers (who were paid twice daily) to receive pay. The relative would then hurry to the grocery store in order to buy goods before the afternoon bout of inflation.

Note that as money starts to lose its usefulness as a store of value, it deteriorates as a medium of exchange as well. People become reluctant to accept it as payment for real goods. It also starts to lose its value as a standard of deferred payment— and therefore as a unit of accounting.

Still, it is easy to exaggerate the influence that hyperinflation has on the destruction of money. Instances in which hyperinflation has induced people to return to a barter system are very rare; even Germany clung to a monetary system throughout its inflationary episode. Moreover, people are reluctant to shift to a *new* medium of exchange. Perhaps this is because it is difficult to get general agreement as to what the new "money" will be, and considerable time may be required before the new money medium is generally accepted. Thus, even though people try to hold as little money as possible for as short a period as possible during hyperinflation, they cling to the current *monetary system*. Apparently money needs to retain its use as a store of value just long enough for people to run to stores with their wages and to convert them into goods.

THE DISTINCTION BETWEEN MONEY AND CREDIT

You must be clear about the distinction between money and credit. Money is the most liquid asset in which people choose to hold part of their wealth. Credit, on the other hand, consists of purchasing power lent or made available to borrowers. The credit market makes it possible for those individuals who are unwilling to wait for goods or purchasing power to have at a cost (an interest rate) more goods or purchasing power now.

To further demonstrate the distinction between money and credit, consider a society in which no money exists, where, nonetheless, credit can indeed exist. In such an economy, Mr. Jones could loan Mrs. Smith one of his machines for a year. Mrs. Smith could promise to return the machine to Jones at the end of one year and pay him five units of the output she produces as interest for the credit that he extended to her. In this situation, the amount of credit clearly does not depend on the existence of or the amount of money in society.

THE DESIRABLE PROPERTIES OF MONEY

At a minimum, money has five requisite properties. They are:

1 *Portability:* Money must be easy to carry around and easy to transfer in order to make purchases in different locations. If money is not portable, it cannot be widely used.

2 *Durability:* Money that does not have the quality of physical durability will lose its value as money. For example, popcorn could be money but it would be difficult to keep it in its current form. It would become stale, soggy, wear out, flake apart, and so on. Money has not always been characterized by durability, however. Roman soldiers were paid in salt (hence the origin of the word "salary"), which certainly is not durable in a humid or wet climate.

3 *Divisibility:* Money must be easily divided into equal parts to allow for purchases of smaller units. However, some monies have been indivisible. In African countries, cows have at various times been used as money in spite of the fact that a fraction of a cow is quite a different entity than a whole cow.

4 *Standardizability:* To be useful, money must be standardized; its units should be of equal quality and physically indistinguishable. Only if money is standardized can individuals be certain of what they are receiving when they make economic exchanges. Counterexamples do nonetheless exist. The American colonists used tobacco as money, but tobacco could never be standardized. Equal quantities by weight were not available to represent

equal value because of the different *qualities* of tobacco; humidity also caused problems on occasion.

5 *Recognizability:* Money must be easily recognized. If it is not easily recognized, individuals will find it difficult to determine whether they are dealing with money or some inferior asset (a counterfeit).

In modern nations today, money typically consists of coins, paper currency, and checking-account balances (upon which checks can be written). All of these types of money have the five desirable properties previously discussed.

In the past, societies have most often chosen a precious metal or coin as money. Silver and gold, for example, have proved to be durable, portable, divisible, standardizable, and recognizable. Precious metals have been designated as money more often in the past than virtually any other commodity which served as money at one time or another. Governments have often stepped in to certify the weights of silver and gold coins and they have charged a price for this service. To obtain revenues, governments typically have charged a **seigniorage.** Whenever the market value of the base metal in the coin is less than the face value of the coin, seigniorage exists: It is the charge levied on the individual for converting the metal into a bona fide coin. (When the charge levied for conversion simply covers the cost of conversion, the process is called ''brassage,'' not seigniorage.)

Societies generally go through trial-and-error procedures before adopting a common medium of exchange. Eventually, individuals will choose the commodity that offers the least costly benefits of a common medium of exchange. Hence, what serves as money in an economy will change as the costs of production of the alternative monies change. Whenever a government chooses an ''appropriate'' money, that money will continue to serve as a medium of exchange only if it is generally worthwhile for individuals to use it. A case in point is the Susan B. Anthony dollar, designed to replace the discontinued Eisenhower dollar in the United States. In 1979, the U.S. Treasury issued the Anthony dollar and believed that it would come into widespread use. Unfortunately for the Treasury, individuals did not take too keenly to the new dollar because of its similarity to the quarter. In spite of its eleven-sided border, it still looked and felt very much like a quarter. Given the availability of dollar bills, few people chose to use the Anthony dollar; it is really not an important part of our circulating coins.

TYPES OF MONEY

History shows that money has existed in diverse forms. Table 2-2 lists some of the different types of money that have existed throughout history.

Most types of money that were used (some are shown in Table 2-2) are commodity monies: They are physical commodities. The history of money has been a movement away from such commodity monies (gold and silver coins)

TABLE 2-2 Different Types of Money

Iron	Red woodpecker scalps	Leather
Copper	Feathers	Gold
Brass	Glass	Silver
Wine	Polished beads (wampum)	Knives
Corn	Rum	Pots
Salt	Molasses	Boats
Horses	Tobacco	Pitch
Sheep	Agricultural implements	Rice
Goats	Round stones with centers	Cows
Tortoise shells	removed	Slaves
Porpoise teeth	Crystal salt bars	Paper
Whale teeth	Snail shells	Cigarettes
Boar tusk	Playing cards	

to credit money, such as checking accounts. To understand this movement let's look at the classifications of money. There are basically two major classifications—commodity money and credit money. Within the classification of commodity money there are two subclassifications, as indicated below. Credit money (which is sometimes called fiat money) contains numerous subclassifications. In outline form, these types of money are as follows:

1 Commodity money
   A Full-bodied money
   B Representative full-bodied money
2 Credit money
   A Issued by governments and central banks
      1 Token coins
      2 Paper
         a Issued by government
         b Issued by central banks
   B Issued by depository institutions
      1 Bank notes
      2 Demand deposits

Commodity Money   Commodity monies are those physical commodities that also have a nonmonetary use. This classification includes full-bodied money and representative full-bodied money.

Full-Bodied Money   Any money whose value as a good in nonmonetary purposes is equivalent to its value as a medium of exchange is called **full-bodied money.** Early commodity monies, such as wool, boats, sheep, and corn, had equivalent monetary and nonmonetary values. In more modern times, nations have minted coins whose metallic content had a value in nonmonetary uses (teeth fillings, jewelry, etc.) equal to its exchange value as money. (A later chapter discusses an economy on the gold standard, in which gold coins are used as full-bodied money.) Full-bodied money coins typically have been issued by governments and could legally be melted for nonmonetary uses.

The fact that full-bodied coins have money value (purchasing power) equivalent to their nonmonetary uses does not mean that they have a *constant* value. The purchasing power of a full-bodied coin will change in terms of other commodities. As the prices of all other goods and services change, so, too, does the purchasing power of a full-bodied money. In other words, the use of full-bodied coins does not prevent inflation or deflation (a decline in the weighted average of all prices through time) from occurring. Consider an example: A country using full-bodied gold coins could still experience inflation if a new discovery of large amounts of gold occurred or if the costs of mining gold fell dramatically. Consider the effects of a discovery of large amounts of gold. With the same amount of goods and services available, but, say, twice the supply of gold money available, the prices of available goods and services in terms of gold would have to rise; the relative price of gold would fall.

Representative Full-Bodied Money A type of money (paper or coin) which is of negligible value but is *backed* by (can be converted into) a commodity such as gold or silver is defined as **representative full-bodied money.** In other words, a paper currency in a representative full-bodied monetary system is the equivalent of full-bodied coins. The paper itself is representative and has no value as a commodity. But it does represent the total amount of full-bodied money in existence. Prior to 1933, for example, in the United States gold certificates were widely circulated. These certificates represented the equivalent amount of gold coin, or bullion, held by the Treasury. Hence, the gold certificates were fully backed by the actual commodity: A fifty-dollar gold certificate was a claim to fifty dollars' worth of gold (at the official, or governmentally guaranteed, exchange price of twenty dollars per ounce of gold) usually stored by the U.S. government in Fort Knox, Kentucky.

Another example is the silver certificates that formerly existed in the United States. They were fully redeemable in silver at the official exchange rate. In the mid-1960s, the world market price of silver rose dramatically. Individuals started exchanging their silver certificates for silver at the official price (the rate at which the government promised to exchange dollars and silver) of $1.29 an ounce of silver. The U.S. Treasury honored its commitment at this exchange rate until June 24, 1968.

Representative full-bodied money saves transactions costs because the transfer of large sums of money in gold or silver (or anything else) is unwieldy. Paper claims on the physical commodity are much easier and cheaper to utilize.

Credit Money An economy uses **credit money** when it uses money that does not have a commodity value, or whose nonmonetary value is less than its value in monetary uses. For example, a copper coin whose copper value melted down is, say, one-tenth of a cent, but whose monetary value is one cent, is credit money. Credit money can be broken down into two major subclassifications: credit money issued by governments and central banks, and that issued by depository institutions.

Credit Money Issued by Governments and Central Banks   Governments and central banks issue much of the credit money that exists in the world today. The copper coin mentioned above was issued by the U.S. government. It was a token coin—one whose metal value was worth less than its numeral, or money, value. In the United States, all token coins are issued by the U.S. Treasury. In other countries, central banks (our central bank is called the Federal Reserve System, or the Fed) also issue token coins.

Governments and central banks also issue paper credit money. Today, the only credit paper of the federal government is the U.S. notes ("greenbacks") that were used to finance the Civil War. About $350 million worth of these promissory notes are still in circulation. The remainder of the paper credit money used today are Federal Reserve notes, issued by the Federal Reserve System. Chances are that all the paper currency in your wallet or purse is in the form of Federal Reserve notes that were issued by the Fed.

Credit Money Issued by Depository Institutions   Numerous financial institutions in this country have the legal right to issue credit money in the form of transaction accounts; they are referred to as depository institutions. Banks, savings and loan associations, credit unions, and the like all offer some form of a transaction account to their customers. Depositors are able to write a check to pay for the purchase of goods and services. All these depository institutions are private, that is, not owned by the government.

In the distant past, private banks have also issued paper currency. These were promissory notes (the banks "promised" to redeem them for a precious metal) of the private banks, and they played an important role in our monetary system. The First and Second Banks of the United States, chartered by the federal government, as well as national banks (also chartered by the federal government), have at times issued paper notes. So, too, have state-chartered banks.

MONETARY STANDARDS, OR WHAT BACKS MONEY

Today in the United States, all of us accept coins, Federal Reserve notes, and transactions balances in exchange for items sold, including labor services. The question remains, Why are we willing to accept for payment something that has no *intrinsic* value? The reason is that in this country the payments arise from a **fiduciary monetary standard.** This means that the value of the payments rests upon the public's confidence that it can be exchanged for goods and services. "Fiduciary" comes from the Latin *fiducia,* which means trust or confidence. In other words, under our fiduciary monetary standard, money,

The Karl Marx Mark. West Germany recently began to mint a five-mark coin bearing the image of Karl Marx, who once described money as the "common whore, the common pimp of peoples and nations." *(Deutsche Bank AG Hamburg.)*

whether in the form of currency or transaction accounts, is not convertible into a fixed quantity of gold or silver or into some other precious commodity. The paper money that people hold in their wallets or purses or transaction account balances cannot be exchanged for a specified quantity of some specific commodity; it is just pieces of paper. Coins have a value stamped on them that is normally greater than the market value of the metal in them. Nevertheless, currency and transaction accounts are money because of their acceptability and their predictability of value.

Acceptability Transaction accounts and currency are money because they are accepted in exchange for goods and services. They are accepted because people have confidence that they can later be exchanged for other goods and services. This confidence is based on the knowledge that such exchanges have occurred in the past without problems.

Predictability of Value For money to have a predictable value, the relationship between the quantity of money supplied and the quantity of money demanded must not change frequently, abruptly, or in great magnitude. In this sense, the value of money is like the economic value of other goods and services. Supply and demand determine what the dollar "sells" for. What is the selling price of a dollar? It is what has to be given up in order to "purchase" a dollar. What have to be given up are the goods and services that could have been obtained instead of the dollar. In other words, in order to own one dollar, an individual must give up the purchasing power inherent in that dollar. That purchasing power might be equal to a used paperback book or a bag of french fries.

The purchasing power of the dollar (that is, its value) therefore varies inversely with the price level. Thus, the more rapid the rate of increase of the price level, the more rapid the decrease in the value, or purchasing power, of the dollar. Money retains its usefulness even if its value—its purchasing

HIGHLIGHT   Bad Money Drives Out Good Money

The financial advisor to Queen Elizabeth I was Sir Thomas Gresham (1519–1579). It is believed that he coined the phrase "Bad money drives good money out of circulation."

To understand *Gresham's law,* as it is called, "bad money" must first be defined. It can be defined by using the dime as an example. Dimes minted after 1965 had a metal content value of less than 10 cents. Pre-1965 minted dimes had a metal content value greater than 10 cents. The dimes minted after 1965 were "bad" money and the dimes minted before 1965 were "good" money. The terms *bad* and *good* refer only to the nonmonetary value of money. Given a choice, individuals prefer to own good money rather than bad money. Owning good money makes the owner richer because the good money is worth more than its face value.

Only when there is a government-fixed exchange rate between two kinds of money can bad money drive out good money. In the case of pre-1965 minted dimes and post-1965 minted dimes, the fixed exchange rate under law was one for one. Had there not been a fixed exchange rate, sellers could have expressed the price of goods two different ways: in terms of old dimes or in terms of new dimes. Consider the purchase of one dollar's worth of goods after 1965. A merchant might have expressed the price of the product as, say, ten post-1965 dimes and seven pre-1965 dimes. If this had been the case, the two dimes would have coexisted in circulation. During the Civil War, for example, both gold dollars and United States paper dollars remained in circulation, even though a tremendous number of paper dollars was printed to finance the war against the south. Why? Because each good or service had two prices: one in terms of gold dollars and one in terms of paper dollars. No governmentally imposed fixed exchange rate existed between gold dollars and greenbacks at that time.

When Sir Thomas Gresham explained to Queen Elizabeth (so the story goes) what had happened to the money supply, he observed that the coins which had the higher silver content were no longer being used as a medium of exchange in England. The coins with the lower silver content were exchanged for goods and services. Henry VIII (Elizabeth's father) had reduced the silver content of silver coins from 92.5 percent pure silver to only about 33 percent in 1545. But the face value of the coin had not been reduced accordingly. It is not surprising that only the one-third-pure silver coins remained in circulation.

power—declines every year. Money can still be used and accepted during periods of inflation because it retains the characteristic of *predictability* of value. If individuals believe that the rate of inflation is going to be 10 percent next year, then they expect that a dollar received a year hence will have approximately 9 percent less purchasing power than the same dollar this year. Individuals will not necessarily refuse to use money or accept it in exchange simply because they know that its value will decline by slightly more than 9 percent over the next year. As will be discussed later, the expectation of a declining value of money will change the amounts and types of financial assets that people want to hold—including the desired amount of money.

THE ROLE OF MONEY IN AN ECONOMY

The importance of studying money was already pointed out at the beginning of this chapter. Money affects important economic variables, such as gross national product (economic activity), the price level, and interest rates. The use of money also allows for specialization and therefore economic efficiency. Perhaps the best way to understand the importance of money in any economy is to look at an economy that doesn't use money. When there is no generally accepted medium of exchange, individuals engage in **barter,** which is the direct exchange of goods and services for other goods and services.

The Problems of a Barter Economy   The major problem facing a barter economy is that a **double coincidence of wants** is required for exchange. This means that if Ms. Hanford wishes to acquire bread, but only has shoes for exchange, then she must seek out someone else (say, Mr. Terry) who is a baker seeking shoes. The search for Mr. Terry involves a use of time; there is an opportunity cost of that time spent searching for a trading partner. It is virtually impossible to find someone in an economy at all times who simultaneously wants the good or service that another individual at that time wants to exchange. In other words, the double coincidence of wants rarely occurs in a complex modern society. Consequently, the absence of a double coincidence of wants requires individuals either to hold goods and services for long periods of time, or to make numerous intermediary exchanges in order to obtain the goods and services they want to have.

Consider an example: Mr. Terry has just produced ten loaves of bread by working all day. In exchange for eight of those loaves of bread, he wishes to acquire a pair of shoes for his daughter. There may be someone out there—Ms. Hanford—who has a pair of girl's shoes and who is in need of bread for her large family. Unless Terry knows about Hanford's situation, he will have to seek her out, which entails the use of his time. If he fails to do so rather quickly, his bread will become stale. He may decide, therefore, to exchange eight loaves of bread for three pots, even though he has enough pots. Then he might find a trading partner who will take the three pots in exchange for ten pounds of apples. Finally, he might find someone willing to take the ten pounds of apples in exchange for the pair of girl's shoes. All of which amounts to a complicated, time-consuming, and costly process, to be sure.

This does not mean that barter has always been inefficient. Some societies produce a limited range of goods and services and little trade transpires. In such societies, barter may have worked well and may continue to do so. However, when the array of goods and services expands and frequent trading with other societies occurs, the cost of barter will greatly exceed its benefits. A new payment mechanism will gradually replace barter, even though limited barter may continue in a fully developed monetary system. Barter still occurs in the United States today.[2]

---

[2]The recent resurgence of barter in the U.S. economy can be attributed to an attempt to avoid taxes more than to anything else.

The Shortcomings of a Pure Barter Society
A pure barter economy has numerous shortcomings. Consider the following:

1 *Absence of a method of storing generalized purchasing power:* With money, individuals and businesses have a store of *generalized* purchasing power (as opposed to specific purchasing power in the form of, say, shoes, pots, pans, and so on). Barter provides only a specific store of purchasing power. It allows individuals to store only specific goods, which may decrease in value due to physical deterioration or a change in tastes.

2 *Absence of a common unit of measure and value:* Under a barter system, the price of every good or service must be expressed in terms of every other good and service. Barter therefore leads to the absence of a standardized way to state the price of commodities. Consider the number of prices that would exist if there were only 1,000 goods in the economy but no money or monetary unit of accounting. Every good could be exchanged for the remaining 999 goods. That means that shoes could be exchanged for haircuts, symphony orchestra tickets, oranges, milk, or other items. In the absence of a monetary unit, the price of shoes could be expressed in terms of the remaining 999 commodities. What is true for shoes would be true for every one of the other 999 commodities. The number of unique exchange rates, or prices, would be found by the formula:

$$\text{Exchange rates (prices)} = [N(N-1)]/2$$

N signifies the number of goods and services being exchanged. In the simple example used here, N equals 1,000; therefore:

$$\text{Exchange rates (prices)} = \frac{1,000(999)}{2} = 499,500$$

Each time a person in this 1,000-good economy tried to make a purchase, he or she would be faced with almost one-half million potential rates of exchange. Switching to a monetary unit of accounting simplifies matters greatly. With one monetary unit of accounting, such as the dollar, the individual in this economy would contend with only $N-1$ rates of exchange or, in this case, 999. In other words, the use of a monetary unit would reduce the number of rates of exchange in this example to one five-hundredths of what they would be without such a system. Clearly, this reduction in the number of relative prices would make economic life less costly and facilitate trade.

Typically, the monetary unit used as a unit of accounting is the same as the medium of exchange. There are exceptions, however. Until recently, in Britain many commodities' values were expressed in guineas. A guinea was a gold coin worth twenty-one shillings, but guineas had not circulated for most of the time during which that common term of value was utilized.

3 *Absence of a designated unit to use in writing contracts requiring future payments:* Many contracts deal with future activities and future

exchanges. In a barter system, it is difficult to write contracts for future payments in a unit readily acceptable to both parties. It is still possible to make such contracts for the future payment of goods or services, but the market value of those agreed-upon goods or services may change drastically by the time the future payment is due.

WHAT FOLLOWS

This chapter has explained the importance of money, and the forms and types of money that have been and are being used today. The rest of Unit 1 will examine the changing definition of the money supply, the history of banks, and the functions of banks in our economy.

Unit 2 looks at interest rates and financial markets. Unit 3 examines the regulation and the management of commercial banks.

Central banking is considered in Unit 4. In that unit, our Federal Reserve System, including its history and structure, is analyzed in detail. Units 5, 6, and 7 can be considered the macroeconomic section of this text, and in this section monetary theory and policy are examined in detail. Finally, Unit 8 treats the important topics of exchange rates and the balance of payments, as well as the history and problems of international finance.

CURRENT CONTROVERSY

Is Money Becoming Obsolete?

In the last few years the notion of what money is has changed dramatically in the United States and elsewhere. This nation and many parts of the world have entered into an era of electronic banking. Instead of using cash or checks, individuals using electronic banking can make deposits and purchases simply by electronic signals. Some individuals think that this means that money is obsolete. The notion of money as expressed in this chapter, however, remains the same. Money has basic functions, as a medium of exchange and as a store of value.

When an individual gets paid for working, does the fact that the individual doesn't see or feel his or her actual money income in the form of a paycheck mean that money is no longer being used? Does a purchase at a store using a sophisticated electronic automatic debit system (in which your account in some financial institution is immediately debited for the purchase) mean that money is no longer being used? The answer must be no. Individuals are still using a means of exchange called the dollar. Rather than using dollar bills or writing out a physical check (which, by the way, is not money itself—only the *account balance* is money), one simply transfers an electronic signal over a telephone line. The electronic signal travels as a change in the line's magnetic field which is interpreted to reduce the available "money" if a purchase has been made or increase the available "money" if a deposit has been made.

Individuals still must make decisions about the amount of money they wish to hold. They must decide what portion of their depository institution transaction account balance should be spent immediately and what part saved, or how much should be used to purchase an income-earning asset, such as a stock or bond. Electronic banking does not mean the death of money. Rather, it means that the *method* of transferring money is changing. The United States still has a system of credit money.

Electronic banking is only one step on a long, sometimes tortuous path in the evolution of a monetary system. If history is any guide, it will not be the last step.

DISCUSSION QUESTIONS

1 What disadvantages do consumers face in a system of electronic banking?

2 Why does electronic banking change only the method of transfer rather than the amount of money?

CHAPTER SUMMARY

1 Money is that which is accepted as such. It is used as a medium of exchange, a store of value, a unit of accounting, and a standard of deferred payment. By definition, money is the most liquid of all assets.

2 Economists study money because it is believed to affect other economic variables. Changes in the money stock are highly correlated with changes in the price level, nominal interest rates, and nominal GNP.

3 Money and credit are not the same thing; credit is the extending of purchasing power to others for a future payment. Credit and interest rates can exist even in a barter economy.

4 In order for something to be useful as money, it must be portable, durable, divisible, standardizable, and recognizable; but exceptions to each of these desirable properties can be found in history. Gold and silver have these properties and have been very popular money forms throughout the ages. In theory and in practice, what is acceptable as money is subject to change.

5 There are two basic types of money: commodity money and credit money. Commodity money includes full-bodied money and representative full-bodied money. The essence of commodity money is that its face value is equal to (or can be exchanged for) its market value. Credit money, on the other hand, has a face value that exceeds its market value. Credit money is issued by governments and central banks and/or by depository institutions.

6 The United States is presently on a fiduciary monetary standard; our money is not "backed" by anything other than the public's faith that it will be accepted as payment for goods and services. As long as money has acceptability and its value is reasonably predictable, a fiduciary monetary standard can operate. Under a gold standard, a nation's currency is defined in terms of a fixed quantity of gold; the government promises to convert this currency into gold at this established rate "on demand." Each of these monetary systems is deemed preferable to a barter system.

GLOSSARY

Barter: Trading a good or service for another without the use of money.

Comparative advantage: The ability to produce something at a lower opportunity cost than others can.

Credit, or fiat, money: Money whose face value is more than its market value; paper money not backed by anything but faith in its universal acceptance, e.g., paper bills and transaction account balances.

Currency: The value of coins and paper money.

Double coincidence of wants: A situation in which a person who has good A to trade and wants good B finds someone with good B to trade and who wants good A.

Fiduciary monetary standard: A monetary standard under which the currency is not backed by anything except the public's confidence, or faith, in the assumption that the currency can be exchanged for goods and services.

Full-bodied money: Money whose face value is equal to its market value, such as gold or silver coins.

Gross national product (GNP): The market value of all final goods and services produced over a period of time (usually a year).

Income: Payment for providing resources to the productive process, per unit of time.

Inflation: A rise in the weighted average of all prices over time.

Liquidity: The degree to which an asset can be sold for cash without a loss in nominal value. Money, by definition, is the most liquid of all assets.

Medium of exchange: Whatever is accepted as payment for purchases of goods or services or for debt; a necessary property of money.

Money: Money is that which is universally acceptable in an economy by sellers of goods and services as payment for the goods and services, and by creditors as payment for debts.

Opportunity cost: The economic cost of any activity, measured by the highest-valued alternative activity.

Representative full-bodied money: Money which is of negligible value as a commodity but is "backed by" (can be converted into, at a fixed nominal price) a valuable commodity, such as gold or silver.

Seigniorage: The process whereby governments gain "profit" by placing a face value on a coin that exceeds its inherent market value.

Standard of deferred payment: A property of an asset that makes it desirable for use as a means of settling debts maturing in the future; an essential property of money.

Store of value: The ability of an item to hold value over time; a necessary property of money.

Unit of accounting: A measure by which prices and values are expressed; the common denominator of the price system; an essential property of money.

Wealth: Net worth; the value of assets minus liabilities (debt), at a given moment in time.

PROBLEMS

2-1 Consider a barter economy in which ten goods and services are produced and exchanged. How many exchange rates exist in that economy?

2-2 Can paper money be more valuable than the market, or intrinsic, value of the paper itself?

2-3 Recently, five economists and a sociologist played poker. The sociologist was losing and, as a last measure, introduced U.S. postage stamps as his "money." Can Gresham's law help predict how the five economists reacted to this?

SELECTED REFERENCES

Angell, Norman, *The Story of Money* (New York: Frederick A. Stokes Co., 1929).

Brunner, Karl, and Allan A. Meltzer, "The Uses of Money: Money in the Theory of an Exchange Economy," *American Economic Review,* vol. 61, December 1971, pp. 784–805.

Einzig, Paul, *Primitive Money,* 2d ed. (New York: Oxford University Press, 1966).

Nussbaum, Arthur, *A History of the Dollar* (New York: Columbia University Press, 1957).

Chapter 3

The Changing Definition of the Money Supply

CHAPTER PREVIEW

1 Why is the money supply so difficult to measure?

2 What are the transactions and liquidity approaches to measuring the money supply?

3 How is money officially defined in the United States?

4 What is the best definition of the money supply?

Money is important. Changes in the total supply of money and changes in the rate at which money is growing affect important economic variables, such as the rate of inflation, interest rates, employment, and national income and output. Although there is widespread agreement among economists that money is important, they have never agreed on how to define and how to measure money. As Chapter 1 suggested, recent technological and regulatory changes have further contributed to the difficulty in defining and measuring money. In this chapter we will

1   Discuss why it is important to define and measure money
2   Analyze the two basic approaches to defining and measuring money
3   Show how money is defined officially by the Fed and relate the official definitions to the basic approaches analyzed in item **2** above
4   Explore how recent financial innovations have compounded the problems of defining and measuring money

WHY IT IS IMPORTANT TO DEFINE AND MEASURE MONEY

Because changes in the total supply and growth rate of money affect important economic variables, they can also affect the attainment of ultimate national economic goals. High employment, price stability (a situation in which neither significant inflation nor significant deflation exists), economic growth, and an equilibrium in international payments are all, directly or indirectly, related to changes in the total supply of money and changes in the growth of money. The optimal quantity and growth of money, therefore, is that which enables the nation to achieve these goals. Later chapters indicate how elusive these concepts of an "optimal" quantity and growth rate of money actually are.

Monetary policy—changing the supply of money by the Fed in order to achieve national economic goals—requires a meaningful definition of the money supply. In particular, monetary policy requires the following[1]:

1   A close correspondence must exist between the *theoretical* definition of money and the *empirical* (or measurable) definition of money. The real world doesn't allow scientists to measure their theoretical constructs perfectly.
2   The Fed must be able to control the empirically defined money supply and to meet the targets that it sets for the money supply with the tools at its disposal. The Fed cannot achieve ultimate national goals directly; what it

---

[1]See Bryan Higgins and Jon Faust, "NOWs and Super NOWs: Implications for Defining and Measuring Money," *Economic Review* (a publication of the Federal Reserve Bank of Kansas City) vol. 68, no. 1, January 1983, pp. 3–18, for an excellent discussion of the main topics in this chapter.

can do is use its powers to alter some "money-like" variables. The problem of setting monetary targets (or goals for the growth rate of money) is discussed in Chapter 26; the tools that the Fed can use to alter the money supply are analyzed in Chapters 14, 15, and 16.

3 The empirical definition of money must be closely and predictably related to ultimate national goals. It is not very useful to the nation if the Fed achieves its monetary-growth-rate targets unless such achievement alters economic variables in a desired direction.

In short, a successful monetary policy requires that the Fed properly measure money and effectively control its growth rate.

TWO APPROACHES TO DEFINING AND MEASURING MONEY

There is honest disagreement as to the proper *definition* of money and the "best" *measure* of money. The two basic approaches to measuring money are the transactions approach, which stresses the role of money as a medium of exchange, and the liquidity approach, which stresses the role of money as a temporary store of value.

The Transactions Approach   The transactions approach to measuring money emphasizes money's function as a medium of exchange. Proponents of this approach claim that the essence of money is that it (and only it) is accepted as a means of payment for other goods and services. They stress that this is an important difference between money and other assets; a qualitative difference exists between those assets that perform as a medium of exchange and all other assets. All assets serve as a store of value; only a few are accepted as a medium of exchange.

Given this theoretical preference for the definition of money, the transactions approach suggests that *only an asset that serves as a medium of exchange be included in the empirical measurement of money.* Such assets would include the coins and paper currency that circulate and are generally accepted as a means of payment. Also included would be transactions accounts, upon which checks can be written.

Regarding the second criterion for monetary policy, proponents of the transactions approach assert that the Fed *can* control the supply of money that is used to make transactions. Finally, many economists (some dating back to the nineteenth century, as Chapters 17 and 18 indicate) believe that money thus defined shows a reliable and predictable relationship to national economic goals. Households and businesses hold money in order to finance anticipated (and regular) expenditures in the near future; people hold "spending money." This is referred to as the *transactions motive* for holding money (discussed in Chapter 18) and is not to be confused with "saving money"— money held due to uncertainty in order to finance an uncertain amount of expenditures at some unknown time. This latter reason for holding money to meet emergencies is referred to as the *precautionary motive* (also discussed in Chapter 18).

Traditionally, assets held in such forms (coins, currency, transactions accounts) have not earned interest and therefore have been subject to an opportunity cost of forgone interest. For that reason, people can be expected to minimize the money they hold as a medium of exchange. If the total money supply were to increase (as a result of monetary authorities' actions or new discoveries of those metals used as money), then the community would be expected to increase its spending. In turn, this increase in spending might well increase national output, national income, employment, and the price level. A decrease in the money supply would lead to a predictable reduction in community spending, with predictable effects on the variables associated with national economic goals. A warning: We have assumed that money-supply changes have not been exactly offset by money-*demand* changes. That is, the relationship between changes in the money supply and changes in economic variables is described holding other things constant.

The Liquidity Approach   The liquidity approach to measuring money stresses that the essential distinguishing property of money is that it is the most liquid of all assets. The liquidity attribute of an asset refers to the ease with which the asset can be sold (or redeemed) at an unknown future time *at a known nominal dollar price* on short notice and with minimum costs.[2]

The Liquidity Continuum   This approach emphasizes the function of money as a store of value, and plays down the medium of exchange role that money plays. In effect, this approach implies that *money is not qualitatively different from other assets;* liquidity is a property of all assets, to some degree. Assets can be ranked along a continuum, ranging from money to financial assets such as stocks and bonds or real (nonfinancial) assets such as cars, stereos, and houses. Each of these assets serves as a store of value, but each is associated with a different degree of liquidity.

Money is the most liquid of all assets; it does not need to be converted into something else in order to be made spendable. Moreover, because the dollar is *the* unit of accounting (the specific measure in which prices and values are expressed), it can neither gain nor lose nominal value. The nominal value of a dollar bill is always $1. By contrast, a house is not a very liquid asset. Real estate prices fluctuate in value; the dollar price of a house in the future is very likely to be different from the dollar price of that house at present. A house, furthermore, may take a long time to sell, and substantial brokerage fees are involved in converting that asset called a house into a spendable asset called money.

---

[2]J. R. Hicks, "Liquidity," *Economic Journal,* vol. 72, no. 288, December 1962, p. 787. Note that for ease of exposition we are equating "money" with the U.S. "dollar"—which holds true only in the United States.

The Determinants of Liquidity   Why are some assets more liquid than others? In general, liquidity depends on two major factors: whether or not a *secondary market* (discussed in Chapter 5) exists for the asset, and the *term to maturity* of the asset.

Consider the financial asset "common stock," which is a piece of paper indicating ownership in a corporation. When a corporation starts out (or wants to expand or to "go public"), it sells stock shares in order to raise funds. The first time the stock is sold it is sold in a primary market; when it is resold (over and over) it is sold in a secondary market. Because secondary markets exist for stocks (and for most other financial assets), stocks are more liquid than they would be were there no organized secondary markets. Think of the transactions costs involved in lost time and effort in trying to sell 100 shares of stock if no secondary market existed. The liquidity of even a nonfinancial asset is increased by a secondary market. Can you see why the liquidity of automobiles is increased due to the existence of used-car lots?

Financial assets have differing terms to reach maturity. Stocks and money have no term to maturity; neither do some bonds (consols are nonmaturing bonds). Most bonds, however, do have a specific term to maturity. A bond is a credit instrument representing a promise made by a corporation or by a government to pay a specific amount of money in specified periods. Typically, a bond pays a specific amount per period for a specific length of time and then the face value is returned to the bond owner when the bond matures. Bonds have terms to maturity varying from 3 to 30 years. Suppose a bond has a face value of $1,000 and pays $100 per year for 3 years and then matures—at which time the bond purchaser gets back $1,000. If the original selling price of the bond were $1,000 (it need not have been), then this bond has had a yield of 10 percent and a 3-year term to maturity. Chapter 6 discusses bonds in more detail, and it indicates that as the rate of interest changes, bond prices (in the secondary market for bonds) also change. This means that it is possible for a person to resell a bond at a higher price than he or she paid for it (realize a capital gain) or resell a bond at a lower price (take a capital loss). The important thing to realize is that a *given* change in the market interest rate changes the price of long-term bonds more than it changes the price of short-term bonds. Because short-term bonds fluctuate in price less than long-term bonds do, short-term bonds are more liquid.

Liquidity and the Measurement of Money   Each person in the community selects some desirable asset portfolio (composition) consisting of money, financial assets, and nonfinancial assets; money is the most liquid of all the assets in the portfolio. The community is in equilibrium when no one has an incentive to rearrange his or her portfolio. Of course, diverse assets have differing degrees of liquidity (and therefore risk), and people have differing feelings about how much risk they wish to assume. Other things being constant, the higher the risk associated with a financial asset, the greater must be the expected rate of return before people will acquire that asset voluntarily. In equilibrium, each individual is satisfied with his or her particular portfolio, which doubtlessly differs among people according to their diverse desires for liquidity and their disparate expectations concerning future events.

If the Fed changes the supply of money (other things being constant), the community's equilibrium is disturbed. An increase in the money supply means (immediately) that the community is now more liquid than it wants to be. It is reasonable to assume that this increase in liquidity—an increase in the proportion of the public's portfolio held in money—will cause further portfolio adjustments until a new equilibrium is established. The community might now be inclined to purchase assets that are less liquid. If it purchases financial assets with its newfound liquidity, a series of events (discussed in detail in Chapter 7) ensues which causes market interest rates to fall. This leads to an increase in investment and to an increase in household expenditures on durable (long-lasting) consumer goods. If the community spends its excess liquidity on nonfinancial assets, community spending will increase directly. In either case, national income, employment, national output, and the price level are potentially increased. One can imagine that the results would be precisely the opposite were the Fed to reduce the community's liquidity (lower its ratio of money to total assets) by reducing the money supply. A warning: Once again we have analyzed changes in the money supply holding other things constant. If money-supply increases lead to offsetting increases in the *demand* for liquidity too, then our conclusions are invalid. We return to this issue in Chapter 24.

Using a liquidity definition of money and a portfolio-adjustment approach to explain the role of money in the economy leads one to broaden the definition of money beyond the transactions approach. The liquidity approach includes in the measurement of money those assets that are highly liquid, i.e., those assets that can be converted to money quickly, without loss of nominal dollar value and without much cost. In general, any asset that guarantees to the holder a fixed nominal dollar value in the future is a candidate for inclusion in the liquidity measure of money. Another way to state this is that any asset for which no nominal capital gain or loss is possible qualifies as a perfectly liquid asset and is therefore money. Those assets for which only slight capital gains or losses are possible are highly liquid and are called **near monies.** Clearly, those assets that serve as mediums of exchange—coins, paper currency, and transactions accounts—meet this requirement. So, too, do passbook savings accounts in thrift institutions. As will be seen shortly, it is not clear where the cutoff point along the asset/liquidity continuum should be.

HOW THE FED MEASURES THE MONEY SUPPLY

The Fed incorporates both the transactions approach and the liquidity approach when it measures the money supply. Each approach is discussed in turn.

M1: The Transactions Approach Consider Table 3-1; it shows what specifically is included in the transactions approach and it gives the specific measurements for each component, as of April 1983. The $137.4 figure in the table represents the value of coins and paper currency outside the U.S. Treasury, the Federal Reserve banks, and the vaults of commercial banks. The paper currency consists of $1, $2, $5, $10, $20, $50, and $100 denominations; $500,

TABLE 3-1 The Fed's Measure of Money as a Medium of Exchange: M1, April 1983

M1 Component	Amount
Currency	$137.4
Transactions accounts	
Demand deposits	242.4
Other checkable deposits	120.3
Traveler's checks	4.4
Total M1	$504.5

*Components do not exactly sum to M1 because of rounding.

$1,000, $5,000, and $10,000 bills were all discontinued in 1945. If high inflation rates return, we might see them again.

Currency Currency consists of the following:

1 *Coins minted by the U.S. Treasury:* Coins are credit money because the value of the metal in each coin is normally less than the face value of the coin. From time to time, the market value of the metal used in coins has risen so high that the coins have disappeared from circulation. (Recall Gresham's law.) Individuals have held the coins or melted them down and sold the metal in spite of the fact that this practice was and still is illegal. For example, in 1950, the market value of the silver in a dime was 7 cents. By 1962, the market value had risen to 10 cents. Dimes minted with a 90 percent silver content disappeared from circulation. Many were melted down for the silver content; many more were kept as collectors' items. When silver was selling for $2 per ounce, a bag of silver coins with a face value of $1,000 had a market value of $1,550 dollars.

2 *Federal Reserve notes issued by the Federal Reserve banks and U.S. notes issued by the U.S. Treasury:* Until 1960, all one-dollar bills were issued by the Treasury and were called silver certificates. There are several hundred million dollars' worth of silver certificates still in circulation. The remainder of the paper bills in circulation are Federal Reserve notes. Federal Reserve notes are printed by the Bureau of Engraving and Printing under contract to the various Federal Reserve banks. As will be shown in Chapter 12, the Federal Reserve System consists of twelve separate banks. Each of these banks issues its own currency. Look at Figure 3-1, which shows a typical one-dollar bill. It was issued by the Federal Reserve Bank of Atlanta, as indicated by the letter F, to the left of Washington's picture. If you look at all of the Federal Reserve notes that you have, you will find that they were

issued by one or more of the twelve Federal Reserve branches. The legend designating each branch is as follows:

A—Boston	G—Chicago
B—New York	H—St. Louis
C—Philadelphia	I —Minneapolis
D—Cleveland	J—Kansas City
E—Richmond	K—Dallas
F—Atlanta	L—San Fransisco

The increased importance of currency in the United States money supply Both on a per capita basis and as a percentage of M1, currency has increased in significance in the United States. In 1973, for example, the amount of currency in circulation per American family was about $325. In 1983 it had risen to about $602. As a percentage of M1, it has risen from 20.5 percent at the end of 1960 to over 28 percent at the end of 1983.

FIGURE 3-1   **A Typical One Dollar Bill.**

Why has there been such a large expansion of the use of currency in the 1970s and 1980s? We're not sure, but one major reason is the increased size of the so-called underground economy.

The growth in the underground economy The **underground, or subterranean, economy** consists of cash transactions that are unreported to the Internal Revenue Service as income. Such cash transactions occur for several reasons, which include but are not limited to drug sales, tax evasion, and payment of wages to illegal immigrants.

Putting illegal activities (such as drug dealing and prostitution) aside, the major increase in the underground economy has been due to individuals' attempts to avoid taxation by federal and state governments. Tax rates in the United States have been rising for some time now. As more and more individuals have been put into higher and higher tax brackets, the incentive to engage in unreported economic exchange has increased. For example, many professional home repairpersons will do the work only if they are paid in cash so that there will be no record of their having received income.

Various estimates of the size of the underground economy have been made. The lowest is around 10 percent of the reported gross national product, and the highest reaches 30 percent.

Transactions Accounts Transactions accounts include demand deposits at commercial banks and other checkable deposits (OCDs).

Demand deposits in commercial banks Older money-and-banking texts emphasized the distinction between **commercial banks** and all other **depository institutions.** The distinction was crucial then because commercial banks were defined as the only type of financial (depository) institution allowed by law to accept demand deposits (checking accounts). This was a reasonable definition until 1981; such is not the case today, however. Demand deposits at commercial banks nevertheless remain the largest component of the M1 money supply.

The term **demand deposit** is used because such a deposit can be converted to currency on demand (immediately) or used to make a payment to a third party. The checking-account deposit itself does not have legal-tender status.[3] Nonetheless, demand deposits are clearly a medium of exchange in this economy. The physical check itself is not money, however; rather, it is the account balance that is money. That is why one talks in terms of demand deposits, or transaction account balances, rather than checks as constituting part of the money supply.

Other checkable deposits Of growing importance in all definitions of the money supply are other checkable deposits in commercial banks and thrift institutions. These consist of the following:

---

[3]Legal-tender status refers to something that, when offered in payment for debt, must be accepted—according to law.

HIGHLIGHT   How Money Enters Circulation

Currency is manufactured at the Bureau of Engraving and Printing and the U.S. Mint. It is then shipped to the U.S. Treasury and to the Federal Reserve for further distribution. It enters circulation, usually, when households and businesses cash checks at depository institutions and withdraw some portion of the check's value. This is an important point, because it indicates that the *public* determines what proportion of M1 is held in currency. The Fed can determine, within limits, what total M1 is, but the public determines its composition. This point will be stressed in Chapter 8 when money deposit expansion multipliers are analyzed.

1   *Negotiable orders of withdrawal (NOW) accounts:* These are interest-bearing savings accounts on which checks may be written, and they are issued by thrift institutions. Until 1981, **NOW accounts** were authorized only in New England, New York, and New Jersey. Since 1981, all states have allowed NOW accounts or their equivalent. Business corporations are not permitted to use NOW accounts.

2   *Super-NOW accounts:* As of July 5, 1983, thrift institutions were allowed to offer **Super-NOW accounts,** which allow unlimited checking. They require a minimum deposit of $2,500 and there is no interest-rate ceiling placed on these accounts.

3   *Automatic-transfer-system (ATS) accounts at commercial banks:* An **ATS account** is a combination of a savings account on which interest is paid on the outstanding balance and a regular checking account on which no interest is paid. Usually, the account holder keeps a relatively small balance in the checking account but writes checks freely. Whenever there is a negative balance in the checking account, an automatic transfer is made from the interest-earning savings account. In effect, the ATS account is the commercial banks' version of the NOW account, although commercial banks can now offer NOWs too. Both offer a way to earn interest on checking account funds and both are prohibited to business corporations.

4   *Credit-union-share-draft **(CUSD)** accounts:* Credit union members usually have the ability to write a type of check called a share draft. A credit union share draft is similar to a negotiable order of withdrawal.

5   *Demand deposits at mutual savings banks:* Mutual savings banks are thrift institutions that are nonprofit-oriented. Any profits remaining after operating expenses are paid are kept in a surplus account or distributed to depositors. They offer savings accounts, time deposits, and NOW accounts; only a few states allow mutual savings banks to offer demand deposits.

Traveler's Checks These checks are paid for by the purchaser at the time of transfer. The total quantity of traveler's checks outstanding issued by institutions other than banks is part of the M1 money supply.[4] American Express, Citibank, Cooks, and other institutions issue traveler's checks.

M2: The Liquidity Approach

The narrowest definition of the money supply, M1, does not include the so-called near monies, which are slightly less liquid assets. To the extent that an individual's willingness to spend depends on his or her total liquidity, the inclusion of near monies in the money supply provides a "better" definition of the money supply for the purpose of explaining changes in economic activity. This somewhat broader definition of the money supply is officially designated as **M2** by the Fed and is outlined in Table 3-2. M2 consists of M1 plus the following:

1 Savings and small denomination time deposits at all depository institutions
2 Overnight repurchase agreements at commercial banks
3 Overnight Eurodollars held by U.S. residents (other than banks) at Caribbean branches of member banks
4 Balances in money market mutual funds
5 Money market deposit accounts

Savings Deposits Savings deposits in all depository institutions (e.g., commercial banks, mutual savings banks, savings and loan associations, and credit unions) are part of the M2 money supply. A savings deposit is a type of **time deposit.** It is called a time deposit because, in principle, the owner of the deposit must give fourteen days' notice prior to withdrawing it or any part of it. Savings deposits also include the money market deposit account (introduced on December 14, 1982), which allows limited checking privileges (six checks per month) and unceilinged interest rates. Savings deposits can be of two kinds—statement or passbook.

Statement savings deposits A statement savings deposit is similar to a checking account because the owner (depositor) receives a monthly statement or record of deposits and withdrawals and the interest earned during the month. With the statement savings account, deposits and withdrawals can be made by mail.

Passbook savings accounts A passbook savings account requires that the owner physically present a paper passbook each time he or she makes a deposit or a withdrawal. The passbook is marked to record the deposits and withdrawals. In the United States, passbook savings deposits are more popular than statement savings deposits.

---

[4]Banks place the funds that are to be used to redeem traveler's checks in a special deposit account and they are therefore already counted as transactions accounts. Nonbank issues, however, do not place these funds in transactions accounts. Improvements in data collection have made it possible to estimate the size of nonbank traveler's checks; in June 1981 they were included in M1.

TABLE 3-2 A Fed Measure of Money as a Temporary Store of Value: M2 April 1983

Components	Amount
M1	504.4
Savings deposits	321.5
Small-denomination time deposits	729.7
Overnight RPs	42.3
Overnight Eurodollars	8.1
Money market mutual funds	146.7
Money market deposit accounts	341.2
Total*	2086.4

*M2 is not equal to the sum of its components for a technical reason. See any H-6 Series, a Federal Reserve statistical release.

Small-Denomination Time Deposits Time deposits include savings certificates and small certificates of deposit. To be included in the M2 definition of the money supply, such time deposits must be less than $100,000—hence the name *small*-denomination time deposits. The owner of a savings certificate, or a certificate of deposit (CD), is given a receipt indicating the amount deposited, the interest rate to be paid, and the maturity date. A CD is an actual certificate that indicates the date of issue, its maturity date, and other relevant contractual matters.

A variety of small-denomination time deposits are available. They include 6-month money market certificates as well as floating-rate (varying with market rates) certificates of $2\frac{1}{2}$ years' maturity or more.

Overnight Repurchase Agreements at Commercial Banks (REPOs, or RPs) A **repurchase agreement** may be made by a bank to sell Treasury or federal-agency securities to its customers, coupled with an agreement to repurchase them at a price that includes accumulated interest. REPOs help to fill a gap because businesses are not allowed to use NOW accounts; REPOs can be thought of as a financial innovation that bypasses regulation. They are discussed in Chapter 5.

Overnight Eurodollars Eurodollars are dollar-denominated deposits in foreign commercial banks and in foreign branches of U.S. banks. The phrase "dollar-denominated" simply means that although the deposit might be held at a Caribbean commercial bank, its value is stated in terms of U.S. dollars rather than in terms of the local currency. The term "Eurodollar" is inaccurate since banks outside continental Europe participate in the so-called Eurodollar market, and also because banks in some countries issue deposits denominated in German marks, Swiss marks, British sterling, and Dutch guilders. Only those deposits made overnight by U.S. residents (other than banks) at Caribbean branches of member banks are included as part of the M2 money supply.

Money Market Mutual Fund Balances   Many individuals and institutions keep part of their assets in the form of shares in **money market mutual funds.**[5] These mutual funds invest only in short-term credit instruments. The majority of these money market funds allow check-writing privileges, provided that the size of the check exceeds some minimum, such as $500 or $1,000.

Money Market Deposit Accounts   These are accounts issued by banks and thrift institutions. They have no minimum maturity, allow limited checking privileges, and pay an interest rate comparable to the money market mutual fund rate.

M3: An Even Broader Definition of the Money Supply   An even broader definition of the money supply officially given by the Federal Reserve system is called **M3**. M3 consists of M2 plus the following:

1   Large-denomination time deposits at all depository institutions
2   Term repurchase agreements at commercial banks and savings and loan associations
3   Institution-only money market mutual fund balances

Large-Denomination Time Deposits   These types of time deposits have face values of over $100,000. A major difference between large-denomination and small-denomination time deposits is that the former are *negotiable;* they can be bought and sold with no problem or penalty. A small-denomination time deposit is not negotiable. The most common name for a large-denomination time deposit is **jumbo certificate of deposit, or jumbo CD.** Most large-denomination CDs are owned by business firms that invest idle funds for short periods of time. Another main feature of large CDs is that since 1973 no interest-rate limitations have been placed on them in any way. (Interest-rate limitations have traditionally been placed on small-denomination time deposits.)

Term Repurchase Agreements at Commercial Banks and Savings and Loan Associations   Term REPOs (or RPs) are like overnight RPs described previously, but they are for longer than overnight. They may be for a week or a month.

---

[5]First introduced by Merrill Lynch in 1975, they are pools of funds contributed by investors. The institution, or "fund," invests the pooled money in short-term instruments such as Treasury bills, bank CDs, and commercial paper (all discussed in Chapter 5).

A Measure of Liquidity: L   The Federal Reserve System uses a broad definition of liquidity and labels it L. **L** consists of M3 plus "other liquid assets such as term Eurodollars held by U.S. residents other than banks, banker's acceptances, commercial paper, Treasury bills and other liquid Treasury securities, and U.S. savings bonds."[6]

WHAT IS THE "BEST" DEFINITION OF THE MONEY SUPPLY?

Is there a "best" definition of the money supply? Is it M1, M2, M3, or L? No answer can be given to such an important question. It turns out that for different purposes, different definitions of the money supply are best. For example, if one wishes to know what definition of the money supply is most controllable by the Federal Reserve System, it is the narrowest definition, or M1. On the other hand, that definition which seems to correlate best with economic activity is one of the broader definitions, M2 or M3—the results are mixed. The appropriate definition depends on the question being asked. Also, the best definition will change as technology changes and as the financial sector of the economy engages in innovation.

CURRENT CONTROVERSY

Is M1 Still a Measure of the Transactions Concept of Money?*

A number of financial innovations that arose in the 1970s seem to have blurred the distinction between M1—the transactions notion of money—and other assets. Money market mutual funds (MMMF), introduced in 1975, had grown to over a $200-million industry by 1983. Repurchase agreements and overnight Eurodollars deposits are now being used extensively by corporations to earn interest on very short-term balances that are used basically for transactions.

   More important, perhaps, are the NOW accounts and the Super-NOWs. The NOW accounts are just like checking accounts, and the Super-NOWs offer limited checking privileges. These instruments prompted the redefinition of the narrowest (transactions) definition of money.

---

[6]*Federal Reserve Bulletin.* These terms are discussed in Chapters 5 and 6.

*See "NOWs and Super NOWs: Implications for Defining and Measuring Money," cited in footnote 1. Also see John A. Tatom, "Money Market Deposit Accounts, Super NOWs and Monetary Policy," *Review*, Federal Reserve Bank of St. Louis, vol. 65, no. 3, March 1983, pp. 5–25.

In 1979 the narrowest definition of money was called M1 and included currency and demand deposits at commercial banks. In 1980 the narrowest definition of money was called M1A; it included the currency, demand deposits at commercial banks, *and* traveler's checks issued by new bank corporations. Also in that year M1B was defined; it included the components of M1A *and* NOW accounts, ATS accounts, and credit-union share accounts. The Fed again has changed its narrowest definition of money; M1 is now the narrowest definition and it is equivalent to M1B (it adds demand deposits at mutual savings banks). In December 1982 the money market deposit account (MMDA) was introduced, and it was included under M2—under money market mutual funds. The MMDA was an immediate success, pulling in more than $138 billion in deposits during the first fourteen weeks it was offered! When Super-NOW accounts were introduced in January 1983, they were included in M1 under "other checkable deposits."

By now it is clear that financial innovations have made the job of defining money difficult. They have also blurred the distinction between transactions accounts and other slightly less liquid assets. Surely a significant portion of M1 consists of money that is *not* used to finance anticipated short-run expenditures; if so, then changes in M1 may not be closely and predictably related to changes in total spending.

What is at issue here is not a mere taxonomical question. It may be that financial innovations, as they arise, cause distortions in the measures of M1, M2, and M3. As people move money from one credit instrument to another (seeking higher interest earnings), the various Ms move in different directions, or some move while others remain constant. Thus we get changes in the various money measures *but nothing essential may be happening to consumer or business behavior*. The interpretation of changes in the various money measures becomes difficult. Equally important, control over the various money measures becomes difficult; if the Fed can't attain its growth-rate targets for M1 or M2, then its ability to reach ultimate national economic goals is thereby hampered. We return to the issue of monetary control in Chapter 26. Right now you need only be aware of the seeds of the problem—the difficulty of separating the transactions definition of money from the liquidity definition, or distinguishing between the function of money as a medium of exchange and its function as a temporary store of value.

CHAPTER SUMMARY

1 Since money is what is *accepted* as money, in practice money assumes different forms. Also, technological changes in the banking industry lead to changes in the form of money. For these reasons, money is difficult to define and measure.

2 There are two basic approaches to measuring the money supply: the transactions approach and the liquidity approach. The transactions approach stresses that money is a medium of exchange. This approach excludes asset forms that cannot directly be used to make transactions; U.S. gov-

ernment securities and savings deposits are excluded by such a strict definition of money because they must first be converted before spending. The liquidity approach stresses that very liquid assets can, by definition, be easily converted into money without loss of nominal value; any capital gains or losses are very small. As such, they represent an asset form that measures *potential* transactions; this approach includes near monies in the definition of money.

3 Today there are several official definitions of money: M1, M2, M3, and L; this is a movement from narrow to broad measures of money. The broader measures include less liquid assets.

4 The best definition of money depends on the purpose to which the definition is put. M1 is the measure of money over which the Fed has most control, but M2 and M3 seem to be more highly correlated with economic activity.

GLOSSARY

ATS accounts: Automatic-transfer-system accounts; a combination of interest-bearing savings accounts and non-interest-bearing checking accounts, by which funds are automatically transferred from savings accounts to checking accounts when the latter are overdrawn.

Commercial bank: A bank that accepts demand deposits, as well as time and savings deposits.

Currency: The value of coins minted by the U.S. Treasury, the Federal Reserve notes issued by the Federal Reserve banks, and the U.S. notes issued by the U.S. Treasury.

CUSD accounts: Credit-union share-drafts accounts; accounts similar to NOW accounts owned by credit-union members.

Demand deposits: A deposit placed in a depository institution, payable on demand and transferable by check.

Depository institutions: Financial institutions that accept deposits for savers and lend those deposits out at interest.

Eurodollar deposits: Deposits denominated in U.S. dollars but held in banks outside the United States, usually (but not always) in overseas branches of U.S. banks.

Fed: The Federal Reserve System; the central banking system of the United States.

Jumbo certificates of deposit (jumbo CD): A large (face value over $100,000) time deposit, issued to businesses, that matures at a specific date; the interest rate depends on market conditions at the time of issuance.

L: M3 plus other liquid assets (such as Treasury bills and U.S. savings bonds).

M1: The value of currency, demand deposits in commercial banks, transactions deposits in thrift institutions, and traveler's checks.

M2: M1 plus (1) savings and small-denomination time deposits at all depository institutions, (2) overnight repurchase agreements at commercial banks, (3) overnight Eurodollars held by U.S. residents (other than banks) at Caribbean branches of member banks, and (4) balances of money market mutual funds.

M3: M2 plus (1) large-denomination (over $100,000) time deposits at all depository institutions, (2) term repurchase agreements at commercial banks and savings and loan associations, and (3) institution-only money market mutual fund balances.

Money market mutual funds: Funds from the public which an investment company accepts and uses to acquire credit instruments. The funds can usually be withdrawn by checks written on the fund.

Near monies: Assets that are highly liquid but are not considered M1 money, such as U.S. Treasury bills and savings deposits in banks and in savings and loan associations; only slight capital gains or losses are likely on near monies.

NOW accounts: Negotiable order of withdrawal accounts; interest-bearing savings accounts on which checks can be written.

Repurchase agreement at a commercial bank (REPO, or RP): An agreement made by a bank to sell Treasury or federal agency securities to its customers, coupled with an agreement to repurchase them at a price that includes accumulated interest.

Thrift institutions: Mutual savings banks, savings and loan associations, and credit unions.

Time deposits: Interest-bearing bank deposits, which require 14 days notice prior to withdrawal.

Transactions accounts: NOW accounts, ATS accounts, CUSD accounts, and demand deposits at mutual savings banks.

Underground, or subterranean, economy: That economy which consists of illegal activities and otherwise legal activities that are unreported to the Internal Revenue Service.

PROBLEMS

3-1 How have technological changes altered the form of money?

3-2 What are the components of M1?

3-3 What are the components of M2?

SELECTED REFERENCES

Higgins, Bryan, and Jon Faust, "NOWs and Super NOWs: Implications for Defining and Measuring Money," *Economic Review,* Federal Reserve Bank of Kansas City, January 1983, pp. 3–18.

Porter, Richard D., Thomas D. Simpson, and Eileen Manskopf, "Financial Innovation and the Monetary Aggregates," *Brookings Papers on Economic Activity,* no. 1, 1979.

Tatom, John A., "Money Market Deposit Accounts, Super NOWs and the Monetary Policy," *Review,* Federal Reserve Bank of St. Louis, March 1983, pp. 5–25.

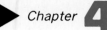

Chapter **4**

Financial Intermediation and the Origins of Banking

CHAPTER PREVIEW

1. How does the existence of money facilitate the separation of the acts of saving and investment?

2. How does money facilitate the transfer of funds from saver to investor?

3. What is financial intermediation, and what are its advantages?

4. Why did the process of coining arise, and how did banking originate in the goldsmith craft?

5. How did fractional reserve banking evolve?

FINANCIAL INTERMEDIATION

Chapter 2 indicated that barter provides only a specific store of purchasing power; people must save by acquiring real goods directly. When people save in a barter economy, they do so by "nonconsuming" (or by not selling) all the goods they produce or all that they earn by offering their services to an employer. In a money economy, **saving** is also defined as nonconsumption of income; saving equals income minus consumption. In a money economy, however, saving takes the form of a *generalized* purchasing power—money. People acquire money instead of goods.

In a barter economy, **investment,** the purchase of productive equipment—such as physical structures, machines, and inventories—can be undertaken through *personal* saving.[1] Would-be investors who want to expand their business operations or start a business do so by consuming less than their income and then trading the real goods that they thereby acquire for investment goods.

When an economy evolves from a barter to a money standard, it becomes easier for people to separate the act of saving from the act of investment.[2] Investors don't have to save personally; they can obtain generalized purchasing power (money) from savers. This is beneficial to savers because they gain a generalized store of value and because they can earn interest on this extension of credit. Savers would not voluntarily make such an exchange unless they perceived a benefit from doing so. Part of the gain is that interest earnings allow them to consume more in the future. Investors perceive a gain because they can start a new business or expand their existing one. If everything works out well, investors can pay savers interest out of the profits they earn from their investments. (Chapter 6 indicates how the market interest rate is determined by the interaction of household saving and business investment.) Because society can now more easily separate the acts of saving and investment, it too is better off: Those who save are not usually the ones who seek to recognize a business opportunity and capitalize on it.

In short, a money economy encourages saving and investment, and it facilitates the transfer of purchasing power from savers to investors. These advantages promote economic growth and a rising living standard for the community.

As economies moved from barter to money, the stage was set for a new business: banking. By connecting savers (ultimate lenders) with investors (ultimate borrowers), banks could facilitate the transferral of purchasing power.

---

[1]Laypersons refer to "investments" in stocks, bonds, and other financial assets. Economists refer to such purchases as mere transfers of claims to real investment goods.

[2]Technically, credit can be extended in a barter economy, but money facilitates the transfer of purchasing power from saver to investor and also permits a more complex system of transference to evolve.

Banks provided a "middleperson" service—for a small fee, of course. The origin of banks is discussed at the end of this chapter.

As the economy and the financial system developed, other **financial institutions** (or financial intermediaries) emerged. Today, commercial banks, savings and loan associations, mutual savings banks, credit unions, insurance companies, pension funds, and mutual funds are all in the business of transferring funds from savers to investors. This process has come to be known as **financial intermediation,** which is analyzed below. The process of financial intermediation has spawned a variety of financial assets (or financial instruments, or credit instruments), such as stocks, bonds, mortgages, mutual funds, purchase agreements, etc. These financial assets are traded in specific *markets;* our financial system has evolved into a complex web wherein various types of financial institutions trade a wide variety of financial assets in many different financial markets, all of which are analyzed in Chapter 5.

CHANNELING SAVING TO INVESTMENTS

Financial markets perform the function of channeling saving funds to business investments. Two basic economic groups are households and businesses. Those households or businesses that spend more than their incomes are net borrowers; those specific households or businesses that spend less than their incomes are net savers. While it is possible for *specific* households or businesses to be net savers or net borrowers, as a *group,* households are net savers and as a *group,* businesses are net borrowers. For ease of exposition, we ignore household borrowing or business saving.

Direct Financing Businesses can start anew or expand by obtaining funds directly from households. One way to do so is by selling **common stock** to the public. A common stock is an evidence of part ownership in a corporation; it entitles the owner to vote on certain corporate decisions and to share in any profits. A share of common stock is a financial asset to the owner and a financial liability to the issuer, or corporation. A business can also obtain funds by issuing (selling) bonds. A **bond** is evidence that a promise has been made by a corporation to pay a specified amount of money in recognition of a loan to the business. The bond is a financial asset to the lender-owner and a financial liability (debt) to the borrower-corporation.

In both these examples, direct financing has occurred; businesses have borrowed directly from households. In turn, businesses use these saving funds to make purchases of plant, equipment, and inventory. Figure 4-1 shows the process of direct financing. Markets have evolved to facilitate direct financing. Stocks and bonds are *originally* sold in *primary markets;* often they are resold (many times), through transactions taking place in *secondary markets.* Primary and secondary markets are analyzed in Chapter 5.

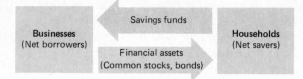

FIGURE 4-1 **Direct Financing.** This figure shows the process of direct financing. Borrowers borrow directly from households by selling them stocks and bonds. No financial intermediaries are used to channel saving into investment.

Financial Intermediation Indirect financing occurs as a result of financial intermediation. Financial institutions, acting as middlepersons, perform the function of channeling saving funds from households (ultimate lenders) to businesses (ultimate borrowers). For example, commercial banks accept monetary liabilities, such as demand deposits and savings deposits; thrift institutions accept monetary liabilities, such as passbook savings and time deposits; and insurance companies accept monetary liabilities, such as premium payments.[3] In turn, financial institutions purchase assets (relend the funds). For example, commercial banks purchase IOUs from businesses, and thrift institutions purchase mortgages from home buyers (this latter transaction implies a relending back to households).

---

[3]Monetary liabilities to financial institutions are simultaneously monetary assets to depositors.

HIGHLIGHT International Comparisons of Saving and Investment

The following table shows international comparisons of saving and investment. The saving rate is defined as the ratio of a nation's personal saving to its disposable income (net national product minus taxes plus transfers). The investment percentage rate equals the ratio of investment expenditures to gross national product (GNP).

The United States apparently has the lowest saving rate and the lowest investment rate.

Some people maintain that these low-saving and investment rates are responsible for the reduction in the United States' economic growth rate.

Country	Saving Rate, %	Investment Rate, %
Japan	20.1	23.5
France	15.6	16.3
United Kingdom	15.1	15.4
West Germany	14.5	15.6
Italy	23.8	14.4
United States	5.6	10.9

Source: Adapted from an editorial in *The Wall Street Journal*, July 6, 1981.

Financial intermediation allows access to funds by smaller businesses (corporate and noncorporate) for whom it is impractical (because of high transactions costs) to sell stocks and bonds. Financial intermediation also benefits smaller *savers;* many small savers can pool their funds in a financial institution which can thereby make larger loans. Finally, financial intermediation allows savers to reduce risk; instead of lending to a specific business, a given household lends to a financial institution. This is a less risky transaction for households because (1) deposits are insured by regulatory agencies and (2) financial institutions gather many funds from many small savers and relend these funds to a variety of borrowers. Each depositor, in effect, has made a very small loan to *many* businesses and households, and the risk therefore has been spread over many types of loans and many different borrowers. It is extremely unlikely that all, or even most, of these loans will not be repaid.

We turn now to a very brief history of the evolution of banks from humble goldsmith shops to powerful modern corporations.

THE ORIGIN OF BANKING

Barter was inconvenient and recognized as such, even in primitive economic systems. Uncoined metals were desirable for religious and ornamental purposes, their durability, and their high value for both nonmoney and monetary uses. Bullion (uncoined bars, or ingots, of gold or silver), however, has serious disadvantages as a medium of exchange. Weighing and assaying apparatus to assure quality was not always available at the site of exchange, and short-weighing and adulteration came to represent an implicit transactions cost. Coinage, however, represented a solution to the problems of using bullion as money. (It also marked the entry of government into monetary matters and that role has, for better or worse, continued.) The king's seal imprinted upon a lump of metal certified a specific weight of metal of a given purity. The names of many present-day monetary units (pounds, lira, and shekels) were originally units of weight.

Although coinage represented an important advancement in the development of money, certain disadvantages remained. Among the more significant were:

1 The possibility of theft of money being transported or stored
2 Transportation costs
3 The absence of an interest return on the coins

The Goldsmith Largely as a result of the danger of theft, the practice arose of leaving precious bullion and coins in the custody of goldsmiths. Since goldsmiths worked with those precious metals, they, of necessity, had established the means to protect them. This made goldsmiths the natural choice to receive and store monetary gold and silver for wary owners. These owners, who were the first "depositors" in banking history, doubtless expected that the custodians of their monetary wealth would hold it all intact. The custodian may have performed this service as a favor for friends, but as the practice of safeguarding others' money became more prevalent, the goldsmith began imposing charges.

At this early stage in the history of banking, a depositor who wanted to make a payment for a transaction would go to the custodian, redeem some of his coins, and use them to make the payment. The inconvenience in this procedure is apparent. It would certainly be much easier to transfer a *claim* against the depositor's coins than to transfer the coins themselves. Warehouse receipts (papers documenting the precious metal coins in storage) signed by the custodian therefore began to be used as payment. These early "goldsmith notes" were acceptable to the payee for one reason—the payee believed that the notes could be exchanged for gold coins at the goldsmith's place of business. A vital step in the evolution of money had occurred. People began to use paper claims (instead of the precious metal coins, or specie, themselves) as a medium of exchange.

The Goldsmith Becomes a Banker

The next step in the development of banking was the goldsmiths' discovery that they need not hold in their vaults all the coins deposited with them. As long as depositors were *confident* that they could convert their warehouse receipts into specie, they were content to make payments with the receipts and leave the gold and silver on deposit. Of course, some withdrawals were made during each business day, but additional precious metal coin deposits were also being received each day. Goldsmiths soon realized that, on average, daily withdrawals were about equal to daily deposits. Nevertheless, there were days when withdrawals exceeded deposits. If goldsmiths could predict those days when withdrawals were likely to exceed deposits, and by how much, then they could hold a contingency **reserve.**

The goldsmiths wrote warehouse receipts for a much larger value than the value of the precious metal coins they were safeguarding. Thus, the value of "money" (or reserves) the goldsmiths had on hand to meet withdrawals in gold and silver coins represented only a fraction of the value of all the warehouse receipts they had issued. The concept of **fractional reserve banking** was born, and goldsmiths were transformed from mere custodians of specie into bankers. If the practice originated surreptitiously (as it doubtlessly did), the secret was soon out. The public could be convinced, however, that a mutual advantage existed in the fractional reserve system. The banker provided safety, convenience, ease of transfer, and bookkeeping services at little or no charge to the public. In exchange, the banker was allowed to use the public's deposits as reserves against lending activity. As is the case in most communities of interest, a way to achieve their mutual advantages was found. Any moral or ethical implications of holding less than 100 percent reserves in order to increase profits have long since been rationalized; the only problem is the possibility of a sporadic failure of confidence and a "run" on the bank (when people rush to get their money out of the bank before reserves are

The Bank of England. The Old Lady of Threadneedle Street, then and now. *(Courtesy of Culver Pictures and United Press International.)*

depleted). Sound, conservative practices and demeanor by banks and bankers helped to alleviate the fears of the public, and fractional reserve banking had arrived.

HIGHLIGHT   Modern Goldsmiths

The following table indicates the vital statistics of the top fifty largest bank holding companies. A bank holding company links together the management of a group of banks or a group of enterprises engaged in banking-related businesses.

Source: Adapted from *Forbes,* April 11, 1983, p. 130.

1983 Annual Banking Survey

50 largest bank holding companies: a statistical profile.

Rank	Total Assets	Total Deposits	Nonperform Assets % Total Assets	Total Loans	Loan Loss Reserves as % of Loans	Total Invest- ments	Standby Letters of Credit	Total Capital	Long- Term Debt % Capital	Total Operating Income	Net Income[4]	Company and Headquarters
1	$129,997	$76,538	1.4%	$86,524	0.9%	$4,771	$15,313	$15,381	68.4%	$17,814	$747.0	Citicorp (NY)
2	122,221	94,342	2.1	74,591	0.9	7,149	6,795	6,761	32.3	14,955	388.8	BankAmerica (Cal)
3	80,863	56,858	1.9	55,156	1.1	4,130	5,300	4,611	28.7	10,171	332.5	Chase Manhattan (NY)
4	64,041	43,825	1.5	42,514	0.9[5]	2,527	7,700	4,278	41.8	7,640	296.3	Mfrs Hanover (NY)
5	58,597	37,910	0.9	31,495	1.1[5]	6,112	5,600	3,419	20.7	6,885	441.7	JP Morgan (NY)
6	48,275	27,998	1.7	29,768	1.1	3,802	6,140	2,546	23.6	5,515	269.1	Chemical New York (NY)
7	42,899	28,175	4.5	32,820	1.1	2,065	4,340	2,982	42.7	5,900	84.4	Continental Illinois (Ill)
8	40,884	30,542	2.8	22,893	1.2	4,164	1,600	2,792	35.9	4,608	228.4	First Interstate Bncp (Cal)
9	40,427	24,493	1.4	21,034	1.2[5]	1,755	5,638	1,996	22.1	4,639	228.5	Bankers Trust NY (NY)
10	36,991	25,848	2.2	24,927	1.3[5]	1,920	2,253	2,806	46.9	4,491	234.1	Security Pacific (Cal)
11	35,876	27,419	2.4	21,830	1.0[5]	1,315	3,233	2,178	31.5	4,402	144.0	First Chicago (Ill)
12	24,939	18,195	3.1	16,131	1.0	703	1,909	1,393	15.3	2,894	71.1	Crocker National (Cal)
13	24,814	18,180	2.3	18,838	1.0	604	824	2,482	55.7	3,290	141.8	Wells Fargo (CAL)
14	21,030	14,405	2.1	12,654	1.3	3,230	1,024	1,627	31.5	2,416	222.9	InterFirst (Tex)
15	20,294	12,328	1.7	11,365	1.6[5]	1,407	929	1,561	31.6	2,355	142.7	Mellon National (Pa)
16	20,239	15,057	2.1	12,182	1.2	1,379	1,055	1,489	40.7	2,412	88.4	Marine Midland Banks (NY)
17	19,514	14,153	1.1	9,975	1.4[5]	1,025	1,109	1,127	30.6	2,277	82.6	Irving Bank (NY)
18	18,267	11,674	1.7	10,335	1.2	1,390	1,013	1,295	31.7	2,745	129.1	First Natl Boston (Mass)
19	18,217	13,212	1.0	9,760	1.3	2,350	490	974	10.5	1,798	170.0	Texas Comm Bancshs (Tex)
20	17,585	11,971	1.6	10,674	1.3	2,554	519	2,183	51.8	2,081	114.1	Northwest Bancorp (Minn)
21	17,218	11,942	1.5	9,950	1.3	2,545	688	1,192	25.5	1,934	156.7	RepublicBank (Tex)
22	16,899	11,877	2.2	9,161	1.1	2,656	1,102	1,352	31.9	1,961	115.9	First Bank System (Minn)
23	16,567	13,355	1.8	9,366	1.4[5]	2,374	900	1,014	12.5	1,729	132.9	First City Bancorp (Tex)
24	12,724	8,873	2.1	7,496	0.9	1,022	561	608	16.9	1,523	74.3	Bank of New York (NY)
25	12,407	8,580	1.3	5,684	1.2	1,809	317	871	13.9	1,406	77.4	NBD Bancorp (Mich)

1982 size measures ($millions)

26	11,611	0.9	5,384	1.5	1,804	566	859	20.1	1,307	115.7	PNC Financial (Pa)
27	11,560	1.3	5,559	1.4	1,955	237	801	33.8	1,073	77.0	NCNB (NC)
28	10,190	1.6	6,612	1.5[5]	1,291	672	725	23.9	1,142	103.3	Mercantile Texas (Tex)
29	10,028	8.0	7,226	2.4	421	285	580	21.1	1,398	−90.2	Seafirst (Wash)
30	9,280	0.5	2,536	1.6	1,229	84	767	38.9	1,249	75.2	Republic New York (NY)
31	8,325	3.6	5,551	1.0	375	1,067	465	23.1	1,061	28.9	European American[6] (NY)
32	7,545	1.3	4,302	1.1	584	405	403	13.6	859	31.0	Union Bank[6,7] (Cal)
33	7,378	1.1	3,088	1.1	1,299	145	412	6.8	752	42.1	Comerica (Mich)
34	7,274	1.1	3,573	1.3	930	111	593	27.4	845	48.7	Southeast Banking (Fla)
35	7,183	1.5	4,211	1.1[5]	1,034	87	411	0.0	807	51.0	Valley National (Ariz)
36	7,137	1.2	3,988	0.9	488	461	408	6.4	918	40.1	Harris Bankcorp (Ill)
37	6,932	0.5	3,385	1.4[5]	1,604	50	511	24.1	791	64.6	Barnett Banks of Fla (Fla)
38	6,927	1.3	3,925	1.2	891	120	503	22.9	773	67.3	Southwest Bancshs (Tex)
39	6,916	1.1	3,668	1.3	919	95	445	3.1	810	77.7	Wachovia (NC)
40	6,823	1.3	2,972	1.5	1,425	272	483	18.2	661	46.7	National City (Ohio)
41	6,807	2.4	4,082	1.1[5]	682	265	386	3.6	818	21.0	Natl Bank N Amer[6,7] (NY)
42	6,647	1.5[8]	4,669	2.9	306	181[8]	1,205	66.8	886	16.4	Walter E Heller Intl[9] (Ill)
43	6,504	3.5	4,406[5]	1.1[5]	647	126	438	21.1	789	3.3	Michigan National (Mich)
44	6,301	1.0	3,154	1.3	571	247	524	24.9	770	60.5	Philadelphia Natl (Pa)
45	6,253	2.2	3,399	1.0	568	325	368	8.1	826	33.6	Northern Trust (Ill)
46	6,168	0.8	2,886	1.6	999	56	357	22.0	663	50.0	First Union (NC)
47	6,011	1.9	3,985	1.9[5]	1,159	143	409	9.8	718	86.7	Allied Bancshares (Tex)
48	6,005	1.0	3,299	1.4[5]	1,127	40	452	26.7	635	51.5	Citizens & Sthrn Ga (Ga)
49	5,865	2.2	4,026	1.2	371	155	439	18.1	732	39.2	Rainier Bancorp (Wash)
50	5,822	2.2	3,062	1.0	1,777	121	352	6.9	661	26.4	BancOhio (Ohio)

[1] Four-year average is a compounded annual rate: 1978/82.

[2] From continuing operations after security gains or losses excluding gain on sale of operations and extraordinary items.

[3] Net interest income on a tax-equivalent basis as a percent of average earning assets.

[4] From continuing operations before security gains or losses excluding gain on sale of operations and extraordinary items.

[5] Includes leases.

[6] Company not publicly traded.

[7] Bank only; not organized as a holding company.

[8] Bank only.

[9] Includes results of nonbank operations where applicable.

CURRENT CONTROVERSY

Does the United States Save and Invest Enough?

In recent years there has been considerable concern about the slowing down of the United States' economic growth rate and the slowing down of its labor productivity growth rate. The economic growth rate is measured by the annual percentage change in real (inflation-adjusted) national output, or real GNP. Labor productivity is measured by the ratio of real GNP to the quantity of labor required to produce that output. One important determinant of both economic growth and labor productivity growth is the rate of capital-goods expansion—that is, investment. As this chapter indicated, saving must take place before investment is possible.

The first Highlight presented in this chapter indicated that, relative to other developed nations, the United States has low saving and investment ratios. Two important questions come to mind: (1) Why are U.S. saving and investment ratios relatively low? (2) Are low saving and investment ratios necessarily bad?

Why are U.S. saving and investment ratios relatively low? Many experts offer different reasons. In a later chapter, we discuss whether federal government borrowing to finance its expenditures competes with business borrowing and therefore reduces the saving funds available for business investment. Here we consider whether high U.S. tax rates adversely affect saving.

It is alleged that higher tax rates reduce saving in the following manner. Interest earnings are taxed. When people decide how to divide their income between present consumption and saving (for future consumption), they are really concerned with the *after-tax* interest rate earnings on saving. At any given real interest rate, the higher the tax rate, the lower the after-tax real interest rate. The lower the after-tax real interest rate, the more people are likely to substitute present consumption for future consumption and the less they are likely to save from a given income level. Higher tax rates, therefore, provide disincentives to save.

While this analysis is fine as far as it goes, it may not go far enough. If people save in order to meet future economic needs (such as retirement), a lower after-tax rate of return may force them to save more. In order to see why, assume zero inflation for ease of exposition and consider a case in which a family has a goal of saving $100,000 for retirement. If tax rates rise and cause the after-tax real interest rate to fall, the family must now save more out of its same income level in order to reach the $100,000 total savings goal.

It seems that we have reasons to believe that higher tax rates, which reduce after-tax interest rates, induce people to save less *and* to save more! It follows that we can't decide theoretically what the *net* effect will be of higher income tax rates that reduce after-tax interest rates.

Is a lower saving and investment ratio necessarily bad? At first blush, it seems that this situation is bad because a lower investment ratio slows down a nation's rate of economic growth. As indicated in earlier chapters, economic growth is one of our national economic goals.

It is important to realize that a trade-off exists between present consumption and future consumption. In order to consume more in the future, the community must save more now—and convert those saving funds in capital expansion. It can't be true that it is *always* better for a nation to increase its growth rate at the expense of present consumption; an optimal growth rate must reflect the community's preferences for present versus future consumption. In short, it is possible that the United States' growth rate has slowed because its residents want it to. People may be inclined to save less now, relative to the past, because they are not as willing to wait to consume in the future. Perhaps they feel that the future has become more uncertain. If so, who can say they are wrong?

CHAPTER SUMMARY

1. People save in a barter economy by nonconsuming all the goods they receive for their work efforts; they thereby acquire real goods. Investment also requires nonconsumption of real-goods income, which then must be traded for plant and equipment.

2. Money makes it easier for people to separate the acts of saving and investment. Saving represents a nonexpenditure out of money income; when people save they accumulate money, or a generalized store of purchasing power. This generalized store of purchasing power, or saving funds, can be turned over to an investor—who need not personally engage in the act of saving. This transfer of purchasing power from savers to investors benefits savers—who benefit by earning interest paid willingly by profit-seeking investors. The transfer also benefits investors, who can now earn profits from which interest payments can be made, because they are not forced to save.

3. The transfer of funds from savers to investors can be made directly, through direct financing. Businesses can sell stocks or bonds directly to the public in primary markets. The public can increase the liquidity of these financial assets by reselling them in secondary markets.

4. Financial institutions, or financial intermediaries, have evolved as middle-persons who channel saving funds from savers to businesses that use the funds to make investments. This process is referred to as financial intermediation, and it is beneficial to society because it allows smaller businesses (for whom stock and bond issuance is impractical) access to saving funds. Financial intermediation also benefits smaller savers because financial institutions can pool their funds and diversify their investments, thereby reducing risk to small savers. Moreover, saving deposits are insured by regulatory agencies.

5. Uncoined metals were probably the first monies to pass the test of time. However, short-weighing and adulteration problems made the transactions costs high for such money. A king's seal imprinted on a specific quantity of metal—coinage—was an improvement over the use of

uncoined metal as money. Still, coinage did not eliminate the problems of (a) the danger of theft, (b) high transportation costs, or (c) an absence of an interest return on the coin.

6 Because coins can easily be stolen, people started leaving them (and their other valuable assets) with goldsmiths who had safe vaults. Before long, people left coins with goldsmiths in return for warehouse receipts, or claims against the deposits. Eventually, these warehouse receipts became a medium of exchange; this was a vital step in the evolution of money because people became accustomed to using paper claims, (instead of gold coins) as a medium of exchange.

7 Eventually, goldsmiths came to realize that it was not necessary to hold 100 percent of the specie deposited in reserve. Most withdrawal requests were met out of current deposits; only a contingency reserve was necessary for the periods when withdrawals exceeded new deposits. Goldsmiths loaned out money not necessary for reserves at interest, and depositors kept their wealth where it was safe. Thus was born the system of fractional reserve banking. The system worked well—except during bank runs.

GLOSSARY

Bond: Evidence that a corporation has received a loan and has promised to pay the lender a specific amount of money at specific future dates.

Common stock: A certificate of part-ownership in a corporation that entitles the owner to certain voting privileges and to a share in any profits.

Financial institutions: Institutions, such as commercial banks, savings and loan associations, insurance companies, pension funds, and so on, that receive funds from households and lend them to businesses and others.

Financial intermediation: The process by which financial institutions accept savings from households and lend these savings to businesses.

Fractional reserve banking: A system in which depository institutions hold reserves equal to less than 100 percent of total deposits.

Investment: Expenditures by businesses for plant and equipment, inventories, and improvements to plant.

Note issuance: The creation of paper money by a government or a central or commercial bank.

Reserves: The portion of total deposits held by depository institutions that is not lent; instead these funds are held to meet day-to-day withdrawals.

Saving: The part of income that is not spent on consumption.

PROBLEMS

4-1 How would you go about deciding the proper reserve ratio if you were an early goldsmith or an early banker? Would the proper ratio be different if a central bank existed to provide liquidity in times of bank runs?

SELECTED REFERENCES

Angell, Norman, *The Story of Money* (New York: Frederick J. Stokes Co., 1929).

Friedman, Milton, and Anna J. Schwartz, *A Monetary History of the United States, 1867–1960* (Princeton, N.J.: Princeton University Press, 1963).

Robertson, D. H., *Money,* 6th ed. (New York: Pitman Publishing Corp., 1948).

Interest Rates and Financial Markets

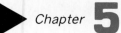
Financial Institutions and Credit Instruments

Up to this point we have discussed financial institutions, or financial intermediaries, in a general way. This chapter discusses the most important financial institutions that have evolved in the United States and elaborates on the process of financial intermediation. It also discusses financial disintermediation, why disintermediation occurs, and why it is unlikely to continue at such a rapid pace. Then the chapter turns to a discussion of credit instruments, the tools that financial institutions use when they perform the process of intermediation. Finally, the markets in which credit instruments are bought and sold are introduced.

FINANCIAL INSTITUTIONS

Table 5-1 shows the most important kinds of financial institutions, ranked by asset size. This table lists financial institutions that perform a common function. Therefore, to some extent these specific institutions are similar. Note, however, the tremendous differences in asset sizes; they perform similar functions but some are more important than others. A mere ranking by asset size, furthermore, *fails to distinguish among these institutions with respect to the types of assets and liabilities they acquire.* Table 5-2 helps to do so.

Commercial Banks   Commercial banks are the most important of all the financial institutions. They are ranked number one in asset size and they are the most diversified with respect to both assets and liabilities, as Table 5-2 indicates. Traditionally, their main sources of funds have been demand deposits. This situation has changed over the past twenty-five years; savings and time deposits (including certificates of deposit, called CDs) have become an even more important source of funds for commercial banks. Table 5-2 shows that commercial banks purchase a wide variety of assets.

TABLE 5-1 Financial Institutions Ranked by Asset Size (End of 1982)	
Financial Institution	**Asset Size***
Commercial banks	$1,972.2
Savings and loan associations	706.0
Life insurance companies	584.3
Private pension funds	336.1
State and local pension funds	253.1
Finance Companies	229.8
Investment Companies	76.8
Mutual savings banks	174.2
Money market funds	206.6
Credit unions	88.8
Total financial assets, in billions of dollars	$4,627.9

Source: '83 Savings and Loan Sourcebook, United States League of Savings Institutes, Chicago, Ill., 1983.

TABLE 5-2 Financial Intermediaries and Their Assets and Liabilities

Financial Intermediary	Liabilities	Assets
Commerical banks	Demand deposits, saving deposits, various other time deposits, NOW accounts	Car loans and other consumer debt, business loans, government securities, home mortgages
Savings and loan associations	Savings and loan shares, transaction accounts, various time deposits	Home mortgages, some consumer and business debt
Mutual savings banks	NOW accounts, savings accounts, and various time deposits	Home mortgages and some consumer and business debt
Credit unions	Credit union shares and transaction accounts	Consumer debt, long-term mortgage loans
Insurance companies	Insurance contracts, annuities, pension plans	Mortgages, stocks, bonds, real estate
Pension and retirement funds	Pension plans	Stocks, bonds, mortgages, time deposits
Money market mutual funds	Fund shares that have limited checking privileges	Short-term credit instruments such as large-size bank CDs, Treasury bills, and high-grade commercial paper

Savings and Loan Associations (S&Ls)   The source of funds for the approximately 500 S&Ls, traditionally, has been savings deposits; traditionally, S&Ls have purchased mortgage loans with those funds. You may recall that Chapter 1 indicated that such was the role of S&Ls—to assure low-cost financing for home buyers. While they still perform this function, recent deregulation has allowed S&Ls to broaden both their liabilities (they can offer NOW accounts and money market certificates—a form of time deposits) and their assets (they can make some consumer and business loans).

Mutual Savings Banks   The 500 or so mutual savings banks are very similar to S&L's with respect to functions. One major difference between them is that mutual savings banks are owned by their depositors, who are shareholders. Deregulation also has permitted these "mutuals" to broaden somewhat their liabilities and assets.

Credit Unions   Credit unions are organized as cooperatives for members who share a common interest—such as employees of a company, unions, a fraternal order, or a church. Members buy shares that make them eligible to borrow from the credit union. Until recently, credit unions were able to offer only savings deposits and purchase consumer debt; deregulation now permits them to offer transactions accounts and to purchase long-term mortgage loans. Along with S&Ls and mutual savings banks, credit unions comprise the category of thrift institutions—or, simply, "thrifts."

Money Market Mutual Funds These institutions sprang up in the mid-1970s and have grown dramatically. People buy shares in a fund and they have limited checking privileges on these shares. Money market mutual funds purchase short-term credit such as large-size bank certificates of deposit, Treasury bills, and high-grade commercial paper—defined later in this chapter.

Insurance Companies These include life insurance and property and casualty insurance companies. Life insurance companies, which rank third in asset size, receive funds (premiums) that insure people against the financial consequences of death. Actuarial tables permit them to predict with great accuracy the number of annual deaths (and therefore the amount of money they must pay to policy beneficiaries) for long periods of time. They, consequently, purchase longer-term assets, such as long-term corporate bonds and long-term commercial (nonresidential) mortgages. Property and casualty insurance companies insure car owners against theft and collision and homeowners against fire and burglary. They are not as certain as to what their annual payments to policy-holders will be; consequently, they purchase highly liquid, short-term assets and high-grade bonds.

Pension and Retirement Funds These institutions are akin to life insurance companies; they can predict with high accuracy what their annual payouts (pensions, annuities) will be for long periods into the future. They invest in long-term corporate bonds, high-grade common stocks, large-denomination time deposits, and long-term mortgages.

Commercial banks, savings and loan associations, credit unions, and mutual savings banks receive special attention in this text because one part of their liabilities—funds they obtain from savers and lend to borrowers—constitutes the major portion of the money supply. These funds are transactions accounts and deposits, NOW accounts, ATSs, and share draft accounts, discussed in Chapter 3.

FINANCIAL INTERMEDIATION

The technical term **financial intermediation** applies only when a financial intermediary comes between the ultimate lender and the ultimate borrower. When a savings and loan association accepts funds from savers for placement in a savings account and then lends those funds as mortgage money to home buyers, the S&L intermediates between savers and home buyers. The ultimate saver (the lender) does not deal directly with the ultimate borrower (the home buyer). In essence, all financial intermediaries *issue their own liabilities* to the public—savings deposits, savings and loan shares, insurance policies, etc.—and use savers' funds *to buy assets*—bonds, mortgages, and consumer debt.

Intermediation and Portfolio Diversification **Financial intermediaries** do more than play the role of intermediaries between ultimate lenders (savers) and ultimate borrowers. They also perform a valuable role by offering savers an asset that

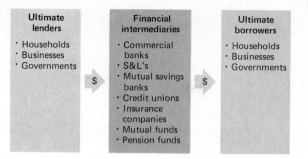

FIGURE 5-1   The Process of Financial Intermediation.   The process of financial intermediation is depicted here. Note that ultimate lenders and ultimate borrowers are the same economic units—households, businesses, and governments—but not necessarily the same individuals. Whereas individual households can be net lenders or borrowers, households as an economic unit are net lenders. Specific businesses or governments, similarly, can be net lenders or borrowers; both, as economic units, are net borrowers.

that is really a well diversified portfolio of assets. For example, if a small saver were required to deal directly with ultimate borrowers, such as perhaps a home buyer seeking mortgage money, the small saver essentially would be "putting all his or her eggs in one basket." The small saver would end up with only one asset—a mortgage contract on one piece of property. Having such a limited number of assets increases the risk of default and of losing the entire asset portfolio. The financial intermediary, such as a savings and loan association, can offer the small saver a reduction in risk through diversification. This is accomplished by pooling the excess funds of numerous small savers in order to purchase a large variety of assets from numerous ultimate borrowers. As a result, the small saver might end up with, say, $20,000 in a savings deposit, but implicitly the saver has "purchased" a small fraction of each of thousands of mortgage contracts. Looked at another way, financial intermediaries allow savers to purchase assets that are relatively safe and more liquid and that also earn interest. When a saver deposits money in his or her account at the local credit union, that saver is implicitly purchasing shares in the credit union. The financial intermediaries in turn purchase assets, such as mortgages and land, which are sold by the ultimate borrowers.

Consider Figure 5-1, which shows the process of intermediation. Note that the ultimate lenders comprise the same economic units as the ultimate borrowers; financial institutions clearly play the role of middlepersons.

FINANCIAL DISINTERMEDIATION

The reverse of the financial intermediation process is **financial disintermediation.** Savers take funds out of deposit accounts and invest directly in, say, a bond issued by the U.S. government. In other words, rather than allowing the financial intermediary to use the saver's deposited funds to purchase U.S. Treasury bonds, the saver does it directly.

Why Disintermediation Occurs   Individuals remove their savings from financial institutions when the direct purchase of financial claims issued by households, corporations, and governments will bring a higher rate of return than a savings account in a financial intermediary. If, for example, a savings account in a thrift institution offers 5.25 percent interest, while securities issued by the U.S. government offer 12 percent interest, some savers will reduce the funds they leave in thrifts or commercial bank saving deposits and increase their holdings of U.S. government securities. Not surprisingly, the amount of disintermediation that occurs depends, in large part, on differences between interest rates offered by financial intermediaries and by such ultimate borrowers as corporations and governments. The most rapid rate of disintermediation in the United States has occurred when nominal rates of interest have risen rapidly because of high rates of inflation (and therefore high anticipated future rates of inflation). *This was possible because the regulations of the Federal government prevented financial intermediaries from offering higher interest rates on normal savings-type accounts.* Other interest rates were unregulated and rose with the rate of inflation.

Conditions for disintermediation existed in 1969, 1973, and 1974. During those periods people predictably transferred their savings deposits from thrifts and financial institutions and purchased financial assets directly; the rate of savings-deposit growth fell dramatically during these episodes.

In 1975, as a reaction to the process of disintermediation, a new financial intermediary sprang up—money market mutual funds. These institutions were unregulated, and they offered interest rates on savings that were competitive with market interest rates. Although this financial innovation helped to stem the tide of disintermediation, it didn't help the thrifts.

By the end of 1977, yields on U.S. Treasury bills (short-term bonds issued by the U.S. Treasury) again rose above the maximum interest rates that commercial banks and thrift institutions were legally permitted to pay on passbook savings deposits. In order to forestall another loss of savings deposits to the disintermediation process and to the mutual funds—an event that would have threatened the very existence of thrift institutions—federal regulators of depository institutions authorized a new category of 6-month time deposits called "money market certificates." Commercial banks, S&Ls, and mutual savings banks were permitted to offer these certificates after June 1, 1978.[1] This new liability and others included in the accompanying Highlight have made the thrift institutions more competitive in the market for saving funds. Of special importance in reversing the *intra*-intermediary movement of funds from thrifts to money market mutual funds accounts is the "money market deposit account," an instrument that competes *directly* with money market mutual funds.

---

[1] R. Alton Gilbert and Jean M. Lovati, "Disintermediation: An Old Disorder with a New Remedy," *Review,* Federal Reserve Bank of St. Louis, January 1979.

CREDIT INSTRUMENTS

When lenders and borrowers transact voluntarily, both parties *perceive* gain; otherwise, the transaction would not take place. Of course, in the final analysis, one party may gain more than the other, or one party may be worse off as a result of the borrower-lender transaction. It is possible, and it is usually the case, for *both* parties to be better off as a result of a loan. A loan is an extension of credit, and a credit instrument is a written evidence of the extension of a loan. Credit instruments are exchanged in credit markets, and such markets facilitate economic growth. In fact, variations in the amount of credit in an economy may affect economic activity as much as variations in the money supply. Chapter 27 discusses the feasibility of the Fed's setting targets for credit extension rather than targets for the growth in the stock of money.

An extension of credit allows the borrower to make expenditures sooner than otherwise; it also allows the lender to earn interest and to purchase more goods in the future. This transferal of purchasing power is an element that is common to all credit instruments. Because all credit instruments can substitute for each other, interest rates earned on the various credit instruments will move up and down together as market conditions change.

If Mr. Smith wanted to borrow a great deal of money for a very long period of time, he would find that there would be few willing to make such a loan. Those few that would be willing to extend credit would insist on a very high interest rate because a good deal of uncertainty would exist. Suppose, however, that it were possible for the original lender to sell Mr. Smith's debt obligation—transfer the extension of credit—to a third party, such as Ms. Johnson. Indeed, suppose further that Johnson could resell the credit instrument to someone else, and so on. The net result of such sales and resales of the original credit instrument would be that many people would have extended smaller amounts of credit to Smith for shorter periods of time. The ability to resell credit instruments, therefore, lowers the risk of credit extension and increases the liquidity of the credit instrument. By increasing the liquidity of credit instruments, the ability to resell debt (or transfer credit extension) permits greater quantities of credit extension, facilitates trade, and lowers interest rates to borrowers.

Credit instruments, in general, convey the following information: the identity of the borrower, the amount of money to be paid when the instrument matures, and the amount of interest and when it is to be paid. Credit instruments take a variety of forms, many of which will be discussed in this chapter. The broadest classification is according to whether the credit instrument is negotiable or nonnegotiable. All credit instruments permit the transfer of credit, but some have the quality of negotiability while others do not. The key difference lies in the rights of those who participate in the transaction when the credit instrument is created and when it is subsequently transferred. Negotiability, therefore, involves a legal rather than an economic concept. A **negotiable credit instrument** is a written and signed unconditional promise to pay a specified sum of money at a specified time; technically, it meets the

HIGHLIGHT: Deregulation That Stems the Tide of Disintermediation and Makes the Thrifts More Competitive

Legislation and Regulation Have Created New Forms of Liabilities

Date in Effect	Maturity	Ceiling* Based on	Minimum Deposit	Comments
June 1, 1978	6 months	6-month Treasury bill†	$10,000§	Called "money market certificate"
July 1, 1979	2½–3½ years	2½-year Treasury security†	No minimum	Called "small savers certificate"
Oct. 1, 1981	1 year	70 percent of 1-year Treasury bill rate	No minimum	Called "all savers certificate"; interest is tax-exempt up to $1,000 for individuals and $2,000 for joint returns; expired Dec. 31, 1982
Dec. 1, 1981	1½ years or more	No ceiling	No minimum	IRA and Keogh accounts only
May 1, 1982	3½ years or more	No ceiling	No minimum	First step in Regulation-Q phase-out schedule
May 1, 1982	91 days	91-day Treasury bill†	$7,500§	
Sept. 1, 1982	7–31 days	91-day Treasury bill†; removed Jan. 5, 1983	$20,000§	
Dec. 14, 1982	Available upon demand	No ceiling	$2,500	This "money market deposit account" allows limited third-party transfers
Jan. 5, 1983	Available upon demand	No ceiling	$2,500	Called "Super-NOW account"; allows unlimited checking, but is subject to a 12% reserve requirement

*The actual calculation of the deposit rate ceiling is quite complicated. For details see table 1.16 in any recent Federal Reserve Bulletin.
†Includes a one-quarter of 1 percentage point advantage for thrifts over commercial banks.
‡Initially the maturity was 4 years or more. It changed several times until it was fixed at 2½–3 years on May 1, 1982.
§Reduced to $2,500 effective Jan. 5, 1983.

Adapted from Jan G. Loeys, "Deregulation: A New Future for Thrifts," *Business Reivew,* Federal Reserve Board of Philadelphia, January–February 1983, p. 23.

TABLE 5-3 Negotiable Credit Instruments (Transactions That Are Covered by Article III of the Uniform Commercial Code)

Government Promissory Notes	Private Promissory Notes	Bills of Exchange

U.S. Treasury Securities
  Bills of 1 year or less
  Notes of 1 to 10 years
  Bonds of 5 years or more
U.S. government agencies
  Bonds
  Certificates
State and local governments
  Bonds
	Commercial paper
	Corporate bonds
		Bank drafts
		  Sight
		  Time
		Trade drafts
		  Sight
		  Time

formal requirements of Section 3 of the Uniform Commercial Code. If a credit instrument is negotiable, it is generally thought to be more easily transferred to third parties. The rights of third parties are often stronger in this case than in a situation where third parties accept a **nonnegotiable credit instrument,** where there is *not* an unconditional promise to pay; nonnegotiable credit instruments do not meet the formal requirements of Section 3 of the Uniform Commercial Code, and any disputes regarding these instruments must be resolved under ordinary contract law. We are more concerned with negotiable credit instruments here because they are more important and because they are more related to money and banking activities. A classification of negotiable credit instruments appears in Table 5-3; you should refer to this diagram as each instrument is discussed in turn. Negotiable credit instruments are further classified into (1) promissory notes, and (2) drafts, or bills of exchange. Each is defined and analyzed below.

Promissory Notes   A **promissory note** is a written instrument signed by the notemaker promising to pay a specific sum of money on a specific date. Two parties are involved in promissory notes, the maker or payer (borrower) who promises to pay, and the payee (lender). Promissory notes are further classified according to *who* makes the promise to pay—governments or private parties.

      Government-Issued Promissory Notes   The U.S. government issues three types of securities:

1 *Treasury bills:* The shortest-term U.S. Treasury securities are **Treasury bills** issued for maturity periods of 3, 6, and 9 months, as well as 1 year. The most often issued are 3- and 6-month bills. The minimum face value on these bills is $10,000. There is no stated interest; rather, they are sold at a discount. A 3-month $10,000 Treasury bill might sell, for example, for $9,700. The discount is $300. Because they are redeemed for $10,000 at

maturity, an implicit interest rate has been earned in the form of a guaranteed capital gain.

2 *Treasury notes:* **Treasury notes** have a stated coupon rate of interest which is paid every 6 months (for most notes). The minimum face value of Treasury notes is $1,000. They are issued for maturity periods of 1 to 3 years.

3 *Treasury bonds:* **Treasury bonds** usually have a maturity of 3 years or more. They too have a coupon rate of interest; it is usually paid semiannually.

Many government agencies also issue credit securities. They are not technically securities of the U.S. government as are U.S. Treasury securities. Some, however, *are* backed by the "full faith and credit of the United States." For example, bonds issued by the Federal Home Loan Bank Board do have such a status.

Municipal and state governments also issue securities. They are grouped under the common name, **munies.** The interest that buyers can earn on municipal and state government-issued credit instruments is exempt from federal income tax.

Private Promissory Notes   Typically, private promissory notes are classified into two categories: short-term, unsecured notes (for which no collateral is required), called **commercial paper,** and longer-term notes called bonds. Commercial paper can be issued by banks, corporations, and financial institutions. The maximum length of maturity is 270 days. Commercial paper does not have to be registered with the Securities and Exchange Commission (a regulatory agency discussed in Chapter 10) provided that its maturity does not exceed 270 days.

There are numerous types of corporate bonds. Some are secured by collateral; others are not. The following are the most common types:

1 *Debentures:* No specific assets of the corporation are pledged as security for these corporate bonds. Rather, the general credit rating of the corporation is at stake, plus any assets that can be seized if the corporation defaults on the bonds.

2 *Mortgage bonds:* These corporate bonds are secured by a mortgage on all or part of the real property owned by the corporation. There are many kinds of mortgage bonds, including first, second, and even third mortgage types. The first mortgage bonds are the "senior" security: First-mortgage bondholders have first claim to the assets of the company if it is liquidated.

3 *Equipment trust bonds:* The backing for this type of secured bond is a specific piece of equipment. The title of the equipment is vested in a trustee, who holds such title for the benefit of the buyers of the bonds.

4 *Collateral trust bonds:* These corporate bonds are secured by collateral not related to real estate. Such collateral may be shares of stock in another corporation or accounts receivable.

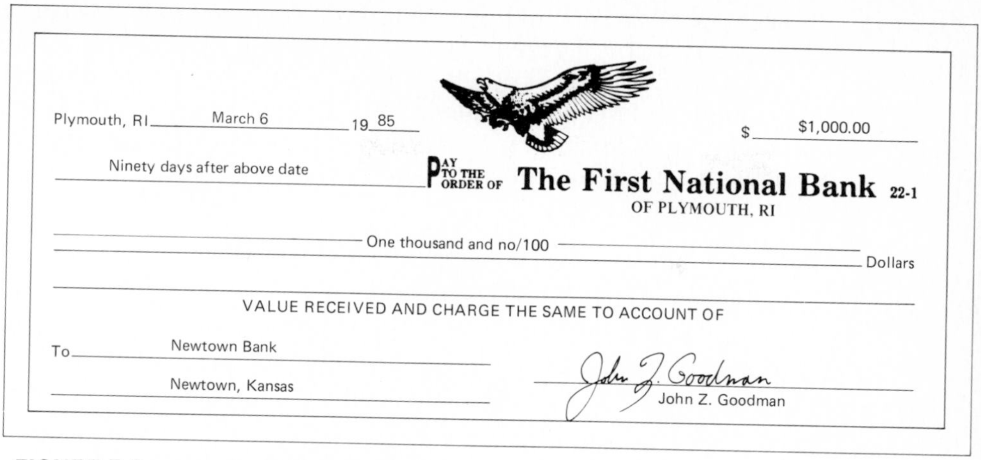

Plymouth, RI_____ March 6 _____ 19 85 _____

Ninety days after above date

PAY TO THE ORDER OF **The First National Bank** 22-1
OF PLYMOUTH, RI

$ _____ $1,000.00 _____

_____ One thousand and no/100 _____ Dollars

VALUE RECEIVED AND CHARGE THE SAME TO ACCOUNT OF

To_____ Newtown Bank _____

Newtown, Kansas

John Z. Goodman
John Z. Goodman

FIGURE 5-2 **Typical Bill of Exchange.**

5   *Convertible bonds:* These bonds can be exchanged for a specified number of shares of common stock, when and if the bondholder so desires. The rate of conversion is not determined until the time the conversion is exercised.

6   *Callable bonds:* A corporation that issues a callable bond may "call it in" and repay the principal at any time. Any of the bonds just described may be issued with this overriding feature.

Drafts   A **draft,** or **bill of exchange,** as shown in Figure 5-2, is an unconditional written order where the party creating it (the drawer) orders another party (the drawee) to pay money, usually to a third party (the payee). Note that drafts, unlike promissory notes, include a third party. Drafts are further classified into bank drafts and trade drafts. The drawee must be obligated to the drawer either by agreement or through a debt relationship before the drawee is obligated to the drawer to honor the order.

Drafts are of two varieties, time and sight. A time draft is a draft that is payable at a definite future time. A sight draft is payable on sight, that is when the holder presents it for payment.[2] A draft can be *both* a time and a sight draft; such a draft is one payable at a stated time after sight.

Bank Drafts   A bank draft is a credit instrument drawn on a bank. It can be either a bank sight draft or a bank time draft. Time bank drafts can become banker's acceptances if the bank guarantees payment; in effect, the banker's

---

[2]Or a sight draft is payable on acceptance. Acceptance is the drawee's written promise (engagement) to pay the draft when it comes due. The usual manner of acceptance is by writing the word "accepted" across the face of the instrument, followed by the date of acceptance and the signature of the drawee.

acceptance makes the time draft more liquid because it substitutes the credit of the bank for the credit of the notemaker.

A **check** is a distinct type of draft, a sight bank draft, drawn on a bank and payable on demand. On certain types of checks, the bank is both the drawer and the drawee. For example, cashier's checks drawn by the bank on itself are payable on demand when issued. Traveler's checks are drawn on the bank or on a financial institution, but they require the payee's authorized signature before becoming payable.

Trade Drafts When the payment of a draft is drawn on a person or institution other than a bank, the draft is referred to as a "trade draft." Like bank drafts, trade drafts are classified either as sight trade drafts or time trade drafts. Time trade drafts can become "trade acceptances" (shown in Figure 5-3), which are important to both domestic and international commerce.

The trade acceptance is a time trade draft that permits sellers of goods to receive payment before the buyer is obligated to pay. The goods seller writes a time trade draft on the purchases, which commits the buyer to pay a specific sum at a specific future date. The seller, or drawer of the draft, can make him- or herself, a bank, or anyone else (a creditor) the payee of the time trade draft. When the goods are taken from the seller by a transporter, the seller receives a receipt that acknowledges this fact, called a bill of lading. This bill of lading, along with the time trade draft, can then be sent by the seller to the buyer's bank, which in turn gives it to the buyer if the buyer accepts the goods. The buyer acknowledges receipt and acceptance of the goods by writing "accepted" on the time trade draft, which thereby becomes a trade acceptance. The seller of the goods can now sell the credit instrument to other creditors; the goods seller can receive payment before the goods purchaser is obligated to pay. Of course, in order to get money sooner, the merchant must pay interest—the rate depending on the creditworthiness of the goods purchaser. If the bank has agreed to guarantee payment to the seller by writing "accepted" in its name, the time draft would be a bank acceptance and probably would be more marketable than an ordinary trade acceptance.

FIGURE 5-3 Typical Trade Acceptance.

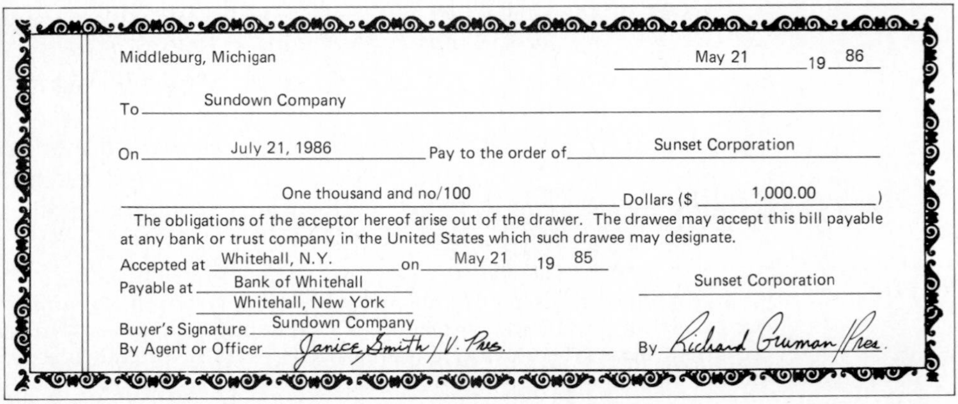
Middleburg, Michigan May 21 19 86

To Sundown Company

On July 21, 1986 Pay to the order of Sunset Corporation

One thousand and no/100 Dollars ($ 1,000.00)

The obligations of the acceptor hereof arise out of the drawer. The drawee may accept this bill payable at any bank or trust company in the United States which such drawee may designate.

Accepted at Whitehall, N.Y. on May 21 19 85

Payable at Bank of Whitehall, Whitehall, New York — Sunset Corporation

Buyer's Signature Sundown Company

By Agent or Officer Janice Smith / V. Pres. — By Richard Gruman / Pres.

PRIMARY AND SECONDARY FINANCIAL MARKETS

Financial transactions occur in both primary and secondary financial markets. A **primary market** is one in which a new security is bought and sold. A **secondary market** is one in which existing securities are exchanged; secondary markets are important to primary markets because they make the instruments traded in the latter markets more liquid. A primary financial market exists for U.S. government securities, corporate bonds, and corporate stocks. Newly issued securities constitute additions to the supply of credit. When the U.S. Treasury sells $1 billion of newly created bonds, they are purchased in what is called the primary securities market. Primary markets also exist for newly issued stocks and bonds of nongovernment corporations.

The issuance of stocks and bonds in the primary securities market is aided by so-called investment bankers (who often also act as brokers and dealers in secondary markets). An investment banker undertakes what is called an underwriting of a new issue. Underwriting means that the investment banker guarantees to the issuing corporations and governments a fixed price and (in the case of a bond) a fixed yield. The underwriting investment banker publicly announces the upcoming new issue in financial publications and elsewhere. Figure 5-4 contains such an example. There are many underwriting investment bankers in this particular case.

Underwriters will attempt to sell all the underwritten stocks or bonds within a day or so of the date of issuance. The investment bankers underwriting the new issues in the primary securities market earn their profit by attempting to "buy cheap and sell dear." They attempt to sell the new issues at a price higher than that price they have guaranteed the issuer. Note, however, that investment bankers are not true bankers and they do not carry out investment spending. Rather, they are simply market makers in the sense that they make sure that a market exists for about-to-be-issued new securities. Investment bankers do not accept deposits nor do they make commercial or consumer loans. In fact, commercial bankers are prohibited from underwriting corporate securities by the Glass-Steagall Act of 1933, which separated commercial banking and investment banking. Commercial banks can and do participate in underwriting the bonds of state and municipal governments because their securities are presumed to be safer.[3] Virtually all types of individuals, households, and businesses buy new issues. Some of the assets owned by financial intermediaries, for example, will have been purchased in the primary securities market.

The actual marketplace for the underwriting of new bonds is the conference suites of investment banking firms, which are linked by telephone with each other and with the corporations or governments that are issuing the new bonds. The investors (for example, large insurance companies and pension

---

[3]Note, however, that at times the governments of New York City, Cleveland, Boston, and the state of Michigan were more or less teetering on the brink of bankruptcy.

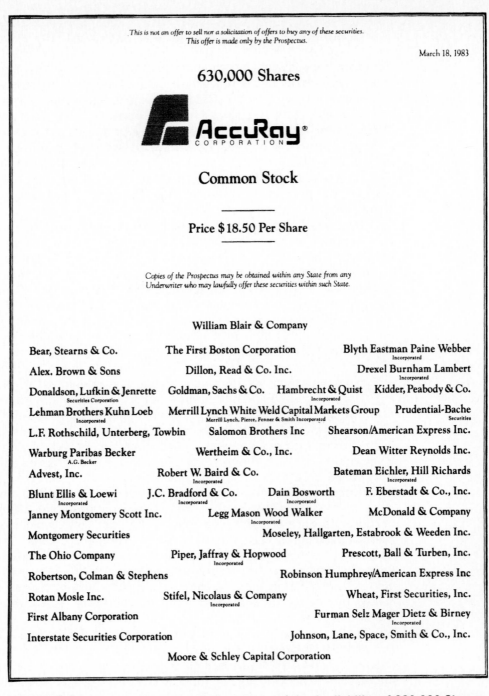

This is not an offer to sell nor a solicitation of offers to buy any of these securities.
This offer is made only by the Prospectus.

March 18, 1983

630,000 Shares

AccuRay ®
CORPORATION

Common Stock

Price $18.50 Per Share

Copies of the Prospectus may be obtained within any State from any
Underwriter who may lawfully offer these securities within such State.

William Blair & Company

Bear, Stearns & Co.	The First Boston Corporation	Blyth Eastman Paine Webber Incorporated
Alex. Brown & Sons	Dillon, Read & Co. Inc.	Drexel Burnham Lambert Incorporated
Donaldson, Lufkin & Jenrette Securities Corporation	Goldman, Sachs & Co. Hambrecht & Quist Incorporated Kidder, Peabody & Co.	
Lehman Brothers Kuhn Loeb Incorporated	Merrill Lynch White Weld Capital Markets Group Merrill Lynch, Pierce, Fenner & Smith Incorporated	Prudential-Bache Securities
L.F. Rothschild, Unterberg, Towbin	Salomon Brothers Inc	Shearson/American Express Inc.
Warburg Paribas Becker A.G. Becker	Wertheim & Co., Inc.	Dean Witter Reynolds Inc.
Advest, Inc.	Robert W. Baird & Co. Incorporated	Bateman Eichler, Hill Richards Incorporated
Blunt Ellis & Loewi Incorporated	J.C. Bradford & Co. Incorporated Dain Bosworth Incorporated	F. Eberstadt & Co., Inc.
Janney Montgomery Scott Inc.	Legg Mason Wood Walker Incorporated	McDonald & Company
Montgomery Securities		Moseley, Hallgarten, Estabrook & Weeden Inc.
The Ohio Company	Piper, Jaffray & Hopwood Incorporated	Prescott, Ball & Turben, Inc.
Robertson, Colman & Stephens		Robinson Humphrey/American Express Inc
Rotan Mosle Inc.	Stifel, Nicolaus & Company Incorporated	Wheat, First Securities, Inc.
First Albany Corporation		Furman Selz Mager Dietz & Birney Incorporated
Interstate Securities Corporation		Johnson, Lane, Space, Smith & Co., Inc.
	Moore & Schley Capital Corporation	

FIGURE 5-4   Anno' ncement, by Underwriters, of the Availability of 630,000 Shares of AccuRay Corpo' tion.

plans) will also be in communication via telephone with the underwriting investment banking firms. By far, the most important commodity sold by investment banking firms is information about the yield required to sell an issue and the identity of prospective buyers.

Investment bankers are able to underwrite new issues not because they have acquired funds from deposits, but rather because they have enough of their own capital to buy up what is not sold to buyers at the guaranteed price. Consider an example: The Big Investment Banking Firm underwrites XYZ Corporation's issuance of 1,000 bonds with a face value of $10,000, offering a coupon rate of 10 percent per year for 10 years. The Big Investment Banking Firm guarantees that the bonds will sell for at least their face value of $10,000 apiece. As it turns out, the bonds can only be sold at a discount. The average price is $9,000. The Big Investment Banking Firm will incur a loss of $1,000 on each bond, for a total loss of $100,000.

CAPITAL AND MONEY MARKETS

Capital Markets **Capital markets** include the purchase and sale of securities with a maturity of one year or more—that is, long-term securities. The stock market is arbitrarily included as part of the capital market. In a sense, a share of stock is a long-term security because it has no maturity date. As long as the corporation exists, the share of stock can remain in existence.

The stock market is by far the largest capital market in terms of the dollar value of the securities outstanding. About 35 percent of all stocks outstanding are owned by individuals; the remainder are owned indirectly by individuals through their pension plans and insurance companies.

The second largest component of the capital market by dollar value is the mortgage market. There are two categories of mortgages:

1 Residential, for from one- to four-family homes
2 Agricultural and commercial

Table 5-4 shows the dollar value of mortgages owned by commercial banks, savings and loan associations, mutual savings banks, and life insurance companies. Only recently have commercial banks expanded into the home and commercial mortgage market.

The third largest component of the capital market is the market for corporate bonds. Life insurance companies are the main owners of corporate bonds; they own slightly more than one-third of all corporate bonds.

Finally, long-term U.S. government securities and those issued by federal government agencies, as well as state and local governments, are purchased by a broad spectrum of institutions and individuals. The attractiveness of U.S. government notes and bonds to the private investor lies in their insulation from default risk.

TABLE 5-4 Dollar Volume of Mortgages Owned by Commercial Banks, Savings and Loan Associations, Mutual Savings Banks, and Life Insurance Companies, 1982

Total Major Financial Institutions	$1,021,225*
Commercial banks	301,742
Mutual savings banks	93,882
Savings & loan associations	484,297
Life insurance companies	141,304

*In millions of dollars.
Source: Board of Governors of the Federal Reserve System, *Federal Reserve Bulletin*.

Secondary Capital Markets In the past, an active secondary capital market existed only for U.S. government securities and stocks listed on major exchanges. Smaller secondary markets did exist for corporate, state, and local bonds, but they were inactive most of the time. During the last decade, the secondary markets for corporate, state, and local bonds have expanded. Additionally, secondary markets have developed for consumer credit and bank business loans.

The Money Markets Capital markets consist of securities issued in principal for one year or more. The term **money market** typically applies to the trading of credit instruments issued for less than one year. Money market instruments are highly liquid and readily marketable.

The largest sector of the money market is the market for U.S. Treasury bills of less than one-year maturity (T-bills). These very important securities will be discussed in Chapter 7.

Large-denomination certificates of deposit (CDs), defined in Chapter 3, are negotiable. They were "invented" simultaneously by several aggressive U.S. commercial banks in 1961. All negotiable CDs are of $100,000 denominations or more. They are deposits in the issuing institution. A commercial bank carries a CD on its accounting books as a liability. Purchasers of CDs, of course, consider them assets.

Negotiable CDs play an increasingly important role in money market transactions. They comprise an important source of funds for medium- and large-sized banks. Corporate treasurers purchase CDs because they provide earnings with a high degree of liquidity and because there is an active resale (secondary) market.

In addition to the CDs and T-bills discussed above, the markets for commercial paper and bankers' acceptances are other important parts of the money market.

Repurchase agreements, defined in Chapter 3, make up an important part of today's money market. REPOs enable a holder of securities to acquire funds by selling the securities and simultaneously agreeing to repurchase them at a later date. They are a means of facilitating borrowing and lending for short periods of time and for providing the lender with liquidity. REPOs typically involve a commercial bank and a corporation. The bank sells securities (often U.S. Treasury bills) to a corporate treasurer and promises to buy them back (often the next day) at a predetermined price. The difference between today's selling price and tomorrow's repurchase price is the implicit interest payment.

Another relatively new form of money market trading is in the **federal funds market,** where banks borrow from and lend to each other the deposits (reserves) they have at the Fed. Most banks use the federal funds market to meet reserve requirements or earn interest over short accounting periods. Chapter 6 discusses the federal funds market in more detail.

Still another new part of the money market consists of money market mutual funds. These funds provide "shareholders" with an interest return tied very closely to short-term money market rates. After being introduced in 1975, these funds tended to languish until the upward movement of interest rates that began in 1979. Money market funds are typically invested in such short-term instruments as CDs, T-bills, and bankers' acceptances that are issued in large denominations. The attractive feature of money market funds is that they can be redeemed quickly by the fund shareholder, either by check or wire transfer. During the 1970s, the small saver had usually been able to earn a higher rate of return on money market mutual funds than in other equally liquid savings instruments. Money market mutual funds are currently meeting stiff competition from money market deposit accounts, which thrift institutions are now permitted to offer.

CURRENT CONTROVERSY

Should There Be Credit Controls?

Can barriers against a normal ebb and flow of credit, in order to direct it to more "socially acceptable" uses, achieve a better use of credit? Can they do so in times of unstable credit conditions? Every time interest rates rise or business is bad, this controversy emerges. In 1969, Congress passed the Credit Control Act (Public Law 91–151), which authorized the President to instruct the Federal Reserve to "regulate and control any or all extension of credit." The Fed was allowed to "utilize the services of any other agencies, federal or state, where available and appropriate." During the period of the act's existence (until June 30, 1982), the Fed had the power to license people to borrow or to lend, to set loan limits for any purchases of new or used goods, to prescribe maximum interest rates and credit terms, to set maximum ratios of loan-to-deposits or assets, and to prohibit or limit any extension of credit under any circumstances that the Board deemed appropriate. (Talk about broad and sweeping powers!)

Such credit controls have a wide appeal. Why should credit go only to individuals and corporations that can afford to pay the going rate of interest? Should not those most worthy and productive among us be first in line to receive credit?

The basic problem inherent in these opinions is the difficulty in defining productivity and creditworthiness. Does a business needing funds to develop a new computer deserve special access to credit markets compared to a business wanting to borrow the same quantity of money to develop a new type of hybrid corn seed?

Even if that problem were surmounted, a more important problem remains. Once credit is allocated specifically to a business or household for a specific "worthy" purpose, there is no guarantee that the borrowed dollars will be used for that purpose. A dollar is a dollar is a dollar. It would be difficult, if not impossible, to prove that the dollars allocated to a given company for plant modernization were not spent instead on a string of polo ponies for the chairperson of the board.

Actually, this controversy existed only on an intellectual level until 1980, when President Carter invoked the Credit Control Act of 1969. Under the powers of that act, the Federal Reserve implemented the Carter Credit Control Package on March 24, 1980. Among other things, the program consisted of special credit constraints which provided guidelines for loans made by commercial banks, finance companies, and other lenders. The Fed was directed to restrict loans that were "unproductive"; it set a 9 percent annual limit on the growth of total domestic loans *at each bank* and established a specific level of certain bank borrowings. The Fed also established reserve requirements on money market mutual funds. Many believe that this contraction of credit contributed to the 1980 recession. By July 1980 the credit-control program was eliminated. The whole incident has convinced many that credit controls are a crude tool for exercising monetary restraint.

CHAPTER SUMMARY

1   Financial intermediaries are financial institutions that borrow funds (accept deposits) from people who willingly surrender current purchasing power. Financial intermediaries then lend these funds to (or buy securities from) those who wish to use the funds for current expenditures. In effect, financial intermediaries act as middlepersons who accept household saving and lend it to businesses that use the saving for investment purposes.

2   Financial disintermediation occurs when people remove funds from financial intermediaries and lend those funds directly to ultimate borrowers. Disintermediation often occurs when financial intermediaries are perceived as requiring too high a spread between the rates at which they borrow and the rates at which they lend. This occurs when market interest rates exceed interest-rate ceilings placed on savings deposits. Financial disintermediation is an attempt to eliminate the middleperson. Recent deregulation measures are expected to reduce disintermediation.

3   Financial institutions, corporations, and governments issue a variety of credit instruments. A partial list of credit instruments includes convertible and callable bonds, time and sight drafts and checks, U.S. government bonds, notes and certificates, and commercial paper.

4   A primary market is one in which a *new* issue is bought and sold. Secondary markets

are those in which previously issued securities are bought and sold. U.S. government agencies also issue bonds. Municipal and state governments issue securities which are referred to as "munies." Corporations issue commercial paper and bonds.

5 The market in which long-term securities (those that mature in one year or more) are traded is called the capital market. The capital market includes the stock market, the mortgage market, the corporate bond market, and the market for long-term U.S. government securities.

6 The market in which short-term securities (those that mature in less than one year) are traded is called the money market. The money market includes the markets for U.S. Treasury bills, negotiable CDs, commercial paper, bankers' acceptances, federal funds, and money market mutual funds.

7 Credit controls authorize the president to instruct the Fed to "regulate and control any or all extension of credit." These controls have wide appeal, but in practice they are difficult to administer and enforce.

GLOSSARY

Capital market: A market in which securities with a maturity of one year or more (long-term) are exchanged.

Check: A sight bank draft payable on demand.

Commercial paper: Unsecured short-term promissory notes issued by banks, corporations, and finance companies.

Draft, or bill of exchange: A negotiable credit instrument by which the drawer orders another party (the drawee) to pay a certain sum of money to a third party.

Federal funds market: A market in which very short-term (usually overnight) funds are exchanged between financial institutions; the funds borrowed and lent are usually reserves on deposit with a Federal Reserve district bank.

Financial disintermediation: The process by which ultimate lenders remove funds from financial intermediaries and lend funds directly to ultimate borrowers.

Financial intermediary: A financial institution that borrows funds (or accepts deposits) from parties that willingly give up current purchasing power and lends to (or buys securities from) those who wish to use the funds for current expenditures.

Financial intermediation: The process by which a financial intermediary acts between an ultimate borrower and an ultimate lender, serving each of their interests.

Money market: A market in which securities with a maturity of less than one year (short-term) are exchanged.

Munies: Municipal bonds which are issued by state and local governments, the earnings on which are exempt from federal income taxes.

Negotiable credit instrument: A written and signed unconditional promise to pay a specified sum of money at a specified time that meets the requirements of Article III of the Uniform Commercial Code.

Nonnegotiable credit instrument: A contract that indicates evidence of credit extension and is transferable, but not negotiable, to third parties because it doesn't meet the requirements of Article III of the Uniform Commercial Code.

Primary market: A market in which the purchases and sales of a newly issued credit instrument are made.

Promissory note: A written instrument signed by the notemaker promising to pay a specific sum of money at a specific date.

Secondary market: A market in which previously issued credit instruments are bought and sold.

Treasury bond: A long-term (three or more years) promissory note issued by the U.S. Treasury and secured by the "full faith and credit of the United States."

Treasury note: A medium-term (one- to three-year) promissory note issued by the U.S. Treasury and secured by the "full faith and credit of the United States."

PROBLEMS

5-1 List the following markets under the money market and the capital market headings:

   a Money market mutual funds

   b T-bills

   c Mortgage market

   d Corporate bond market

   e Federal funds

   f Long-term U.S. Treasury securities

   g Commercial paper

SELECTED REFERENCES

Cook, Timothy R., and Bruce J. Summers (eds.), *Instruments of the Money Market* (Richmond, Va.: Federal Reserve Bank of Richmond, 1981).

Gilbert, R. Alton, and Jean M. Lovati "Disintermediation: An Old Disorder with a New Remedy," *Review,* Federal Reserve Bank of St. Louis, January 1979, pp. 10–15.

Goldsmith, Raymond W., *Financial Intermediaries in the American Economy since 1900* (Princeton, N.J.: Princeton University Press, 1958).

Hurley, Evelyn H., "The Commercial Paper Market," *Federal Reserve Bulletin,* June 1977, pp. 523–536.

Polakoff, Murray E., and Thomas Durkin, et al., *Financial Institutions and Markets,* 2d ed. (Boston: Houghton Mifflin, 1981).

Zwick, Burton, "The Market for Corporate Bonds," *Quarterly Review,* Federal Reserve Bank of New York, Autumn 1977, pp. 27–36.

Chapter **6**

Interest Rates

It is instructive to consider a money economy in which no credit markets exist. Under a creditless system income recipients have two options. They can exchange their money income for goods and services (consume) or they can save some of their income and hold money, a generalized store of purchasing power. The money they hold can be spent at a later date and it can buy, assuming no inflation, the same bundle of goods and services at any time in the future.[1]

If credit markets emerge in an economy, income recipients now have a third option—they can lend some of their saving and earn interest. In short, income recipients can consume and save as before, but now they can save by holding *or by lending it to others.* Credit markets allow people to hold their savings in a nonmoney form—credit instruments.

INTEREST AND THE INTEREST RATE

Interest is the amount of money that lenders receive when they extend credit; the **interest rate** is the ratio of interest to the amount lent. For example, suppose that $100 is lent and, at the end of one year, $110 must be paid back. The interest paid is $10 and the interest rate is 10 percent (because $10/$100 = .10).

In a money economy, credit markets will arise because (1) different households have different personalities—they have different preferences for present versus future consumption, and (2) businesses can make investments in plant, equipment, and/or inventory that are profitable enough to enable them to pay back interest. At a given rate of interest (say, 5 percent), some households will prefer to be net savers or net lenders. Given their personal tastes for trading off present for future consumption, they will prefer to save and lend out some percentage of their income. At that same rate of interest some households will prefer to be net borrowers. They will prefer to consume more than their income in the present, knowing that they must forgo future consumption because they must pay back interest and principal (the amount they borrow). At a 5 percent rate of interest, some businesses prefer to be net lenders because they believe that the rate of return (profit rate) on their investment is less than the 5 percent interest rate they can earn. On the other hand, some businesses feel that they can earn more than 5 percent on their investment, so they will be net borrowers. In short, at any interest rate there will be net lenders and net borrowers, and credit markets will emerge to accommodate them. Governments, too, can be net lenders or borrowers, but we delay the discussion of their role in the credit markets until the next chapter.

---

[1]To be more precise, the purchase of an identical bundle of goods and services in the future also requires the assumption of no *relative* price changes in the future.

THE TRADE-OFF BETWEEN PRESENT AND FUTURE CONSUMPTION

At the heart of the interest-rate phenomenon lies the trade-off between present purchasing power and future purchasing power. The interest rate is the price that must be paid for credit and, like other prices, it performs an allocating (or rationing) function. The interest rate helps society decide how to allocate goods and services through time.

Also, like other prices, it provides information. At a national level, the rate of interest reflects the community's rate of time preference for goods and services. Other things constant, a relatively high interest rate indicates a community that is impatient and wants to consume more in the present. For ease of exposition, we will refer to this type of community as present-oriented. Other things constant, a relatively low rate of interest reflects a patient, future-oriented society that is willing to forgo present consumption. Future-oriented societies tend to grow more rapidly than present-oriented societies. In future-oriented societies, the national saving and investment ratios are relatively high and the economic growth rate will reflect this capital expansion.

At the individual level, the interest rate provides essential information. The market rate of interest indicates the rate at which a household can trade present for future purchasing power. For example, if the market rate of interest is 5 percent, each household has the option of choosing, say, $100 worth of purchasing power today or $105 worth of purchasing power next year ($100 × 1.05) or $110.25 worth of purchasing power two years from now ($100 × 1.05 × 1.05), and so on into the future. If Mr. Patullo values $1.00 of today's consumption so highly that he requires $1.06 worth of consumption one year from now to make him indifferent to spending the $1.00 now or one year hence, he will spend the $1.00 now; his *personal* trade-off between present and future consumption (6 percent) is greater than society's trade-off (the 5 percent market interest rate), so he will spend the $1.00 now. If Ms. Oliver is indifferent to $1.00 of consumption today and $1.03 of consumption one year from now, her personal interest rate is 3 percent. She will save the $1.00 and purchase $1.05 worth of goods next year.

Similarly, if the market rate of interest is 5 percent, Corporation X will *borrow* if it expects to earn a profit rate greater than 5 percent and *lend* if it expects to earn a profit rate of less than 5 percent.

The interest rate, therefore, allows people to compare present values to future values because, by its very nature, it reflects the trade-off between present purchasing power and future purchasing power. Because different households have different time preferences for consumption and because different businesses have different profit expectations, at a given rate of interest some economic units will be net lenders and others will be net borrowers.

DETERMINATION OF THE MARKET RATE OF INTEREST

Net savers, or net lenders, will supply funds to the credit market. Net borrowers will demand funds from the credit market.

The Supply of Credit   The supply of credit curve is positively sloped; it rises from left to right. At higher interest rates more households and businesses will become net lenders. As the rate of interest increases, more households observe a market rate of interest that exceeds their personal trade-off between present and future consumption. At some very high interest rate, even the extremely present-oriented, "live-for-today" individuals will find it worthwhile to save more of their incomes. Similarly, at some very high interest rate even very profitable businesses will find that they cannot repay interest out of earnings; they can earn a better rate of return by becoming net savers. Figure 6-1 shows a community's probable supply-of-credit curve.

The Demand for Credit   The community's demand-for-credit curve will be negatively sloped; it falls from left to right. As the rate of interest falls, more people prefer to become net borrowers. As the interest rate decreases, more households discover that the market rate of interest is below their personal rate of interest. They decide to reduce their saving rate. At some very low rate of interest (for some it may be *negative*), even future-oriented people find that they prefer to consume more in the present and save less. For businesses, lower interest rates mean that more investment projects exist for which they can borrow funds, pay the interest, and keep some net profit. In short, as the rate of interest falls, other things constant, the quantity demanded of credit rises. A probable community demand-for-credit curve is depicted in Figure 6-2.

FIGURE 6-1   The Supply of Credit.   This curve indicates that at higher interest rates more households and businesses prefer to become net lenders. Higher market interest rates create a situation in which more households face a market rate of interest that exceeds their personal rate of interest, and more businesses face a market rate of interest that exceeds the profit rate that they expect to earn on investment projects.

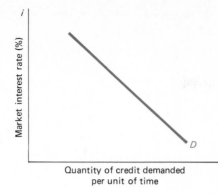

FIGURE 6-2 The Demand for Credit. The demand-for-credit curve is negatively sloped, indicating that as the rate of interest falls the quantity demanded for credit rises. This is because at lower interest rates more investment projects are profitable than at higher rates. Also, at lower interest rates more households face market interest rates that are below their personal interest rates. In short, as the rate of interest falls, more households and businesses find it worthwhile to become net borrowers.

The Market Rate of Interest Figure 6-3 indicates how the community supply of and demand for credit determine the market rate of interest. For the economy depicted, the market rate of interest will be 10 percent.

At a rate of interest above 10 percent (at 12 percent, for example), the quantity of credit supplied exceeds the quantity demanded for credit; a sur-

FIGURE 6-3 The Supply of, and Demand for, Credit. Given the supply and demand curves below, the market rate of interest will be established at 10%, where the curves intersect. At a 12% market rate of interest, the quantity of credit supplied exceeds the quantity of credit demanded and a surplus of credit exists. Some net lenders will not be able to earn any interest and will offer to accept less interest for their savings. Their competition for borrowers causes the market rate of interest to fall toward 10%. At an 8% interest rate, the quantity demanded exceeds the quantity of credit supplied; therefore a shortage of credit exists. Some borrowers will be unable to obtain funds; competition among borrowers will drive interest rates toward 10%.

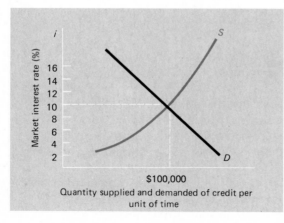

plus of credit exists. Lenders, competing with each other for borrowers, will force the interest rate down toward 10 percent.

On the other hand, at 8 percent a shortage of credit exists; the quantity demanded for credit exceeds the quantity supplied at that interest rate. Borrowers, competing with each other for credit, will drive the interest rate up toward 10 percent.

Eventually, the market rate of interest will be established at 10 percent, at which point the quantity of credit supplied and the quantity demanded for credit are both equal to $100,000,000. Equilibrium is said to exist, because neither suppliers nor demanders of credit have any incentive to change their behavior.

THE ALLOCATIVE ROLE OF INTEREST

Any study of a market system involves the realization that prices allocate resources in the economy. Interest is the price that allocates loanable funds (credit) to consumers and to businesses. Businesses compete with each other for loanable funds, and the interest rate allocates loanable funds to different firms and therefore to the investment projects of those firms. Those investment, or capital, projects whose rates of return are higher than the market rate of interest in the credit market will be undertaken, given an unrestricted, or free, market for loanable funds. For example, if the expected rate of return on the purchase of a new factory in an industry is 20 percent and loanable funds can be acquired for 15 percent, then that investment project—the new factory—will be purchased. If, on the other hand, that same project has an expected rate of return of 9 percent, it will not be undertaken. The funds will go to the highest bidders—those who are willing and able to pay the highest interest rates. In practice, the funds will go to those firms that are the most profitable. By this method, profitable firms are allowed to expand and unprofitable firms are forced to contract or go bankrupt. This allocation of credit among businesses can be considered efficient if efficiency is defined in terms of consumer sovereignty. If it is "good" for consumers to influence output by their dollar votes in the marketplace, then it is "good" to allow profitable businesses to expand and force unprofitable (or less profitable) businesses to contract.

Consumers also compete with each other for credit. By allowing credit to go to the highest bidder, the interest rate allocates consumption through time. It allows present-oriented people, who are willing to pay high interest rates, to consume more now and less later. Allowing credit to go to the highest bidder also allows future-oriented people to substitute more future consumption for less present consumption. If it is "good" to allow people to choose their rate of consumption through time, then it is "good" to allow the rate of interest to allocate credit among competing households.

NOMINAL VERSUS REAL INTEREST RATES

A **nominal interest rate** is defined as the rate of exchange between a dollar today and a dollar at some future time. For example, if the market, or nominal, rate of interest is 10 percent per year, then a dollar today can be exchanged for $1.10 one year from now.

The **real interest rate,** on the other hand, is the rate of exchange between goods and services (real things) today and goods and services at some future date. In a world of no inflation or deflation, the nominal rate of interest is equal to the real rate of interest. A 10 percent annual rate of interest with no inflation guarantees a rate of exchange of $1.00 in money terms with $1.10 in money terms a year from now, and vice versa. Since, in our hypothetical example, there is no inflation in real terms (purchasing power terms), the rate of exchange is between $1.00 of real goods and services today and $1.10 of real goods and services a year from now.

But what about a world in which inflation (or deflation) is anticipated? Assume that everyone anticipates a 10 percent annual rate of inflation and leave aside the complications of taxes. A nominal rate of interest of 10 percent per year will still mean that the rate of exchange between dollars today and dollars a year from now is 1 to 1.1. But $1.10 in dollar terms a year from now will buy only $1.00 worth of the goods and services that can be purchased today. If everyone anticipates a 10 percent annual inflation rate, then in real terms the 10 percent annual nominal rate of interest effectively means a *zero* real rate of interest.

An Equation Relating Real and Nominal Interest Rates   A simple equation can be used to show the relationship between the nominal rate of interest and the real rate of interest. It is as follows:[2]

Nominal rate of interest

= real rate of interest + expected rate of inflation

This equation can be rearranged to show that:

Real rate of interest

= nominal rate of interest − expected rate of inflation

---

[2]The exact equation is:

$$i_{nominal} = i_{real} + \text{expected inflation rate} + (i_{real} \times \text{expected inflation rate})$$

Normally, the product in the parentheses is small and can be ignored. Such is not the case, however, during periods of very high inflation; it certainly is not during hyperinflation.

Needless to say, the real rate of interest is very difficult to measure because the expected rate of inflation cannot be measured. Only nominal rates of interest are published. Some economists have attempted to estimate the expected rate of inflation by looking at past rates of inflation. However, these attempts have been unsuccessful because there is no way of knowing people's actual expectations. In fact, the St. Louis Federal Reserve used to publish an estimated real rate of interest, but it stopped doing so when it realized how inaccurate these estimates turned out to be. Nonetheless, the distinction between nominal and real rates of interest is crucial in a world of inflation and expected inflation when trying to predict household and business behavior, as later chapters will emphasize.

The Demand for and Supply of Credit, or Loanable Funds, Revisited

Earlier in this chapter, demand and supply curves for loanable funds were given in Figure 6-3. This diagram is now redone; remember, it was originally drawn under the implicit assumption that there were no inflationary expectations. Those same demand and supply curves are shown in Figure 6-4 as *DD* and *SS*. Now assume that demanders have inflationary expectations of 10 percent per year. The demand curve will shift upward by that amount to *D'D'*. Assume further that the suppliers of credit have the same expectations. The supply curve will also shift up by 10 percent to *S'S'*. If (as is assumed) the expectations of demanders and suppliers of credit are the same, the nominal rate of interest will rise by that expected rate of inflation to $i_e + 10$ percent.

The historical evidence of the relationship between the actual rates of inflation and nominal rates of interest is compelling. Figure 6-5 indicates what

FIGURE 6-4 This figure shows the result of inflationary expectations. If both lenders (suppliers) and borrowers (demanders) of loanable funds expect an annual rate of inflation of 10%, the demand curve will shift to the right (from *DD* to *D'D'*, an increase) and the supply curve will shift to the left (from *SS* to *S'S'*, a decrease). The new nominal interest rate will rise by approximately ten percentage points, from 10% to 20%.

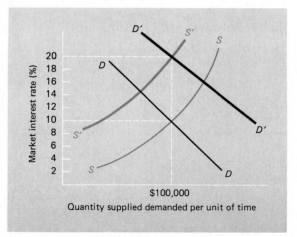

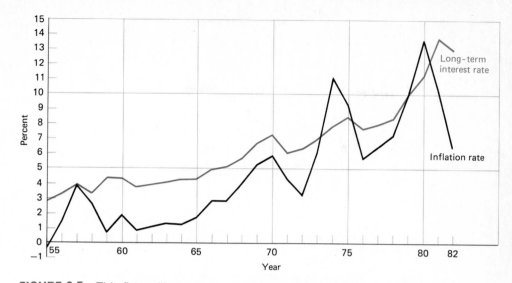

FIGURE 6-5 This figure illustrates the relation between long-term interest rates (as measured by the interest rate on 10-year government securities) and the rate of inflation (as measured by the consumer price index) from 1955 to 1982.

has happened to long-term nominal rates of interest in the United States since 1955 and what has happened to the actual rate of inflation over the same period. As the rate of inflation began to rise in 1965, so, too, did nominal interest rates. The relationship is not exact, however, because the nominal rate of interest consists of a nonobserved variable—the *anticipated* rate of inflation. Data, unfortunately, exist only for the *actual* rate of inflation. However, it can be said that during periods of inflation, nominal interest rates tend to be higher than during periods of zero inflation because individuals expect prices to continue to rise in the future. It takes time for people to adjust, however, to rates of inflation that are higher than those experienced in the past. Thus, when rates of inflation rise relatively rapidly compared to the past, nominal rates will not rise so rapidly. Only after individuals fully expect the new higher rate of inflation to continue will nominal interest rates fully compensate for the inflation.

DIFFERENT TYPES OF NOMINAL INTEREST RATES

Every lending market has its own interest rate. There is a mortgage market, a short-term business loan market, and a government securities market. For every type of market lending instrument—such as a government bond or a mortgage—there is a particular interest rate. In the sections that follow, some of the most important interest rates are discussed. Other, equally important interest rates are analyzed in Chapter 7.

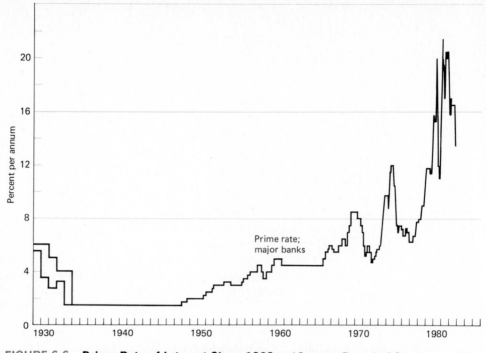

FIGURE 6-6 **Prime Rate of Interest Since 1929.** (*Source:* Board of Governors of the Federal Reserve System, *1982 Historical Chart Book,* p. 99.)

The Prime Rate Perhaps the most frequently quoted interest rate is the **prime rate.** This is the rate banks charge on short-term loans made to large corporations with impeccable financial credentials—their "most creditworthy customers," as the newspapers refer to them. The published prime rate is typically the lowest interest rate that such creditworthy businesses pay for short-term loans. Such business transactions are characterized by relatively little risk of nonrepayment. Fewer expenses are incurred by the lending bank to investigate the creditworthiness of the borrowing company. In Figure 6-6 the prime rate is shown for a fifty-two-year period. Notice that it changes in discrete jumps. It is usually a fixed rate posted by the majority of lending banks.

Prior to 1972, the prime rate had been constant for a long period of time. After that year, the prime rate began to change more often and became known as a variable prime rate. The interest rate actually paid by borrowing corporations is sometimes much higher than the published prime rate.[3] The banks require borrowers to leave a **compensating balance** to obtain a loan.

---

[3]And sometimes lower. According to some reports, banks may have *discounted* from prime for some customers when the prime rate reached levels of $21\frac{1}{2}$ percent in early 1981.

The compensating balance is a checking account balance of some specified amount earning zero interest.

Consider an example: U.S. Steel desires to borrow $10 million from the ABC Bank. ABC agrees to make the loan at the published 10 percent annual prime rate but requires that U.S. Steel leave $2.5 million in a non-interest-bearing corporate checking account. U.S. Steel is really not getting its $10 million loan at a 10 percent interest rate, since it can withdraw only $7.5 million from the bank. What, then, is the true interest payment for borrowing the $10 million? U.S. Steel pays 10 percent on $10 million (or $1 million per year), but it gets the use of only $7.5 million. It is therefore actually paying $1 million on a yearly basis to borrow $7.5 million. U.S. Steel ends up paying not a 10 percent, but a $13\frac{1}{3}$ percent annual rate. Thus, unless the compensating balance is publicly known, the actual interest rate paid cannot be determined by anyone but the involved parties.

There is another method used by banks to get borrowers to pay interest rates above the apparent prime rate. Sometimes banks switch their most creditworthy borrowers into a less creditworthy category, requiring them to pay a higher interest rate. Banks do this to raise the actual rates paid without raising their posted, or published, interest-rate schedule.

The Corporate Bond Rate   Another important interest rate is the one paid on high-grade (low-risk) corporate bonds. Suppose a corporation, such as International Chemical & Nuclear (ICN), wants to expand its production facilities and must borrow money to do this. One way to raise that money is to borrow by issuing IOUs in the form of ICN corporate bonds. It sells these bonds, say, for $1,000 apiece and agrees to pay back the principal to the lenders at the end of ten years. During those years, ICN also promises to pay annual interest on the loan. That annual interest payment, divided by the price of the bond, is the corporate bond rate. Different corporations borrow at different bond rates, depending on the financial soundness (creditworthiness) of the institution backing the rate.

Bond-Rating Services   Risk ratings for corporate (and state and local government) bonds are provided by Moody's Investors Service and Standard & Poor's Corporation. The Moody's ratings consist of nine different classes or grades, ranging from Aaa (best quality) to Baa (lower-medium quality) to Caa (poor standing) to C (extremely poor prospect). The ratings are based on detailed studies designed to assess the financial soundness of a particular corporation (or government) to determine how risky its bonds are for investors. More precisely, the studies are designed to assess the ability of a government or corporation to make its interest and principal payments on schedule. Each corporate issue is given a particular rating.

Published corporate bond rates are usually given only for the highest-grade bonds—those that are rated Aaa by Moody's or AAA by Standard & Poor's. Look at Figure 6-7, which indicates that average corporate bond rates moved up and down until about the 1950s. Since the 1950s, there seems to have been an upward trend in *nominal* corporate bond rates.

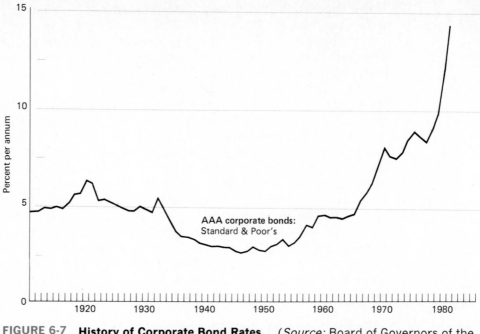

FIGURE 6-7 **History of Corporate Bond Rates.** (*Source:* Board of Governors of the Federal Reserve System, *1982 Historical Chart Book,* p. 96.)

THE CALCULATION OF INTEREST YIELDS

Nominal Yield If a bond is issued for $1,000 with an agreement to pay, say, $100 in interest every year, then it has an annual coupon rate of interest of 10 percent. This is also called its **nominal yield** (''yield'' is synonymous with interest rate). The nominal yield is defined as:

$$i_n = \frac{C}{F}$$

where i_n = nominal yield
C = annual coupon interest payment
F = face amount of the bond

There are two other measures of return to a bond—its current yield and its yield-to-maturity (or effective yield).

Current Yield **Current yield** is the dollar annual interest expressed as a percentage of the current market price of the bond. Bonds are often issued (and resold) at a price different from their face value. Thus, a 6 percent bond currently selling at $900 would have a nominal yield of 6 percent ($60 divided by $1,000) but a current yield of 6.67 percent ($60 divided by $900). Thus,

$$i_c = \frac{C}{P}$$

where i_c stands for the current yield and P stands for the price of the bond.

Yield-to-Maturity (or Effective Yield) on Long-Term Bonds[4]   The **yield-to-maturity** on a long-term bond is more difficult to calculate. The difficulty stems from the fact that such bonds typically are sold at a discount—at a price less than their face value—and are redeemed at maturity for their face value. The interest rate, or yield, therefore requires taking into account the value of the automatic capital gain *and* the coupon interest payments. For example, consider a 3-year bond that has a face value of $1,000, pays $50 per year in coupon interest, and is currently selling for $875.65. What is the effective yield on that 3-year bond?

Discounting   In order to answer that question, it is helpful to understand the concept of **discounting**, the process of finding the value today of dollars in the future. We have already indicated that the rate of interest provides a means of translating the value of future purchasing power into present purchasing power; the market interest rate reflects the trade-off between present and future consumption. It should come as no surprise, therefore, that discounting is intimately related to the interest rate.

The value today of any amount of money in the future is given by the equation:

$$P = \frac{R_1}{(1 + i)} + \frac{R_2}{(1 + i)^2} + \frac{R_3}{(1 + i)^3} + \cdots + \frac{R_n}{(1 + i)^n} \qquad \text{(6-1)}$$

where P = present value; the value today, or the market price of the asset (Today's market price of an asset will reflect the asset's present value.)
R_1 = the amount of money to be received one year hence
R_2 = the amount of money to be received two years hence
R_n = the amount of money to be received n years hence
i = the market rate of interest

The first thing to note is that there is a *direct* relationship between P and a given future stream of revenues, R. Other things constant, the higher the coupon interest the higher will be the selling price of the bond, P. Next, notice that an *inverse* relationship exists between the price of the bond and the mar-

---

[4]We calculate yield-to-maturity on short-term bonds (bills) in the next chapter.

ket interest rate. For a given R-stream, the higher the market rate of interest, the less the bond will sell for today; the lower the interest rate the higher the value today of a given future R-stream.

Suppose that a bond with a face value of $1,000 pays $50 per annum and matures in three years. If the market rate of interest is 10 percent, what will be the selling price of that bond today? According to our equation (remembering that in the third year the bond owner receives $50 coupon interest *and* the face value of the bond),

$$P = \frac{\$50}{(1.1)} + \frac{\$50}{(1.1)^2} + \frac{\$1,050}{(1.1)^3}$$

$$P = \$45.45 + \$41.32 + \$788.88 = \$875.65$$

(6-2)

Because the present value of that bond is $875.65, a competitive market will price that bond precisely at its economic value.[5]

It might be helpful to interpret what the value $875.65 means in this context. If someone were to place $875.65 today in an investment program that earns 10 percent per annum coupon interest, she could draw out $50 in year 1, $50 in year 2, and $1,050 in year 3 and then there would be nothing left in the investment account. For that reason, a bond that gives $50 per year for 3 years and pays a $1,000 face value at the end of 3 years has a present value of $875.65 *when the market rate of interest is 10 percent.*

Yield-to-Maturity and Discounting   We are now ready to return to our original question. What is the yield-to-maturity of a 3-year bond that has a face value of $1,000, pays $50 per annum in coupon interest (has a nominal yield of 5 percent), and is currently selling for $875.65? We can use Equation (6-1) to help us calculate the yield-to-maturity of this bond. Note that $P = \$875.65$, $R_1 = R_2 = \$50$, $R_3 = \$1,050$, and i is the unknown. Thus,

$$\$875.65 = \frac{\$50}{(1 + i)} + \frac{\$50}{(1 + i)^2} + \frac{\$1,050}{(1 + i)^3}$$

By now you can see that solving for i will give

$$i = i_m = 10\%$$

where i_m stands for the yield-to-maturity. Because i_m calculations are so complicated, yield-to-maturity is best determined by using a bond table. Table 6-1, a portion of an actual bond table, shows the yield-to-maturity of bonds with different maturities, given a face value of $1,000 and a nominal yield of 6 percent.

---

[5]In practice, coupon interest is paid semiannually, so Equation (6-2) is only a close approximation.

TABLE 6-1 Portion of Bond Table for 6% Nominal Yield

Assume that a bond with a face value of $1,000 and a nominal yield of 6 percent, and a maturity date of $7\frac{1}{2}$ years, can be purchased for approximately $900. The owner is paid $1,000 at the end of that period. To find the yield-to-maturity, or total effective yield, look for the number closest to 90.00 under the years to maturity column of $7\frac{1}{2}$. That number is 89.92, or $899.20, which is closest to $900. In the extreme left-hand column, the yield-to-maturity is 7.8 percent for a 6 percent coupon, or nominal, yield on a bond with a face value of $1,000.

Yield-to-Maturity (6% annual yield)	Years to Maturity				
	6	$6\frac{1}{2}$	7	$7\frac{1}{2}$	8
7.00%	95.17	94.85	94.54	94.24	93.95
7.20%	94.24	93.86	93.49	93.14	92.80
7.40%	93.31	92.88	92.46	92.05	91.66
7.60%	92.40	91.91	91.44	90.98	90.54
7.80%	91.50	90.96	90.43	89.92	89.44
8.00%	90.61	90.01	89.44	88.88	88.35

The Market for Long-term Bonds Bonds are credit instruments and buyers and sellers of bonds exchange in bond markets. As is usually the case, supply and demand determine price; the price of a bond is determined at the point of intersection of the supply and demand curves. Consider Figure 6-8, which indicates the supply of and demand for 3-year bonds that have a nominal yield of 5 percent.

The demand for bonds reflects the intentions of *suppliers* of credit; bond purchasers are lenders and they will purchase more bonds at a lower price than they will at a higher price. This is because bonds yield a fixed and determined *R*-stream. The lower the price of a bond, the higher the yield-to-maturity; the higher the yield-to-maturity, the more people are willing to lend. Note that this demand-for-bonds curve is equivalent to the supply-of-credit curve illustrated in Figures 6-1 and 6-3.

The supply of bonds curve reflects the intentions of demanders of credit; bond sellers are borrowers and they will offer more bonds at a higher price than at a lower price. As implied in the paragraph above, because the *R*-stream of bonds is constant, higher bond prices mean lower yields-to-maturity. Bond suppliers are willing to supply more bonds (borrow more) at lower interest rates than at higher interest rates.

Consider Figure 6-8 and compare it to Figure 6-3. A bond price of $922.69 is equivalent to a yield-to-maturity of $922.69 (for a 3-year bond with a nominal yield of 5 percent). Such a situation implies a surplus of bonds in Figure 6-8 and a shortage of credit in Figure 6-3. A surplus of bonds implies that bond sellers (borrowers) cannot find sufficient buyers (lenders). Hence, a shortage of credit exists and interest rates will rise—bond prices will fall.

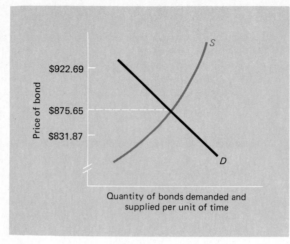

FIGURE 6-8 **The Supply of and Demand for 3-Year Bonds with a 5% Nominal Yield.** This graph indicates that the equilibrium price will be established at $875.65 when the market rate of interest is 10%. At a higher price of, say, $922.69, a surplus of bonds exists. This bond price is equivalent to an 8% yield-to-maturity, so this situation corresponds to a shortage in Figure 6-3. A surplus of bonds means that a shortage of funds exists for borrowers. At a lower price of, say, $831.87, a shortage of bonds exists. At that bond price, the yield-to-maturity is 12%, and as Figure 6-3 indicates, a surplus of credit exists. A shortage of bonds implies that lenders cannot find a sufficient quantity of borrowers at the going bond price.

At a price of $831.87, which is equivalent to a yield-to-maturity of 12 percent, a shortage of bonds exists in Figure 6-8 and a surplus of credit exists in Figure 6-3. A shortage of bonds implies that bond buyers (lenders) cannot find enough sellers (borrowers). If lenders cannot find enough borrowers at the going interest rate, a surplus of credit exists and interest rates will fall—bond prices will rise.

The Yield on Nonmaturing Bonds, or Consols Consider an economy in which there is only one interest rate that fluctuates over time depending on the supply of and the demand for credit, or loanable funds. Also assume that only one bond exists. It is issued by the government every January 1 with a face value of $1,000. The coupon rate of interest (yield) is whatever the market rate of interest is on that date. Also, the bond has an infinite lifetime; it can never be turned in for $1,000. (Actually, this type of bond exists; it is called a **consol** and is issued by the British government.)

Now suppose that on January 1 the market rate of interest in the economy is 10 percent. The consol issued to you, if you give the government $1,000, has a large (infinite!) number of coupons that you can turn in at the end of each year to obtain $100 in interest payments. In other words, you send in the coupon at the end of each year and a short time later you receive

HIGHLIGHT Understanding the Financial Press: Reading Bond Market Quotations

Bonds normally have a face value of $1,000; but they can sell for more or less than that amount. In other words, they sell at a premium or a discount from their face value. Prices for bonds are listed as a percentage of their face value. A figure of $79\frac{5}{8}$, for example, means that a $1,000 bond is selling for $796.25.

The following table is a listing of sample bond quotes from the New York Bond Exchange. Actually, the majority of bonds, including all tax-exempt bonds, are traded in the over-the-counter market. Listings of over-the-counter bond transactions are similar to those for over-the-counter

stocks in that the listing will include a bid and ask price. Often there will be more than one listing of bonds for a particular company. This simply means that the company has different bond issues, each maturing at a different date or having different characteristics.

Reading Bond Quotes

A	B	C	D	E	F	G	H
Bonds		Cur. Yld.	Vol.	High	Low	Close	Net Chg.
A Airl	11s88	14.	11	$79\frac{5}{8}$	$79\frac{5}{8}$	$79\frac{5}{8}$	$-1\frac{1}{2}$
A Airl	$5\frac{1}{4}$ 98	CV	341	57	53	53	-2
A Brnd	$5\frac{7}{8}$ 92	11.	5	$55\frac{7}{8}$	$55\frac{7}{8}$	$55\frac{7}{8}$	
A Can	6s97	13.	2	$45\frac{5}{8}$	$45\frac{5}{8}$	$45\frac{5}{8}$	$-\frac{1}{2}$
An Mot	6s88	CV	5	55	53	55	$+2$
A Sug	5.3s93	10.	1	$50\frac{5}{8}$	$50\frac{5}{8}$	$50\frac{5}{8}$	$-\frac{3}{8}$
ATT	$2\frac{7}{8}$ s87	4.2	25	69	$68\frac{1}{2}$	69	$+\frac{1}{2}$
ATT	$13\frac{1}{4}$ 91	14.	234	$96\frac{3}{4}$	$96\frac{1}{4}$	$96\frac{3}{4}$	$+\frac{1}{8}$
Anhr	9s05	CV	15	124	124	124	-2

A   Name of the company.
B   Coupon or nominal interest rate of the bond and its due or maturity date.
C   Current yield, or the coupon rate divided by the current selling price. Where "CV" appears, the bond is convertible into the company's stock. The price of the conversion is not given, however. Rather, a *Standard and Poor's* or a *Moody's Bond Book* or the financial statement of the corporation will give such information.
D   Number of bonds sold.
E.   Highest selling price of the bond that trading day. (Corporate bonds are quoted in $\frac{1}{8}$ points. A bond selling at $79\frac{5}{8}$ has a price of $796.25.)
F   Lowest price paid for that bond that trading day.
G   Closing price.
H   Net change from the previous trading day's closing price.

$100 in the mail. The nominal yield on the bond is 10 percent per year. Suppose that by the beginning of the following year, the market rate of interest in the economy rises from 10 percent to 20 percent. Let's say that you decide to sell your consol on January 1 of the following year. Would anyone be willing to pay you $1,000 for that bond with its coupon rate of 10 percent? Probably not. After all, anyone could purchase a newly issued government consol with a coupon rate of 20 percent a year since, by assumption, the government issues each bond at the market rate of interest. What is the highest price you could get for your bond? You would have to give the buyer a deal comparable to the one he or she would receive on a new bond. Thus, with a coupon rate giving only $100 a year in an economy with a 20 percent interest rate, you would only be able to obtain $500 if you sold your consol ($100 is equal to 20 percent of $500).

This simple example illustrates a key point that will be used throughout the rest of this book: *The market value or price of existing (old) bonds is inversely related to the market rate of interest in the economy.*

There is a simple formula for consols (bonds) with an infinite lifetime (no maturity date). The value of $1 in interest payments per year *forever* is equal to $1 divided by *i*, where *i* is the market (nominal) rate of interest (in decimal form).[6] Otherwise stated:

Value of $1 in interest payments forever $= \$1/i$

In the above example, the amount of dollars paid out per year was $100. With a market rate of interest of 10 percent, the formula indicates that the market price of the bond would be $100 divided by 0.10 or $1,000. With a market rate of interest of 20 percent, the formula indicates that the market price of the existing consols would equal $100 divided by 0.20, or $500. Thus, even in the absence of risk of interest payment (or principal with a bond that does have a specified life, or maturity), one can never be certain that the market price of an existing bond will remain the same as it was when the bond was purchased. Whenever interest rates in the economy rise, the price of existing bonds will fall because bonds, by definition, are typically fixed, nominal income-producing assets, in terms of dollars per year. Conversely, if interest rates fall, the market price of existing bonds will rise. In other words, owners of bonds can incur capital losses or obtain capital gains due to the changing market value of such assets.

Figure 6-9 shows the supply of and demand for consols; like Figure 6-8, it is equivalent to Figure 6-3. Figure 6-9 shows the price of consols that pay $50 per annum, forever, to the consol owners. At a price of $500, which is equivalent to a yield of 10 percent, equilibrium exists. At any lower price, a shortage of consols (and a surplus of credit in Figure 6-3) exists, which causes consol prices to rise and interest rates to fall. At any price above $500 for consols, a

---

[6]More generally, $P = \dfrac{R}{i}$, where P = price, or present value, and R = annual coupon interest.

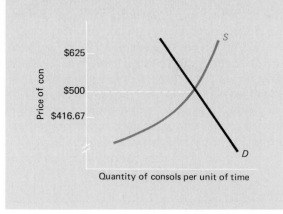

FIGURE 6-9 **The Supply of and Demand for Consols.** This figure shows the supply of and demand for consols that pay $50 per annum. Equilibrium exists at a price of $500, which is equivalent to a market yield of 10%. At a consol price of $625, which is equivalent to a yield of 8%, a surplus of consols and a shortage of credit exist. At a consol price of $416.67, a shortage of consols and a surplus of credit exist. After surpluses and shortages are eliminated in competitive markets, the consol price will be established at $500, where equilibrium exists.

surplus of consols and a shortage of credit exist, causing consol prices to fall and interest rates to rise.

Interest Rate Changes and Bond Price Changes You can understand why an inverse relationship exists between bond prices and interest rates (given fixed coupon interest payments) by recalling Equation (6-1):

$$P = \frac{R_1}{(1 + i)} + \frac{R_2}{(1 + i)^2} + \frac{R_3}{(1 + i)^3} + \cdots + \frac{R_n}{(1 + i)^n}$$

For a bond the Rs are given. If i rises, P must fall; if i falls, P must rise.

Throughout this chapter we have made calculations on yields and bond prices. Consider Table 6-2, which shows various market interest rates and the corresponding bond prices for bonds of differing maturities. For both the

TABLE 6-2		
Market Interest Rate, %	**Price of 3-Year Bond**	**Price of Consol**
12	$831.87	$416.67
10	$875.65	$500.00
8	$922.69	$625.00

three-year bonds and the consols, the coupon interest is $50 per annum. Note that a given change in the rate of interest generates a much less dramatic change in the price of the bonds with a three-year maturity.

In the next chapter, when we discuss the yields on short-term bonds, or bills, we will again have occasion to note that the shorter the term-to-maturity of a bond, the smaller will be the price change of the bond—for a given change in the market rate of interest. Bonds, therefore, are capable of bestowing capital gains and losses on their owners. Furthermore, longer-term bonds bestow greater capital gains or losses than do short-term bonds, for given interest-rate changes. This important conclusion implies that long-term bonds are less liquid than short-term bonds, an implication that will loom large in later chapters.

THE TERM STRUCTURE OF INTEREST RATES

Usually, the rate of interest on short-term loans is different from the rate of interest on long-term loans. A 3-month Treasury bill (analyzed in the next chapter) rarely has the same effective yield as a 5-year U.S. government bond. As indicated earlier, bonds with a maturity of less than 1 year (bills) are considered short-term; those with a maturity of from 1 to 3 years (notes), medium-term; and those over 3 years, long-term. The relationship between short-term interest rates and longer-term interest rates has been designated the **term structure of interest rates.** When a single borrower looks to the range of possibilities, that borrower is faced with a potentially confusing menu of rates, maturities, quotations, terms, and charges.

To understand the relationship between short-term and longer-term rates, first consider securities issued by the U.S. Treasury. Such securities have, for all practical purposes, a zero risk of default of interest payment or principal. Consequently, the only major difference between the different types of securities issued by the U.S. Treasury will be the coupon rate (discount rate, on Treasury bills) and the maturity.[7] On October 31, 1982, there were 156 different U.S. Treasury issues outstanding. An issue is a group of securities that has the same combination of coupon rate (discount rate on bills) and maturity. Approximately 34 percent of these issues were due to mature in one year or less and are therefore considered short-term. Most of these short-term issues were 3- or 6-month Treasury bills. Now look at Figure 6-10. On the vertical axis is the interest rate, or yield-to-maturity (effective yield). On the horizontal axis is the maturity date. The farther into the future the maturity date is, the longer the term-to-maturity of the security. The curve connecting the yields of the securities of differing maturity is called the **yield curve.** It gives in graphic form the term structure of interest rates on October 29, 1982. The particular term structure of interest rates represented by these actual

---

[7]Treasury bills pay no coupons; interest is earned only by discounting, or paying a price less than the face value. At maturity, the buyer receives the face value.

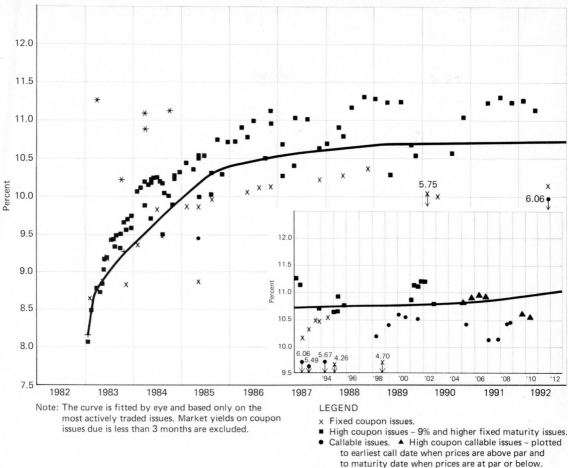

Note: The curve is fitted by eye and based only on the
most actively traded issues. Market yields on coupon
issues due is less than 3 months are excluded.

LEGEND

x Fixed coupon issues.
■ High coupon issues – 9% and higher fixed maturity issues.
● Callable issues. ▲ High coupon callable issues – plotted
      to earliest call date when prices are above par and
      to maturity date when prices are at par or below.
* 1½% exchange notes.
+ Bills – coupon equivalent of 3 mo., 6 mo., and 1 yr. bills.

FIGURE 6-10   A Yield Curve of Treasury Securities, Beginning Oct. 29, 1982. This
is based on closing bid quotations. (*Source:* U.S. Treasury Dept., *Treasury Bulletin,*
November 1982, p. 56.)

data does not constitute the only term structure that can occur. The yield
curve can take on one of the four possible constructions represented in panels
(*a*), (*b*), (*c*), and (*d*) in Figure 6-11. The one closest to that represented by the
real data in Figure 6-10 is in panel (*a*). It is an upward-sloping yield curve. A
yield curve is drawn as of a particular date and, therefore, can be expected to
shift through time. The following analysis offers theories as to why a yield
curve takes a particular shape at a given moment in time.

Why the Term Structure of Interest Rates Exists   What explains the various yield
curves that have existed throughout the history of this economy? There are
several theories. The most commonly used theory is the expectations theory.

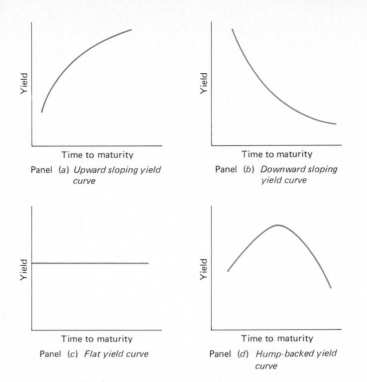

FIGURE 6-11   Panel (*a*) upward-sloping yield curve; panel (*b*) downward-sloping yield curve, panel (*c*) flat yield curve, panel (*d*) hump-backed yield curve.

Analysis of the effects of investor expectations concerning *future* market rates of interest is the basis for determining why the yield curve takes a given shape.

Expections of Rising Market Interest Rates   Consider a world in which the dominant expectation is that market rates of interest will rise in the future. Assume that an investor purchases a bond with a three-year maturity and an effective yield of, say, 10 percent. If market rates of interest were expected to rise to 20 percent gradually over the next three years, and if the investor tried to sell that bond in, say, a year and a half, he or she would sustain a capital loss; at that time, the price of the bond would be less than the purchase price.

Remember, as market rates of interest rise, the market price of existing bonds falls. If all yields on bonds from one year to three years' maturity are the same, rational investors expecting higher market rates of interest in the future will attempt to sell their longer-term bonds to avoid the anticipated capital losses as market rates of interest rise. They will seek out short-term bonds of, say, one year. In the process, as investors sell off long-term bonds and buy short-term bonds to avoid anticipated capital losses, the market price of long-term bonds will fall and the market price of short-term bonds will rise. Why? With any given supply of these different issues, a reduction in the demand for long-term bonds and an increase in the demand for short-term bonds will reduce the price of the former and increase the price of the latter. But, because the amount of coupon interest paid on any bond is fixed in dollars, the effective yield will rise on long-term bonds as their prices fall, and it will fall on short-term bonds as their prices rise. The result is an upward-sloping yield curve similar to the one represented in panel (*a*) of Figure 6-11. The process that has just been described is loosely called **arbitrage.**[8] Buyers will switch between long- and short-term markets until a long-term bond provides the same yield as a series of short-term securities held over the same period of time. Note, however, that future short-term interest rates are always unknown; they can only be predicted or estimated. Thus, it is the expectations concerning future short-term rates that determine what current long-term rates will be.

Also note that the expectations-theory model of yield curves assumes that long-term and short-term debt instruments are perfect substitutes. Therefore, the rate on long-term bonds will equal the average of successive short-term rates that are expected over the same period of time. This assumption simplifies away the reality that individuals will pay a premium for owning short-term bonds because they are more liquid than long-term bonds.

Expectations of Falling Market Rates of Interest in the Future   What if investors believe that market rates of interest will fall in the future? Those who own short-term bonds will see the possibility of obtaining a capital gain if they buy long-term bonds that have the same yield as short-term bonds. After all, if market rates of interest do fall in the future, the market price of existing bonds will rise. The demand for long-term bonds will rise and the demand for short-term bonds will fall. The price of long-term bonds will rise and the price of short-term bonds will fall. The effective yield on long-term bonds will go down and the effective yield on short-term bonds will rise. The result will be a downward-sloping yield curve, as shown in panel (*b*) of Figure 6-11.

Another way of looking at this situation is that with an expectation of lower future market interest rates, lenders will want to obtain the high current rate of interest for as long a period of time as possible. They will therefore increase their demand for long-term debt instruments. Conversely, borrowers will want to meet their borrowing needs for as short a time as possible in the anticipation of being able to borrow at a lower rate of interest in the future.

Interest-Rate Expectations That Generate Flat and Hump-backed Yield Curves   A flat yield curve, as illustrated in panel (*c*) of Figure 6-11, can be explained by the expectations theory under the supposition that money and capital market participants expect market interest rates to remain constant throughout the future.

---

[8]We use the word ''loosely'' because technically arbitrage refers to the *simultaneous* purchase and sale of an item in order to take advantage of artificial price differences.

The hump-backed yield curve, as illustrated in panel (*d*) of Figure 6-11, can similarly be explained by prevailing expectations that the market rate of interest will first rise in the immediate future and fall after that.

The Segmented-Markets Theory   An alternative explanation of the term structure of interest is the segmented-markets theory, which maintains that buyers and sellers of credit instruments specialize in different term maturities. To these specialists, credit instruments of different maturities are not good substitutes. Commercial banks tend to have short-term liabilities, and therefore tend to acquire short-term assets. Life insurance companies have very predictable, long-term liabilities (policy payments) and therefore tend to purchase long-term credit instruments. Because credit instruments of differing terms-to-maturity are traded in segmented markets, the yield curve can take *any* shape.

The existence of segmented markets raises the possibility of a monetary policy conducted so as to raise short-term interest rates (to encourage foreign money inflows or to reduce money outflows that could earn higher interest rates in foreign countries; to lessen a balance of payments problem) and lower long-term interest rates (to encourage domestic capital expansion). If markets are truly segmented, the Fed need only sell short-term bills and buy long-term bonds; such a policy will raise short-term interest rates and lower long-term rates. Indeed, during 1960 to 1961 the Fed tried precisely that, in a maneuver referred to as "operation twist" (because of the attempt to "twist" the yield curve). The Treasury was to cooperate by decreasing its issues of long-term bonds and increasing its issues of short-term credit instruments.

Unfortunately, the Treasury didn't cooperate—it continued to sell long-term securities during that period. The operation was not a success and was abandoned. Whether the fault lies with the segmented-markets theory or with the Treasury has not yet been determined.

Why the Term Structure of Interest Rates Is Important

Understanding the term structure of interest rates is important not only from an intellectual but also from a practical point of view. Corporate treasurers must make decisions at all times about what to do with available cash and about how to finance expansion. In both instances, a decision about the purchase or sale of short-term versus long-term securities is crucial. The U.S. Treasury also must decide how to manage the $1-trillion-plus debt of the U.S. government. When some of those bonds mature, should the Treasury refund them by selling new short-term bonds or new long-term bonds? Armed with an understanding of the term structure of interest rates, a policymaker can make a reasonably sound decision in such circumstances.

A last note will close this section. Any explanation of the term structure of interest rates describes a pattern of interest rates only at a *given* moment in time. Do not get the impression that the term sturcture of interest rates can explain why interest rates in general either rise or fall through time. That topic will be discussed in a later chapter. Right now, the relationship between risk and rate of return will be examined in more detail.

RISK AND RATE OF RETURN

To explain as simply as possible the notion of the term structure of interest rates, we eliminated the risk of default (nonpayment) from the discussion by concentrating only on U.S. government securities. For other issues, the risk of default is not zero. It turns out that there is a relationship between risk and a bond's actual rate of return, or yield-to-maturity.

Market Risk No matter what the purpose of the borrowed funds, all annual interest rates paid or received represent the price that the lender charges for giving the borrower immediate command over goods and services. In a world of imperfect information about future market annual rates of interest, a lender will typically charge a higher rate of interest the longer the length of the loan because the lender incurs a greater market risk. The lender incurs the risk that as general rates of interest rise in the economy, there could have been a higher rate of return from alternative uses of the loaned funds. For example, consider what happened to the net worth of savings and loan associations in the late 1970s and early 1980s. During the early 1970s, many of these financial institutions loaned funds for purchases of real estate at 7, 8, and 9 percent interest on twenty- to thirty-year terms. When interest rates rose to 15 and even 18 percent in the mortgage market in the late 1970s and early 1980s, the value of those loans dropped dramatically. The net worth of savings and loans was reduced accordingly because their assets fell by more than their liabilities. Those lenders that lent funds at such low interest rates for one- or two- or three-year periods were able to withstand the rise in interest rates much better than savings and loan associations. Short-term lenders had all their loans come due during the period of rising interest rates and were able to relend the money at the higher market rates.

Risk of Default An additional factor affecting interest rates is the differences in the risk of receiving interest and repayment of principal from the borrower. Suppose a financial institution lends money to General Motors for a five-year period. The probability that General Motors will default on the loan is (at least for now) very close to zero. On the other hand, consider a new mini-micro computer company in business for only six months. The risk incurred by the financial institution willing to lend money to this company for five years is much greater. The probability of that fledgling company defaulting on its interest and principal payments is certainly greater than zero.

To compensate for the higher risk of default, lending institutions typically charge a higher price. That higher price is in the form of a higher interest rate charged on loans to less creditworthy customers. A loan to General Motors for a five-year period might be made at, say, 10 percent, but a loan to the computer company might be made at 18 percent.

The same analysis holds when investors consider purchasing debt securities from corporations and local and state governments. The more financially sound the corporation or government issuing the bond, the more willing investors will be to purchase those bonds without requiring additional compensation for risk. Now look at Table 6-3, which shows yields-to-maturity for selected bonds over time. That table shows a positive relationship between risk and rate of return, or yield. This relationship is also presented in Figure 6-12, where the vertical axis is labeled interest rate, or yield. The term *interest rate* is used when considering borrowing money; the term *yield* is customarily used when considering the purchase of a bond.

The fact that risk and rate of return go hand in hand is an important factor in the investment decisions of businesses and households. No one can expect to receive a relatively high yield on any investment without incurring a relatively higher risk. If you put your savings into an insured savings account at a commercial bank, you will earn a relatively low rate of interest. Putting your savings into a Moody's-rated C bond *may* result in a much higher rate of return. But the corporation (or government) issuing that bond certainly stands a substantial chance of defaulting on the payment of interest and principal. Figure 6-12 is relevant here. Actually, the positive relationship between risk and rate of return reflects the old economic adage "There ain't no such thing as a free lunch." It is impossible, in a world of competition among market participants, to obtain consistently a higher-than-normal rate of return without incurring a higher-than-normal risk.

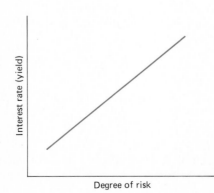

FIGURE 6-12 This curve indicates that, other things constant, higher degrees of risk require higher interest rates, or yields.

TABLE 6-3 Yield-to-Maturity for Selected Bonds over Time

This table shows that (1) effective yields fluctuate over time; (2) the longer the maturity, the greater the effective yield on average; and (3) the greater the risk, the greater the effective yield.

Bond and Rating	Yield-to-maturity										
	1972	1973	1974	1975	1976	1977	1978	1979	1980	1981	1982
U.S. Treasury bills (3 months)	4.07	4.04	4.89	5.84	4.99	5.27	7.22	10.04	11.51	14.08	10.69
U.S. government bonds (3 years)	5.72	6.95	7.82	7.49	6.77	6.69	8.29	9.71	11.55	14.44	12.92
State & local government bonds (Aaa)	5.02	4.99	5.89	6.42	5.66	5.20	5.52	5.92	7.85	10.43	10.88
State & local government bonds (Baa)	5.49	7.74	6.53	7.62	7.49	6.12	6.27	6.73	9.01	11.76	12.48
Corporate bonds (Aaa)	7.21	7.44	8.57	8.83	8.43	8.02	8.73	9.63	11.94	14.17	13.79
Corporate bonds (Baa)	8.16	8.24	9.50	10.61	9.75	8.97	9.49	10.69	13.67	16.04	16.11

CURRENT CONTROVERSY

Can Usury Laws Help Consumers?

A positive rate of interest has been condemned, legally prohibited, and limited throughout recorded history. Aristotle, for example, declared money to be "sterile" and therefore undeserving of earning interest in return for its use. Medieval Christianity condemned the charging of interest as a venial sin. The stigma attached to lending money has been so great that dominant ethnic groups have historically shunned the occupation and left it to minorities to serve borrowing needs.

Laws against lending that requires payment plus interest have been called usury laws. More recently, usury laws specify a maximum interest rate at which loans can be made. Usury laws can be traced back to early Babylonians who permitted credit but limited the rate of interest. The Bible tells us that "Thou shalt not lend upon usury to thy brother . . ." (*Deut.* 23:19:20). In the Roman republic, interest charges were explicitly forbidden, but they were permitted later during the period of the Roman Empire. By the fifteenth century, it was recognized that humans are not perfect. Martin Luther, along with other reformers, began to concede that creditors could not explicitly be prevented from charging interest. In the eighteenth century, restrictions on charging interest were relaxed, but most nations did have maximum legal rates at so-called "reasonable" levels. Usury laws in the United States were inherited from Britain. They remained in force in this country even after they were repealed in Great Britain in 1854. Most states still have on their books prohibitions against "usurist" rates of interest. The intent of these laws is to hold down the cost of borrowing.

If market rates of interest are below the usury rate in a particular state, there is no problem. For example, if a state specifies that consumer credit cannot be given at higher than 18 percent, but the market interest rate for such credit is generally 12 percent, then the usury rate is a nonaffected price ceiling. However, as the nominal interest rate pushes up to and above the usury rate, trouble occurs. Loanable funds are the most mobile of all commodities. Lenders unable to obtain a market rate of interest due to a usury ceiling will simply transfer their funds to other markets within the same state where the usury law does not apply or to other states that have a more liberal usury law. Borrowers in the affected state are therefore faced with the confusing circumstance of having a right *not* to pay higher than a ceiling rate but with no funds available to borrow at that rate! A simple supply-demand analysis can show why.

Look at Figure 1. Here the market for consumer credit in state X is shown. There is a supply curve for loanable funds and a demand curve. The market-clearing rate of interest is 18 percent. At that rate, both the quantity demanded and supplied is Q_e. Now assume that a usury law is passed by the legislature limiting creditors to charge 15 percent. At that rate, the quantity of credit demanded will increase to Q_d, but the quantity supplied will decrease to Q_s. The difference is called a "shortage," but it is only a shortage at the price of credit of 15 percent per annum.

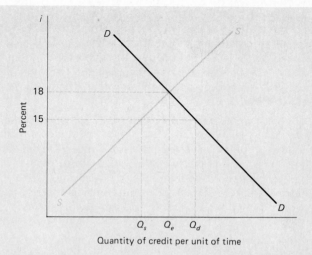

FIGURE 1 This figure shows the shortage of funds that occurs when the usury ceiling is 15% and the equilibrium rate is higher.

One of the results of the usury law in this example is that lenders will be more restrictive in their lending practices. That is, they will attempt to reduce the cost of lending by reducing the number of late payers and defaulters. This will be done by refusing credit to the less creditworthy demanders of credit. Those people are typically the ones on welfare, with unstable working histories, students, and the like. In other words, those who are hurt most by effective usury laws are often the very groups that were supposed to be helped by the usury laws.

CHAPTER SUMMARY

1   In the simplest model, the market rate of interest is established at the point of intersection of the supply of and the demand for credit, or loanable funds. The demand for loanable funds consists of the demand for consumer loans (consumption) and business loans (investment); each varies inversely as the rate of interest rises or falls. The supply of loanable funds consists mostly of household saving; it is directly related to the rate of interest.

2   The rate of interest is the price of credit. As such, it performs the *allocative* function that all prices do. It allocates scarce loanable funds to the highest bidders. By doing so, it allocates physical capital to the most profitable businesses and durable consumer goods to those households that are more present oriented.

3   The nominal interest rate is the *market* rate of interest. It is the rate of exchange between a dollar today and a dollar in the future. The real rate of interest is adjusted for expected future price-level changes; it is the rate of exchange between goods and services today and goods and services in the future.

4 Various yields can be calculated for a given bond. The nominal yield is equal to the coupon interest divided by the face amount of the bond. The current yield equals the coupon interest divided by the market price of the bond. The yield-to-maturity of the same bond is also expressed as a percentage, and it is the effective annual rate of return that would be earned by holding the bond to maturity; it reflects the bond price, its coupon interest earnings, and any capital gain or loss resulting from holding the bond to maturity.

5 The nature of a bond is such that it offers a fixed nominal coupon value to the holder at specific future dates. However, its selling price can differ from its face value. When market interest rates change, the prices of bonds will change. More specifically, if interest rates rise, the prices of bonds will fall; if interest rates fall, the prices of bonds will rise. Hence, general interest-rate rises generate capital losses for bond owners; reductions in the rate of interest create capital gains for bond owners. The longer the term-to-maturity of the bond the greater the possibility of capital gain or loss.

6 Given a level of risk, the rate of interest on short-term loans differs from the rate of interest on long-term loans. The relationship between long- and short-term interest rates for securities of comparable risk is referred to as the term structure of interest rates. Yield curves reflect yields *at a given moment in time* on comparable-risk securities maturing at different future dates. Depending on what future interest rates are expected to be, yield curves can be upward-sloping, downward-sloping, flat, or hump-backed.

7 In general, riskier securities require higher interest rates. Other things constant, long-term securities are riskier than short-term securities; hence, for long-term bonds buyers (lenders) require a higher interest rate. Also, for those securities that are subject to a higher risk of default on interest or principal, buyers (lenders) will require a higher interest yield.

8 Usury laws limit the rate of interest that can be charged to borrowers. The laws are usually passed to protect low-income and minority groups. In practice, usury laws that are set below market-clearing levels encourage lenders to allocate loanable funds (for which a shortage has been created) to low-risk borrowers. In general, low-income and minority groups are considered high-risk borrowers.

GLOSSARY

Arbitrage: The simultaneous purchase and sale of an item in order to take advantage of price differences.

Compensating balance: Funds that a borrower agrees to maintain in its checking account (earning no interest) as a condition for obtaining a loan; a way to charge a rate of interest higher than the apparent rate.

Consol: A nonmaturing bond, issued (usually) by the British government, that pays coupon interest but is not redeemable.

Current yield: The annual coupon rate of interest divided by the current market price of a bond.

Discounting A method of charging interest in which the borrower receives less than

the principal amount of the loan; interest paid equals the difference between the amount borrowed and the amount actually received.

Interest: A payment for obtaining credit.

Interest rate: The annual percentage rate of return received from lending or investing money.

Nominal interest rate: The

rate of exchange between a dollar today and a dollar at some future date.

Nominal yield: The annual coupon rate of interest divided by the face amount of a bond.

Prime rate: The interest rate charged by banks on short-term loans to the most creditworthy corporations.

Real interest rate: The rate of exchange between real things (goods and services) today and real things at some future period; an interest rate that has been adjusted for expected price-level changes.

Term structure of interest rates: The relationship on a specific date between short-term and long-term interest rates for credit instruments that have similar risk.

Yield curve: The relationship that exists on a specific date between nominal interest rates earned by different credit instruments with similar risk but with different maturities.

Yield-to-maturity: The rate of return that would be earned by holding a bond to maturity. It reflects the bond price, coupon interest earnings, and any capital gain or loss resulting from holding the bond to maturity.

PROBLEMS

6-1 What is the value of a consol that promises to pay $100 per year to the holder forever if the rate of interest is

a 5 percent

b 10 percent

c 20 percent

6-2 Turn to Table 6-1 and estimate the yield-to-maturity of a bond that has a face value of $1,000, matures in 6 years, has a nominal yield of 6 percent, and is currently selling for $906.10.

6-3 A 4-year bond has a face value of $1,000 and a nominal yield of 7 percent. If the market rate of interest is currently 10 percent, what is the present value (or market price) of that bond?

SELECTED REFERENCES

Clayton, Gary E., and Christopher B. Spivey, *The Time Value of Money* (Philadelphia, Pa.: W. G. Saunders, 1978).

Fischer, Irving, *The Theory of Interest* (New York: Augustus M. Kelley, 1965).

Garley, John G., "Financial Institutions in the Saving-Investment Process," *Proceedings of the 1959 Conference on Saving and Residential Financing,* 1959.

Humphrey, Thomas M., "The Early History of the Real/Nominal Interest Rate Relationship," *Economic Review,* Federal Reserve Bank of Richmond, May–June 1983, pp. 2–10.

————, "Can the Central Bank Peg Real Interest Rates? A Survey of Classical and Neoclassical Opinion," *Economic Review,* Federal Reserve Bank of Richmond, September–October 1983, pp. 12–21.

Malkiel, Burton G., *The Term Structure of Interest Rates: Theory, Empirical Evidence and Application* (Silver Burdett Co., 1970). Reprinted in Thomas M. Havrilesky and J. T. Boorman (eds.), *Current Issues in Monetary Theory and Policy,* 2d ed. (Arlington Heights, Ill.: AHM Publishing Corp., 1980), pp. 395–418.

Chapter 7

Government Securities and Debt Management

CHAPTER PREVIEW

1 What exactly is the national debt?

2 What are Treasury bills and how are they auctioned?

3 How are the Treasury-bill rate and yield calculated?

4 Why are T-bills so popular?

5 What are the principles of federal government debt management?

6 What off-budget federal government activities affect credit markets?

7 What is the function of a futures market for securities?

The U.S. Treasury Department is the fiscal agent for the federal government. It is responsible for collecting revenues (primarily through the Internal Revenue Service) and subsequently spending those funds as authorized by Congress and approved by the President. The main sources of revenue collected by the U.S. Treasury are personal and corporate taxes; other sources are miscellaneous taxes and fees. When these funds are insufficient to meet annual federal government expenditures, the U.S. Treasury incurs a deficit and must borrow. The amount of the accumulated borrowing not yet paid off is called the **national debt.**

To get an idea of the extent of the Treasury's financing of federal government deficits, look at Figure 7-1. It shows the federal government deficits (and occasional surpluses) for the last twenty-eight years. In fiscal 1983 alone (October 1, 1982, to September 30, 1983), the U.S. Treasury had to sell approximately $200 billion of new federal government debt securities to cover the deficit.

To understand the significance of the national debt, consider Figure 7-2 and Table 7-1. Figure 7-2 shows nominal gross national debt from 1967 to 1983. Table 7-1 indicates the amount of debt outstanding on September 30,

FIGURE 7-1 **Federal Government Deficits and Surpluses.** Beginning in October 1976, the federal government shifted from a fiscal year of July 1 to June 30 to a fiscal year of October 1 to September 30. The 3-month period from July 1, 1976, to September 30, 1976, is a separate fiscal period known as the transition quarter. Hence, the break in the graph during that period. (*Source:* Council of Economic Advisors, *Economic Report of the President.*)

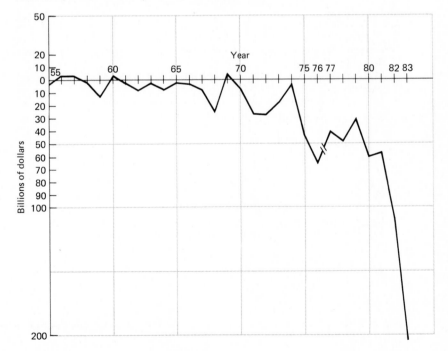

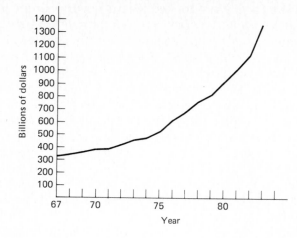

FIGURE 7-2 Nominal Gross National Debt from 1967 to 1983. The nominal (not inflation-adjusted) national debt has increased steadily from 1967 to 1983. (*Source:* U.S. Treasury Dept., *Treasury Bulletin.*)

1982, by maturity and classification of investors. Even if a miracle occurred and no *further* government deficits had to be financed, Table 7-1 shows that the U.S. Treasury must continually refinance the maturing *existing* debt—or retire it (pay it off).

TABLE 7-1 Amount of Marketable Interest-Bearing Debt

Outstanding by maturity and by owner, end of fiscal 1982, in millions of dollars.

Panel (*a*)
Maturity distribution of marketable interest-bearing public debt held by private investors

Amount outstanding privately held	$682,043
Within 1 year	314,436
1–5 years	221,783
5–10 years	75,749
10–20 years	33,017
20 years and over	37,058

Panel (*b*)
Distribution of marketable interest-bearing securities by class of investors

Total	$824,422
U.S. government accounts	7,944
Federal Reserve banks	134,393
Private investors	682,085

Source: U.S. Treasury Dept., *Treasury Bulletin.*

SECURITIES ISSUED BY THE UNITED STATES GOVERNMENT

The U.S. government issues three types of securities, or credit instruments.[1]

1 *Treasury bills:* The shortest-term U.S. Treasury securities are Treasury bills issued for periods of 3, 6, and 9 months, as well as 1 year. The most often issued are 3- and 6-month bills. The minimum face value on these bills is $10,000. There is no stated interest; rather, bills are sold at a discount. A $10,000, 3-month Treasury bill might sell, for example, for $9,700. The discount is $300; the buyer earns interest by purchasing the bill for $9,700 and redeeming it for $10,000 on the maturity date.

2 *Treasury notes:* Treasury notes have a stated coupon rate of interest, and the interest is most often paid every 6 months. The minimum face value of Treasury notes is $1,000. They are issued for periods of 1 to 10 years. Notes are also usually sold at a discount, making the yield-to-maturity higher than the stated coupon rate of interest.

3 *Treasury bonds:* These bonds usually have a maturity of 5 years or more. They, too, have a coupon rate of interest that is usually paid semiannually. The coupon rate is set by law at a maximum of $4\frac{1}{4}$ percent, although the Tax Equity and Fiscal Responsibility Act of 1982 increased the allowable exceptions to this rate to $110 billion. That is, the Treasury is permitted to have $110 billion of debt issued at a stated coupon rate above $4\frac{1}{4}$ percent. All of which is irrelevant, of course, because the $4\frac{1}{4}$ percent coupon interest-rate bonds can be sold at discount; their yields-to-maturity, therefore, will reflect market (not coupon) rates.

THE PRIMARY MARKET FOR TREASURY BILLS

A primary market is one in which the borrower sells debt directly to the lender; when the debt is sold, the borrower creates a new credit instrument, thus expanding the supply of credit.

The primary market for Treasury bills is the auction held every Monday (unless the Monday is a federal holiday, in which case it is held on the previous Friday). The most popular T-bills auctioned have 91-day and 182-day maturities; these bills are auctioned each week. They are the most liquid credit

---

[1]Since January 1983, all notes and bonds are issued in registered form; only bills are issued in bearer form. The maturity payment on bills, therefore, is made to the *holder*. For notes and bonds, the name and address of the current owner are registered with the Treasury; any ownership change must be recorded with the Treasury.

instruments of the U.S. government and are therefore the most popular. Less popular T-bill auctions of the 9-month and 1-year varieties are held at various times. On a typical Monday, $6.2 billion of 91-day T-bills and $6.2 billion of 182-day T-bills are auctioned.

The Auction   Two types of bids may be tendered in the auction for T-bills: a competitive bid and a noncompetitive bid.

A **competitive bid** specifies the number of bills a buyer is willing to purchase at a stipulated price. The bid is "put in the hopper" along with all the other bids. The bills are sold to the highest bidders.

A **noncompetitive bid** contains an offer to buy a specific quantity of T-bills at the average price paid for all the bills sold in that day's competitive auction. Usually, noncompetitive bids are made by small investors who may not have much experience in bidding. A noncompetitive bid ensures that the bidder will get to buy T-bills on the day of the bid, although without knowing the exact price to be paid. By contrast, a competitive bidder may not get to make a purchase at an auction, but for competitive bidders whose bids are accepted, the exact price to be paid is known. Any one noncompetitive bidder is not allowed to purchase more than $200,000 in total face value for T-bills of any kind at any one auction.

The mechanics of the auction require the U.S. Treasury first to subtract the amount of noncompetitive bids from the total amount of the bills to be sold. For example, if T-bills totaling $1 billion in face value are to be auctioned, and noncompetitive bids total $250 million, that means that $750 million is available to competitive bidders in the order of their bids—highest bidders buy first, second highest bidders buy second, and so on. If, for example, there is a total of $2 billion worth of bids from competitive bidders, only those offering the highest prices for the T-bills will get a crack at the amount of bills available after the noncompetitive bidders' total has been subtracted, or $750 million in this case. This process assures the Treasury of receiving the highest possible revenues from the sale of the bills. After the assignment of the bills available for competitive bidding, the noncompetitive bids are automatically accepted at the weighted average price of the competitive bids. If, for example, the weighted average price of the competitive bids on the $750 million of T-bills is $9,700 per $10,000 face value of 3-month T-bills, then *all* of the $250 million in T-bills going to noncompetitive bidders will be sold at $9,700 each.

The T-Bill Rate and the Yield on T-Bills   Ninety-one-day and 182-day T-bills have a minimum face value of $10,000; that is, they are redeemable for $10,000 or multiples thereof. Longer-term U.S. Treasury issues (notes and bonds) have smaller minimum face values.

Calculating Published Treasury Bill Rates   Published **Treasury bill rates** are discount rates based on a 360-day year for ease of calculation. Consider the following example: A $10,000, 91-day T-bill is sold at auction for $9,685. The T-bill rate is calculated from the following equation:

$$i_B = \left(\frac{F - P}{F}\right) \times \left(\frac{360}{n}\right) \qquad \text{(7-1)}$$

where i_B = the T-bill rate
  P = the price paid for the T-bill
  F = the face value of the T-bill
  n = the number of days to maturity

In the example,

$$R_B = \left(\frac{\$10,000 - \$9,685}{\$10,000}\right) \times \left(\frac{360}{91}\right) \qquad \text{(7-2)}$$

The Treasury would therefore list the T-bill rate for this auction at 12.462 percent.

Calculating a Treasury Bill Equivalent Coupon Yield   Published Treasury bill rates are based on a 360-day year and the face value of the investment. To obtain a **coupon yield equivalent,** or an approximation to the *true* annual yield, substitute a *365-day* year and the *actual purchase price* of the T-bill at the beginning of the period in Equation (7-1). The formula for an approximate coupon yield equivalent[2] is:

$$i_Y = \left|\left(\frac{F - P}{P}\right)\right| \times \left(\frac{365}{n}\right) \qquad \text{(7-3)}$$

Here, i_Y equals the approximate coupon yield, P equals the price paid for the T-bill, and n is the number of days to maturity. Using the above example for a 91-day, $10,000 T-bill sold at auction for $9,685, the simplified formula becomes:

$$i_Y = \left[\left(\frac{100 - 96.850}{96.850}\right)\right] \times \left(\frac{365}{91}\right) = 0.13046 \qquad \text{(7-4)}$$

The coupon yield on this T-bill is 13.046 percent. It is higher than the published T-bill rate because it takes into account: (1) the actual number of days

---

[2]$(F - P)/P$ gives the interest rate *per period,* and $365/n$ gives the number of periods per year. By multiplying the former by the latter an annualized interest rate results, so the rate can be made comparable to annual yields on longer-term credit instruments. Hence the term "equivalent" yield. This calculated rate is considered to be an "approximate" annual rate because it assumes that the market conditions don't change over the periods—an unlikely happenstance.

in a year and (2) that the interest is earned on the price paid for the T-bill rather than its face value.

THE SECONDARY MARKET FOR TREASURY BILLS

Treasury bills are traded actively in a secondary market, because some buyers (households, businesses, banks, the Fed) prefer to sell their 91-day (or other) Treasury bills before the maturity date. The existence of a large secondary market in T-bills allows for their transfer prior to maturity. This secondary market makes T-bills the most liquid, next to money itself, of all financial assets. There are specialized dealers in government securities who are ready to buy and sell existing T-bills to ultimate lenders at all times.

These dealers compile information about the bid and ask T-bill (discount) rates for currently outstanding T-bills. These discount rates are not the same as the already indicated approximate coupon yields which give the rates in the primary market. Rather, they are a means of determining the prices at which *existing* T-bills will be traded in the secondary market. For example, consider a T-bill due to mature in 73 days. The **asked price** for this security is 96.785. That means that, if purchased, the buyer must give the dealer $9,678.50. In turn, the buyer will receive a $10,000 T-bill that will mature in 73 days. The formula for calculating the approximate coupon yield is:

$$i_Y = \left(\frac{F - P}{P}\right) \times \left(\frac{365}{n}\right) \tag{7-5}$$

where, as before, P represents the asked price and n represents the number of days remaining before the T-bill matures. The yield-to-maturity for this T-bill is computed to be:[3]

$$i_Y = \left[\left(\frac{10,000 - 9,678.50}{9,678.50}\right)\right] \times \left(\frac{365}{73}\right)$$
$$= 0.16608 \tag{7-6}$$

The approximate coupon yield is therefore 16.608 percent per year. This figure represents the approximate annual return to a buyer who purchases this existing bill and holds it to maturity (73 days later) and then redeems it with the U.S. Treasury for $10,000. On the other side of the coin, the seller forgoes a rate of return of 16.608 percent per year by selling the bill.

Liquidity and T-bills Note that the approximate equivalent coupon yields for T-bills in the secondary market bear no necessary relationship to either the published T-bill rate when the T-bills were sold at auction or the approximate equivalent

---

[3]Note that now, because we are not dealing with the primary market, n need not be just 91 or 282; it represents the *remaining* days to maturity for the bill in question.

coupon rate on that auction day. If demand and supply conditions for the new T-bills sold on the market change abruptly, the equivalent coupon rates in the secondary market can differ significantly from the rate on the date of issue. However, the shorter the length of the T-bill, the less the actual price that bill will change in the secondary market for any given interest-rate change in the economy. After all, once sold at auction, a 91-day T-bill has only 90 days to maturity. Even if general interest rates in the economy were to rise dramatically, say, 10 days after the T-bill was sold, its value in the secondary market would not fall significantly because owners would merely have to wait 81 days to exchange the proceeds of the T-bill for higher-interest-earning assets.

To make this clear, consider an extreme example: Suppose that one day after a large number of T-bills were sold at auction at a coupon yield equivalent of 10 percent, all interest rates in the economy doubled. Remember from Chapter 6 that in this situation the market value of outstanding consols (a bond with no maturity) would fall to half their original value on the day after *they* were issued. What would happen to the market price of T-bills that had, say, 90 days left to run? Let's first determine their price on the day of issue, then their price on the next day. If these T-bills were earning a 10 percent effective coupon yield on the day they were issued, their price on that day could be found by using the formula:

$$i_Y = \frac{F - P}{P} \times \frac{365}{n} \tag{7-7}$$

Solving for P gives:[4]

$$P = \frac{F}{(i_Y \times n/365) + 1} \tag{7-8}$$

Therefore,

$$P = \frac{\$10,000}{[.10(91/365)] + 1} \tag{7-9}$$

So,

$$P = \$9,756.75$$

In other words, when sold, the $10,000, 91-day T-bill will command a market price of $9,756.75.

---

[4](1) $i_Y = [(F - P)/P] \times (365/n)$ (4) $P(i_Y \times n/365) + P = F$
(2) $i_Y \times n/365 = (F - P)/P$ (5) $P(i_Y \times n/365 + 1) = F$
(3) $P(i_Y \times n/365) = F - P$ (6) $P = F(i_Y \times n/365 + 1)$

If interest rates everywhere double overnight, yesterday's *new* issue of T-bills would now sell on the secondary market at a price that reflects the new market conditions. The equivalent coupon yield would now be 20 percent. Let's calculate the value of those T-bills that were sold yesterday and have 90 days to maturity. Substituting the new values into Equation (7-8) gives:

$$P = \frac{\$10,000}{[.20(90/365)] + 1} \tag{7-10}$$

Therefore,

$$P = \$9,530.03$$

The market value of the T-bill would fall from its issue price of $9,756.75 to $9,530.03 on the next day. That represents a reduction in value of only 2.3 percent, *even though interest rates have doubled.*

Now calculate the change in the market price of a 5-year bond when interest rates double. Recalling the equation in Chapter 6 that indicates the value of long-term bonds, we know that at issue, if interest rates are 10 percent, 5-year bonds that have a nominal yield of 5 percent and a face value of $10,000 will be priced at:

$$P = \frac{\$500}{1.1} + \frac{\$500}{(1.1)^2} + \frac{\$500}{(1.1)^3} + \frac{\$500}{(1.1)^4} + \frac{\$10,500}{(1.1)^5} \tag{7-11}$$

Therefore,

$$P = \$454.55 + \$413.22 + \$375.66 + \$341.51 + \$6,519.67$$

$$P = \$8,104.61$$

If interest rates were to double to 20 percent, that bond now will sell for:

$$P = \frac{\$500}{1.2} + \frac{\$500}{(1.2)^2} + \frac{\$500}{(1.2)^3} + \frac{\$500}{(1.2)^4} + \frac{\$10,500}{(1.2)^5}$$

$$P = \$416.67 + \$347.22 + \$289.35 + \$241.12 + \$4,219.71$$

$$P = \$5,514.07$$

The price of this bond would fall from $8,104.66 to $5,514.07. If you bought a newly issued 5-year bond with a 5 percent nominal yield, and the next day interest rates doubled, your bond would be worth $2,590.59 less than the day before—a drop in value of 31.96 percent.

This result confirms the conclusion in Chapter 6: The shorter the term-to-maturity of a bond or bill, the less its price will fluctuate for a given change in market interest rates. T-bills are extremely liquid because they are of short duration and because they can be traded in secondary markets.

HIGHLIGHT   The Coming Age of INSTINET

Public auctions cannot handle the large volume of T-bills traded by large institutional investors such as insurance companies, pension plans, and money market mutual funds. To facilitate the trading of T-bills among themselves, these large institutional investors have become linked through a computerized brokerage service called INSTINET. Institutions interested in buying or selling have their bids and offers recorded via terminals in their own offices. These terminals transmit the information on bids and offers to a central computer where they are compared with the bids and offers of other subscribing institutions. When a match between buyer and seller is electronically recognized, the trade is automatically recorded and executed.

All participants in this particular market prefer buying and selling electronically. Unfortunately, however, it seems that technology has displaced brokers. (Maybe they can be retrained as computer programmers.)

PRIMARY AND SECONDARY MARKETS FOR TREASURY NOTES AND BONDS

The Primary Market for Treasury Notes and Bills   Treasury notes and bonds differ from Treasury bills in that bills pay no coupon rate of interest. The minimum par (face) value on T-bills is $10,000; on Treasury notes it is $1,000; on Treasury bonds it can be as low as $500. Treasury bonds can have any maturity; usually, however, they are used for borrowing for five or more years. Treasury bonds are similar to Treasury notes in that they have a contractual coupon rate of interest that is usually paid semiannually. As with Treasury notes, bonds can be sold at auction, by cash subscription, and in exchange for maturing securities.

Both notes and bonds can be sold by **subscription** in a manner that is not available to purchasers of Treasury bills. When selling by subscription, the Treasury simply announces the coupon rate that it will offer, as well as the maturity of the issue, and so on. This announcement is made one to three weeks before the issue date. During the intervening time, investors subscribe for the total quantity of the issue they wish at par value. Investors typically offer to purchase a much larger quantity than is being issued, in which case they each receive a *pro rata* share of the issue. The entire issue is therefore always sold, but no one purchaser obtains the entire amount offered for purchase.

The Secondary Market in Notes and Bonds   There is a large secondary market in U.S. Treasury notes and bonds. The published information about the secondary market in notes and bonds is a little more complicated than it is for T-bills; the market information must contain the coupon rate, and the maturity date, as well as the bid and asked prices and the yield-to-maturity. Look at Table 6-

2, which shows a typical set of quotes for U.S. Treasury notes and bonds. Note that bid and asked prices are quoted as a percentage of maturity value, with the decimal places used to express thirty-secondths instead of hundredths. (This is different from the method of price quotation used for T-bills.) Thus, a 99.24 asked price indicates that dealers are selling the note or bond at $99\frac{24}{32}$ per $100 par value. Otherwise stated, the bond or note is selling for $99.75 per $100 of par value. Thus, a $10,000 Treasury note with this asked price would be selling at $9,975.

DEBT MANAGEMENT BY THE U.S. TREASURY

About $250 billion in government debt matures each year and is paid by refinancing. The main treasury management decision is what kind of debt to reissue: short-term, intermediate-term, long-term, or a combination of the different terms. The composition of the refinancing may affect output, employment, and the price level. Thus, government-debt refinancing requires careful consideration. The principles that the Treasury must take into account in its management of the debt are:

1   Stabilization
2   Minimizing the frequency of issuing new debt
3   Minimizing cost

Stabilization   It has often been suggested that the U.S. Treasury should manage the maturity of the debt in such a way as to counter the business cycle. In response to inflation, for example, the Treasury should, according to this stabilization principle, issue longer-term debt. Those who argue this way believe that total spending in the economy will then be restrained by two influences. First, the issuance of long-term debt drives up long-term interest rates, and this inhibits private borrowing and investment spending. Second, the replacement of short-term issues with longer-term issues reduces the total supply of more liquid assets and replaces it with less liquid assets. This tends to reduce current spending.

The latter contention warrants further explanation. Many students of macroeconomics believe that the community's total desired amount of spending depends, at least in part, on the amount of liquid assets in the hands of the nonbanking public. If the amount of liquid assets is reduced by the Treasury's exchange of short-term debt for long-term debt, then the community's desired level of spending presumably will fall. One way for people to increase their liquidity is to spend less on goods and services.

If the economy is in a recession, the stabilization principle calls for the U.S. Treasury to exchange maturing long-term debt with short-term debt. In so doing, total spending is encouraged by two influences:

1   Long-term interest rates fall, encouraging private borrowing and investment spending.

2   Replacing long-term issues with short-term issues increases the total supply of the more liquid assets and thus tends to increase current spending.

Minimizing the Frequency of Issuing New Debt

The easiest way to reduce how frequently securities are issued is to lengthen the average term-to-maturity of the national debt. If all the outstanding national debt were converted to long-term bonds with, say, with a fifteen-year maturity, the Treasury would not have to refinance it so frequently—it would only have to refinance the debt once every fifteen years! Few students of Treasury debt management take this principle seriously. Most believe that a countercyclical policy which follows the stabilization principle is more important. Or, they believe that minimizing the interest cost on the national debt is wiser.

Minimizing Cost

Interest paid on the borrowing to finance the national debt is a substantial cost to the federal government. In 1982, for example, interest paid on the national debt was $99 billion, and 13.6 percent of the federal government budget. Proponents of the principle of cost minimization, as applied to debt management, believe that the Treasury should refund the national debt so that interest paid is as low as possible. Typically, this involves exchanging long-term debt for short-term debt because the term structure of the interest rate curve typically has been upward-sloping. Short-term rates have been lower than long-term rates. If the Treasury follows the principle of cost minimization when faced with an ascending yield curve, it will exchange long-term debt for short-term debt. On the other hand, descending yield curves have existed; yields have fallen as term-to-maturity has increased. Under the cost minimization rule, the Treasury would have to replace short-term debt with long-term debt. Note, however, that even when the Treasury does want to issue more long-term bonds, it may be restricted by limits imposed by Congress.

HIGHLIGHT   The "Permanent" Debt Ceiling

Webster's Seventh New Collegiate Dictionary defines *permanent* as "continuing or enduring without fundamental or marked change: stable." The "permanent" debt ceiling for the U.S. Treasury is the maximum amount of national debt mandated by Congress and, as such, it represents the maximum federal debt under U.S. law.

In 1947, the permanent debt ceiling was $100 billion. In 1961, the permanent debt ceiling was $300 billion. In 1971, the permanent debt ceiling was $400 billion.

Since 1971, there has been a temporary debt ceiling; in 1981, it was $1 trillion and in 1983, $1.3 trillion. Presumably, these temporary debt ceilings will revert to the permanent debt ceiling if Congress does not pass an increasingly higher temporary ceiling each year.

If you're confused about the meaning of the word "permanent" (and even "temporary"), *Webster's Seventh New Collegiate Dictionary* will certainly not be of much help. However, with respect to the national debt, if what is supposed to be temporary looks like it is going to be permanent, then Congress will eventually call it permanent. See what we mean?

DIRECT GOVERNMENT LOANS AND GOVERNMENT-GUARANTEED LOANS

Each year the federal government budget is verified by the Treasury and published in detail in various government publications. The budget shows that in 1982 the federal government spent $111 billion more than it received. That deficit presumably represented the amount of credit demanded by the federal government in that year. Actually, however, the impact of federal government activity on the financial markets is not restricted to the published federal budget deficit. The federal government's presence in the credit markets has three other sources: (1) activities of "off-budget" agencies, (2) operation of government-sponsored enterprises, and (3) provision of federally guaranteed loans, each discussed presently.

It is crucial to understand that none of these three major activities directly affects the federal budget. Congress does not vote on appropriations and expenditures involved in these activities. This is particularly true of "off-budget" agencies, whose deficits are, for the most part, financed by loans from the U.S. Treasury. The operations of one of these agencies—the Federal Financing Bank—have significant effects on the federal budget.

Table 7-2 shows the effect of adding the outlays of the off-budget federal agencies to the federal deficit. Column (2) indicates the size of the federal deficit—that is, expenditures minus receipts. Now look at column (4), which includes column (3), expenditures of the off-budget agencies (which are ulti-

TABLE 7-2	Federal Deficit or Surplus, Including Off-Budget Outlays		
(Billions of dollars)			
(1) Fiscal Year	(2) Budget Surplus or Deficit (−)	(3) Off-Budget Outlays	(4) Total Surplus or Deficit (−)
1972	− 23.4		− 23.4
1973	− 14.8	.1	− 14.9
1974	− 4.7	1.4	− 6.1
1975	− 45.2	8.1	− 53.2
1976	− 66.4	7.3	− 73.7
Transition quarter	− 13.0	1.8	− 14.7
1977	− 44.9	8.7	− 53.6
1978	− 48.8	10.4	− 59.2
1979	− 27.7	12.5	− 40.2
1980	− 59.6	14.2	− 73.8
1981	− 57.9	21.0	− 78.9
1982	−110.6	17.3	−127.9
1983 (est.)	−207.7	17.0	−224.8

Source: Council of Economic Advisors, *Economic Indicators*, February 1983.

mately financed by the Treasury). The deficit that includes the off-budget agencies is much larger. The published federal deficit shows only *part* of the impact of the federal government on the credit markets. Let's take a closer look at off-budget agencies.

Off-Budget Agencies   All off-budget agencies are owned and controlled by the federal government. Examples of off-budget agencies include the Federal Financing Bank, the Pension Benefit Guaranty Program, and the Rural Electrification and Telephone Revolving Fund. By law, their transactions are *excluded* from the federal budget. Appropriations for these agencies are not included in the budget totals, nor are the outlays of these off-budget agencies subject to ceilings set by congressional budget resolutions. Off-budget borrowing has grown from $1 billion in 1974 to $21.2 billion in 1981; since then it has fallen to $15.2 billion. Table 7-3 shows off-budget agency outlays from 1973 through 1983.

   The Federal Financing Bank   The most important off-budget agency is the Federal Financing Bank (FFB), which began operation in 1974. Today it provides most of the financing for off-budget agencies and also for certain on-budget agencies. The FFB lends by three methods:

1   Purchasing agency debt (bonds)

TABLE 7-3   Off-Budget Outlays by Agency

(Billions of dollars)

	1973	1974	1975	1976	TQ[f]	1977	1978	1979	1980	1981[d]	1982	1983[ae]
Federal Financing Bank		.1	6.4	5.9	2.6	8.2	10.6	13.2	14.5	23.1	14.1	14.3
Rural Electrification and Telephone Revolving Fund[c]	.1	.5	.5	.2	−.1	.4	.1	[b]	[b]			
Rural Telephone Bank	[b]	.1	.1	.1	[b]	.1	.1	.1	.2	.2		
Pension Benefit Guaranty Corporation[d]			[b]	[b]	[b]	[b]	[b]	[b]				
United States Postal Service Fund		.8	1.1	1.1	−.7	−.2	−.5	−.9	−.4	.2	−.5	.9
United States Railway Association		[b]	[b]	.1	[b]	.2	.1	.1	[b]	.3		
United States Synthetic Fuels Corporation												
Total off-budget outlays	0.1	1.4	8.1	7.3	1.8	8.7	10.3	12.4	14.3	23.2	13.6	15.2

[a]Estimate—Office of Management and Budget estimate in fiscal 1982 budget document.
[b]Less than $50 million.
[c]No net outlays are authorized after fiscal 1980.
[d]Put on-budget by PL 96-364, September 26, 1980—retroactively included in fiscal 1980 budget.
[e]The USSFC was created by the 1980 Energy Security Act.
[f]TQ—In calendar year 1976, the federal fiscal year was converted from a July 1–June 30 basis to an October 1–September 30 basis. The TQ refers to the transition quarter from July 1 to September 30, 1976.
Detail may not add to total because of rounding.
Source: Stephen Pollock, ''Off Budget Federal Outlays,'' *Economic Review,* Federal Reserve Bank of Kansas City, March 1981.

2   Purchasing loans and loan assets

3   Purchasing loan guarantees

All these purchases are financed with funds borrowed directly from the Treasury. The original purpose of the FFB was to coordinate and to consolidate the borrowing of a number of federal agencies. The FFB was designed to act as an intermediary—buying securities issued by off-budget agencies and paying for them with funds borrowed from the Treasury. Funds lent by the FFB to off-budget agencies do not show up in the budget totals voted and authorized by Congress.[5]

The purchase of guaranteed loans by the FFB   Federal agencies often guarantee loans to insure the lender against any loss resulting from default by the borrower. Some of the most famous cases of loan guarantees involve New York City, Chrysler, and Lockheed. When the FFB purchases a guaranteed loan at the request of a federal agency, that purchase is ultimately paid for by the Treasury, which will probably sell securities to cover the expense.

Such an action is an indirect loan from the Treasury to the private sector borrower, but it is a ''loan'' that will not show up anywhere in the federal budget or deficit. Nonetheless, total borrowing by the Treasury has increased to finance the purchase. The crucial thing about all this is that Congress has no direct control over the increases in federal spending that are financed by FFB purchases of guaranteed loans.

Government-Sponsored Enterprises   Another way the federal government affects credit markets without showing up in the federal budget is by lending to government-sponsored enterprises which were originally established to perform specific credit functions but are now privately owned. Although the transactions of these enterprises are not included in the federal budget, they are subject to government supervision. Three of these agencies operate under the watchful eye of the Farm Credit Administration; they are Banks for Cooperatives, Federal Intermediate Credit Banks, and Federal Land Banks. Three other agencies support the housing market; they are the Federal National Mortgage Association (Fannie Mae), the Federal Home Loan Banks, and the Federal Home Loan Mortgage Corporation (Freddie Mac).

---

[5]By purchasing the debt of other agencies, the FFB accomplishes what it was originally created to do—consolidate and coordinate the borrowing of various federal agencies. Prior to the start of FFB operations in May 1974, these other agencies obtained credit by independently marketing their own securities. Their offerings were usually small and irregular and because the public was unfamiliar with these agencies and their securities, they had to pay interest rates significantly higher than the rates on U.S. Treasury issues. In an effort to eliminate this high interest premium, the FFB was authorized to buy agency issues at one-eighth of a percent over the Treasury's cost of borrowing. Originally, the FFB was to obtain its funds at this rate by direct borrowing from the public. However, the rates that the FFB paid on its first offering were considerably higher than rates on Treasury borrowing. Since then, the FFB has obtained its funds by borrowing directly from the Treasury.

Guaranteed Loans or Mortgage Pools The third category of federal government activities that affects the credit markets but doesn't affect the federal budget is the guaranteed mortgage pool. Guaranteed mortgage pools are loans which the federal government insures wholly or partly, or guarantees the payment of principal or interest, or both. Like the off-budget agencies and federally sponsored agencies, federal loan guarantees do not show up in the federal budget. The bulk of loan guarantees has been used to support housing. However, in recent years, guarantees have been used increasingly for other purposes, such as the loan guarantees involving Chrysler and the City of New York.

STATE AND LOCAL GOVERNMENT SECURITIES

State and local governments issue debt (borrow) in the form of state and local bonds. These bonds are called municipal bonds, or simply "munies." The chief characteristic of munies is that they are tax-exempt; that is, interest income earned on munies is exempt from federal income taxes.

There are two types of municipal bonds: general obligation bonds and revenue bonds. **General obligation bonds** are secured by the taxing power of the issuing municipality. **Revenue bonds** are secured by the revenues to be obtained from the specific project that the bonds are used to finance (e.g., a toll bridge).

The range of default risk for munies is wide. The bond-rating services, such as Moody's and Standard & Poor's, may give different divisions of the same municipality different ratings, depending on the soundness of the financial structure of the rated division. For example, on February 1, 1983, Moody's rated Cleveland, Ohio, general obligations at Ba, and at the same time it rated Cleveland's Electric Light Mortgage revenue bonds at Caa, a significantly lower rating.

CURRENT CONTROVERSY

Tax-Exempt Municipal Bonds: Whom Do They Benefit?

Congress created the tax-exempt status for municipal-bond interest income in order to lower the cost of borrowing for municipal governments. But a side effect has been that certain groups in society have benefitted. In order to determine which groups benefit—besides municipal governments—it is important to understand that the personal income tax system of the federal government is progressive. In this system, as one is pushed into higher tax brackets, a higher tax rate is applied to the last dollars earned. Keep this in mind during the following discussion.

Interest paid to holders of municipal bonds is a form of tax shelter because such interest income need not be reported on federal income tax returns. What is the benefit to the owner of the tax-exempt bond? Before the question can be answered, the investor's marginal tax rate must be known. Assume that it is 50 percent. Every dollar the investor obtains in tax-exempt interest (as opposed to taxable income) is a dollar on which he or she will *not* have to pay taxes. Therefore, the tax saving for the investor in the 50 percent tax bracket is 50 percent. On the other hand, if the investor's marginal tax bracket is 20 percent, the benefit of the tax-exempt interest status is only 20 cents on every dollar of tax-exempt income.

Bond buyers are well aware of these facts. In their competition to obtain tax savings (that is, tax-exempt income) from these bonds, buyers will bid up their prices and cause the yield to be relatively low. A look at the financial pages of a newspaper will demonstrate the difference in yields between tax-exempt and non-tax-exempt bonds of similar quality and maturity. Typically, the difference represents the implicit taxes that the high-marginal-tax-bracket investor pays when buying such a bond.

Consider a specific example. Assume that munies are selling at a price that yields 7 percent per year and that non-tax-exempt bonds of equivalent risk and maturity are selling at a price that yields 10 percent a year. Which is the appropriate one to purchase, all other things held constant? The decision is based on the investor's marginal tax bracket. Investors in relatively high tax brackets are probably better off buying the tax-exempt bonds; investors in lower tax brackets may not be. To see why, refer to the table below during the following discussion.

Tax-Exempt Bonds: To Buy or Not to Buy?

The answer depends on your marginal tax rate.

		Low tax bracket (20%)		High tax bracket (50%)	
		(1) Non-Tax-Exempt Bond	(2) Tax-Exempt Bond	(3) Non-tax- Exempt Bond	(4) Tax-Exempt Bond
A	Federal tax rate	20%	20%	50%	50%
B	Interest rate payable from a *non-tax-exempt bond*	10%	—	10%	—
C1	Interest rate payable from a *tax-exempt bond*	—	7%	—	7%
C2	Percentage points you must pay in taxes	2%	0%	5%	0
D	Percentage points you get to keep	8%	7%	5%	7%
E	After paying taxes, which bond pays more interest and by how much?	Non-tax-exempt pays 8% − 7% = 1% point more than tax-exempt			Tax-exempt pays 7% − 5% = 2% points more than non-tax-exempt
F	Which to buy?	In low tax bracket, buy *non*-tax-exempt bonds			In high tax bracket, buy tax-exempt bonds

Assume that the investor is in the 20-percent tax bracket. If this investor buys a non-tax-exempt bond yielding 10 percent, the after-tax yield will be 8 percent (10% − 20% of 10% = 8%). As shown in column (2), the before- and after-tax yield on the munie is 7 percent, because no taxes are paid on the interest (see rows C1 and D). This investor is better off buying the non-tax-exempt bond.

A person in the 50 percent tax bracket, on the other hand, would be better off buying the 7 percent tax-exempt munie [see columns (3) and (4)]. The after-tax yield on the non-tax-exempt 10 percent bond is 50 percent of 10 percent, or 5 percent (row D). On the other hand, all the interest on the tax-exempt municipal bond can be kept, and that is equal to 7 percent, or two percentage points more (row E).

Who benefits most from the tax-exempt status of municipal bonds? This simple example demonstrates that because of our progressive tax system, only those in higher income tax brackets are really able to benefit from the tax-exempt status of the asset.

THE SECURITIES FUTURES MARKET

In the last few years, an active futures market in securities has developed. In any **futures market,** buyers and sellers agree to trade a certain quantity of a commodity, for a specific price, at a specified date in the future. Many people engage in such common future delivery contracts as ordering next year's model of a Chevrolet from the local Chevrolet dealer two months before the car is scheduled to arrive, or ordering a book from the bookstore that will not be delivered for three weeks. As another example: A farmer may make a contract to deliver 1 million bushels of grain to the operator of a grain elevator at a specific month in the future at a price agreed upon by both parties today. All these contracts are called forward contracts.

A forward contract is not, strictly speaking, the same as a futures contract; the latter applies only to those contracts executed in formal commodities exchange markets. Until recently, agricultural commodities were the most well-known goods for which futures contracts were traded. These were traded on the Chicago Board of Trade, the Chicago Mercantile Exchange, and other exchanges. Now, however, there are futures contracts for T-bills, T-bonds, and government-insured mortgages. These financial futures are traded primarily on the Chicago Board of Trade, the International Monetary Market of the Chicago Mercantile Exchange, the New York Futures Exchange, and the New York Commodity Exchange. The bulk of financial futures is traded on the two Chicago exchanges. The difference between a forward and a futures contract is more complicated than this simple explanation has indicated. In a futures market, the dealings are strictly impersonal; buyers and sellers know nothing but the price, a few characteristics of the product, and the date and the place of delivery. Unlike forward contracts, futures contracts rarely result in actual delivery. Buyers usually settle their contracts by purchasing offsetting contracts before the last day of trading. For example, a contract to deliver can be settled (or closed) by purchasing an offsetting contract (in effect promising to receive delivery).

A purchaser of a futures contract today in effect agrees to accept delivery of, say, $1 million of T-bills at a specific date in the future at a specific price (or implicit coupon yield). The price specified in the futures contract is called the **futures price.** Table 7-4 gives some futures prices and other information on T-bills for February 15, 1983. A **spot price** is the price that the commodity can be purchased for today, or "on the spot." It is also called today's cash price. The *spot* or cash discount rate on the March 1983, 91-day Treasury bill (not shown) is 7.85 percent. In contrast, the *futures* settlement discount rate on the March 1983 contract is 8.20 percent, as shown in Table 7-4.

On the other side of the exchange, it is possible to sell a futures contract. When an investor sells a futures contract, he or she in effect agrees to deliver a specified amount of a commodity at a specified date and price. Those who have agreed to deliver commodities in the future at a stated price are said to have a **short position,** or to be short, or to have gone short; they have sold

TABLE 7-4 Futures Prices for Treasury Bills as of February 15, 1983

This table shows the implicit discount rate at which different contracts of 91-day Treasury bills traded.* Column (1) shows the month in which the contract matures; column (2), the implicit rate at which the contract opened; column (3), the high for the day; column (4), the low for the day; and column (5), the change from the preceding day. Columns (6) and (7) show the settlement and change in discount rates directly (so that they need not be implied from the index); column (8) shows the open interest (or number of contracts which have not been closed by offsetting contracts).

Treasury bills (IMM) — $1 mil.; pts. of 100%

(1)	Open (2)	High (3)	Low (4)	Settle	Chg (5)	Settle (6)	Chg (7)	Open interest (8)
Mar 83	91.86	91.89	91.78	91.80−	.03	8.20+	.03	26,599
June	91.77	91.83	91.62	91.64−	.02	8.36+	.02	12,523
Sept	91.36	91.38	91.29	91.32		8.68		4,179
Dec	91.05	91.05	90.99	90.99		9.01		1,941
Mar 84	90.74	90.75	90.66	90.69−	.03	9.31+	.03	751
June	90.50	90.50	90.42	90.42−	.06	9.58	.06	497
Sept	90.20	90.31	90.20	90.20−	.07	9.80	.07	170
Dec	90.04	90.04	90.01	90.01−	.05	9.99+	.05	59

*The International Monetary Market (IMM) developed a method of quoting T-bill discount rates for futures that conforms to the conventional methods of trading in stocks and commodities futures. The IMM system is an index based on the difference between the actual T-bill discount rate and 100. A T-bill discount rate of 6.00 percent would be quoted as 94.00 on the IMM in terms of the index. (Note 94.00 is *not* the price; the price of a 90-day T-bill is $985.00.)
Source: Adapted from *The Wall Street Journal,* Feb. 16, 1983.

futures contracts. Those who agree to buy a certain quantity at a stated price in the future are said to have a **long position,** or to have gone long.

The Why of Securities Futures
Financial futures provide an opportunity for bond purchasers to protect themselves against rises in the market rate of interest that reduce the market price of bonds. Bond purchasers guarantee themselves an interest rate (bond price) in the future, thereby reducing the risk—and potential profit—of purchasing bonds. The risk is placed on speculators who accept it voluntarily (by guaranteeing the future bond price to the futures seller), hoping to earn large profits.

This risk transfer is akin to the situation where farmers sell their growing products for a guaranteed price in the future (because they fear that market prices will fall by the time the crops are ready for market) to speculators who are betting on a future price rise. The farmer is guaranteed a modest profit and the speculator is liable for big gains or losses.

It's interesting that a T-bill, which is already quite liquid because it is of short maturity and because it is traded in secondary markets, can be made *simultaneously* more liquid (to hedgers) and less liquid (to speculators) due to the emergence of a T-bill futures market.

The T-Bill Futures Market
One of the most active financial futures markets is that for 3-month (91-day) T-bills. An investor could buy a contract today to take delivery of (and pay for) $1 million of 3-month T-bills 91 days from today. After a seller of a contract to make delivery has been located in the trading pits by open outcry (quite unlike the sedate telephone conversations in the markets for the T-bills themselves), the trade is concluded with an agreement on the price. At this point, a clearinghouse interposes itself in the transaction in the following way: The buyer's contract and the seller's contract are now with the clearinghouse and not with the other party in the transaction.

The key role of the clearinghouse is to administer the different requirements imposed on the transactors in futures contracts. For example, certain **margin requirements** are created by the exchanges, such as the Chicago Board of Trade or the Chicago Mercantile Exchange.[6] An initial margin of, say, .0012 percent, or $1,200, per $1 million contract in T-bills is imposed on the buyer. This margin may be posted in the form of cash, eligible securities, or bank letters of credit.

For as long as the contract is outstanding, it will be "marked to market." That is, a buyer of a contract to take delivery in 91 days will have his or her margin account credited with the profit if the market price of the contract rises, or debited with a loss if its price declines. Profits in the margin account may be withdrawn immediately; but when sufficient losses occur to reduce the margin below $1,200 per contract, the buyer must pay the difference in cash into his or her account before trading opens the next day.

---

[6]A margin requirement of, say, 20 percent means that a purchaser must "put up" 20 percent of the purchasing price—in effect, the purchaser can borrow only 80 percent of the purchase price. Higher margin requirements presumably reduce the degree of risk in such transactions.

When the customer wishes to get out of the contract before maturity, he or she must take an offsetting position. That is, in order for a buyer to get out of the futures contract to take delivery of $1 million of T-bills on some day in the future, he or she must sell a futures contract for delivery of $1 million of T-bills on that same date. The order is sent to the trading pit, and a sales contract is executed (not with the party who sold it in the first place). Once again, the clearinghouse interposes itself between the two parties, and the latest sale is offset against the original purchase. If T-bill futures contract prices go up after the customer purchases a futures contract, the customer obtains a profit; and conversely, a loss occurs if T-bill futures prices fall.

CHAPTER SUMMARY

1 When the U.S. Treasury collects revenues that are insufficient to cover federal government expenditures, it must borrow. The total amount of U.S. government securities outstanding is called the national debt; the national debt results from federal government deficit spending.

2 A primary market exists for Treasury bills; every week an auction for T-bills is conducted. Competitive and noncompetitive bids are tendered in these auctions.

3 No coupon interest payments are made on T-bills. T-bills are sold at a discount; therefore, interest earned is represented by the difference between what is paid for the T-bill at auction and the face value for which the bill is redeemed at maturity. Published T-bill rates are discount rates that are based on a 360-day year. The T-bill equivalent coupon yield takes into account a 365-day year and the fact that interest is earned on the price of the bill and not its face value. It follows that the T-bill equivalent coupon yield exceeds the published T-bill rate.

4 A secondary market exists for T-bills. Because these T-bills mature in less than a year, the approximate coupon yield formula must take this into account. Because T-bills are of such a short duration, even very large changes in the market interest rate cause only slight changes in the prices of T-bills. As a consequence, they are considered very safe and very liquid.

5 Over $250 billion in government debt matures each year and is repaid by borrowing again. Since this is an enormous undertaking, debt-management principles have been developed. The principles that the Treasury might take into account in its management of the debt include stabilization, minimization of the frequency of issue, and cost minimization.

6 The federal government deficit only partially reflects the impact of federal government influence on the financial market. Federal government loan activities that do not show up directly on the federal budget are off-budget agency activities, operation of government-sponsored enterprises, and provision of federally guaranteed loans. Inclusion of off-budget agency borrowing and lending, in effect, increases the *actual* budget deficit.

7 Tax-exempt municipal bonds benefit only those people in high marginal tax brackets; they are tax-free but their yield has been bid down by high-income individuals seeking tax shelters.

8 A futures market for securities provides lenders with an opportunity to protect themselves against changes in the market rate of interest. Of course, decreased

risk is obtained only by sacrificing potential capital gains. In effect, traders who wish to avoid risk are able to earn modest returns, while others are allowed to speculate and try for higher returns.

GLOSSARY

Asked price: The price at which a dealer is willing to sell credit instruments in a secondary market.

Bid price: The price at which a dealer is willing to purchase credit instruments in a secondary market.

Competitive bid: An offer to purchase a specific dollar amount of T-bills at a specified price in the primary market for T-bills.

Coupon yield equivalent: The yield on a T-bill when it is adjusted for a 365-day year, using the bond's market price instead of its face value.

Futures market: A market in which people presently agree to exchange a specific commodity at a specified price on some specific future date.

Futures price: The price specified in a futures contract.

General obligation bonds: Municipal bonds that are secured by the taxing power of the issuing municipality.

Long position: An agreement to buy a specific quantity of some commodity in the future at a stated price.

Margin requirement: The percentage of the purchase price of stocks or bonds that a customer must pay when funds are borrowed to finance the purchase.

National debt: The total market value of all U.S. government securities outstanding.

Noncompetitive bid: An offer to purchase a specific dollar amount of T-bills at the average price in the competitive

auction in the primary market for T-bills.

Revenue bonds: Municipal bonds that are secured by the earnings of the project financed by the bond sales.

Short position: An agreement to deliver a specific quantity of some commodity in the future at a stated price.

Spot price: The price at which a commodity can be purchased right now; today's cash price.

Subscription: An offering of new issues of U.S. Treasury notes or bonds at announced coupon rates.

Treasury bill rate: The percent discounted from the par value of a T-bill, calculated on a 360-day year.

PROBLEMS

7-1 Calculate the published T-bill rate for a $10,000, 91-day bill that is sold at auction for $9,700.

7-2 Calculate the approximate coupon yield equivalent of the T-bill indicated in problem 7-1.

7-3 Calculate the approximate coupon yield equivalent of a 91-day T-bill purchased in a secondary market for $9,700 that matures in 79 days.

7-4 Assume a 10 percent effective coupon yield on the date of issuance of a 91-day T-bill that has a face value of $10,000.

a What is its selling price?

b What is its selling price 10 days later if interest rates rise to 25 percent?

SELECTED REFERENCES

First Boston Corporation, *Handbook of Securities of the United States Government and Federal Agencies;* published every second year.

Robbins, Sidney, *The Securities Markets: Operations and Issues* (New York: The Free Press, 1966).

Webster, Charles E., Jr., "The Effects of Deficits on Interest Rates," *Economic Review,* Federal Reserve Bank of Kansas City, May 1983, pp. 19–28.

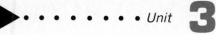

Commercial Banking

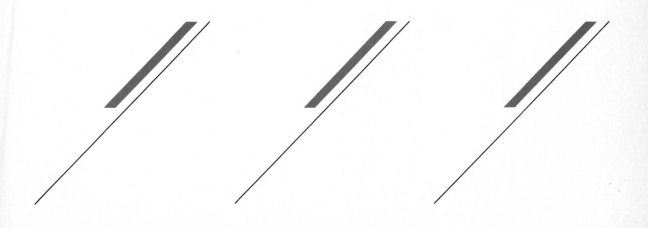

Chapter 8

Deposit Creation

CHAPTER PREVIEW

1 What happens when someone deposits in a depository institution a check that is written on another depository institution?

2 What happens when someone deposits in a depository institution a check that is written on the Fed?

3 How does a depository institution react to an increase in its reserves?

4 What is the maximum deposit expansion multiplier?

5 What reduces the size of the deposit expansion multiplier?

Many depository institutions accept transactions deposits, which mean that they will hold your money and pay it out as you order them to do so. These institutions—commercial banks and thrift institutions—need not hold a 100 percent reserve on their transactions-balance liabilities. Rather, they are required to hold only fractional reserves; they lend out part and keep part on deposit at all times. As this chapter will show, the requirement of fractional reserves for transactions balances leads to a multiple expansion (or contraction) of the money supply (however defined) when the reserves of these institutions increase (or decrease). For example, when a U.S. government security is purchased from the public by the Fed, the new funds are deposited in depository institutions, but only a fraction of them need be held as reserves. The remainder can be lent. In turn, those funds are redeposited in the system and again a fraction of them is held as reserves; the remainder can be lent once more. Thus, there is a multiple expansion of the money supply.

In the analysis that follows, we examine the relationship between the level of reserves and the size of the money supply. This analysis shows that whatever affects reserves also affects the money supply. We show first that when someone deposits a check in one bank, *that is written on another bank,* the two banks involved are individually affected—but the overall money supply does not change. Then we show that when someone deposits a check in a depository institution that is written on the *Fed,* a multiple expansion in the money supply results.

THE RELATIONSHIP BETWEEN RESERVES AND TOTAL DEPOSITS IN DEPOSITORY INSTITUTIONS

To show the relationship between reserves and depository institution deposits, we first analyze a single bank (existing alongside many others).

This single bank is required to hold reserves, in the form of vault cash or in its reserve account with a Fed district bank; any reserves held above the **required reserves** are referred to as **excess reserves.** For example, if you deposit a $1,000 check in bank A, which is subject to a 10 percent reserve requirement, when bank A receives credit for this check by the Fed (the Fed increases bank A's reserve account by $1,000), it receives an increase in reserves of $1,000—$100 of which are required and $900 of which are excess.

A single bank is able to make loans to its customers only to the extent that it has reserves above the level legally required to cover the new deposits. When an individual bank has (has no) excess reserves, it can (cannot) make loans and change the money supply. Only the banking system as a whole can alter the amount of deposits and hence the money supply. This will become obvious as the T-accounts of an isolated bank are compared to the T-accounts of several banks that we will use to represent the complete banking system.

How a Single Bank Reacts to an Increase in Reserves To examine the behavior of a single bank after its reserves are increased, the following assumptions are made.

1 The **required reserve ratio** is 12 percent for all transactions deposits: The government requires that an amount equal to 12 percent of all demand deposits be held on reserve in a district Federal Reserve bank, or in vault cash.

2 Transactions deposits are the bank's only liability; reserves at the district Federal Reserve bank and loans are the bank's only assets. Loans are promises made by customers to repay some amount in the future; that is, they are IOUs.

3 There is such a ready loan demand that the bank has no trouble lending additional money.

4 Every time a loan is made to an individual (consumer or business), all of the proceeds from the loan are put into a transactions deposit; no cash (paper currency or coins) is withdrawn.

5 Depository institutions desire to keep their excess reserves at a zero level because reserves at the district Federal Reserve bank do not earn interest. Depository institutions will wish to convert excess reserves into interest-bearing assets such as loans.

Look at the initial positon of the bank in Figure 8-1. Liabilities consist of $1 million in demand deposits. Assets consist of $120,000 in reserves, which you can see are required reserves in the form of vault cash or in the depository institution's reserve account at the district Federal Reserve branch, and $880,000 in loans to customers. Total assets of $1 million equal total liabilities of $1 million.[1] With a 12 percent reserve requirement and $1 million in demand deposits, the bank has required reserves of $120,000 (12 percent of $1 million), actual reserves of $120,000, and no excess reserves.

Assume that a *new* depositor writes a $100,000 check drawn on another depository institution and deposits it in bank 1. Demand deposits in bank 1, therefore, immediately increase by $100,000, bringing the total to $1.1 million. At the same time, total reserves of bank 1 increase to $220,000. A $1.1 million total in demand deposits means that required reserves will have to be $132,000. Bank 1 *now has* excess reserves equal to $220,000 minus $132,000, or $88,000. This is shown in the **T-account** in Figure 8-2.

Look at excess reserves in Figure 8-2. Excess reserves were zero before the $100,000 deposit and after they are $88,000—that's $88,000 worth of

---

[1]The simplifying assumption here is that assets equal liabilities and that the bank has a zero net worth. Actually, a depository institution rarely has a net worth of more than a small percentage of its total assets. In fact, in the 1980s, a number of depository institutions had a net worth approaching zero. Many of those institutions were forced to merge with financially stronger institutions.

Assets		Liabilities	
Total reserves	$120,000	Demand deposits	$1,000,000
Required reserves ($120,000)			
Excess reserves (−0)			
Loans	$880,000		
Total	$1,000,000	Total	$1,000,000

FIGURE 8-1 **Bank 1.**

Assets		Liabilities	
Total reserves	$220,000	Demand deposits	$1,100,000
Required reserves ($132,000)			
Excess reserves ($88,000)			
Loans	$880,000		
Total	$1,100,000	Total	$1,100,000

FIGURE 8-2 **Bank 1.**

assets not earning any income. Bank 1 will now lend out this $88,000 in excess reserves in order to obtain income. Loans will increase to $968,000. The borrowers who receive the loans will not leave them on deposit in bank 1. They borrow money to spend it. As they spend it, actual reserves eventually will fall to $132,000 (as required), and excess reserves will again become zero, as indicated in Figure 8-3.

In this example, a person came in and deposited an additional $100,000 check drawn on another bank. That $100,000 became part of the reserves of

FIGURE 8-3 **Bank 1.**

Assets		Liabilities	
Total reserves	$132,000	Demand deposits	$1,100,000
Required reserves ($132,000)			
Excess reserves (−0)			
Loans	$968,000		
Total	$1,100,000	Total	$1,100,000

bank 1. Because that deposit immediately created excess reserves, further loans were possible for bank 1. The excess reserves were lent out to earn interest. A bank will not lend more than its excess reserves because, by law, it must hold a certain amount of required reserves.

What Has Happened to the Money Supply?   A look at the T-accounts for bank 1 might give the impression that the money supply increased because of the new customer's $100,000 deposit. Remember, though, that the deposit was a check written on another bank. Therefore, the other bank suffered a *decline* in its demand deposits and its reserves. While total assets and liabilities in bank 1 have increased by $100,000, they have decreased in the other bank by $100,000. Thus, the *total* amount of money and credit in the economy is unaffected by the transfer of funds from one depository institution to another.

Each individual depository institution can create loans (and deposits) only to the extent that it has excess reserves. In the above example, bank 1 had $88,000 of excess reserves after the deposit of the $100,000. On the other hand, the bank on which the check was written found that its excess reserves were now a *negative* $88,000 (assuming it had zero excess reserves previously). That bank now has less reserves than required by law; it has deficit reserves.[2] It will have to call in loans in order to make actual reserves meet required reserves.

The thing to remember is that new reserves are not created when checks written on one bank are deposited in another bank. The Federal Reserve System, however, can create new reserves; that is the subject of the next section.

THE FED'S DIRECT EFFECT ON THE OVERALL LEVEL OF RESERVES

This section examines the *Fed's* direct effect on the level of reserves. Following it is an explanation of how a change in the level of reserves causes a multiple change in the total money supply. First consider the Federal Open Market Committee (FOMC), whose decisions essentially determine the level of reserves in the monetary system.

Federal Open Market Committee (FOMC)   Open-market operations are the buying and selling of U.S. government securities in the open market (the private secondary U.S. securities market) by the FOMC in order to change the money supply. If the FOMC decides that the Fed should buy or sell bonds, it instructs the New York Federal Reserve Bank trading desk to do so.[3]

---

[2]If bank 2 held zero excess reserves, it held $12 in required reserves for every $100 in demand deposit liabilities. If a $1 loss in demand deposit liabilities led to a 12-cent reduction in total reserves, bank 2 would still have zero excess reserves. A $1 reduction in demand deposit liabilities, however, leads to a $1 loss in total reserves; therefore, bank 2 will experience an 88-cent net reduction for every $1 it loses in demand deposit liabilities.

[3]Actually, the Fed usually deals in Treasury *bills*.

FEDERAL RESERVE SYSTEM		DEPOSITORY INSTITUTION	
Assets	Liabilities	Assets	Liabilities
+$100,000 U.S. government securities	+$100,000 Depository institution's reserves	+$100,000 Reserves	+$100,000 Transactions deposit owned by broker

FIGURE 8-4   T-Accounts for the Federal Reserve and the Depository Institution When a U.S. Government Security Is Purchased by the Fed.

A Sample Transaction   Assume that the trading desk at the New York Fed has received an order to purchase $100,000 worth of U.S. government securities.[4]

The Fed pays for these securities by writing a check on itself for $100,000. This check is given to the bond dealer in exchange for the $100,000 worth of bonds. The bond dealer deposits a $100,000 check in its transactions account at a bank, which then sends the $100,000 check back to the Federal Reserve. When the Fed receives the check, it adds $100,000 to the reserve account of the bank that sent it the check. Thus, the Fed has created $100,000 of reserves. The Fed can create reserves because it has the ability to "write up" (that is, add to) the reserve accounts of depository institutions whenever it buys U.S. securities. When the Fed buys a U.S. government security in the open market, it expands total reserves and the money supply (initially) by the amount of the purchase.

Using T-Accounts   Consider the T-accounts of the Fed and of the depository institution receiving the check. Figure 8-4 shows the T-accounts for the Federal Reserve after the bond purchase and for the depository institution after the bond dealer deposits the $100,000 check. The Fed's T-account (which here deals only with changes) shows that after the purchase, the Fed's assets have increased by $100,000 in the form of U.S. government securities. Liabilities have also increased by $100,000, in the form of an increase in the reserve account of the depository institution. The T-account for the depository institution shows an increase in assets of $100,000 in the form of reserves with its district Federal Reserve bank. The depository institution also has an increase in its liabilities in the form of $100,000 in the transaction account of the bond broker; this is an immediate $100,000 increase in the money supply.

---

[4]In practice, the trading desk is never given a specific dollar amount to purchase or sell. The account manager uses personal discretion in determining what amount should be purchased or sold in order to satisfy the FOMC's latest directive. For expositional purposes, assume nonetheless that the account manager is directed to make a specific transaction.

The Sale of a $100,000 U.S. Government Security by the Fed   The process is reversed when the account manager at the New York Fed trading desk sells a U.S. government security from the portfolio of the Fed. When the individual or institution buying the security from the Fed writes a check for $100,000, the Fed reduces the reserves of the depository institution on which the check was written. Thus, the $100,000 sale of the U.S. government security leads to a reduction in reserves in the banking system.

Using T-Accounts   Figure 8-5 shows the T-accounts for the sale of a U.S. government security by the Fed. On the left-hand side, the T-account for the Federal Reserve is shown. When the $100,000 check goes to the Federal Reserve System, the Federal Reserve reduces by $100,000 the reserve account of the depository institution on which the check is written. The Fed's assets are also reduced by $100,000 because it no longer owns the U.S. government security. The depository institution's liabilities are reduced by $100,000 when that amount is deducted from the account of the bond purchaser, and the money supply is thereby reduced by that amount. The depository institution's assets are also reduced by $100,000 because the Fed has reduced its reserves by that amount.

Adjusting the Price of the U.S. Government Securities   No one is forced to deal with the Fed; it sells or purchases government securities in the open market. The Fed merely adjusts the price it offers or asks until it can buy or sell what it wants. For example, if the Fed wants to sell a U.S. government security for $100,000 and no one wants to buy it, the Fed can lower the selling price (thereby increasing the yield). If the Fed wants to buy a $100,000 U.S. security and no one wants to sell it, it raises its offered price until sellers are willing to sell at the price offered (thereby reducing the yield).

Remember that the Fed can purchase as large an amount of U.S. government securities as it wishes because it is empowered to pay for them by writing a check on itself. Also, it can adjust the price of bonds to achieve its objective because, unlike private securities dealers, it does not have to worry about minimizing capital losses or maximizing capital gains. The Fed is operated for social benefit, not for private gains. In any event, every time the Fed purchases

FIGURE 8-5   **T-Accounts after the Fed Has Sold $100,000 of U.S. Government Securities.**

FEDERAL RESERVE SYSTEM		DEPOSITORY INSTITUTION	
Assets	Liabilities	Assets	Liabilities
−$100,000 Reduction in U.S. government securities	−$100,000 Depository institution's reserves	−$100,000 Reserves	−$100,000 Transactions account balances

U.S. government securities, it increases reserves in the system. We will now consider the relationship between the resulting money supply and reserves.

MONEY (DEPOSIT) EXPANSION BY THE BANKING SYSTEM

Consider now the entire banking system. For all practical purposes, we can look at all depository institutions (we will refer to them as banks) taken as a whole. While they do not all have the same reserve requirements and their different liabilities do not have the same reserve requirements, for the purpose of exposition, these real-world details may be ignored. To understand how money is created, we must understand how depository institutions respond to Fed actions that increase reserves in the entire system.

The Fed Purchases U.S. Government Securities Assume that the Fed purchases a $100,000 U.S. government security from a bond broker. The bond broker deposits the $100,000 check in bank 1 (which started out in the position depicted in Figure 8-1). The check, however, is not written on another depository institution. Rather, it is written on the Fed itself.

Look at the T-account for bank 1 shown in Figure 8-6. If this figure looks familiar, it is because it is exactly the same as Figure 8-2. Reserves have been increased by $100,000 to $220,000, and demand deposits have also been increased by $100,000. Because required reserves on $1.1 million of demand deposits are only $132,000 ($1,100,000 $\times$ .12 = $132,000), there are $88,000 ($220,000 − $132,000 = $88,000) of excess reserves.

What Has Happened to the Money Supply? The major difference between this example and the one given previously is that *here the money supply increased by $100,000 immediately.* Why? Because demand deposits held by the public—the bond brokers—are part of the money supply *and no other bank has lost reserves.* Thus, the purchase of a $100,000 U.S. government

FIGURE 8-6 Bank 1.

Assets		Liabilities	
Total reserves	$220,000	Demand deposits	$1,100,000
Required reserves ($132,000)			
Excess reserves ($88,000)			
Loans	$880,000		
Total	$1,100,000	Total	$1,100,000

Assets		Liabilities	
Total reserves	$132,000	Demand deposits	$1,100,000
Required reserves ($132,000)			
Excess reserves (−0)			
Loans	$968,000		
Total	$1,100,000	Total	$1,100,000

FIGURE 8-7   **Bank 1.**

security by the Federal Reserve from the public increases the money supply immediately by $100,000.

The Process Does Not Stop   The process of money creation does not stop here. Look again at the T-account in Figure 8-6. Bank 1 has excess reserves of $88,000. No other depository institution (or combination of depository institutions) has negative excess reserves of $88,000 as a result of the Fed's bond purchase.

Bank 1 will not wish to hold non-interest-bearing excess reserves. It will expand its loans by $88,000, as shown in Figure 8-7. Figure 8-7 is exactly like Figure 8-3, but there has been no corresponding reduction in loans at any other depository institution.

The individuals who have received the $88,000 of new loans will spend these funds, which will then be deposited in other banks. To make this example simple, assume that the $88,000 in excess reserves was lent to a single firm for the purpose of buying a Burger King franchise. After the firm buys the Burger King franchise, Burger King deposits the $88,000 in its account at bank 2. For the purpose of simplicity, ignore the previous assets and liabilities in bank 2 and concentrate only on the T-account *changes* resulting from this new deposit, as shown in Figure 8-8. A plus sign indicates that the T-account has increased, and a minus sign indicates that the entry has decreased. For bank 2, the $88,000 deposit, after the check has been sent to the Fed, becomes an

FIGURE 8-8   **Bank 2.**

Assets		Liabilities	
Total reserves	$88,000	New demand deposits	$88,000
Required reserves ($10,500)			
Excess reserves ($77,440)			
Total	$88,000	Total	$88,000

Assets		Liabilities	
Total reserves	$10,560	Demand deposits	$88,000
Required reserves ($90,000)			
Excess reserves (−0)			
Loans	$77,440		
Total	**$88,000**	**Total**	**$88,000**

FIGURE 8-9   Bank 2.

increase in reserves (assets) as well as an increase in demand deposits (liabilities). Because the reserve requirement is assumed to be 12 percent, or $10,560, bank 2 will have excess reserves of $77,440. But, of course, excess reserves are not income-producing, so bank 2 will reduce them to zero by making loans of $77,440 (which will earn interest income), as Figure 8-9 shows.

Remember that in this example the original $100,000 deposit was a check issued by a Federal Reserve bank. That $100,000 constituted an immediate increase in the money supply of $100,000. The money-creation process (in addition to the original $100,000) occurs because of the fractional reserve banking system, coupled with the desire of depository institutions to maintain zero excess reserves (given a sufficient loan demand).

A Continuation of the Money Creation Process   Assume that another firm has received a $77,440 loan from bank 2 because it wants to buy into an oil-drilling firm. This oil-drilling firm has an account at bank 3. Look at bank 3's simplified T-account in Figure 8-10, where, again, only increases in the assets and liabilities are shown. When the firm borrowing from bank 2 pays the $77,440 to the oil-drilling firm's manager, the manager deposits the check at bank 3. Total reserves at bank 3 go up by that amount when the check is sent to the Fed.

FIGURE 8-10   Bank 3.

Assets		Liabilities	
Total reserves	$77,440	New demand deposits	$77,440
Required reserves ($9,292.80)			
Excess reserves ($68,147.20)			
Total	**$77,440**	**Total**	**$77,440**

Assets		Liabilities	
Total reserves	$ 9,292.80	Demand deposits	$77,440.00
Required reserves ($9,292.80)			
Excess reserves (− 0)			
Loans	$68,147.20		
Total	$77,440.00	Total	$77,440.00

FIGURE 8-11   Bank 3.

Because the reserve requirement is 12 percent, required reserves rise by $9,292.80 and excess reserves are therefore $68,147.20. Bank 3 also will want to lend those non-interest-earning assets (excess reserves). When it does, loans will increase by $68,147.20. Total reserves will fall to $9,292.80; excess reserves become zero as the oil-drilling firm's manager writes checks on the new deposits. The money supply has thereby increased by another $68,147.20, as indicated in Figure 8-11.

The Process Continues to Banks 4, 5, 6, Etc.   This process will continue. Each bank obtains smaller and smaller increases in deposits because 12 percent of each deposit must be held in reserve; therefore, each succeeding depository institution makes correspondingly smaller loans. Table 8-1 shows the new deposits, possible loans, and required reserves for the remaining depository institutions in the system.

TABLE 8-1   The Maximum Potential Effect on the Money Supply of an Increase in Reserves of $100,000 with a 12% Required Reserve

Bank	New Deposits	Possible Loans & Investments (Excess Reserves)	Required Reserves
1	$100,000	$ 88,000	$ 12,000
2	88,000	77,440	10,560
3	77,440	68,147	9,293
4	68,147	59,970	8,178
5	59,970	52,773	7,196
6	52,773	46,440	6,333
7	46,440	40,868	5,573
8	40,868	35,963	4,904
All other banks	$299,695	$263,732	$ 35,963
Total	$833,333	$733,333	$100,000

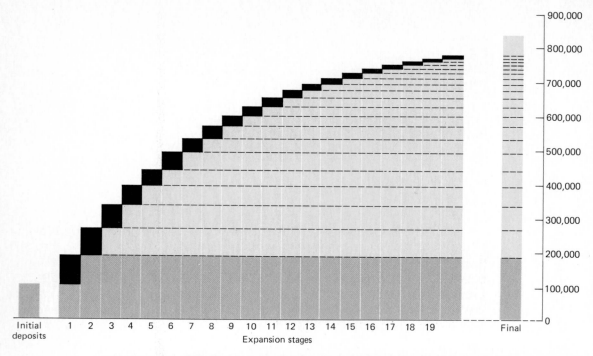

FIGURE 8-12 The Multiple Expansion in the Money Supply Due to $100,000 in New Reserves, When the Required Reserve Ratio Is 12%. The banks are all aligned in decreasing order of new deposits created. This is merely a graphical representation of Table 8-1.

What Has Happened to the Total Money Supply? In this simple example, the money supply increased initially by the $100,000 that the Fed paid to the bond broker in exchange for a bond. It was further increased by an $88,000 deposit in bank 2. And it was again increased by a $77,440 deposit in bank 3. Eventually the money supply will increase by a total approaching $833,333.33. This is shown in Table 8-1 and graphically represented in Figure 8-12.

Overall Reserves Must Increase for the Multiple Expansion to Occur Even with fractional reserve banking and zero excess reserves, the money supply cannot multiply unless overall reserves are increased. The original new deposit in bank 1 in the previous example was in the form of a check written on a Federal Reserve district bank. It therefore represented *new* reserves to the banking system. Had that check been written on bank 3, for example, nothing would have happened to the total amount of demand deposits; there would have been no change in the total money supply. To repeat: Checks written on banks within the system represent assets and liabilities which simply cancel each other out. Only when excess reserves are created by the Federal Reserve System can the money supply increase.

The example would work the same way if depository institutions used their excess reserves to acquire interest-earning securities instead of to make loans. The owners of those securities would receive checks from the purchasing depository institution; the securities sellers would then deposit these checks into their own depository institutions. The deposit expansion process would continue in the same manner.

THE MONEY (DEPOSIT) MULTIPLIER

In the example just given, a $100,000 increase in excess reserves generated by the Fed's purchase of a security yielded an $833,333 increase in the money supply; the money supply increased by an $8\frac{1}{3}$ multiple of the initial $100,000 increase in overall reserves. The relationship between the *maximum* increase in demand deposits and the change in reserves can be derived mathematically. Again assume that there are only demand deposits in the system and that the required reserve ratio is the same for all depository institutions, and that banks hold zero excess reserves. Consider the following equation:

$$R = r \times D \tag{8-1}$$

where R = total reserves
r = required reserve ratio
D = demand deposits

In other words, total reserves in the system equal the required reserve ratio times total demand deposits.

Now divide each side of Equation (8-1) by the required reserve ratio, r.

$$R/r = (r \times D)/r = rD/r \tag{8-2}$$

The right-hand side of this equation can be simplified by eliminating r, so that

$$R/r = D \tag{8-3}$$

and

$$R \times 1/r = D \tag{8-4}$$

Now multiply the left-hand and right-hand sides of this equation by a small change, which we denote by Δ, so that

$$\Delta R \cdot 1/r = \Delta D \tag{8-5}$$

Equation (8-4) shows that a change in reserves that produces excess reserves will increase demand deposits by the factor $1/r$ times the change in reserves; $1/r$ is the money multiplier.[5] Consider the example used earlier. The Fed increased reserves by $100,000 and the required reserve ratio was 12 percent. Putting those values into Equation (8-4) yields:

$$\$100,000 \times 1/.12 = \$100,000 \times 8\tfrac{1}{3} = \$833,333 \qquad \text{(8-6)}$$

In this example, the money multiplier was $8\tfrac{1}{3}$; $1/.12 = 8\tfrac{1}{3}$.

The *money multiplier* given in Equation (8-4) can also be used for deposit *contraction.* If the Fed sells a $100,000 T-bill, excess reserves in the system are reduced by $100,000. Given a required reserve ratio of 12 percent, demand deposits (and hence the money supply) will decrease by $833,333.

This formula gives the *maximum* that the money supply will change for a specific change in reserves, or the maximum deposit multiplier. It is a formula for a very simplified world in which all depository institutions have the same required reserve ratio and all deposits are demand deposits, and the public wants neither more nor less cash on hand. In reality, different depository institutions have different reserve ratios, depending on their total assets. Also, the reserve ratio for demand deposits is different from that for time deposits. Finally, when the community wants to hold more or less cash, then the money multiplier will change. We now turn to a discussion of forces that reduce the size of the money multiplier.

Forces That Reduce the Size of the Money Multiplier   A number of simplified assumptions were made originally to derive the maximum money multiplier. The expansion (or contraction) multiplier in the real world is considerably smaller. Several factors account for this:

Leakages   The entire loan from one depository institution is not typically deposited in another depository institution. There are at least two leakages that may occur:

1 *Currency Drains:*   When deposits increase, the public may wish to hold more currency. Currency that is kept in a person's wallet or purse or stashed in a safe deposit box or hidden underneath a mattress remains outside banks. The greater the amount of cash leakage, the smaller will be the money multiplier. To the extent that there are cash leakages in each step, the amount of deposits in the next depository institution will be smaller than otherwise; therefore, the excess reserves in those depository institutions will be smaller. The creation of new loans will hence be smaller.

---

[5]You may have observed, from Figure 8-12, that the deposit expansion process can be expressed as the sum of a geometric series. In particular, $1 + b + b^2 + \cdots + b^{n-1} + \cdots = 1/(1 - b)$, if $0 < b < 1$. In our example, $b = .88$, which represents the percentage of a change in deposits that can be used to create new deposits; $r = 1 - b = .12$, which equals the required reserve ratio. Thus, $1 + (.88) + (.88)^2 + \cdots + (.88)^{n-1} + \cdots = 1/.12 = 8\tfrac{1}{3}$. Thus $\Delta D = \Delta R(1 + b + b^2 + b^{n-1} + \cdots) = \Delta R \times 1/r$.

2 *Excess Reserves:* Depository institutions may maintain excess reserves above zero. Depository institutions do not in fact always keep zero excess reserves. For example, when they fear significant future rises in interest rates (which would lower the prices of bonds they purchase) or if the economy appears to be headed for a recession (which would increase the risk of borrower default on principal and interest), they may keep reserves above the required level. To the extent that depository institutions wish to keep positive excess reserves (sometimes called **prudential reserves**), the money multiplier will be smaller. Assuming a 12 percent required reserve, a depository institution receiving $100,000 in new deposits might keep more than $12,000 in additional reserves. The greater the desire for excess reserves, the smaller the deposit expansion multiplier.

The currency-drain effect is believed to be more significant than the effect of excess reserves.

Demand versus Time Deposits In the real world, time deposits typically carry a lower reserve requirement ratio than demand deposits do. The Depository Institutions Deregulation and Monetary Control Act of 1980 mandates the minimum and maximum reserve-requirement ratios that the Fed can set on demand deposits at 3 and 14 percent, respectively; on time deposits (other than savings), the minimum and maximum are 0 and 9 percent. Therefore, if some of the new deposits created are converted into time deposits, the money multiplier will actually increase.

Changes in the Amount of Currency Held by the Public[6] The public acquires currency from depository institutions by "cashing" checks, and rids itself of undesired currency accumulation by placing the currency with depository institutions, in return for increases in its transactions accounts. While currency withdrawals and deposits are an everyday occurrence, *major* withdrawals are made prior to Christmas and other holidays; the currency is returned after the holidays. Later in the text we show how such major withdrawals and deposits of currency are a force that the Fed must reckon with when it conducts monetary policy. Here we are concerned only with showing how currency deposits and withdrawals affect the reserves of depository institutions under a fractional reserve system. A 12 percent required reserve ratio is assumed.

When Currency Is Deposited in a Bank When the public is holding more currency than it wants to hold, it can deposit the currency at its local bank in its transactions accounts. Suppose Mrs. Romano deposits $100 in currency in her demand deposit account. The bank can keep the currency in its vault cash, which counts as a reserve for its reserve requirement. Figure 8-13 shows the

---

[6]Derived from *Modern Money Mechanics,* Federal Reserve Bank of Chicago, October 1982, pp. 16–17.

Assets		Liabilities	
Vault cash	+$100	Deposits	+$100
Reserves			
Required ($12)			
Excess ($88)			
Total	$100	Total	$100

FIGURE 8-13 **The Bound Brook Bank.**

position of the Bound Brook Bank, which incurs a $100 liability in the form of demand deposits to Mrs. Romano, and a $100 increase in vault cash. Because vault cash can be used as a reserve, the Bound Brook Bank now has $88 in excess reserves and $12 in required reserves. The banking system has just received a net reserve increase. One dollar in the form of currency in circulation represents only one dollar of money; that *same* one dollar if placed in a transactions account can "support" *several* dollars of expansion of bank deposits and of bank loans and investments. A required reserve ratio of 12 percent means that, at a maximum, the money multiplier will be $8\frac{1}{3}$. In our example, the $88 increase in excess reserves that results when $100 of currency is placed in a transactions account can potentially increase the money supply by $88 \times 8\frac{1}{3} = \$733.33$.

Suppose the Bound Brook Bank decides to ship Mrs. Romano's $100 currency deposit to its regional Federal Reserve bank. Consider Figure 8-14. The Fed's T-account indicates a $100 increase in its liabilities to the Bound Brook Bank, in the form of reserves now held in its account at the Fed. Simultaneously, the Fed loses $100 in liabilities, because Federal Reserve notes (paper currency) are a liability to the Fed.

The shipment of currency from the Bound Brook Bank to its regional Federal Reserve bank shows up on the asset side of the Bound Brook Bank's T-

FIGURE 8-14

Federal Reserve Bank		Bound Brook Bank	
Assets	Liabilities	Assets	Liabilities
	+$100 Bank reserve accounts	−$100 Vault cash	
	−$100 Federal Reserve notes outstanding	+$100 Reserves with the Fed	

account. The bank loses $100 in vault cash but gains $100 in its reserve account at the Fed.

Whether the Bound Brook Bank decides to hold Mrs. Romano's $100 currency deposit or decides to ship it to the Fed, the net result is the same: The banking system experiences an $88 net increase in reserves, which is subject to a money multiplier.

When Currency Is Withdrawn from a Bank   Precisely the opposite occurs when currency is withdrawn from a bank. Suppose Mr. Ritter withdraws $100 in currency from the New Brunswick Bank by "cashing" his own (or anyone else's) $100 check there. Figure 8-15 shows the T-account of the New Brunswick Bank; as expected, that bank loses $100 in vault cash. The New Brunswick Bank experiences a $100 decrease in its assets (vault cash) and a $100 decrease in liabilities (it owes $100 less to Mr. Ritter). If the bank had previously held zero excess reserves, it now has a deficit of $88 in reserves; *total* reserves fell by $100 but its *required* reserves fell by only $12. Because the reserve requirement is 12 percent, a given amount of bank reserves can "support" deposits $8\frac{1}{3}$ times as great; when currency is withdrawn from transactions accounts, a net loss in reserves occurs. A $100 increase in currency withdrawal uses up $100 in reserves. Because an $88 decrease in the banking system's overall reserves has resulted, a money multiplier contraction can be expected. At a maximum, the money supply would fall by $733.33.

Figure 8-16 shows what happens if the New Brunswick Bank replenishes its cash by drawing down $100 in new Federal Reserve notes issued by the Federal Reserve. The Federal Reserve bank receives a $100 decrease in liabilities because it charges the New Brunswick Bank for the currency by decreasing its reserve; simultaneously, the Fed receives an increase of $100 in its liabilities because Federal Reserve notes are a liability to the Fed.

The New Brunswick Bank T-account indicates changes on the asset side; vault cash rises by $100 and its reserves with the Federal Reserve bank fall by $100.

Whether the New Brunswick Bank decides to lose vault cash or replenish it with Federal Reserve notes obtained by the Fed, the result is the same: The banking system loses $88 in net reserves, and a potential multiple contraction in the money supply occurs.

FIGURE 8-15   **The New Brunswick Bank.**

Assets		Liabilities	
Vault cash	−$100	Deposits	−$100
Reserves			
Required			
(−$12)			
Deficit			
($88)			

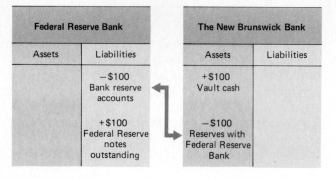

FIGURE 8-16

Empirical Estimates of the Money Multiplier
Depending on what the required reserve ratio is, the maximum money multiplier is determined; the reciprocal of the required reserve ratio indicates the maximum money multiplier. This maximum is never attained, however, because of the desire for depository institutions to hold excess reserves and the desire of the public to withdraw currency. The maximum money multiplier is further complicated by the fact that reserve requirements set on transactions accounts deposits vary with:[7]

1   The size of the depository institutions' total transactions accounts liabilities. Between $0 and $26.3 million the reserve requirement is 3 percent; over $26.3 million, the reserve requirement is 12 percent.

2   The maturity of nonpersonal time deposits (time deposits that are not transactions accounts and in which the interest is held by a depositor that is not a "natural person"). For a maturity of less than $2\frac{1}{2}$ years, the reserve ratio is 3 percent; for $2\frac{1}{2}$ years or more, the reserve requirement is 0.

Furthermore, Eurocurrency liabilities of all types have a required reserve ratio of 3 percent.

Even the potential, or maximum, money multiplier is difficult to estimate. One cannot merely average the 12 percent reserve requirement to the 3 percent reserve requirement and obtain a $7\frac{1}{2}$ percent requirement, because some of these accounts should be weighted more heavily than others due to their relative magnitudes. To compound the problem, we have several definitions of money.

Empirical estimates of money multipliers (MM) are derived by calculating the ratio of the money supply (M1 or M2) to the sum of depository institution reserves (R) and currency (C) that support this money supply. Thus,

$$MM = M1/(R + C)$$

[7]Before the Monetary Control Act of 1980, the reserve requirements were even more complicated and varied.

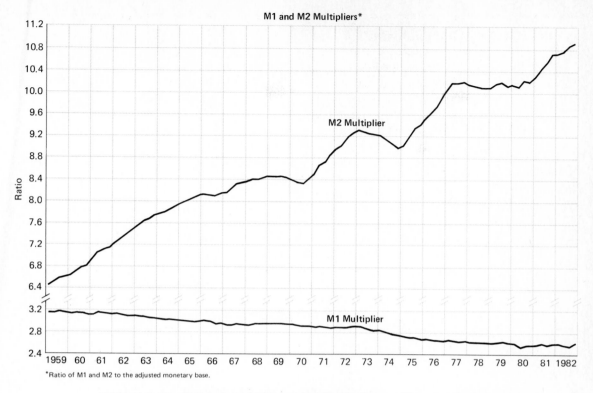

*Ratio of M1 and M2 to the adjusted monetary base.

FIGURE 8-17 Estimates of M1 and M2 Multipliers. (*Source: Review,* Federal Reserve Bank of St. Louis, March 1983, p. 15.)

and

$$MM = M2/(R + C)$$

Figure 8-17 shows empirical estimates of M1 and M2 money multipliers from 1959 to 1982. As is to be expected, the M2 multiplier is greater than the M1 multiplier (it has a larger numerator and the same denominator); the M2 multiplier is rising through time while the M1 multiplier is quite stable.

From 1980 to June 1983, while the reserve ratios indicated above have been in force, the M1 multiplier has been very stable, ranging between 2.41 and 2.64. If we make the simplifying assumption that the reserve requirement ratio was 12 percent for *all* deposits during that period, the maximum money multiplier would have been $8\frac{1}{3}$. Once we realize further that for many deposits the reserve-requirement ratio is only 3 percent, it is easy to see that the *actual* M1 money multiplier is significantly less than the maximum money multiplier. Cash withdrawals and excess reserves are important inhibitors of deposit expansion.

CHAPTER SUMMARY

1 A fractional reserve banking system leads to the possibility of a multiple expansion (contraction) of the money supply as a result of an increase (decrease) in reserves.

2 When a depository institution receives an increase in reserves over and above its required reserve level, it has an incentive to increase its lending or to purchase interest-earning securities. It can do so only to the extent that it has *excess* reserves.

3 No new reserves are created when checks written on one depository institution are deposited in another; one depository institution gets an increase in reserves that is offset by the other's loss in reserves.

4 The Fed can create or destroy depository institution reserves; as a consequence, the Fed can change the money supply. If the Fed purchases T-bills from a depository institution or from a household that deposits the Fed's check in a depository institution, *total* reserves in the banking system will rise by the price of the T-bills. Excess reserves rise (by a smaller amount) and depository institutions have an incentive to increase lending by creating transactions deposits. As a result, the money supply increases.

5 If the Fed sells T-bills to a depository institution or to a household that pays for them with a check written on a depository institution, *total* reserves in the banking system decrease. If, prior to this transaction, excess reserves were zero for the depository institutions involved, then this transaction will cause excess reserves to be negative; actual reserves will be less than required reserves. The depository institution must call in loans and not renew maturing loans. As a consequence, the money supply falls.

6 No one is forced to deal with the Fed when the Fed wishes to buy or sell in the open market; the Fed induces households and depository institutions to buy from it (or sell to it) by offering a lower price (or a higher price) for the securities. Because it is not concerned with profit maximization (and because it can purchase government securities merely by writing a check on itself), the Fed can perform as many open-market operations as necessary to achieve its objectives.

7 Fed open-market transactions directly change *overall* reserves in the banking system; therefore, the Fed can change the money supply. The relationship between changes in total reserves and changes in the public's deposits—the money supply—is defined by the deposit expansion multiplier. In order to determine the maximum deposit expansion, the change in reserves is multiplied by the reciprocal of the required-reserve ratio; the reciprocal of the required-reserve ratio is called the maximum deposit expansion multiplier. Because the United States has a fractional reserve banking system, the required-reserve ratio is less than 1 and the maximum deposit expansion multiplier is greater than 1. In other words, it is possible for the money supply to change by a multiple of a change in total reserves.

8 The real-world money multiplier is only about one-third of the maximum money multiplier, partly because depository institutions actually hold some excess reserves, but mostly because of currency drains. A currency drain occurs when the public does not deposit the *entire* amount of a check in a depository institution; the public withholds some of the check in the form of currency.

9 Time deposits typically carry a lower reserve requirement than do demand depos-

its. If some of the newly created demand deposits are subsequently transferred into time deposits, the money multiplier increases.

GLOSSARY

Excess reserves: Reserves that a depository institution, or the whole banking system, holds above required reserves; total reserves minus required reserves.

Money multiplier: The number by which a change in reserves is multiplied in order to calculate the ultimate change in deposits; the reciprocal of the required-reserve ratio.

Prudential reserves: Reserves that depository institutions voluntarily hold above required reserves in order to remain liquid to prepare for troubled times.

Required-reserve ratio: The percentage of total reserves that the Fed requires depository institutions to hold in the form of vault cash or in a reserve account with the Fed.

Required reserves: The value of reserves that a depository institution must hold in the form of vault cash or in a reserve account with the Fed; required reserves are equal to some percentage of total deposits.

T-account: A simplified balance sheet that includes only the assets and liabilities (or their changes) under discussion.

PROBLEMS

8-1 Assume a 5 percent required-reserve ratio, zero excess reserves, no cash drain, and a ready loan demand. The Fed buys a $1 million T-bill from a depository institution.

a What is the maximum money multiplier?

b By how much will total deposits rise?

8-2 The Fed purchases a $1 million T-bill from Mr. Mondrone, who deposits it in bank 1. Using T-accounts, show the immediate effects of this transaction on the Fed and bank 1.

8-3 Continuing the example from problem 8-2:

a Indicate bank 1's position more precisely using a T-account, if required reserves equal 5 percent of demand deposits.

b By how much can bank 1 increase its lending?

SELECTED REFERENCES

Nichols, Dorothy M., *Modern Money Mechanics: A Workbook on Deposits, Currency, and Bank Reserves,* Federal Reserve Bank of Chicago, 1961; revised in 1968, 1971, 1975, and 1982.

Tobin, James, "Commercial Banks as Creators of 'Money,'" in D. Carson (ed.), *Banking and Monetary Studies* (Homewood, Ill.: Irwin, 1963), pp. 408–419.

Chapter **9**

The Management of Depository Institutions

CHAPTER PREVIEW

1 Why do banks have a liquidity problem?

2 How do banks select their assets?

3 How do banks manage their liabilities?

4 How have banks changed the structure of their liabilities in recent years?

5 Are bank asset management and liability management policies interrelated?

6 Does deposit insurance increase the probability of bank failure?

The preceding chapters have shown that depository institutions are becoming more and more alike. Indeed, the blurring of distinctions among them is proceeding at an accelerated pace. For the sake of brevity, the word "bank" in this chapter refers to any of the depository institutions in our banking system.

Banks are business firms. They hire inputs and produce products or services for sale, and they aim to obtain profits. As financial intermediaries, they create short-term, highly liquid liabilities in the form of transactions and time deposits and "sell" these created liabilities to savers. The proceeds obtained are then used by the intermediaries to buy longer-term, less liquid assets (such as bonds, mortgages, consumer loans, and so on) in the financial markets.

This chapter examines the theories of managing banks. The concern of bank management theories is with the management of inputs and the management of assets. This chapter also discusses check clearing, a service that the banking industry provides for its customers.

ASSETS MANAGEMENT

There are three theories of how a bank should manage the asset side of its balance sheet—that is, how to manage the output of the bank:

1 The **commercial loan theory,** or **real bills doctrine**
2 The **shiftability theory**
3 The **anticipated income theory**

The Commercial Loan Theory, or Real Bills Doctrine A bank has a problem that is best described as the liquidity-earnings dilemma. If a bank desired to be a totally safe haven for all its depositors' funds, it would simply hold all those funds in its vault (i.e., as a perfectly liquid asset). Then, whenever a depositor requested cash from his or her bank, the banker would merely let down the drawbridge, cross the moat to the vault, and return to place the cash in the customer's hand. The problem is that no earnings would be generated for the bank if it were only a storehouse of cash.

Bankers could take a position at the other extreme. They could employ all the funds deposited with them to buy stock in Bismuth Mining, a company that will operate on the planet Uranus. The opportunity for substantial earnings might be large in that venture, but these earnings would probably not be obtained tomorrow (or indeed for quite some time). The investment has an earnings potential that is great, but the mining stock is not liquid. It would be difficult to liquidate (sell) the assets to obtain cash when depositors wanted to make withdrawals.

To resolve the liquidity-earnings problem, bankers long ago recognized the advantage of making *self-liquidating loans* (otherwise known as real bills). A loan was considered self-liquidating if it was secured by goods in the process of production, or by finished goods in transit to their final destination for resale. When the goods were sold, the loan could be repaid. Loans of this type could ensure the banks continuous liquidity and earn profits. Thus, liquidity and earnings were simultaneously gained. (Note, however, that no loan is truly automatically self-liquidating because there may not be a market for the goods produced.) Banks that limit themselves to making self-liquidating loans subscribe to the commercial loan theory of bank management (or the real bills doctrine).

Another perceived advantage of this theory of bank management was that the money supply was thought to expand and contract automatically with the "needs of trade." As business activity increased, more self-liquidating loans would be made, and this would increase the money supply. If business activity declined, fewer such loans would be made and the money supply would decline.

The commercial loan theory has two flaws. First, no loan is automatically self-liquidating. Second, loans are secured by the money value of the goods the loan helped pay for in some way. During periods of prosperity and inflation, the size of the loans, and hence the money supply, will increase and raise prices still more. During a period of recession and deflation, the opposite will occur. As the prices of goods fall, the dollar volume of loans will decline and the money supply will fall. This is not exactly the appropriate monetary policy in periods of recession. As a consequence, if the commercial loan theory were put into practice, a third party (such as a central bank) would be necessary to correct for excessive or insufficient growths in the money supply. (We return to the commercial loan theory of bank management and its relation to monetary policy in Chapter 15.)

Although commercial loans continue to be an important component of banks' asset portfolios, the development of other uses of their funds has caused the modus operandi of modern banks to change considerably.

The Shiftability Theory   Prior to the 1920s, bankers looked to their *loan* portfolios for liquidity. That is, they wanted to make sure that they could easily liquidate some of their loans to obtain needed funds for unexpected net withdrawals. Today, banks look to their *securities* portfolios for liquidity. Securities portfolios consist of U.S. government securities, municipal securities, and privately issued securities. A bank's securities portfolio consists primarily of T-bills, which were introduced in 1929. By the end of World War II, T-bills and other money market securities (short-term securities) had virtually supplanted the loan portfolio as a source of bank liquidity by selling them.

This shifting of assets from less liquid loans to more liquid money market instruments is effective only if all banks are not at the same time selling liquid money market instruments in order to obtain cash. Everyone cannot be a seller of T-bills simultaneously. Someone must be a buyer. An attempt to increase the *total* liquidity of the banking system through this process is doomed to failure unless an institution such as a central bank will *purchase* T-bills when all banks are attempting to increase their liquidity.

The shiftability theory, then, contains the same defect that plagues the commercial loan theory. Both must rely on a third party, such as the Fed, to increase the supply of *total* liquidity when necessary. What will provide instant liquidity for one or a few banks at most cannot provide a source of increased liquidity for the banking system as a whole. The Fed must be a ready buyer of securities from any and all banks for total liquidity to increase.

The Anticipated Income Theory The third theory of bank management of assets was developed in the 1950s in reaction to the apparent insufficient liquidity provided by the making of commercial loans and the holding of money market securities. Using the doctrine of anticipated income, bankers again began to look at their *loan* portfolios as a source of liquidity. The anticipated income theory encouraged bankers to treat long-term loans as potential sources of liquidity.

How can a banker consider a mortgage loan as a source of liquidity when, typically, it has such a long maturity? Using the theory of anticipated income, these loans are typically paid off by the borrower in a *series* of installments. Viewed in this way, the bank's loan portfolio provides the bank with a *continuous* flow of funds that adds to the bank's liquidity. Moreover, even though the loans are long-term, in a liquidity crisis the bank can sell the loans to obtain needed cash in secondary markets.

In a sense, mortgage loans (as well as consumer and business loans for some specified period of time) are now considered to be equivalent to short-term business loans that finance inventories. Basically, the anticipated income theory is much like the commercial loan theory except that it embraces a broader base of securities from which liquidity may be obtained. That broader base now includes longer-maturity loans which contribute *regularly* to liquidity.

The Selection of Assets: Risk and Portfolio Diversification

Bank managements select assets by weighing their profitability against their risk. Traditionally, this has been done quite conservatively. A bank's portfolio is selected with risk avoidance in mind. Managers attempt to maximize the rate of return at an *acceptable* level of risk rather than to choose a preferred rate of return and minimize the risk consistent with that preferred profit rate. The term "risk" is employed to include both default risk and market risk. Default risk is the likelihood of nonrepayment of the loan; market risk is the result of unexpected changes in interest rates in the economy. Remember that there is an inverse relationship between the rate of interest and the market value of previously issued bonds or other fixed money income-yielding assets (which are the types of assets that banks own).

Asset Acquisition and Expected Rates of Return The determination by banks of which assets to acquire is based on *expected* rates of return rather than on current rates. If interest rates are expected to rise in the near future, it is likely that cash and very short-term assets (such as overnight federal funds) will be held in order to avoid capital losses that would result from holding fixed money income-earning securities when interest rates rise. (Bank management behavior would be the opposite if interest rates were expected to fall.) A bank holding cash and overnight federal funds, for example, cannot be seriously affected by an increase in market interest rates. But a bank holding 6-month T-bills will be affected adversely by a rise in market rates of interest because the value of the T-bills will fall significantly.

To minimize risk but still achieve a relatively fixed level of earnings, banks attempt to diversify their asset portfolios. The aim of diversification is to acquire a portfolio consisting of some assets that increase in value when other assets decrease in value, so that the net changes in values approach zero. In the optimal situation, the variable rates of return on diversified assets will act to stabilize the *average overall* rate of return on the total portfolio and thus decrease risk resulting from changes in market activities.

A numerical example Suppose that two assets are available to a portfolio manager. Asset *A* has a rate of return of 20 percent half the time and 12 percent the other half. Similarly, asset *Y* has likely returns of 24 and 8 percent. Both assets have an average expected rate of return of 16 percent. The expected rate of return is obtained by multiplying each rate of return by the probability of obtaining it. Therefore, the expected rate of return of asset *A* equals

$$(0.5 \times .2) + (0.5 \times .12) = .16$$

The expected rate of return of asset *Y* equals

$$(0.5 \times .24) + (0.5 \times .08) = .16$$

While the average expected rate of return is the same for both assets, the variability (relative to the average) in the rates of return on asset *Y* is greater than on asset *A*. Given this greater variability in rates of return, asset *Y* is said to be riskier than asset *A*. The point is that a potential investor cannot determine the degree of risk simply by looking at the *expected* rate of return.

Suppose a recession occurred and the rate of return on one asset increased and the rate of return on the other asset decreased. How would these changes affect the rate of return for a portfolio containing both asset *A* and asset *Y*? If the rates of return of two assets change in opposite directions, the change in the average rate of return of a portfolio containing the two will be less than the change in the rate of return from a portfolio consisting of only one of the assets.

Let's assume the following:

1   Asset *A* has a *high* rate of return (20 percent) during the period when asset *Y* has a *low* rate of return (8 percent).

2   Asset *Y* has a *high* rate of return (24 percent) during the period that asset *A* has a *low* rate of return (12 percent).

3   Given these individual variabilities, a portfolio can be acquired that will have no variability in return (i.e., zero risk) all the time.

That portfolio will consist of two-thirds of asset A and one-third of asset Y ($2 of A for every $1 of Y). It will have a constant return of 16 percent. The calculation is as follows:

$$(2/3 \times .20) + (1/3 \times .08) = .13333 + 0.02667$$
$$= .16, \text{ or } 16 \text{ percent (half the time)}$$
$$(2/3 \times .12) + (1/3 \times .24) = 0.08 + 0.08$$
$$= .16, \text{ or } 16 \text{ percent (half the time)}$$

Fully offsetting assets are not of course readily available; but to the extent that long-term and short-term assets move in different directions at the same time, asset acquisitions similar to those found in the above example are possible.

An Examination of Depository Institution Assets in More Detail   Bank assets fall into three broadly defined categories:

1 Vault cash, balances at other banks, and federal funds sold
2 Investments
3 Loans

Vault Cash, Balances at Other Banks, and Federal Funds Sold   Vault cash, the coins and paper money in the bank's vault and cash drawers, is held because banks are legally obligated to pay their deposit liabilities in cash when requested. Banks also maintain balances with other banks; these are typically called **correspondent balances.** Banks hold deposits with each other to aid in check clearing. We return to a discussion of correspondent balances later in this chapter when we analyze check clearing.

Federal funds "sold" really consist of reserves that a bank has lent in the short run in the federal funds market. Banks can lend excess reserves at any time. Typically, the services of federal funds are sold only for overnight.

Investments   Investments (not to be confused with business investments) is a name given by bankers to the securities of governments or their agencies, certificates of deposit from other banks, and (to a small extent) the commercial paper and corporate bonds they hold. Banks are not allowed to invest in common stock. This regulatory prohibition is a carry-over from the bank failures of the late 1920s and early 1930s.[1]

---

[1]Banks cannot own stock for their own accounts (except for bank holding companies owning stock of another bank). But banks can and do buy stocks for the trust accounts that they manage. Also, they can and do lend to brokers, who in turn lend to customers on "margin." Banks, therefore, still have an indirect exposure to downturns in the stock market.

Bank asset	Liquidity ranking	Earnings ranking
Vault cash; balances at other banks; federal funds sold	Highest	Lowest
Investments	Intermediate	Intermediate
Loans	Lowest	Highest

FIGURE 9-1   **The Liquidity-Earning Spectrum.**

Loans   Loans are the assets which most distinguish banks from other businesses. Loans represent the main product or output of a bank. They fall into several categories, based on the uses for which the loans are made. The major categories of loans are:

1   Commercial and industrial
2   Real estate
3   Consumer
4   To other financial institutions
5   Agricultural
6   To securities brokers and dealers to carry securities

Liquidity versus Earnings   The distinctions among these fundamental asset categories are based on their liquidity and earnings. Vault cash, for example, is perfectly liquid but earns no return. Neither do balances at other banks. Federal funds sold (lent) do earn returns, but they have been placed in the first category because of their very high liquidity and relatively low earnings.

Investments are intermediate on the liquidity-earning spectrum, as shown in Figure 9-1. They are less liquid than cash and earn a greater return, but they are not as illiquid as loans and they earn less.

Loans are the most important source of earnings in the bank's asset portfolio. Other things equal, the larger the loan portfolio, the higher the earnings and the greater the default and market risks.

LIABILITY MANAGEMENT

The theories examined thus far are theories of the management of the *asset* side of a bank's balance sheet. For many years it appeared to bankers that only assets could be managed. The choice seemed to them to be limited to what types of loans to make and what types of securities to buy. Liabilities were, from the bankers' point of view, passive. Bankers did not believe they could determine what kinds of liabilities the bank had; their liabilities were equal to whatever savers deposited in transactions or time accounts.

Over time, bank liquidity practices have changed markedly. No longer is the asset side of the balance sheet considered the sole source of liquidity. *Because banks' assets are less liquid today than in the past, banks are more reliant on liabilities for liquidity.* Banks can obtain funds by selling repurchase agreements and large negotiable certificates of deposit, and by borrowing on the federal funds market or from the Eurodollar market or from the Fed. Each of these sources of funds provides banks the option of managing their liabilities. They can also offer NOW accounts, Super-NOW accounts, and money market accounts to the public.

A bank seeks to attract funds to buy assets such as loans and securities by issuing financial claims against itself. The two traditional types of claims issued by banks against themselves are demand deposits and time deposits. These claims compete with other financial claims for the favor of nonbank asset holders. For example, a bank's demand and time deposits vie with currency, claims of other banks, and primary securities of varying yields and maturity lengths issued by both governments and the private sector. Bankers are somewhat restricted by law with respect to price and the maturity characteristics of the demand and time deposits which they can issue against themselves; but the regulators have not been able to keep pace with the ingenuity and innovativeness of aggressive bank managers.

Depository institutions obtain only a small percentage of their total funds from their owners, or stockholders (actually no more than 10 percent). They must rely largely on debt claims, the great majority of which are demand or time deposit liabilities, for over 90 percent of their total funds on which they can earn profits. Until the 1950s, the reliance was largely on demand deposits. Since the early 1960s, however, banks have increasingly sought savings and time deposits. For the majority of banks today and for the economy as a whole, time and savings deposits significantly exceed demand deposits.

The distinction between time deposits and savings deposits is based on maturity dates. Savings deposits have no maturity date and may be withdrawn from the bank at (almost) any time. Time deposits do have specific maturity dates and carry significant interest forfeitures for early withdrawal. Today, the most important time deposit is the certificate of deposit (see Chapter 5). Especially important are negotiable CDs, which are for $100,000 or more (jumbo CDs). The negotiable certificates have fixed maturities and interest rates, but they are payable to "bearer" and do not even require endorsement. An extensive secondary market in these negotiable CDs flourishes, and the holder can exchange them for money at any time.

Although deposit liabilities make up part of total bank debt, banks also create other types of claims. Some of the nondeposit items are short-term in nature; others are long-term. For example, some banks have issued bonds that have several years to maturity, and bank holding companies have sold commercial paper of very short duration and transferred the funds to subsidiary banks. Table 9-1 shows the changing structure of bank liabilities over the last three decades.

TABLE 9-1 The Changing Structure of Bank Liabilities, 1950 to Present

Deposit and nondeposit sources of funds as a percent of bank liabilities

Year	Deposits as a Percent of Liabilities	Nondeposit Sources of Funds as a Percent of Liabilities
1950	99	1
1955	98	2
1960	97	3
1965	96	4
1970	90	10
1975	89	11
1976	89	11
1977	88	12
1978	86	14
1979	84	16
1980	83	17
1981	81	19
1982*	75	25

*September date; all other years reflect end of December dates.
Source: Board of Governors of the Federal Reserve System, *Federal Reserve Bulletin.*

In recent years, along with the growth in large time deposits, including negotiable CDs of over $100,000, there has been an equally remarkable growth in so-called nondeposit liabilities. Nondeposit liabilities include borrowed overnight federal funds, REPOs, and Eurodollar borrowings.

BANK LIABILITY MANAGEMENT

Because deposits are the major sources of bank funds and because they remain relatively stable in total value, they are not a source of new liquidity. Without additional sources of funds, any decline in deposit liabilities would force a contraction in bank assets.

To compensate for deposit drains and to provide additional liquidity, banks in recent years have begun to engage in short-term borrowing. Banks now borrow from new sources, by selling promissory notes, commercial paper, and Eurodollars. These do not have the same legal classification as deposits, and they do not have reserve requirements and interest-rate ceilings attached to them. Realizing that these alternative sources of lendable funds could seriously hamper monetary policy, regulators have attempted to restrict them. Thus has begun a cat-and-mouse game in which creative acts of bank liability management have been countered by a series of regulatory

HIGHLIGHT The Revolution in Money and Bank Robbing

The revolution in money and banking has led to a parallel revolution in money and bank robbing. Willie Sutton allegedly said that he robbed banks because that "was where the money was." Would-be Willie Suttons today, however, must be well versed in computer technology and electronic transfer systems.

Most financial transactions move unencoded over telephone wires; over $400 billion is transmitted daily in the United States over a complex financial network. It is possible for a savvy modern-day bank robber, using several hundred dollars' worth of electronics equipment, to wiretap a telephone line to automated teller machines (ATMs). Then, by recording and playing back computer instructions sent to the machine, the robber can send the message to "stick 'em up."

Banks have attempted to beef up their security to prevent such computer heists. One way is by encrypting the data, or scrambling the personal identification numbers (or entire instructions) of the customers by computer according to some mathematical equation. The U.S. government's Data Encryption Standard, the most widely used equation, is apparently so effective that it has not been possible for bank robbers to crack it—at least not yet. The hardware necessary for such encryption, however, can add $5,000 to the cost of a single ATM; only a few banks have been willing to pay the price.

While it may not be feasible for a computer whiz bank robber to tap into the ATM system, it certainly would be worth the time to go after the money moved between banks via the electronic fund transfer (EFT) networks, where last year some $64 trillion was moved between the Fed and member banks. Such funds, moreover, were only *partially* encrypted. Hmm.

Source: Based on Susan Dentzer and William J. Cook "Tapping the Bank's Wires," *Newsweek,* Apr. 25, 1983.

changes. Despite these regulatory attempts, the innovativeness of banks seeking additional funds has not been stifled. Even today, the interest rates on federal funds, repurchase agreements, jumbo CDs, and Eurodollar borrowings are market-determined and not regulated rates. Banking authorities have attempted some innovative regulation in this area. In October 1979, the Federal Reserve attached an 8 percent marginal reserve requirement on managed liabilities (including large time deposits, Eurodollar borrowings, REPOs, and federal funds borrowing from non-Federal Reserve member institutions). Note that this was a *marginal* requirement and applied only to nondeposit liabilities in excess of some base amount. This requirement was changed several times and reduced to zero in 1980.

Bail-outs and Riskier Bank Portfolios

During the early 1980s, more than a few depository institutions found themselves on the brink of failure. In some instances, federal authorities stepped in to save them. There is controversy, however, concerning whether or not monetary authorities should help financial institutions that are in trouble. *In fact, some argue that the public interest is better served by allowing more financial institutions to fail in the short run in order to ensure the stability and the viability of the overall monetary system in the long run.*

Originally, regulation of the banking industry was meant to apply to the banking system as a whole. Some regulatory agencies have unilaterally expanded their mandates from Congress, however. Instead of protecting the banking *system,* these agencies have attempted to protect each and every *member* of the system: They have bailed out failing banks.

The danger inherent in the success of such agencies [e.g., the Federal Deposit Insurance Corporation (FDIC) and the Federal Savings and Loan Insurance Corporation (FSLIC)] is that by insuring all banks equally for a flat percentage fee of total deposits, they have allowed the weak and poorly managed financial institutions to prosper along with the strong. This danger manifests itself in the tendency for lenders to undertake greater risks than they would in a free, unregulated market. The managers of financial institutions can assume that even if their institutions should become insolvent (liabilities exceed assets) because of excessive risk-taking, regulatory agencies will either arrange an "assistant merger" or secure a fresh infusion of capital.

The real costs of such "bail-out banking" are twofold:

1 *De facto* 100 percent insurance for all failures fosters a public perception that all bank liabilities are riskless.

2 Bail-out banking fosters in managers the presumption that their banking operations will be backstopped by the federal government no matter how recklessly they manage their portfolios.

Perhaps one way out of this dilemma is to charge to financial institutions a variable percentage fee which depends on the riskiness of their asset portfolios. Those banks that choose to earn higher rates of return by assuming more risk would be forced to pay a higher fee to the insuring institution.

Note that in the most blatant cases of bank mismanagement, banks have been allowed to fail. In 1982, for example, the Penn Square Bank in Oklahoma City failed at a cost of almost $1.5 million to some of its depositors whose deposits exceeded the FDIC insured limit. Some of these losses are likely to be recovered, however, in the ensuing liquidation process that the FDIC will conduct.

Mismanagement in the Penn Square Bank case was attributed to two main factors:

1 The continued extension and renewal of energy loans to oil and natural gas developers in the face of an energy market whose relative prices and profits were falling

2 The failure of other banks that were co-lenders with Penn Square to energy developers, to scrutinize Penn Square's (and their own) loan portfolio; they failed to recognize that the loans were shaky and were not being repaid.

THE RELATIONSHIP BETWEEN ASSET MANAGEMENT AND LIABILITY MANAGEMENT

To explain the theories of bank asset management and bank liability management we have separated them. In the real world they are interdependent. For example, the rates that a bank is able to pay on its deposit liabilities depend largely upon the yields realized from its asset portfolio. Consider what happened to savings and loan associations during the early 1980s. On the asset side of their balance sheet were mostly long-term mortgage loans made at relatively low rates of interest in the 1960s and 1970s. To continue to attract funds (prevent the withdrawal of funds, or disintermediation), savings and loan associations had to offer liabilities at higher rates of interest than they were earning on their assets. As their expenses exceeded their revenues, a large number of savings and loan associations became financially unsound in the early 1980s, and that led to governmental bail-out solutions. The banks that remained had to seek out higher returns on assets that were, therefore, riskier.

CHECK CLEARING

Banks are in the business of earning profits by making loans and purchasing securities. The primary sources of their funds are the deposits that they accept. Because banks compete for customer deposits, they must offer depositors something in return. Customers receive interest or "free" services for their deposits. In recent years, financial innovation and deregulation have permitted *explicit* interest payments on transactions balances. Depositors also receive *implicit* interest in the form of ease in transferring their deposits to others—check writing and check clearing.

Intrabank Check Clearing If a depositor wants to withdraw cash from a transactions account for personal use, the bank surrenders vault cash and reduces the depositor's transactions balance by an equal amount (see Chapter 9).

If Monica writes a $100 check to Lester, and they both have transactions accounts in the First Federal Bank, the transaction is easily recorded. First Federal subtracts $100 from Monica's account and adds it to Lester's account.

Interbank Check Clearing
In the United States, three methods of check clearing are used:

1 Correspondent banking
2 Local clearinghousing
3 Fed check clearing

Correspondent Banking Earlier in this chapter we indicated that banks hold deposits with each other, called correspondent balances.[2] Two banks located in a particular geographic area realize that many check-writing activities will involve them both. In order to facilitate check clearing and provide a service to their depositors, each bank will hold deposits with the other.

Suppose Tommie banks with First Federal and Rachel deals with Franklin National Bank. Rachel writes Tommie a $200 check that Tommie deposits in First Federal, which adds $200 to its own assets as "cash items in the process of collection" and credits Tommie's account with the same amount (a liability to First Federal). Note, however, that First Federal may not allow Tommie to spend the $200 until the check is *cleared*—when payment has actually been made after it has been verified that Rachel indeed can cover the $200 check (see the Highlight, "Playing the Float").

Rachel's check will be presented to her bank, Franklin National. If Rachel's account does not contain the $200, the check will be stamped "insufficient funds," and the transaction will be canceled. In the happy event that Rachel's account does have sufficient funds, Franklin National will deduct the money from her account *and* subtract $200 from the account it has with First Federal. Tommie's bank then reduces its liabilities by $200 (Franklin National's deposit) and its assets by $200 (cash items in the process of collection).

Clearly, banks in the same area will make many such bookkeeping transactions daily. By exchanging checks drawn on each other, correspondent banks can clear checks without actually physically transferring cash. If the sum of the values of the checks drawn on each bank is not the same (i.e., if the values of the checks are not exactly offsetting), the difference is made up by an interbank deposit transfer. Note that if Franklin National's balances at First Federal become depleted, it must transfer funds to First Federal. This will increase First Federal's reserves and increase its lending ability; it will decrease Franklin National's reserves and decrease its lending ability.

Local Clearinghousing In an area in which many banks exist and interbank transactions are large, local clearinghouses for the clearing of checks become feasible.

---

[2]Some interbank deposits are, in effect, compensatory balances. A small bank voluntarily will hold balances in a large bank for non-check-clearing purposes because it receives such services as securities purchases and sales and foreign transactions.

HIGHLIGHT Playing the Float*

Banks typically collect money from checks sooner than they credit it to their customers' accounts. To receive payment for a check a bank sends it to a local clearinghouse or a Federal Reserve district bank. The bank receives credit for the check within a few days, but it usually takes the clearing agency longer to collect from the bank on which the check was drawn.

The bank, having already been paid for the check, *may wait several days* (sometimes weeks) *before allowing the customer to use his or her own funds*. In the meantime, the bank can use the money to earn interest, a practice that is

known as "playing the float." The customer, in effect, is giving the bank a free loan for a short period.

Bankers maintain that the check credited to them by the Fed is only *provisional;* if the check eventually "bounces," the Fed debits the bank's reserve account accordingly. This argument is somewhat undercut, however, when one considers the magnitudes involved. Lee Falls, a vice president of San Franciso's Bank of America, estimates that his bank earns $3.35 million daily by playing the float; it suffers only $3 million of bad check losses *per year.* In defense of his bank's practices,

however, Falls argues that the number of bad checks would rise prohibitively if the banks eliminated waiting periods.

California State Assembly Speaker Willie Brown has introduced a bill in the assembly that would require banks to clear checks within five days. In the U.S. Congress, Senators Christopher Dodd of Connecticut and William Proxmire of Wisconsin have proposed a new law that would require banks to publish their check-clearing schedules— hoping that as depositors become aware of banks that play the float, competition will reduce check-clearing delays.

*Inspired by a similarly entitled article by the *Time* business staff, *Time,* May 16, 1983, p. 59.

A clearinghouse is a location at which many banks exchange checks drawn on each other. At the end of the day, the *net* payments made among banks is tallied, and an *overall* settling-up is made. Note that *individual* transactions are not processed.

For example, suppose that during one day First Federal received a total of $200 million in checks from two other banks and had to pay $150 million to them; Franklin National received $100 million from the other two banks and had to pay $100 million to them; the Somerville Bank received $50 million from the other two banks and had to pay $100 million. In the summing up, all that is necessary is that the Somerville Bank pay $50 million to First Federal.[3] The time, effort, and paperwork saved is enormous when only overall net payments are calculated and individual transactions are ignored.

[3]Probably with a check drawn on the Federal Reserve district bank; actual currency is almost never transferred.

Fed Check Clearing   The establishment of a nationwide check-clearing system was one of the original reasons for creating the Fed. The country was divided into twelve districts (each with a Federal Reserve district bank) for the express purpose of check clearing. As the economy advanced and the number of checks to be cleared increased, the twelve districts were further divided into smaller regions that contained check-clearing facilities.

Consider first check clearing within a Federal Reserve district. Bob in Bowling Green writes a $1,000 check to Jean in St. Louis. Jean deposits the check in the St. Louis Bank, which credits her account and sends the check (along with many others) to the Federal Reserve Bank of St. Louis. The St. Louis Federal Reserve Bank then sends the check to Bowling Green, which deducts $1,000 from Bob's transactions account. After it is verified that Bob has funds sufficient to cover the $1,000 check, the St. Louis Federal Reserve Bank deducts the $1,000 from the Bowling Green bank's account with it; the St. Louis Federal Reserve Bank also adds $1,000 to the St. Louis bank's reserve account. The check is usually cleared within a few days, with no actual shipment of currency necessary.

Consider now an example in which a check must be cleared between banks in two different districts. Bob in Bowling Green writes a $200 check to his son, Gary, in Cambridge, Massachusetts. Gary deposits the $200 in the Cambridge bank, which credits his account and sends the check (with others) to the Federal Reserve Bank of Boston. In turn, the Boston Fed sends the check (via airmail, with others) to the Federal Reserve Bank of St. Louis, which in turn sends it to the Bowling Green bank. If the St. Louis Fed is not notified within a specific period that the check has ''bounced,'' the Fed deducts the amount of the check from the Bowling Green bank's reserve account with it. The Boston Federal Reserve Bank adds the $200 to the Cambridge bank's reserve account. To this point, all *non-Fed* accounts are settled; in effect, the Bowling Green bank has paid the Cambridge bank and Bob has paid Gary. But reading carefully, you know that the St. Louis Fed still ''owes'' $200 to the Boston Fed.

The St. Louis Fed pays the Boston Fed the $200 through the Interdistrict Settlement Fund in Washington, D.C. Each district bank has an account at the Interdistrict Settlement Fund, which acts as an interdistrict clearinghouse. At the end of the day, Bob's check will be added to many others and net balances will be credited or deducted from each district.

By the procedures analyzed here—intrabank clearing, correspondent banking, local clearinghousing, and Federal Reserve check clearing—over 35 billion checks a year are paid and cleared quickly, with low transactions costs and with virtually no actual transferals of currency.

CURRENT CONTROVERSY

Pricing of the Fed's Services

Prior to the passage of the Depository Institutions Deregulation and Monetary Control Act of 1980, only members of the Federal Reserve System were allowed access to most of the services offered by the Federal Reserve: check clearing and collection and borrowing from the Fed. Now all depository institutions must hold reserves with Federal Reserve district banks, but all such depository institutions have access to the Fed's services, which are priced according to cost. In principle, the Fed must calculate the cost of its services by adding up the following:

1   Production costs
2   Prorated allocated overhead expenses
3   A 16 percent markup (presumably to cover taxes that would have been paid by a private company offering the services, and a normal return to capital to a private entrepreneur)

After its first year of operation, the Fed's business in check clearing declined, as Figure 1 indicates. It became less costly for banks and large money market centers to contract privately for check-clearing services. As a result, the Fed was running an accounting loss in its check-clearing function.

To counter this loss in business, beginning in late fall of 1982, the Fed started aggressively competing with commercial clearinghouses in an effort to get a larger share of the market. The commercial clearinghouses reacted negatively and accused the Fed of abusing its power as a regulator to enhance itself as a competitor.

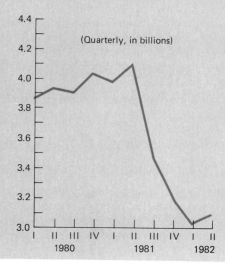

(Quarterly, in billions)

FIGURE 1   Check Processing by the Federal Reserve. (*Source:* Based on John Helyar, "Fed Irritates Big Banks by Fighting to Regain Share of Check-Clearing," *Wall Street Journal,* Oct. 26, 1982, p. 35.)

The numbers are quite fascinating. A commercial clearing bank receives about 8 cents per check processed. When 8 cents is multiplied by hundreds of millions of checks, that's big business! Fighting for its "fair share" of the action, the Fed in 1982 revised its jet courier transportation system and offered to change its price schedule. Competing commercial clearinghouses estimate that if the Fed actually makes these price changes, it will increase its business by 50 percent or more.

The fact is that some of the big banks had made large investments in check-processing operations, figuring that the Fed would not compete as if it were a private firm. Those big banks continue to fight the Fed tooth and nail, but small banks don't share this concern. Indeed, the nation's thousands of community banks typically defend the Fed. The controversy undoubtedly will continue. Critics of the Fed contend that because it is a government agency, it shouldn't be concerned about its percentage of the total check-clearing business. But any student of government bureaucracy knows that powerful vested interests are behind the battle. The Fed employs numerous check processors who want job security. An organization of 20,000 employees does not want to be driven out of business.

CHAPTER SUMMARY

1 Banks create short-term, highly liquid liabilities by accepting demand and time deposits; they then use them to buy longer-term, less liquid assets. As a consequence, banks have a potential liquidity problem: Their liabilities are more liquid than are their assets.

2 There are various theories about how banks should solve their liquidity problem. The commercial loan theory is that banks can solve their liquidity problem by making only short-term, self-liquidating loans that are secured by goods in the process of production or goods in transit. There are two flaws in this theory: (a) No loan is truly automatically self-liquidating because there may not be a market for the goods produced; and (b) such a policy entails automatic destabilizing changes in the money supply because the money supply automatically increases during periods of inflation and contracts during periods of recession.

3 Another theory of how banks can solve their liquidity problem is the shiftability theory. This theory is that banks should purchase assets that are highly liquid. It follows that *both* bank assets and bank liabilities will then be highly liquid. The problem with this theory is that the entire financial system cannot simultaneously increase its liquidity; a third party such as a central bank is required to increase liquidity for the entire financial community in times of financial crisis.

4 A third theory about how banks can resolve liquidity problems is the anticipated income theory. This theory is that banks will have sufficient liquidity even if they make *long-term* loans, if those loans are repaid in a series of installments that provides banks with predictable inflows of funds. Moreover, these long-term loans can be sold in secondary markets to meet liquidity problems.

5 A trade-off exists between profitability and security; assets that yield higher rates of return are usually riskier. Banks have typically selected conservative asset portfolios; bank managers usually select an acceptable degree of risk and then attempt to maximize earnings subject to that risk level. Asset acquisition is determined by expected future rates of return and not by current rates of return. If interest rates are expected to rise in the near future, banks will purchase very short-term assets. If interest rates are expected to fall, banks will purchase longer-term assets in order to realize capital gains. Bank assets can be classified into (a) vault cash, balances at other banks, and federal funds sold—all highly liquid, with no earnings; (b) investments—moderately liquid, moderate earnings; and (c) loans—low liquidity, high earnings.

6 Banks can also provide for liquidity by managing their *liabilities.* Since the 1960s, banks in need of liquidity have offered to customers such less liquid liabilities as saving certificates and various certificates of deposit. Today, time and saving deposits significantly exceed demand deposits in most depository institutions. In other words, depository institutions have reduced the liquidity of their liabilities.

7 Asset management and liability management, although usually analyzed separately, are interrelated in the real world. For example, the rates that a bank is able to pay on its deposit liabilities depend largely upon the yields that it can realize on its asset portfolio.

8 Financial institutions are bailed out by their insurers when they are in trouble. The probability of a bail-out, combined with deposit insurance, provides incentives for bank managers to acquire high-risk portfolios to increase a bank's rate of return.

GLOSSARY

Anticipated income theory: The theory that banks can solve their liquidity problem even by making long-term loans if borrowers repay the loans in a series of continuous installments.

Commercial loan theory, or real bills doctrine: The the-ory that banks can provide needed liquidity by making only short-term, self-liquidating loans secured by goods in the process of production or goods in transit.

Correspondent balances: Balances held by one bank (usually a smaller one) in another bank for ease of check clearing; some depositing banks do so to receive advice and special services.

Shiftability theory: The theory that banks can solve their liquidity problem by purchasing assets that are highly liquid.

PROBLEMS

9-1 **(a)** Calculate the expected rate of return on asset *A* and asset *Y* when asset *A* yields 10 percent half the time and 8 percent half the time and asset *Y* yields 16 percent half the time and 2 percent half the time.

(b) Which asset is considered riskier?

9-2 Assume that the five Federal Reserve district banks listed below paid and received the following amounts (in millions of dollars) on a given day:

District Bank	Received	Paid	Net Receipts
Dallas	500	490	+ 10
Richmond	400	500	−100
Atlanta	500	540	− 40
St. Louis	450	420	+ 30
San Francisco	600	500	+100
Totals	2,450	2,450	0

How would the Interdistrict Settlement Fund settle the accounts among these districts?

SELECTED REFERENCES

Federal Reserve Bank of Chicago, *Proceedings of a Conference on Bank Structure and Competition,* 1982.

Lovati, Jean M., "The Growing Similarity among Financial Institutions," *Review,* Federal Reserve Bank of St. Louis, October 1977, pp. 2–11.

Robinson, Roland, *The Management of Bank Funds* (New York: McGraw-Hill, 1962).

Silber, William L., *Commercial Bank Liability Management* (Chicago: Association of Reserve City Bankers, 1978).

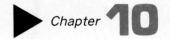
The Regulation of Depository Institutions

CHAPTER PREVIEW

1 Why does the failure of a bank have a greater effect on the economy than the failure of any other business of comparable size?

2 Why are commercial banks not permitted to be investment banks?

3 Until recently banks were not permitted to pay interest on demand deposits. Why now and not before?

4 What harmful effects has regulation had on the banking industry?

5 Why and how has branch banking been discouraged in the United States?

6 What are the main provisions of the Depository Institutions Deregulation and Monetary Control Act of 1980?

The days of free banking ended during the early part of this century. Since then a plethora of operating constraints have been imposed on existing depository institutions and on the entrepreneurs who would like to create new depository institutions. During most of the twentieth century, banking has been one of the most highly regulated industries in the United States. To understand why there has been so much banking regulation during the past fifty years, let's take a quick glance at the 1930s to see what caused the concern about banking operations.

THE EVOLUTION OF BANKING REGULATION

Businesses fail (go bankrupt) often. They fail for many different reasons, and when they do fail they cause all kinds of hardships to creditors, to owners, to workers, and to customers. But, perhaps, the greatest hardships result when a depository institution fails because so many individuals depend on the safety and security of banks—indeed, that is why they place their deposits in depository institutions in the first place.

Look at Figure 10-1, which indicates that during the 1920s an average of about 600 banks failed each year. In the early 1930s, that average soared to 2,000 failures each year. It was in 1933, at the height of such bank failures, that the **Federal Deposit Insurance Corporation (FDIC)** was founded; the FDIC insured the funds of depositors and removed the reason for ruinous "runs"

FIGURE 10-1   Banks Closed, 1921–1981 (The Federal Deposit Insurance Corporation Was Created in 1934).   (*Source:* Milton Friedman and Anna Jacobson Schwartz, *A Monetary History of the United States 1867–1960* (Princeton: p. 439; and Federal Deposit Insurance Corporation, *1981 Annual Report*, p. 70.)

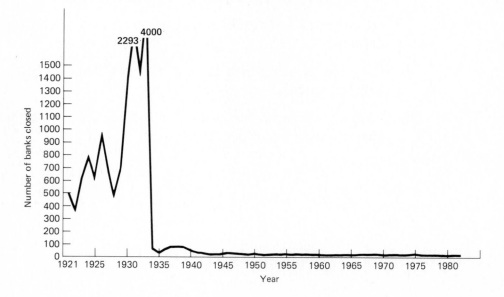

on banks. When a bank is forced out of business the FDIC pays back deposi-tors. Since the FDIC was created the number of bank failures has averaged only twelve per year. In the last fifty years, only some 600 banks have failed. This tremendous drop in bank-failure rates came after the passage of the fed-eral legislation to regulate and insure banks as part of the New Deal philosophy of the 1930s.

At the heart of banking regulation was the desire to prevent future bank failures. The Great Depression of the 1930s induced regulators to trade an efficient, competitive banking system for one which was somewhat less effi-cient but much safer with respect to bank failures and runs on banks.

As this chapter will show, however, banking regulation became so perva-sive that many traditional depository institutions (especially the S&Ls) were unable to compete with other (more innovative) institutions, such as the money market mutual funds, in the climate of rising interest rates in the 1970s and 1980s. Subsequently, some regulations were removed to give those depository institutions greater freedom to respond to changing market con-ditions. In particular, the Depository Institutions Deregulation and Monetary Control Act of 1980 and later laws passed by Congress have put the various depository institutions—commercial banks, savings and loan associations, mutual savings banks, and credit unions—on a more equal footing with each other. These traditional financial intermediaries now also find themselves fac-ing competition from stock brokerage companies that now offer a variety of banking-type services. Even retail store chains such as Sears have joined forces with brokerage firms to offer investment and banking services to their customers.

To understand the evolution of banking regulation in this country, we will quickly review a short history of the more important banking acts.

THE GLASS-STEAGALL BANKING ACT OF 1933

The Banking Act of 1933, also known as the Glass-Steagall Act, was passed by Congress and signed into law by President Roosevelt on July 16, 1933. The act was authored by Senator Carter Glass (Democrat, Virginia) and Congress-man Henry Steagall (Democrat, Alabama), the chairpersons of the Senate and House Banking Committees, respectively. This landmark legislation contained the following key provisions.

1   The Federal Deposit Insurance Corporation (FDIC)[1] was created. The FDIC was designed to give depositors confidence in a bank, even if the bank appeared to be weak and about to fail. With the confidence that their deposits were insured, depositors would not run to withdraw their funds

---

[1]The Federal Home Loan Bank Board (FHLBB) was established in 1932 to supervise savings and loan associations, and in 1934 the Federal Savings and Loan Insurance Corporation (FSLIC) was created to insure their depositors' funds.

from their local bank for fear of losing their money. Thus, the FDIC helped reduce the probability of bank failures.

2   Commercial banks were prohibited from engaging in investment banking (underwriting).[2] Because investment banking requires underwriters to guarantee a minimum total purchase price for the stocks or bonds they are underwriting, there is a possibility of tremendous losses if the under-written stock or bond issue does not sell well. By divorcing commercial banking from investment banking, Congress felt that it was removing a tempting but risky business activity from commercial banks—commercial bank losses, after all, would be losses of depositors' money.

3   Commercial banks were prohibited from paying interest on any deposit that is payable on demand. It was thought that this prohibition would pre-vent banks from engaging in cutthroat competition for deposits, which (allegedly) would force banks to earn higher interest rates by making ris-kier investments and riskier loans.

4   The Fed was given the authority to establish ceilings on interest rates that member banks could pay on time and on savings deposits. It also was empowered to use government securities as collateral for the Federal Reserve notes it issued. We elaborate on interest-rate ceilings later in this chapter in the section entitled "Interest-Rate Ceilings Revisited."

The Banking Act of 1935 reorganized the Fed and granted increased authority to its Board of Governors. The legislation passed during the early 1930s provided the framework for the regulation of our banking system for the next fifty years.

The Federal Deposit Insurance Corporation   The Federal Deposit Insurance Corpo-ration is a government agency that guarantees the deposits of each depositor (in commercial banks) up to a specified limit, even though the bank that accepts those deposits may fail. Currently, this limit is $100,000. Deposits in savings and loan associations are usually insured up to the same amount by the **Federal Savings and Loan Insurance Corporation (FSLIC);** credit-union deposits are usually insured by the **National Credit Union Administration (NCUA),** which supervises the National Credit Union Shareholders Insurance Fund.

The FDIC was established to mitigate the primary cause of bank failures— the simultaneous rush of depositors to convert their demand deposits or sav-ings deposits into currency.

Consider the following scenario. A bank begins to look shaky; its assets may not seem sufficient to cover its liabilities. If the bank has no deposit insur-ance, depositors in this shaky bank (and any banks associated with it) will all

---

[2]A distinction between commercial banking and investment banking was made in Chapter 5.

HIGHLIGHT

How to Have Insured Deposits in Excess of $100,000

The current $100,000 maximum protection on deposits applies to the total deposits a single depositor has under his or her name *within a single bank*. Thus, if an individual has $70,000 in a savings account in one bank and $40,000 in a checking account in the same name at the same bank, that individual would be insured up to $100,000, not $110,000. Moreover, if an individual has accounts in the same name in the main office and in one or more branch offices of the insured bank, the accounts are added together to determine the insured amount.

It is possible, however, to be insured for more than $100,000 by splitting funds among different banks and accounts. An individual whose savings account balance reaches the maximum limitation on insurability can split the funds, either among a number of banks or among a number of accounts. For example, if married, the individual can have an account, his or her spouse can have an account, and the two of them can have a joint account. Thus, the maximum insurability of a household unit increases to $300,000. If this couple has two children, they can set up guardian or trustee accounts, which are also insured separately.

want to withdraw their money from the bank at the same time. Their concern is that this shaky bank will not have enough money to return their deposits to them in the form of currency. Indeed, this is what happens in a bank failure when insurance doesn't exist. Just as with the failure of a regular business, the creditors of the bank may not all get paid, or, if they do, they will get paid less than 100 percent of what they are owed. Depositors are creditors of a bank because their deposits are liabilities of the bank. In a fractional reserve banking system, banks do not have 100 percent of their depositors' money in the form of vault cash. All depositors, therefore, cannot simultaneously withdraw all their money. It is therefore necessary to assure depositors that they can have their deposits converted into cash, when they wish, no matter how serious the financial situation of the bank.

The FDIC provided this assurance. By insuring deposits, the FDIC bolstered depositors' trust in the banking system and provided depositors with the incentive to leave their deposits with the bank, even in the face of widespread talk of bank failures. In 1933, it was sufficient for the FDIC to cover each account up to $2,500.

Even though the FDIC was created by the federal government and is considered a federal agency, it is not funded out of federal taxes. Like any private insurance fund, the total of the insurance premiums paid by the insured is the source of the funds. The FDIC insurance is funded by an assessment of insured commercial banks. That assessment is one-twelfth of 1 percent of commercial banks' total deposits. In recent years, the actual assessment fee turned out to be less than half the original assessment fee. The banks have paid fees of only about one twenty-seventh of 1 percent of their total deposits.

The Separation of Commercial Banking from Investment Banking   Chapter 5
pointed out that the activity called investment banking has virtually nothing to do with banking. An investment banker underwrites a new issue of corporate or municipal bonds or an issue of a private corporation's shares of stock. By "underwriting" the investment banker guarantees that the entire issue will be sold at a minimum price per bond or per share of stock. Commercial banking, on the other hand, involves the acceptance of deposits by savers and the purchase of assets from borrowers. Commercial banking is at the heart of the process of financial intermediation between savers and borrowers. Investment banking is a brokerage service.

The separation of commercial and investment banking was mandated because of the then prevailing opinion that many commercial banks up to 1935 had been involved in the underwriting of risky securities. When some of those securities did not sell at the promised minimum price, the commercial bank that was underwriting the issue simply added the securities to its own asset portfolio. Its asset portfolio would end up being too risky because it contained too many risky securities.

Consider an example. Prior to the 1935 act, the XYZ Bank agrees to underwrite a new issue of $1 million in bonds being sold by the Acme Corporation. The underwriting department of the bank estimates that the bonds can be sold at par at a yield to the purchaser of, say, 3 percent. (Remember, this example is illustrating what occurred in the 1920s when interest rates were much lower than they are today.) As fate would have it, the bond market does not assess the bonds in a similar manner, and they cannot all be sold at the guaranteed price. The bank sells what it can at that price and places the remainder at an overvalued price (in the sense that it couldn't sell all the bonds at par and is now valuing the bonds at par in its own portfolio). This makes the bank itself less financially secure. It also provides an incentive for the bank to purchase the bonds for the portfolios that it is managing in trust for its customers; the bank might be inclined to give investment advice that is not objective.

The Prohibition of Interest on Demand Deposits   Prohibiting interest on demand
deposits seemed reasonable in the early 1930s when banks were trying to attract customers by paying high interest rates. Otherwise stated, banks were paying an increasingly higher price for their inputs—deposit liabilities.

In order to pay high interest rates on deposit liabilities, banks had to earn high rates from the assets of their balance sheet. So they used depositors' money in investments that promised high returns. However, high return and high risk go hand in hand. When business activity slowed, the value of riskier assets declined substantially. Many banks were not able to sell them at their earlier values when they tried to cover deposit withdrawals. The specter of insolvency and bank failure loomed large. To prevent failures resulting from this kind of competition, banks were forbidden to pay interest on demand deposits. Note, however, that recent research indicates little basis for this theory of bank failures.

RESTRICTIONS ON BANK ENTRY

One of the conditions that results from regulating an industry is the creation of barriers to entry. Indeed, the concern with overcompetition in the banking industry led very early to an entry-restricting philosophy. A convincing case for worthiness or need is necessary before a commercial bank can obtain a federal or state charter. Before a bank will be granted a charter, the bank's founders must give proof of their integrity and ability to manage a bank. Additionally (particularly during the 1960s and early 1970s), state and federal regulatory banking agencies required evidence of "need" for a new bank before they would issue a charter. Obviously, the term "need" is difficult to define objectively. For many years, "unworthy" would-be bankers were detected and prevented from entering the industry. Existing banks were making higher-than-normal rates of return (in certain geographic areas) while regulatory agencies prevented new competition from entering the industry.

Some studies indicate that the Federal Deposit Insurance Corporation has been responsible for restricting entry into banking. For example, Sam Peltzman claims that from the period 1936 to 1962, the FDIC restricted entry such that only 60 percent of the banks that would have existed without FDIC restriction did exist. Peltzman described the key method used to restrict entry into banking as the establishment of a federally administered "needs" criterion for entry in the National Banking Act of 1935.[3]

Specifically the Act requires the Federal Reserve System before admitting a new state bank to membership and the Comptroller of the Currency before chartering a new national bank to pass on . . . the financial history and condition of the bank, the adequacy of its capital structure, its future earnings prospects . . . the convenience and needs of the community to be served by the bank. . . .[4]

Most important, however, the Act makes the same requirement of the Federal Deposit Insurance Corporation (the FDIC) before it may insure a new nonmember state bank.[5] Administrative decisions (by the FDIC and the other agencies) based on this needs criterion are nonreviewable. Given the relative attractiveness of deposit insurance, the vesting of this discretionary power in the FDIC gives the Federal authorities an effective veto over the chartering policies of the individual states.

---

[3]Sam Peltzman, "Entry in Commercial Banking," *Journal of Law and Economics,* October 1965, p. 12.

[4]12 U.S.C. §§ 1814(a), 1816 64 Stat. 1876 (1950), 12 U.S.C. §§ 1814(a), 1816 (1964). (Peltzman's citation.)

[5]12 U.S.C. § 1815 64 Stat. 876 (1950), 12 U.S.C. § 1815 (1964). (Peltzman's citation.)

THE CHOICE OF A BANK
CHARTER—OUR DUAL BANKING SYSTEM

Since 1864, commercial bank founders have been able to choose between seeking a state charter (from a state banking authority) or a federal charter (from the federal government through the **comptroller of the currency**). This option has led to the coexistence of national banks and state banks. Thus, the United States has a dual banking system. As of 1983, 68 percent of all banks had state charters; however, they accounted for only 43 percent of the total assets of all banks. To further confuse the issue, membership in the Federal Reserve System and the FDIC is optional for state banks; 18 percent of all member banks are state-chartered. But membership in the Federal Reserve System and the Federal Deposit Insurance Corporation is required for all nationally chartered banks.

The Overlap of Regulation and Supervision   In principle, the dual banking system allows for an overlapping of supervision and regulation by several authorities. There are four sources of regulation, supervision, and control:

1   The comptroller of the currency
2   The Federal Reserve
3   The FDIC
4   State banking authorities

Figure 10-2 shows the jurisdiction over commercial banks as of December 31, 1981.

The three federal agencies listed above each have their own way of examining, scrutinizing, and appraising the activities of a federally chartered bank. In principle, each agency can conduct its own examination of a federally chartered commercial bank, and thus such banks are subject to triple scrutiny. Only state-chartered banks (if they remain outside the Federal Reserve System and the FDIC) can be subjected to the supervision and examination procedures of a single state agency. In reality, since 1981, state banking commissions have had sole jurisdiction over only 480 *uninsured* non-Federal Reserve member banks. The comptroller of the currency, on the other hand, maintains chartering, supervisory, and examining powers over some 4,555 national banks. Even though the Fed has supervisory power over all national banks and state-chartered member (of the Fed) banks, it examines only state-chartered member banks. National banks are examined by the comptroller of the currency.

Because almost all commercial banks have FDIC insurance, the FDIC has examining powers over most state-chartered banks and all nationally chartered banks. In practice, however, the FDIC examines only nonmember state-insured banks.

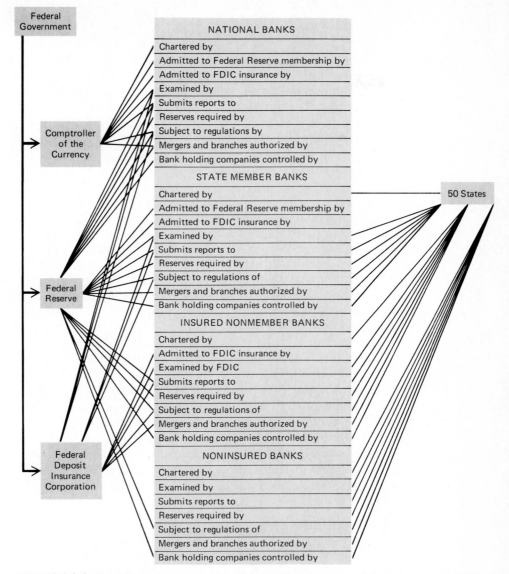

FIGURE 10-2   The Overlapping Regulation and Supervision of Commercial Banks.
(*Source:* Adapted from hearings on financial structure and regulation, Subcommittee on Financial Institutions of the Senate Committee on Banking, Housing and Urban Affairs, 93d Congress, 1st session, 1973. Cited in Murray E. Polakoff, Thomas A. Durkin, et al., *Financial Institutions and Markets,* 2d ed., Boston: Houghton Mifflin, 1981; and *Economic Review,* Federal Reserve Bank of Atlanta, December 1982, p. 46.)

UNIT VERSUS BRANCH BANKING

Most countries have a few large banks, each bank with many branches located throughout the nation. The United States, on the other hand, has a large number of distinct and separate depository institutions throughout the country. The reason there are so many banks in the United States is that depositors and politicians distrust large banks. Consequently, various state laws have allowed only **unit banking,** which is a system that permits each bank to have only a single geographic location; thus, many states have prevented **branch banking.** A branch bank, as its name suggests, is one of two or more banking offices owned and operated by a single banking corporation. Branch banking comprises a banking corporation having two or more "branches" or offices within a geographic area; branch offices can be newly opened or they can be existing banks that are acquired and merged into the corporation. In states where branch banking is allowed, banking authorities have continued to deny the opening of new branch banks when they are acquired from existing banks; however, they do allow branch offices "built from scratch." State-bank regulators have prevented the acquisition of existing bank offices by banking corporations for fear that competition in the banking industry will be reduced.

Table 10-1 shows that branch banking has grown in the last two decades. Of course, more growth would have occurred if all states had no restrictions against branch banking. As of 1980, for example, twenty-two states allowed statewide branching, seventeen permitted limited branching (mainly within one county), and the remaining eleven permitted no branching at all (they are unit banking states). In principle, branching across state lines has not been allowed by any of the states, although in practice *interstate* banking does occur. This important topic is treated later in the chapter.

State law, not federal law, governs branch banking. Federal law does not prohibit national banks from branching, but national banks must obey the

TABLE 10-1 Branch Banking Since 1960			
	Number of states with		
Year	**Statewide Branching**	**Limited Branching**	**Unit Banking**
1960	16	17	18
1965	18	16	17
1970	20	16	15
1975	22	14	15
1980	22	17	11

Source: Board of Governors of the Federal Reserve System, *Federal Reserve Bulletin.*

TABLE 10-2   Multi-Bank Holding Companies

Year	No. of Multi-Bank Holding Cos.	No. of Banks	No. of Branches	Assets*	Deposits*
1960	47	426	1,037	20	18
1965	53	468	1,486	31	28
1970	121	895	3,260	93	78
1975	289	2,264	9,896	371	297
1981	407	2,607	14,121	678	480

*Billions of dollars.

Source: Board of Governors of the Federal Reserve System, *Annual Statistical Digest.* Includes only domestic data.

branching law of the states in which they are located. At the federal level, however, some doors to branch banking have been opened in states that prohibit it. For example, in 1974, the comptroller of the currency ruled that customer-bank communications terminals (CBCTs) do not qualify as branch banks. Taken in its broadest perspective, this ruling suggests the possibility that robot branches (no people) may be forthcoming regardless of a state's restrictions on branching.[6]

Multi-Bank Holding Companies   In addition to branching, there is another mechanism for establishing multiple-office banking. Through **multi-bank holding companies** (sometimes called group banking), a corporation can obtain ownership or control of two or more independently incorporated banks. Such an arrangement may cross state lines and, in fact, some holding companies do operate in several states.

As in many matters pertaining to bank regulation, state laws relative to multi-bank holding companies differ. About a dozen states specifically prohibit any kind of activity which results in a multi-bank holding company. However, many states have no specific legislation in this area. Multi-bank holding companies have greatly expanded in the last three decades. Table 10-2 shows the rapid growth since 1965 in deposits effectively controlled by these multi-bank companies. This rapid expansion of group banking can be attributed to the legal limitations on branching. To a considerable degree, group banking has served as a way to evade the intrastate branching laws; most multi-bank holding companies are located in unit-banking states. Moreover, because under certain circumstances these groups can operate across state lines, group

---

[6]On the other hand, the Fed and the courts have ruled that whether or not CBCTs are branches depends on state law. Thus in some states (Texas, for one) CBCTs were ruled to be branches, and because Texas outlaws branches the machines had to be removed. Such are the problems of a multiple regulatory system.

banking has become an attractive device for circumventing state rules against interstate banking as well.

Distinguishing between a One-Bank Holding Company and a Multi-Bank Holding Company

While multi-bank holding companies are of relatively recent origin, the one-bank holding company is not. A **one-bank holding company** is defined as a business organization that is involved in numerous activities, including banking. For example, Macy's Department Store has owned a bank for many years. So, too, have the Goodyear Tire & Rubber Company, Montgomery-Ward, and the United Mine Workers. The original purpose of the one-bank holding company was to allow a nonbanking enterprise to engage legally in banking. Since the 1970s, however, this device has been used by commercial banks to enter nonbanking commercial activities. Table 10-3 shows the growth in one-bank holding companies from 1973 to 1981.

The Bank Holding Company Act of 1956 did not specifically prohibit banks from engaging in a multitude of nonbanking commercial activities. Consequently, as one-bank holding companies, commercial banks could engage in bookkeeping and data-processing services, insurance, courier services, management services, and the like. Perhaps more importantly, as one-bank hold-

---

TABLE 10-3 One-Bank Holding Companies†

Year	No. of One-Bank Holding Cos.	No. of Banks	No. of Branches	Assets*	Deposits*
1973	1,282	1,282	7,861	262	207
1975	1,419	1,410	8,486	290	230
1977	1,607	1,602	10,241	496	403
1979	2,028	2,019	11,920	693	541
1981	3,093	3,082	14,329	756	587

*Billions of dollars.

†Prior to 1971, there were only multi-bank holding companies. Following an amendment in 1970 to the Bank Holding Company Act, one-bank holding companies were formed as well. The first year for which the Board of Governors of the Federal Reserve System (in the *Annual Statistical Digest 1971–1975*) distinguished between multi-bank and one-bank holding companies was 1973. We can infer, however, that there were at least 1,316 one-bank holding companies by the end of 1971 and 1,356 by the end of 1972. The estimate was derived as follows: The number of multi-bank holding companies grew from 121 in 1970 to 251 in 1973 and there was a total of 1,567 multi- and one-bank holding companies combined in 1971, and 1,607 in 1972. This suggests there were *at least* 1,316 (1567−251) one-bank holding companies by the end of 1971 and 1,356 (1607−251) in 1972.

Source: Board of Governors of the Federal Reserve System, *Annual Statistical Digest*. Data after 1975 includes foreign data.

ing companies, commercial banks were able to raise funds more easily (instead of attracting deposits) by selling the holding company's commercial paper. Thus, one-bank holding companies could obtain funds in the unregulated commercial market and then channel those funds to the parent bank, where they could be used to offset partially restrictive Fed actions designed to reduce bank reserves, lending, and the money supply. The one-bank holding companies also enabled commercial banks to evade the implications of interest-rate restrictions imposed by federal legislation and Federal Reserve regulations because the banks were able to raise nondeposit funds for loans and investments and forestall disintermediation.

Regulators and members of Congress shared concern about the activities of one-bank holding companies. Could a holding company's sale of unregulated commercial paper affect the soundness of the bank? Could conflicts of interest and increased concentration of financial power arise because of the growth of one-bank holding companies? Questions like these led to the passage of the 1970 Bank Holding Company Act. This act brought one-bank holding companies under the same restrictions as multi-bank holding companies (pursuant to the 1956 Bank Holding Company Act). A major worry of regulators of the nonbanking activities of one-bank holding companies is the fear of industrial and financial concentration in America. Other countries have allowed gigantic one-bank holding companies to operate in various commercial areas, including banking. One such one-bank holding company is the Japanese *zaibatsu,* a vast financial industrial commercial enterprise.

HIGHLIGHT   The *Zaibatsu*

Imagine the merger of the First National City Bank, the Prudential Insurance Company, and International Telephone and Telegraph. In Japan, such a concentration of financial and industrial concerns, called a *zaibatsu,* is not unusual and is encouraged by the government. These *zaibatsus* presumably can reap economies of scale—lower unit costs for larger-scale operations—in the production, marketing, and financing of new products for both industry and consumers. These economies of scale are realized, however, at the cost of relatively high concentration in the financial and industrial sectors; a large percentage of banking services and industrial output is accounted for by a very small percentage of the total number of businesses in the country.

In the late 1960s in the United States, one-bank holding companies were suspected of trying to become *zaibatsus.* As with most suspicions of conspiracy, this one was unfounded. Recent experience (and research) shows that one-bank holding companies in this country were interested in such important ancillary services as data processing and communications. One-bank holding companies were also formed in an attempt to avoid limitations imposed on commercial banks.

INTERSTATE BANKING

Each bank in this country initially served only its own particular community. It was not allowed to extend its services to other communities. As transportation systems improved, communications expanded, and population increased and became more mobile, banks sought to extend their services beyond the limits represented by the geographic boundary of its community. In the early 1900s, some banks (following their migrating customers) established branches across state lines. To counter interstate branching, the McFadden Act was passed in 1927. It subjects national banks to the branch-banking regulations of the state in which they operate. The McFadden Act thus precluded branch banking across state lines, although the act allowed existing branches to continue operating (and they do to this day). As pointed out earlier, some branch banking has continued through multi-bank holding companies, but those activities were partially curtailed by the Bank Holding Company Act of 1956.

Banking in the 1980s has become more complex. Unstable interest rates, new forms of interest-earning demand deposits, and competition from nontraditional rivals (stockbrokerage companies, such as Kidder-Peabody and Dean Whitter, and retailers, such as Sears) have changed the scope of banking operations. The ability to attract depositors from regional and national markets has become important for small regional banks, as well as for large city banks. Although the interstate expansion of full-service banking (the acceptance of demand and time deposits, and loans to consumers and businesses) is still prohibited, multi-bank holding companies have aggressively begun to diversify their operations across state lines, particularly in the loan and consumer-finance markets.

Recently twenty-six banks, including such giants as the Bank of America, Chase Manhattan, and Continental Illinois Bank & Trust, joined together to establish the **PLUS SYSTEM,** a nationwide automated teller-machine network. This network will enable customers of participating banks to withdraw cash, transfer funds from one account to another, and verify deposit balances anywhere around the country. Although the network technically will enable customers to bank across state lines, current banking laws prohibit banks from accepting deposits outside their own states.[7]

Other attempts to create interstate banking are occurring on almost a daily basis. For example, Western Bancorp, a large multi-bank holding company, operates in eleven western states. In 1981, all its banks were renamed the First Interstate Bank, and it has applied in every state in the union to use

---

[7]This is true except for certain subsidiaries of some U.S. commercial banks that have been set up under the Edge Act. This act was passed in 1919 and allows limited acceptance of deposits by banks, provided these deposits are related to international transactions. Deposits also may be accepted across state lines if they are used to finance the production of goods intended primarily for export.

that name for its banks. At present, even though the Western Bancorp banks in Idaho and California have the same name, the owner of a deposit account in an Idaho First Interstate Bank cannot make a deposit or a withdrawal in a California First Interstate Bank.

Another recent arrangement with definite implications for interstate banking is the network established by a group of banks in the western United States. These banks have combined to create a system of bank franchises. The idea was developed by the Los Angeles–based Trust Interstate Bank Corp. This group anticipates that small regional banks will eventually compete against the PLUS SYSTEM mentioned above and against the interstate banking activities of such rapidly growing giants as the First Interstate Bank (if Congress changes interstate banking laws). When the network is fully developed, participating banks will hook up to a common automatic teller system in a satellite data network and will combine their marketing and advertising functions.

INTEREST-RATE CEILINGS REVISITED

Most economists agree that the main problems with our financial system are the result of interest-rate restrictions. The restrictions on the maximum rates payable on demand deposits and time deposits (created during the 1960s and 1970s) cannot endure in an era of inflation, which generates rising nominal interest rates. Remember that the Banking Act of 1933 prohibited any interest payments on *demand* deposits. Prior to that time, banks had offered interest on such deposits. The Banking Act of 1933 and the Banking Act of 1935 authorized the Federal Reserve Board and the Federal Deposit Insurance Corporation to set maximum rates of interest payable on bank *time* deposits. (In 1966, Congress gave the **Federal Home Loan Bank Board** (**FHLBB**) the authority to set interest-rate ceilings on funds held at savings and loan associations.) Table 10-4 is a sample of the various maximum or Regulation-Q interest rates that have been in effect over time.[8]

Recall that disallowing interest payments on demand deposits was supposed to prevent "ruinous competition" among commercial banks. Interest-rate limitations were extended to savings and loan associations in 1966 primarily to ensure an inexpensive flow of funds into the residential housing market. The idea was that the maximum rate of interest payable by savings and loan associations would remain low even during periods of high market rates of interest, and allow S&Ls to continue lending money for mortgages at low rates.

---

[8]Since the Banking Act of 1933, Regulation Q of the Federal Reserve Code has placed ceilings on time and savings deposits. Regulation Q will be phased out, as provided by the Monetary Control Act, discussed later in the chapter.

TABLE 10-4 Maximum Regulation Q Rates: Maximum Interest Rates Payable on Time and Savings Deposits at Federally Insured Institutions

Percent per annum

Type and Maturity of Deposit	Commercial banks		Savings and loan associations and mutual savings banks (thrift institutions)	
	In effect Jan. 31, 1983		In effect Jan. 31, 1983	
	Percent	Effective Date	Percent	Effective Date
Savings	$5\frac{1}{4}$	7/1/79	$5\frac{1}{2}$	7/1/79
Negotiable-order-of-withdrawal accounts	$5\frac{1}{4}$	12/31/80	$5\frac{1}{4}$	12/31/80
Time accounts				
Fixed ceiling rates by maturity				
14–89 days	$5\frac{1}{4}$	8/1/79		
90 days to 1 year	$5\frac{3}{4}$	1/1/80	6	1/1/80
1 to 2 years	6	7/1/73	$6\frac{1}{2}$	
2 to $2\frac{1}{2}$ years				
$2\frac{1}{2}$ to 4 years	$6\frac{1}{2}$	7/1/73	$6\frac{3}{4}$	
4 to 6 years	$7\frac{1}{4}$	11/1/73	$7\frac{1}{2}$	11/1/73
6 to 8 years	$7\frac{1}{2}$	12/23/74	$7\frac{3}{4}$	12/23/74
8 years or more	$7\frac{3}{4}$	6/1/78	8	6/1/78
Issued to governmental units (all maturities)	8	6/1/78	8	6/1/78
IRAs and Keogh (H.R. 10) plans (3 years or more)	8	6/1/78	8	6/1/78

Source: Adapted from Board of Governors of the Federal Reserve System, *Federal Reserve Bulletin*, February 1983, p. A9.

Disintermediation Rears Its Head So much for good intentions. As market rates of interest rose above the rates that thrift institutions (particularly savings and loan associations) were allowed to pay, disintermediation occurred. Disintermediation, you will recall, is the withdrawal of funds from a financial intermediary by a saver and the subsequent loan of those funds to such ultimate borrowers as a corporation or a government. For example, market interest rates payable on T-bills and commercial paper exceeded the maximum interest rate paid by thrift institutions; depositors withdrew their time deposits and placed them directly in these higher-interest-paying investments. Not surprisingly, there have been years when time deposits held by commercial banks and thrift institutions actually declined.

Figure 10-3 shows the "yield spread" between the T-bill rate and the max-

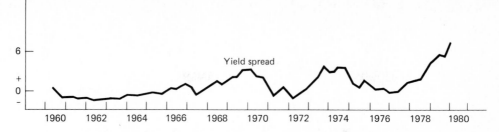

FIGURE 10-3 **Yield Spread: Treasury Bill Rate Minus Ceiling Rate on Passbook Savings Accounts.** This figure shows how the yield spread, defined as the T-bill interest rate minus the maximum allowable interest rate payable on passbook savings deposits, varied between 1960 and 1980. The yield spread was at its highest level during the last three years of the 1970s; not coincidentally, the greatest reduction in commercial bank and S&L time deposits also occurred during that three-year period. (*Source: Federal Reserve Bulletin,* Washington, D.C., February 1980, p. 106.)

imum allowable interest rate payable on passbook savings deposits. This yield spread widened considerably at the end of the 1960s, narrowed for the first few years of the 1970s, widened again in 1974, narrowed until about 1976, and then at the end of the 1970s became the widest ever. As expected, the greatest reduction in commercial bank and savings and loan time deposits occurred during the last three years of the 1970s, when the yield spread was the highest.

Interest-rate ceilings, particularly on deposits at savings and loan associations, led to sometimes disastrous problems in the housing industry. As savings and loan associations lost deposits as a result of disintermediation, the housing industry experienced credit crunches. The effect of interest-rate limitations on the distribution of income also became clear during the late 1970s; depositors with *large* accounts quickly took advantage of such market alternatives as T-bills (with a minimum unit size of $10,000), banker's acceptances (typically with a minimum unit size of $5,000), and other types of savings outlets that offered higher market yields but which required higher initial deposits. During much of the later 1970s, there were no restrictions on the maximum interest rates payable on jumbo CDs (those with face values of $100,000 or more). The people who suffered the most from interest-rate limitations during the 1970s and the early 1980s were clearly the *smaller* savers who were not able to meet the minimum deposit requirements.

Money market mutual funds requiring relatively small minimum initial deposits ($500, for example) have provided an alternative savings outlet to small savers. These funds compete with commercial-bank and thrift-institution time deposits that offer market rates of interest. Figure 10-4 shows the growth in money-market mutual funds; that growth is clearly related to the yield spread indicated in Figure 10-1; during the last part of the 1970s, many people withdrew their funds from time deposits and placed them in money market mutual funds.

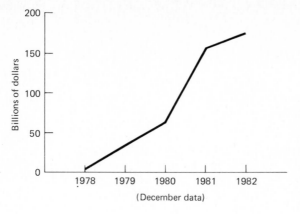

FIGURE 10-4 **Growth in Money Market Mutual Funds.** These are broker/dealer and general purpose money market mutual funds. (*Source:* Board of Governors of the Federal Reserve System, *Federal Reserve Bulletin.*)

The Hunt Commission   Interest-rate restrictions, as well as other regulations, caused fundamental problems in the financial system. Recognition of these problems led to the formation of a presidential commission on financial structure and regulation, called the Hunt Commission, in 1970. This commission recommended sweeping changes in banking regulation. Despite attempts in 1973 and again in 1975, these recommendations were not enacted into law. The Hunt Commission advocated a financial system with fewer restrictions on how financial institutions may operate. The commission made some eighty-nine recommendations aimed at unburdening the financial sector of the economy from "overregulation." The four most important recommendations were that:

1   All Regulation Q interest-rate ceilings be gradually removed
2   Depository institutions, including savings and loan associations, credit unions, and savings banks, be allowed to offer checking accounts
3   Thrift institutions be permitted a wider range of investment opportunities
4   Restrictions on entry into banking and other financial markets be reduced

Nine years after the publication of the Hunt Commission's report, Congress passed the 1980 Depository Institutions Deregulation and Monetary Control Act. That act did in fact put into effect the four major recommendations outlined above.

SUMMARY OF MAJOR REGULATORY CHANGES THROUGH 1980

The history of regulatory and institutional changes within the financial sector is instructive because it shows how institutions adapted to changing market conditions and how regulations had to be altered to reflect institutional changes. Table 10-5 shows selected regulatory and institutional changes within the financial sector.

TABLE 10-5 Selected Regulatory and Institutional Changes

Date	Commercial Banks	Other Financial Institutions
Sept. 1970		Savings and loan associations (S&Ls) are permitted to make nonnegotiable transfers from savings accounts for household-related expenses.
June 1972		Massachusetts mutual savings banks (MSBs) begin to offer negotiable order of withdrawal (NOW) accounts.
Sept. 1972		New Hampshire MSBs begin to offer NOW accounts.
Jan. 1974	All depository institutions in Massachusetts and New Hampshire (except credit unions) are authorized by congressional actions to offer NOW accounts. This action limited interest-bearing negotiable deposits to these two states. Thus, interest-bearing negotiable transfer accounts at banks began on an experimental basis.	
Jan. 1974		Nebraska S&L begins point-of-sale (POS) electronic funds transfer system. First Federal S&L of Lincoln, Nebraska, places an electronic terminal in a Hinky Dinky Supermarket. The terminal allows customers of the S&L to pay for groceries, make deposits to or withdrawals from their savings accounts.
Apr. 1974	State of Washington enacts legislation that allows state-chartered commercial banks, MSBs, S&Ls to establish any number of automated facilities throughout the state, provided that those operating these facilities share the cost and operations of the terminals when asked to do so by the state authorities. Commercial banks are required to share facilities with other commercial banks and have the option of sharing them with thrift institutions. Thrifts are permitted but not required to share the facilities.	
May 1974		Experimental 24-hour electronic facility opens on a shared basis by 15 Washington MSBs and S&Ls.
June 1974		New York state banking regulation permits MSB to offer non-interest-bearing NOW accounts (NINOWs).
Aug. 1974		Administrator of the National Credit Union Administration grants 3 Federal credit unions temporary authority to begin offering share drafts. These 3 credit unions were joined by 2 state credit unions in a 6-month pilot program (launched October 1974).
Sept. 1974		Pennsylvania attorney general rules MSB may legally offer a form of negotiable-order-of-withdrawal account.
Dec. 1974	Comptroller of the currency's interpretive ruling permits national banks to operate customer-bank communication terminals (CBCTs).	Federal Home Loan Bank Board (FHLBB) adopts a regulation which gives depositors traveling more than 50 miles from their homes access to their savings account balances through any other federally insured S&L by means of a traveler's convenience withdrawal (wire or telephone access).

TABLE 10-5   Selected Regulatory and Institutional Changes (*Continued*)

Date	Commercial Banks	Other Financial Institutions
Jan. 1975		California state-chartered S&L offers variable-rate mortgages (VRMs). Minnesota MSB introduces ''pay-by-phone'' service.
Apr. 1975	Commercial banks are authorized to make transfers from a customer's savings account to a demand deposit account upon telephone order from the customer.	FLBBB adopts two regulations: 1 Authorizes federal S&Ls to offer their customers bill-paying service from interest-bearing savings accounts. 2 Allows federal S&L service corporations and companies to make consumer loans (limited to states which allow such activity and subject to state restrictions)
May 1975	CBCT operated exclusively by a national bank is subjected to a 50-mile geographical restriction unless CBCT is available to be shared with one or more deposit institutions. A national bank may use a CBCT established and operated by some other institution and may participate in a statewide EFTS system.	
June 1975		Oregon governor signs into law legislation which allows the state's only MSB to offer checking accounts.
June 31, 1975	U.S. District Court Judge Robinson rules CBCTs authorized for national banks by the comptroller of the currency are illegal and must be shut down. (About 72 CBCTs, owned by national banks, have been installed in various parts of the country under the interpretive ruling issued by comptroller, Dec. 12, 1974.) Robinson's decision directly attacks the Dec. 12, 1974, interpretation, calling the terminals branches, both as defined by the U.S. Supreme Court in its 1969 Plant City case and as construed by Congress when it passed the McFadden Act in 1927.	
Sept. 1975	Commercial banks are allowed to make preauthorized nonnegotiable transfers from a customer's savings account for any purpose. Previously (since 1962), such transfers were limited to mortgage-related payments.	Massachusetts MSB introduces VRM program.
Oct. 1975		State legislation permits state-chartered thrift institutions in Maine to offer personal checking accounts.
Nov. 1975	Federal Reserve amends definition of savings deposits in Regulations D and Q to permit business savings accounts, up to $150,000, at member banks.	
Dec. 1975		State legislation permits thrift institutions in Connecticut to offer personal checking accounts.

TABLE 10-5 Selected Regulatory and Institutional Changes (*Continued*)

Date	Commercial Banks	Other Financial Institutions
Jan. 1976		While the authority to offer share drafts was still officially temporary, additional credit unions begin to offer share-draft accounts following the end of the 6-month pilot program initiated in the fall of 1974.
		As of year-end, 222 credit unions (roughly 1%) in 44 states have been approved to offer share drafts to their shareholders.
		Federal Reserve System adopts a policy for automated check-clearing systems (ACHs) to offer their services on a nondiscriminatory basis to all types of financial institutions.
Feb. 1976		Illinois S&Ls begin offering non-interest-bearing NOW accounts.
		Congress authorizes all depository institutions in New England to offer interest-paying NOW accounts (effective Mar. 1, 1976).
May 1976	U.S. Court of Appeals for the District of Columbia upholds earlier ruling by the U.S. District Court for the District of Columbia that national banks' CBCTs are branches under the McFadden Act.	New York governor signs legislation permitting checking accounts, including overdraft privileges, at state-chartered MSBs and S&Ls.
Oct. 4, 1976	U.S. Supreme Court lets stand ruling that CBCTs are bank branches.	
Feb. 14, 1977	Iowa statewide electronic banking system begins operating and represents the nation's first shared statewide network, encompassing a broad range of large and small banks in Iowa. (At last count, the system had 33 participating banks; 92 merchant terminals operate through a switch or central computer.)	
Apr. 1977		All but 15 of the nation's 470 MSBs have either NOW accounts, traditional checking accounts, or a combination of the two.
		Legislation enacted to expand credit-union lending authority, including authority to make 30-year mortgage loans.

Lovati, Jean M. "The Growing Similarity among Financial Institutions," *Review,* Federal Reserve Bank of St. Louis, Oct. 27, 1977, vol. 59, pp. 6–7.

THE DEPOSITORY INSTITUTIONS DEREGULATION AND MONETARY CONTROL ACT OF 1980

During the 1970s, disintermediation hurt savings and loan associations and the housing industry. During the same time, many state-chartered member banks also abandoned the Federal Reserve System because (1) the Fed required member banks to hold higher reserves than most state banking authorities required of nonmember state-chartered banks and (2) some non-member state-chartered banks were allowed to hold high-quality interest-earning assets as reserves. As nominal interest rates rose, the cost of Fed membership grew higher for state-chartered banks.[9] The Fed became concerned about its ability to control and regulate the banking sector and the money supply as more banks abandoned the Federal Reserve System.

The tremendous growth in money market mutual funds also caused great harm to thrift institutions because the thrift institutions were not allowed to offer market interest rates to depositors.

To eliminate or to reduce these and other problems, the Federal Reserve provided detailed suggestions to Congress for a new financial environment. The end result was the Depository Institutions Deregulation and Monetary Control Act (DIDMCA) of 1980. Table 10-6 summarizes the most important effects of this wide-ranging act.

Two provisions in the DIDMCA of 1980 eliminated the Federal Reserve System's problem of declining membership. Because *all* depository institutions of similar size are now required to hold the same quantity of reserves with the Federal Reserve System, membership no longer affects a depository institution's profitability. All depository institutions now have equal access to Federal Reserve services and they pay the same price for services (e.g., check clearing and collection).

This new law, as Table 10-6 documents, covers a lot of new ground. The 1980 act is Congress's mandate to regulatory agencies to simplify all preceding monetary and banking regulations enacted by Congress. Note, however, that although the act does reduce regulation in a number of areas, it also increases regulation in others. Many nonmember state banks will now be subject to *more* regulation than they were prior to 1980.

THE GROWING SIMILARITY AMONG FINANCIAL INSTITUTIONS

It was possible until recently to distinguish clearly between a commercial bank and any other type of thrift institution. The basic difference was that commercial banks were legally permitted to accept demand deposits (checking

---

[9]And for national banks, some of whom surrendered their charters to become state chartered.

TABLE 10-6 Primary Provisions and the Effects of the Depository Institutions Deregulation and Monetary Control Act of 1980

Provision	Effect
Phases out deposit interest ceilings	Interest rate ceiling on deposits is to be phased out over a period of 6 years. A depository institutions deregulation committee was set up to do this.
Nationwide NOW accounts permitted	Any depository institution after Dec. 31, 1980, was allowed to offer NOW accounts; that is, interest-bearing checking accounts to individuals and nonprofit organizations. Automatic transfer services (ATSs) were also allowed in all commercial banks. Savings and loan associations can use remote service units, and credit unions that are federally insured can offer share draft accounts (CUSDs).
Reserves required on all transactions accounts at depository institutions	Gradually, reserve requirements are to be uniformly applied to all transactions accounts which are defined as demand (checking) deposits, NOW accounts, ATS accounts, and credit union share drafts. This required reserve system is to be phased in over 8 years for all depository institutions that are not Federal Reserve members. For Federal Reserve members, the act meant a reduction in reserve requirements; those reductions would be phased in over 4 years.
Increased access to the discount window	All depository institutions issuing transactions accounts and nonpersonal time deposits now have the same borrowing privileges at the Federal Reserve discount window just as if they were member commercial banks.
Fees established for Federal Reserve services	A fee schedule for the Federal Reserve "chores" such as check clearing and collection, wire transfers, and the like was to be established by Oct. 1, 1981.
Power of thrift institutions expanded	Federally insured credit unions were allowed to make residential real estate loans. Savings and loan associations had higher loan ceilings and some ability to make consumer loans, and the power to issue credit cards.
The imposition of supplemental reserves	The Federal Reserve Board, under extraordinary circumstances, can impose additional reserve requirements on any depository institution of up to 4 percent of its transactions accounts. This supplementary reserve, if imposed, must earn interest.
Increased level federally insured deposits	Previously, federally insured deposits had a ceiling of $40,000; that ceiling was increased to $100,000.

Source: Economic Review, Federal Reserve Bank of Atlanta, vol. LXV, no. 2, March–April 1980, pp. 4–5.

accounts), and they made commercial business loans. This distinction remained until 1972 when mutual savings banks in Connecticut and New Hampshire began to offer negotiable-order-of-withdrawal (NOW) accounts. Since then, other changes have occurred in all types of depository institutions and the distinction among them is blurring. Virtually all depository institutions can offer some form of interest-earning transactions account. As a result, the other depository institutions now have checkable deposit liabilities; and this has caused a change in the structure of their assets and their liabilities. Savings and loan associations now include shorter-term assets in their portfolios; mutual savings banks and credit unions, which once invested only in such long-term assets such as mortgages, are now allowed to make various types of consumer loans (e.g., for cars and furniture). While at first the shift in the asset composition of these depository institutions was not significant, the shift can be expected to be large in the future. There are some lags on the part of regulators with respect to adjusting to financial innovation, and there is also a learning lag on the part of bank management with respect to financial innovation.

Thus, the different kinds of depository institutions are competing in both directions—for deposits on one side and for assets on the other side. As a result, consumers have more alternatives for "banking" services. Past regulation created artificial specialization in deposits and services offered by specific institutions. Deregulation will create opportunities and incentives for depository institutions to enter all financial markets. Soon all kinds of financial intermediaries will be indistinguishable. Someday they will all be "banks."

DEPOSITOR PROTECTION AND THE TREATMENT OF FAILING BANKS

Since the FDIC was created to insure deposits at the commercial banks, the FSLIC to insure deposits at S&Ls and mutual savings banks, and the NCUA to insure deposits at credit unions, not many of these depository institutions have failed. More importantly, depositors at the institutions which did fail did not lose any substantial part of their deposits.

The insuring agencies have established procedures to handle banks that become insolvent. There are three possible ways an insuring agency may resolve a depository institution's pending or actual failure.

1 The depository institution may be allowed to go into receivership—the so-called pay-off method. The insurer sends its agents to the institution, verifies the deposit records, and immediately pays funds directly to each depositor, up to the $100,000 limit. After this is done, the insuring agency liquidates that institution's assets. The insuring agency divides the institution's remaining assets on a prorated basis among the depositors who have claims in excess of their insurance, and among other creditors. About 60 percent of the insured institutions that have failed in recent years have paid off depositors and then been liquidated by this method.

2 The insuring agency can arrange for a "marriage" between the failing institution and a sound institution. This alternative is used in some 40 percent of the instances of failed institutions. The acquiring institution assumes the failed bank's deposits and its other liabilities and its assets. During the early

1980s, the insuring agency has often subsidized the acquiring institution by absorbing *all* of the liabilities of the failing institution.

3 The third way of resolving the problem of a failed bank has thus far been used only for *commercial bank* failures. The FDIC takes over the failed commercial bank and establishes a Deposit Insurance National Bank to provide temporary service to customers. Deposit Insurance National Banks offer limited services (they are not full-service banks) and operate for a maximum of two years. It is hoped that in the meantime some other commercial bank will acquire the Deposit Insurance National Bank and continue its operation. Between 1935 and 1980, only five Deposit Insurance National Banks were created.

Examination Procedures to Prevent Failure of a Depository Institution   Because insuring agencies guarantee an institution's deposits, they feel they should have some say in the way these institutions operate. Insuring agencies therefore require examinations of the institutions they insure. The idea of examination is to head off trouble before it snowballs into insolvency and failure. The insuring agencies maintain guidelines for the appropriate assets that insured institutions may purchase. By forcing commercial banks, S&Ls, savings banks, and credit unions to lend conservatively, the agencies hope to prevent potential insolvency problems from bad loans.

Some critics of regulation contend that the examination practices of insuring agencies and their requirements for conservative asset portfolio selection have stifled innovation. The recent success of noninsured financial intermediaries, in particular money market mutual funds, is in no small way due to the absence of such strict examination procedures.

CURRENT CONTROVERSY

How Many Regulatory Agencies Are Necessary?

The distinctions among financial institutions are disappearing. The combination of financial innovations and deregulation has largely erased the boundaries separating commercial banks and thrift institutions. In 1983, South Dakota decided to let banks own insurance companies; in April 1983, Prudential Insurance arranged to buy a bank in Georgia; Merrill Lynch, which pioneered money market mutual funds in which limited checking privileges exist, agreed to purchase a savings and loan association and American Express indicated similar intentions; Citibank now sells stocks and bonds; Sears has among its subsidiaries an insurance company, a brokerage house (Dean Witter), and a California depository institution.

As financial institutions become more similar, more people are asking such searching questions as:*

1 Why are eight agencies needed to regulate the securities market?
2 Why are three agencies (the FDIC, the Fed, and the office of the comptroller of the currency) needed to regulate commercial banks?
3 Can't we just have *one* regulatory agency for all financial institutions?

John Shad, the Securities and Exchange Commission (SEC) chairperson, has indicated that financial institutions playing the same game "ought to be subject to the same referees and rules." Not surprisingly, individual regulators are in favor of combining the *other* regulatory agencies and leaving *theirs* alone. For example, William Isaac, head of the FDIC, favors joining the regulatory functions of the Fed, the comptroller of the currency, and the Federal Home Loan Bank Board under one agency, but he wants to retain the FDIC and broaden its jurisdiction to *all* depository institutions, including S&Ls. The Home Loan Bank Board, which supervises the S&Ls, agrees in principle that regulatory agencies should be joined, but it wants S&L regulators to have a separate identity.

In general, the big banks want a single, new, financial-institution regulatory agency. The Fed would shed its regulatory powers and have one function—to control the money supply. The big banks have the support of the FDIC, the comptroller's office, and the Treasury.

Smaller banks, which are not without influence in Congress, prefer that the Fed retain its regulatory powers because the Fed has been a foot-dragger in deregulation. The Fed has been slow in approving nonbanking acquisitions, and it has refused to permit bank holding companies to engage in underwriting securities and in real-estate development. Smaller banks have an ally in Paul Volcker, the newly reappointed chairperson of the Fed, who maintains that regulatory power over financial institutions is important to the Fed if it is to control the money supply.

This issue was brought to a head in the fall of 1983, when a White House task force (chaired by Vice President Bush) convened to recommend reforms in financial regulation. The task force includes all the top financial regulators and the heads of the Treasury, Office of Management and Budget (OMB), Justice Department, and the White House Policy Development Office.

---

*Based on Peter Bernstein, Anna Cifelli, Richard I. Kirkland, Jr., and Craig C. Carter, "Big Banks Want to Shed the Fed," *Fortune,* May 2, 1983, pp. 29–30.

CHAPTER SUMMARY

1 The failure of a depository institution is an event of special importance because many people depend on the safety and security of such institutions. Moreover, when one bank fails the soundness of other banks becomes suspect. If all banks

are on a fractional reserve system, *no* bank can survive a situation in which all or most depositors attempt to withdraw their money at the same time. During the Great Depression bank runs were contagious and many banks toppled; many economists believe that widespread bank failures contributed significantly to the severity of the Great Depression.

2   The Banking Act of 1933 (the Glass-Steagall Act) was a landmark in banking regulation. It was passed as a reaction to the collapse of the banking system during the Great Depression. The key provisions of the Glass-Steagall Act were (a) the creation of the FDIC, (b) the separation of commercial banking from investment banking, and (c) a prohibition of payment of interest on demand deposits.

3   The FDIC insures the deposits of commercial banks. The FDIC has eliminated the fragile nature inherent in a fractional reserve banking system; by providing depositor confidence in even shaky banks, the "bank run" has been eliminated.

4   It was deemed important to separate commercial banking from investment banking because investment banking was believed to increase the riskiness of a commercial bank's portfolio.

5   If banks were allowed to pay interest on demand deposits, they might be inclined to use depositors' money to acquire assets that pay higher rates of return—and which therefore are riskier—than assets they might otherwise have acquired. Thus, the Glass-Steagall Act prohibited the payment of interest on demand deposits.

6   The preoccupation with excessive competition in the banking industry led to an entry-restricting policy: Potential entrants to the banking industry are required to provide a convincing case for the "need" for another bank before they can obtain a charter. This preoccupation, it is believed, has led to reduced competition in the banking industry.

7   The dual banking system in the United States has contributed to overlapping supervision and regulation of banks. There are four sources of regulation, supervision, and control: the comptroller of the currency, the Federal Reserve, the FDIC, and state banking authorities.

8   Historically, the U.S. public has distrusted large banks. As a consequence, there is a large number of distinct and separate depository institutions. Interstate banking has been prohibited, and individual states have encouraged a unit banking system and discouraged branch banking. In recent years, technological and legal innovations have helped to reverse this trend. In 1974, the comptroller of the currency ruled that customer-bank communications terminals are not branch banks. Attempts to create interstate banking are commonplace: Multi-bank holding companies are crossing state lines and are also circumventing unit-banking laws; one-bank holding companies are also circumventing laws that separate commercial banks from noncommercial bank activities.

9   The problems resulting from the overregulation of the banking industry led the 1970 Hunt Commission to recommend that: all Regulation-Q ceilings on interest rates be gradually removed, all depository institutions be permitted to offer demand deposits, thrift institutions be permitted a wider range of investment opportunities, and entry restrictions into banking and other financial markets be reduced.

10   In 1980, the Depository Institutions Deregulation and Monetary Control Act was passed and the four major Hunt Commission recommendations were put into

effect. All depository institutions are now required to hold reserves with the Fed and now have access to Federal Reserve services on an equal basis and pay the same price for these services. The 1980 act represented Congress's mandate to the regulatory agencies to simplify all existing regulations. The main result of this act is that the distinction among financial institutions is disappearing; they are all competing for deposits on one side of the balance sheet and for investments on the other side. Past regulation had created artificial specialization among financial institutions; the 1980 act will remove them.

11 The FDIC, FSLIC, and NCUA have insured deposits and have contributed greatly to financial stability in this country. When a depository institution becomes insolvent, there are three possible ways in which the insuring agency can handle the problem: (a) the depository institution may be allowed to go into receivership, (b) the insuring agency can arrange for a "marriage" of the failing institution to a sound one, or (c) in the case of a commercial bank, the failed institution can be taken over by the FDIC temporarily, with the hope that it will be acquired by another commercial bank in the future.

GLOSSARY

Branch banking: A system that allows banks to operate at more than one location.

Comptroller of the currency: The office in the U.S. Treasury Department that supervises the regulation and examination of national banks.

Federal Deposit Insurance Corporation (FDIC): A government agency that insures the deposits held in member banks; all members of the Fed and other banks that qualify can join.

Federal Home Loan Bank Board (FHLBB): A committee of three appointed by the President of the United States to regulate members of the Federal Home Loan Bank System. It also regulates FSLIC and the Federal Home Loan Mortgage Corporation.

Federal Savings and Loan Insurance Corporation (FSLIC): A government agency that insures deposits held in member savings and loan associations.

Multi-bank holding companies: Corporations that own and control two or more independently incorporated banks; also called group banking.

National Credit Union Administration (NCUA): A federal agency that insures credit-union deposits.

One-bank holding company: A business organization that owns one bank and is involved in other commercial activities.

PLUS SYSTEM: A nationwide automated teller-machine network that joins twenty-six banks.

Unit banking: A restriction preventing banks from operating at more than one location; a prohibition against branch banking.

PROBLEMS

10-1 What criteria might a federal or state regulatory commission use to decide whether a bank is "needed" in a specific area?

10-2 How would an unregulated free market decide if a bank is needed in a specific area?

SELECTED REFERENCES

Alhadett, David, *Monopoly and Competition in Banking* (Berkeley, Calif.: University of California Press, 1954).

Benston, George, *Bank Examination. The Bulletin* (New York University Graduate School of Business Administration, 1973).

Brown, Donald M., "Bank Holding Company Performance Studies and the Public Interest: Normative Uses for Positive Analysis?" *Review* (Federal Reserve Bank of St. Louis), March 1983, pp. 26–34.

Cargill, Thomas F., and Gillian G. Garcia, *Financial Deregulation and Monetary Control* (Stanford, Calif.: Hoover Institution Press, 1982).

Golembe, Carter H., and David S. Holland, *Federal Regulation of Banking* (Washington: Golembe Associates, 1981).

Spong, Kenneth, *Banking Regulation: Its Purposes, Implementation, and Effects* (Federal Reserve Bank of Kansas City, 1983).

West, Robert Craig, "The Depository Institutions Deregulating Act of 1980: A Historical Perspective," *Economic Review* (Federal Reserve Bank of Kansas City), February 1982.

Central Banking

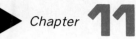
The Beginnings: A Short History of National Banking

CHAPTER PREVIEW

1 How did the dual banking system in the United States originate?

2 Why does inflation usually occur during wartime?

3 What caused the growth of wildcat banking and did this phenomenon cause inflation?

4 Why did Confederate dollars become worthless?

5 Why didn't greenbacks drive convertible paper money out of circulation?

No other country has a banking system as extensive and complex as the system in the United States. Other countries typically have a central bank and only ten to twenty commercial banks (each with many branches). The United States, on the other hand, has a dual banking system which includes both state-chartered banks and federally chartered banks. This two-tiered chartering arrangement accounts for the relatively large number of banks in this country. The best way to understand this dual banking system is through an historical review of the separate forces that have molded our financial world.

THE REVOLUTIONARY WAR

In your American history classes, you learned that one thing the American colonists agreed on was that they wanted independence and were willing to fight for it. They disagreed on just about everything else. Two major controversies arose concerning governmental power (whether to have a strong central government or strong state governments framed within a federal system) and financial power (whether to have a strong central bank concentrating financial power or many independent banks, none more financially powerful than the others).

During the War of Independence, the Continental Congress confronted these controversies. It also faced the problem of financing the War of Independence.

Financing the War of Independence Even though the total cost of the war to the United States was only $100 million and probably less than 10 percent of national income per year from 1775 to 1783, the Continental Congress had difficulty raising this sum. The Articles of Confederation were quite weak and did not authorize the Continental Congress to tax citizens. Congress, however, was able to borrow almost $8 million in gold from abroad; over three-fourths of it came from France, the rest from Holland and Spain. About $2 million was raised by borrowing from individuals and businesses. Requests from the Congress for state contributions brought only $6 million. From the viewpoint of any particular state, it often seemed wise to hold back and let the other states pay. When each state acted this way, little revenue was raised.

Continental Dollars The Continental Congress authorized an issue of almost $200 million in paper currency during the four-year period commencing in 1775. During that period this paper money was actually worth little more than $40 million in gold. Few individuals had confidence that this paper currency, called "Continentals," would be redeemed in specie (gold or silver) after the revo-

---

Continental Currency. In order to finance the Revolutionary War, the Continental Congress issued so much of this paper money that worthless items were referred to as being "not worth a Continental." *(Smithsonian Institution.)*

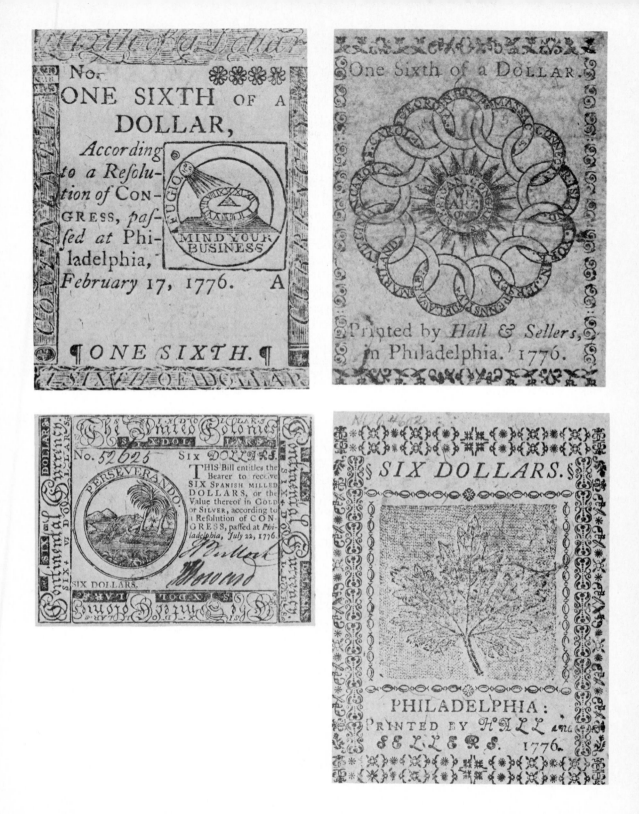

lution. Given a lack of faith in the future exchange value of Continentals, their current exchange value in terms of gold declined steadily. Congress did not have the power at that time to declare Continentals to be legal tender (currency which, by law, must be accepted as payment for debt obligations). Instead, Congress asked the states to penalize persons who refused to take them in exchange for goods and services.

By 1781, Continentals were worth one five-hundredth of their face value. There were two reasons for this extremely low exchange value: (1) the public's lack of faith in the government; and (2) the tremendous increase in the number of Continentals issued. The relationship between the supply of money in circulation and its price (purchasing power) became quite clear during this period with the expression "not worth a Continental." As with all commodities, when the supply expands more rapidly than the demand, the equilibrium, or market-clearing, price falls. The "price" of a dollar is its purchasing power. The rapid increase in the supply of Continentals led to a decline in their purchasing power. This is otherwise known as an inflationary situation; it takes more units of money to buy the same units of goods and services.

THE EARLY YEARS OF THE REPUBLIC

Following the ratification of the U.S. Constitution in 1789, the new federal government was empowered to "coin money, regulate the value thereof, and mint coins, in addition to fixing the standard of weights and measures." Implicit in this section of the Constitution was the ability of the federal government to create a national currency. This was important for the future development of commercial activities and capital markets (markets in which the buying and selling of debts and shares in companies take place). The Constitution also allowed the federal government to redeem the debts of the "several" (individual) states. This further aided the development of capital markets.

The Views of Hamilton   A key provision of the Constitution is that the federal government is empowered to regulate (control the size of) the money supply. Initial efforts to regulate the money supply were lacking, but some important attempts to provide a stable monetary system were made in the early years of the republic. Alexander Hamilton was appointed Secretary of the Treasury in 1791 at the age of thirty-four. The powers granted to him by this office were second only to those of the President. Hamilton's financial program reflected his belief in a powerful national government (as opposed to powerful separate state governments). Hamilton was adamant about the establishment of a basic unit of value in the monetary system. At his prodding, the Mint Act of 1792 was passed. The dollar was to be the basic unit of value, and the decimal system was to replace the British system of pounds, shillings, and pence.

Consistent with his view that the national government should be powerful, Hamilton was in favor of a national bank: "The tendency of a national bank is to increase public and private credit. Industries increase, commodities will multiply, agriculture and manufacturing flourishes, and herein consists the true wealth and prosperity of a state."[1]

An Alternative View While Alexander Hamilton was an ardent proponent of a strong commercial banking sector, Thomas Jefferson wanted the United States to remain a largely agricultural country. Jefferson was thus generally opposed to banks because he believed they were mainly associated with industrial and commercial activity.

Alexander Hamilton belonged to that group of federalists that favored centralization of political power in the federal government. This included the ability to control, charter, and supervise banks. Indeed, the federalists did not believe that the Constitution allowed state regulation of banking. The antifederalists, led by Jefferson, championed states' rights. Not only did they argue for state chartering and supervision of banks, but they also fought for laws which would prevent the involvement of the federal government in any of these activities.

The important thing to realize is that during this period (from the beginning of the republic to the end of the 1780s), the main function of a bank was to issue **bank notes.** Bank notes were pieces of paper representing a liability on the part of the issuing bank; these notes were easily transferred from one person to another. The feature distinguishing a bank note from a bank deposit was that the bank note did not require the payer to specify the payee. Bank notes, then, were similar to coins; but the notes were more portable because, in principle, any amount of money could be specified and printed on a bank note.[2] As a means of payment, bank notes were much more important than demand deposits. Checking accounts were used only in cities from the period 1781 to 1811, during which time the number of banks grew from twenty to more than ninety. During this period few towns existed, travel was slow, and communication was difficult.

By 1789, the year the U.S. Constitution was ratified, the United States had three incorporated banks. These were the Bank of North America and Philadelphia, established in 1782; the Bank of New York, established in 1784; and the Bank of Massachusetts, established in 1784. A number of *un*incorporated, or private, banks had also been formed. At that time, common law provided that individuals could engage in any business of their choice, including banking. Not until the 1800s did the states attempt to limit banking by these private, unincorporated firms.

---

[1]Letter to Robert Morris, 1781.

[2]Historians believe that the issuance of bank notes started during the Renaissance in Florence. Several centuries later, when the Bank of England and the Bank of Amsterdam started the practice in earnest, however, bank notes took on much more importance. In both Amsterdam and England, citizens assumed that bank notes would be convertible to specie (gold or silver).

THE BANKS OF THE UNITED STATES

After the ratification of the Constitution and prior to the American Civil War, the federal government chartered two banks to serve the public interest.

The First Bank of the United States   For a number of years Hamilton lobbied for a national bank. His lobbying eventually paid off, and Congress chartered the First Bank of the United States in 1791. Its charter specified that the bank would last for a period of twenty years. The First Bank of the United States was a private corporation governed by twenty-five directors. It had a capital stock of $10 million, of which the federal government provided 20 percent. That may seem like a small amount, but in its time it was the largest bank and, indeed, the largest private corporation in the United States. Its head office was in Philadelphia and it had branches in major cities throughout the country. In effect, it was a nationwide branch-banking system that was owned by private investors and the federal government.

The First Bank of the United States served as the federal government's depository; it would receive funds from the federal government and transfer them to designated payees. The bank issued demand deposits as well as bank notes. Because of its many branch offices, it was able to lend funds and transfer payments to and from various parts of the country.

To some extent, the First Bank of the United States took on many of the functions of a central bank. It was able to control the power that state banks had to issue notes and to lend funds. When the First Bank decided to lend more to private parties, the reserves of state banks expanded. When it reduced its loans, the reserves of state banks contracted. It also exerted power over state banks in another way. If the First Bank of the United States came into possession of state bank notes, it could hold the notes (or pay them out) and the issuing state banks were not required to draw down on their reserves of gold or silver. On the other hand, if the First Bank presented state bank notes for redemption at the banks that issued them, the issuing banks had to pay in gold or silver; thus their reserves fell.

The End of the First Bank of the United States   The First Bank of the United States was profitable. It averaged an 8 percent per year rate of return for its investors. When its charter came up for renewal in 1811, however, it was not renewed. There were many reasons why Congress refused to renew the charter. One of the most important reasons was that during the twenty years, the ownership of some of the bank's stock had shifted to foreigners. As today, Americans feared excessive foreign control over the economy. This view was particularly prevalent during the attempt to make the First Bank a central bank.

The antifederalists also fought the First Bank on the ground that the Constitution contained no specific provision for bank charters. The antifederalists were worried about the centralization of power in the federal government at the expense of the states' powers. They contended that the First Bank of the

United States would discourage the growth of state banks by regularly presenting state bank notes for redemption in specie.

The First Bank's closing in 1811 came at an unfortunate time. During the War of 1812, Treasury finances were in poor condition and no central depository existed. Additionally, as a consequence of the First Bank's demise, a great increase in unregulated local banking ensued. The absence of the restraining influence of the First Bank allowed for a rapid increase in the amount of state-bank-note issues. From 1812 to 1817, state-bank-note issues rose from about $50 million to over $100 million. Specie payment was abandoned. That is, banks were not willing to redeem their bank notes in gold or silver. Because of the chaotic banking system that existed at that time, the cry went up for a second U.S. bank, again to be chartered by the federal government.

The Second Bank of the United States   In 1816, the federal government gave a twenty-year charter to the Second Bank of the United States. This bank resembled the First Bank in many respects but it was larger and had a capital stock of $35 million. The federal government again provided 20 percent of its capital. The remaining 80 percent was purchased by individuals, private companies, private corporations, and state governments. The board of directors consisted of twenty-five members, five of whom were appointed by the President; the remainder were appointed by the private stockholders. As with the First Bank, the Second Bank had branches in major cities throughout the country.

The Second Bank provided commercial banking services to the economy as well as central banking services to the banking system. As with the First Bank, it regulated state banks by presenting their notes for redemption in specie and by controlling the amount of credit it created.

Soon after the Second Bank was chartered, a number of economic difficulties arose. For example, the price of cotton dropped and farmers began to have financial troubles. Instead of countering these troubles with such expansionary activities as increasing loans and not requiring state banks to redeem bank notes, the Second Bank of the United States contracted its deposits from 1818 to 1819. Especially hard hit were the banks in the west that were having trouble collecting the loans due them. At the same time, the U.S. government had to pay the debt incurred for the Louisiana Purchase. As a result, quite a bit of specie flowed overseas and helped contract further the American money supply. (Chapter 29 analyzes how gold outflows reduce the domestic money supply and increase the money supply of the countries receiving the gold.)

The ultimate result was the so-called panic of 1819. The Second Bank of the United States halted the payment of specie to its depositors; there were numerous simultaneous state-bank failures throughout the economy. As a result, the money supply contracted and the price level (CPI) fell by 22 percent from 1816 to 1821. The extent of this particular financial and economic crisis should not be exaggerated, however. The United States was still a highly agricultural nation, with 93 percent of the population living in rural areas. Thus, the nonfarming sector of the economy was relatively small, and even

HIGHLIGHT Banker's Biography: Nicholas Biddle (1786–1884), President, Second Bank of the United States (1823–1836)

Faulty strategy in his fight against President Jackson and the Jacksonians was not in keeping with the brilliant career that Nicholas Biddle had carved for himself. Biddle came from a prominent Philadelphia family. James Biddle, his father, was a U.S. Naval officer, commander of the *Ontario,* and the man who took formal possession of Oregon Country for the United States in 1818.

Young Nicholas was a precocious student; he entered the University of Pennsylvania at the tender age of ten and graduated at thirteen. He also received a degree from the College of New Jersey (now Princeton) at age fifteeen. He was a student of the classics and French literature and became the editor of America's first literary periodical, *Port Folio.* In 1815, he helped prepare Pennsylvania's reply to the Hartford Convention, in which numerous proposed amendments to the Constitution had been offered. Most of these proposals attempted to limit the powers of Congress and the executive branch of the government. Biddle later compiled for the State Department a digest of

foreign legislation affecting U.S. trade.

Among his published works was *A History of the Expedition under the Command of Captains Lewis and Clark,* which he prepared from the explorers' notes and journals.

By the time Biddle was appointed a director of the Second Bank of the United States, he was considered brilliant, debonaire, and versatile. At the age of thirty-seven he had already been a writer, a lawyer, a state senator, and a diplomat. To these traits, Biddle added tremendous pride and an uncompromising attitude toward others. These two qualities served him well when he took over the presidency of the Second Bank.

As president, Biddle showed that he could discipline any other bank by requiring it to pay debts to the Second Bank of the United States in hard specie. But such behavior did not win Biddle many friends in the newer sections of the country or in the Old South.

Biddle's cavalier demeanor did not enhance his chances of overriding President Jackson's veto of the bank's charter in

1832. Jackson claimed the bank was unconstitutional and a monopoly that used public funds to enrich a few already wealthy men. Jackson's veto prevailed and from 1834 to 1836, Biddle concentrated on liquidating the bank.

After the charter of the Second Bank of the United States had expired, Biddle applied to the Pennsylvania legislature for incorporation of the bank's Philadelphia branch. It cost Biddle nearly $6 million to secure the charter, and, to compound the private bank's liquidity problems, Biddle borrowed heavily in Europe in an attempt to corner the cotton market. As cotton prices continued to fall in world markets, however, the bank was forced to seek more credit time and again—at ever higher interest rates. Soon Biddle found difficulty in getting credit at *any* interest rate. He then resorted to increasingly dubious Wall Street operations, which lessened even more Biddle's (and his bank's) reputation and prestige. With its credit and reputation ruined, Biddle's private bank closed its doors in 1836, dragging several other banks down with it.*

*In 1981, the Texas billionaire Hunt brothers and some wealthy Arabs relearned the lesson of how difficult it is to corner a market when they lost a fortune in the silver market.

Nicholas Biddle. The controversial president of the Second Bank of the United States. *(National Portrait Gallery, Smithsonian Institution.)*

Biddle died disgraced and discredited by many, but he left behind principles that would be used later in the formulation of a true central banking system in the United States. Some observers believe that the monetary and banking reforms of Franklin Delano Roosevelt and the Federal Reserve System were in part based on principles established by Biddle.

though it was hit very hard by the panic of 1819 and the subsequent reduction in business activity, the largely self-sufficient agricultural sector did not suffer greatly.

As a result of the panic of 1819, the first president of the Second Bank, William Jones, was ousted. The second president was Langdon Sheves (1819–1823), who in turn was replaced by the highly esteemed Nicholas Biddle (1823–1836). Biddle eventually ran into difficulties, however.

The Demise of the Second Bank of the United States
Toward the end of Biddle's appointment, there were strong political forces at work to make sure that the charter of the Second Bank lapsed. When Andrew Jackson was elected to the presidency of the United States in 1828, the Second Bank's troubles were

magnified. During the campaign, the majority of the directors and officers of the Second Bank publicly opposed Jackson and his party. In particular, Biddle openly opposed Jackson's reelection in 1832.

Jackson attacked the Second Bank on the ground of unconstitutionality. He wanted to close it, but a committee was formed in the House of Representatives that eventually affirmed the constitutionality of the bank. During the 1820s, the bank had provided the economy with a national currency. Because it had a large number of branches, U.S. bank notes were in circulation everywhere. The rate of exchange between U.S. bank notes and all other bank notes was basically stable throughout the nation. Congress apparently saw this as a good thing, and Jackson's attempt to block recharter of the bank on the ground of unconstitutionality failed.

In fact, the recharter of the Second Bank was one of the major political campaign issues in the 1832 election. Soon after winning the election, Jackson withdrew all federal deposits from the bank and placed them in selected state banks, often called "pet" banks.

Ultimately, Biddle's biggest political mistake was to apply for a recharter four years before the 1836 expiration date of the original charter. His intention was to secure a recharter and at the same time embarrass Jackson in the 1832 election. The recharter was in fact passed by Congress in July 1832, but it was vetoed by Jackson upon his reelection. Congress did not override this veto. Biddle's scheme backfired and the Second Bank of the United States closed its doors in 1836.

Inflation after the Demise of the Second Bank of the United States

The demise of the Second Bank of the United States in 1836 brought with it many changes on the American banking scene. Inflation increased and it continued from 1835 through 1837. A depression occurred from 1839 to 1843. Many historians believe that the inflation was caused by the fall of the Second Bank of the United States. They feel that the absence of the Second Bank's restraining forces on state banks led to a rapid increase in the amount of paper currency available (resulting from the proliferation of "wildcat banks," so called because their locations were said to be so remote that only wildcats frequented them). Historically, large increases in the supply of money have led to a reduction in the price of money. But the price of money is its purchasing power, and so large increases in the supply of money have typically led to increases in the rate of inflation. Figure 11-1 shows that the money supply did increase after Jackson's veto of the act to recharter the Second Bank in 1832.

The increase of wildcat banking was not the major cause of the increase in the money supply from 1832 to 1836. The ratio of bank-held reserves to credit outstanding did not fall during that period because, on the whole, banks were fairly cautious. The increase in the money supply was due mainly to an increase in the amount of specie—gold and silver—in the U.S. economy. After all, the United States was part of an international economy. It adhered to a specie standard that involved shipments of specie into and out of the country. Gold and silver formed the basis of the circulating money supply. During this time, there was a large increase in specie imports from Mexico as well as from

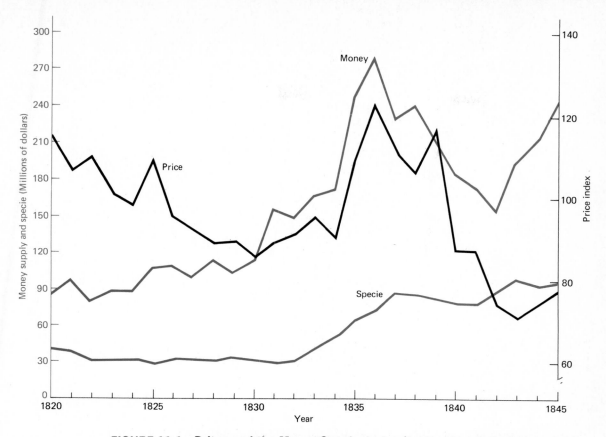

FIGURE 11-1 Prices and the Money Supply during the Demise of the Second Bank.
Prices rose sharply during 1835 and from 1829 to 1836. Although this price rise has
generally been attributed to the demise of the Second Bank and the proliferation of
money emanating from wildcat banks, much of it was in fact due to the influx of
specie into the United States, as indicated on the bottom line. A 100% increase in
specie had occurred in the eight years prior to 1835. (*Source:* Hugh Rockoff,
"Money, Prices, and Banks in the Jacksonian Era," in R. W. Fogel and S. L.
Engerman, eds., *The Reinterpretation of American Economic History,* New York:
Harper & Row, 1971, table 1, p. 451.)

Britain and France. The bottom line of Figure 11-1 shows that the amount of
specie flowing into the United States increased dramatically from 1832 until
about 1837. This inflow of specie is attributed largely to three causes:

1 The increase in U.S. exports of cotton to England
2 Foreign investment in the developing U.S. transportation system
3 The reestablishment of Anglo-American commercial ties which had been
   interrupted by the War of 1812 between the United States and England.
   From 1821 to 1837 the British invested more than $125 million in United
   States' transportation and other social overhead facilities

Thus, the demise of the Second Bank of the United States alone was not responsible for the inflation from 1835 to 1836.

A Decline in the Public's Confidence in Banks In the early 1830s, public confidence in banks increased, largely because the Second Bank helped maintain sound banking practices throughout the nation. This confidence led to a sharp reduction in the proportion of money that individuals and businesses held in specie; during that time, the amount of specie held in banks increased. Paper money would serve just as well, people believed, as long as the banks were sound. But after the demise of the Second Bank, public confidence in banks again declined. The proportion of money that individuals wished to hold in specie increased, and the specie holdings of banks declined. The Specie Circular Act of 1836 required that (most) federal land sales be paid in gold, and this also increased specie holdings by individuals. When depositors requested specie from the banks and some banks could not redeem bank notes with specie, banking panics occurred. The high demand for specie at this time put great strains on the banking system. The end result was the worst depression of the century; the depression lasted from 1839 to 1843.

STATE BANKING AND ITS ABUSES PRIOR TO THE CIVIL WAR

Between 1836 and the establishment of the national banking system in 1863, there were two sets of banks in the United States. There were first the private, unincorporated banks, and second the banks that were incorporated with charters from state governments. The private banks (companies) acted in a manner similar to the incorporated banks throughout this period.

Free Banking State legislatures in Michigan and in New York passed **free banking laws** in 1837 and 1838, respectively. After these dates, most other states followed suit. Prior to this time, a bank could obtain a corporate charter from a state only by an act of the legislature of that state. Free banking laws ended this practice; anyone or any group could now secure a corporate charter and engage in banking if it complied with the provisions of the general bank incorporation law. The requirements for obtaining a charter varied from state to state.

According to critics of the day, the requirements were inadequate to protect depositors and the general public. Critics of free banking claimed that state banks had inadequate capital and inadequate reserves against their notes and deposits. Many state banks at that time made risky loans. Problems with state banks resulted in the practice of circulating state bank notes of different values. Some state bank notes could be redeemed in gold and silver; they circulated at face value. That is, if a state bank note had $10 printed on it, it was just as good as having $10 in gold or silver. Other state bank notes circulated at small discounts; still others circulated at huge discounts. Not an insignificant portion of circulating state bank notes became completely worthless. Counterfeiters often made particular state bank notes valueless. By the end of the 1860s, for example, there were over 5,000 types of counterfeited notes in circulation. For the Bank of Delaware alone, there were approximately three dozen counterfeit issues in circulation.

New York enacted and implemented a highly restrictive banking law in order to avoid such abuses. Banks in that state were supervised and examined. It is not surprising, then, that the legislation which established the national banking system in 1863 was modeled to a large extent on New York law.

Inflationary Finance in the Confederacy

Inflationary Finance in the Confederacy   From 1861 on, the Confederate government had to use part of the south's resources to fight the war. Foreigners were unwilling to lend large sums to the Confederacy and after the northern blockade on trade came into effect in 1862, very few import duties could be used to support the war effort. The south did obtain a certain amount of the property of the federal government and of Union citizens when the war broke out. (The most noteworthy acquisitions were the Harper's Ferry Arsenal and the naval shipyards at Norfolk.) There was a certain amount of confiscation of goods, in addition to internal taxes and loans. But these sources of income accounted for less than one-half the total outlays of the Confederate government during the Civil War. At that time, these outlays were valued at about $3 billion. The remaining half of the total outlays was financed by inflation. The Confederacy issued large amounts of paper notes. Figure 11-2 shows that an index of prices in the south rose from 100 in January 1861 to 9,210 in April 1865. The index of the stock of money in circulation in the Confederacy grew from 100 in January 1861 to 2,000 in April 1865.

What occurred was a typical hyperinflation, a dramatic increase in the price level over a short period of time. As prices began to rise rapidly, consumers anticipated further increases. They realized that Confederate notes would lose purchasing power because of inflation, so they attempted to spend the notes before they lost value. In this way, Confederate citizens bid up prices even faster than would have otherwise been the case and faster than would seem appropriate for the increase in the money supply.[3] During the period from October 1863 to April 1865, the price level rose at a much more rapid rate than the rate of increase in the Confederacy's money supply.

The Confederacy also faced a problem not encountered by most countries during hyperinflation: Toward the end of the war, everyone assumed that the Confederate notes would have a zero exchange value if the Union forces prevailed. Clearly, a Confederate dollar would be worth nothing if the south

---

[3]That is, the velocity of circulation increased; the rate at which money was spent and respent, per year, increased because people believed that the value of a unit of money was falling. We discuss the concept of the velocity of money in more detail in Chapter 18.

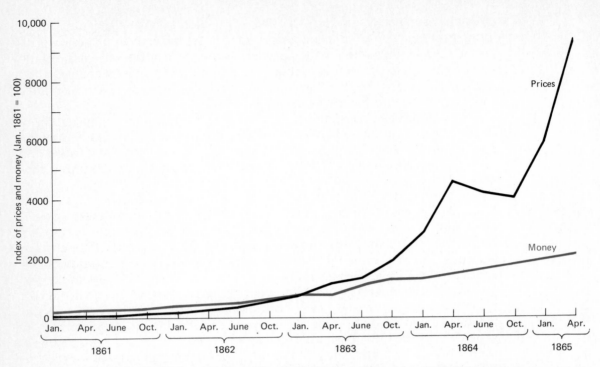

FIGURE 11-2 **Inflation in the Confederacy.** The rate of inflation was not very great initially, but by the end of the Civil War the value of a Confederate dollar had depreciated to about 1% of its original value. (*Source:* E. M. Lerner, "Money, Prices, and Wages in the Confederacy, 1861–1865," *Journal of Political Economy,* vol. 63, February 1955, p. 29.)

lost. Thus, for two reasons, inflation in the Confederacy was astronomical by the end of 1864.

Financing the Northern Effort   With the outbreak of war in 1861, there was an immediate financial panic in the north as banks suspended specie payments. The number of business failures rose. The federal treasury was almost empty, and federal credit diminished when the government itself suspended specie payments. After all, the Union, too, had to finance the war. It did so by taxing and issuing paper money.

    Borrowing   With respect to the first form of war finance, J. Cooke, a Philadelphia banker, floated many loans for the government. He popularized bond issues by emphasizing the advantages of the investment and the patriotic duty of the citizens in the north. Over $2 billion was raised in this manner. Cooke's fee was 1 percent on sales up to $10 million and three-eighths of 1 percent on sales that exceeded that figure. Cooke acted as an investment banker acts today. The only difference was that the bond issuer was the government rather than a private corporation.

Taxation   The north used taxation to raise funds more extensively than the south did:

1   Excise taxes were raised in 1862, were extended to numerous goods and services, and yielded about $300 million.
2   The Morrill tariff was passed in 1861, and it raised another $300 million.
3   An income tax produced about $55 million.

Money Creation   As in the south, large amounts of paper money were created to help finance the north's war effort. About $330 million in U.S. notes, otherwise called "greenbacks," were issued. **Greenbacks** were a form of fiduciary currency that was nonredeemable paper money. Being nonredeemable meant that the U.S. government did not agree to exchange it at any point in time for gold or silver. It was fiduciary in the sense that the government was trusted not to increase significantly the total number of greenbacks in circulation so that their purchasing power would remain constant. During the Civil War, the nonredeemable fiduciary greenbacks circulated alongside the existing gold and silver coins and other forms of redeemable currency, such as state bank notes.

It is interesting to note that Gresham's law did not seem to apply to greenbacks. Gresham's law states that, "Bad money drives out good money." Presumably, greenbacks were bad money and all other paper currencies redeemable in gold were good money. *But Gresham's law applies only to situations in which the rate of exchange between the so-called good money and bad money is fixed.* During the Civil War, this rate of exchange was *not* fixed; greenbacks did not exchange one-for-one for dollar bills that were redeemable in specie. All money redeemable in gold, as well as the price of gold, fluctuated in price in terms of greenbacks. In 1864, it took $2 in greenbacks to get one gold dollar. The rate of inflation, as measured by prices in terms of greenbacks, depended on the amount of note issues. Figure 11-3 shows what happened to the Consumer Price Index (CPI) during the period 1861 to 1865.

Enactment of the National Banking Act

Prior to the federal legislation of 1863 and 1864 which established a national banking system, state bank charters were easily obtained in just about any state. The main intent of the National Banking Act—at least that which was offered to the public—was to establish a national system that would unify all the banks in the United States, with respect to who was eligible to start one, what type of paper currency could be issued, what type and how many reserves were to be held, and so on. However, with *several exceptions,* the original legislation was based on the free-banking philosophy of the day: that anyone could open and operate a bank and that banks were no different from any other business. The several exceptions to the free-banking philosophy, however, made all the difference in the world, as will be explained below. The result was far from a national banking system, and no national institution able to expand credit markets and credit availability actually came into being.

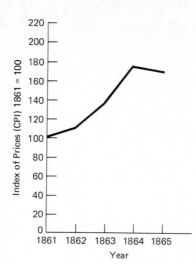

FIGURE 11-3 **Inflation in the Union.** Between 1861 and 1865, prices in the Union rose by 70%.

The War and the Need for More Money Congress enacted the banking legislation primarily, although not exclusively, to increase the government's borrowing power during the Civil War. It did this by requiring all national banks to invest a portion of their capital in U.S. government securities. The capital necessary to open a national bank was substantially greater than most banks (especially those in rural areas) actually had. And besides, in the agricultural areas of the country, the average capital required of nonnational, or state, banks was less than the minimum required of a national bank. Moreover, national banks were forbidden to make real-estate loans. As a result of these requirements and restrictions, a system of national banks did not arise and become the one and only institution for banking throughout the United States.

Since the National Banking Act was not successful in inducing state banks to take up federal charters and to comply with all the requirements of the act, the act failed in one of its purposes. Congress then decided to reduce the number of state banks by levying a 10 percent tax on any bank or individual that paid with or used state bank notes. The goal was to force state banks to become nationally chartered banks. This congressional action was successful in reducing the number of state banks from about 1,000 in 1864 to only 250 in 1868. But the success of the note tax was not permanent. By 1914, for example, there were over 17,000 state banks and only about 7,000 national banks. State banks not only survived the 10 percent note tax but thrived. They did this in an era when bank deposits (usually in the form of checking accounts, or demand deposits) became the more prominent means of payment. Because state banks could create *checking deposits,* they could exist profitably without issuing bank notes. And since there were fewer restrictions on state-chartered banks than on federally chartered banks, it is not surprising that state-chartered banks enjoyed a greater growth rate than federally chartered banks.

The Benefits of the National Banking Act Even though the National Banking Act did not create a unified banking system, it did give the country's banks a link to a reserve system that provided a legally sanctioned and formal mechanism for transferring funds between banks. This mechanism for funds transferal was a result of the fact that the National Banking Act required that banks hold reserves in one of three forms: specie, Treasury currency, or as deposits in larger banks. This third provision for reserves generally meant that the banking system's reserves would concentrate (pyramid) in the larger city banks in the money market centers, because these centers required more funds and paid higher interest rates. This system tended to promote an efficient allocation of loanable funds throughout the country. It was now easier for funds to go to areas where they would yield the highest rate of return. This generally meant (during that period) the transfer of bank funds from agricultural to industrial uses; this helped funnel credit to areas requiring large amounts of capital, such as railroad investment and large-scale industry.

On the other hand, this reserve system had its problems. Periodically, the smaller rural banks would call upon the larger city banks for cash to satisfy their own depositors' liquidity needs. The larger city banks, finding that their reserves fell correspondingly, cut back on their own lending, thereby contributing to a general scarcity of credit. As a consequence, this system that allowed a pyramiding of reserves caused financial crises to spread quickly throughout the financial community. *Under the national banking system there was no "lender of last resort" to supply additional funds during such "credit crunches";* because holders of reserves (large city banks) were themselves commercial banks, they were subject to the identical credit crunches that the smaller banks were. That is one reason for the creation of the Federal Reserve System in 1913.

CHAPTER SUMMARY

1 The United States has a dual banking system; banks are chartered either by the federal government or by a state. This dual system exists partly because of the long controversy regarding states' rights versus the federal government's rights, and partly because of a desire to keep financial power diffused.

2 Because wars must be financed and because people have always been reluctant to pay taxes, it has often been politic for governments to increase the money supply during wartime. During the Revolutionary War, the Continental Congress was not empowered to tax; the War of Independence was financed partly by borrowing gold from abroad and partly by borrowing from the states. However, it was financed mostly by issuing paper currency called "Continentals." Predictably, a rapid increase in the supply of Continentals led to inflation. During the Civil War, the south had difficulty borrowing from foreign nations, and the north's blockade greatly reduced the value of import duties as a source of tax revenues. As a consequence, the south financed its struggle largely by issuing Confederate paper money; hyperinflation resulted. This inflation was further fueled when it became apparent that the south would lose; the *velocity* of Confederate money increased along with its

supply. The north financed the war by taxing, borrowing, and issuing greenbacks—fiduciary paper currency that was nonredeemable in gold. These greenbacks circulated along with paper money that *was* redeemable in gold, but greenbacks did not drive out the hard currency, as suggested by Gresham's law. This was because the rate of exchange between greenbacks and redeemable paper dollars was not fixed by law; an increase in the supply of greenbacks relative to redeemable paper currency merely increased the greenback price of redeemable paper money.

3 The U.S. Constitution, ratified in 1779, empowered the federal government to issue a national currency and to redeem the debts of state governments. This allowed capital markets to develop. Alexander Hamilton used his considerable powers to advance the course of a strong central government in general, and a national bank with important powers in particular. Thomas Jefferson was a powerful foe of Hamilton on both these issues.

4 After the ratification of the Constitution, and prior to the Civil War, the federal government chartered two national banks. The First Bank of the United States was chartered in 1791; its charter specified that it was to last only twenty years. It was a private corporation financed partially by the federal government. In practice, it was a nationwide branch-banking system that accepted demand deposits and issued bank notes. It served as the federal government's bank and performed other central banking functions as well; in particular, it was able to control the note-issuing and lending powers of the various state banks and indirectly influence state bank reserves by expanding or contracting its own loans. It also was able to influence state bank reserves *directly* by redeeming or not redeeming state bank notes for specie. The charter of the First Bank of the United States was not renewed; those who feared the power of a central government were able to block rechartering in 1811.

5 In 1816, the federal government granted a twenty-year charter to the Second Bank of the United States; in many respects, it was like the First Bank of the United States. Unfortunately, the Second Bank of the United States pursued a contractionary monetary policy during a period when cotton prices were falling and farmers were in financial straits. The Panic of 1819 ensued and the Second Bank halted the payment of specie to its depositors. Many state banks failed; this caused a contraction of the money supply, deflation, and a financial and economic crisis. The bank was given a second charter but President Andrew Jackson vetoed it; the bank closed in 1836.

6 The demise of the Second Bank of the United States was followed by a period of inflation; this was widely interpreted as having resulted from the proliferation of wildcat banks and a concomitant increase in the paper currency they issued. However, closer inspection of that period indicates that much of the increase in the money supply was brought on by a rapid growth in gold and silver *specie* imported from abroad. Moreover, the ratio of bank-held reserves to credit outstanding did not fall during that period.

7 Between 1836 and the establishment of the national banking system in 1863, two types of banks operated in the United States: private, unincorporated banks and state-chartered banks. This was the period of free banking and a bank need only comply with the provisions of a general bank incorporation law to obtain a charter; an act of state legislation was not required. It was perceived that free banking was inflationary and not in the interests of depositor safety.

8 In 1863 and 1864, federal legislation created a national banking system which was expected to establish a national system that would unify all the banks in the United States. This legislation was passed primarily to facilitate government borrowing during the Civil War. As a consequence, all *national* banks were required to invest a portion of their capital in U.S. government securities. Also, the capital necessary to establish a national bank was substantially greater than that required to open a state bank. National banks were disallowed from making real-estate loans. As a consequence, state banks were not induced to request national charters and to comply with national regulations. Failing to convert state banks into national banks by this legislative route, Congress levied a 10 percent tax on banks and individuals that paid with or used state notes. The number of state banks fell dramatically as a result. However, a rebirth of state banks occurred when state banks began issuing *demand deposits* aggressively—relative to the taxed bank notes.

9 Even though the National Banking Act did not create the hoped-for unified banking system, it did link all banking to a formal system of interbank transfers. Thus, loanable funds were reallocated through banks toward their most productive use.

GLOSSARY

Bank note: A piece of paper that represents a liability on the part of the issuing bank to the holder—and not to a *specific* payee.

Free banking laws: Laws (existing during the 1800s) that facilitated the formation of banks; businesses could obtain banking charters by complying with a general bank incorporation law; an act of government legislation was not necessary to create a bank.

Greenbacks: A fiduciary nonredeemable paper money issued by the United States (the north) during the Civil War.

PROBLEMS

11-1 Assume that when first issued each greenback $1 bill was equal in value to one-half of $1's worth of a paper dollar that was redeemable in gold. Assume further that $20 of redeemable paper money had a market value of one ounce of gold.

a What is the exchange rate of greenbacks per $1 of gold-redeemable paper money?

b How many greenbacks were required to purchase one ounce of gold?

11-2 Continuing problem 11-1, assume now that the supply of greenbacks increases twice as fast as the supply of redeemable paper currency, and that the supply of redeemable paper currency doubles while the quantity of gold remains constant. Other things constant, calculate:

a The gold price of redeemable paper currency

b The exchange rate of greenbacks for redeemable paper currency

c The number of greenbacks required to purchase one ounce of gold

SELECTED REFERENCES

Friedman, Milton, and Anna J. Schwartz, *A Monetary History of the United States, 1867–1960* (Princeton, N.J.: Princeton University Press, 1963).

Lerner, E. M., ''Money, Prices, and Wages in the Confederacy, 1861–1865,'' *Journal of Political Economy,* vol. 63, February 1955.

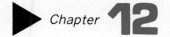
The History and Structure of the Federal Reserve System

The United States was one of the last major countries to establish a central bank. The Bank of Sweden was established in 1656, the Bank of England in 1694, the Bank of France in 1800, the Netherlands Bank in 1814, the Bank of Belgium in 1835, and the Bank of Japan in 1888. It was not until the Federal Reserve Act was signed into law on December 23, 1913, that a central bank—Federal Reserve System—was established in this country.

THE FIRST AND SECOND BANKS OF THE UNITED STATES REVISITED

A short history of the First and Second Banks of the United States was presented in Chapter 11. As pointed out, both those banks performed certain central banking functions.[1] They were both partially owned by the federal government and had branches in major cities. Both were depositories for federal government funds. They were able to regulate the money supply by changing the amount of credit they offered to the nonbanking sector, and thereby change reserves in all banks. Furthermore, the First and Second Banks of the United States could affect the money supply by changing the amount of bank notes in circulation. When those banks wanted to contract the money supply, they would exchange state bank notes for specie. When they did not want to contract the money supply, they would either hold the notes or use them as payment.

From 1836 (when the charter of the Second Bank of the United States expired) until the Civil War, the federal government had little to do with banking. The passage of the Currency Act in 1863 and the National Banking Act in 1864 brought the federal government back into the banking business. Although the hoped-for national banking system did not result, banks were increasingly able to transfer funds from one part of the country to the other.

From about 1900 until 1914, the Treasury engaged in certain activities normally associated with a central bank. For example, the Treasury could increase reserves in the banking system by purchasing previously issued government bonds or by expanding government deposits in various banks. Additionally, the Treasury could use moral suasion to induce national banks to increase the amount of national bank notes in circulation.

THE ALDRICH-VREELAND ACT

The U.S. economy has periodically experienced banking panics. When a banking panic has occurred, many banks have refused to make payment in specie or currency. A severe banking panic occurred in 1907. In New York City a small

---

[1]While there are many possible functions that a central bank can perform, economists generally believe that the most crucial functions—the ones that define a central bank—are: (1) regulating the money supply; and (2) acting as a "lender of last resort," that is, providing liquidity to banks during financially troubled times.

number of relatively large banks were on the verge of failing; that is, they were almost insolvent (their liabilities nearly exceeded their assets). When word got out, there was a run on those banks as well as on other banks. Banks in outlying areas attempted to obtain currency from their correspondent banks in major cities. They could not obtain the currency, however, unless they paid a premium. This reduction in available currency for commercial activities seriously inconvenienced both retailers and employees because at that time currency constituted a higher percentage of the total money supply. In 1907, the ratio of currency to the *sum* of demand deposits and time deposits was 15 percent.[2]

As a direct result of the panic of 1907, Congress passed the Aldrich-Vreeland Act in 1908. This act required that Congress appoint a National Monetary Commission. The Commission was to recommend reforms necessary for the establishment of a central bank. Nine congressional representatives and nine senators held extensive hearings. Some of the more important recommendations from the National Monetary Commission were:

1 The creation of a central institution that would hold *and* create bank reserves through its credit-creating powers

2 The establishment of a coordinated system of check clearing and collection

3 The creation of an efficient fiscal agent to assist the Treasury in its debt management and with its receipts, disbursals, and foreign-exchange transactions

THE FEDERAL RESERVE ACT ESTABLISHES THE U.S. CENTRAL BANK

Even after the panic of 1907 and the recommendations of the 1908 National Monetary Commission, strong opposition to a central bank continued. From the inception of the United States as a nation, antifederalist sentiment often prevailed. When it became apparent that a central bank was to be established, there was a controversy as to who should control it. Naturally, the federal government wanted control. So, too, did the business sector and potential member banks (i.e., national banks). Finally, a compromise was reached among the contending factions. The federal government, the business community, and member banks would each have representation in the control of the U.S. central bank. There was to be a division of control between the central authorities in Washington, D.C., and regional district Federal Reserve banks.

The historic legislation creating the U.S. central banking system was signed into law on December 23, 1913, by President Woodrow Wilson. As orig-

---

[2]The data available before 1915 are not broken down into time deposits and demand deposits; the ratio of currency to demand deposits was, of course, higher than 15 percent.

inally conceived, the Federal Reserve System was to be a type of cooperative among businesses, consumers, bankers, and the federal government. It was hoped that the Fed, as it has come to be called, was now empowered to prevent financial panics—such as the one that occurred in 1907—because it could lend funds (and thereby provide liquidity) to banks during monetary crises. The Fed was *not* conceived as an institution that would control the money supply, interest rates, and credit. Rather, it was to give "elasticity" to money and bank reserves. Money elasticity existed if the money supply could change substantially, over short periods of time, in response to the public's changes in the demand for it. *Thus, the Fed was not viewed as an institution that would actively alter the money supply to achieve economic goals, but rather as an institution that would change the money supply at the public's will.*

"Elasticity" was to be obtained via a discounting, or lending, mechanism. Through this mechanism, member banks were allowed to borrow funds temporarily from the Fed. In the United States no such discounting mechanism existed at that time. The amount of elasticity actually providable by the Fed was limited, however, because the Federal Reserve Act was very specific in terms of assets that could be rediscounted. The term **rediscounting** applies to the process of central banks lending reserves on the basis of collateral that may have already been discounted. For example, if a member bank is in need of reserves and has in its asset portfolio private paper that it has already discounted, the Fed will extend a loan to the member bank (in the form of reserves) at a discount—thus the notion of Fed *re*discounting. The process of discounting and rediscounting is discussed in greater detail in Chapter 15.

The Federal Reserve Act specified what collateral would be eligible for rediscounting.[3] Eligible collateral consisted mostly of high-grade, self-liquidating commercial paper. Over the years, however, the eligibility for discounting has been expanded—as specified in Regulation A of the Federal Reserve Code. Most important, a 1916 amendment authorized advances (loans) to member banks on the bank's own 15-day notes, secured either by eligible paper or by government securities. In 1932, the Fed was authorized to make advances to member banks on *any* asset.

The Federal Reserve Act also defined reserves to member banks in a way different from the way in which they had been defined for national banks up to that time. Only deposits of member banks in Federal Reserve district banks were to be used as reserves in the Federal Reserve System.

For the most part, the Fed was viewed as a passive service agency. It engaged in day-to-day activities that are currently called **chores.** These include check clearing and collection, regulation of member banks, and providing currency. At its inception, the Fed's function did not include engaging

---

[3]The money supply could also change with changes in the amount of gold and by Fed purchases and sales of government securities, banker's acceptances, and bills of exchange.

in countercyclical monetary policy—that is, the Fed was not expecte
expand the money supply in order to counteract a recession and decrease
money supply in order to counteract a period of inflation. (Neither was c
tercyclical monetary policy a function of the First and Second Banks of
United States.) The Fed did not perform open-market operations for a num
of years; nor was the Fed empowered to change the reserve requirem
fixed by Congress.

The Question of Capitalization for the Federal Reserve Banks   Who should pro-
vide the capital for the Federal Reserve banks? Recall that the First and Second Banks of the United States were owned in part (20 percent) by the federal
government, and the remainder was owned by the private sector. Many
argued that a similar system should be used for the new central bank. Others
favored selling stock to the general public. Still others thought stock should
be sold only to member banks. Ultimately, each member bank at that time
(national bank) was required to subscribe to (buy) the stock of its district Federal Reserve bank. A mandatory subscription was to equal 3 percent of each
national bank's net worth (called capital and surplus). Another 3 percent was
due at the Fed's request. In *actuality,* each member bank paid only the 3 percent of its net worth as a subscription to the Federal Reserve System. Because
the member banks own the stock of each Federal Reserve district bank, these
district banks are properly designated as wholly owned by the member banks.
*Ownership does not mean, however, that private banks control the Fed or
even receive its earnings (except for an insignificant amount).*

The Relationship between the Twelve Federal Reserve Banks and the Board
of Governors   The Federal Reserve Act of 1913 left much unsaid about
what should be the relationship between the twelve Federal Reserve district
banks and the Federal Reserve Board (renamed the Board of Governors of the
Federal Reserve System pursuant to the Banking Act of 1933) in Washington,
D.C. To a large extent, the district banks handled their chores independently
of each other. Additionally, they engaged in discounting (almost) independently of each other. At that time, the New York Fed was still the most important district bank because it held the largest percentage of the Federal
Reserve bank's total reserves. This is still the case today.

From its inception until 1922, Fed policy was determined by the officials
of the twelve district banks. In other words, the Federal Reserve Board had
little power. Indeed, the most powerful leadership came from the president of
the Federal Reserve Bank of New York, Benjamin Strong. During this period,
there was a conflict between the Federal Reserve Board and the twelve Federal Reserve banks because the Board wanted to dominate policymaking. It
was not until the Banking Act of 1935 that the Board obtained complete control over policymaking. There was a gradual shift of power within the system
from district banks to the Board of Governors. Today that power is centralized
in the Board of Governors.

HIGHLIGHT **Banker's Biography: Allan Sproul (1896–1978), President, Federal Reserve Bank of New York (1941–1956)**

Allan Sproul was the third chief executive officer of the Federal Reserve Bank of New York and was considered one of history's most talented central bankers. During his presidency of the New York Fed he stimulated a whole generation of Federal Reserve officials. He is known as the person who fostered monetary stability in this country and international economic cooperation. Sproul was a ruggedly built, 200-pound man, slightly under six feet tall. He looked as solid, someone once said, as the Federal Reserve bank itself. Sproul was born in San Francisco, where he spent his youth and early adulthood. He attended the University of California at Berkeley, from which, after having spent a short time as a pilot in World War I, he graduated in 1919 with a degree in agriculture. After having worked as an agricultural advisor for two small banks in southern California, he accepted a position as head of the research department at the Fed in San Francisco. He stayed with the Fed for thirty-six years. By 1924 he had become secretary of the San Francisco Fed. During his tenure as secretary he had to travel to Washington

Allan Sproul. The respected third president of the Federal Reserve Bank of New York. *(Courtesy of United Press International.)*

for monetary policy conferences. Benjamin Strong, then head of the Federal Reserve Bank of New York, was impressed with Sproul. By 1928, Strong was asking Sproul if he would be interested in transferring to the New York Fed.

In 1930, with the stock market in shambles and the economy quickly sliding downhill, Sproul decided to get into the "thick of things"—he moved to New York. After a few years as secretary there, he was assigned to the foreign department and became deeply involved in international monetary affairs, which became a lifelong major interest. By 1936 he was promoted to first vice president, and then his biggest step, to manager of the system open-market account, a position he took in 1938. When Sproul took over as head of the New York Fed in 1941, he also became vice chairperson of the Federal Open Market Committee (FOMC). Then he became involved in the complexities of war finance. He went along with the Fed's pegging of interest rates to help the Treasury finance the war. The result, of course, was not Treasury financing but monetary-creation financing, as the Fed continued to purchase U.S. securities in the open market in order to maintain low interest rates.

As the war came to a head, Sproul devoted his attention to the postwar plans for domestic and international economic reform. He was against most of them. He opposed, for example, the Full Employment Act because he did not want to see excessive government interference in the economy: "Just as there seems to be a limit of tolerance of the woes and evils of alternate boom and depression, there is probably also a limit of tolerance of Government intervention into what we call private enterprise, if it is to remain private enterprise."*

Although he was against the proposed International Monetary Fund, he did endorse the International Bank for Reconstruction and Development (the World Bank) because he viewed the latter as simply a way of easing the severe dislocation problems after the war. Then in 1946 he was offered the presidency of the World Bank, but he decided to remain at the Fed. He felt that the World Bank's operations would be more political than economic.

The Fed and the Treasury were at odds over the continuing desire by the Treasury to peg interest rates after the war ended. The controversy was resolved on Wednesday, January 31, 1951, when President Truman requested that members of the Federal Open Market Committee (of which Sproul was still vice chairperson) meet with him. FOMC members felt that the result of the meeting was that they no longer had to peg interest rates. Nonetheless, White House and Treasury sources indicated that the Fed had agreed to the President's request to support government securities prices. Difficult negotiations ensued. Finally, on March 4, 1951, the famous Treasury–Federal Reserve "accord" was announced. Sproul and the chairperson of the board, Thomas B. McCabe, had met with Truman over and over again. Sproul developed a stomach ulcer during those trying times.

Now that the Fed was no longer constrained by the pegging operation of the war, its Open Market Committee could conduct open-market policy with a free hand. But most of the members were still of the "real bills" school—they wanted to deal only in short-term U.S. securities. Allan Sproul disagreed. He felt that the government securities market would develop on its own, learning how best to adapt to open-market operations in all areas, not just short-term securities. He viewed the bills-only doctrine as philosophically in league with the proponents of pegging: It was just another monetary straitjacket. The struggles over this issue caused Sproul's ulcers to flare up. It would take a week of milk and bland food after every Open Market Committee meeting before he could function normally again.

Finally, sometime during 1955, Sproul started thinking seriously about leaving the Fed.

He could no longer tell whether his role was helpful or harmful to the system's objectives. His resignation was effective June 30, 1956.

Although he retired at the age of sixty, the following twenty years saw him involved in the banking industry as a director of Wells Fargo, then as a

consultant. He gave mc talks about monetary a al policies and internatior financial affairs. He w: banker to the end.

*Hearings on Full Employment Act of 1945, United States Senate Committee on Banking an cy, p. 1219.

THE FORMAL STRUCTURE OF THE FEDERAL RESERVE SYSTEM

Currently the Federal Reserve System consists of:

1 The Board of Governors
2 Twelve Federal Reserve banks
3 Member banks
4 Other depository institutions

Within the system itself, there are two major committees:

1 The Federal Open Market Committee (FOMC)
2 The Federal Advisory Council (FAC)

The Board of Governors   The Board of Governors consists of seven members and each member serves a fourteen-year term. The terms are staggered so that one of the seven members is retired at the end of every two years. The governors are appointed by the President. Neither the comptroller of the currency nor the secretary of the Treasury is eligible to be a governor. No member of the Board can be reappointed if he or she has served a full term. At any one time, no more than one member can be selected from any of the twelve Federal Reserve districts.[4] One of the members is designated by the President as chairperson and another as vice chairperson. Each appointment of the seven members is accomplished with the advice and consent of the Senate. Although each governor can serve a fourteen-year term, the chairperson of the Board of Governors serves a four-year term.

The Board of Governors does not need to go to Congress to obtain its operating revenues. Nor does the General Accounting Office (GAO) perform a full audit of the Board's activities, because the Board's operating funds are

[4]Although, in practice, considerable leeway is given in determining a potential governor's home district.

obtained from the "earnings" of the twelve Federal Reserve banks and therefore are presumably not under the control of Congress or the GAO.

In principle, the Federal Reserve System maintains its independence on three levels: (1) the Board's independent source of revenues; (2) the staggered terms of the governors; and (3) freedom of accountability to the GAO. The Congress decided that in order for the Fed to carry out its functions effectively, it should be independent of both the executive and the legislative branches of government. Whether this independence has been abused and should be terminated is the subject of the Current Controversy at the end of this chapter.

Among its many powers, the Board of Governors can:

1 Approve or disapprove discount rates established by the various district banks

2 Establish within the limits set by Congress reserve requirements for all depository institutions

3 Permit one district reserve bank to lend to another, and *require* such a loan if at least five members of the Board agree

4 Determine the types of loans that the Federal Reserve district banks shall make

5 Supervise the Federal Reserve district banks by examining their accounts

---

HIGHLIGHT The Fed's Game Plan in Case of Nuclear Attack

Nuclear attack by an enemy nation is improbable but not impossible. The federal government has developed a complicated plan for carrying out essential activities if such an attack were to occur. All regional offices of important federal agencies are required to establish emergency operating teams. For example, the Federal Reserve Bank of Kansas City has such a team and its activities would be carried out from the bottom of the Carey Salt Mine near Hutchinson, Kansas. The Kansas City Fed leases two underground rooms from Underground Vaults and Storage Company. The rooms are 650 feet below the ground. The eleven other Federal Reserve banks have similar emergency relocation centers, but not all are so well protected.

In case of an "advanced alert" indicating the possibility of imminent nuclear attack, 150 employees from the Kansas City bank and its three branches are under standing orders to rush to the salt mine. People from every department—check collection, auditing, and so on—would come. This is consistent with the federal government's national plan for "emergency preparedness," which states that following a nuclear attack, provision is to be made for "the clearance of checks, including those drawn on destroyed banks."

To ensure that the bank's employees show up, the plan has made provisions for the dependents of the bank's employees. There is enough food in the shelter to supply 400 people for about a month.

The Federal Reserve System believes strongly in

Underground Vault Company Located in Kansas, this is one of twelve underground storage vaults that will help to maintain monetary stability even after a nuclear war. *(Underground Vault Company)*

reestablishing a monetary system as soon after a nuclear attack as possible. The Fed has stated that "Victory in a nuclear war will belong to the country that recovers first and the financial community will bear a heavy burden of responsibility in effecting a rapid recovery."

Every Federal Reserve district bank has issued "emergency operating letters and bulletins." These directives include a copy of the Treasury Department's Emergency Banking Regulation Number One. This regulation attempts to head off a potential run on banks by banning cash withdrawals "except for the purposes, and not in excess of those amounts, for which cash is customarily used." It goes on to state that banks are to be encouraged to continue selling U.S. savings bonds. However, banks that are holding government securities but are short of funds should borrow against the securities rather than try to sell them "in an unfavorable market."

The Fed is well aware of the inefficiencies of a barter system, and post-attack financial planners want to make sure that barter does not replace the monetary economy. To ensure that there is sufficient currency, should an attack destroy the Bureau of Engraving and Printing, banks are instructed not to remove worn and damaged bills from circulation after a nuclear war. The Fed has a large stockpile of currency at its main relocation site near Culpeper, Virginia. The stockpile goal was originally $5 billion in notes. When that seemed excessive, it was reduced to $700 million.

Federal Reserve District Banks   The original Federal Reserve Act authorized twelve separate Federal Reserve districts, each with its own Federal Reserve bank. Figure 12-1 shows the location of the twelve Federal Reserve banks and the twenty-six branches.

Each Federal Reserve district bank is a federally chartered corporation. It has stockholders, directors, and a president. In each of the twelve geographical districts, the member banks are the stockholders of the Reserve bank.[5] They select six of the nine directors for each district bank. Currently, each member bank purchases stock in the Federal Reserve bank equal to 3 percent of its net worth. As the net worth of the member bank increases, it must purchase additional Federal Reserve bank stock.

The nine directors of each Federal Reserve district bank are categorized as class A in the banking sector, class B in the business sector, and class C in the public sector. Class A directors are elected by the member banks. Of the class A directors, one is supposed to represent a small bank, one a medium-sized bank, and one a large bank. Member banks also elect the class B directors, who are not necessarily bankers. Rather, they typically are prominent individuals from the business or agricultural sectors.

Finally, class C directors are directly appointed by the board of governors of the Federal Reserve System in Washington, D.C. These directors cannot be officers of any bank; they are to be from the public sector. Each director

---

[5]The Federal Reserve district banks realize substantial earnings despite the fact that they are not in the business of profit-making. The commercial bank stockholders in a Fed district are paid a 6-percent "dividend" in the amount of their subscription for Fed membership; any excess earnings of the Fed are turned over to the U.S. Treasury at the end of each fiscal year.

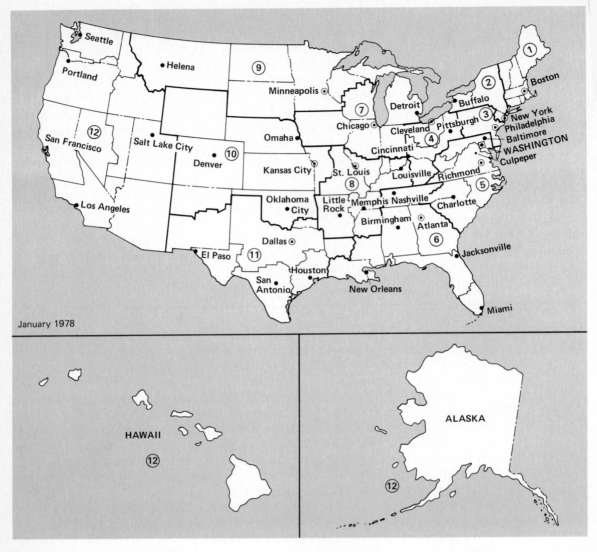

January 1978

LEGEND

—— Boundaries of Federal Reserve Districts

—— Boundaries of Federal Reserve Branch Territories

▣ Board of Governors of the Federal Reserve System

⊙ Federal Reserve Bank Cities

• Federal Reserve Branch Cities

· Federal Reserve Bank Facilities

FIGURE 12-1 Geographical Locations of Federal Reserve District Banks. (*Source:* Board of Governors of the Federal Reserve System, *The Federal Reserve System— Purposes and Functions,* 1974, p. 16.)

serves a three-year term. These terms are staggered such that one director of each of the three categories is elected or appointed each year.

An important power of the Board of Governors is to select the chairperson and the deputy chairperson of the Board of Directors of each district Federal Reserve bank. These two individuals are selected from the three class C directors.

The Federal Reserve district banks are privately owned by the member banks; however, control by member banks is limited. Also the degree to which the district banks' profits are remitted to the member banks is strictly controlled. The Federal Reserve district banks are not chartered to earn profits, but rather to supervise member banks and to engage in the implementation of the monetary policy set forth by the Board of Governors of the Federal Reserve System.

In this age of rapid communications technology, there has been some discussion about the actual need for district banks. Is their continuing existence simply another case of a government agency outliving its usefulness? It is safe to say that the vested interests of those who work for and with each district bank will remain sufficiently strong to prevent the demise of district banks, even if they are no longer needed.

Member Banks   As Chapter 11 pointed out, the United States has a dual banking system consisting of nationally chartered banks and state-chartered banks. All national banks are required to be members of the Federal Reserve System. State banks can become members if they wish. Prior to the passage of the Depository Institutions Deregulation and Monetary Control Act of 1980, membership in the Federal Reserve System offered major benefits. Member banks were allowed to use the Fed's check-clearing facilities as well as its transfer wire service for transferring funds from one bank to another. In order to be a depository of the U.S. Treasury (to have a U.S. Treasury tax and loan account), a bank had to be a member of the Federal Reserve System. There was and perhaps continues to be some prestige attached to membership in the Fed. As of 1981, however, all depository institutions can avail themselves of the Fed's services if they pay the fees charged by the Fed. In other words, any depository institution can use the Fed's check-clearing and collection process if it is willing to pay a service charge. By 1986, virtually all depository institutions will be required to hold non-interest-bearing reserves with Federal Reserve district banks; this will further diminish the distinction between member and nonmember banks.

Nonmember Depository Institutions   The diagram of the Federal Reserve System in Figure 12-2 shows no category labeled nonmember depository institutions. Prior to the passage of the Monetary Control Act of 1980, this category had no place in a diagram of the Fed. But because all depository institutions must (or will by 1986) hold reserves with district Federal Reserve banks, nonmember state commercial banks, savings and loan associations, mutual savings banks, and credit unions must eventually be included in the organizational chart of the Federal Reserve System.

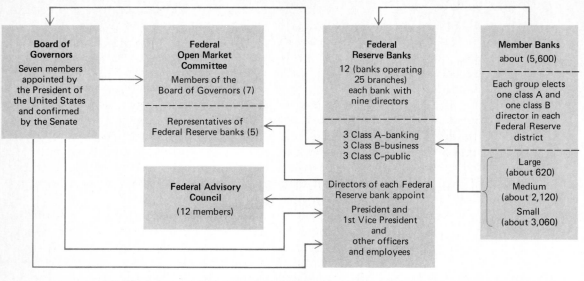

FIGURE 12-2 **The Organizational Structure of the Federal Reserve System.**
(*Source:* Board of Governors of the Federal Reserve System.)

The Federal Open Market Committee The banking acts of 1933 and 1935 created, among other things, a **Federal Open Market Committee (FOMC),** composed of the seven members of the Board of Governors of the Federal Reserve and five Fed district bank presidents. The FOMC was created to formulate and to execute policies with respect to the purchase and sale of government securities (to pursue monetary policies) for the Federal Reserve System as a whole. These transactions in government securities are normally referred to as **open-market operations.** After the FOMC was put into operation, individual district reserve banks were no longer allowed to pursue their own transactions in government securities without FOMC permission. Because the twelve-member FOMC is controlled by the seven Federal Reserve governors, its establishment further strengthened the leadership role of the Board of Governors.

The chairperson of the Board of Governors is also the chairperson of the FOMC. The president of the Federal Reserve Bank of New York is the only permanent member of the FOMC and is always the FOMC vice chairperson.[6]

The four remaining positions on the FOMC are rotated among the presidents of the district banks. In reality, all twelve presidents attend virtually every meeting of the FOMC. They all take part in discussion, but only five of them are voting members. The FOMC meets thirteen times a year in Washington, D.C. A detailed discussion of FOMC operating procedures is provided in Chapter 15.

---

[6]The president of the New York Fed earns about twice as much as the chairperson of the Board of Governors. Paul Volcker took a pay cut of $50,000 in 1979 when he moved from the leadership of the New York Fed to chair the Board of Governors.

At the meeting of the FOMC, the actual quantity and nature of future open-market operations are not rigidly set. A general **FOMC directive** is given to the person in charge of the trading desk at the New York Fed. This person is called the FOMC account manager, or simply the account manager. The account manager confers daily by telephone with some of the FOMC members. The purchase and sale of U.S. government securities by the New York Fed is done through a system of dealers. Note that the Fed deals in the secondary U.S. government securities market. That is, it buys and sells *already existing* U.S. government securities.

The Federal Advisory Council The Federal Reserve Act of 1913 established the Federal Advisory Council (FAC). Its establishment was part of the compromise concerning who should control the Federal Reserve System. The FAC is composed of twelve individuals, each from the twelve Federal Reserve districts. It was originally designed to promote communication between the banking industry and the Fed. Virtually all members of the FAC have been prominent bankers.

The FAC meets quarterly with the Board of Governors of the Federal Reserve System. As its name implies, the FAC's role is strictly advisory; the Board of Governors is under no obligation to follow FAC advice. Indeed, Fed insiders say that the FAC is virtually powerless (and perhaps even useless). It is simply a medium for public relations.

THE REALITIES OF POWER WITHIN THE FEDERAL RESERVE SYSTEM

Clearly, the chairperson of the Board of Governors is a powerful figure in the formation and execution of monetary policy. The chairperson is not only the most important member of the board but also the most important member of the FOMC. And it is the chairperson who speaks for the entire system at all times. A careful reading of the original Federal Reserve Act of 1913 gives the impression that all seven members of the Board of Governors were intended to be equal. But as is often the case, some are more equal than others. On various occasions the chairperson has been an advisor to the President of the United States, and the chairperson informs the Congress of the Fed's actions.

In principle, the United States has a central banking system consisting of twelve banks and twenty-six branches. In actuality, there is one central bank in Washington, D.C., with twelve major field offices and twenty-six minor field offices scattered throughout the country. Geographically, all policy decisions are made in Washington. The various field offices have virtually no impact on Federal Reserve policy. One exception may be the New York field office because its president is the permanent vice chairperson of the FOMC. Additionally, the role that district bank presidents play in the FOMC does give them some limited power.

The Professional Staff   Not often discussed, but definitely important, is the Federal Reserve System's professional staff. The Board of Governors relies heavily on the professional staff to interpret economic events and to predict the impact of potential monetary policy changes. Many senior staff members have been with the Federal Reserve System for decades, and several governors have been appointed from the professional staff, although none has been chosen as chairperson. They are the permanent bureaucracy of the Fed and have been known to have great influence on the thinking of Board members. At every meeting of the FOMC, staff personnel make written and oral presentations about the state of the economy and potential policy issues.

THE FOMC

In principle, the 1935 legislation establishing the FOMC confined its purposes to open-market operations. Over the last decade, however, virtually all policy matters have been brought up for review at the thirteen annual FOMC meetings in Washington. Discussion of reserve-requirement changes, discount-rate changes, and the like, are often added to the agenda. Indeed, originally each individual district bank had the authority to set its own discount rates. That authority was gradually shifted to the Board of Governors. Although the discount rate usually changes only a few times a year, the Board of Directors of each district bank must reestablish or change the existing discount rate every fourteen days. Whenever a change in the discount rate is desired by a district bank Board, the recommended change must be reported to the Board of Governors in Washington, D.C. It is the Washington, D.C. Board that can veto or approve the recommended rate. In reality, there is normally no difference among the discount rates charged by the twelve district banks.

The Account Manager   To some extent, the account manager has discretionary control. Because the FOMC's directives are presented in broad language, it is up to the account manager to translate these directives into daily open-market-operation decisions. However, it is important to note that the account manager consults almost daily with the chairperson of the Board.

The President of the New York Fed   At various times, the president of the New York Fed has become a prominent figure within the Federal Reserve System. On occasion, the president of the New York Fed has even challenged the leadership and wisdom of the chairperson of the Board of Governors. The biography of Allan Sproul in this chapter indicates how important the president of the New York Fed can be.

The Rest of the Players   If the impression has been given that the remaining players within the Fed—directors of the Federal Reserve district banks, the FAC, member banks, and nonmember depository institutions—have little power, that impression is correct. In reality, the power in the system does not extend to any of them.

CURRENT CONTROVERSY

Should the Fed Remain Independent?

The Federal Reserve System was originally set up as an independent agency of the federal government. It is legally an agent of Congress, but it is not controlled by the Congress or the President. The independence of the agency has already been emphasized in this chapter. Indeed, if you look in the *Congressional Directory,* the Federal Reserve is listed along with the American National Red Cross and the Appalachian Regional Commission. The independence of the Fed has been cherished and assumed immutable by the chairpersons of the Board of Governors.*

THE EXECUTIVE BRANCH'S CONTROL OVER THE FED

Originally, the Secretary of the Treasury was the chairperson of the Federal Reserve Board (now called the Board of Governors). At that time, the Fed was simply an arm of the White House. Because the Fed was not engaged in discretionary monetary policy, however, its lack of independence was not important. Until the mid-1930s, both the Secretary of the Treasury and the comptroller of the currency were *ex officio* (that is, by virtue of holding official position) members of the Federal Reserve Board. But in 1935, both offices were dropped from the Board. Congress suspected the Treasury had had too much influence on the Fed. The Treasury nonetheless retained some of its influence, particularly during World War II. The Treasury forced the Fed to agree to peg interest rates to keep the cost of borrowing as low as possible during the war effort. Fed policy from 1942 to 1951 was therefore guided by a commitment to stabilize the price of U.S. securities.

Throughout the years, there has been some evidence that the executive branch has had a more than inconsequential influence over Fed operations. For example, in 1953, when Dwight Eisenhower won the office of President on a platform to curb inflation, the Fed reduced the rate of growth of the money supply. When President Lyndon Johnson wanted expansionary monetary policies to finance the Vietnam war, along with the expansion of his Great Society programs, the Fed apparently cooperated (although there was a conflict in 1966 when the Fed severely cut back on the rate of growth of the money supply and caused a credit crunch). By the end of LBJ's tenure, the rate of growth in the money supply was 8 percent annually. Evidence indicates that during the Nixon years, the Fed changed the money-supply growth rate to correspond with the administration's shifts in domestic policy; the money supply increased when the Nixon administration pursued expansionary policies, and it grew less rapidly when the administration pursued contractionary policies. Dr. Robert Weintraub, a senior congressional economist, has been quoted as saying about

Arthur Burns, a former chairperson of the Board of Governors, that "there were three Arthur Burnses, one for Nixon, one for Ford, and one for Carter. The Fed has always done pretty much what the administration wants."†

COMPLAINTS ABOUT THE FED'S ACTIONS

Critics of the Federal Reserve System have blamed many undesirable events in U.S. economic history on the Fed; these events include:

1 The Great Depression
2 The recession of 1960
3 The credit crunch of 1966
4 Virtually every other recession and monetary problem

Perhaps because of these and other complaints, in the 1970s Congress passed resolutions directing that the Fed's activities be monitored by Congress. This had never before occurred in the history of the Federal Reserve System. In 1975, Congress passed a resolution introduced by Senator William Proxmire directing the Fed to take appropriate action in the last half of the year to increase the money supply at a rate substantially higher than in the recent past. Additionally, this joint congressional resolution required that the Fed report to Congress every six months to indicate its goals in terms of the growth rate in the money supply. Prior to this resolution, the desires of the FOMC were first known ninety days after the meetings took place; this was later changed to forty-five days and still later to thirty days. Congress has also proposed that the Fed be subjected to a government accounting audit on a regular basis; ostensibly to monitor the Fed's internal business practices, this proposal likely has only nuisance value. This resolution has not yet been passed by Congress.

Critics of the Fed believe that the congressional resolution requiring it to report to Congress every six months may turn out to be one of the most important congressional actions affecting the Fed in particular and the banking system in general. The Fed chairperson now must report to both houses of Congress twice a year. The chairperson of the Fed outlines the explicit goals of the Fed in terms of the rate of growth of the money supply and how well it has succeeded in reaching its money supply growth goals in the past. Some observers believe that such explicit reporting of goals and accomplishments will prevent the Fed from greatly overshooting or undershooting some "reasonable" long-run growth rate in the money supply.

MERGING THE FED WITH THE TREASURY

As an alternative to increased congressional control, some critics of the Fed have argued that the Fed should be merged directly with the Treasury. Proponents of such a view argue that it is a viable alternative to complete congressional control. After all, there are many divergent views among the 535 members of Congress. Turning over the Fed to the Treasury would not, however, be a simple matter. In the Federal Reserve Act of 1913 Congress delegated its power "to coin money, regulate the value thereof" from Article I, Section 8 of the Constitution, to the Fed. It would now have to repeal that section of the 1913 act, and it seems unlikely that Congress is willing to do so.

Proponents of a merger between the Fed and the Treasury believe that such a move would improve coordination of the monetary and fiscal policies of the government. Additionally, there would be only *one* place to put the blame for monetary policy that is too restrictive or too expansionary. Today, it is possible for the President to blame the Fed *and* Congress, for the Congress to blame the Fed, and for the Fed to deny everything.

*Except from 1942 to 1951 when the Fed agreed to keep the yield on government bonds pegged.

†*Time*, July 5, 1982, p. 43.

CHAPTER SUMMARY

1   The First and Second Banks of the United States performed several central banking functions, although neither was a formal central bank.

2   The Aldrich-Vreeland Act of 1908 was passed as a direct result of a banking crisis—the panic of 1907. The act required that Congress appoint a National Monetary Commission to study reforms necessary for the establishment of a central bank.

3   On December 23, 1913, the Federal Reserve Act was passed; it created a central bank called the Federal Reserve System. Its main function was to provide liquidity to the banking system (by rediscounting) in order to prevent future banking panics. The act specified the collateral that was eligible for rediscounting and that only funds of member banks deposited in Federal Reserve district banks would be counted as reserves. The chores of the Federal Reserve include check clearing and collection, supervising the regulation of member banks, and providing currency. It was not envisioned at that time that the Fed would engage in monetary policy to stabilize the economy. Member banks are the sole owners of the Fed; this fact, however, does not mean that member banks control the Fed or receive all its earnings. Twelve Federal Reserve district banks were also created; initially each was like an independent central bank. A policy struggle between the Federal Reserve Board of Governors and the twelve Federal Reserve banks ensued and the Board eventually won; the Board now has near complete control over the Fed's actions.

4   The formal structure of the Federal Reserve System consists of a Board of Governors, twelve Federal Reserve banks, member banks, and other depository institutions. Two major committees include the Federal Open Market Committee (FOMC) and the Federal Advisory Council (FAC). The FAC is largely a public relations agency for the Fed.

5   The Board of Governors consists of seven members; each governor is appointed to a fourteen-year term by the President of the United States with the approval of the

Senate. The board is somewhat politically independent because it does not rely on Congress to obtain its funds and because it is not accountable to the General Accounting Office. Another major source of the Board's independence stems from the fact that each member is appointed for a fourteen-year term. Currently, the Board has the power to approve or disapprove discount rates established by the district banks, establish reserve requirements for depository institutions, permit or require interdistrict reserve lending, determine the types of loans that the district banks can make, and supervise the district banks.

6   Each of the twelve Federal Reserve district banks is a federally chartered corporation, with stockholders, a director, and a president. Each director serves a three-year term. The district banks are privately *owned* by member banks, but member-bank *control* is very limited. District banks are chartered to supervise member banks, and not to earn profits.

7   The FOMC is the most important Fed committee; it was created in the 1933 to 1935 period to formulate and engage in open-market operations. After the FOMC was created, individual district banks were no longer permitted to engage in independent open-market operations. The FOMC issues general directives to an account manager who carries out FOMC policy through a system of government securities dealers. Open-market operations are carried out in a secondary market.

8   In recent years, the Fed has come under much criticism. It has been blamed for the Great Depression and subsequent recessions and credit crunches. The Fed's independence has been challenged; some think that it is not really independent of politics, others think it is too independent. Since 1975 the Fed has been required to report to Congress every six months to indicate its goals; it has recently been proposed that the Fed be audited on a regular basis. Some critics of the Fed have suggested that the Fed be merged with the Treasury; it is alleged that a merger would facilitate stabilization policies.

GLOSSARY

Chores: Day-to-day Fed activities such as check clearing and collection, supervision of the regulation of member banks, and providing currency.

Federal Open Market Committee (FOMC): A major policy-making unit of the Fed that directs open-market operations.

FOMC directive: A written or verbal instruction from the FOMC to the system's open-market account managers regarding the conduct of open-market operations.

Open-market operations: The purchase or sale of U.S. Treasury securities or federal-government-agency securities by the Fed; a method of monetary control.

Rediscounting: The process of discounting by central banks to member banks that borrow reserves on the basis of collateral that has already been discounted once.

PROBLEMS

12-1   Franklin National Bank purchases a one-year, $100,000 Treasury security for $90,000. What is the discount rate on this security?

12-2 Continuing problem 12-1, assume that Franklin National then borrows $100,000 in reserves from the Fed. The Fed credits Franklin National's account with $95,000. What is the rediscount rate that the Fed charged Franklin National? (Assume a one-year borrowing term for simplicity.)

SELECTED REFERENCES

Board of Governors of the Federal Reserve, *The Federal Reserve System—Purposes and Functions* (Washington, D.C., 1974).

Eastburn, David P., *The Federal Reserve on Record: Readings on Current Issues from Statements by Federal Reserve Officials* (Federal Reserve Bank of Philadelphia, 1965).

Eccles, Marriner, *Beckoning Frontiers (New York: Knopf, 1951).*

Friedman, Milton, and Anna J. Schwartz: *A Monetary History of the United States, 1867–1960* (Princeton, N.J.: Princeton University Press, 1963).

Selected Papers of Allan Sproul (Federal Reserve Bank of New York, 1980).

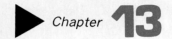

The Fed's Balance Sheet

The Federal Reserve System is the central bank in the United States, and its primary function is monetary policy. To be sure, the twelve separate Federal Reserve banks perform other services (their "chores"), but the ultimate job of the Fed is monetary management. The Fed is responsible for controlling (1) the money supply, and (2) the supply of funds for loans (the supply of credit) to businesses, households, and governments.

The Fed manages the money supply by means of:

1   Open-market operations in which the Fed buys from or sells to depository institutions, or the public, short-term government securities.

2   Changing the discount rate, which is the interest rate that the Fed charges depository institutions that borrow from it.

3   Varying (within limits specified by Congress) the reserve requirement ratio, which is the fraction of total deposits that must be held by depository institutions to satisfy reserve requirements with their Federal Reserve district banks. Depository institutions can use only vault cash or their deposits at the Federal Reserve to meet legal reserve requirements.

While this third means is potentially powerful, the Fed has chosen to regulate the money supply chiefly by open-market operations and, to a lesser degree, by encouraging or discouraging borrowing from the Fed by depository institutions.

In short, the Fed manages the money stock mostly by open-market operations and somewhat by changing the discount rate. Each of these activities directly affects depository institution reserves.

This chapter explains how these and other Fed (and U.S. Treasury) activities change depository institution reserves. It also shows that actions taken by Federal Reserve banks to increase or decrease their own assets can alter depository institution reserves. To begin, we must first examine the consolidated balance sheet of the twelve Federal Reserve banks. In the process of doing so we will:

1   Review a few general accounting terms and principles

2   Examine briefly the main entries on the asset side of the Fed's balance sheet

3   Look briefly at the main entries on the liabilities and capital accounts side of the Fed's balance sheet

4   Rearrange the Fed's balance sheet and incorporate Treasury activities to indicate sources and competing uses of depository institution reserves

5   Analyze the effects of specific Fed or Treasury activities on depository institution reserves

SOME ACCOUNTING PRINCIPLES

An asset is defined as anything of value that is *owned* by the person, corporation, or institution in question. A liability is debt *owed* by that same person, corporation, or institution. Net worth, otherwise known as owner's equity, stockholder's equity, or capital and surplus, is whatever is left over after the value of debts is subtracted from the value of assets. Thus:

$$\text{Net worth} = \text{assets} - \text{liabilities} \qquad \textbf{(13-1)}$$

Or, rearranging:

$$\text{Assets} = \text{liabilities} + \text{net worth} \qquad \textbf{(13-2)}$$

A balance sheet is merely an arithmetic statement representing the relationship among the assets. liabilities, and net worth of an economic entity at a *specific point in time.* It is the balance sheet that specifies that assets are equal to liabilities plus net worth.

THE FED'S BALANCE SHEET

Consider Table 13-1, which shows a consolidated balance sheet of the Federal Reserve on April 28, 1982. This table indicates that the assets ($180.629 billion) are equal to the liabilities ($177.721 billion) plus the capital accounts ($2.908 billion).

The Fed's Assets   As Table 13-1 indicates, the Fed's largest assets are:

1   U.S. government securities
2   Loans to depository institutions
3   Acceptances
4   Gold certificates
5   Special drawing rights (SDRs)
6   Assets denominated in foreign currencies
7   Cash items in the process of collection

These assets will be grouped and discussed individually in the following sections; the other assets will be ignored because they are relatively small and their exclusion will not change the conclusions of this chapter.

U.S. Government Securities and Federal Agency Obligations   U.S. government securities are by far the largest Fed asset; they total over $130 billion, as line 14 in Table 13-1 indicates. As the table shows in lines 9 through

TABLE 13-1 A Consolidated Balance Sheet for the Federal Reserve Banks on April 28, 1982

Federal Reserve Banks: Condition and Federal Reserve note statements (millions of dollars)

Account	Apr. 28 1982 Condition Statements
Assets	
1 Gold certificate account	11,150
2 Special drawing rights certificate account	3,818
3 Coin	403
Loans:	
4 To depository institutions	6,180
5 Other	0
Acceptances:	
6 Held under repurchase agreements	192
Federal agency obligations:	
7 Bought outright	9,008
8 Held under repurchase agreements	348
U.S. government securities bought outright:	
9 Bills	49,687
10 Notes	60,389
11 Bonds*	18,090
12 Total*	128,166
13 Held under repurchase agreements	2,205
14 Total U.S. government securities	130,371
15 **Total loans and securities**	**149,099**
16 Cash items in process of collection	9,427
17 Bank premises	515
Other assets:	
18 Denominated in foreign currencies†	4,981
19 All other‡	4,236
20 **Total assets**	**180,629**
Liabilities	
21 Federal Reserve notes	130,500
Deposits:	
22 Depository institutions	26,673
23 U.S. Treasury—general account	10,869
24 Foreign—official accounts	264
25 Other	484
26 **Total deposits**	**38,290**
27 Deferred availability cash items	6,557
28 Other liabilities and accrued dividends§	2,374
29 **Total liabilities**	**177,721**
Capital Accounts	
30 Capital paid in	1,308
31 Surplus	1,278
32 Other capital accounts	322
33 **Total liabilities and capital accounts**	**180,629**
34 Memo: Marketable U.S. government securities held in custody for foreign and international account	90,775

TABLE 13-1 A Consolidated Balance Sheet for the Federal Reserve Banks on April 28, 1982 (*Continued*)

		Note Statements
35	Federal Reserve notes outstanding (issued to bank)	152,898
36	Less: Held by bank¶	22,398
37	Federal Reserve notes, net	130,500
	Collateral for Federal Reserve notes:	
38	Gold certificate account	11,150
39	Special drawing rights certificate account	3,818
40	Other eligible assets	0
41	U.S. government and agency securities	115,532
42	**Total collateral**	**130,500**

*Includes securities loaned—fully guaranteed by U.S. government securities pledged with Federal Reserve banks—and *excludes* (if any) securities sold and scheduled to be bought back under matched sale-purchase transactions.
†Includes U.S. government securities held under repurchase agreement against receipt of foreign currencies and foreign currencies warehoused for the U.S. Treasury. Assets shown in this line are revalued monthly at market exchange rates.
‡Includes special investment account at Chicago of Treasury bills maturing within 90 days.
§Includes exchange-translation account reflecting the monthly revaluation at market exchange rates of foreign-exchange commitments.
¶Beginning September 1980, Federal Reserve notes held by the Reserve bank are exempt from the collateral requirement.
Source: Adapted from *Federal Reserve Bulletin,* May 1982, p. A11.

13, U.S. government securities consist of bills, notes, and bonds owned outright by the Fed and some held under repurchase agreements. They amount to about 72 percent of the Fed's total assets.

The Fed also owns the obligations of various U.S. government agencies, such as the Federal National Mortgage Association, Farm Credit System, Export-Import Bank, Federal Home Loan Banks, and the United States Postal Service. The table indicates on lines 7 and 8 that the Fed held almost $9.5 billion of these obligations on April 20, 1982. United States government securities *and* federal agency obligations owned by the Fed can be placed under the rubric of "U.S. government obligations." This classification is important not only because of the magnitude of these entries, but because the purchases and sales of these securities (open-market operations) are also the Fed's most important tool for changing depository institution reserves.

Loans to Depository Institutions Loans to depository institutions, represented on line 4 in Table 13-1, also are a policy tool of the Fed. This category can alternatively be thought of as depository institution borrowings; the rate that the Fed charges depository institutions for borrowing is the discount rate.

This asset category is the means by which the Fed can influence the cost and therefore the quantity of depository institution reserves.

Acceptances   As pointed out in Chapter 5, an acceptance (lines 6, 7, and 8 in Table 13-1) is a bill of exchange (used primarily in international trade). Acceptances are marked "accepted" by the depository institution on which they are drawn. When the depository institution writes *accepted* on the draft, it commits itself to honoring that draft, thereby allowing the customer to substitute the bank's credit for his or her own credit. The Fed routinely purchases banker's acceptances at prevailing interest rates in order to stimulate their use in international trade.

The Fed is able to influence depository institution reserves by purchasing or selling in this market for banker's acceptances. The Fed's activities in this market are similar to its open-market operations in the U.S. government securities market.

International Reserve Assets   Certain **international reserve assets** are included in the Fed's asset portfolio. These are gold certificates (line 1 in Table 13-1); special drawing rights (line 2); and assets denominated in foreign currencies (line 18).

Gold certificates: These certificates are Fed claims against the monetary gold which is held by the Treasury. The Treasury monetizes the gold stock when it sells gold certificates for each dollar's worth of gold it holds; gold is currently valued at the "official" price of $42.22 per ounce. Because the market price of gold is much higher, $11.15 billion (line 1 in the table) vastly understates this Fed asset. These **gold certificates** are listed as an asset of the Fed, but the gold itself is held by the U.S. Treasury (for the most part at Fort Knox, Kentucky).

Before the Federal Reserve System was established in 1913, the majority of gold certificates were owned by commercial banks. They were used by commercial banks as part of their legal reserves. After 1914, the majority of gold certificates were acquired by the Federal Reserve. Between 1914 and 1971, the U.S. Treasury bought and sold gold bullion; therefore, the amount of gold certificates varied with purchases and sales of gold by the U.S. Treasury.

Special drawing rights (SDRs): SDRs are Fed claims against the special drawing rights created by the **International Monetary Fund (IMF)** and held by the Treasury. SDRs have existed since January 1970, when the IMF issued them to member countries. They are a type of international money and may be used by the Treasury to obtain foreign currency. When the Treasury obtains an SDR from the IMF or from another country, it issues an SDR certificate to the Federal Reserve bank in exchange for a special Treasury deposit. SDRs are owned only by the Fed; the total issued by the Treasury is limited to the total amount of SDRs that the Treasury owns. In the Fed's balance sheet, the SDR certificate account is simply a record of the certificates owned by the Fed. This account is handled the same way as the gold certificate account. When the Fed and the Treasury transact on the SDR certificate account, the changes occur in book entries rather than in actual paper certificates.

Foreign currency assets: Assets denominated in foreign currencies are mostly **foreign exchange** or foreign currency holdings, but U.S. government securities held under repurchase agreements which were purchased in foreign currencies are also included. Typically, these foreign currencies are held in the form of bank balances in foreign banks. They are normally held for the purpose of influencing **foreign exchange rates,** particularly with respect to the dollar. The IMF, foreign exchange, and foreign exchange rates are discussed in detail in Chapter 29.

Cash Items in Process of Collection   The Fed provides a check-collecting and clearing service for depository institutions; every day billions of dollars worth of checks flow to the Fed for collection. The Fed "clears" these checks by crediting the reserve accounts of the depository institutions that present the checks for collection and by debiting the accounts of the depository institutions on which the checks are drawn. Cash items in the process of collection (CIIPC) indicate the value of those checks that are in the Fed's possession, but that have not yet been "collected" by debiting the value from the proper depository institution's reserve account.

Suppose that a $1,000 check is written on bank A and deposited in bank B, which sends it to the Fed for collecting and clearing. The Fed doesn't credit bank B's reserve account and debit bank A's reserve account *immediately.* Instead, it treats the $1,000 check as its own asset, in the CIIPC category; at the same time the Fed realizes that it has an obligation to bank B because it eventually must credit bank B's reserve account $1,000. This $1,000 obligation is a Fed liability and is referred to as a deferred availability cash item (DACI), which appears in the next section, under Fed liabilities.

The Fed's Liabilities and Capital Accounts   In Table 13-1, the Fed's liabilities and its capital accounts are listed. The capital accounts are strictly equivalent to net worth in Equation (13-1). Sometimes the capital accounts are called capital and surplus accounts.

The Fed's chief liabilities consist of:

1   Federal Reserve notes
2   Deposits of depository institutions, the U.S. Treasury, and foreign governments
3   Deferred availability cash items

There are certain other liabilities and accrued dividends liabilities; we shall discuss each.

Federal Reserve Notes   Federal Reserve notes are a very large part of the paper currency used in the United States and are what most people think of as "money." Look at a dollar bill. The words "Federal Reserve Note" are printed across the top. Federal Reserve notes, or paper currency, are debts of (claims against) the Federal Reserve banks. Anyone unhappy with the state of the economy may take his or her Federal Reserve notes to a local bank to do something about it. The employees there will cheerfully replace such notes with *other* Federal Reserve notes. But more on this in the next Highlight.

Deposits at the Fed Depository institutions are forced to meet their reserve requirements either by holding vault cash or by maintaining deposits at the Federal Reserve district bank. These deposits (line 22 of Table 13-1) are assets of the depository institutions but liabilities of the Fed.

The U.S. Treasury also maintains deposits at the Fed (line 23), for the Fed is the government's principal bank. These Treasury assets are the Fed's liabilities. Similarly, foreign central banks and the International Monetary Fund hold assets in the form of deposits at the Fed (line 24); these assets are also the Fed's liabilities.

It should be stressed that the Fed is very selective in issuing deposit claims against itself; it accepts deposits only from depository institutions, the U.S. government, foreign central banks, and the IMF. This means that individuals, nondepository businesses, and state and local governments are not allowed to maintain deposits with the Fed.

HIGHLIGHT   The "Backing" of Paper Money

Many students believe that the U.S. dollar is "backed" by gold. This is not true; any attempt to demand replacement of a Federal Reserve note with gold will be unsuccessful. After taking an economics course or two, you learn that the U.S. dollar is not backed by anything other than people's faith in the Fed's ability to maintain the dollar's command over goods and services.

Still, a reading of Table 13-1 shows that collateral for Federal Reserve notes does exist. Each Federal Reserve bank must maintain collateral to match the volume of its outstanding Federal Reserve notes. Actually, each Federal Reserve bank issues its own notes. This was discussed in Chapter 2, where the code of each of the twelve Federal Reserve banks was given. This code is identified above the serial number on the left-hand side of each Federal Reserve note. The name of the issuing Federal Reserve bank is written within the small circle surrounding the code letter of the issuing bank.

Assets that qualify as collateral for Federal Reserve notes include gold certificates, SDRs, collateral received by the Fed in making loans to depository institutions, and U.S. government securities. Because the Fed can increase its holdings of government securities almost at will, it is apparent that the Fed has no problem matching collateral to the value of Federal Reserve notes. The ability of the Fed to purchase U.S. government securities through open-market operations presumably allows the Fed to increase Federal Reserve notes without limit (although this is highly unlikely).

Deferred Availability Cash Items (DACI)   This entry was mentioned in an earlier discussion of the Fed asset, CIIPC. DACI represents the value of checks that the Fed has not yet "paid." Because the value of each check will become a Fed liability when it is credited to the appropriate bank's reserve account, DACI represent a *future* obligation of the Fed. Therefore, they are properly listed as a Fed liability in the Fed's balance sheet in Table 13-1 (line 27).

Other Liabilities and Accrued Dividends   This liability category includes an exchange-transaction account that reflects the monthly revaluation in dollars and at market exchange rates of the foreign exchange holdings of the Fed. These are basically liabilities of the Fed with respect to foreign central banks. This item also includes other operating obligations that the Federal Reserve banks have incurred but have not yet paid.

HIGHLIGHT   Who Owns the Fed?

Each Federal Reserve district bank is owned by the member banks in that district; the member banks subscribe an amount equal to 3 percent of the member's paid-in capital plus surplus. Another 3 percent is subject to "call" by the district Federal Reserve bank; the Federal Reserve bank can request the money at any time. Unlike its member banks, the Fed is a nonprofit organization. In principle, it is a nongovernmental institution.

The member-bank owners of the Federal Reserve banks receive a 6 percent annual dividend on their stock in their district bank. Federal Reserve banks typically earn more than necessary to pay the 6 percent to member banks, because Fed earnings (on government securities, and lending and check-clearing charges)

generate a surplus above the dividends granted to member-bank owners. This surplus is turned over to the U.S. Treasury and, on occasion, is quite substantial. For example, in 1980, the surplus amounted to $57 million.

Technically, the Fed is owned by the member banks. Yet, ownership of an asset ultimately rests with those who control it. A person who is legally a minor, for example, may have clear title to a car, but if that minor's parents will not let him or her drive it, sell it, or rent it to others, does the minor really "own" it? So it is with the Fed. Through time, the control of the Fed has moved from the district banks to the Board of Governors in Washington, D.C. While it is generally believed that the Fed

is independent of the government, this independence is a bit of a sham. After all, the Federal Reserve Act was passed by Congress and Congress is free to amend it—as it has done several times. Congress has not been shy about letting the Board of Governors know that it has amendment powers. As pointed out in Chapter 10, Congress now requires that the Fed report annually its actions and policies for the coming year. While the Fed still has room to make significant decisions, it is on notice that its actions are under close congressional scrutiny. To the extent that the Congress and the President are able to influence and control the Fed's policies, ownership in any meaningful sense does not lie with its figurehead owners.

Capital Accounts As Table 13-1 indicates, the capital accounts include paid-in capital, surplus, and other capital accounts. Capital accounts represent ownership claims on the Fed. In principle, these ownership claims are from the member banks. This topic will be discussed further in the next Highlight.

ADDITIONAL REMARKS ABOUT THE FED BALANCE SHEET

A balance sheet must balance: Assets must equal liabilities plus net worth (capital accounts). At any given moment, therefore, an economic entity such as the Fed must have a total of debt claims (liabilities) plus ownership claims (capital accounts) that equal the value of assets. It follows that for the Fed (or any economic agent):

1 Net increases in assets must be paid for by creating and issuing a net increase in debt and/or ownership claims.

2 Conversely, net decreases in asset holdings must be accomplished by the destruction and withdrawal of an equal amount of outstanding debt and/ or ownership claims.

Consider Table 13-1 again and note that total Fed assets on April 28, 1982, were over $180 billion (line 20) and that ownership claims were therefore less than $3 billion (lines 30–32). Ownership claims, therefore, represented only about 1.67 percent of total assets. It follows that the Fed paid for its assets mostly by issuing debt against itself.[1] Similarly, when the Fed decreases these assets, it will retire debt claims against itself.

DISTINGUISHING BETWEEN FED TRANSACTIONS WITH DEPOSITORY INSTITUTIONS AND WITH THE PUBLIC

It is important to distinguish between transactions that the Fed undertakes with depository institutions and those that it undertakes with the public. When the Fed deals with depository institutions, it alters the depository institution's reserve account by the value of the transaction. For example, if the Fed purchases $1 million in Treasury bills from depository institution Z, it pays Z by crediting Z's reserve account with $1 million. A sale of $1 million of Treasury bills to depository institution N will lead to a $1 million deduction from N's reserve account.

---

[1] An individual who purchases a house does the same thing. The value of the liabilities plus the equity in the house (the down payment) is equal to the price of the house.

Transactions undertaken by the Fed with the public are more complicated. Suppose Mrs. Ritter buys a $1 million T-bill from the Fed. She pays for it by writing a check on depository institution Z. The Fed will deduct the amount of the check from Z's reserve account and send the check back to Z. Z will then deduct $1 million from Mrs. Ritter's checking account. This process is shown in panel (a) of Figure 13-1.

Complementary reasoning indicates that if Mr. Price sells the Fed a T-bill, the Fed will pay with a check drawn on a Federal Reserve bank. Mr. Price will then deposit this check at his local depository institution P. In turn, P will credit Mr. Price's account (this will be a liability for P) and send the check to

FIGURE 13-1 Fed Transactions with the Public. (a) Purchase of T-bills from the Fed: Mrs. Ritter buys $1 million ($1M) of T-bills from the Fed and pays for them by a check drawn on depository institution Z. (b) Sale of T-bills to the Fed: Mr. Price sells $1 million ($1M) of T-bills to the Fed and deposits the proceeds in depository institution P.

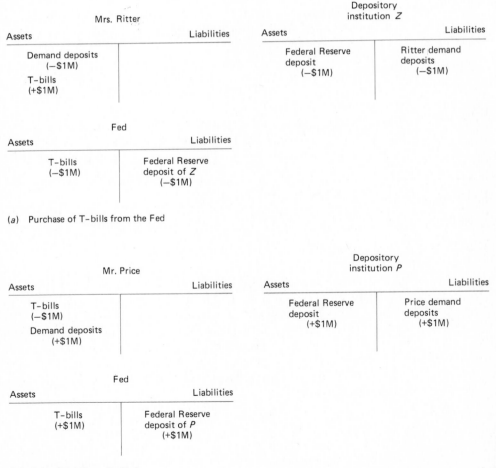

(a) Purchase of T-bills from the Fed

(b) Sale of T-bills to the Fed

the Fed. The Fed will then add the amount of the check to P's reserve account and thereby increase P's assets and the Fed's liabilities by an equal amount. This is shown in panel (b) of Figure 13-1.

Note that in each of the transactions, the Fed has affected depository institution reserves. When the Fed buys a security from a depository institution or the public, depository institution reserves will rise. When the Fed sells a security to a depository institution or to the public, depository institution reserves will fall. Fed transactions with the public have the additional effect of *directly* changing the money supply; Fed transactions with depository institutions only indirectly alter the money supply, when depository institutions react to the altered status of their reserve accounts with the Fed.

Previous chapters have emphasized the importance of bank reserves (defined as the value of bank deposits in a reserve account with the Fed plus bank vault cash) and of changes in bank reserves. An individual bank cannot increase its lending (given zero excess reserves) unless it somehow receives an increase in reserves; it must contract lending if its reserves are below the required level. Similarly, the *banking system* cannot expand unless overall excess reserves are positive; the banking system will be forced to contract if overall excess reserves are negative. Monetary policy itself is conducted by the process of the Fed's altering overall bank reserves. Because changes in reserves are so important, we devote the next section to an analysis of the ways in which reserves in the banking system can be changed.

HOW BANK RESERVES ARE CHANGED

In order to understand better the way in which the Fed's balance sheet is affected by its transactions, consider the Fed's asset and liability structure using the following notations:

a = U.S. government securities and federal agency obligations

b = Loans to depository institutions

c = Acceptances

d = Gold certificates

e = SDRs

f = Foreign currency assets

g = Cash items in process of collection

h = Other Fed assets

i = Federal Reserve notes, excluding bank vault cash (i.e., circulating Federal Reserve notes)

j = Depository institution deposits with the Fed plus Federal Reserve notes held as bank vault cash (i.e., bank reserves)

k = U.S. Treasury deposits with the Fed

l = Foreign central bank and IMF deposits with the Fed

m = Deferred availability cash items

n = Other liabilities and accrued dividends

o = Capital account

$t = g - m$, where t equals "float" (discussed later); t is a Fed asset

x = Federal Reserve holdings of Treasury-issued cash

Remembering the basic accounting identity that:

Assets = liabilities + capital account

Then:

$$a + b + c + d + e + f + t + h + x = i + j + k + l + n + o \quad \textbf{(13-3)}$$

Solving for j, bank reserves, yields

$$j = (a + b + c + d + e + f + t + h + x) - (i + k + l + n + o) \quad \textbf{(13-4)}$$

Equation (13-4) is very instructive; it indicates that any increase in the Fed's *assets* (a through x) will increase bank reserves and potentially cause the money supply to rise—unless offset by an equal increase in Fed liabilities or capital account. Conversely, any decrease in the Fed's assets will decrease bank reserves and cause the money supply to contract—again, unless the decrease is offset by an equal decrease in the rest of the Fed's balance sheet. Every Fed asset is a potential source of depository institution reserves because the Fed can, in one way or another, pay for these assets by crediting a depository institution's reserve account with the purchase price. When the Fed sells one of these assets, it can eventually "charge" a depository institution for the asset by reducing that institution's reserve account by the sale price.

Equation (13-4) also indicates that a change in Fed *liabilities* (i through n) will also change bank reserves, unless offset by an equal change in Fed assets. Other things constant, an increase in circulating Federal Reserve notes—due to an increase in the public's desire for currency—will cause bank reserves to fall, as Chapter 8 indicated.

Other United States Treasury Activities We have already indicated that U.S. Treasury activities can affect bank reserves; consider letters d, x and k in Equation (13-4). A detailed account of U.S. Treasury sales and purchases of gold is made in the next section.

Other Treasury activities can also affect bank reserves. The Treasury, like the Fed, also issues currency, and the impact on bank reserves of changes in Treasury currency outstanding is the same as the effects of changes in Federal Reserve notes. As a consequence we treat Treasury currency outstanding as a *source* of bank reserves, and we use the letter y to represent Treasury-issued currency held in cash by depository institutions, and p to represent "Treasury currency outstanding where $p = x + y + q$". It includes all Treasury-issued coin and paper currency regardless of who holds it—the public, commercial banks, the Fed, or the Treasury itself. In order to take account of the fact that some U.S. Treasury currency also circulates, we introduce the letter q, which represents Treasury currency in circulation. Then add p to the left-hand side of (13-3) and $x + y + q$ to the right-hand side; then subtract x from both sides. This gives

$$a + b + c + d + e + f + t + h + p$$
$$= i + j + k + l + n + o + y + q \qquad \textbf{(13-5)}$$

Letting Treasury-issued circulating currency (q) plus circulating Federal Reserve notes (i) represent "currency in circulation" (r) yields the equation:

$$r = q + i \qquad \textbf{(13-6)}$$

Then:

$$a + b + c + d + e + f + t + h + p = r + j + l + n + o + y \qquad \textbf{(13-7)}$$

Note that currency in circulation is a *use* of reserves; it is one form in which bank reserves can be used or absorbed by the economy. An increase in either q or i, other things constant, leads to an increase in r and a *decrease* in bank reserves; when the public increases its holdings of currency of either type, bank reserves fall.

THE BANK RESERVE EQUATION

We can now rewrite Equation (13-4), taking into account these additional Treasury activities, in a way that clearly indicates the sources and uses of bank reserves. Now $i + R$ denotes the reserves of depository institutions the bank reserve equation can be rewritten as:

$$R = j + y \qquad \textbf{(13-8)}$$

and

$$R = y + j = (a + b + c + d + e + f + t + h + p)$$
$$- (r + k + l + n + o) \qquad \textbf{13-9}$$

Alternatively stated:

Depository Institution Reserves	Equals	Sources of Reserves	Minus	Alternative Uses of Reserves
(R = Bank deposits at the Fed + bank vault cash in the form of Federal Reserve Notes and Treasury Notes)		a = U.S. government and federal agency obligations $+b$ = Loans to depository institutions $+c$ = Acceptances $+d$ = Gold certificates $+e$ = SDRs $+f$ = Foreign currency accounts $+t$ = Float $+h$ = Other Fed assets $+x$ = Treasury currency held by the Fed		r = Currency in circulation $+k$ = Treasury deposits $+l$ = Foreign deposits $+n$ = Other liabilities $+o$ = Capital account

Equation (13-9) is quite similar to Equation (13-4), but it takes into account additional U.S. Treasury activities that offset bank reserves. To understand the relationships in Equation (13-7), let's consider the following three important examples.

Changes in Federal Reserve Bank Float A high percentage of checks drawn on banks and deposited in other banks is cleared or collected through the Fed. Checks that are drawn on banks located near Federal Reserve district banks are credited immediately to the depository bank's reserve account and are collected the same day by debiting the reserve account of the bank on which the checks are written. All checks are *credited* to the accounts of the depository bank according to a published schedule, but the Fed never takes more than two days to credit a depository bank after it receives a check. Some checks, however, take the Fed *more* than two days to collect because of processing or transportation delays. In effect, the Fed gives banks that sends it checks to clear a reserve credit for checks not yet collected. This reserve credit is called float and is defined as the difference between cash items in process of collection (CIIPC) and deferred availability cash items (DACI). Float is always positive, because there are always checks that cannot be collected and verified as being good within the Fed's published crediting schedule. Changes in the amount of float change bank reserves.

An Increase in Reserve Bank Float Increases Bank Reserves Consider the case in which bank A receives checks totaling $1,000, drawn on banks B,

C, and D, all located in distant cities. Bank A sends the checks to a Federal Reserve bank for collection and bank A's assets immediately rise by $1,000 in the form of DACI; bank A's liabilities also rise by $1,000 in the form of deposits to its customers. The Fed receives the check and treats it as a $1,000 asset (CIIPC) and a $1,000 liability (DACI). Figure 13-2 shows these transactions in panel (*a*). At this point, float has not arisen because, for the Fed, CIIPC and DACI both equal $1,000.

Assume that bank A receives credit in two days. At the end of that period the Federal Reserve bank reduces its DACI liability by crediting bank A's reserve account by $1,000. If the checks from B, C, and D actually take longer than two days to collect, CIIPC *in the interim* are not reduced, and float now equals $1,000. In effect, bank A has been extended credit for that interim period by the Fed. As panel (*b*) shows, bank A's reserves have increased by $1,000, $880 of which are excess reserves (assuming a 12 percent required reserve ratio). Because no other bank has, *at this point,* lost reserves, *overall* bank reserves have increased. In terms of Equation (13-9), if t rises and no other term changes, R will rise.

A Decrease in Reserve Bank Float Reduces Bank Reserves All good things come to an end, however, and as panel (*c*) shows, when the $1,000 of checks are actually collected by the Fed from banks B, C, and D, float disap-

FIGURE 13-2

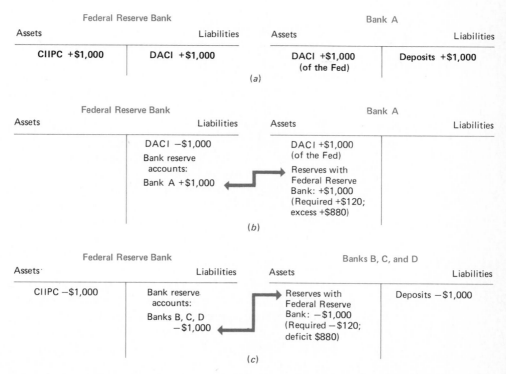

Fed's CIIPC falls by $1,000) and the reserve balances of banks B, C, and D fall by $1,000. In total, the three banks have now lost $1,000 of reserves, just offsetting bank A's increase that was indicated in panel (*b*).

This example shows that increases in Federal Reserve bank float cause bank reserves to rise, and decreases in Federal Reserve bank float cause bank reserves to fall. The volume of float is quite stable on an annual average, but it often fluctuates sharply over short periods of time. The volume of float changes significantly and predictably at midmonth and at the end of the year, when an increase in checkwriting occurs. Anything that causes delays in the delivery of mail—such as bad weather or transportation strikes—can increase float significantly, as checks sent by the Fed for collection are slowed down en route to paying banks. As Chapter 16 indicates, significant changes in float that lead to undesirable changes in bank reserves can be offset by Fed open-market operations.

Monetary Policy and the Reserve Equation   In the next three chapters we discuss the Fed's three principal monetary policy tools. These tools can be classified in two ways:

1   As they affect the magnitude and cost of depository reserves.
2   As they affect depository institution reserve requirements.

Discount-rate changes and open-market operations fall into the first category; required reserve ratio changes fall into the second.

The Fed Buys or Sells a U.S. Government Security   Suppose that the Fed buys a U.S. government security for $1 million from a depository institution. As Equation (13-9) indicates, a rise in *a* will increase *R* as long as there are no offsetting changes in the rest of the balance sheet. How does this come about? The Fed buys the security for $1 million from the depository institution by crediting that institution's reserve account with $1 million. The Fed obtains the $1 million asset (the U.S. government security) and simultaneously incurs a $1 million liability to the depository institution in the form of reserves or deposits at the Fed. The depository institution merely trades asset forms; it gives up a $1 million U.S. government security for $1 million in reserves at the Fed. The depository institution's liabilities at this stage are unaffected. See Figure 13-3.

Complementary reasoning indicates that if the Fed buys the $1 million security from the *public,* the process is a bit more involved but the results are the same in terms of the Fed's balance sheet. The Fed buys the security with a check drawn on a Federal Reserve bank. The nonbank seller of the $1 million security places the check in his or her depository institution, which in turn sends a check to the Federal Reserve bank in its district. The Fed then credits that depository institution's reserve account with $1 million. The Fed again has purchased an asset by crediting a depository institution's reserve account with the purchase price. The government security is now an asset of the Fed and it is offset by an equal liability of the Fed to the depository institution. The

Depository institution		Fed	
Securities (−$1M) Federal Reserve deposit (+$1M)		Securities (+$1M)	Federal Reserve deposit (+$1M)

FIGURE 13-3   The Fed Buys U.S. Government Securities from a Depository Institution.   The Fed buys $1 million ($1M) of securities from a depository institution by crediting its reserve account.

depository institution has obtained a $1 million asset in the form of reserves; this asset has been offset by an equal increase in the depository institution's liabilities, in the form of an increased demand deposit owned by the original nonbank, private seller of the security to the Fed. This private seller has merely changed asset forms; he or she surrendered a $1 million government security for a demand deposit (asset) at a depository institution. Although it may appear that only the asset's form has changed, the following has *also* occurred:

1   The money supply has increased because the private citizen traded a government security (nonmoney asset) for a demand deposit (a money asset).

2   Total reserves, R in Equation (13-9), have increased; this could cause the money supply to increase even more. By complementary reasoning, a Fed sale of securities to either depository institutions or to the public will cause depository institution reserves and the money supply to fall. See Figure 13-4.

FIGURE 13-4   The Fed Buys Securities from the Public.   The Fed buys $1 million ($1M) of the U.S. government securities from a nonbank seller and pays for them with a check drawn on the Fed. The nonbank seller deposits the check in a depository institution.

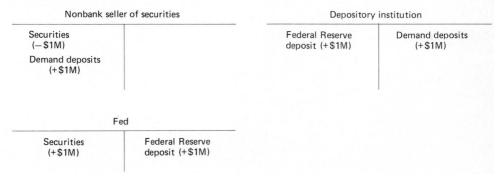

Nonbank seller of securities		Depository institution	
Securities (−$1M) Demand deposits (+$1M)		Federal Reserve deposit (+$1M)	Demand deposits (+$1M)

Fed	
Securities (+$1M)	Federal Reserve deposit (+$1M)

FIGURE 13-5   **The Fed Lends $1 Million ($1M) to a Depository Institution.**

A similar series of transactions would occur if the Fed bought or sold in the market for acceptances. Equation (13-9) indicates that if the Fed increases or decreases acceptances, c, then depository institution reserves, R, will rise or fall. In either case, the Fed can purchase or sell an asset by crediting or debiting a depository institution's reserve account. The Fed's assets and liabilities change equally, but changes in a depository institution's reserves normally induce the institution to alter its lending capacity; usually the money supply will change accordingly.

The Fed Lends to a Depository Institution   In Equation (13-9), if the Fed increased its lending to a depository institution and this action is not counteracted by another change in the Fed's balance sheet, reserves will rise: An increase in b is accompanied by an increase in R, other things held constant. How does this occur? The Fed can acquire an asset—a depository institution's debt obligation—by increasing that depository institution's reserve account. The Fed acquires the asset in the form of a depository institution's IOU, and an equal liability in the form of reserves of that same depository institution. The depository institution has received an equal increase in assets (reserves with the Fed) and liabilities (a debt to the Fed). The depository institution, however, now has an increase in its reserves and its potential to make loans is thereby increased.[2] On occasion, depository institutions may increase their loans outstanding and then borrow needed reserves from the Fed, even though in principle they are not supposed to do this.

Figure 13-5 shows the steps involved in the above analysis. The reader should be able to redo Figure 13-5 to show the steps involved when the depository institution repays its debt to the Fed.

---

[2]As will be indicated in Chapter 15, the Fed has not used this tool aggressively in recent years to change the money supply. Still, this analysis (and experience in this country and others) indicates that this tool could be effective.

CURRENT CONTROVERSY

Should Federal Reserve Float Be Eliminated?*

Federal Reserve float arises because the Fed's time schedule of crediting one bank's reserve account (the availability schedule) is short relative to the *actual* time it takes the Fed to clear checks and debit the reserve account of the bank on which the check is drawn. Lags in Fed check collection come from unexpected processing delays and equipment malfunctions within the Fed offices, transportation delays, and computer or communications breakdowns.

The value of Federal Reserve float can be determined by the market value of the bank reserves created by float. The market value of those reserves can be estimated by using the federal funds interest rate (the interest rate that banks charge each other for overnight reserve loans). Figure 1 shows the annual amount of Federal Reserve float (in billions of dollars, on the solid line) and the annual value at the federal funds rate of that float (in millions of dollars, on the dashed line) for the period 1965 to 1982. To banks the value of float is significant; it reached a peak of nearly $800 million in 1979 and thereafter declined. Federal Reserve float has fallen since 1979 because the Monetary Control Act of 1980 required the Fed to eliminate float or charge banks for this extension of credit.

Clearly, Federal Reserve float benefits banks, but who pays for this "subsidy" to banks? The cost of Federal Reserve float is borne by the U.S. Treasury. Banks *do not* earn interest on required reserves, and therefore the Fed imposes an implicit tax on banks for maintaining them. In effect, the banks extend an interest-free loan to the Fed, the implicit value of which is equal to the earnings that banks *could have* earned on required reserves. Other things constant, Fed earnings are higher. Because

FIGURE 1 Federal Reserve Float.

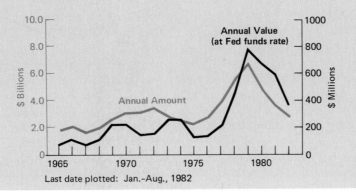

Last date plotted: Jan.-Aug., 1982

the Fed turns most of its profits over to the U.S. Treasury, the Treasury bears the cost of Federal Reserve float.

On the other hand, the "subsidy" of float that the Fed extends to banks can be seen as a *partial offset* to the implicit tax that the Fed imposes on banks by not paying interest on required reserves. As such, some feel that the elimination of float is unfair.

Fair or unfair, the Fed is committed to eliminating float, and, as Figure 1 shows, it has reduced float significantly. Most of the reduction since 1979 is the direct result of Fed investments in faster check processing. Float could be totally eliminated if the Fed were to move toward an electronic payment system in which debits, credits, and information flows (confirmations that the checks are good) are simultaneously recorded. It is believed that a fully electronic payments system won't be available until the distant future. In the meantime, the Fed is committed to reducing float further; Congress mandated that from July 1, 1983, the Fed must charge for float. Whether the Fed *should* charge for or reduce float is another issue, one that involves value judgments and considerations of fairness.

*From Jack H. Beebe, "Float," *The Weekly Newsletter,* Federal Reserve Bank of San Francisco, Dec. 3, 1982, pp. 1–3.

CHAPTER SUMMARY

1   The Fed manages the money supply (1) mostly through open-market operations, (2) somewhat by changing the discount rate, and (3) occasionally by changing depository institution reserve requirements. The first two tools directly affect total depository institution reserves.

2   The fundamental accounting identity states that:

Assets = liabilities + net worth

A balance sheet indicates that this relationship holds true at any specific moment in time.

3   The Fed's largest assets are gold certificates, special drawing rights, loans to depository institutions, acceptances, U.S. government securities, cash items in the process of collection, and assets denominated in foreign currencies.

4   The Fed's largest liabilities are Federal Reserve notes, deposits of (a) depository institutions, (b) the U.S. Treasury, and (c) foreign governments, and deferred availability cash items. Individuals, nondepository businesses, and state and local governments are not allowed to maintain deposits with the Fed.

5   Technically, the Fed is owned by member banks; however, the President and Congress have traditionally been able to exert some control over the Fed. In recent years, the Fed has come under even closer scrutiny by Congress.

6   The Fed (or any other economic agent) can (a) increase its assets by increasing its debts or increasing ownership claims, and (b) decrease its assets by destroying its liabilities or reducing ownership claims. Because ownership claims of the Fed represent less than 2 percent of its total assets, the Fed pays for most of its assets by issuing debt claims against itself.

7   When the Fed deals with a depository institution, it directly alters the latter's reserve account by the value of the transaction. Transactions between the Fed and the public are more complicated because depository institution reserves are altered *indirectly,* as the public draws down on or increases its deposits with depository institutions. Moreover, Fed purchases or sales of government securities to the public directly increase or decrease the money supply; Fed purchases or sales of government securities to depository institutions indirectly increase or decrease the money supply as a result of banks' reactions to the altered state of their reserves.

8   The bank reserve equation is an algebraic manipulation of the fundamental accounting identity; it isolates depository institution reserves and states that they are equal to the sum of the Fed's individual asset entries (sources of funds) minus the Fed's individual liability entries (alternative uses of funds) other than the depository institution reserves. The reserve equation indicates that each Fed asset is a potential source of depository institution reserves because the Fed can pay for these (or any other) assets by crediting a depository institution's reserve account by an amount equal to the price of the asset. Fed sales of assets potentially reduce depository institution reserves because the Fed can "charge" a depository institution by reducing its reserve account by the amount of the sales price. The bank reserve equation also indicates that U.S. Treasury activities also affect bank reserves.

9   Float is defined as cash items in the process of collection (a Fed asset) minus deferred availability cash items (a Fed liability). Float is a Fed credit to depository institutions and results from the fact that there is a time lag between when the Fed credits and debits reserve accounts and when it performs its check-collecting chore; float would be zero if the Fed credited and debited reserve accounts simultaneously as it collected checks. Increases in float increase bank reserves, and decreases in float decrease bank reserves.

GLOSSARY

Cash items in process of collection (CIIPC): An asset on the Fed's balance sheet representing the value of those checks that are in the Fed's possession, but that have not yet been collected by debiting the value from the proper depository institution's reserve accounts.

Deferred availability cash items (DACI): A liability on the Fed's balance sheet representing the value of checks not yet paid; a future obligation of the Fed.

Float: Cash items in process of collection minus deferred availability cash items; Fed credit that results from the fact that the Fed does not credit and debit reserve accounts simultaneously when it collects checks.

Foreign exchange: An international reserve asset of the Fed in the form of foreign currency.

Foreign exchange rates: The prices of units of foreign

money expressed in terms of units of domestic money.

Gold certificates: A type of paper currency that represents gold bullion owned by the U.S. government; gold certificates are a claim against this gold and are listed as a Fed asset when the U.S. Treasury sells them to the Fed in exchange for Treasury deposits at the Fed.

International Monetary Fund (IMF): An international agency that helps nations settle their payments imbalances.

International reserve assets: The assets in the Fed's portfolio (gold certificates, special drawing rights, and assets denominated in foreign currencies) which can be used to settle international payments.

PROBLEMS

13-1 Write the bank reserve equation, using the symbols used in this chapter.

13-2 Classify the following under the headings "Fed assets" and "Fed liabilities": Federal Reserve notes, deferred availability cash items, U.S. government securities and federal agency obligations, foreign central bank and IMF deposits with the Fed, cash items in process of collection, gold certificates, float.

SELECTED REFERENCES

Beebe, Jack H., "Float," *Weekly Newsletter,* Federal Reserve Bank of San Francisco, Dec. 3, 1982, pp. 1–3.

Nichols, Dorothy M., *Modern Money Mechanics: A Workbook on Deposits, Currency, and Bank Reserves* (Federal Reserve Bank of Chicago, 1961; revised in 1968, 1971, 1975, and 1982).

Roosa, Robert V., *Federal Reserve Operations in the Money and Government Securities Markets* (Federal Reserve Bank of New York, 1956).

Samansky, Arthur, *Stat Facts* (Federal Reserve Bank of New York, 1981).

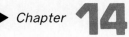
Reserve Requirements

The previous chapter stressed the importance of depository institution deposits at the Fed. Depository institutions keep all their reserves except for their vault cash at Federal Reserve district banks. These depository institution deposits are a Fed liability. Chapter 8 showed that changes in overall reserves may lead to a multiple change in the money supply. Indeed, the maximum deposit expansion multiplier was found to be the reciprocal of the required reserve ratio.

This chapter will examine the following:

1 Reserve requirements in greater detail, including a brief history of U.S. reserve requirements
2 How reserve requirements are calculated
3 How depository institutions meet these requirements
4 How different kinds of reserves are defined
5 Why reserve requirements were imposed, the implications of zero required reserves, and how the Fed uses changes in reserve requirements as a monetary policy tool

REQUIRED RESERVES

Congress gives the Fed the power to set legal reserve requirements—within limits—for depository institutions. Only a depository institution's vault cash and its deposits at the Fed are eligible to satisfy these legal reserve requirements.

Before we analyze reserve requirements, let's look at a short history of reserve requirements in the United States.

A Brief History of Reserve Requirements in the United States The reserve requirements for national banks were originally not set by the Fed but by the U.S. Congress. It was widely believed by members of Congress, bankers, and the public that reserve requirements were necessary to ensure the safety of deposits and the soundness of the banking system. On the other hand, some astute observers noted that setting reserve requirement ratios at low percentages was akin to preparing for future fires by requiring each house to hold a pail of water on reserve. Today we realize that a better system for assuring the safety of depositors' money exists—deposit insurance (federal or private). As a consequence, reserve requirements are maintained today not as a means of protecting depositors' money, but as an instrument of monetary policy.

The Banking Act of 1935 gave the Federal Reserve Board of Governors the power, within the limits prescribed by Congress, to set reserve requirements. The purpose as specified in the act was to allow the Fed greater control over credit markets.

In 1936, the Fed raised reserve requirements to counteract the great quantities of excess reserves (representing nearly 27 percent of total demand

TABLE 14-1 Required Reserve Ratios Imposed by the Federal Reserve

This table shows how the Fed increased the required reserve ratio dramatically during the period from Aug. 16, 1936 to May 1, 1937. By May of 1937, the various required reserve ratios were twice as high as they were in 1917.

Effective Date	June 21, 1917	Aug. 16, 1936	Mar. 1, 1937	May 1, 1937
Designation of Deposit and Bank				
On net demand deposits in				
Central reserve city	13	$19\frac{1}{2}$	$22\frac{3}{4}$	26
Reserve city	10	15	$17\frac{1}{2}$	20
Country	7	$10\frac{1}{2}$	$12\frac{1}{4}$	14
On time deposits	3	$4\frac{1}{2}$	$5\frac{1}{4}$	6

Source: Adapted from Board of Governors of the Federal Reserve, *Banking and Monetary Statistics,* 1943, p. 400.

deposits and over 5 percent of total overall deposits) that the Fed feared was potentially inflationary. The Fed believed that nothing adverse would happen if it raised reserve requirements. With the advantage of hindsight, however, it is now obvious that member banks then *wished* to remain highly liquid. They felt that high liquidity in the form of excess reserves was necessary to prevent a recurrence of the bank disaster of 1929 to 1933. After the Fed increased reserve requirements in 1936, member banks *still* wanted to maintain excess reserves. This desire for liquidity caused member banks to curtail lending even more. The Fed increased reserve requirements again. Reserve requirements finally reached the upper limit permitted by Congress. On May 1, 1937, the required reserve ratio was twice as high as it was on June 21, 1917. Table 14-1 shows the required reserve ratio for net demand deposits at central reserve city banks (the difference in bank types is explained in footnote 1) was 13 percent in 1917. On May 1, 1937, it was 26 percent. The Fed eventually was successful in reducing excess reserves, but in the process it caused the money supply to contract dramatically.

Differentials in Reserve Requirements From the time reserve requirements were first set by the Fed in 1936 until the early 1970s, the Fed set different reserve requirements for different banks. The requirements for any bank depended on the location of the bank. There were three categories: central reserve city banks, reserve city banks, and country banks.[1] Higher reserve requirements were imposed on central reserve city banks and reserve city banks to insure more liquidity in case country banks holding correspondent

---

[1]Central reserve city banks are those banks located in Chicago and New York; reserve city banks are those located in about sixty other specified large cities; country banks are located elsewhere.

TABLE 14-2

Type of Deposit, and Deposit Interval in Millions of Dollars	Member bank requirements before implementation of the Monetary Control Act	
	Percent	Effective Date
Net demand*		
0–2	7	12/30/76
2–10	$9\frac{1}{2}$	12/30/76
10–100	$11\frac{3}{4}$	12/30/76
100–400	$12\frac{3}{4}$	12/30/76
Over 400	$16\frac{1}{4}$	12/30/76
Time and savings*†		
Savings	3	3/16/67
Time‡		
0–5, by maturity		
30–179 days	3	3/16/67
180 days to 4 years	$2\frac{1}{2}$	1/8/76
4 years or more	1	10/30/75
Over 5, by maturity		
30–179 days	6	12/12/74
180 days to 4 years	$2\frac{1}{2}$	1/8/76
4 years or more	1	10/30/75

Note: For changes in reserve requirements beginning 1963, see Board's *Annual Statistical Digest, 1971–1975* and for prior changes, see Board's *Annual Report* for 1976, table 13. Under provisions of the Monetary Control Act, depository institutions include commercial banks, mutual savings banks, savings and loan associations, credit unions, agencies and branches of foreign banks, and Edge Act corporations.

*(a) Requirement schedules are graduated, and each deposit interval applies to that part of the deposits of each bank. Demand deposits subject to reserve requirements were gross demand deposits minus cash items in process of collection and demand balances due from domestic banks.

(b) The Federal Reserve Act as amended through 1978 specified different ranges of requirements for reserve city banks and for other banks. Reserve cities were designated under a criterion adopted effective Nov. 9, 1972, by which a bank having net demand deposits of more than $400 million was considered to have the character of business of a reserve city bank. The presence of the head office of such a bank constituted designation of that place as a reserve city. Cities in which there were Federal Reserve banks or branches were also reserve cities. Any banks having net demand deposits of $400 million or less were considered to have the character of business of banks outside of reserve cities and were permitted to maintain reserves at ratios set for banks not in reserve cities.

(c) Effective Aug. 24, 1978, the Regulation M reserve requirements on net balances due from domestic banks to their foreign branches and on deposits that foreign branches lend to U.S. residents were reduced to zero from 4% and 1% respectively. The Regulation D reserve requirement on borrowings from unrelated banks abroad was also reduced to zero from 4%.

(d) Effective with the reserve computation period beginning Nov. 16, 1978, domestic deposits of Edge corporations were subject to the same reserve requirements as deposits of member banks.

†(a) Negotiable order of withdrawal (NOW) accounts and time deposits such as Christmas and vacation club accounts were subject to the same requirements as savings deposits.

TABLE 14-2   *(Continued)*

(b) The average reserve requirement on savings and other time deposits before implementation of the Monetary Control Act had to be at least 3%, the minimum specified by law.

‡(a) Effective No. 2, 1978, a supplementary reserve requirement of 2% was imposed on large time deposits of $100,000 or more, obligations of affiliates, and ineligible acceptances. This supplementary requirement was eliminated with the maintenance period beginning July 24, 1980.

(b) Effective with the reserve maintenance period beginning Oct. 25, 1979, a marginal reserve requirement of 8% was added to managed liabilities in excess of a base amount. This marginal requirement was increased to 10% beginning Apr. 3, 1980, was decreased to 5% beginning June 12, 1980, and was reduced to zero beginning July 24, 1980. Managed liabilities are defined as large time deposits, Eurodollar borrowings, repurchase agreements against U.S. government and federal agency securities, federal funds borrowings from nonmember institutions, and certain other obligations. In general, the base for the marginal reserve requirement was originally the greater of (a) $100 million or (b) the average amount of the managed liabilities held by a member bank. Edge Corporation, or family of U.S. branches and agencies of a foreign bank for the two statement weeks ending Sept. 26, 1979. For the computation period beginning Mar. 20, 1980, the base was lowered by (a) 7% or (b) the decrease in an institution's U.S. office gross loans to foreigners and gross balances due from foreign offices of other institutions between the base period (Sept. 13–26, 1979) and the week ending Mar. 12, 1980, whichever was greater. For the computation period beginning May 29, 1980, the base was increased by $7\frac{1}{2}$% above the base used to calculate the marginal reserve in the statement week of May 14–21, 1980. In addition, beginning Mar. 19, 1980, the base was reduced to the extent that foreign loans and balances declined.

Source: Adapted from *Federal Reserve Bulletin,* May 1982, reprinted from p. A-8.

balances in such banks wished to withdraw funds from them. In 1972, the Fed changed its policy of setting reserve requirements according to the size or classification of the city in which a bank was located to one of setting reserve requirements based only on the size of the bank's deposits.

Banks were reclassified into five categories based on net amount of demand deposits. Table 14-2 shows the categories and their reserve requirement percentages. This policy was again changed as a result of the Depository Institutions Deregulation and Monetary Control Act of 1980. The change is shown in Table 14-3. This act also brought about other changes in reserve requirements; under it, the Fed's reserve requirements are eventually to be imposed on all depository institutions.

CALCULATING RESERVE REQUIREMENTS

Member banks (today *all* depository institutions) do not have to satisfy reserve requirements on a *daily* basis; instead their reserves are averaged over a seven-day period. Prior to 1978, a member bank calculated its reserve requirements using a **contemporaneous reserve accounting system (CRA).** The CRA system required Fed member banks to calculate their required reserves in any week on the basis of their total net deposits in the same week.

TABLE 14-3		

Type of Deposit, and Deposit Interval	Depository institution requirements after implementation of the Monetary Control Act*	
	Percent	Effective Date
Net transaction accounts†‡		
$0–$26 million	3	11/13/80
Over $26 million	12	11/13/80
Nonpersonal time deposits§		
By original maturity		
Less than 4 years	3	11/13/80
4 years or more	0	11/13/80
Eurocurrency liabilities		
All types	3	11/13/80

*For existing nonmember banks and thrift institutions at the time of implementation of the Monetary Control Act, the phase-in period ends Sept. 3, 1987. For existing member banks the phase-in period is about 3 years, depending on whether their new reserve requirements are greater or less than the old requirements. For existing agencies and branches of foreign banks, the phase-in ends Aug. 12, 1982. All new institutions will have a 2-year phase-in beginning with the date that they open for business.

†Transaction accounts include all deposits on which the account holder is permitted to make withdrawals by negotiable or transferable instruments, payment orders of withdrawal, and telephone and preauthorized transfers (in excess of 3 per month) for the purpose of making payments to third persons or others.

‡The Monetary Control Act of 1980 requires that the amount of transaction accounts against which the 3% reserve requirement will apply be modified annually to 80% of the percentage increase in transaction accounts held by all depository institutions on the previous June 30. At the beginning of 1982 the amount was accordingly increased from $25 million to $26 million.

§In general, nonpersonal time deposits are time deposits, including savings deposits, that are not transaction accounts and in which the beneficial interest is held by a depositor that is not a natural person. All included are certain transferable time deposits held by natural persons, and certain obligations issued to depository institution offices located outside the United States. For details, see section 204.2 of Regulation D.

Note: Required reserves must be held in the form of deposits with Federal Reserve banks or vault cash. After implementation of the Monetary Control Act, nonmembers may maintain reserves on a pass-through basis with certain approved institutions.

Source: Adapted from *Federal Reserve Bulletin,* May 1982, reprinted from p. A-8.

Net demand deposits are gross demand deposits minus the sum of cash items in the process of collection and demand balances due other banks. Deposits and required reserves were calculated on a weekly basis, but the so-called statement week ran from each Thursday through the following Wednesday. During any statement week, the daily average of *required* reserves was equal to a percentage of the average net deposits in the bank during that week.

From 1978 until February 1984, member banks (all depository institutions today) were subject to a **lagged reserve accounting system (LRA).** Average net deposits *two weeks earlier* were used to determine the required reserves for the *current* week; they were calculated by adding cash in the vault two weeks ago to the average net reserve deposit balance at the Fed district bank for the current week.

Consider a numerical example. A depository institution has an average of $50 million of net demand deposits during a statement week and no other deposit liabilities. It also has a $1 million daily average in vault cash. Assume the reserve ratio is 10 percent. Thus, required reserves are $5 million two weeks later. This depository institution must have actual reserves equal to $4 million in the form of deposits with the Federal Reserve district bank two weeks later, which when added to the $1 million of vault cash in the statement week satisfies the legal reserve requirement.

Suppose that two weeks later the depository institution has a deficit or surplus in its deposits at the Fed of no more than 2 percent of required reserves. This deficit or surplus can be carried forward to the next week; the deficit can be offset by a surplus in the next week and the surplus can be used to offset a deficit in the next week. If a deficit *exceeds* more than 2 percent of required reserves, the depository institution is subject to a penalty equal to the discount rate, plus 2 percent times its shortage.

The lagged reserve accounting system was designed to allow member banks to reduce their excess reserves and thereby increase their earnings. The idea was that if member banks could always predict precisely what their required deposits at the Fed would be in two weeks, they could make sure they did not have an overabundance of non-interest-earning excess reserves in two weeks. The LRA system seemed to be effective; the average excess reserves of all member banks fell from $400 million in 1978 to approximately $250 million by 1980.

Criticism of LRA   While the institution of lagged reserve accounting may have benefited member banks (and more recently all depository institutions holding reserves) by reducing average excess reserves, it seemed to hamper monetary policy. The problems resulting from using lagged reserve requirements will be taken up in Chapter 27. Suffice it to say that in July 1982, in response to heavy criticism of LRA, the Fed agreed to return to a form of contemporaneous reserve accounting and this went into effect in February 1984.

PLEDGED ASSETS

Thus far we have examined reserve requirements only in the form of vault cash or deposits at the Federal Reserve district bank. Yet depository institutions are also subject to another requirement—**pledged assets.** Banks are required (by the depositing institution) to hold U.S. government securities or high-quality municipal securities as collateral against the deposits of federal, state, and local governments. In other words, if a depository institution has a transactions deposit of the state of California or the city of Sacramento or of the federal government, the state or city requires the depository institution to

pledge as collateral an equal amount of U.S. securities or high-quality municipal securities. The U.S. Treasury also requires banks to hold T-bills as a condition for the Treasury to maintain deposits at that bank. Pledged assets represent a tie-in clause; in order for a depository institution to obtain the
deposits of a government agency, the depository institution must agree to
hold government securities.

MEETING RESERVE REQUIREMENTS

A depository institution can obtain funds to meet its reserve requirements by
selling securities (or other assets) to other depository institutions or by borrowing from other depository institutions in the federal funds market. Note,
however, that while *one* depository institution can avail itself of these opportunities to increase reserves, *all* depository institutions cannot *simultaneously*
satisfy their reserve requirements by doing so. The total amount of reserves
in existence cannot be changed by one depository institution, or even by all
depository institutions exchanging assets and reserves with each other.

On the other hand, depository institutions in general can increase overall
reserves by borrowing from the Fed or from the Eurodollar market, or by selling securities to the Fed. Depository institutions in general also have the
option of meeting reserve requirements by making fewer loans and by not
renewing loans as they mature.[2]

DEFINING DIFFERENT TYPES OF
RESERVES AND THE MONETARY BASE

The Fed's key to monetary policy is its ability to affect depository institution
reserves. Total reserves, however, do not tell the whole story. For this reason,
several other measures of reserves have been developed. Some definitions for
these concepts are offered here.

1   *The monetary base:*   The **monetary base,** or simply the base or the
    reserve base, has also been called high-powered money. The monetary
    base consists of total depository institution reserves plus currency in cir-
    culation. Currency in circulation is currency in the hands of the public and
    not in the Fed, the U.S. Treasury, or bank vaults. This sum is referred to
    as high-powered money because a dollar's worth of it can support several
    dollars for transactions accounts in a fractional reserve system, as you will
    recall from Chapter 8. The higher the required reserve ratio, the less
    power each dollar in the monetary base has; the lower the required
    reserve ratio, the more power each dollar in the monetary base has. In

---

[2]See the "Bank Reserve Equation" in Chapter 13 for an overview of how total bank reserves can
be altered.

HIGHLIGHT   The Federal Funds Market

Federal funds are deposits (usually held at the Fed) that one depository institution "purchases" (borrows) from another. They are referred to as "federal funds" because they are electronically transferred from one depository institution's reserve account to another's over a facility leased from the Federal Reserve System, called the "Fed wire." When one depository institution purchases deposits from another, the transfer is recorded by the Fed on the same day—although the Fed normally takes at least one day to clear a check. Although the federal funds market is used mostly by commercial banks, other depository institutions such as mutual savings banks, federal government agencies, and savings and loan associations are also active participants.

Depository institutions also use the federal funds market for purposes other than meeting reserve requirements. Some large banks buy federal funds in order to resell them to country correspondent banks, as a service to the smaller banks. The growth in this market from 1967 to the present is shown in Table 1.

Some institutions borrow beyond their required reserves, so they must be using the federal funds market to obtain funds to relend, as well as to meet their reserve requirements. Note that the market nearly doubled from 1978 to 1979. This occurred because the rate of inflation increased dramatically, and with it so did interest rates. These higher interest rates

attracted many previously idle excess reserves from smaller rural banks.

The interest rate that selling depository institutions charge the buyer is called the **federal funds rate.** This rate can be *influenced* by the Fed, as will be shown in later chapters, but it is not set by the Fed. The Fed uses this rate to gauge its success in achieving short-term interest rate targets.

TABLE 1   Federal Funds Market Growth Since 1967

Year*	Federal Funds Purchased by Domestic Commercial Banks (Billions of Dollars)
1967	$2.3
1968	2.1
1969	3.4
1970	8.1
1971	7.9
1972	8.0
1973	9.2
1974	16.1
1975	20.2
1976	16.2
1977	22.3
1978	23.5
1979	45.2
1980	44.4
1982	54.2
1983	58.7

*Midyear.
Source: Federal Reserve Bank of New York, *Quarterly Review,* Summer 1977, vol. 2, p. 40, and *Federal Reserve Bulletins,* 1978–1983.

other words, the monetary base consists of those assets available to the public which, if held by depository institutions, *could* be used to satisfy Federal Reserve requirements. (Remember currency in the vaults of depository institutions can be used to satisfy reserve requirements.)

2   *The adjusted monetary base:* When we adjust the monetary base to reflect changes in reserve requirements, we call that the **adjusted monetary base.** It is the monetary base adjusted by the dollar equivalent of the change in the average reserve requirement ratio; it reflects the implicit change in the money multiplier. The adjusted monetary base takes into account the fact that a given monetary base can support differing maximum levels of the total money supply—depending on what the required reserve ratio is. The higher the required reserve ratio, the smaller the total money supply that a given monetary base can support.

3   *Excess reserves:*   **Excess reserves** are those reserves above the reserves required by law: Excess reserves = actual reserves − required reserves.

4   *Borrowed reserves:*   **Borrowed reserves** are those reserves that have been borrowed by depository institutions from the Fed.

5   *Nonborrowed reserves:*   It is widely believed that depository institutions are reluctant to make loans or purchase securities with borrowed reserves. To reflect the *willingness* of depository institutions to lend or purchase securities, borrowed reserves are subtracted from total reserves, which gives **nonborrowed reserves.**

With reference to the monetary base, when borrowed reserves are subtracted from the monetary base, the **nonborrowed base** is derived. Presumably, the nonborrowed base better reflects the potential maximum money supply than does the monetary base.

6   *Free Reserves:*   **Free reserves** are obtained by subtracting borrowed reserves from excess reserves, or: Free reserves = excess reserves − borrowed reserves.

Depository institutions tend to use these free reserves to repay the Fed the amount of reserves borrowed from the Fed before they purchase securities or make loans. If so, then free reserves are a good measure of the degree to which depository institutions are able to expand their assets.

WHY A RESERVE REQUIREMENT?

Early in the banking history of this country, certain states imposed reserve requirements on state-chartered banks. National banks also have had a reserve requirement since 1863. Today virtually all depository institutions have some type of reserve requirement. Why are reserve requirements imposed on depository institutions?

One way to determine how important something is, is to try to determine what life would be like without it. What would be the economic effects of a zero required reserve system? It might appear that such a system would be disastrous. Actually, it seems likely that depository institutions would *voluntarily* hold reserves based on some percentage of their deposits. Depository institutions have sufficient experience to indicate the amount of funds they need to have on reserve to meet cash and deposit withdrawals. Continued profitability would require sufficient liquidity to satisfy depositors. Thus, depository institutions would doubtless hold reserves to cover normal expected net withdrawals. These might be called prudent reserves. So, even in a world of zero reserve requirements, prudent reserves would not be zero.

Can the Fed and Congress determine for all institutions in general "the best" reserve ratio better than each depository institution can determine what its own "best" reserve ratio should be? Can the Fed and Congress determine the appropriate reserve ratio during abnormal times?

Do Reserve Requirements Protect the Depositor?   Only if the required reserve ratio were set at 100 percent could depositors be assured of liquidity on demand. The closing of so many banks that met the Fed's reserve requirements during the Great Depression is proof positive that even with required reserves (at less than 100 percent), banks can and do fail.

Actually, the argument that reserve requirements are necessary to protect depositors is irrelevant today. Deposit insurance has eliminated the concern of a run on banks. Why, then, have reserve requirements?

The Reason for Reserve Requirements   Reserve requirements must be viewed as a monetary policy tool of the Fed. The Fed can directly alter required reserves (within the limits set by Congress) and thereby alter the size of the money supply. (Remember that the maximum expansion deposit multiplier is a function of the reciprocal of the required reserve ratio.) Rarely in recent times has the Fed used changes in reserve requirements to affect monetary policy. Rather, the argument in favor of required reserves relates to the *stability* of the money multiplier. If required reserves are stable, then the money multiplier will, within certain bounds, be stable. This means that the Fed can control the money supply with greater accuracy when it engages in open-market operations. A voluntary reserve ratio would certainly be less stable than a required reserve ratio, and control over the money supply would therefore be more difficult.

Reserve Requirement Changes as a Monetary Policy Tool Examined in More Detail   A change in reserve requirements affects the money supply in two ways; it changes (1) the level of excess reserves and (2) the money (or deposit expansion) multiplier.

When the required reserve ratio falls, a depository institution's *actual reserves are not immediately affected.* But excess reserves rise. A lower reserve ratio will also increase the size of the money multiplier because these increased excess reserves can be turned into loans and deposits. For example, as Figure 14-1 shows, given an average reserve requirement of 12 percent, $12 of reserves would be required to support $100 of deposits. But, as Figure 14-2 shows, a reduction in the legal reserve requirement to 10 percent would "tie up" only $10 for reserves, freeing $2 out of each $12 of reserves for use in creating additional bank loans and deposits. Note that the total amount of reserves is unaffected initially. Excess reserves rise; therefore, the bank can increase its lending. The money expansion multiplier would rise from $8\frac{1}{3}$ to 10.

Bank A

Assets		Liabilities	
Loans and investments	$88	Deposits	$100
Reserves	$12		
(Required, $12; excess, $0)			

FIGURE 14-1

Federal Reserve Bank			Bank A		
Assets		Liabilities	Assets		Liabilities
	No	change	Reserves $12	Deposits $100	
			(Required, $10; excess, $2		

FIGURE 14-2

An *increase* in reserve requirements, on the other hand, absorbs additional reserve funds, and banks that previously had zero excess reserves would be forced to acquire more reserves or reduce their loans or investments, because actual reserves are unaffected by changes in the required reserve ratio initially.

Consider Figure 14-3, which indicates the initial result of an increase in the required reserve ratio from 12 percent to 14 percent. Total reserves are initially unaffected, but required reserves rise from $12 to $14 for each $100 deposit. Assuming bank A had zero excess reserves prior to the change in the required reserve ratio, it must now reduce its loans and investments until its deposits fall in line with the existing amount of reserves. The money expansion multiplier falls from $8\frac{1}{3}$ to $7\frac{1}{7}$.

The Fed has been reluctant to use a change in the reserve ratio as a monetary policy tool for at least two reasons:

1 It considers this tool "too powerful." Even small changes in reserve requirements could have an enormous effect on excess reserves and

FIGURE 14-3

Federal Reserve Bank			Bank A		
Assets		Liabilities	Assets		Liabilities
	No	change	Reserves $12	Deposits $100	
			(Required, $14; deficit, $2)		

therefore on deposit creation and the money supply. The Fed maintains that this tool is crude and unnecessary, because open-market operations can be carried out with facility and refinement. Still it is hard to see why the Fed can't change reserve requirements by very small amounts.

2 The Fed feels that member banks would be put at a competitive disadvantage if the reserve ratio were increased relative to other depository institutions. This concern is no longer relevant because with the passage of the Depository Institutions Deregulation and Monetary Control Act of 1980, both member and nonmember banks of the same size are subject to exactly the same reserve requirements. For this reason, it is possible that the Fed will use reserve requirement changes as a monetary policy tool more often in the future.

CURRENT CONTROVERSY

Depository Institutions Should Have a 100 Percent Reserve Requirement

Required reserve ratios are supposedly more stable and predictable than voluntary reserve ratios; hence they permit easier and more consistent monetary control by the Fed. If this is true, it would seem to follow that a 100 percent reserve requirement would allow the monetary authorities even better control over the money supply. Whether a system of mandatory reserve requirement ratios causes depository institutions to vary their reserve ratio less often than would a system of voluntary reserve requirement ratios is unknown. But it is known that a 100 percent reserve requirement system definitely allows the monetary authorities to have better control over the money supply.

A 100 percent reserve requirement would abolish multiple deposit expansion by the banking system—the money expansion multiplier would be equal to 1. Such a requirement was proposed by Irving Fisher in 1935 and it represented Fisher's notion of how to stop runs on banks.*

Milton Friedman, unhappy with the fractional reserve banking system, has also proposed a 100 percent reserve requirement with slight variations.† Recognizing that banks would be displeased because bank earnings would fall, Friedman has suggested that the Fed pay interest at a rate equivalent to the yield on T-bills, on bank reserves held at Federal Reserve district banks.

The major advantage of a 100 percent reserve requirement today is that it would allow the Fed more precise control over the money supply. However, it would not necessarily improve the position of depositors in terms of whether or not they had to worry about runs on banks. Deposit insurance has eliminated that possibility for the most part. In any event, with a 100 percent reserve requirement, the Fed would no longer have to be concerned about the unpredictability of excess reserves and leakages into currency. Perhaps another advantage is that with 100 percent reserves, the Fed and Congress could reduce substantially the regulation of depository institutions.

OPEN-MARKET OPERATIONS

Under a 100 percent reserve requirement system, open-market operations would work as follows: If the Fed bought $1 million of T-bills from depository institution A, A's reserves would rise by that much. Institution A could then increase its lending by $1 million and the money supply would rise by $1 million. However, when the $1 million is spent and deposited in, say, depository institution B, B must hold the whole $1 million to meet its reserve requirement. It follows that no more lending is possible; therefore, no further increase in deposits and the money supply will occur. The effect of a $1 million Fed security purchase is a $1 million increase in the money supply. The money multiplier is 1.

With a 100 percent reserve requirement, the Fed can change the money supply with more precision than it does today. This appeals to those who want the Fed to use its discretion in changing the money supply, *and* also to those who wish the Fed to follow a monetary rule that increases the money supply at a steady rate.

Will a 100 percent reserve requirement be applied in the future? The probability of this is small because it represents a radical change. It would be disruptive and confusing to the banking community; and the Fed would also run into the problem of properly defining the money supply and of determining which items of a depository institution's liabilities are considered deposits subject to a 100 percent reserve requirement.

*Irving Fisher, *One Hundred Percent Money* (New York: Adelphia Co., 1935).

†Milton Friedman, *A Program for Monetary Stability* (New York: Fordham University Press, 1960).

CHAPTER SUMMARY

1 Originally reserve requirements for banks were set by Congress. In 1935 Congress gave the Fed the power to set, within broad limits, reserve requirements for depository institutions. Only vault cash and deposits at a Fed district bank can be used to meet the Fed's reserve requirement.

2 Until the 1970s, the Fed set a bank's reserve requirements according to the size or classification of the city in which it was located; after that a depository institution's reserves were determined by the size of the bank's deposits.

3 Each depository institution is obligated to calculate its reserve requirement, which is based on the Fed's requirement. Prior to 1978, a contemporaneous reserve accounting system (CRA) was used. Under a CRA system, during any given statement week the daily average of required reserves must equal the required percent-

ages of average *net* deposits held by the bank. From 1978 until August 1983, depository institutions were allowed to use a lagged reserve accounting system (LRA), so that they could better predict their reserve requirements and thereby hold fewer costly (non-interest-earning) excess reserves. Under an LRA system, a bank is required to calculate its current required deposits at the Fed based on its average daily net deposits for the statement week two weeks earlier. Current required deposits at the Fed are determined by multiplying the required reserve ratio times the average daily net deposit value for the statement week two weeks earlier, and subtracting from that amount the average daily value of vault cash in the bank for the statement week two weeks earlier. After February 1984, depository institutions were again forced to use a form of the CRA system.

4   Depository institutions are also required to have a reserve requirement referred to as pledged assets; depository institutions are required to hold U.S. government securities (or high-quality municipal securities) as collateral against deposits made by federal, state, and local governments.

5   A depository institution can meet its reserve requirement by selling securities to the Fed or other depository institutions, borrowing from other depository institutions in the federal funds market, borrowing in the Eurodollar market, making fewer loans, and not renewing loans that mature.

6   All depository institutions are *forced* to hold reserves, but it is apparent that they would do so *voluntarily* in order to remain in business. They would probably hold a smaller percentage of deposits in reserve, but it is not apparent that the legally mandated reserve requirement provides more protection to depositors in abnormal times. Moreover, the FDIC now protects depositors; a mandatory reserve requirement seems redundant. Reserve requirements must be viewed as a monetary policy tool; if the required reserve ratio is stable, the money multiplier will also be stable. As a consequence, the Fed can control the money supply more accurately through open-market operations; a voluntary reserve requirement would be less stable and monetary control would be more difficult.

7   Changes in reserve requirements, a more direct monetary tool, have not been used aggressively by the Fed in the past. Because *all* depository institutions are now forced to meet reserve requirements by the Fed; member banks have lost their competitive disadvantage; and therefore, changes in reserve requirements might be used more often by the Fed in the future.

8   A 100 percent reserve requirement on depository institutions would eliminate the need for the FDIC and for much depository institution regulation. It would also increase the Fed's control over the money supply; the Fed's concern over currency leakages and excess reserves would disappear and the deposit expansion multiplier would equal 1.

GLOSSARY

Borrowed reserves: Reserves borrowed by depository institutions from the Fed through the discount window.

Contemporaneous reserve accounting system (CRA): A method of calculating a depository institution's required reserves in any week based on the institution's current week's daily average of net deposits.

Excess reserves: Actual reserves minus required reserves.

Federal funds: Deposits, usually held at the Fed, that one depository institution borrows from another.

Federal funds rate: The rate that lending depository institutions charge borrowing depository institutions for the use of excess reserves.

Free reserves: Excess reserves minus borrowed reserves.

Lagged reserve accounting system (LRA): A method of calculating a depository institution's current required deposits at the Fed based on the institution's average daily net deposits for the week that was two weeks earlier.

Monetary base: Total bank reserves plus currency in circulation outside depository institutions; also called the reserve base, or high-powered money.

Nonborrowed base: The monetary base minus borrowed reserves.

Nonborrowed reserves: Total reserves minus borrowed reserves.

Pledged assets: Assets, usually in the form of T-bills, that depository institutions are required to hold as collateral against deposits made by federal, state, and local governments.

PROBLEMS

14-1 The Bound Brook Bank has daily net deposits that average $10,000,000 and daily vault cash that averages $10,000 during a statement week. Under a lagged reserve accounting system, what must be the Bound Brook Bank's deposits at the Fed two weeks hence, assuming that it is subject to an average reserve requirement of 12 percent?

14-2 Study the T-account below and answer the following questions:

a What is the required reserve ratio for this bank?

b If all depository institutions were subject to this required reserve ratio, what is the value of the maximum money expansion multiplier?

Bank A			
Assets		**Liabilities**	
Loans and investments	$176,000	Deposits	$200,000
Reserves	24,000		
(Required $24,000 Excess 0)			
	$200,000		$200,000

14-3 Assume that bank A in problem 14-2 is suddenly subject to an 8 percent required reserve ratio.

a What happens immediately to bank A's total reserves?

b What is the value of bank A's excess reserves?

c What is bank A likely to do now?

d If all depository institutions are now subject to an 8 percent required reserve ratio, what is the value of the maximum money expansion multiplier?

SELECTED REFERENCES

Adkerson, Richard C., "Can Reserve Recognition Accounting Work?" *Journal of Accountancy,* September 1979.

Berger, Albert, *The Money Supply Process* (Belmont, Calif.: Wadsworth Publishing Co., 1971).

Burger, Albert E., "Does the Federal Reserve Invest Member Bank Reserves?" *Review,* Federal Reserve Bank of St. Louis, July 1978.

Federal Reserve Bank of St. Louis, "Contemporaneous Reserve Requirements to Begin February 1984," in *Banking and Finance,* Fall 1983.

Fisher, Irving, *One Hundred Percent Money* (New York: Adelphia Co., 1935).

Friedman, Milton, *A Program for Monetary Stability* (New York: Fordham University Press, 1960).

Poole, William, and Charles Lieberman, "Improving Monetary Control," *Brookings Papers on Economic Activity,* 1972.

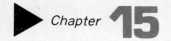

Chapter **15**

Discounting

CHAPTER PREVIEW

1 What is Fed discount policy?

2 Why would a policy that followed the commercial loan theory worsen both recessions and inflations?

3 Why has the discount rate not been an important Fed monetary policy tool?

4 The discount rate tends to lag behind changes in other interest rates. What implications does this have?

5 Should the Fed be a lender of last resort?

Chapter 13 explained how changes in any Fed asset affect depository institution reserves. Increased Fed lending to depository institutions directly increases the depository institution's reserves (if other balance sheet items are constant). Chapter 8 explained how increases in excess reserves lead to a multiple increase in the money supply. Monetary policy, therefore, can be conducted by changing the lending, or discount, policy of the Fed. This chapter develops the theory of discount policy and presents a brief history of U.S. discount policy. It ends with a Current Controversy about setting the discount rate below market rates.

THE THEORY OF DISCOUNT POLICY

Discounting is defined as the lending by the Federal Reserve System to depository institutions. As explained in Chapter 4, the term "discounting" gets its name from the method by which depository institutions obtain loans from the Fed. Depository institutions discount commercial loans that are eligible by selling those loans to the Fed for a short time, in exchange for an increase in the depository institution's reserve account. The Fed "discounts" the asset (loan) by increasing the depository institution's reserve account by a value that is less than the amount of the IOU. The depository institution, in a short period of time, then buys the asset back at the face value of the loan. In practice, however, the most common type of depository institution borrowing from the Fed is in the form of an **advance,** which is a promissory note signed by an official of the depository institution with U.S. government securities as collateral. Nonetheless, all Fed lending to member banks is usually called discounting.

Discount Policy **Discount policy** refers to the terms and conditions under which the Fed lends to depository institutions. It has, of necessity, both a price dimension—the discount rate—and a quantity dimension—the amount of lending that the Fed chooses to do.

The Fed's discount rate is the "price dimension" of discount policy; it is the rate that the Fed charges on its loans to depository institutions. If the Fed were ready to lend unlimited quantities of reserves at any given discount rate, it could directly control (even dictate) short-term interest rates. For example, if the Fed wished to lower short-term interest rates, through its discount policy it could agree to lend unlimited reserves to depository institutions at a discount rate below market rates. Depository institutions would be able to obtain reserves at an interest rate below the rate at which they could lend those reserves. Competition among depository institutions would then cause all short-term interest rates to fall when all depository institutions were allowed to borrow from the Fed at below-market interest rates. The Fed thus can make borrowing from it a more profitable source of funds than such alternatives as selling CDs, selling the securities it owns, or borrowing in the federal funds market or in the Eurodollar markets. A discount rate that is set with no restriction on the quantity of Fed lending, however, would require the Fed to relinquish its control over the money supply.

The quantity dimension of discount policy refers to the amount of reserves the Fed is *willing* to lend at any given discount rate to depository institutions. Because the Fed can lend whatever amount it wishes and because increased lending directly increases reserves, the Fed can choose the money supply it prefers by selecting the amount it will lend. For example, if the Fed knew the amount of currency the public desired to hold and if it knew the amount of excess reserves depository institutions were prepared to hold (prudential reserves), then (given the required reserve ratios) it could determine the money supply or its rate of growth simply by adjusting its quantity of lending. But in so doing, it gives up control over the interest rates. The Fed would have to increase or decrease its lending regardless of what happened to interest rates if it wanted to affect the money supply in a particular way. This chapter will emphasize that *the Fed cannot simultaneously set short-term interest rates and the rates of growth of the money supply*. The Fed must choose one goal or the other. In fact, throughout its history, the Fed *has* typically targeted either interest rates or the rate of growth of the money supply. Figure 15-1 shows how the Fed is forced to choose either an interest rate or the quantity of money. Given the community's demand for money curve, D_M, if the Fed wants the market interest rate to be at i_e, it must maintain a money supply equal to MM; a larger supply of money will cause interest rates to fall below i_e, and a smaller money supply will cause interest rates to rise above i_e. On the other hand, if the Fed desires money supply MM, it must accept interest rate i_e; if the Fed desires a higher interest rate or a lower one, it must reduce or increase the money supply. Given the demand for money curve, D_M, the Fed cannot simultaneously choose, for example, interest rate i_1 and money supply MM. We derive the demand for money curve systematically in Chapter 20.

FIGURE 15-1   The Fed cannot simultaneously determine an interest rate and the money supply—given a demand for money function. If the Fed wants the interest rate to be i_1 it must reduce the money supply from MM. If the Fed wants to change the money supply from MM, it must accept a change in the interest rate from i_e.

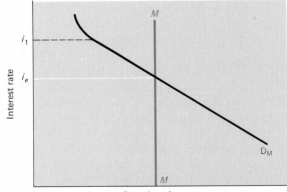

To reiterate, the price dimension of discount policy—the discount rate—determines the quantity of borrowing demanded from the Fed. The Fed then determines the quantity supplied as part of the quantity dimension of discount policy. Only when the quantity demanded is equal to the quantity supplied will a zero change in discount policy be appropriate. However, if at a given discount rate the quantity of borrowing demanded exceeds the quantity of loans the Fed is willing to supply, a shortage will exist. The Fed will then have to ration or even refuse to lend to some depository institutions. Thus, the quantity dimension of discount policy may have to include rationing or outright refusal.[1]

The Effect of Borrowing from and Repaying the Fed on Bank Reserves   The bank reserve equation in Chapter 13 indicates that bank reserves can change if depository institutions increase or decrease their borrowing from the Fed, if other items in the equation remain constant. In this section we show how this is done, using T-accounts.

When a bank borrows from the Fed it borrows reserves; a bank usually borrows to make up for reserve deficiencies, not to obtain excess reserves. As a consequence (and unlike the other cases in which a depository institution obtains more reserves), a bank borrows reserves to finance an expansion that has *already* taken place.

In order to accommodate loan demands and to maximize total profits, banks normally make loans with the expectation that they will soon acquire funds from new deposits or from borrowing in the money market. When the bank makes a loan with such an expectation, it creates demand deposits liabilities *but not reserves*. In the absence of excess reserves, insufficient reserves will exist to meet reserve requirements on the newly extended loans. Similarly, *individual* banks may incur reserve deficiencies via unexpected withdrawals and corresponding losses of reserves when the checks are cleared.[2] Under these circumstances, a bank may borrow reserves temporarily from its reserve bank.

Suppose that the Bowling Green Bank makes a $100 loan to one of its customers but discovers that its reserves are not sufficient to cover the newly extended loan. For simplicity, assume that the Bowling Green Bank had exactly zero excess reserves when it made the $100 loan. Figure 15-2 shows the results. The Bowling Green Bank receives a $100 liability increase in the form of new deposits. Its assets also rise by $100, in the form of loan IOU's. Its actual reserves are unaffected, but its *required* reserves have risen by $12 (assuming a 12 percent required reserve ratio) and it therefore incurs a $12 reserve deficit.

---

[1]The Fed might employ "moral suasion" and implore depository institutions to ignore the fact that borrowing from it would be profitable; it would state that such borrowing would be adverse to the "common good"—presumably defined as the Fed's achieving one or another of its many goals. To date, moral suasion has not been a notable success.

[2]Of course, other banks will receive these deposits and have their reserve accounts credited when the checks clear.

Bowling Green Bank

Assets		Liabilities	
Loans	+$100	Deposits	$100
Reserves (no change)			
(Required, +$12; deficit, $12)			

FIGURE 15-2 The Bowling Green Bank makes a $100 loan when it has zero excess reserves. Assuming a 12% reserve requirement, it now has a reserve deficit; it has $12 in negative reserves.

The Bowling Green Bank may temporarily borrow $12 from its Federal Reserve bank, which extends a loan by crediting the Bowling Green Bank's reserve account (a new $12 liability to the Federal Reserve bank) and crediting its own assets with a $12 increase in "discounts and advances." The Bowling Green Bank gains a $12 asset in the form of reserves and receives a corresponding liability "borrowings from Federal Reserve bank." Figure 15-3 indicates how a $12 loan from the Federal Reserve bank to the Bowling Green Bank appears in T-accounts. Note that *no further expansion can take place on the new reserves* because they are all needed by the Bowling Green Bank to cover its newly created loan shown in the previous figure.

In order to repay its $12 loan from its Federal Reserve bank, the Bowling Green Bank must gain reserves through either deposit growth or by selling assets. Figure 15-4 indicates what happens to the Bowling Green Bank's balance sheet when it sells securities. Assume that the Bowling Green Bank sells $12 worth of assets to Mrs. Proctor, who pays for them by check. The $12 check is sent to the Federal Reserve bank for clearing, and the Fed credits the bank's reserve account accordingly. Figure 15-4 shows the changes in the Bowling Green Bank's balance sheet. When the bank changes asset forms, its assets rise by $12 in the form of reserves with the Federal Reserve bank, and its assets fall by $12 because it sold the security to Mrs. Proctor.

Now that the Bowling Green Bank has increased its reserves it is in a position to repay its loan from the Fed. It does so by authorizing a debit to its reserve account at the Federal Reserve bank. The Bowling Green Bank

FIGURE 15-3 In order to cover its reserve deficit, the Bowling Green Bank borrows from a Federal Reserve bank. The Bowling Green Bank's assets and liabilities rise by the amount of the borrowing ($12 here). The bank is now exactly meeting its reserve requirements and no further expansion can take place.

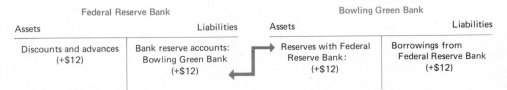

Bowling Green Bank

Assets		Liabilities
Securities	−$12	
Reserves with Federal Reserve Bank	+$12	

FIGURE 15-4   The Bowling Green Bank increases its reserves by selling $12 worth of securities to Mrs. Proctor. The bank's assets have changed merely in form; its liabilities are unaffected.

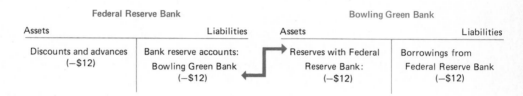

FIGURE 15-5   This figure shows how the balance sheets of the Federal Reserve bank and the Bowling Green Bank change when the Bowling Green Bank repays the $12 that it borrowed from its Federal Reserve bank.

thereby reduces its assets (reserves with the Federal Reserve bank) and its liabilities (borrowings from the Federal Reserve bank) by $12. The Federal Reserve bank, in turn, also reduces its assets—discounts and advances—by $12 and reduces its liabilities—reserves owed to the Bowling Green Bank resulting from the clearing of Mrs. Proctor's check—by $12. Figure 15-5 shows how Bowling Green Bank's repayment of the $12 it borrowed from its Federal Reserve bank changes the balance sheet of both institutions.

A SHORT HISTORY OF DISCOUNT POLICY

Discounting was the main instrument of monetary control in Great Britain during the nineteenth century. In the United States, however, this tool was not available until the Federal Reserve System was established in 1913. Until that time, the money supply was determined by the availability of specie (gold or silver) and national bank note issues (which were secured by U.S. Treasury securities deposited with the comptroller of the currency). No mechanism existed to change systematically the availability of credit and the money supply in response to economic conditions.

In the early 1900s, the need to remedy that situation was recognized. It was hoped that some system of monetary control could be developed to prevent the periodic monetary panics that had plagued this country throughout the nineteenth century and the early part of the twentieth century. It was expected that such a system of monetary control would provide sufficient liquidity to service the "needs of trade" *and* to establish an institution that would act as a "lender of last resort" in emergencies. The institution acting as a **lender of last resort** provided that a federal government agency would be available to lend funds to banks that could not obtain funds from any of the conventional private sources.

At that time, the commercial loan theory (discussed in Chapter 9) dominated the thinking about central banking. Recall that the commercial loan theory was a theory of how the asset side of commercial bank balance sheets should look. Commercial banks were to make short-term, self-liquidating loans that served the needs of production. The principal liabilities of commercial banks were deposits that were payable on demand; therefore, these liabilities were short-term. It seemed prudent for bankers to match short-term liabilities with short-term assets in order to avoid liquidity problems.

From this reasoning, it followed that a central bank should lend to commercial banks only on the collateral of such short-term, self-liquidating debt. In order to qualify as a borrower from the central bank, the commercial bank must have collateral (obtained from the original borrower) indicating that short-term, self-liquidating productive loans were made. Unfortunately, this system calls for a money supply that expands and contracts with the business cycle. As production expands, businesses require more funds to finance their activities; they obtain loans from commercial banks. In turn, if a commercial bank needs more funds, it can borrow them from the central bank. Thus, as output expands, the money supply expands and the needs of trade are served.

When production falls, the need for borrowing falls and banks reduce their lending or do not renew maturing loans. Consequently, few commercial banks require additional funds; they do not borrow from the central bank. Thus, a declining output is matched by a reduced money supply.

It was believed that such a system would provide ample (but not too much) liquidity. Monetary policy is not discretionary; that is, control of the money supply is not determined by the actions of the central bank. Rather, the central bank "policy" is initiated by the borrower, not by the central bank itself. This is a **pro-cyclical** monetary policy. Under such a central banking system, the money supply will expand in boom periods and contract in recessions; thus it pushes the economy in a direction in which it is already heading. Those who believe that changes in the money supply exert independent and significant effects on output and employment consider such a monetary system inappropriate.

Another flaw in the commercial loan theory as applied to central banking is that changes in central-bank lending lead to *multiple* changes in the money supply (see Chapter 8). This means that the pro-cyclical effects of increases and decreases in commercial bank borrowing from the central bank are expanded; and deposit creation in the second, third, and following rounds may well appear in depository institutions over which the central bank has little or no control. These institutions may well feel free to make long-term, non-self-liquidating loans and loans considered to be "unproductive," such as consumer loans or real estate loans. In short, a commercial loan theory that asks a central bank to control the money supply by controlling the kinds of loans that banks extend gives the central bank no control over the money supply *or* over the kinds of loans extended by the banks!

Unfortunately, the Federal Reserve Act of 1913 was greatly influenced by the commercial loan theory. Basically, the only monetary control tool provided by that act was discount policy. Open-market operations were unknown and did not come into use until the 1920s. Reserve requirements, moreover, were set by Congress; and it wasn't until the 1930s that the Fed was empowered to change reserve requirements within congressionally defined limits.

Because of the influence of the commercial loan theory, the Federal Reserve Act specified that (regardless of the financial condition of the member bank) only certain kinds of collateral were eligible for discount. This was clearly inconsistent with the Fed's role as a lender of last resort.

Discount Policy during the 1920s   In the 1920s, the Board of Governors of the Federal Reserve System indicated a preference for setting the discount rate *higher* than the rates on short-term government securities and banker's acceptances. The implication was that the Fed wanted to impose a penalty on member banks that borrowed from it. In practice, however, the 1921 to 1929 period was characterized as one in which the discount rate was set below even that of the **call-money** market rate, a virtually riskless rate of return because of the creditworthiness of the borrower and the very short period of the loan. Call money, or call loans, were typically made on the stock shares of reputable corporations. The shares were lent for very short periods and (theoretically) were repayable on "call"—or whenever demanded back by the lender.

It was profitable during these years for member banks to borrow continuously from the Fed. In fact, after World War I, member bank borrowings were greater than their unborrowed reserve balances. In its annual report in 1928, the Federal Reserve Board indicated that "continuous indebtedness at the reserve banks, except under unusual circumstances, is an abuse of reserve bank facilities." Even earlier, in its 1925 report, the Board had indicated that "the proper occasion for borrowing at the reserve bank is for the purpose of meeting temporary and seasonal needs." The Fed was attempting to set the tone for its discount policy, in terms of the price dimension and the quantity dimension, by its words rather than its act. The discount rate was to be set below other short-term rates, but the resulting shortage of funds available from the Fed at this attractive discount rate was *not* going to be met in the future by increased Fed lending. The Fed's contention that use of the discount window was a privilege and not a right had become a cliché even at this early date. (In practice, however, during this period the Fed permitted continuous borrowing.)

Discount Policy since the 1930s   Prior to the 1930s the Fed merely *talked* about disallowing continuous borrowing, but during the Great Depression and World War II the Fed, by rationing its lending, *in fact* allowed very little borrowing.

The policy of setting a relatively low discount rate and discouraging member bank borrowing has had a major implication: Open-market operations replaced discount policies as the Fed's most important monetary tool. In principle, the Fed can conduct monetary policy by raising and lowering the discount rate, which has the effect of discouraging or encouraging bank borrowing. In turn, changes in the amount of bank borrowing from the Fed will affect bank reserves, and ultimately this will change the money supply. If the Fed insists on relegating a small role to the discount policy tool, however, it must then opt for another tool to conduct its monetary policy. In such a way, the road was paved for the rise of open-market operations, discussed in the next chapter.

Remember that the Federal Reserve Act contained a discount policy that was to provide sufficient reserves and liquidity to the banking system, and to allow the Fed to act as a lender of last resort. What evolved, however, was a discount policy with much more modest objectives. In general, the Fed attempted to restrict member bank borrowing to a small percentage of member bank reserves by keeping the discount rate close to other short-term interest rates and by requiring member banks to reduce their borrowing when borrowing exceeded certain Fed (formal or informal) guidelines.

In 1955, the Fed revised its Regulation A, which defines the procedures and terms for extending loans to member banks. Between then and 1979, discounts and advances averaged only 2 to 4 percent of member bank reserves and were 3 percent or more in only eight years.

In 1973, the Fed broadened its lending policies by adding a seasonal borrowing privilege directed to the seasonal reserve needs of the 2,000 small member banks that had less than $50 million in total deposits. These small depository institutions generally lack reliable access to national money markets. Financial institutions eligible for seasonal borrowing are expected to provide part of their own seasonal needs—up to 5 percent of their average total deposits in the preceding calendar year. Additional seasonal needs can be met by borrowing from the Fed, for up to ninety days.

The 1980 Depository Institutions Deregulation and Monetary Control Act extended borrowing privileges to nonmember banks and to thrift institutions having transactions accounts. Today, the Federal Reserve Act has been amended to permit lending on any collateral. But if the collateral is not government securities or other eligible collateral, as defined by the amended Regulation A, then the discount rate will be one-half of 1 percent higher than the basic discount rate. The Fed still insists that continuous borrowing in a noncrisis situation is "a privilege and not a right."[3]

Currently, there are three categories of borrowing from the Fed:

1 The basic borrowing privilege, which is routine and can be transacted by telephone. A borrower can borrow up to a specific percentage of its reserve requirements.[4] Such borrowing is for a very short period of time, however.

---

[3]In 1977, as rumor had it, the Fed reprimanded several large New York banks for borrowing from the Fed at $5\frac{3}{4}$ percent and relending at $6\frac{1}{2}$ percent in the federal funds market.

[4]The percentage allowable is higher for smaller institutions.

2 Seasonal borrowing privileges. Smaller- and medium-sized banks in resort or agricultural areas that experience heavy seasonal changes in deposits or loan demands can borrow, if they arrange to do so in advance.

3 Other adjustment credits with priority for large and longer-term lending to meet such emergencies as a natural disaster or a financial panic.

DISCOUNT RATE (PRICE) POLICY REVISITED

It has been noted that a change in the discount rate can directly affect short-term interest rates and depository institution reserves, and can indirectly affect lending and the money supply.

The Demonstration Effect   Another possible effect of a change in the discount rate is referred to as the **demonstration effect.** This means that by changing the discount rate the Fed can signal its intentions and the financial community will react accordingly. Unfortunately, it is not clear what "reacting accordingly" entails. A Fed increase in the discount rate could be interpreted as either (1) the intent of the Fed to tighten monetary policy, or (2) an admission by the Fed that it is unable to contain inflation and that it is keeping the discount rate in line with increases in other short-term rates. An act which can be interpreted in two entirely different ways can hardly be useful as a "demonstration effect" tool. Moreover, it would appear that the Fed could demonstrate its intentions by using its other tools or by simply stating its intentions without using any of its tools. Because a change in the discount rate will be interpreted in at least two different (and contradictory) ways, any demonstration effect is likely to be, on net, quite small.

A Sluggish Discount Rate Policy   When the Fed changes the discount rate, it is usually criticized. If it raises the discount rate, the press and politicians invariably interpret this as a tight money policy; and a tight money policy is usually quite unpopular. If the Fed lowers the discount rate, foreign bankers view the move as an attempt to lower the price of the dollar on foreign exchange markets and to give the United States a competitive advantage in foreign trade. After all, when interest rates fall in the United States relative to the rest of the world, capital flows out of the United States, reducing the demand for dollars from foreigners. This will cause a reduction in the price of dollars expressed in terms of other currencies and cause other countries' citizens to view U.S. purchases as "better deals," and American exporters find that they now have a competitive advantage in world markets for goods. We elaborate on all this in Chapter 29.

It is not surprising, therefore, that for the most part the discount rate has been sluggish in response to changes in economic conditions. The Fed in the past has not wanted to "rock the boat."

During boom times, interest rates normally rise along with most other prices. If the Fed does not raise the discount rate, its "price" for borrowed reserves will be relatively lower than other short-term rates. The Fed, therefore, will be lending at precisely the time a policy to counter inflation (**countercyclical policy**) calls for a restrictive monetary stance. At best, a lagging, or sluggish, discount rate change interferes with monetary policy; at worst, it is destabilizing. Nonetheless, it is probably safe to say that most economists do not worry about this problem because the Fed does not have to lend a specified quantity at the discount window. And even if it does lend, such lending can be offset by open-market sales of T-bills.

Changes in the Discount Rate   The board of directors of each Federal Reserve bank is required either to reestablish or to change the current discount rate every fourteen days. The recommended change (usually it's a nonchange) is reported to the Board of Governors, who may either approve or veto it. Consider the following data on discount rate changes: From January 1, 1960, to January 1, 1970, the New York Fed changed its discount rate thirteen times.

FIGURE 15-6   Member Bank Borrowings and Short-Term Interest Rate Differential. (*Source:* R. Alton Gilbert, "Benefits of Borrowing from the Federal Reserve When the Discount Rate Is Below Market Interest Rates," *Review,* Federal Reserve Bank of St. Louis, vol. 61, no. 3, March 1979, p. 27.)

From January 1, 1970, to January 1, 1980, the New York Fed changed it thirty-six times.[5]

This increase in the frequency of discount rate changes did not, however, reflect a more aggressive use of discount policy. Close examination reveals that these changes in the discount rate *followed* changes in the federal funds rate. Figure 15-6 indicates that member bank borrowing is indeed responsive to *relative changes* in the discount rate. Despite the fact that the Fed allegedly disallows borrowing for profit, member borrowings are closely and positively related to the difference between the federal funds rate and the discount rate. As this difference rises, the discount rate falls relatively and member banks react predictably: They borrow more from the Fed. This indicates that in practice it is difficult to allow borrowing only for specific needs. Depository institutions apparently "need" to borrow more when it is more profitable to do so.

In actuality, the observed changes in the discount rate that have followed changes in the federal funds rates represent passive actions on the part of the Fed. The Fed has attempted to keep the relative discount rate constant.

QUANTITATIVE DISCOUNT POLICY REVISITED

As noted earlier, since the 1930s the Fed has been reluctant to lend continuously to a given institution. Yet it does lend, and its lending policy is not without its critics. From one point of view, this policy of lending to depository institutions undoes with the left hand what other Fed policies have done with the right hand. Restrictive monetary policy, for example, can be offset by Fed lending to depository institutions that "need" the funds to meet their reserve requirements. Lending by the Fed can be used to avoid intentional tight open-market policy. From another point of view, depository institution borrowing from the Fed is a safety valve. If the Fed has been too restrictive and has created a severe shortage of reserves, discounting offers a short-term solution; it allows sufficient time for depository institutions to meet reserve requirements.

In recent years, the Fed has taken a more aggressive role as a lender of last resort to specific institutions facing emergencies. Two dramatic examples are the Penn Central Railroad and the Franklin National Bank.

The Case of Penn Central In 1970, the Penn Central Railroad went bankrupt when it defaulted on its outstanding commercial paper (IOUs). This action led to serious repercussions in the commercial-paper market, and other firms had trouble selling their commercial paper. These firms, in turn, sought bank loans and created an increase in the demand for funds. In order to prevent a sharp rise

---

[5]Although these data are reported for the New York Fed, the discount rate for the various Federal Reserve banks may, in fact, vary. In actuality, under virtually all circumstances, the discount rates at all Federal Reserve district banks are the same.

in interest rates for commercial paper, the Fed stepped in and lent funds to the banks involved by allowing them special borrowing privileges.

The Case of Franklin National Bank In 1965 and again in 1970, the Fed recognized that Franklin National Bank, an aggressive Long Island, New York, bank that speculated in the foreign exchange market, was a problem bank. Then in the last three months of 1974, Franklin National lost $30 million in foreign exchange transactions (most of these transactions were not authorized by regulatory agencies and violated the limits set by the bank itself). When word leaked about Franklin National Bank's financial condition, the bank found it difficult to obtain short-term funds. For example, it was unable to borrow reserves in the federal funds market. In effect, the creditors or potential creditors of Franklin National were causing a "run" on this bank. In the past, a typical run on a bank was done by household depositors; now it was being led by depository institutions. In any event, the Fed wanted to prevent an international incident, as well as chaotic conditions that would provoke depositors of Franklin National to withdraw their funds. The Fed began lending Franklin National reserves at a bargain rate; it lent more than $1.5 billion at a rate of 7.5 percent. This was a bargain considering Franklin National's credit rating and the fact that during the lending period, the federal funds rate was between 10.5 percent and 12.9 percent. In the meantime, the Fed arranged for this bank to be merged with the European-American Bank and Trust, a New York

Franklin National Bank. A large New York bank that was "bailed out" by the Fed. In 1974 the Fed "married" Franklin National to the European-American Bank & Trust Company. *(Courtesy of United Press International.)*

state-chartered bank owned by an association of European banks. The forced merger came about on October 8, 1974. In effect, the Franklin National Bank failed, but the failure was covered up by this "marriage."

The Fed Regains Its Role of Lender of Last Resort   The Fed's actions during the Penn Central and Franklin National crises did much to restore confidence in it as a lender of last resort. Some critics maintain that *too much* confidence is now placed in the Fed. Some economists believe that if a national bank can rest secure in the knowledge that the Fed will bail it out, it will try to increase profits by increasing the riskiness (and rate of return) of its asset portfolio. If this is true, an increased Fed role as a lender of last resort may lead paradoxically to a higher rate of bank failures.

CURRENT CONTROVERSY

What Should the Discount Rate Be?

The Fed insists that depository institutions are to use the "discount window" (borrow from the Fed) only for need, not for profit. As Figure 15-6 showed, depository institutions (previously only member banks) apparently "need" to borrow from the Fed more often when the discount rate is significantly lower than the federal funds rate. That is, depository institutions seem to need to borrow more from the Fed when it is profitable to borrow.

One student of discount rate policy has asked: Who benefits when the Fed sets the discount rate below other comparable risk short-term interest rates?*

In general, the benefit is defined as the interest expense avoided by borrowing institutions when the discount rate is below interest rates on alternative competitive sources of funds. In this case, the benefit is the interest expense saved by borrowing reserves at the discount rate instead of borrowing the same amount at the federal funds rate. We can calculate the ratio of this interest saved to the average reserve balances held at the Fed by each institution. The higher this ratio, the greater the benefit.

R. Alton Gilbert used a statistical analysis of these benefits to come to the following conclusions:

1   Because most member banks had never borrowed, the benefits were concentrated in a small percentage of member banks.

2   Because the percentage of member banks that borrow was higher for large banks than for small banks, in general large banks have benefited more than small banks have.

3   The relatively small banks that *did* borrow benefited as much or more than the large banks did.

Should the capricious nature of the benefits of discount rate policy be allowed to continue? Many critics say no. They argue that the discount rate should be a penalty rate. That is, they argue that the discount rate should be set at two percentage points above the federal funds rate so that when depository institutions go to the discount window, they are in fact punished for having to do so. After all, borrowing from the Federal Reserve System should be to meet an emergency and not to make a profit. If the discount rate were routinely set at two percentage points above the federal funds rate, there would be no question about the use of such borrowed reserves. Also, there would no longer be a need for a discount rate policy. One aspect of Federal Reserve policy could be eliminated completely.

*See R. Alton Gilbert, "Benefits of Borrowing from the Federal Reserve When the Discount Rate Is Below Market Interest Rates," *Review,* Federal Reserve Bank of St. Louis, March 1969, vol. 61, no. 3, pp. 25–32.

CHAPTER SUMMARY

1 The Fed lends to depository institutions by a process called discounting. In principle, discounting can be an important monetary policy tool; in England it is.

2 Discount policy refers to the terms and conditions under which the Fed lends to depository institutions. Such policy has a price dimension (the discount rate) and a quantity dimension (the amount of lending that the Fed chooses to do).

3 If the Fed were prepared to lend unlimited quantities at any given discount rate, it could directly control short-term interest rates. It could do so by setting the discount rate below market interest rates and lending unlimited reserves to depository institutions. To do so, however, the Fed would be forced to give up its control over the money supply; the money supply would be determined by the willingness of depository institutions to borrow from the Fed and to make loans.

4 The real-bills doctrine is a theory that maintains that by controlling the *types* of loans that depository institutions make, it is possible to adjust the money supply automatically to the needs of trade. The real-bills doctrine predicts that a central bank can control the money supply by controlling the kinds of loans that depository institutions extend. In practice, such a policy leaves the central bank with control over neither the money supply nor the kinds of loans that are made.

5 The practice of setting the discount rate below the market rate of interest and discouraging member banks from borrowing helped to eliminate discounting as a major policy tool. It was replaced by open-market operations as the Fed's primary instrument of monetary control. To this day the Fed still insists that continuous borrowing from it in a noncrisis situation is a privilege and not a right.

6 Currently there are three categories of borrowing from the Fed: (a) the basic borrowing privilege, which is routine but short-term; (b) seasonal borrowing privileges for smaller- and medium-sized banks that reside in resort or farm areas; and (c) emergency borrowing in case of natural disasters or financial panics.

7 In practice, changes in the discount rate have lagged behind changes in market interest rates. In principle, this can interfere with monetary policy or even be destabilizing.

8 Empirical evidence shows that in the past, member banks have indeed used the discount window more frequently when the discount rate has been significantly lower than the T-bill rate, and less frequently when the spread between the two rates has been insignificant. This indicates that member banks have felt a stronger "need" to borrow from the Fed when it was profitable to do so. In general, the benefits of the Fed policy of setting the discount rate below market interest rates accrue to those who do in fact borrow more often from the Fed. In practice, it is usually the larger depository institutions that borrow from the Fed most often.

9 In the 1970s, the Fed bailed out the Penn Central Railroad and the Franklin National Bank; both actions did much to restore confidence in the Fed as a lender of last resort.

GLOSSARY

Advance A promissory note signed by an official of a depository institution; the depository institution uses U.S. government securities as collateral to borrow from the Fed.

Countercyclical policies: Policies that push the economy in a direction away from the direction in which it is headed.

Demonstration effect: The effect on economic activity of changes in, say, the discount rate that results when the community interprets the changes as an indication of a change in monetary policy.

Discount policy: The terms and conditions under which the Fed lends to depository institutions.

Lender of last resort: A government institution that agrees to provide funds to depository institutions that cannot obtain funds from more traditional sources.

Pro-cyclical activities: Activities that push an economy further in the direction in which it is already heading.

PROBLEMS

15-1 Suppose that bank A makes a $1,000 loan when it has zero excess reserves; it must satisfy a 12 percent reserve requirement. What happens to bank A's

a Liabilities?

b Actual reserves?

c Required reserves?

d Reserve position (excess or deficit)?

15-2 Continuing problem 15-1, suppose that bank A sells $120 of securities to one of its customers in order to pay back its Federal Reserve bank. Immediately after it sells $120 of securities, what happens to bank A's

a Liabilities?

b Assets?

SELECTED REFERENCES

Gilbert, Alton R., "Benefits of Borrowing from the Federal Reserve when the Discount Rate Is Below Market Interest Rates," *Review,* Federal Reserve Bank of St. Louis, March 1979, pp. 25–32.

Goodfriend, Marvin, and Monica Hargraves, "A Historical Assessment of the Rationales and Functions of Reserve Requirements," *Economic Review,* Federal Reserve Bank of Richmond, March–April 1983, pp. 3–21.

Humphrey, Thomas M., "The Classical Concept of the Lender of Last Resort," *Economic Review,* Federal Reserve Bank of Richmond, January–February 1975.

Nichols, Dorothy M., *Modern Money Mechanics: A Workbook on Deposits, Currency, and Bank Reserves* (Federal Reserve Bank of Chicago, 1961; revised in 1968, 1971, 1975, and 1982).

Polakoft, Murray E., "Federal Reserve Discount Policy and Its Critics," in Deane Carson (ed.), *Banking and Monetary Studies* (Homewood, Ill.: Irwin, 1963).

Smith, Warren L., "The Discount Rate as a Credit Control Weapon," *Journal of Political Economy,* April 1958.

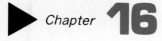
Open-Market Operations

The preceding two chapters examined required reserves and discounting. Those chapters indicated that monetary policy can be conducted by changing either the reserve ratio or the discount rate. The third monetary tool, and the one that has become the most important, is open-market operations (OMO).

Open-market operations are defined as the Fed's purchase and sale of U.S. government securities. United States government securities were defined in Chapter 7 as Treasury bills, Treasury notes, and Treasury bonds. Actually, OMO are usually conducted by the purchase and sale of T-bills. Additionally, OMO involve the purchase and sale of federal agency securities, such as those issued by the Federal National Mortgage Association (so-called Fannie Mae) and, in minor amounts, banker's acceptances.

THREE DIRECT EFFECTS OF OPEN-MARKET OPERATIONS

When the Fed purchases or sells securities on the open market, the economy is affected in three *direct* ways:

1 Depository-institution reserves change.
2 The price (and, therefore, yield) of securities changes.
3 Economywide expectations change.

Changes in Reserves Chapter 8 pointed out how Fed purchases of T-bills from a depository institution change that depository-institution's reserves. Briefly, if the Fed purchases $1 million worth of T-bills from a depository institution, the Fed eventually pays for them by increasing the reserve account of that institution. That means that the depository institution changes its asset portfolio's structure. It now has $1 million less in T-bills and $1 million more in reserve deposits at the Fed. The Fed has a $1-million increase in its assets—the T-bill—and in its liabilities—in deposit obligations to the selling depository institution.

A depository-institution's reserves also increase if the Fed purchases the $1 million T-bill from the private sector. Thus, whenever the Fed purchases U.S. government securities, depository-institution reserves increase by exactly the amount of the purchase. Furthermore, other things being constant, the money supply will expand by some multiple of the original Fed purchase. This increase in the money supply will, ultimately, lead to an increase in the level of economic activity.

Complementary reasoning indicates that the sale of a T-bill by the Fed to a depository institution or to the nonbanking public decreases overall depository-institution reserves and normally leads to a multiple contraction in the money supply. This contraction in the money supply eventually will lead to a reduction in economic activity.

Interest-Rate Changes As indicated in Chapter 6, as the price of a bill or bond changes, so, too, does its yield. An increase in the purchase of bonds will cause bond prices to rise, which amounts to a decrease in bond yields. A decrease in bond purchases causes bond prices to fall and bond yields to rise.

Because the Fed is a large buyer/seller relative to all other buyers/sellers of U.S. Government securities, the Fed can (usually) affect directly the price of a bill or bond. It follows that the Fed can also affect interest rates. In principle, the Fed can change short-, medium-, or long-term interest rates by buying or selling securities aggressively in any of these markets. To maintain a given price (and therefore interest rate) for a bill, all the Fed need do is to be prepared to buy or to sell as much as the rest of the traders care to sell or to buy at that "going" security price (interest rate).

Change in Expectations A "demonstration effect" exists for OMO, as well as for the other monetary tools. "Fed watchers"[1] monitor OMO and make their predictions about the future effects of OMO on such economic variables as interest rates and inflation—and on their own lives. Unfortunately, no general agreement exists among economists as to how expectations change specifically when specific OMO changes occur. For example, an increase in Fed purchases of securities can be interpreted as an expansionary monetary policy that will cause lower interest rates, increased business production and investment, and increased consumer spending. On the other hand, expansionary monetary policy might induce expectations of still higher future increases in the money supply and the anticipation of inflation. The expectation of higher rates of inflation will encourage money lenders to place an inflationary premium on interest rates; nominal interest rates will rise. Moreover, an expectation of increased inflation may well discourage business investment and consumer spending.

In short, changes in OMO will probably lead to expectational changes, but specific expectational changes are not easy to predict.

OMO, Interest Rates, and the Money Supply Chapter 15 indicated that the Fed's discount-rate policy enables it to control either the short-term interest rate or the money supply; it cannot do both. In order to realize its short-term interest-rate target, the Fed cannot independently alter the money supply; and, in order to achieve its money-supply growth-rate target, the Fed cannot control the interest rate.

It turns out that, even though OMO are pursued on the Fed's initiative (unlike depository-institution borrowing), OMO present the same dilemma to the Fed. The Fed can "peg" a security price (interest rate) by being prepared to buy or to sell an unlimited quantity of the security at that price. Suppose that the "natural" rate of interest, or the market-determined rate of interest,

---

[1]Fed watchers include stock market analysts, brokerage house employees, general investors, corporate treasurers, and a host of other individuals (including university professors) who are concerned about the future course of interest rates, credit availability, and inflation.

is 7 percent.[2] If the Fed wants the short-term rate to be 5 percent, it must be prepared to buy as many T-bills as necessary to drive the price of the bills upward until their price is consistent with the 5 percent interest rate. Presumably, the Fed can accomplish this goal. By doing so, however, it will increase depository-institution reserves and it *must* accept an increase in the money supply.

Complementary reasoning indicates that if the Fed wishes to peg short-term interest rates *above* the market-determined rate, it must be prepared to sell a large enough quantity of T-bills to drive the price of bills far enough down to raise the interest rate to the desired level. Unfortunately, the Fed *must* accept an overall decrease in reserves and a smaller money supply when it uses this policy. The conclusion is that OMO do not permit the Fed to peg an interest rate *and* to peg the growth of the money supply at a rate that is inconsistent with the pegged interest rate.

Similarly, the Fed can use OMO to change the money supply in desired directions, but by doing so it must allow the interest rate to "go where it will go." If the Fed increases the money supply by purchasing T-bills on the open market, it will directly increase the price of T-bills and lower their yield. Banking reserves also will increase as a direct result of increased OMO purchases. If banks now have excess reserves, they will increase their lending; increased lending, given the demand for household and business loans, will cause interest rates to fall as banks compete for borrowers. Similarly, if the Fed sells T-bills on the open market, the prices of T-bills will fall and their yields will rise. Fed sales of T-bills will also decrease depository-institution reserves and decrease the amount of funds available for lending. This will put an upward pressure on interest rates as borrowers compete for scarcer loanable funds.

Interest-Rate Interaction via Portfolio Adjustments   When the Fed affects OMO, it directly affects the price of T-bills and the interest rate on T-bills. This will lead to changes in other short-term interest rates. For example, suppose that the Fed sells a large quantity of T-bills, the effect of which is to cause interest rates on T-bills to rise, as T-bill prices fall. Other things constant, interest rates now are relatively higher on T-bills and relatively lower on comparable short-term credit instruments, such as 4- to 6-month prime commercial paper and banker's acceptances. Lenders in the commercial-paper and banker's-acceptances markets will be attracted to the relatively higher yields on T-bills. They will increase their purchases of T-bills and finance these purchases by selling some of their holdings of commercial paper and banker's acceptances; lenders will make portfolio adjustments that reflect the now relatively higher yield on T-bills. The net result of these sales of commercial paper and banker's acceptances is that the yields on these short-term credit instruments will rise as their prices fall. A rise in T-bill rates, therefore, will lead to a rise in the yields

---

[2]The natural rate of interest is an important concept and one that will be developed in more detail in a later chapter. For now, suffice it to say that it is a real rate, is market-determined, and is set by forces *outside* the Fed.

of comparable short-term credit instruments as lenders make portfolio adjustments in order to increase their earnings.

Similarly, if the Fed buys a large quantity of T-bills, their prices will rise and their yields will fall. Lenders will now be attracted to T-bill substitutes; they will sell T-bills and purchase commercial paper and banker's acceptances, which now have relatively higher yields. This lender portfolio adjustment will cause the prices of T-bill substitutes to rise, and the yields on these substitutes will, therefore, fall.

In summary, portfolio adjustments that attempt to increase earnings for lenders will cause short-term interest rates to rise and fall together. When the Fed changes the T-bill rate in conducting OMO, it automatically affects the yields on T-bill substitutes—in the same direction.

THE MECHANICS OF OPEN-MARKET OPERATIONS

Thirteen times a year the Federal Open Market Committee meets in Washington, D.C. Its staff briefs the committee on current economic conditions and future projections in what is referred to as the "chart show." The FOMC then issues a *directive,* which is an instruction to the two managers of the open-market accounts. One manager heads domestic operations; the other heads foreign operations. Both managers are vice presidents of the New York Fed. The New York Fed serves as the agent of the twelve Federal Reserve banks in conducting OMO, and the two managers take their orders from the FOMC.

The FOMC Directive   The **FOMC directive** to the account managers consists of three parts:

1   Part A contains the qualitative statements of the stabilization goals; for example, higher employment, lower inflation, stable growth of real output, and a balance-of-payments improvement.

2   Part B includes the specific target ranges for the next year (from the current quarter to the corresponding quarter one year later). These targets have varied over the years, but usually they are stated in terms of credit conditions, interest rates, or monetary aggregates (the various money-supply measures).

3   Part C lists short-term (two-month) targets that take into account special calendar events (such as Christmas, when currency leakages are unusually large) but are consistent with the goals in part B.

It is important to realize that the FOMC directive does *not* set specific targets for reserves in the system. It is up to the account managers to decide the dollar value of the securities to be bought or sold on the open market in order to achieve the results mandated in the directive. Of course, the discretionary power of the managers is not unlimited. If the FOMC changes its mind or feels that its directives are not being carried out properly, it can issue additional verbal instructions to the account managers before the next meeting of the FOMC. Figure 16-1 is a copy of one page of such a FOMC directive.

Although the directive eventually is made public (currently at the end of thirty days), it is not made public immediately. The reason for keeping the directive secret for three or four weeks is that some people are in a position to act upon this information more rapidly than others and thus can earn profits at the expense of others. Carrying this policy of secrecy to the extreme, the domestic account manager at the New York Fed actually places buy and sell orders simultaneously with different dealers, so that it is not immediately apparent whether the Fed is a net buyer or a net seller. This attitude of secrecy is not without its critics; some feel that in this day of modern electronic communications, the Fed should announce its directive immediately and publicly. It is difficult to understand how immediate disclosure could help some and

FIGURE 16-1   **The Minutes of A Typical FOMC Meeting.**   This is the first page of a policy directive that was issued to the Federal Reserve Bank of New York following the November 16, 1982, FOMC meeting. (*Source:* Board of Governors of the Federal Reserve System, *Federal Reserve Bulletin,* January 1983, pp. 20–21.)

MEETING HELD ON NOVEMBER 16, 1982

1. Domestic Policy Directive

The information reviewed at this meeting suggested that real GNP would change little in the fourth quarter, after increasing at an annual rate of ¾ percent in the third quarter according to preliminary estimates of the Commerce Department. Average prices, as measured by the fixed-weight price index for gross domestic business product, were continuing to rise at a much less rapid pace than in 1981.

The nominal value of retail sales rose 0.6 percent in October, but the level was little higher than in the second and third quarters. Sales increased at automotive outlets and furniture and appliance stores, but edged down at nondurable goods stores. Unit sales of new domestic automobiles fell back to an annual rate of 5.3 million units, after having increased to an annual rate of 6.2 million units in September in response to special promotions aimed at reducing excess stocks of 1982 models.

The index of industrial production declined 0.8 percent in October, a little more than in both August and September, and was about 11½ percent below its recent peak in July 1981. Output of business equipment fell substantially further in October, and as in other recent months, defense and space equipment was the only major category of final products showing strength. Capacity utilization in manufacturing fell 0.8 percentage point to 68.4 percent, the lowest level in the postwar period.

Nonfarm payroll employment fell further in October, declining slightly more than the average over the previous four months. Cutbacks in employment were widespread and were especially marked in durables manufacturing. The unemployment rate rose an additional 0.3 percentage hurt others in any systematic fashion. But, it is easy to see how a policy of secrecy places high premiums on inside information.

Day-to-Day Operations Once the account managers have received their directive, they brief the members of their trading staffs and the action begins. In particular, the domestic account manager contacts the three dozen or so special dealers in government securities who are located in New York City; the securities dealers in turn deal with the public. As a semipublic institution (it is owned by member banks but controlled governmentally), the Fed's activities are under scrutiny; therefore, it strives to sell at the highest price and buy at the lowest price in its open-market operations.

It is often true that no physical paper check is necessary for an open-market transaction. A computer links the district reserve banks to commercial banks, which act as clearing agents for the special dealers in government securities. A given transaction is debited and credited to the reserve accounts of the depository institutions in question; this is often done on the same day as the transaction. The open-market operations of any day last only about a half hour.

A BRIEF HISTORY OF OPEN-MARKET OPERATIONS

The Emergence of Open-Market Operations as a Tool for Monetary Control The Federal Reserve Act of 1913 provided that changes in the discount rate would be the main monetary control tool. Almost immediately after the federal district banks were formed, however, they began purchasing government securities (that earned interest) in the New York money markets, to obtain income. In the early 1920s, an informal committee of Federal Reserve bank officers began to coordinate the actions of the twelve reserve banks. More or less by accident, they discovered that by buying and selling securities in the open market they were able to change bank reserves, overall credit conditions, and the supply of money. Relatively large government deficits (financed by sales of government bonds) during World War I added to the stock of government securities and led to the formation of secondary markets for these securities. (The deficits occurring during and after World War II further increased the quantity of these securities outstanding.) By 1923, the Fed consciously was using OMO to accommodate commerce and trade. But early in the 1930s, the Fed did not buy government securities because those securities weren't usable as collateral for Federal Reserve notes. The Glass-Steagall Act of 1932 permitted the Fed to use government securities as collateral for its Federal Reserve notes, and the problem was solved. Because Treasury securities were eligible for collateral by the Fed, and because they were widely accepted by banks and the public due to their "riskless" nature, a lively market for Treasury securities developed. This market helped to pave the way for the Fed's wide use of OMO to effect monetary policy; OMO were on their way to becoming the primary instrument of monetary control.

In 1935, the FOMC was organized and it has become the most important policy unit in the Fed. From 1935 to 1957, the FOMC limited OMO to bills and other securities maturing in one year or less; but this policy was criticized as being too restrictive. In the early 1960s, the Fed attempted to "twist" the yield curve via **operation twist.** As pointed out in Chapter 6, the so-called normal yield curve is one in which short-term rates are lower than long-term rates. In order to twist this curve, the Fed pursued a policy of generating high short-term rates by selling short-term securities aggressively and generating lower long-term rates by buying long-term securities aggressively. High short-term interest rates at that time seemed necessary to encourage foreigners to invest their dollar earnings in the United States and to reduce America's balance-of-payments deficit. Low long-run interest rates were considered beneficial because they would promote capital investment, economic growth, and full employment in the United States. This "twist" policy was not particularly successful; short-term rates did not rise significantly. Although long-term government security interest rates did fall, mortgages and corporate bond yields did not.

In 1962, the Fed began to buy and sell foreign currencies. Its intention was to stabilize foreign exchange rates with respect to the dollar. The acquisition of foreign currencies in its portfolio allowed the Fed to "support" the dollar on foreign exchange markets by buying U.S. dollars with foreign currency. After 1971, the United States dollar was allowed to "float" and the Fed's activity in this area diminished. In 1983, however, the Fed again began to intervene in the foreign exchange markets in order to help "stabilize" currencies. This issue is discussed in Chapter 29.

Credit Conditions versus Reserves as a Fed Monetary Policy Target FOMC directives have historically been couched in terms of "tighter" or "easier" credit conditions. These terms have proved difficult to define in practice. Credit conditions were supposedly reflected by interest rates, member bank reserves, and overall loans. Until 1966, policy was established around desired levels of free reserves (defined in Chapter 14 as excess reserves minus borrowed reserves) and short-term interest rates. But in 1966 the "proviso clause" was added—monetary policy was to be conducted toward tighter money market conditions (restrictive monetary growth and higher interest rates) *provided* that *bank credit* did not deviate significantly from projections. And then, in 1970, a money-supply measure was added to bank credit as a proviso for the FOMC directive. The Fed wanted to make sure that the growth of the money supply remained within well-defined boundaries.

Since that time, target ranges have been given for the federal funds rate and for various definitions of the money supply. For most of the 1970s the federal-funds-rate target range was very narrow, whereas the target range for the monetary aggregates was quite large. To make matters even more confusing, the Fed announced in 1972 that it was going to use **reserves available to support private deposits (RPDs)** as an operating target. RPDs are obtained by subtracting from total reserves the sum of reserves required against U.S. government deposits and interbank deposits. RPDs can support private, non-bank deposits both for demand deposits and time deposits.

In 1976, the Fed announced that it would abandon RPDs as a monetary target and instead look at the monetary base. Defined in Chapter 14, the base is equal to the total amount of currency that *would be* in circulation if everyone withdrew money from his or her deposits in currency. In other words, the monetary base is equal to currency held by the nonbank public plus the reserves of the depository institutions, either in vault cash or as deposits at the district Federal Reserve banks. In addition to the monetary base, total reserves and nonborrowed reserves were to be targeted. At that time, the Fed did not announce which of these three indicators it preferred.

A significant change occurred in October 1979. The Fed indicated that it would put more emphasis on targeting a narrow rate of growth in the different monetary aggregates rather than concern itself with interest rates and, in particular, the federal funds rate. The target range for federal funds rates was broadened considerably, but the target range for the monetary growth rates was narrowed considerably. Critics of FOMC actions maintain that this was only a change in emphasis and not really a change in targets. History shows that the Fed's ability to keep its rate of growth of the money supply within its target range has been relatively poor.[3]

TYPES OF OPEN-MARKET OPERATIONS

There are two basic types of OMO transactions:

1   Outright purchases or sales
2   Purchases under repurchase agreements (REPOs) and sales under match sale repurchase agreements (reverse REPOs, also known as matched transactions).

Outright Purchases or Sales   Outright purchases or sales are what might be expected—the Fed buys or sells securities in the open market and no strings are attached to the transactions. If the Fed purchases a security, it is not obligated to sell it back at a later date. If the Fed sells a security to a buyer, the buyer is not obligated to resell it to the Fed at a later date.

Repurchase Agreements and Reverse Repurchase Agreements   In a repurchase agreement the Fed buys securities from a dealer and the dealer agrees to repurchase the securities at a specified date and price. In effect, such a trans-

---

[3]Some argue that the reason for the Fed's poor showing between October 1979 and 1984 was that it was using lag reserve accounting. The switch to contemporaneous reserve accounting on February 2, 1984, was supposed to improve the Fed's ability to achieve its monetary aggregate growth rate targets. This issue is discussed in Chapter 27.

action is a loan by the Fed to the dealer; the interest rate is set by auction among the dealers. A Fed purchase under a repurchase agreement by the dealer is referred to as a REPO.

The counterpart to the REPO is the reverse REPO, or match sales-pur-

---

HIGHLIGHT   REPOs Bite the Dust: A Case Study in the Failure of Drysdale

On May 17, 1982, Drysdale Government Securities, Inc., defaulted on $160 million in interest payments owed on $2 billion worth of borrowed government securities. This default threatened the existence of several financial institutions, including the Chase Manhattan Bank, the third largest bank in the country. The ability of a relatively small government securities dealer (capital of $35 million) to imperil significantly the nation's financial stability is due to two recent phenomena:

1 The large and increasing volume of Treasury borrowing ($135 billion in fiscal 1982, absorbing more than 79 percent of the economy's net private saving).

2 The innovation of the financial instrument called the REPO.

Drysdale's "REPO strategy" was an attempt to take advantage of the fact that (before the Drysdale default) accumulated *coupon interest* was paid to the seller of securities *only* when securities were sold outright. REPO sales are temporary sales, and the provider of coupon-bearing securities (the REPO seller) generally was not paid the value of the interest that had accrued since the last coupon payment. Drysdale, therefore, was able to raise a substantial amount of temporary capital (money)—in the form of coupon interest—by *buying* REPOs without paying for the accrued interest, and then selling them outright and obtaining the accrued interest. With high coupon securities, the amount of temporary capital raised could be substantial.

The capital raised in this way was used to finance other forms of trading in the government securities market. Drysdale speculated in this market by "selling short," which involves the current borrowing of securities which the short seller hopes to replace in the future with securities purchased at a lower price. You can earn $50 of profit if you *now* borrow ten shares of securities valued at $200 and replace the ten shares next week if their value falls to $150 in the meantime.

Unfortunately for Drysdale, government bond prices increased in the spring of 1982, reflecting general interest rate reductions. Drysdale then found itself in the position of having to pay back borrowed securities that were worth *more*—not less—than they had been at the time they were borrowed.

The Drysdale collapse led to a widespread review and tightening of credit procedures. Another securities dealer firm, Lombard-Walls, went bankrupt, and the legal status of the REPO was called into question. During Lombard-Walls's bankruptcy proceeding, some of their customers were unable to liquidate holdings obtained from the firm under REPO arrangements; others met delays in getting back securities that had been provided to the firm under REPO arrangements.

REPO activity declined after these two security firm failures. Just before the Drysdale default, there were about $103 billion in REPOs outstanding; during the next five weeks, the volume outstanding fell to $87 billion. REPOs were now perceived as being riskier.

TABLE 16-1 Federal Reserve Open-Market Transactions—1982	
Types of Transactions*	
Outright transactions:	
Gross purchases	19,870
Gross sales	8,369
Redemptions	3,189
Matched transactions:	
Gross purchases	543,804
Gross sales	543,173
Repurchase agreements:	
Gross purchases	149,731
Gross sales	148,286
Total change in system:	
Open market account from 1981†	9,773

*In millions of dollars. Includes U.S. government securities and federal agency obligations and excludes banker's acceptances. $1,285 million net repurchase agreements.
†Total includes banker's acceptances.
Source: Board of Governors of the Federal Reserve System, *Federal Reserve Bulletin.*

chase transaction. In such a transaction, the Fed sells securities to a dealer and also agrees to buy back the securities at a specified price and date. This amounts to a loan to the Fed by the dealer.

REPOs and reverse REPOs are typically very short-term contracts. REPOs are usually conducted for fewer than fifteen days (typically seven days), and reverse REPOs are usually terminated in seven or fewer days. *The duration of REPOs and reverse REPOs indicates that they are used only when the Fed wants to alter depository-institution reserves temporarily.* Table 16-1 shows that REPOs and reverse REPOs are by far the greatest part of the gross volume of Fed open-market transactions. Furthermore, they are becoming an increasingly higher percentage of the gross value of open-market operations.

DEFENSIVE AND DYNAMIC OPEN-MARKET TRANSACTIONS

At first sight, Table 16-1 appears rather startling. The net change of Fed holdings of governmental securities (and to a lesser extent, banker's acceptances) is a very small percentage of the total transactions. In terms of the volume of gross transactions, REPOs and reverse REPOs are about twenty-two times greater than outright purchases or sales of government securities and agency obligations.

In order to understand Table 16-1, it is crucial to distinguish between dynamic and defensive open-market operations. **Dynamic OMO** are designed to *change* the level of depository-institution reserves. Outright purchases or sales of government securities or of agency obligations, which are more or less

HIGHLIGHT   Federal Reserve Data

Every Monday, *The Wall Street Journal* publishes a compilation of important financial indicators in the financial section of the paper in a table labeled Federal Reserve Data. An example is shown here. This table is divided into four sections showing: (1) key assets and liabilities of ten large weekly reporting banks in New York City; (2) changes in member bank reserves and the composition of those changes; (3) money supply (M1) and reserve aggregates; and (4) key interest rates on a week-to-week basis.

Specific entries in this table may be appropriate indicators of future movements in the variables. The level of commercial and industrial loans, for example, is a good indicator of the demand for credit; the borrowings from the Fed category indicate recent changes in the use of the discount privilege and correlate well with the free reserves series also contained in the table.

Although extreme caution should be employed in attempting to assess monetary policy on the basis of weekly movements in money-supply figures and monetary aggregates, an examination of Federal Reserve-data tables over an *extended* period of time does enable one to identify trends and to predict future values.

The data published in this table are released on Friday afternoons by the Fed, and frequently stock- and bond-

Federal Reserve Data

KEY ASSETS AND LIABILITIES OF 10 WEEKLY REPORTING MEMBER BANKS IN NEW YORK CITY
(in millions of dollars)

	July 13, 1983	Change from July 6, 1983
ASSETS:		
Total assets	232,979	− 8,067
Total loans and investments	143,658	− 3,385
Includes:		
Commercial and industrial loans	57,437	+ 55
Domestic	55,784	− 7
Foreign	1,653	+ 62
Acceptances, comm'l paper	1,324	+ 248
Finance company loans	3,859	+ 59
Personal loans	11,810	− 12
Loan loss reserve	2,527	− 9
U.S. Treasury securities	8,265	− 844
Federal agency securities	1,532	+ 5
Municipal issues	11,978	+ 102
Due in one year or less	1,530	− 18
Longer term	10,448	+ 120
LIABILITIES:		
Demand deposits	121,446	− 4,601
Demand deposits adjusted (a)	26,075	− 2,218
Time and savings deposits	73,124	+ 238
Negotiable CDs ($100,000 and up)	22,207	− 149
Borrowings	57,810	− 3,298

a-Excludes government and bank deposits and cash items being collected.

MEMBER BANK RESERVE CHANGES
Changes in weekly averages of reserves and related items during the week and year ended July 20, 1983 were as follows (in millions of dollars)-b

	July 20 1983	Chg fm July 13 1983	wk end July 21 1982
Reserve bank credit:			
U.S. Gov't securities:			
Bought outright	142,841	− 322	+ 9,627
Held under repurch agreemt	2,620	+ 2,620	+ 1,679
Federal agency issues:			
Bought outright	8,880	− 6	− 121
Held under repurch agreemt	156	+ 156	− 155
Acceptances—bought outright			
Held under repurch agreemt	129	+ 129	− 359
Borrowings from Fed	1,233	+ 86	+ 639
Seasonal borrowings	179	+ 35	− 60
Extended credit	460	+ 26	+ 427
Float	1,621	− 1,045	− 367

Other Federal Reserve Assets	8,764	+ 127	− 152
Total Reserve Bank Credit	166,244	+ 1,746	+10,790
Gold Stock	11,131	....	− 18
SDR certificates	4,618	....	+ 743
Treasury currency outstanding	13,786		....
Total	195,779	+ 1,746	+11,515
Currency in circulation	160,707	− 958	+12,791
Treasury cash holdings	526	− 2	+ 102
Treasury dpts with F.R. Bnks	3,309	− 1,189	+ 128
Foreign dpts with F.R. Bnks	262	+ 53	− 16
Other deposits with F.R. Bnks	690	+ 45	+ 127
Other F.R. liabilities & capital	5,313	+ 225	− 136
Total	171,695	− 1,751	+13,669
Reserves			
With F.R. Banks	24,083	+ 3,496	− 2,155
Total inc. cash	39,856	+ 2,139	− 799
Required reserves	39,514	+ 2,269	− 874
Excess reserves	342	− 130	+ 75
Free reserves	−252	− 155	....

b-The figures reflect adjustment for new Federal Reserve rules that impose reserve requirements on most deposit-taking institutions, including non-member commercial banks, mutual savings banks and savings and loan associations.

MONETARY AND RESERVE AGGREGATES
(daily average in billions)

	One week ended:	
	July 13	July 6
Money supply (M1) sa	514.6	514.3
Money supply (M1) nsa	520.4	524.0
	July 20	July 13
Monetary base	185.45	183.86
Total Reserves	42.52	41.05
Nonborrowed Reserves	41.28	39.90
Required Reserves	42.18	40.58
	Four weeks ended:	
	July 13	June 15
Money supply (M1) sa	512.2	510.8

sa-Seasonally adjusted. nsa-Not seasonally adjusted.

KEY INTEREST RATES
(weekly average)

	July 20	July 13
Federal funds	9.43	9.21
Treasury bill (90 day)	9.11	9.10
Commercial paper (dealer, 90 day)	9.30	9.24
Certfs of Deposit (resale, 90 day)	9.55	9.50
Eurodollars (90 days)	10.04	10.05

market movements of some significance are attributed to the money-supply (M1) figure. Most economists would agree that this behavior does not

indicate an appropriate response to such a short-term phenomenon. Indeed, there is some pressure both from within the Fed and from without to

discontinue publication of M1 figures on a weekly basis because of the inappropriate way in which this single weekly number has been used.

---

permanent, will accomplish that end. On the other hand, **defensive OMO** are balancing adjustments intended to *maintain* the current level of total depository-institution reserves. From time to time, the economy encounters foreseen and unforeseen events that automatically and temporarily change total reserves and/or the money supply. In order to keep the economy on an even keel and to maintain the desired level of total reserves, short-term defensive actions are necessary. REPOs and reverse REPOs, because of their short-term nature, are designed to do precisely that. REPOs provide temporary reserves, and reverse REPOs sop up temporary excess reserves. Consider two examples.

At Christmas time, there are enormous currency drains from depository institutions, causing depository-institution reserves to shrink—as Chapter 8 indicated. The Fed counters currency drainage via REPO transactions; the Fed buys securities with the arrangement that it can sell them back after Christmas. The initial Fed purchase creates reserves for the Yuletide season; then, around January 1, the Fed sells back the securities to offset the enormous quantity of currency that the public is redepositing in depository institutions.

Similarly, around April 15, when income-tax-payment time rolls around, the reserve position of depository institutions falls and the money supply falls with it, as taxpayers send checks to the IRS (which is a branch of the U.S. Treasury). The Treasury's account at the Fed is therefore increased by the same amount by which public deposit accounts in depository-institution reserves are decreased. This temporary reduction in the public's total deposits and depository-institution reserves can be, and often is, offset by REPOs.

CURRENT CONTROVERSY

The Thorny Question of Fed Churning

As Table 16-1 indicates, the Fed engages in a large number of open-market operations designed to change the total level of reserves by relatively small amounts. This process is aptly referred to as **churning**. Churning has generated a considerable amount of controversy. Some have complained that the only beneficiaries of churning are three dozen or so special securities dealers that earn enormous brokerage fees.

(Note that when stockbrokers encourage excessive buying and selling of securities in order to increase their own profits, they are subject to prosecution.)

Federal Reserve officials claim that much of the supposed churning is really not churning at all. They contend that temporary transactions and those arranged on behalf of foreign central banks do not constitute churning. In particular, to provide reserves on a temporary basis, the Fed engages in repurchase agreements with dealers. When there is a "need" to *drain* reserves temporarily, the Fed arranges reverse repurchase agreements. Federal Reserve officials believe that such transactions should not be included in the computation of the gross open-market purchases of securities indicated in Table 16-1.*

Officials at the Federal Reserve System maintain that the bulk of System open-market operations are defensive in nature and do no more than accommodate seasonal variations in the demand for currency and deposits. The churning is necessary to accommodate these seasonal variations in currency and deposit demand. The resolution of this controversy is therefore not straightforward. Any type of fixed rate of growth of reserves in the banking system would eliminate the defensive nature of OMO operations. Because seasonal swings in the demand for cash balances are quite large over a one-year period, depository institutions might find themselves with temporary large short-run changes in reserves. For example, if the Fed did not engage in defensive open-market operations, there would be a sharp contraction in the *supply* of deposits each December and a sharp expansion each January, just the opposite of what would happen to the *demand* for cash balances.

---

*See, for example, Fred J. Levin and Ann-Marie Meulendyke, "Monetary Policy: Theory and Practice, A Comment," *Journal of Money, Credit, and Banking,* vol. 14, no. 3, August 1982, pp. 399–403.

CHAPTER SUMMARY

1　Open-market operations (OMO) are the purchase and sale by the Fed of U.S. government securities; in practice, OMO are conducted through Fed purchases and sales of T-bills and federal agency securities.

2　When the Fed conducts OMO, it affects the economy in three ways: depository-institution reserves change, interest rates on securities change, and economywide expectations change.

3　Because the Fed can purchase or sell a relatively large amount of T-bills, it can affect the price of these securities—and therefore it can affect their yields. In particular, when the Fed purchases T-bills aggressively it can increase their prices and thereby lower their yields; aggressive Fed sales of T-bills will lower their prices and increase their yields. In principle, the Fed can change short-, medium-, or long-term interest rates by buying or selling securities aggressively in any of those markets.

4　OMO can also affect the economy by changing expectations about future interest rates. Unfortunately, economists do not agree as to *how* expectations change when OMO change.

5   The Fed can peg a securities price or yield only by being prepared to buy or sell an unlimited quantity of the security to all concerned at the pegged rate. However, if the Fed attempts to peg a securities yield above or below the natural rate, the Fed must surrender control over depository-institution reserves and over the money supply.

6   The FOMC directive to account managers consists of three parts. Part A contains a qualitative stabilization goal; part B includes specific target ranges for credit conditions, interest rates, and monetary aggregates over the next year; part C lists short-term (two-month) targets that take into account special seasonal events. The FOMC directive does not set specific targets for reserves in the banking system. The account managers decide on the specific quantity of securities to be bought and sold in order to comply with the general directive. In practice, the FOMC has considerable control over account managers. Moreover, the FOMC directive is not made public immediately, although the benefits of such a policy are not obvious.

7   In the 1920s, the Fed discovered, more or less by accident, that its purchases or sales in the open market could affect bank reserves, overall credit conditions, and the supply of money. By 1923, the Fed was using OMO consciously to accommodate commerce and trade. The Glass-Steagall Act of 1932 permitted the Fed to use government securities as collateral for Federal Reserve notes, and OMO became the prime instrument of monetary control.

8   In the early 1960s, the Fed experimented with operation twist, a conscious attempt to raise short-term interest rates (by selling short-term securities) and lower long-term interest rates (by buying long-term securities). The operation was not successful. In 1962, the Fed began to buy and sell foreign currencies in the foreign exchange market in order to "support" the dollar, but in 1981 the attempt was abandoned and the dollar was allowed to float to its equilibrium position vis à vis other currencies. In 1983 Fed intervention in the foreign exchange market again became an issue.

9   Until 1966 Fed policy was established around desired levels of free reserves; in 1966 the proviso clause was added. Firmer money conditions were to be pursued, provided that bank credit did not deviate significantly from projections. In 1970, a money-supply measure was added to bank credit as an additional proviso to the FOMC directive. Since then, target ranges have been given for the federal funds rate and for various monetary aggregates. In 1972, the Fed began targeting RPDs but changed to a monetary base target in 1976. During most of the 1970s, the Fed set a very narrow range for the federal funds target and a broad range for the monetary aggregates target. Reflecting a fundamental policy change, in 1979 the Fed narrowed the target growth rates for the monetary aggregates and broadened the range for the federal-funds-rate target. The Fed has not been notably successful in achieving its monetary aggregates targets.

10 There are two basic types of open-market operations: (a) outright purchase or sales, and (b) REPOs and reverse REPOs. Because REPOs and reverse REPOs are very short-term agreements, the Fed uses them only when it wants to alter depository-institution reserves temporarily; REPOs and reverse REPOs are used by the Fed when it engages in defensive OMO. REPOs provide temporary reserves and reverse REPOs sop up temporary excess reserves; defensive OMO are intended to maintain the current level of depository-institution reserves. Dynamic OMO, on the other hand, are intended to *change* the level of depository-institution reserves,

and outright purchases or sales of T-bills by the Fed are best suited for that function.

11 The Fed engages in a large volume of OMO in order to change the total level of reserves by relatively small amounts. This is referred to as Fed churning. The Fed maintains that defensive OMO and actions on behalf of foreign central banks are necessary and therefore should not be considered as churning.

GLOSSARY

Churning: The process of engaging in a large number of offsetting OMO which change the total level of reserves by relatively small amounts.

Defensive OMO: Open-market operations in which REPOs and reverse REPOs are used to maintain the current level of total depository-institution reserves.

Dynamic OMO: Open-market operations in which outright purchases and sales of T-bills are designed to change the level of depository-institution reserves.

FOMC directive: Federal Open Market Committee instructions to account managers that include (1) a qualitative stabilization goal; (2) specific target ranges in terms of credit conditions, interest rates, and monetary aggregates; and (3) two-month targets that take into account special calendar events.

Operation twist: A 1960s Fed attempt to alter the yield curve so that short-term interest rates are relatively high and long-term interest rates are relatively low.

Reserves available to support private deposits (RPDs): Total reserves minus reserves held against U.S. government deposits and interbank deposits; a Fed-targeted statistic during the 1972-to-1976 period.

PROBLEMS

16-1 The Fed sells T-bills to the public. What happens to the balance sheet of

   a The public?

   b The Fed?

   c The depository institution on which a check is drawn by the public?

16-2 The Fed buys T-bills from a depository institution. What happens to

   a The Fed's balance sheet?

   b The depository institution's balance sheet?

   c The money supply?

SELECTED REFERENCES

Levin, Fred J., and Ann-Marie Meulendyke, "Monetary Policy: Theory and Practice, A Comment," *Journal of Money, Credit, and Banking,* vol. 14, August 1982, pp. 399–403.

Meek, Paul, *Open Market Operations* (Federal Reserve Bank of New York, 1969).

Roosa, Robert V., *Federal Reserve Operations in the Money and Government Securities Markets* (Federal Reserve Bank of New York, 1956).

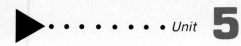

Monetary Theory

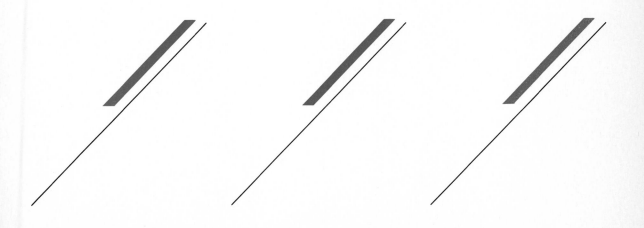

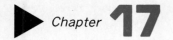

The Classical Model

The evidence indicates that too much money in the economy causes inflation and not enough money causes recession; monetary policy is an attempt to provide just the right amount of money. The optimal amount of money, however, is very difficult to define, as we shall learn throughout the remainder of this text.

A successful monetary policy requires *at least* two things.

1 A theory, or model, of how the economy works. It is important in order to determine what the optimal money supply is, to show how the national levels of income, consumption, investment, and employment—as well as the price level—are determined. It is also crucial to have a model that explains how these economic variables are *interrelated.*

2 A theory that explains how changes in the money supply affect these economic variables.

AN OVERVIEW OF THE NEXT TEN CHAPTERS

The classical model was the first systematic and rigorous attempt to explain the determinants of such important economywide, or aggregate, economic variables as the price level and the national levels of output, income, employment, consumption, saving, and investment. The classical model also attempted to show how these variables were interrelated, and how and where money fit in.

Classical economics covers the time span from the 1770s to the 1930s. Included in the ranks of the classical economists are such intellectual giants as Adam Smith, David Hume, David Ricardo, James and John Stuart Mill, Thomas Malthus, Karl Marx, and A. C. Pigou and other such later "neoclassical" ("neo" means new) economists as Walras, Marshall, and Wicksell. Even Copernicus, the astronomer, contributed to the classical model, and there is strong evidence that Malthus influenced Charles Darwin's thinking about evolution.

The classical model, as presented in this chapter and the next, is a combination of the Cambridge University oral tradition of macroeconomics and a reconstruction by John Maynard Keynes, who will be discussed later.

The conclusion of the classical model was that inherent in capitalism are mechanisms that drive the economy toward full employment; capitalism is a self-regulating economic system. The classical economist recognized the existence of temporary unemployment in the form of frictional unemployment, where people are between full-time jobs, but felt that *eventually* there would be no involuntary unemployment. Widespread unemployment would cause wages to fall, and the surplus of labor would disappear as buyers of labor bought more labor time and sellers of labor offered less time on labor markets. As a consequence, a full-employment output would be *produced.* The classical model also predicted that a full-employment output would be *purchased;* as goods were supplied, the income to purchase the goods would automatically be forthcoming in the form of wages, rents, interest payments, and profits. If people saved "too much"—a surplus of saving—interest rates would fall and this, in turn, would induce households to save less and businesses to invest more. The classical economist summarized these two mechanisms that assumed that a full-employment output would be produced (flexible wage rates) and that a full-employment output would be purchased (flexible interest rates) in the dictum: "Supply creates its own demand." Just by producing goods and services, purchasing power is generated that will be sufficient to purchase those goods.

It is not surprising that such an optimistic outlook left little or no role for governmental intervention in the economy. Chapter 18 indicates why fiscal policy and monetary policy were not advocated by most classical economists. What role did money play in the economy, according to the classical economists? To them, money was merely a medium of exchange; people hold as little money as possible, for as short a period of time as possible, in order to make transactions. The classical economists believed that changes in the money supply were "neutral." Increases in the money supply cause all prices to rise at the same rate; decreases in the money supply cause all prices to fall at the same rate. Because all prices change at the same rate, changes in the money supply leave *relative* prices unaltered. Because consumer-spending and business-spending decisions depend on relative prices, changes in the money supply do not affect real variables such as employment, output, and real (price-level-adjusted) income, real consumption, and real saving. In short, changes in the money supply affect nominal or money variables, but not real variables; money is neutral.

The Great Depression of the 1930s did much to destroy the notion of a self-regulating economy. Prices and wages fell, but so did output and employment; real national income fell by 25 percent during the period of 1929 to 1933, and the unemployment rate was recorded at nearly 25 percent at the depth of the Depression. Economic events have a way of changing economic models, and the Great Depression inspired John Maynard Keynes to launch a revolution in macroeconomic thinking.[1] Keynes ridiculed the notion of a self-regulating economy and stressed that active governmental policies were necessary to assure full employment. In general, Keynes's theory was that "Demand creates its own supply"; Keynes turned the classical dictum upside down. By judicious use of fiscal policy (and, to a lesser extent, monetary policy), the total demand for goods and services (Keynes called it aggregate demand) by households, businesses, and governments could be manipulated to achieve the twin goals of full employment and price stability.

The post-World War II period, especially since the early 1960s, can be thought of as a social experiment in demand management, à la Keynes. While demand management has worked reasonably well, in the 1970s the problem of "stagflation"—the simultaneous existence of both high levels of inflation

---

[1]Macroeconomics, you will recall, is the analysis of broad aggregates in the economy, such as the level of national income, the price level, and the employment-unemployment levels. Microeconomics is concerned with individual economic units such as one consumer or one firm.

and high unemployment—arose. Stagflation eventually may prove as damaging to the Keynesian model as the Great Depression was to the classical model.

In the 1970s, the existence of stagflation launched new economic models. The Friedman-Phelps model (discussed in Chapter 25) develops the notion of a natural rate of unemployment to which an economy returns in the long run. The natural rate of unemployment consists of frictional unemployment plus a host of laws and institutional arrangements (such as unions and monopolies) that interfere with price-wage reductions. It is believed that these price-wage rigidities create unemployment. The Friedman-Phelps model stresses that monetary and fiscal policy can reduce unemployment only by *fooling* buyers and sellers of labor. Buyers and sellers of labor are tricked into lowering the duration of unemployment, and therefore frictional unemployment falls. After adjusting to monetary and fiscal policy, however, people are no longer fooled and the duration of unemployment and the unemployment rate rise. Eventually, therefore, the unemployment rate returns to the natural rate of unemployment; the national output rate, similarly, returns to that rate consistent with the natural rate of unemployment. Note that the Friedman-Phelps model is reminiscent of the classical model because it suggests (1) a self-regulating economy, or at least an economy that eventually returns to some "natural" employment level, and (2) changes in the money supply do not affect real variables such as employment and output *after an adjustment period,* or in the "long run."

A more recent theory, the rational-expectations hypothesis, suggests that monetary and fiscal policy cannot *systematically* fool people. For example, monetary policy cannot cause people systematically to underestimate the rate of inflation. Recall that the Friedman-Phelps model predicts that monetary policy can affect real variables only in the short run, because you can't fool people in the long run. The rational-expectations hypothesis suggests that you can't fool people systematically even in the short run. The conclusion is that monetary and fiscal policy cannot affect real variables *systematically* even in the short run! One implication of this conclusion is that monetary and fiscal policy are useless. In fact, some argue that monetary and fiscal policy themselves can worsen the state of the economy; governmental attempts to stabilize an economy are *themselves* destabilizing. The rational-expectations hypothesis is not widely accepted. It nevertheless is an hypothesis that is an open challenge to would-be advocates of governmental stabilization (monetary and fiscal) policy.

We now can see the reasons for discussing the classical model at length in a money and banking text. The classical model is a theory of how the macroeconomy works; it explains the determinants of and the relationships among the crucial macroeconomic variables. Moreover, recent innovations in economic analysis suggest that the conclusions of the classical model (especially with respect to the role of monetary policy) are still valid. We turn now to a detailed analysis of the classical model. If you lose your perspective anywhere in the next ten chapters, it might be helpful to reread this overview.

Jean Baptiste Say. A nineteenth-century French economist who popularized the classical model and coined "Say's law." *(Courtesy of Historical Pictures Service, Inc.)*

SAY'S LAW

The fundamental conclusion of the classical model is usually summarized in what is referred to as **Say's law.** Jean Baptiste Say (1767–1832) was a popularizer of classical thinking, and he immortalized the classical model (and himself) by coining the dictum: *Supply creates its own demand.* A catchy phrase. But what does it mean?

Say's law asserts that the very process of producing specific goods (supply) is proof that other goods are desired (demand); people produce more goods than they want because they want to trade them for other goods. The implication of this, according to Say, is that no general[2] glut (or overproduction) is possible in a capitalistic, or market, economy. From this it seems to

---

[2]Specific gluts (surpluses) are possible, but surpluses are no more likely than are specific shortages. Both result from imperfect information, and both are resolved by relative price changes. Implicit in Say's law is the generalization that for every surplus there is an equal shortage—at current prices. Those goods for which a surplus exists will experience a relative price reduction; a relative price rise will occur for those goods for which a shortage exists.

follow that the full employment of labor (and other resources) is the norm in such economies.

Underlying Say's law is the premise that wants are unlimited and, further, that the primary goal of economic activity is consumption for oneself or for one's family—either in the present or in the future. Thus, an increase in the supply of one commodity can be interpreted as an increase in the demand for another. If a more or less self-sufficient family wants to increase its consumption, it can do so by producing more and trading off its surplus of one good in order to get more of another.

All this seems reasonable enough in a simple barter economy, in which households produce most of the goods they need and trade for the rest, but what about a more sophisticated economy in which people work for others? Can this complication create the possibility of unemployment? And does the fact that laborers receive money income, some of which can be *saved*, lead to unemployment? No, said the classical economist to these last two questions. The remainder of this chapter is devoted to an analysis of how the classical model, which indeed predicts the full employment of resources for a capitalist economy, justifies this answer.

ASSUMPTIONS OF THE CLASSICAL MODEL

The major assumptions of the classical model are:

1 **Pure competition** exists. No single buyer or seller of an output or input can set price by its own actions. As a consequence, each transactor is a price taker. Another consequence (and a seemingly paradoxical one) is that prices, interest rates, and wages are free to move to whatever levels supply and demand dictate. In other words, although no *individual* buyer can set a price, the community of buyers or sellers can cause prices to rise or to fall to any equilibrium level.

2 Economic agents are motivated by self-interest. One implication of this second assumption is that businesses want to maximize their total profits, and households (consumers and workers) want to maximize their total economic well-being (classical economists referred to this as utility-maximization behavior).

3 Economic agents do not suffer from **money illusions.** That is, buyers and sellers react to changes in relative (not absolute) prices, and to changes in real (price-level-adjusted) wages and interest rates, and not to nominal-value changes. For example, suppose a given consumer had purchased a specific basket of goods and services over the year, and that in the next year *all* prices—including his income—tripled. Because relative prices have not changed, the classical model predicts that he will buy the identical basket of goods and services—other things constant.

Armed with these assumptions, classical economists were able to develop the two foundation blocks on which Say's law rests: the classical theory of the aggregate demand for and supply of labor, and the theory of the level of effective aggregate demand.

THE AGGREGATE DEMAND FOR AND SUPPLY OF LABOR

In sophisticated, highly specialized economies, most laborers work for an employer; relatively small percentages of the population are self-employed. Consequently, a labor market evolves in which buyers and sellers of labor transact voluntarily. The following analysis of the aggregate (or total, or summed) demand for and supply of labor involves a money-using economy; but buyers and sellers of labor are concerned with *real* wages. Recall that real wages are inflation-adjusted; real wages = nominal wages/price level. A rise in real wages occurs if nominal wages rise more rapidly than the price level or fall more slowly than the price level is falling. The real wages fall when nominal wages rise less rapidly than the price level, or fall more rapidly than the price level is falling.

For ease of exposition, a national market for only one skill will be considered; hence, a national wage rate will be established. The aggregate demand for labor curve can be derived by summing all the individual firm labor demand curves; the aggregate supply of labor curve can be derived by summing all the individual labor supply curves.

The Aggregate Demand for Labor

The Firm's Demand for Labor   Assuming that labor is the firm's only variable input, output can be increased only by adding more labor to fixed capital and land services. According to the **law of diminishing returns** (which classical economists deduced), the marginal physical product of labor eventually will fall as a firm employs more labor, other inputs constant.

A profit-maximizing firm purchasing labor will continue to expand its employment of labor until the marginal benefit equals the marginal cost of doing so. The marginal cost of hiring labor services for the competitive firm is the going wage rate. The firm has a constant marginal cost for purchasing labor services equal to the going nominal wage rate, W.

What is the marginal benefit to the firm when it purchases labor services? Is it the **marginal physical product of labor** (the change in total output resulting from a one-unit change in labor)? Not exactly, because the marginal physical product is in physical units and the wage rate is in money units. We must compare apples with apples, money with money. The marginal benefit is equal to the **value of the marginal product of labor,** which equals the marginal product of labor multiplied by the selling price of the output. Note that now the marginal benefit, like the marginal cost, is in money units. That is,

$$MB = VMP_n = MPP_n \times P \tag{17-1}$$

where   MB = marginal benefit
   VMP_n = value of the marginal product of labor, where the subscript
      n represents labor
   MPP_n = marginal physical product of labor
      P = selling price of the good produced

The VMP_n curve eventually will slope downward. As the firm hires more labor, MPP_n eventually falls (due to the law of diminishing returns); P is constant (because the firm is a perfectly competitive seller, or a price taker); and the VMP_n will, therefore, fall.

Having identified the firm's marginal benefit and marginal cost of hiring labor services, it is necessary to explain how much labor the firm will employ to maximize its profit. The firm will hire labor up to the quantity at which its marginal cost (equal to the constant money wage) equals its marginal benefit (equal to the decreasing VMP_n) from doing so. Algebraically,

$$W = MPP_n \times P \tag{17-2}$$

Equation (17-2) can be rewritten as

$$W/P = MPP_n \tag{17-3}$$

This last equation indicates that the equilibrium (profit-maximizing) condition is that the real wage (W/P) must equal the marginal physical product of labor. This is the equilibrium condition in a *barter* economy: In this sense, "Money doesn't matter"; the same quantity of labor would be hired in a barter economy as in a money economy, other things constant.

Suppose the nominal wage rate were now to fall by one-half. What would happen to the quantity of labor demanded? The classical economist would reply, "That depends on what happens to the price of the commodity in question." If the price of the good produced by the firm is also reduced by one-half, the firm would not hire more laborers; because both sides of Equation (17-2) are multiplied by one-half, and the left side of Equation (17-3) does not change, neither equation is affected. Neither, therefore, is the equilibrium of the firm. Before the firm can be induced to hire more labor services per unit of time, the VMP_n must exceed W. This will happen only if price rises *relative* to the wage.

If the nominal wage were to rise, the firm's equilibrium would be disturbed only if the price of the good produced were to rise at a different rate. If the nominal wage rises more rapidly than the price of the good produced is rising, the real wage rises and the employer will purchase less labor. As less labor is employed, the MPP$_n$ will rise, and the VMP$_n$ will rise; the employer will hire less labor until the VMP$_n$ is driven up sufficiently to equal the new, higher real wage.

In short, the firm's quantity demanded for labor is inversely related to W^*, the *real wage;* the firm does not suffer a money illusion. One way to interpret this relationship is as follows: Before the firm voluntarily will hire more labor hours per unit of time (other things constant), the real wage must fall in order to offset the declining marginal product of labor. In fact, the firm's marginal physical product curve *is* its demand for labor curve. The inverse relationship between real wages and a firm's demand for labor curve is indicated in Figure 17-1. Note that each asterisked letter (such as W^*) represents a *real* value (whereas W represents a nominal value). Since $W^* = W/P$, it is clear that the real wage rises when W increases relative to P, and falls when P rises relative to W.

Each point on this demand for labor curve represents a *potential* equilibrium (profit-maximizing) position for the employer. The curve shows the equilibrium quantity of labor that will be purchased, per unit of time, at every real wage. Note that the curve indicates that the quantity demanded depends on the real wage rate and not the nominal wage rate.

The Economy's Demand for Labor The horizontal summation of all demand curves for labor yields the aggregate demand for labor curve in this highly simplified economy. This curve shows that for all firms in the economy a reduction in the real wage is required to induce an increase in the quantity

FIGURE 17-1 **A Firm's Demand for Labor Services.** Because employers are concerned with real, not nominal, wages, the quantity demanded of labor depends on the real wage. This graph indicates an inverse relationship between the real wage and the quantity demanded (N_{q_d}) of labor by the firm per unit of time and reflects the law of diminishing returns. The decreasing marginal physical product of labor and the profit-maximization behavior of employers imply that employers require lower real wages before they will hire more labor per unit of time. In fact, the firm's demand-for-labor curve is the marginal-physical-product-of-labor curve. Each point on this demand curve represents a potential equilibrium position for the employer of labor; each point shows the profit-maximizing quantity of labor the firm will hire at a given real wage rate.

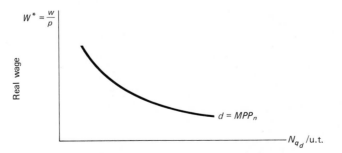

Quantity of labor demanded per unit of time

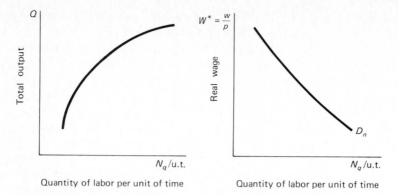

(a) *The Aggregate Production Function*   (b) *The Aggregate Demand for Labor Curve*

FIGURE 17-2   (a) The Aggregate Production Function; (b) The Aggregate-Demand-for-Labor Curve.   Panel (*a*) depicts the aggregate production for the economy. It relates the total output of final goods and services, *Q*, to the quantity of labor (N_q) per unit of time. Other factors of production and technology are held constant. This curve rises (from left to right) at a *decreasing rate,* and therefore reflects the law of diminishing returns.

Panel (*b*) shows the aggregate demand for labor. It is derived by horizontally summing all the individual firm demand (or marginal physical product) curves. Alternatively, it is the first derivative of the aggregate production function indicated in panel (*a*).

demanded of labor, per unit of time, other things constant. What was true for the individual firm is true for all firms collectively. This negatively sloped aggregate demand for labor curve results from the diminishing marginal product of labor (the law of diminishing returns). In a one-commodity world, this demand curve would be the MPP_n curve. Those of you who have studied calculus will realize that MPP_n is the first derivative of the aggregate production function relating labor to total output, other inputs constant. The relationship between these two curves is indicated in Figure 17-2.

The Aggregate Supply of Labor   According to the classical theoreticians (and most of us, too), work is irksome. Indeed, a laborer experiences *increasing marginal disutility* (or irksomeness) as he or she works more hours per day, week, or month. If this is so, then why do people work? Because they receive income which can be used to buy goods and services that have utility.

The rational seller of labor, therefore, compares the marginal disutility (or cost) of working one more unit of time to the marginal utility (or benefit) that can be obtained by spending (or saving) the income derived from working one more unit of time—at the going wage rate. In equilibrium, the rational worker will suppy labor time up to the quantity at which the marginal utility obtained from the (constant) wage rate is just equal to the marginal disutility incurred by working that last unit of time.

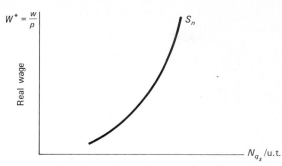

FIGURE 17-3 **An Individual's Supply-of-Labor Curve.** This figure indicates that the quantity supplied of labor by an individual is directly related to the real wage, W^*; which equals the money wage, W, divided by the price level, P; $W^* = W/P$. Because a worker experiences increasing marginal disutility from working more, he or she requires higher real wages before voluntarily working more per unit of time.

Suppose the going money wage doubles. Will a laborer previously in equilibrium work more? The answer, according to the classical economist, depends on what happens to the price level; if the price level also doubles, the worker will not work more because to do so would leave him or her worse off economically. Why? The increasing marginal disutility of working one more unit of time would be greater than the constant marginal utility gained from working that additional unit. (Because prices have doubled, the marginal utility of a doubled money wage has not changed.)

The only way that a rational worker can be induced to work more hours per unit of time is for the *real* wage to rise. Thus, the quantity of labor offered by the representative worker in this model is directly related to the real wage; laborers do not suffer from money illusions. One interpretation of such a relationship is: Before a worker voluntarily will work more hours per unit of time (other things constant), the real wage *must rise* to offset the increasing marginal disutility from working. At every point along the supply of labor curve, the laborer will work up to the point where the marginal benefit (extra utility from income) from working the last hour is exactly equal to the marginal cost (extra disutility) from doing so. This is depicted in Figure 17-3.

The Economy's Supply of Labor By summing all the individual supply of labor curves horizontally, an aggregate supply of labor curve can be derived.

Determination of the Equilibrium Wage Rate

Figure 17-4 shows both the aggregate supply of and the aggregate demand for labor. In a purely competitive labor market, the equilibrium "price" will be at a point of intersection of the supply and demand curves. Consider real wage W_1^* in Figure 17-4. Why will it not be the equilibrium wage rate? Inspection of Figure 17-4 indicates that at W_1^*, the quantity of labor supplied (3,000 units of labor per unit of time) exceeds the quantity of labor demanded (2,000 units of labor per unit of time); hence, a surplus of labor exists at W_1^*. A surplus of labor is more commonly referred to as unemployment. What will happen? Buyers of labor are maximizing total profits at W_1^*; they have hired labor up to the quantity at which the real wage W_1^*

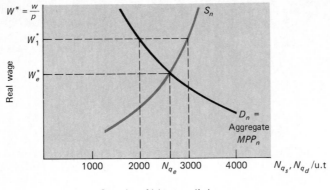

Quantity of labor supplied
and demanded per unit of time

FIGURE 17-4 **Wage Rate Determination.** This figure indicates that the equilibrium real wage will be at W_e^*, the point of intersection of the aggregate-supply-of-labor curve and the aggregate-demand-for-labor curve. At any higher real wage, a surplus of labor (unemployment) exists; laborers competing for jobs will offer to work for less and drive overall real wages down toward W_e^*. At any real wage below W_e^*, a shortage of labor will exist and employers competing for labor will bid wage rates up toward W_e^*. At W_e^*, both buyers and sellers of labor are able to realize their intentions; since both groups are maximizing, neither has an incentive to change its behavior, and equilibrium exists. To the classical economist, N_{qe} represents full employment; those remaining unemployed are idle *voluntarily:* They are unwilling to work at the going real wage rate.

just equals the MPP_n—at 2,000 units of labor.[3] On the other hand, sellers of labor are not able to realize their intentions; they want to sell 3,000 units of labor but can only sell 2,000 units per unit of time. For some laborers, the marginal benefit of the real wage will exceed the (negative of the) marginal disutility for working the last unit of time. These involuntarily unemployed laborers will compete with employed laborers for jobs and drive money wage rates downward; this decrease in W will force real wages W^* down toward W_e^*. Unemployment will exist at any real wage rate above W_e^*; therefore, classical economists reasoned that any real wage rate above W_e^* could only be temporary.

At any wage rate below W_e^*, the quantity of labor demanded exceeds the quantity of labor supplied and a shortage of labor exists. Sellers will be able to realize their intentions; they will (and can) work up to the quantity at which the marginal utility obtained from the last unit of time worked is just offset by the marginal disutility suffered from working it. On the other hand, buyers will not be able to realize their intentions and hence will not be able to maximize

---

[3]Or the money wage, W, just equals the VMP_n. Thus, if $W = MPP_n \times P$, then $W/P = MPP_n$; in a one-commodity world, P is the price of the commodity. In a multi-commodity world, P is a weighted average of all the prices of the goods and services produced in the economy.

total profits. For buyers, the real wage will be less than the MPP_n; alternatively stated, the money wage will be less than the VMP_n.[4] Buyers of labor, competing for labor, will drive wage rates upward, until W_e^* is reached.

Labor for Hire and Full Employment What is the implication of the classical analysis of the aggregate supply of and demand for labor? Full employment is achieved. Why? In Figure 17-4, N_{qe} represents full employment; all those labor hours which might be offered by laborers (beyond N_{qe}) are *voluntarily* withheld. For those extra hours, workers feel that the marginal disutility outweighs any marginal utility derivable from the real wage W_e^*. Any involuntarily unemployed laborers *eventually* (watch out for that word) will find jobs because such a surplus of labor will cause real wages to fall until the quantity of labor demanded rises (and the quantity of labor supplied falls). Full employment of labor results.

Consider Figure 17-5, which shows the aggregate production function in panel (*a*) and the aggregate supply of and demand for labor in panel (*b*). In panel (*b*), the equilibrium quantity of labor, N_{qe}, is established at real wage W_e^*; N_{qe} units of labor are offered and purchased per unit of time. That equilibrium quantity of labor is consistent with an economywide maximum rate of output of Q_e, as panel (*a*) indicates. Thus, the classical theory of the aggregate supply of and the aggregate demand for labor implies that businesses will produce an output requiring the full-employment of labor. *Wage rate flexibility assures that in a competitive market a full-employment output will be produced by business.*

THE LEVEL OF EFFECTIVE AGGREGATE DEMAND

The previous section indicated how the classical economists demonstrated (at least to their own satisfaction) why a full-employment output will be produced even in an economy where laborers rent their services to entrepreneurs for money. But what assures that this full-employment output will be *purchased?* This question is addressed now.

Say's Law and National Income Accounting To be sure, national income accounting demonstrates that the market value of all final goods and services produced during the income period is identical to the incomes generated from their production. Because income forms the basis of the demand for final goods and services, national income accounting provides at least some superficial support for Say's law. Even in a money economy, supply creates its own *potential* demand: Any output supply automatically will create sufficient purchasing power to clear markets.

---

[4]Can you verify this? *Hint:* Pick a real wage below W_e^* and show how many units of labor will be offered by sellers. Then determine what the MPP_n is for that quantity of labor, and compare it to the real wage you selected. Note that the demand for labor curve *is* the MPP_n curve.

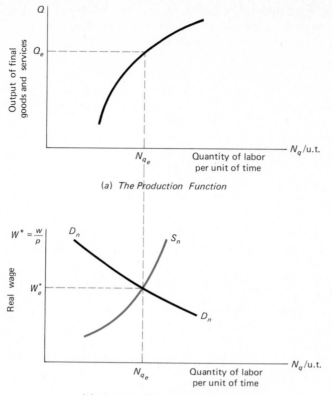

(a) The Production Function

(b) Aggregate Supply and Demand for Labor

FIGURE 17-5 (**a**) **The Production Function;** (**b**) **Aggregate Supply of and Demand for Labor.** Panel (b) shows that in a competitive labor market full employment will be established. Panel (a) shows that the maximum rate of output consistent with this rate of employment is Q_e. The conclusion is that wage rate flexibility assures that a full-employment output will be produced by businesses.

Consider Figure 17-5 again. A competitive labor market assures full employment in panel (b), and the maximum output rate consistent with that full-employment rate is Q_e. Business will produce Q_e because that is the most profitable output rate. Given a set of prices for these final goods and services (represented by Q_e), the value of national income is determined. Weighting final goods and services (Q_e) by their respective prices yields national income (NNP, assuming investment is measured in net terms). Thus, by establishing equilibrium in the labor market, national output of final goods and services is automatically determined. Weighting those final goods by their respective market prices automatically generates sufficient income—and hence purchasing power—to clear markets of those goods.

A nagging question persists, however. What guarantees that this purchasing power will actually be *expended?* In short, what if people *save* a part of their income?

Saving   First, it is necessary to interpret saving. Why do people save? Saving represents a provision for future consumption. People save for their retirement, to accumulate down payments for expensive durable goods, for future emergencies, and so on. People save to "even out" their consumption over time; they save to free themselves from the discipline of consuming only what their income happens to be in a particular period. Individuals typically have varying incomes over their lifetimes—both expected and unexpected (temporarily positive or negative windfalls lead to unexpected income changes). Saving permits them to have a more nearly constant level of consumption through time.

Even granting that saving will ultimately be spent, there is still a short-run problem. *During the period in which some income is saved,* the supply-created potential demand (the purchasing power or income) is not fully expended. The result is that the aggregate demand for consumer goods and services is insufficient to purchase all the goods and services produced. Unemployment results, as producers react to rising inventories by producing less and employing fewer workers.

Saving creates a situation in which purchasing power, generated in the form of income derived from producing goods and services, is not all spent on those goods and services. Consequently, saving represents a leakage from the circular flow of income and it contracts the economy. Saving seems to be a formidable foe of Say's law; if not offset, it can lead to unemployment.

Investment   The classical economists were aware of the potential danger of saving. Classical theoreticians believed, however, that *investment* has precisely the opposite effect on the economy as saving has.

Investment spending is the demand for additional plant and equipment. When investment takes place, incomes and purchasing power are created, but there is no corresponding (at least in the short run) increase in the output of final *consumer* goods and services. Investment, therefore, is potentially an effective antidote to saving. Investment is an injection into the circular flow of income and is a potentially expansionary element in an economy. Indeed, a fully employed economy that suddenly allocates massive resources to investment goods' production will experience inflation, unless saving plans by households increase accordingly. This is because in a full-employment situation, an increase in investment-goods output necessitates a reduction in the output of consumer goods. Households will have the same purchasing power—they were paid to produce investment goods—but they will have fewer consumer goods to purchase. They compete for consumer goods by bidding prices higher, inflation results.

Saving and Investment   The problem, then, is not that people save. *What is at issue is the extent to which household saving plans are offset by business investment plans.* If saving plans exceed investment plans, the economy will contract and unemployment will occur. If investment plans exceed saving plans, then short-run inflation will result. If saving plans are exactly equated with investment plans, however, full employment and price stability will result.[5] The key variables, then, are the saving plans of households and the investment plans of businesses. The classical economists felt that these were both determined primarily by the rate of interest. In turn, the rate of interest is the mechanism in market economies that assures that saving and investment plans are equated.

The Saving Curve   Given income, the main determinant of saving plans per unit of time is the real rate of interest. How are saving plans and the real interest rate related? According to classical economists, if the real interest rate rises, individual households will save more and consume less out of a given level of income. If the real interest rate falls, a household will save less and consume more out of a given level of income.

The classical economists maintained that households would prefer to consume now rather than later because of the uncertainties of life: Spend now because you may not be around later, or you may not be able to enjoy consumption later. Interest is an inducement to households to forgo present consumption; households are offered *more* future consumption if they forgo consumption now. The higher the real interest rate, the more a given amount of saving will enable a household to consume in the future. Therefore, as the real rate of interest rises, households will consume less and save more; lower real interest rates induce households to consume more and save less.

Consider an example. If the real interest rate is zero, a consumer can exchange $100 worth of consumption today for $100 worth of consumption next year. If the real interest rate rises to 3 percent per annum he or she can exchange $100 of consumption today for $103 of consumption one year hence; a real interest rate of 7 percent per annum allows him or her to consume $107 worth of goods next year if he or she forgoes $100 of consumption this year. Clearly, a consumer has more of an incentive to save at higher interest rates than at lower interest rates.

We can assume that this direct relationship between saving per unit of time and real interest rates will also exist for the whole community. Consider Figure 17-6, which shows the community's aggregate saving curve.

Note that this saving curve was derived by holding the level of income constant. This curve will shift to the right if real national income rises; it will shift to the left if the real national income falls. That is, if real income rises, we would expect the community to save more (and consume more) at every real interest rate. If the community's real income falls, we would expect it to save less (and consume less) at every real interest rate.

Loanable funds and saving   The classical economists felt that the saving curve could be considered as a loanable funds curve. That is, they felt that dollars saved would automatically become a part of the supply of funds that could be lent to borrower-businesses. The classical position is that money is merely a medium of exchange; hence, people do not want to hold it. Dollars saved *and held* forgo interest; **hoarding** therefore is irrational in normal times.

---

[5]Assuming the money supply is fixed, as indicated in the next section.

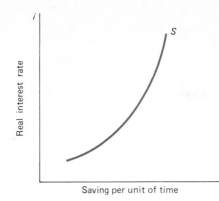

FIGURE 17-6 **The Aggregate Saving Curve.** This graph indicates a direct relationship between the interest rate and the amount of saving per unit of time. The community requires higher interest rates before it will save more from a given national income.

It is one thing to hold dollars for a short period in order to make transactions; it is quite another to hold dollars in idle balances indefinitely.

Finally, it should be stressed that the classical economists viewed interest as consumers' reward for abstinence from present consumption. Therefore, it is legitimate to ask: Who would be willing to reward households for their abstinence? The answer is: Businesses that wish to spend more than their income in order to invest in plant and equipment. We now turn to this matter.

The Investment Curve Given profit expectations of businesses, the most important determinant of business investment is the rate of interest. Rational, profit-maximizing businesses will borrow money to carry out investment projects up to the quantity at which the marginal benefit equals the marginal cost of doing so. What is the marginal cost and what is the marginal benefit?

The marginal cost of borrowing money is, of course, the rate of interest. For any individual firm, the rate of interest is a constant.

The marginal benefit of borrowing money is the expected rate of return on the investment project. Given an interest rate of, say, 10 percent, a firm will carry on investment projects up to the point where the expected rate of return is 10 percent. If an investment project is expected to yield 12 percent, the project will be carried out and "abnormal" profits of 2 percent will be earned, after the 10 percent interest has been paid. For that project yielding exactly 10 percent, normal profits will be earned and all costs will be covered, after interest has been paid. But if an investment project is expected to yield only 8 percent, the project won't be undertaken; it can't even pay off the principal on the loan.

The classical economists maintained that the marginal profitability of investment projects declines as firms in an industry carry out more investment projects.[6] Why? Because the first few investment projects have locational or other advantages. Or, as more and more of a given type of investment is carried out, the supply of the final product increases. Given the demand for the

---

[6]The classical economists referred to this phenomenon as decreasing marginal productivity of capital.

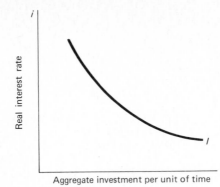

FIGURE 17-7   Industry Demand Curve for Loanable Funds.   This graph shows the inverse relationship between interest rates and the quantity demanded of loanable funds for investment projects. Before firms will voluntarily borrow more funds (to carry out more investment projects), the rate of interest must fall—to offset the declining marginal profitability of investment projects. This curve will shift to the right if profit expectations rise and to the left if they fall.

final product, price falls and therefore so does the profitability of marginal investment projects. Also, as an industry gets larger and larger (as firms carry on more and more investment projects), the prices of inputs specific to the industry rise. Other things constant, marginal profits fall.

The demand for loanable funds to carry out investments is inversely related to the rate of interest. One way to interpret this demand curve is as follows: Before firms will voluntarily carry out more investment projects, the rate of interest must fall to offset decreasing marginal profitability. An aggregate demand curve for loanable funds is indicated in Figure 17-7.

Note that at every point on that curve firms have carried out investment projects up to the quantity at which the expected rate of return on borrowed money is just equal to the interest rate. Hence, every point on the curve is a potential profit-maximizing or equilibrium point.

This curve shifts if profit expectations change. An increase in profit expectations shifts the curve in Figure 17-7 to the right; the quantity of loanable funds demanded is higher at every rate of interest. A decrease in profit expectations shifts the investment curve to the left, since there is a decrease in the quantity of loanable funds demanded at every rate of interest.

Aggregate Saving and Aggregate Investment Curves and Say's Law   Consider Figure 17-8, which shows the aggregate saving and aggregate investment (or the aggregate supply of and aggregate demand for loanable funds) curve.

At i_4, the quantity of loanable funds supplied (500) exceeds the quantity of loanable funds demanded (400). In other words, a surplus of loanable funds exists at i_4. While borrowers are able to realize their intentions (they are maximizing total profits), lenders are not. Competition among lenders, some of whom can't earn any interest at all on their saving, will drive interest rates down toward i_e. As a result, investment will rise (because more investment projects are profitable at lower interest rates) and the quantity of saving will fall.

At any interest rate below i_e, the quantity of loanable funds demanded exceeds the quantity supplied, and a shortage of loanable funds exists. Lenders are able to realize their intentions, but borrowers cannot. Competition

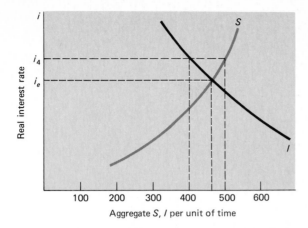

FIGURE 17-8 **The Aggregate Saving and Investment Curves: (*a*) The Aggregate Production Function; (*b*) The Aggregate Supply and Demand for Labor.** This graph shows how the interest rate brings aggregate saving and aggregate investment plans—the supply and the demand for loanable funds—into equality. If saving plans exceed investment plans, the market interest rate will exceed the equilibrium interest rate and a surplus of loanable funds exists. Lenders, competing with each other for interest earnings, will offer to accept lower interest rates, and thereby encourage a smaller quantity saved and a larger quantity invested. This process continues until i_e is established. Complementary reasoning indicates the equilibrium interest rate cannot be less than i_e, since a shortage of loanable funds would then exist. As a by-product, the classical theory of the rate of interest is explained: The equilibrium rate of interest is at the point of intersection of the aggregate saving and aggregate investment curves.

among borrowers will force interest rates up, and scarce loanable funds will go to the highest bidders—presumably the most profitable businesses.

Note that we have also just explained the classical theory of the interest rate. The equilibrium rate of interest will be set at the point of intersection of the aggregate supply of and the aggregate demand for loanable funds curves. Alternatively, the interaction of aggregate saving and investment plans determines the interest rate.

Saving and Investment Plans and Say's Law Before we lose the forest for the trees, we should recapitulate. It has just been demonstrated that interest-rate fluctuations establish the equality of saving and investment plans. Every dollar that leaves the income stream as a dollar saved (and is a potential drag on the economy) automatically reenters as a dollar invested. Hence, saving does not refute Say's law; dollars saved by households are spent by businesses for investment. With respect to full employment, it does not matter why expenditures are made; full employment merely requires that sufficient expenditures be made by some group or combination of groups. Thus, the saving-investment analysis concludes that the full-employment output will indeed be purchased. Say's law remains valid even when the possibility of household saving in a money economy is considered.

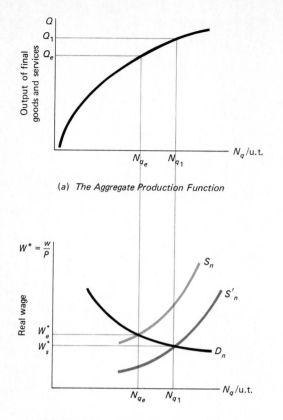

(a) *The Aggregate Production Function*

(b) *The Aggregate Supply and Demand for Labor* **FIGURE 17-9**

MALTHUS AND THE LAW OF DIMINISHING RETURNS

The classical economists deduced the law of diminishing returns, and they didn't shy away from what they thought its implications were. In particular, the Reverend Thomas Robert Malthus (1766–1834), in his earlier writings, maintained that this law relegated most people to a life of economic misery. Malthus contended that whereas population increases geometrically, the food supply (or output in general) increases only arithmetically due to the law of diminishing returns. According to Malthus, without positive checks to increase the death rate (wars, pestilence, famine) or preventive checks to decrease the birth rate (late marriage, sexual abstinence, birth control),[7] most people will live at near-subsistence levels or they will starve.

To see how Malthus's position is related to the classical model, consider Figure 17-9. Panel (a) shows an aggregate production function relating output

---

[7]The last of which Malthus found morally repugnant.

to various employment levels, other things constant. Output increases at a decreasing rate (arithmetically) due to the law of diminishing returns.

Panel (*b*) indicates the aggregate demand for labor, D_n, and the aggregate supply of labor, S_n. Note that as population rises, the supply of labor curve increases—it shifts from S_n to S'_n.

In panel (*b*), an increase in the supply of labor causes the real wage to fall from W_e^* to W_s^*. Note that this population increase causes output to increase at a decreasing rate, from Q_e to Q_1, in panel (a).

Assuming that W_s^* represents the subsistence real wage, Malthus predicted that departures above or below W_s^* lead to movements back to W_s^*. Why? If the real wage drops below W_s^*, many in the population will starve and cause the supply of labor curve to decrease. If real wage rates rise above W_s^*, people will propagate (due to the "passion between the sexes"); this will increase the supply of labor and drive wage rates down again toward W_s^*.

HIGHLIGHT   Charles Darwin and Thomas Robert Malthus

It is well known that Charles Darwin (1800–1882) was one of the early proponents of the doctrine of evolution. What is less known, however, is that Darwin was influenced by the classical model. In particular, Darwin read Malthus's works, corresponded with him, and was profoundly influenced by him.

Darwin felt that deviant characteristics of offspring are the key to the origin of species, but he was at a loss to explain how. The creationists maintained that God created species that were perfect; hence, new species do not evolve. Some believed that deviant offspring surely will not survive since species are already perfectly adapted to their environment. Others noted that climatic changes occur, and that those species that are no longer suited die out. Then Darwin read Malthus's book and suddenly the pieces of the evolutionary puzzle fitted together in his mind.

In effect, Darwin generalized to all living things the theories that Malthus had believed true for people. Being a particularly astute botanist, Darwin noted that *all* living things have the potential to propagate beyond their means of subsistence. One oyster can produce over 60 million eggs in one season! Many other species, although they are not quite so prolific, have the capability of covering the earth in just eight to ten generations—if every offspring survived and begat others. "If every offspring survived"—but that was the rub. They *don't* all survive, and the question becomes: Which will survive? The real competition for life is not among species, but *within* species; the more serious enemy of the zebra is not the lion, but other zebras that compete for the limited means of subsistence.

And so, deviant offspring, if they have characteristics that give them a competitive advantage in a fiercely combative world and a constantly changing environment, will survive and beget offspring with similar competitive advantages. The others won't. Thus Darwin, the botanist, explained the origin of new species with a bit of help from Malthus, the classical economist.

At least for the western nations, Malthus's predictions did not come to pass. The demand for labor increased due to technological changes in industry and agriculture. Moreover, the economically successful nations have stabilized their populations. Presumably, as nations develop from primarily rural to primarily urban societies, the economic status of children changes from assets to liabilities, and rational parents respond accordingly: They have fewer children.

CHAPTER SUMMARY

1   The classical model is an edited and modernized version of the writings of nineteenth-century and early twentieth-century economists.

2   The fundamental conclusion of the classical model is summarized in Say's law, which states that "supply creates its own demand." The implication is that a competitive, capitalistic system has within it mechanisms that assure full employment of labor and other resources.

3   Three important assumptions that underlie the classical model are (a) pure competition exists in all markets, (b) economic agents are motivated by self-interest, and (c) economic agents don't suffer from money illusions.

4   The classical theory of the aggregate demand for and the aggregate supply of labor predicts that a full-employment output level will be produced, other things constant. An individual firm's demand for labor curve is downward-sloping, reflecting the law of diminishing returns. The aggregate demand for labor is derived by summing horizontally all the individual firms' demand for labor curves. An individual laborer's supply of labor curve is upward-sloping, reflecting an assumption of increasing marginal disutility from working longer hours. The aggregate supply of labor curve is derived by summing horizontally all the individual labor supply curves. The interaction of the aggregate supply of labor curve with the aggregate demand for labor curve determines the real wage rate. A full-employment output prevails eventually because if unemployment exists (a surplus of labor), the unemployed compete for jobs and the real wage falls. A reduction in the real wage leads to an increase in the quantity of labor demanded and a decrease in the quantity of labor supplied. In equilibrium, only involuntary unemployment exists.

5   The classical theory of the level of effective aggregate demand assures that a full-employment output will be purchased. If saving plans by households are equal to investment plans by businesses, neither unemployment nor inflation will result.

6   An individual household's saving is directly related to the real interest rate. Holding income constant, an individual will save more at higher real interest rates and save less at lower real interest rates.

7   The aggregate saving curve is derived by summing individual household saving curves; it can be thought of as the primary component of an aggregate supply of loanable funds curve—because hoarding is considered unlikely.

8   A firm carries on investment projects up to the point where the expected marginal rate of return is just offset by the market interest rate.

9   A firm's demand for loanable funds is inversely related to the interest rate.

10   An aggregate demand for loanable funds curve is derived by summing horizontally all the firms' demand for loanable funds curves.

11   The real market rate of interest is established at the point of intersection of the aggregate demand for and the aggregate supply of loanable funds curves.

12   In equilibrium, saving plans and investment plans are equated; leakages are exactly offset by injections, and a full-employment output is purchased.

GLOSSARY

Hoarding: Money saved but not used to earn interest.

Law of diminishing returns: If the total output of a commodity is increased by adding equal units of variable input while other input quantities are held constant, then eventually the marginal product of the variable input falls.

Marginal physical product of labor: The change in total output resulting from a unit change in labor; MPP_n.

Money illusion: An individual or firm suffers from a money illusion if it reacts to absolute and not to relative price changes.

Pure competition: A market structure in which there are many firms in an industry producing a perfectly substitutable product. Pure competitors are price takers; they cannot affect price by their own actions.

Say's law: Supply creates its own demand; wage-rate flexibility assumes that a full-employment output will be produced, and interest-rate flexibility assumes that a full-employment output will be purchased.

Value of marginal product of labor: The MPP_n times the selling price of output; $VMP = MPP_n \times P$.

PROBLEMS

17-1   Assume that Mr. Colacci has an income of $100 per week and that he saves $10 and spends $90 on consumer goods. He works 38 hours per week. Assume now that *all* prices double; all goods and services cost twice as much, wages are two times higher, and nominal interest rates are doubled.

a   Will Mr. Colacci save a higher percentage of his income?

b   Will he work more than 38 hours per week now?

c   Under what conditions would he save more than 10 percent and work more than 38 hours per week, assuming that the price level had doubled?

SELECTED REFERENCES

Fisher, Irving, *The Theory of Interest* (London: Macmillan, 1930).

Hicks, J. R., *Theory of Wages* (London: Macmillan, 1932).

Keynes, J. M., *The General Theory of Employment, Interest, and Money* (New York: Harcourt Brace, 1936).

Say, J. B., *A Treatise on Political Economy* (London: Langmans, 1821).

Schumpeter, Joseph A., *History of Economic Analysis* (Oxford: Oxford University Press, 1954).

Skinner, A. S., "Say's Law: Origins and Content," *Economica,* vol. 34, May 1967, pp. 153–166.

Wicksell, Knute, *Lectures on Political Economy,* vol. III, Lionel Robbins (trans.) (London: Routledge and Kegan Paul, 1934).

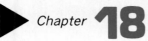
Applications and Criticisms of the Classical Model

Chapter 17 presented the classical model; this chapter discusses the applications and the criticisms of that model. In particular, it explores the implications of the classical model by assuming an increase in general thriftiness and then tracing out the effects of this on aggregate employment. Then the classical theory of the price level is developed, by using the classical predictions generated from Chapter 17. Finally, a discussion of the criticisms of the classical model is presented.

AN INCREASE IN THE POPULACE'S THRIFTINESS

Let's put the classical model to the ultimate test. If saving is a drag on the economy, full employment should be jeopardized when there is a general increase in thriftiness. If all income recipients wish to save more of their incomes and spend less of it, what will happen?

Consider Figure 18-1, and suppose that those who receive incomes decide to save more than before, at any rate of interest. Graphically, this results in a shift to the right in the aggregate saving (or aggregate supply of loanable funds) curve, from S to S'. Other things constant, the interest rate

FIGURE 18-1 An Increase in General Thriftiness. If income recipients decide to save more, the aggregate saving, or supply of loanable funds, curve will shift to the right. That is, households now want to save more at any interest rate. This is indicated as a shift from S to S'. At the previous equilibrium interest rate, i_e, a surplus of loanable funds now exists. This causes the equilibrium interest rate to fall to i_2; in the new equilibrium position, both the quantity saved and the quantity invested have increased. Quantity saved has increased from S_1 to S_2, by exactly the amount that the quantity consumed has fallen—graphically represented by the distance $B–A$. The increase in quantity saved has been offset by the increase in quantity invested that results from the lower interest rate. The full-employment output and expenditure rates do not change, but the composition of output has changed (fewer consumer goods and more investment goods now result). Some laborers have been reallocated from the consumer goods sector to the investment goods sector. The equilibrium position, A, has moved to B. At B, the interest rate is lower, and saving and investment quantities are both higher.

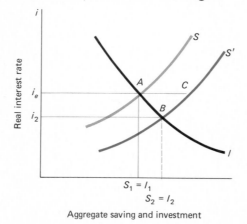

Aggregate saving and investment

falls from i_e to i_2, the new equilibrium rate. With the increase in saving, there would be a surplus of loanable funds at i_e. As a result of the lower interest rate, the quantity of investment rises as more investment projects become profitable. Quantity saved rises from S_1 to S_2, and quantity consumed falls by an identical amount, because income is assumed to remain constant. A surplus of consumer goods now exists, and the consumer-goods sector contracts. Does unemployment in the consumer-goods sector imply general unemployment? No, because those idled workers find jobs in the now-expanding investment goods sector. *An increase in saving leads to an offsetting increase in investment.* Of course, classical economists recognized that *temporary* unemployment could exist, since adjustment lags are probable; it takes time for laborers to transfer from an industry that is contracting to one that is expanding. Still, classical economists essentially believed that in the long run full employment returns.

The net result? Equilibrium moves from A to B. The composition of output changes (more investment goods, fewer consumer goods), but output remains at the full-employment level. Similarly, although the employment level remains full, some laborers are reallocated. The conclusion is that a general increase in saving does not lead to unemployment—if interest rates are free to fall.

THE CLASSICAL THEORY OF THE PRICE LEVEL

Irving Fisher's Equation of Exchange Armed with Say's law, we are now ready to discuss the classical theory of the price level. This theory can be explained by the so-called **equation of exchange** (developed by Irving Fisher, a classical economist who taught at Yale). According to the equation of exchange:

$$MV = PQ = Y \qquad\qquad \textbf{(18-1)}$$

where M = the money supply—coins, currency, and demand deposits actually held by the nonbanking public[1]

V = the income velocity of money—the average number of times each monetary unit is spent on final goods and services per unit of time (usually one year)

P = the average price level

Q = the output of final (consumer and net investment) goods and services

Y = national income

A moment's reflection indicates that MV is equal to total expenditures on final goods and services; the money stock multiplied by the average number

---

[1]Note that this definition of the money supply is a very narrow one; until recently, it was an official definition of money in the United States. As we shall see, this definition is consistent with the transactions-balances notion of money.

of times each monetary unit is spent must be total expenditures. PQ can be thought of as total business receipts from the sales of final goods and services. Thus, $MV = PQ$ says that total expenditures on final goods and services by households and businesses equal total business receipts, a statement that is definitionally true.[2] National income accounting indicates that the market value of final goods and services is identical to the income of the economy: $PQ = Y$.

Alfred Marshall's Formulation Across the Atlantic from Yale, Alfred Marshall and his colleagues at Cambridge University in England had an insight that is mathematically equivalent to Fisher's equation. The Cambridge formulation is:

$$M = kY, \text{ or } M = k(PQ) \tag{18-2}$$

where M = the money supply actually held
   Y = nominal national income, or PQ
   k = the ratio of money actually held to nominal national income

---

[2]The equation of exchange, as formulated, is not a theory but rather a truism, because V is defined *ex post* (after the fact) as being that number obtained when PQ (or Y) is divided by M; M and Y are readily observable and $V = Y/M$, or $V = PQ/M$.

Alfred Marshall. A Cambridge University teacher of J. M. Keynes who synthesized the classical model and pioneered much of modern economics. *(Courtesy of Historical Pictures Service, Inc., Chicago.)*

This equation is also true by definition; k is that ratio obtained, *ex post*, after dividing M by Y (or PQ). Thus, $k = M/Y$. Footnote 2 indicates that $V = Y/M$; therefore, k and V are the reciprocal of each other; $V = 1/k$ and $k = 1/V$.

Both the American and British formulations of the equation of exchange can be transformed from identities into testable theories. *If it can be demonstrated that V and k are ratios desired by the community, and that they are stable—or that they at least change predictably, then the truism has become a theory.*

The Classical Theory of the Demand for Money   Since it lends itself readily to a theory of the demand for money, consider the Cambridge (or Marshallian) version. Let k now represent the community's *desired* ratio of money balances to the level of nominal (not real) national income. The classical economists believed this ratio to be stable. Why? To them, money is merely useful as a medium of exchange; since it is non-interest-bearing, money is not desired for its own sake. Since money produces nothing and earns no interest, rational people use it only to make transactions for goods and services. They called this the **transactions motive** for holding money. Actually, both Fisher and Marshall also recognized the existence of a **precautionary motive** for holding money—meaning that people hold a pool of readily available purchasing power in order to meet emergencies. But, for ease of exposition, economists typically lump these two motives together and refer only to the transactions motive.

Rational businesses and rational households try to keep their individual k's to a minimum,[3] because holding idle money balances imposes an opportunity cost on holders—forgone interest earnings. Why do people hold money at all? Businesses and households typically *receive* money in periods that do not necessarily correspond to the times they want to *spend* it. Were there a perfect coincidence of money receipts and payments, money would be received and spent instantaneously.[4] An imperfect coincidence means that people want to hold money in order to make transactions; households and businesses receive benefit in the form of transactions convenience. Moreover, because people want to hold a pool of readily available purchasing power in order to meet emergencies, by holding money they receive precautionary security. By assumption, the *extra* benefit of holding additional dollars for these motives declines eventually. If so, an individual's optimal k will be established where the decreasing marginal benefit of holding one more unit of money is just offset by the constant marginal cost (forgone interest earnings) from doing so. Holding one more dollar beyond the optimal k leaves an indi-

---

[3]This is equivalent to a *maximum V* in the American equation of exchange approach. Minimally held money balances held for minimum periods (a minimum k) translate into a maximum annual turnover rate for money (a maximum V).

[4]If nonmoney interest-earning assets, such as bonds, could be purchased and sold at zero transactions costs, money would also be held for only very short periods—according to the classical economists, that is.

vidual economically worse off, because beyond that point the marginal benefit is less than the marginal cost.

Each individual probably has a different k. An individual's k depends on frequency of income,[5] credit arrangements with creditors, use of credit cards, and the individual's degree of insecurity. According to the classical economist, however, an overall, stable k is found for the community *as a whole.* That is, the determinants of k do not change significantly in the long run. Classical economists believed the community k to be somewhere between one-fifth and one-fourth.

The conclusion of the previous chapter was that price, wage, and interest-rate flexibility assure full employment. This chapter has demonstrated that an increase in saving by the whole population does not result in unemployment. As a consequence, the economywide output rate of final goods and services is equal to its maximum potential rate. It follows that the classical economists would have predicted a constant Q in the long run; Q is constant at the full-employment level. Thus, we let $Q = \overline{Q}$.[6]

Equation (18-2), which is an identity, can now be rewritten as a *theory* of the demand for money. Let

$$L_1 = kY \tag{18-3}$$

where L_1 represents the desired demand for money to hold for transactions and precautionary balances. Now k is the *desired* ratio of cash balances to the level of nominal (not real) national income, Y. This equation can also be rewritten as:

$$L_1 = k(PQ) \tag{18-4}$$

where PQ is equal to Y, and k and Q are constants. To be sure, this is a simple theory of the demand for money—but it is a theory.[7] The theory indicates that, as nominal income rises, the community will want to hold proportionally more in money balances. For example, assume that nominal national income is $100 per annum and that the community wants to hold a $20 cash balance—$15 to satisfy its transactions motive and $5 to meet its precautionary motive. This means that $k = .2$. If the price level doubles while Q (the flow of final goods and services) remains constant, then L_1 will double to 40. Why? In order to make the same transactions at a price level that is twice as high, $30

---

[5] The more often one gets paid, the less the reason for a transactions motive; hence, the lower is k.

[6] A bar over a letter means that it is held constant.

[7] The American version also can be made into a theory, by indicating that $M\overline{V} = P\overline{Q}$, or $\overline{V} = (P\overline{Q})/M = Y/M$. This formulation clearly indicates that Y is *nominal* income, because $Y = P\overline{Q}$. In principle, a different level of nominal income exists for every possible price level, P. *Real* income is constant in the classical model, however, because Q is constant. Thus, if $Y = P\overline{Q}$, and nominal Y is converted into real national income (Y) in the usual way (dividing by a price index), then $Y^* = Y/P = P\overline{Q}/P = Q$. Because $Q = \overline{Q}$ in the classical model, real national income is also constant.

is now required. Moreover, the community will now require $10 in money balances in order to remain equally secure; a higher price level lowers the purchasing power of a constant stock of money. In short, a doubling of the price level causes nominal national income to double to $200; in turn, desired money balances also double, to $40. Real income and k remain constant. Consider Figure 18-2.

Writing the Cambridge demand for money equation as $L_1 = \overline{k}(P\overline{Q})$ and setting $L_1 = M$ (the quantity demanded for money equals the supply of money) yields the classical theory of the price level. Consider Figure 18-3. This graph indicates that increases in the money supply, given the demand for money, cause the price level to rise. By implication, decreases in the money supply cause the price level to fall. The American quantity theory shows this readily. If $M\overline{V} = P\overline{Q}$, then pure arithmetic indicates that changes in M will lead to proportional changes in P. Thus if the money supply is tripled, prices will triple; a halving of the money supply will cause the price level to be halved.

Why do money-supply changes lead only to long-run price-level changes? Suppose gold is discovered. Because in the nineteenth century many transactions were actually made with gold, gold was a part of the money supply and the money supply therefore instantaneously increases (a shift from M to M' in Figure 18-3). Money holders soon discover that (at Y_A) $M > L_1$ and that they have a surplus of money (at point A in Figure 18-3); people are holding more money than they want to hold in order to meet transactions and precautionary motives. Individuals will rid themselves of excess money balances by increasing their spending for goods and services. Because output is already at its maximum, more money is now chasing the same quantity of goods and services; the increased money expenditures for goods and services cause the price level to rise.

This process can be viewed in another way. Equilibrium requires that the community voluntarily hold the existing money supply, whatever its level might be. An increase in the money supply temporarily upsets this equilibrium; the community is temporarily holding more than it desires in order to make transactions and to remain secure. While it is possible for an individual to spend excess balances, the whole community cannot. As the price level and

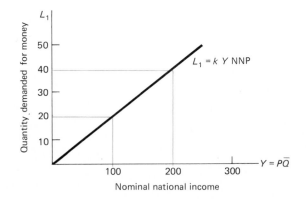

FIGURE 18-2 The Classical Theory of the Price Level. This graph indicates that increases in the level of nominal national income lead to proportional increases in the demand for money balances. Movements from left to right along the horizontal axis result purely from changes in the price level, because Q is predicted to be constant.

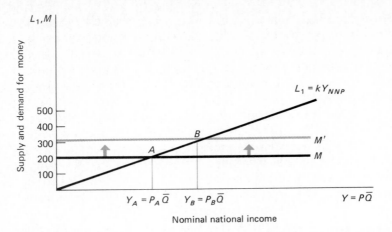

FIGURE 18-3 Start from point A, where the supply of and demand for money both equal 200, and the level of nominal national income equals Y_A. Y_A is the product of a constant Q and P_A—the price level consistent with M = 200. Now increase the money supply from M to M', or from 200 to 300. The new level of nominal national income equals Y_B. The product of the constant Q and P_B is the price level unique to money stock M' or 300.

nominal income rise, however, the quantity of money demanded will rise proportionally. More money is required to make the *same* transactions, which are now higher-priced, and to remain equally secure.

The Neutrality of Money To the classical economist, "Money does not matter" since it serves only as a medium of exchange. One way to explain that expression is to note that changes in the money supply (given the demand for money) change the price level, leaving relative prices unaltered.[8] This situation is referred to as the **neutrality of money;** money-supply changes affect monetary, and not real, phenomena.

The quantities of labor supplied and demanded are functions of the real wage. If neither the supply curve nor the demand curve shifts, the real wage won't change. Changes in labor productivity or in labor attitudes toward work shift the demand for and the supply of labor, but mere money supply changes will not do so in any apparent way. Because money is only a medium of exchange, money supply increases lead to increases in money income, which in turn lead to an increase in the demand for goods and services. Increases in the prices of goods and services, given money wages, lower the real wage. Recall Figure 17-4 from the previous chapter. *Given* the supply of and the

---

[8]Changes in the demand for money, given supply, can also change the price level. An increase in the frequency of payments to income recipients or a closer coincidence of payments and receipts will lower k. As k falls, V rises; given M and Q, the price level rises. Hence, the supply *and* the demand for money determine the price level in the classical model. Changes in k or v were considered stable—over the long run.

demand for labor curves, a reduction in the real wage resulting from an increase in the price level causes a shortage of labor. Unfettered (free) labor markets will, therefore, experience increases in money wages until equilibrium is again restored. Increases in the money supply lead to proportional increases in price and wage levels, but real wages and employment are unaltered.

Because the supply of and the demand for all inputs and outputs are determined in real terms, similar analysis indicates that, while money-supply changes shift monetary curves, real curves remain unaltered. If relative price changes temporarily result from money supply changes, shortages or surpluses will arise and competitive markets will then restore equilibrium at the original relative prices. Money is neutral—what else can one expect from a mere medium of exchange?

MONETARY AND FISCAL POLICIES IN THE CLASSICAL MODEL

Because the classical model predicts full employment, it would appear that the role of monetary and fiscal policies is limited. This conclusion is consistent with the classical tradition's desire for limited governmental activities in the economic system. Still, some early classical economists (Hume, for one) and later neoclassical economists (Pigou, for example) recognized that prices and wages do not readily fall. The "sticky downward" nature of prices and wages and the time lags (in reaching equilibrium) inherent in an economy in disequilibrium may make monetary and fiscal policies desirable. Let's examine those roles.

Monetary Policy in the Classical Model An increase in thriftiness or a relative increase in the demand for imports over exports, or some other such disequilibrium-creating situation (shock) that could create frictional unemployment does not lead to an immediate adjustment when prices and wages are sticky downward. Ultimately, after an adjustment period, the new equilibrium position again results in full employment with (perhaps) a compositional output change (more or less investment goods relative to consumer goods) and a reallocation of labor from one sector of the economy to another. But is comparative statics (comparing one equilibrium position with another and ignoring the process of moving from one to the other) the relevant analytical tool when prices and wages are sticky downward? Probably not. During the adjustment period, the time lag between disequilibrium and adjustment could be shortened (the duration of unemployment lessened) by judicious increases in the money supply. Therefore, a modest role exists for governmental stabilization policy generally, and monetary policy specifically. Starting from a disequilibrium unemployment situation, an increase in the money supply increases total spending, and wages will rise less rapidly (relative wages fall) in the surplus areas.

Fiscal Policy in the Classical Model Fiscal policy, on the other hand, is viewed less favorably in the classical model; its potential as a stabilizer of the economy is slight or redundant. Suppose the government attempts to offset the unemployment resulting from a disequilibrium-creating change in the economy— prolonged by price-wage stickiness downward—by increasing public expenditures.

If these expenditures are financed by higher taxes, the *net* effect is small because the private sector shrinks at the expense of the public sector. If governmental expenditures are financed by selling bonds to the public, the money supply remains constant but the increased demand for loanable funds (due to increased government borrowing, other things constant) causes real interest rates to rise. Higher real interest rates choke off (crowd out) private investment; the public sector expands at the expense of an equal contraction in the private sector. If increased governmental expenditures are financed by printing money to pay for them, output and employment will expand. But these real benefits come from increasing the *money supply.* So why use fiscal policy? Such a combination of fiscal and monetary policy (printing money to pay for public goods) results in an expanded public sector relative to the private sector. While such a change in the composition of national output might be desirable on other grounds, it isn't apparent that it is desirable when the goal is *stabilization of the economy.* Different goals should be separated conceptually. Increasing the employment level is one goal; increasing the proportion of resources allocated to the public sector is quite another.

CRITICISMS OF THE CLASSICAL MODEL

Economic events have a way of changing economic theory. Economists (and other theoreticians as well) cling to their models with an almost religious fervor when those models predict reasonably well. Recurrent doubts and theoretical inelegance are rationalized unless economists are confronted with overwhelming evidence that something is woefully amiss. The Great Depression, which was worldwide and lasted from 1929 until the late 1930s, provided such evidence. Indeed, in Great Britain, a deep recession and high unemployment existed for approximately five years *before* the Great Depression.

In 1936, John Maynard Keynes published a book[9] that was to revolutionize economic thinking. In his book (commonly referred to as *The General Theory*), Keynes criticized previous economic thinking (which he called "the classical model") on empirical and theoretical grounds. He then replaced it with his own version of how the macroeconomy works. The remainder of this chapter will focus on Keynesian and post-Keynesian criticisms of the classical model. The next two chapters present a brief (and modern) version of the Keynesian model.

[9]*The General Theory of Employment, Interest and Money* (London: Macmillan, 1936).

A Brief Overview The most fundamental criticism of any model is an assertion that the model doesn't work; when a model fails to explain or predict, it rightfully is attacked. Moreover, a model can properly be criticized if it is logically inconsistent. Keynes made no secret of his desire to bring about a revolution in economic thinking, and he knew that such a revolution must first take place in the ivory towers of academia. As a consequence, Keynes was not content merely to point out where the classical model failed as a predictor of economic reality. As a shrewd tactician in the game of intellectual warfare, he realized that he must also show how the model is logically flawed and then replace it with a better one.

Recall that the classical model rested on two foundation blocks:

1 Wage-rate adjustments assure that labor surpluses (involuntary unemployment) are eliminated.

2 Interest-rate adjustments bring saving and investment plans into equality, and as a result no general insufficiency of aggregate spending exists.

We now turn to Keynesian and post-Keynesian criticisms of these foundation blocks. If they can be shaken loose, the classical model will fall.

Aggregate Demand for and Supply of Labor Keynes had no serious quarrel with the classical theory of the aggregate demand for labor. Buyers of labor suffer from no "money illusion" and are concerned only with the money wage rate *relative* to output price: Businesses purchase more labor only if the real wage falls. On the other hand, Keynes rejected the classical formulation of the aggregate supply of labor curve. Recall that classical theory states that the aggregate supply of labor curve is upward-sloping and reflects the direct relationship between the real wage and the overall quantity of labor supplied. Such a formulation predicts that during periods when wages are relatively constant and prices are rising, some laborers will withdraw some (or all) of their labor— because the *real* wage is falling. Keynes noted that actual observation did not support this prediction.

Keynes then offered some theoretical reasons to explain why the supply of labor is not directly related to the real wage. For one thing, people are "locked in" to mortgage and other long-term debt payments. It simply won't do for a person to withdraw *some* labor just because the going real wage now has a marginal benefit insufficient to outweigh the marginal disutility. Such considerations must be suspended when fixed debt payments must be made. Keynes also rejected the notion that laborers can bargain for the length of the workweek; surely some rigidity exists with respect to the workweek. Yet, this point can be oversold, as the accompanying Highlight indicates. Finally, according to Keynes, individual unions are concerned largely with their unions' wages relative to *other* unions' wages. In periods of generally rising prices, all unions are equally adversely affected and, hence, will not withdraw their labor.

For these reasons, rising prices, given money wages, will not induce a reduction in total hours of labor offered per week, even though the real wage falls. A *rational* money illusion exists for the supply of labor, and the classical supply of labor curve is suspect;[10] it appears that the quantity of labor supplied is *not* determined by the *real* wage. Added to this is the fact that in the *real world,* prices and wages are sticky downward. This makes involuntary unemployment a distinct possibility. Even the classical economist would have agreed with this last point. And so Keynes dismissed the classical theory of the aggregate supply of and demand for labor on both empirical and theoretical grounds. In his model, he made the assumption of downward price-wage rigidity (as is shown in the following chapters).

The Saving and Investment Curves

Having crumbled one foundation block of the classical model, Keynes then turned on the other. Remember that it is the interest rate that brings saving and investment into equality. Recall the classical position:

1   Saving is directly related to the real interest rate and investment is inversely related to the real interest rate.
2   Saving (and therefore consumption) and investment are (implicitly) *primarily* determined by the real interest rate, and thus these curves are stable.

Keynes rejected both these assertions.

Saving and the Interest Rate

Suppose that individuals set a target for retirement. Let's say that Mr. Smith wants to have $50,000 when he retires. If the interest rate rises (or falls), Mr. Smith must save less (or more) to achieve his saving goal. Thus, a theoretical reason exists for assuming that saving and interest rates are *inversely* related! Moreover, said Keynes, saving (and consumption) is not primarily determined by the interest rate but is a function of real income. In effect, the classical economist held constant the most important determinant of the consumption-saving decision—real income. If full employment usually prevails, then it is legitimate to hold income constant and to claim that saving and consumption are primarily determined by the interest rate. But because the issue is whether or not there can be full employment, it is not proper to hold income constant. To assume a constant

---

[10]Modern economists derive labor supply curves by discussing the trade-off between leisure and income. Such a technique presents the possibility of labor supply curves that are perfectly inelastic (vertical) or even backward-bending (showing fewer labor hours offered at very high real wages as wealthier laborers now can afford to "buy" more leisure). Vertical or backward-bending labor supply curves may exist for individuals, but they are unlikely to exist for aggregate labor supply curves—which incorporate higher participation rates for women and children at high real wages. Thus, while some individuals might prefer to work less at higher wages, this effect will be offset as more women and children respond to higher real wages.

HIGHLIGHT   Wage Rates and the Workweek

According to the classical model, within broad limits, laborers can choose their workweek. Keynes attacked this assumption by noting that most laborers are given the option of working the "normal" workweek or not working at all.

Obviously some workers can choose their workweek, and presumably they do so on the basis of real after-tax earnings compared to forgone leisure. This group includes the self-employed, businesspeople, and professionals (physicians, dentists, and lawyers, to name a few). College teachers can do varying amounts of consulting work; skilled laborers such as carpenters, plumbers, and masons can always moonlight. It appears, therefore, that a significant minority of the work force does have some control over its labor supply.

However, what about industrial factory workers? Surely they must work the standard workweek or not at all, right? Wrong, at least according to the implications of a *Wall Street Journal* article written by Assar Lindbeck, a professor of economics at the University of Stockholm. According to Lindbeck, high marginal tax rates in Sweden have created a situation in which the "actual working time of full-time workers in the mechanical industry is not 40 hours per week, as the statutory rules would suggest, but approximately 29 hours, which is probably the lowest figure among industrial countries."* Lindbeck attributes this reduced workweek to "various kinds of absenteeism." Apparently, even industrial workers can make significant marginal adjustments in the length of their workweek.

Keynesians will doubtlessly reply that such workweek adjustments might be possible when the economy is expanding, but are unlikely during a recession or depression.

*Assar Lindbeck, *The Wall Street Journal*, Sept. 9, 1981, p. 25.

---

national income because full employment is assumed is to assume one's conclusions.

Thus, every time that community real income changes (and it can, if unemployment exists), the classical saving (and consumption) function will shift. In short, according to Keynes, the saving curve is volatile (it fluctuates) because the most important determinant of saving—income—is held constant. When the Keynesian model is discussed in later chapters, you will observe that real saving and real consumption are functions of real disposable income, and not the real interest rate.

Investment and the Interest Rate   Here, again, said Keynes, the classical economist held constant the most important determinant of investment—profit expectations. An inverse relationship exists between investment and the interest rate, *other things constant*. What is held constant is profit expectations, which are subject to quick and violent change. As a consequence, the investment curve also fluctuates—it shifts every time profit expectations change.

Saving, investment, and the interest rate If neither saving nor investment is primarily determined by the interest rate, how can interest-rate fluctuations bring them into equality? If both schedules fluctuate, can one be sure saving-investment equality assures full employment? Keynes answered "They can't" to the first question and "No, one can't be sure" to the second. For example, assume that a recession is brought on by, say, an increase in general thriftiness. According to the classical model, saving increases are offset by investment increases that result from a decline in the real interest rate. But it is not legitimate to hold profit expectations constant during a recession. If profit expectations fall, significant interest-rate reductions might be ignored by business investors. In short, will businesses invest more in plant and equipment at precisely the time they have excess capacity due to a recession? To Keynes the answer to this question is evident and it weakens the classical model. This topic is considered again in the Current Controversy at the end of this chapter. Moreover, a more modern derivation of the investment–interest rate relationship is developed in the following chapter.

Money Supply and Money Demand

Recall that the supply of and the demand for money determine the price level in the classical model, because the annual output of final goods and services (Q) is constant (due to the classical prediction of full employment). In addition, because money is only a medium of exchange, the income velocity of money (V) is also constant. In a basic version of the equation of exchange,

$$M\overline{V} = P\overline{Q} \tag{18-5}$$

It follows that M and P are proportionally related; this is the **crude quantity theory of money.** However, if the assumption of a constant Q is rejected, it no longer follows that M and P vary proportionally. It is possible that changes in M can change P or Q (or both) and therefore, such changes can also change real income, even if V *is relatively constant.* Hence, "Money might matter"; this is a more modern, **sophisticated quantity theory of money.**

Actually, as will be shown in Chapter 20, Keynes also indicated that V (or k) is not constant. Indeed, he showed how changes in M may lead to changes in V in the *opposite* direction. Hence, changes in M might not affect either P or Q—this paved the way back to the notion that "Money doesn't matter." In fact, such a formulation implies that money supply changes may not even affect *nominal* income—in the short run. This implication goes beyond even the classical model in belittling the influence of money.

The Long and the Short of It

Keynes and his legion of followers criticized the patience (some would say insensitivity) of classical (and modern) economists who are prepared to wait for relative price changes to drive the economy toward full employment. In the meantime, what about all the human suffering endured by the unemployed, by the bankrupt, and by their families? This is a question guaranteed to discomfit those who believe in a "self-regulating economy." How long do people have to wait? How long is the long run? Frustrated with classical prescriptions to leave the economy to its own devices and wait for long-run adjustments, Keynes was prompted to offer his oft-quoted dictum "In the long run we are all dead." This dictum has become almost as famous as Say's law.

A Self-Regulating Economy?   The classical economists clung (as do their modern-day intellectual descendants) tenaciously to a belief in a self-regulating economy. Apparently, the Great Depression left no impression on some of them. Nor did three other worldwide depressions and thirteen smaller recessions that occurred between 1870 and 1929—the heyday of free enterprise in the United States. Table 18-1 indicates the time intervals of these business-cycle contractions, as established "officially" by the National Bureau of Economic Research. In the face of business-cycle evidence, one can only marvel at the ability of theory to resist contradiction.

TABLE 18-1   Business-Cycle Expansions (Peaks) and Contractions (Troughs), 1870–1929

Business-cycle reference dates	
Trough	**Peak**
December 1870	October 1873
March 1879	March 1882
May 1885	March 1887
April 1888	July 1890
May 1891	January 1893
June 1894	December 1895
June 1897	June 1899
December 1900	September 1902
August 1904	May 1907
June 1908	January 1910
January 1912	January 1913
December 1914	August 1918
March 1919	January 1920
July 1921	May 1923
July 1924	October 1926
November 1927	August 1929

Source: U.S. Department of Commerce, Bureau of Economic Analysis, *Business Conditions Digest*, July 1982, p. 105.

CURRENT CONTROVERSY

Investment and Excess Capacity

Keynes doubted that businesses are willing to purchase plant and equipment during a recession, even though interest rates are relatively low, because profit expectations also are low. It does not seem sensible to expect businesses to increase investments and expand their capacity at a time when they have excess capacity. Keynes expected businesses to wait until better times come along.

Still, the classical economists are not necessarily *illogical* here. After all, a recession is not expected to last forever. An increase in saving may mean an increase in future spending. Thus, the more discerning entrepreneurs can increase their capacity (which, after all, takes time) and be ready when demand picks up again. By doing so, they can obtain increased market shares and profits at the expense of their competitors who have less foresight. The entrepreneurs who guess correctly and take advantage of low interest rates during a recession can thereby earn abnormal profits. Risky business? Perhaps, but according to the classical economists, that is precisely the *function* of entrepreneurs: to earn abnormal profits (or suffer losses) by taking risks. On the other hand, it is open to question whether a sufficient number of entrepreneurs will respond positively to a lower interest rate to pull the economy out of a recession.

This issue is ultimately an empirical question. While the evidence supports Keynes on this score, in all fairness it should be reemphasized that the classical economists are not necessarily illogical regarding this issue.

CHAPTER SUMMARY

1 Suppose that the whole community decides to consume less and to save more. According to the classical economists, eventually the consumer-goods sector contracts and the investment-goods sector expands; the output level remains at the full-employment level, but the composition of output changes. Similarly, employment remains at the full-employment level, but some laborers are reallocated from the consumer-goods to the investment-goods sector.

2 The equation of exchange, formulated by Irving Fisher, is an identity that states that total expenditures on final goods and services is equal to total business receipts, or $MV = PQ$. The classical economists predicted that the long-run rate of output of final goods and services remains constant at the full-employment level. They also assumed that velocity was stable because the payment habits of the community change very slowly.

3 Because the classical theorists maintained that Q and V are constant in the equation of exchange, their conclusion is that the price level is determined by the supply of and the demand for money. Changes in the money supply lead to proportional

changes in the price level. The classical economists believed that money is only a medium of exchange, and that, therefore, changes in the stock of money change absolute, not relative, prices. As a consequence, real variables such as output and employment are (in the long run) unaffected by money-supply changes; money is neutral.

4 Recognizing that frictional unemployment does exist, some classical economists maintained that the impact of disequilibrium-creating events can be lessened and shortened by judicious use of monetary policy. They were less sanguine about the prospects of fiscal policy.

5 Keynes criticized the foundations of the classical model. He pointed out that the model does not predict well and that it is logically flawed. Keynes's position was that, while the classical demand for labor function is acceptable, its supply of labor function is invalid. Also, he attacked the classical theory of the level of effective aggregate demand. His position was that the relationship between saving and the interest rate, and the relationship between investment and the interest rate, is not so strong as the classical economists believed. Real saving and real consumption are determined primarily by real income, not by the real interest rate.

6 Also, he pointed out that profit expectations—not the real interest rate—are the primary determinant of net investment. If neither saving nor investment is determined primarily by the interest rate, changes in the interest rate cannot bring them into equality. Hence, nothing assured Keynes that a full-employment output would be purchased. Once the credibility of a constant full-employment level of output is questioned, then the crude quantity theory of money becomes doubtful. That is, changes in the money supply may lead to less-than-proportional changes in the price level.

7 Finally, even if the classical conclusion of a long-run-attained full-employment position is accepted (a conclusion which many find unlikely), it must be asked: How long is the long run? Those who are concerned with the human problems concomitant to "adjustment lags" to disequilibrium are not prepared to wait for a self-adjusting economy to attain full employment.

GLOSSARY

Crude quantity theory of money: Changes in the money stock lead to proportional changes in the price level; this proposition follows if velocity and the rate of output are constant.

Equation of exchange: An identity that states that the money stock times the number of times each money unit is spent on final goods and services is equal to the rate of final output multiplied by the respective prices of the final outputs; $MV = PQ$.

Frictional unemployment: Unemployment that occurs when people are between steady jobs; people quit or are laid off and take time to find another job.

Neutrality of money: If changes in the stock of money change only absolute prices, but leave relative prices unaltered, money is said to be neutral; money-supply changes do not affect real phenomena such as output and employment.

Precautionary motive: A motive for holding money that arises because people want to hold a pool of readily available purchasing power in order to meet emergencies.

Sophisticated quantity theory of money: Changes in the money stock lead to changes in national income; whether the national income change is in nominal (P) or real (Q) terms depends on how close the economy is to full employment; this proposition follows if velocity is constant or changes predictably.

Transactions motive: A motive for holding money that arises because people receive income at discrete intervals but want to make expenditures more or less continuously.

PROBLEMS

18-1 Using the equation of exchange, $MV = PQ = Y$, calculate velocity for an economy that has a national income of $3 trillion and a money supply of $500 billion.

18-2 Mrs. Kulcyski has an annual income of $20,000 and holds, on average, $3,000 to meet her transactions motive and $1,000 to meet her precautionary motive. Using the classical demand for money equation, $L_1 = kY$, calculate:

a Her k at a nominal income of $20,000 per year

b How much she will hold for transactions and precautionary motives if the price level and her money income triple

c Her k at a nominal income of $60,000 per year

SELECTED REFERENCES

Fisher, Irving, *The Purchasing Power of Money* (London: Macmillan, 1911).

Friedman, Milton, "The Quantity Theory of Money—A Restatement," in *Studies in the Quantity Theory of Money* (Chicago: University of Chicago Press, 1956).

————, "The Role of Monetary Policy," *American Economic Review*, vol. 58, March 1968, pp. 1–17.

Patinkin, Don, *Money, Interest, and Prices,* 2d ed. (New York: Harper & Row, 1965).

Wicksell, Knute, *Interest and Prices* (New York: Augustus M. Kelley, 1965).

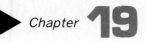

Chapter 19

The Simple Keynesian Model

CHAPTER PREVIEW

1 What is Keynes's theory of the consumption function?

2 What is Keynes's theory of the determination of the short-run level of national income and national employment?

3 What happens if aggregate demand does not equal aggregate supply?

4 Is it possible for equilibrium and unemployment to exist simultaneously?

5 Why do shifts in the aggregate demand curve lead to multiple changes in the equilibrium level of national income?

6 Is there a role for fiscal policy in the Keynesian model?

Before monetary policy can be effective, policymakers must have a model or theory about how the economy operates; they must have a clear idea of what the key economic variables are and how these variables are interrelated. Monetary policy also requires a theory of how money fits into an economy and how changes in the money supply affect the important economic variables. The classical model provided both these necessary ingredients. The classical economists concluded that the economy was self-regulating and that monetary (and fiscal) policy is largely unnecessary.

The Great Depression of the 1930s provided incontrovertible proof that there were no mechanisms within capitalism that brought the economy back to full employment—at least, not in the short run. It was apparent to Keynes and his followers that a new way of looking at the economy was necessary. Keynes was tired of waiting for full employment to return and was interested in what could be done in the meantime. Keynes's analysis dealt also with the determinants of *net national product* (or NNP)—the market value of final goods and services produced during the year—in the short run, especially when the economy was entrenched in a serious recession or depression.

This chapter is concerned with how NNP is determined and how it changes at production levels below the full-employment level. Two important implications result from concentrating economic analysis on those periods when high unemployment of labor and considerable excess capacity exist.[1] These two implications are:

1 National output can be increased over broad ranges without causing the price level to rise; increases in national output cause the price level to rise during periods of low unemployment and low excess capacity. In this chapter, therefore, we assume that the price level remains constant and that all variables are measured in real terms; a change in nominal NNP, I_n, C, S, or i *also* represents a real change in these variables.

2 Keynes was led to concentrate on the aggregate demand for goods and services, or the aggregate expenditures on goods and services, as the prime mover in the economy. As total expenditures change, NNP will change in the same direction.

In this chapter, we discuss Keynes's short-run theory of the equilibrium level of NNP and how NNP changes—at less than full-employment levels. We then discuss the role of fiscal policy in the Keynesian model. In the next chapter, we will analyze monetary policy in the Keynesian model.

According to Keynes, any level of national income is possible in the short run, up to and including full employment, and there are no mechanisms to assure full employment of labor. The key question is: What determines the equilibrium level of national income or employment? Because Keynesian analysis deals with the short run, a functional relationship exists between national

---

[1]A considerable amount of excess capacity exists when the economy is producing only 70 percent—or less—of what it is capable of producing; much labor and much capital are idle.

output and the employment level; in the short run, output can be changed only by varying the amount of labor. Because national income equals the value of output, national income and national output are by definition the same. Output levels are directly related to the unemployment level; therefore, a short-run functional relationship exists between the level of employment and *net national product,* or Y. And so a theory of the determination of the equilibrium employment level is a theory of the determination of the equilibrium national income level, and vice versa.[2] This chapter develops Keynes's theory of the equilibrium level of national income and employment.

AGGREGATE DEMAND

According to Keynes, out of all the possible output and employment levels, businesses select that level that is the most profitable. The most profitable level depends on the **aggregate demand (AD)** for goods and services. Since businesses attempt to maximize profits, they are prepared to adjust output levels to whatever level aggregate demand makes most profitable. The essence of Keynes's model is that the prime mover in the macroeconomy is aggregate demand; aggregate output is passive and dances to the tune of changes in aggregate demand.

What specifically is aggregate demand? It is the sum of the real value of expenditures on final goods and services by each sector of the economy at each level of real national income. Household demand for final goods and services is consumption demand (C); business demand for final goods and services is investment demand (I), and the demand for publicly provided goods and services is government demand (G). Ignoring the international sector,

$$AD = C + I + G \qquad \qquad \textbf{(19-1)}$$

Aggregate demand in a closed, *private* economy (which ignores government demand) is derived as follows:[3]

$$AD = C + I \qquad \qquad \textbf{(19-2)}$$

In these equations, I can represent gross investment (I_g) or net investment (I_n), in which case GNP or NNP, respectively, is derived.[4] This chapter derives *real* NNP, which is denoted as Y. All variables, unless otherwise indicated, are in

---

[2]Keynes solved for the equilibrium employment level and derived from it the equilibrium level of net national product. Modern economists find it convenient to solve for the equilibrium level of Y and deduce from it the equilibrium employment level. Clearly, if indeed a short-run functional relationship does exist between employment and Y, no conflict exists between these two approaches. This text follows the convention of modern economists and determines the equilibrium level of Y.

[3]C represents real consumption *plans* and I represents real investment *plans.*

[4]You will recall that I_g minus depreciation equals I_n.

real values because we assume a constant price level for all output levels until full employment is reached.

THE MODEL

Because Keynes's theory of how income and employment are determined is essentially a theory of aggregate demand, each of the individual components of aggregate demand is discussed in turn.

The Consumption Function Keynes realized that annual community (or individual) consumption is determined by many variables, but he chose to emphasize just one—real disposable income. As a result, Keynesians have derived a rather simple consumption function. Keynes's theory contains three propositions regarding the consumption function, and each is testable.

1 *Real consumption (and real saving) is a stable function of real disposable income.* Since consumption (or saving) and income are related in *real* terms, no money illusion exists; consumers buy an identical bundle of goods and services if national income and all prices change at the same

John Maynard Keynes. The world-famous Cambridge University economist who criticized the classical model and revolutionized macroeconomics. *(Courtesy of United Press International.)*

rate. Note that real consumption or saving depends on real disposable income (Yd). In a closed, private economy $Yd = Y$ because taxes and transfers are ignored; Yd and Y therefore can be used interchangeably in a closed, private economy. Finally, Keynes assumed a *stable* (nonfluctuating) relationship between real consumption (and real saving) and real disposable income. This proposition is a radical departure from the classical model, which assumed that income was constant and that real saving and real consumption are determined primarily by the real interest rate. So far, Keynes's relationship between real consumption and real income has not been specified. The test for proposition 1 is whether or not there is a high correlation between real income and real consumption (and real saving).

2 *As real disposable income rises (for the group or for the individual), both real consumption and real saving also rise.* In effect, this means that income increases will be partially consumed and partially saved. Keynes referred to the ratio of a change in consumption to a change in income as the **marginal propensity to consume (MPC)**:

$$MPC = \Delta C / \Delta Y$$

The **marginal propensity to save (MPS)** is defined similarly:

$$MPS = \Delta S / \Delta Y$$

Proposition 2 can be restated as follows: The MPC and the MPS must be between zero and one. That is, $0 < MPC < 1$ and $0 < MPS < 1$. Because income changes can be only spent or saved, $MPC + MPS = 1$.

Consider an example. Disposable income rises from $100 billion to $110 billion and consumption rises from $80 billion to $87 billion. A $10 billion increase in disposable incomes leads to a $7 billion increase in consumption (and therefore to a $3 billion increase in saving). The $MPC = \Delta C / \Delta Y =$ $7 billion/$10 billion = 0.7, and the $MPS = \Delta S / \Delta Y =$ $3 billion/$10 billion = 0.3. Note that $MPC + MPS = 1$.

3 *As real disposable income rises, the percentage of income devoted to consumption (C/Y), or the **average propensity to consume (APC)**, falls, and the percentage of income devoted to saving (S/Y), or the **average propensity to save (APS)**, rises.* Note that $1 = APC + APS$, since disposable income can be only spent or saved.

Keynes's third proposition currently is referred to as the **absolute income hypothesis;** it says that the APC is inversely related to the absolute level of real disposable income. This hypothesis reflects Keynes's belief that present wants are relatively limited; higher and higher incomes eventually allow people to satisfy their basic current needs, and further income increases won't lead to very much additional consumption. Only so many goods can be consumed currently; thus Keynes was an "underconsumptionist" (following Malthus and Marx).

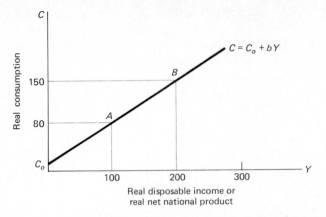

FIGURE 19-1   A Typical Keynesian Consumption Function.   This graph indicates a typical Keynesian consumption function. It is upward-sloping from left to right; as real disposable income rises, so does real consumption. The slope of this straight line is less than 1; income increases are partially saved. The function has a positive vertical intercept ($C_o > 0$), because the APC falls as real national income rises.

Note that the MPC = $\Delta C/\Delta Y$ = 7/10 = 0.7, and that the MPC is mathematically equal to the slope of the consumption function. (Check the slope from A to B.) Also, the APC falls from A to B; it falls from .80 to .75. Can you calculate the APS at points A and B?

Assuming a linear consumption function, Keynes's consumption function can be specified mathematically. The simple Keynesian consumption function can be written as

$$C = C_o + bY, \text{ where } C_o > 0 \text{ and } 0 < b < 1 \tag{19-3}$$

for a closed, private economy in which $Yd = Y$. C_o is the vertical intercept of the consumption function (it is the value of consumption at zero income),[5] and according to Keynes's proposition 3, C_o must be positive.[6] Note that b is the slope of the consumption function and is the MPC; according to Keynes's second hypothesis, b must be between zero and one. A typical Keynesian consumption function is illustrated in Figure 19-1.

The Investment Function   Real net investment is either related to the level of real net national product or it is not. If related, real net national product increases probably induce more net investment. Boom times are associated with high

[5]This intercept value recognizes that there are nonincome determinants of consumption, such as wealth; a change in wealth will change the vertical intercept, and the consumption curve will shift.

[6]Dividing Equation (19-3) by Y yields $C/Y = (C_o/Y) + b$. If $C_o = 0$, then the APC (C/Y) equals the MPC (b), which is a constant. Thus, a zero vertical intercept implies a constant APC (equal to the MPC) as Y rises. Can you verify that C_o/Y falls as Y rises if $C_o > 0$ in the derived equation?

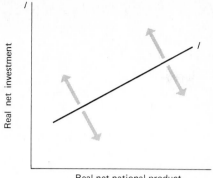

FIGURE 19-2 Induced Investment.   In this graph, higher levels of real net national product induce higher levels of real net investment, and a systematic relationship exists between them. This curve is volatile; it shifts every time interest rates or profit expectations change, as the arrows indicate.

real national income and high real net investment; recessions are associated with relatively low levels of *I* and *Y*. A direct relationship between *I* and *Y* exists. This **induced investment** relationship appears in Figure 19-2.

On the other hand, it is possible to conceive of a situation in which the level of real national income is high but the business outlook is bleak; a high *Y* and a low *I* then coexist. Or, a low *Y* can be associated with high business confidence; then a low *Y* and a high *I* appear. The real relationship might, therefore, be between *I* and the *expected rate of change* of *Y*. If so, no systematic relationship exists between *I* and the *level* of *Y; I* is then *autonomous* (independent) of *Y*. An **autonomous investment** curve appears in Figure 19-3.

What is important to note about the induced and autonomous investment curves is that both are extremely volatile. According to Keynes, the *I* function, unlike the consumption function, shifts significantly and often because net investment depends on subjective evaluations of the future. Are we headed for boom or bust, inflation or recession? Every time businesses change their profit expectations, the investment function shifts (upward if the profit expectations become more favorable, downward if they become less favorable). Technological changes also affect the net investment curve, and they are hardly systematic or predictable. It is hard to exaggerate, according to

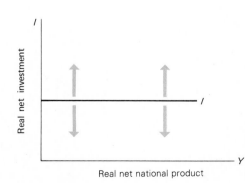

FIGURE 19-3 Autonomous Net Investment.   This graph indicates that no systematic relationship exists between real net investment and real net national product. The *I* function is parallel to the horizontal axis. This *I* curve lies above the horizontal axis; hence, *I* is positive. If *I* = 0, the *I* curve lies on the horizontal axis; a negative *I* implies an *I* curve below the horizontal axis. The curve shifts as profit expectations change and as interest rates change; hence, it is very volatile, as the arrows indicate.

Keynes, the importance of the fact that the investment function is extremely volatile and is therefore subject to violent upward or downward shifts in the short run. As we shall see, such volatility in the I function causes the AD curve to be volatile; in turn, a volatile AD curve makes capitalism itself subject to periods of boom and bust.

Keynes did not quarrel with the classical economists regarding the inverse relationship between real interest rates and net investment. He accepted their argument that the marginal profitability of capital falls, and that businesses carry out investment projects up to the point where the expected marginal rate of return is just offset by the going rate of interest. Thus, interest rates must fall before more investment will be undertaken. How, then, do interest rate changes fit into Keynes's model? If the interest rate falls, the autonomous investment curve in Figure 19-3 shifts upward; net investment is higher at every income level. A higher interest rate shifts that curve downward.[7] Thus, a given autonomous investment curve implicitly holds the interest rate constant.

Aggregate Demand in a Closed, Private Economy   Assuming that real net investment is autonomous, or independent of the level of Y, an aggregate demand curve for a closed, private economy can be derived. Since AD $= C + I$, the aggregate demand function is formed by adding a constant I to the consump-

---

[7] A fall in the interest rate also shifts the induced investment curve in Figure 19-2 upward; a rise in the interest rate shifts it downward.

FIGURE 19-4   Constructing Aggregate Demand in a Closed, Private Economy.   In this graph, positive autonomous net investment is added to the consumption function. Because net investment is autonomous, the aggregate demand curve is parallel to the consumption function. Because net investment is positive, the aggregate demand curve lies above the consumption function. Note that real consumption plans and real investment plans are plotted on the vertical axis; real disposable income is plotted on the horizontal axis.

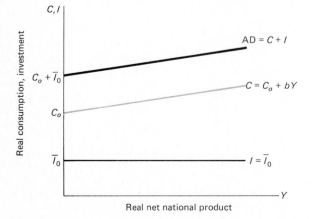

tion function. As long as autonomous investment is nonzero, the aggregate demand curve is parallel to the consumption function.[8] The construction of an AD curve in a closed, private economy is illustrated in Figure 19-4.

AGGREGATE SUPPLY

Aggregate supply (AS) is the total supply schedule for the economy. It shows the various possible levels of aggregate real output values, Y, that businesses produce at every level of real national income. Businesses, as a group, are willing to produce any output level—up to and including full employment—if they expect to be able to sell it. If producers in the aggregate produce $1 trillion worth of goods and services, they thereby generate $1 trillion worth of income in the form of wages, interest, rents, and profits. $2 trillion of goods and services produced will create $2 trillion of income, and so on. Figure 19-5 shows an aggregate supply curve for the economy; the value of real output is plotted on the vertical axis and net national product, or Y, is plotted on the horizontal axis. The AS curve is a 45-degree line—it has a slope equal to one—because the value of output (Y) will be equal to the value of income generated from that production.

AGGREGATE SUPPLY AND AGGREGATE DEMAND DETERMINE EQUILIBRIUM NATIONAL INCOME

All the tools necessary to determine the equilibrium level of national income for a closed, private economy have now been developed. The equilibrium level of national income is at the point of intersection of the aggregate supply and

---

[8]If $C = C_o + bY$ and $I = I_o$ (investment is constant at I_o) and AD = $C + I$, then AD = $C_o + bY + I_o$. Rearranging gives AD = $(C_o + I_o) + bY$. Comparing this function to the consumption function, it is clear that they have the same slope, b (the MPC); if $I_o \neq 0$, then they have different vertical intercepts. Therefore, they are parallel. If $I_o = 0$, then AD equals the consumption function.

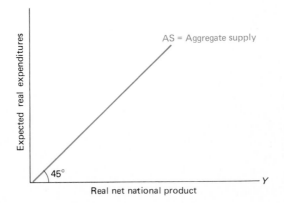

FIGURE 19-5   The Aggregate Supply Curve.   Here the aggregate supply curve is shown as a 45° line, which has a slope of 1. Expected (real) expenditures are on the vertical axis. When moving from left to right along the horizontal axis to higher output rates, real net national product, or Y, also rises.

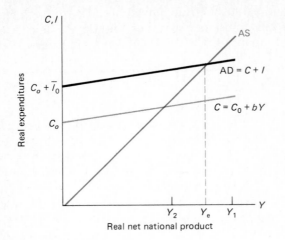

FIGURE 19-6 Equilibrium in a Closed, Private Economy. The most profitable output rate for businesses occurs at real national income Y_e, where aggregate supply and aggregate demand intersect. At a higher rate of output consistent with Y_1, $AS_q > AD_q$ and a surplus of final goods exists. Businesses will react to increased inventories by reducing output and employment. At any level of income less than Y_e, $AD_q > AS_q$ and a shortage of final goods and services exists. If full employment does not exist, output rises and causes Y to rise.

aggregate demand curves; that point represents the most profitable (or least unprofitable) output rate for businesses as a whole.

Consider Figure 19-6. The quantity of AD and the quantity of AS are equated at Y_e; hence, it is the most profitable rate of output for businesses. Any higher output rate (such as Y_1) that generates a higher level of Y than Y_e means that business expectations are unfulfilled. Businesses, in the aggregate, have overestimated what they profitably can produce and sell; they have created a surplus of final goods and services. An undesired increase in inventories occurs, and businesses therefore reduce output and employment in order to maximize profits.

Any rate of output consistent with a net national product level less than Y_e creates a shortage of final goods and services; the quantity of AD, AD_q, exceeds the quantity of AS, AS_q. An undesired decrease in inventories occurs because businesses, in the aggregate, have underestimated what they can sell, and they have not, therefore, maximized profits.

Only at Y_e does $AS_q = AD_q$; only at that unique output level is there no unwanted inventory change; Y_e is the most profitable output rate. Note how AS_q adjusts to AD_q. In that sense, AD is the prime mover and AS is passive; AS_q adjusts to whatever AD is.

Equilibrium via Saving and Investment Plans Equilibrium in a closed, private economy can be found in another manner. Recall that $Y = C + S$, by definition. Hence, if Y and C are known, then S is determined, and is equal to $Y - C$. It follows that a saving curve can be derived by subtracting the consumption from the 45-degree AS curve (because AS_q equals Y). Saving always equals $AS_q - C$. A typical Keynesian saving curve and an autonomous investment curve are plotted in panel (b) of Figure 19-7. Can you see how (b) is derived from (a) in that graph?

In Figure 19-7, observe that in a closed, private economy, if $AD_q > AS_q$ (at

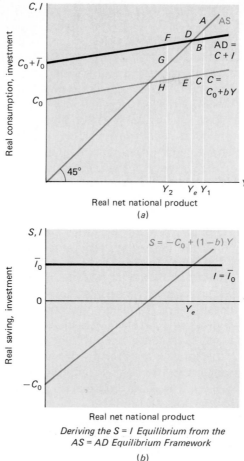

FIGURE 19-7   Deriving the $S = I$ Equilibrium from the AS = AD Equilibrium Framework. Panel (a): AS = AD Framework; Panel (b): Deriving the $S = I$ Equilibrium from the AS = AD Equilibrium Framework.   In panel (b), the saving curve is derived from the 45° AS curve and the C function. At all levels of income greater than Y_e, $AS_q > AD_q$ and $S > I$. At all levels of income less than Y_e, $AD_q > AS_q$ and $I > S$. At Y_e, $AD_q = AS_q$ and therefore $S = I$. In a closed, private economy, the equilibrium condition is that $AD_q = AS_q$ or $S = I$; these are simply two ways of looking at the same phenomenon. The saving curve can also be derived algebraically. Since $Y = C + S$ and $C = C_o + bY$, substituting yields $Y = C_o + bY + S$. Subtracting bY from both sides gives $Y - bY = C_o + S$. Then $(1 - b)Y = C_o + S$. Therefore, $S = -C_o + (1 - b)Y$.

all levels of income less than Y_e), then $I > S$.[9] At all levels of income greater than Y_e, inspection shows that $AS_q > AD_q$ and $S > I$.[10] Only at Y_e does $AS_q = AD_q$ and $S = I$ (saving and investment both equal $D - E$). Therefore, in a closed, private economy, the equilibrium condition is that $AD_q = AS_q$, or $I = S$.

THE MULTIPLIER

Shifts in aggregate demand cause the equilibrium level of national income to change. In this section, this relationship between changes in AD and changes in NNP is explored in detail.

---

[9]At Y_2 in panel (a) of Figure 19-7, saving $= G - H$; investment $= F - H$.

[10]In panel (a) of Figure 19-7, at Y_1 saving $= A - C$; investment $= B - C$.

The **multiplier effect** is the result of *shifts* in the aggregate demand curve. It indicates that every $1 billion shift in aggregate demand causes the equilibrium level of national income to change by more than $1 billion. Every $1 billion shift downward (decrease) in aggregate demand causes the equilibrium level of national income to fall by more than $1 billion.

To understand how the multiplier effect works, consider an equilibrium position that is disturbed by a $1 million increase in autonomous investment for, say, machines.[11] Because one group's expenditure is another group's income, national income has *already* increased by $1 million; the people who built and sold the machine for $1 million have just received an income increase. According to Keynes's theory of the consumption function, they will spend some of this income increase on consumption goods and save some. Assuming a marginal propensity to consume of .75, the machine builders will increase their consumption by $750,000 and their saving by $250,000. Again, because one group's expenditure is another's income, community income now rises by $750,000—for those people who produced the $750,000 worth of goods purchased by the machine builders. Note that *already,* after only two rounds of transactions, total national income has increased by $1.75 million. A $1 million increase in AD, due to an increase in autonomous investment, has caused national income to rise by $1.75 million. Moreover, the process is not yet completed because that group receiving an increase in its income of $750,000 will spend some and save some; the amount that it spends on consumption will become income for still another group, and so on. Thus, every $1 million increase in AD will cause the level of income to rise by more than $1 million. As is demonstrated in the mathematical appendix to this chapter, the multiplier equals $1/(1 - b)$, where b = MPC, the slope of the consumption function. In our example, $b = .75$, so the multiplier is 4; every $1 million shift in aggregate demand causes the level of national income to change by $4 million.

FISCAL POLICY IN THE KEYNESIAN MODEL

Keynes maintained that nothing assures full employment in the short run. Since capitalism contains no mechanisms that move an economy to its full-employment position, it follows that an important stabilizing role exists for government. Keynes's prescription for getting the economy out of high unemployment is fiscal policy. We now depart from a closed, private economy in

---

[11]$AD = (C_o + I_o) + bY$, where $(C_o + I_o)$ is the vertical axis intercept. The AD curve shifts every time that intercept changes. If autonomous net investment changes, or if the vertical intercept of the consumption function (C_o) changes, aggregate demand shifts and Y increases by a multiple of the shift in AD.

order to discuss fiscal policy; the effects on NNP of government expenditures, G, and taxes, T, are now considered.

A Deflationary Gap Consider Figure 19-8. Panel (*a*) indicates a **recessionary gap.** At the full-employment level of income (Y_f), $AS_q > AD_q$ (by the distance $B-C$, the recessionary gap). In panel (*b*), this gap is eliminated by an increase in government expenditures, G. Note that an increase in G shifts the AD curve upward, dollar for dollar; the vertical intercept of the AD curve changes by the amount of the change in G. This is similar to the effect that a shift in consumption and investment has on the AD curve. The AD curve is

$$AD = (C_o + I_o + G) + bY$$

because we now consider a closed (public) economy; we still ignore international transactions. AD will shift dollar for dollar with changes in C_o, I_o, and G. As indicated in the previous section, the investment multiplier, $M_I = 1/(1 - b)$. It follows that the consumption multiplier, which results when the consumption function shifts, is $M_C = 1/(1 - b)$ and that the government expenditure multiplier also is $M_G = 1/(1 - b)$. Thus, $M_I = M_C = M_G = 1/(1 - b)$.

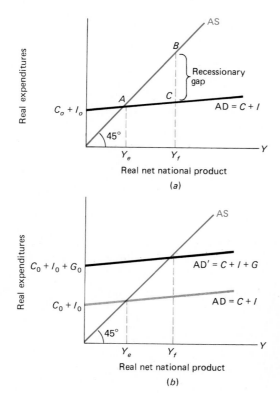

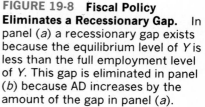

FIGURE 19-8 Fiscal Policy Eliminates a Recessionary Gap. In panel (*a*) a recessionary gap exists because the equilibrium level of Y is less than the full employment level of Y. This gap is eliminated in panel (*b*) because AD increases by the amount of the gap in panel (*a*).

HIGHLIGHT   Pedagogy and History

Economics textbooks typically first discuss the consumption function and then derive the multiplier effect. This is a reasonable approach and makes pedagogical sense. Yet, in the history of ideas, the multiplier was born first and then came the consumption function.

During the Great Depression, Keynes and his followers worked on a very practical problem: how to reduce unemployment. Can unemployment be reduced if government expenditures increase? As noted in the previous chapter, the classical answer is "no"; the public sector can expand only at the expense of the private sector.

Still, in the face of massive unemployment such a trade-off simply didn't make sense. Surely income rises for those people who provide the public goods, someone pointed out. Someone else then noted that if those people *in turn* spend a portion of their income increase, national income rises again. In short, successive rounds of respending would cause income to rise continuously toward infinity! Observers had started out wondering if increased *G* had *any* effect; now it seemed that it had an infinite effect.

Cooler heads prevailed, however, and it took Keynes's colleague R. F. Kahn (to whom Keynes gave credit for a

1931 journal article) to point out that they were dealing with an infinite geometric progression to be sure, but that it would *converge* if the respending percentage (now called the MPC) were between zero and one. It is just one step further to note that consumption is a function of income (not the interest rate) and that the MPC must be between zero and one—as Keynes's proposition 2 clearly states.

Thus, in the history of ideas, the multiplier effect was born as a result of a practical problem, and the consumption function was an important consequence.

CURRENT CONTROVERSY

Does the APC Fall as Real Income Rises?

Keynes's third proposition, known as the absolute income hypothesis, posits an inverse relationship between the APC and real disposable income. Implicitly, this suggests that current wants are relatively limited; after basic "needs" are satisfied, people consume smaller percentages of higher real income levels.* After all, there is only so much that one can eat or spend in a given day, right?

Maybe, maybe not. Under the rubric of food is included gruel, rice, beans, steak, lobster, food in a French restaurant, or food in France at a French restaurant. Housing, too, covers a broad range of possible expenditure levels—from a box (literally), to a shack, to a mansion. Dresses can range in price from $3 to $30,000! In short, there seems to be no lack of ways in which people can spend income. If at a real income level of $10,000 a family reaches equilibrium by spending 80 percent and saving 20 percent, why should these percentages change if real income doubles (or triples or quadruples)? If the income change is perceived as being permanent and the family has had sufficient time to become adjusted to this higher level, the family probably will again consume 80 percent of its income.

It seems, therefore, that theoretical reasons exist for assuming that the APC doesn't fall as real disposable income increases. What do the data show? The facts are somewhat mixed, although the weight of evidence supports the notion that the APC remains constant as real disposable income rises. Short-run time series data (data collected over time) indicate a falling APC as real disposable income rises; hence, Keynes's absolute income hypothesis cannot be rejected by that data. However, studies by Simon Kuznets (a Nobel prize winner) and others indicate that over very long periods (from 1896 to 1929, and from 1929 to the present, in the United States), the APC has shown no trend. That is, despite the tremendous increases in real incomes of people in the United States, the APC has not fallen. It has remained amazingly stable at about 90 percent; long-run time series data indicate a consumption function that is a ray from the origin (a zero vertical intercept) with a slope of about .9. These data clearly contradict Keynes's third hypothesis—although they confirm the first two.

It appears, therefore, that wants may be truly unlimited; once income changes are perceived as being permanent and people become fully adjusted to these higher real income levels, the *percentage* of income devoted to consumption returns to its former level.

---

*Of course, as income rises, people spend more on consumption—as Keynes's second hypothesis indicates. The third hypothesis is concerned with the *percentage* of total income that is consumed as income rises, and not with the *total* amount that is consumed as income rises.

Taxes   Of course, with government expenditures come the inevitable taxes (T). Assume, for ease of exposition, that taxes are autonomous or independent of the level of national income. Thus, as the analysis moves from a closed, private economy to a closed (public) economy the consumption function becomes

$$C = C_o + b\,(Y - T) \tag{19-4}$$

Removing the parentheses and rearranging,

$$C = C_o + bY - bT = (C_o - bT) + bY \tag{19-5}$$

Thus, the vertical axis intercept of the consumption function falls by bT, or by the MPC times autonomous taxes.[12]

Figure 19-9 indicates the effect on the AD curve after both taxes and government expenditures are considered. It is crucial to realize that changes in G

---

[12]Assume that the original consumption function is $C = 100 + .9Y$, and that taxes now equal 20 at every income level. From Equation (19-2), $C = 100 + .9Y - .9(20) = 82 + .9Y$; the vertical intercept has fallen by 18, or bT.

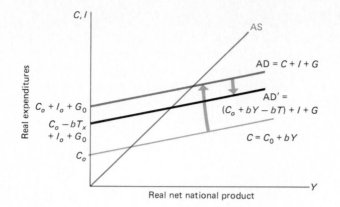

FIGURE 19-9 This graph indicates that the AD' curve, which takes into account both taxes and government expenditures (and sets them equal to each other), lies between the consumption function and the AD curve, which ignores taxes. In other words, a balanced budget is more expansionary than no government activity and less expansionary than government expenditures that are not financed by taxes.

shift the AD curve upward *dollar for dollar,* but that changes in taxes shift AD only by bT. It follows that the AD curve, which incorporates a balanced budget $(G = T)$ lies above the consumption function.[13]

Thus, fiscal policy geared to eliminate deflationary gaps calls for increased G and decreased T. Specifically, some combination of increased G and decreased T shifts the AD curve upward sufficiently to eliminate deflationary gaps. If a balanced budget existed previously, a deficit is called for to eliminate the deflationary gap. Keynes flew to the United States and told President Franklin Delano Roosevelt precisely that: Run budget deficits.[14]

An Inflationary Gap An **inflationary gap** exists if at a full-employment level of income, $AD_q > AS_q$. Presumably, inflationary gaps can also be eliminated by using fiscal policy; stabilization policy requires a reduction in G and/or an increase in T. In other words, the government should run a surplus in times of inflation in order to cool down the economy. In practice, politicians have been more enthusiastic about deficit spending than they have been about running budget surpluses. (Reread footnote 14.)

Figure 19-10 shows an inflationary gap in panel (*a*), and fiscal policy actions that eliminate this inflationary gap in panel (*b*). Thus, AD shifts down-

---

[13]It also follows that the tax multiplier is less than the government expenditure multiplier; it also is of a different sign, because increases in taxes cause NNP to *fall.*

[14]This created somewhat of a problem for President Roosevelt, who ran for office on a balanced-budget platform. Roosevelt eventually got the hang of it though—as has virtually every U.S. President since. The federal government has run deficits in all but five years since the mid-1930s.

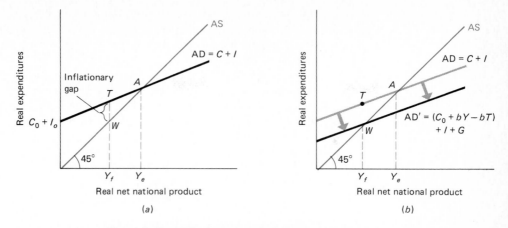

FIGURE 19-10 **Fiscal Policy Eliminates an Inflationary Gap.** In panel (a), an inflationary gap ($T-W$) exists. At Y_f, $AD_q > AS_q$; therefore, community spending exceeds its productive ability. As a consequence, the price level rises and only *nominal* income rises—to Y_e.

In panel (b), aggregate demand shifts downward, from AD to AD', as a result of some combination of decreased G and increased T. If the budget were initially balanced, fiscal policy would require government surpluses to fight inflation.

ward, through point W, and the inflationary gap is eliminated by a government budget surplus.

MONETARY POLICY IN THE KEYNESIAN MODEL

Did Keynes think that monetary policy could help to eliminate inflationary and deflationary gaps? In order to answer this question, it is necessary to discuss the role of money in the Keynesian model. That is the subject of the next chapter, which also compares the classical and the Keynesian models.

CHAPTER SUMMARY

1   The classical model is unable to explain short-run changes in the level of national output, national income, and national employment. Keynes maintained that businesses produce that level of national output (and generate that level of national income and hire that quantity of labor) that is the most profitable. The most profitable output rate depends on aggregate demand; aggregate supply adjusts to aggregate demand. Aggregate demand is equal to the total real value of all planned expenditures on final goods and service at every level of real national income; AD $= C + I + G$ in a closed economy.

2 The simple Keynesian consumption function states that (a) real consumption is a stable function of real disposable income, (b) the marginal propensity to consume is between zero and one, and (c) as real disposable income rises, the average propensity to consume falls.

3 If household consumption and business net investment expenditures are summed, aggregate demand for a closed, private economy is determined; $AD = C + I_n$. Aggregate supply is equal to the total real value of all final goods and services produced at every level of real national income. The equilibrium level of national output (national income) is found at that level at which aggregate supply intersects aggregate demand; the most profitable national output level is where $AS_q = AD_q$. Alternatively, the equilibrium level of national output is established where saving equals investment (in a closed, private economy).

4 If $AD_q > AS_q$, then businesses have underestimated what can profitably be produced and sold; inventories fall involuntarily and profits are not maximized. Businesses respond by increasing output. If $AS_q > AD_q$, then businesses have underestimated what can profitably be produced and sold; inventories rise involuntarily. Businesses respond by reducing output.

5 Shifts in the AD curve cause multiplier effects in an economy; every $1 shift in AD changes the level of national income by more than $1. The multiplier effect occurs because one group's expenditures equal another's income and because income increases resulting from shifts in the AD curve lead to secondary and tertiary (and so on) rounds of respending. The multiplier effect varies directly with the marginal propensity to consume.

6 Keynes believed that capitalism contains no mechanisms that assure full employment and price stability. If full employment and price stability are deemed worthwhile goals, it follows that a stabilization role for the government is necessary. According to Keynes, fiscal policy can play a central role in the stabilization of an economy. During periods of inflation, governments should incur budget surpluses; a budget surplus can eliminate an inflationary gap. During periods of recession, governments should incur budget deficits; a budget deficit can eliminate a recessionary gap. In practice, governments have found it politic to incur budget deficits and impolitic to have budget surpluses—regardless of the state of the economy.

GLOSSARY

Absolute income hypothesis: The APC is inversely related to the level of real disposable income.

Aggregate demand (AD): The total value of all planned real expenditures on final goods and services at every level of real national income.

Aggregate supply (AS): The total real value of all final goods and services produced at every level of real national income. AS_q is identical to net national product.

Autonomous investment: Investment that is independent of the level of national income.

Average propensity to consume (APC): Total consumption divided by total income; the percentage of income devoted to consumption.

Average propensity to save (APS): Total saving divided by total income; the percentage of income devoted to saving.

Induced investment: Investment that varies directly with the level of national income.

Inflationary gap: If at a full-employment level of national income, $AD_q > AS_q$, an inflationary gap exists and is equal to the amount by which AD must shift downward in order to achieve a full-employment, price-stable, equilibrium NNP.

Marginal propensity to consume (MPC): The percentage of a change in income that is consumed; the change in consumption divided by the change in income.

Marginal propensity to save (MPS): The percentage of a change in income that is saved; the change in saving divided by the change in income.

Multiplier effect: Every $1 million shift in aggregate demand changes the level of national income by more than $1 million; the ratio of a change in the equilibrium level of national income to a shift in the AD curve.

Recessionary gap: If at a full-employment level of national income, $AS_q > AD_q$, a deflationary gap exists and is equal to the amount by which AD must shift upward in order to achieve a full-employment, price-stable, equilibrium NNP.

PROBLEMS

19-1 Consider a closed private economy that is characterized by the following equations:

$$C = 30 + .75Y$$
$$I = 10$$

a What is the equilibrium level of national income for the economy above?

b If autonomous net investment falls by 5, what is the new equilibrium level of national income? What is the multiplier?

c If the consumption function shifts so that it now becomes $C = 25 + .75Y$ and autonomous net investment remains at 10, what is the new equilibrium level of national income?

19-2 Consider again a closed private economy characterized by:

$$C = 30 + .75Y \text{ and}$$
$$I = 10$$

If government activities are taken into account and government expenditures equal 4 and taxes equal 4,

a By how much will AD shift?

b By how much will the level of net national product change?

19-3 Consider a closed, private economy characterized by

$$C = 30 + .9Y$$
$$I = 10$$

If government activities are considered and government expenditures equal 4 and taxes equal 4,

    a By how much will AD shift?

    b By how much will national income change?

SELECTED REFERENCES

Ackley, Gardner, *Macroeconomics: Theory and Policy* (New York: Macmillan, 1978).

Blaug, Mark (ed.), *Economic Theory in Retrospect* (Homewood, Ill.: Irwin, 1968).

Breit, William, and Roger L. Ransom, *The Academic Scribblers,* 2d ed. (New York: Holt, Rinehart and Winston, 1982).

Hansen, Alvin, *A Guide to Keynes* (New York: McGraw-Hill, 1953).

Keynes, J. M., *The General Theory of Employment, Interest, and Money* (London: Macmillan, 1936).

MATHEMATICAL APPENDIX

Equilibrium Determination

Given the typical Keynesian consumption function,

$$C = C_o + bY \tag{A-1}$$

where $C_o > 0$ and $0 < b < 1$ and C_o and b are both known, and

$$I = I_o \tag{A-2}$$

Where I_o is the (known) level of autonomous investment, the equilibrium level of income cannot be determined. As things now stand, this system of equations is indeterminate; it has two equations and three variables (C, I, and Y), and a third equation is necessary. As is often the case, the missing equation is the equilibrium condition. Equilibrium requires that

$$AS_q = AD_q \tag{A-3}$$

Since $AS_q = Y$ and $AD_q = C + I$, substitution yields

$$Y = (C_o + bY) + I_o \tag{A-4}$$

Subtracting bY from both sides gives

$$Y - bY = C_o + I_o \tag{A-5}$$

Factoring gives

$$(1 - b)Y = C_o + I_o \tag{A-6}$$

Dividing both sides by $1 - b$ yields

$$Y = \frac{C_o + I_o}{1 - b} \tag{A-7}$$

where b, C_o, and I_o are known constants, and Y is the equilibrium level of income.

The Multiplier

Equation (A-7) says that in a closed, private economy, the equilibrium level of real national income equals the sum of autonomous consumption plus autonomous investment, divided by $1 - b$. If investment changes by ΔI_o, income will also change, by ΔY. Thus

$$Y + \Delta Y = \frac{C_o + I_o + \Delta I_o}{1 - b} \tag{A-8}$$

and

$$Y + \Delta Y = \frac{C_o + I_o}{1 - b} + \frac{\Delta I_o}{1 - b} \tag{A-9}$$

Subtracting (A-7) from (A-9) gives

$$\Delta Y = \frac{\Delta I_o}{1 - b} \tag{A-10}$$

$$\Delta Y / \Delta I = 1/(1 - b) \tag{A-11}$$

and

$$M_I = \frac{\Delta Y}{\Delta I} = \frac{1}{1 - b} \tag{A-12}$$

or the investment multiplier. A moment's reflection will indicate that $M_I = M_C$, where M_C is the consumption multiplier.

Note that since $0 < b < 1$ (by assumption), then $0 < 1 - b < 1$ and therefore $1/(1 - b) > 1$. Thus, an increase in I leads to a larger increase in Y, and a decrease in I leads to a larger decrease in Y.

Saving and Investment

In equilibrium,

$$AS_q = Y = C + I = AD_q \tag{A-13}$$

in a closed, private economy. It also follows that

$$Y - C = S = I \tag{A-14}$$

in equilibrium; thus, the equilibrium condition can be stated alternatively as

$$S = I \tag{A-15}$$

Note that if $AS_q = Y > C + I = AD_q$, then $Y - C > I$ and therefore $S > I$. Similarly, if $AS_q = Y < C + I = AD_q$, then $Y - C < I$, and therefore $S < I$.

The Expanded Keynesian Model

Chapter 17 contained a simplified version of the classical demand for money function. It maintained that money was only a medium of exchange, and, therefore, businesses and households held as little money as possible and for as short a time as possible. The ratio of desired money balances to nominal national income was believed to be constant at its minimum; and, therefore, velocity was a constant at its maximum. To the classical economists, the public held a constant (minimum) fraction of its nominal income in non-interest-earning cash balances; the quantity of money demanded was directly related to the price level.[1] It was considered irrational to *hoard*—hold money above the minimum desired for transactions purposes—because money per se had no value.

Because for the classical economists money was no more than a medium of exchange, they believed that the size of the money supply determined only the price level; it did not affect relative prices. Money was neutral; and, therefore, it did not affect such variables as output and employment. These variables were determined, however, at the full-employment level, according to the dictates of Say's law. Unemployment was defined as a surplus of labor at the current real wage rate. In a free market, this surplus would be eliminated as the real wage was driven down by laborers competing for jobs. Lower real wages increased the quantity of labor demanded and decreased the quantity of labor supplied. The real wage would fall until equilibrium—full employment—was restored. As a consequence, a full-employment output rate was assured. Similarly, an insufficient level of effective aggregate demand for goods and services was interpreted as indicative that a surplus of loanable funds existed. If saving plans exceeded investment plans, a surplus of loanable funds existed at the prevailing real interest rate—an unfettered loanable funds market would result in a falling real interest rate that decreased the quantity saved and increased the quantity invested. This process continued until equilibrium—an equality of saving and investment plans—was restored. As a consequence, the full-employment output would be purchased.

Keynes assigned a more important role to money in the economy. This chapter explores Keynes's demand for money theory and develops his theory of the interest rate. It then reveals an important Keynesian insight: The interest rate is the link between the real world and the money world. This analysis evolves toward a Keynesian-classical synthesis that will require a more elaborate model. This more complicated model will "cost" in terms of intellectual effort, but it will yield a high return because it provides an efficient means to:

1 Demonstrate aggregate equilibrium (a simultaneous equilibrium in both the money and the product markets)
2 Discuss monetary and fiscal policies and their interaction
3 Compare the Keynesian and the classical models

---

[1]If output is constant. If output varies, then the quantity demanded for money varies directly with *both P and Q*—or with their product, nominal NNP.

As was the case for the previous chapter, the price level is assumed to be constant because the economy remains within the range of high unemployment and excess capacity for producers. As a consequence, we need not distinguish between real and nominal values for NNP, interest rates, the supply and demand for money, and other pertinent variables.

KEYNES'S DEMAND FOR MONEY FUNCTION

The Precautionary Motive   Irving Fisher of Yale University and Alfred Marshall of Cambridge University were aware that there also existed the *precautionary motive* for holding money. According to them (and emphasized by Keynes), people want to hold a pool of readily available purchasing power to meet unexpected financial obligations. Rather than be forced to sell a bond or wait for the bond market to open in such a financial emergency, businesses and households voluntarily forgo some interest earnings in order to gain a measure of security. The rational individual therefore compares the marginal cost of forgone interest income to the marginal benefit of security resulting from holding additional money.

Fisher and Marshall believed that, like the nominal transaction demand for money, the nominal precautionary demand for money was a function of the level of nominal income. After all, as the price level rises, a constant amount of cash balances is worth less; the degree of security of money holders will fall. A doubling of the price level will lead to a doubling of the nominal quantity of cash balances demanded to meet *each* motive—the transactions and precautionary motives. For this reason, early twentieth-century neoclassical ("neo" means new) and modern economists such as Marshall and Fisher and their followers typically lump the transactions and the precautionary demands for money together and refer to them as L_1. The equation is:

$$L_1 = kY \tag{20-1}$$

where
L_1 = the desired quantity of money to hold for nominal transactions and precautionary motives
k = the ratio of desired nominal cash balances to nominal national income
Y = nominal national income

Some neoclassical economists also recognized that the precautionary demand for money *might* be inversely related to the interest rate. That is, higher interest rates increase the marginal cost of holding money, and rational individuals might be inclined to economize on their cash balances by forgoing some security or by paying the brokerage and search costs necessary to earn interest.

Keynes's Speculative Demand for Money

Keynes was intrigued by the precautionary demand for money and its implications for the notion that money is used other than as a medium of exchange. If the precautionary demand for money is one exception to the "money is only a medium of exchange" rule, then might there not be another exception?

Keynes developed another entirely different motive for holding money and called it the **speculative demand for money,** which maintains that rational people voluntarily hold money above that desired for L_1. Why would Keynes call "rational" that behavior that the classical economists called *ir*rational?

Financial assets are available in many forms: money, bonds, common stocks, commodities futures, and so on. Until quite recently, interest earnings were not available on money; this is *still* the case for currency, but interest earnings are possible for some transactions accounts. Nonetheless, it is typically true that the interest rate that can be earned on transactions accounts is less than that which can be earned on nonmoney financial assets. It is thus meaningful to distinguish between money and nonmoney financial assets. A more important reason to distinguish between these two types of financial assets is that *capital gains or losses are possible for holders of nonmoney financial assets;* no capital gains or losses are possible on money itself, which is, by definition, the most liquid of all assets. A \$100 bill represents a claim on 100 nominal dollars today or in the future; \$100 worth of bonds can change *in nominal value* over time as market interest rates change. Following tradition, we find it convenient to refer to all these assets for which one can have a capital gain or loss as bonds. Thus, you should be aware that we are using the term "bonds" in a much wider context than we did in previous chapters.

The essence of the speculative demand for money motive is that at certain times money is a financial asset superior to bonds.[2] Why might money be superior to bonds? Because there is an element of risk involved in bondholding (capital loss) and at certain times the cost of the risk outweighs the benefit of interest earnings. Let us examine this proposition in more detail before we derive Keynes's speculative demand for money function.

Recall from Chapter 6 that the yield on a bond is inversely related to its price. The nature of a bond is that it yields a fixed, predetermined, nominal revenue stream (for example, \$100 per month for ten years, at which time the face value is returned to the holder). Thus, as the supply of and the demand for a bond change, its price will change—and so will its yield. Conversely, as interest rates change, so will bond prices. That is, as interest rates change, the present value of a bond changes, and the price of a bond will equal its new present value. A given revenue stream from a bond has a market value that varies inversely with the current market interest rate. The interest rate reflects the opportunity cost of purchasing a particular revenue stream associated with the given bond.

---

[2]If wealth is constant, then a change in the demand for money is an opposite change in the demand for bonds. For example, if the community wants to hold more money, it must do so by selling bonds; if it wants more bonds, it must purchase them with money.

Because bonds offer fixed income streams, their prices vary inversely with the rate of interest. When interest rates rise, bond prices fall and bondholders experience capital losses. It is the possibility of a capital gain or loss—that is, risk—that distinguishes bonds from money. Note again that money yields a zero interest return (if held in coins or currency) and a small interest return (if held in some interest-earning transactions deposit forms), but that no capital gain or loss is possible. Money is the medium of exchange. Bonds, on the other hand, can (and frequently do) change value in terms of the medium of exchange. Bonds are less liquid than money. They may have to be converted into money at a lower value than the original purchase price. Moreover, such conversion requires brokerage fees and a bond market that is in session.[3]

Armed with this information concerning the riskiness of bonds, it is now possible to derive Keynes's speculative demand for money theory. According to Keynes, people voluntarily hold or demand money above and beyond that desired for L_1 (transactions and precautionary motives) because money is, on occasion, a safer form (than bonds) in which to store wealth. Let us refer to this second demand for money (beyond L_1 motives) as **L_2**. But when are bonds risky, and when are they safe? When will L_2 rise or fall?

According to Keynes, people cling to the notion of a **natural rate of interest;** that natural rate of interest is that rate to which the interest rate usually returns.[4] The essence of Keynes's theory is that (other things constant) the further actual rates depart from a "natural rate," the greater are the expectations that the actual rate will return to the natural rate. Thus, relatively high interest rates lead many to expect that those rates will fall; relatively low interest rates lead many to suspect that soon interest rates will rise.

Because the price of bonds varies inversely with the interest rate, people believe they know when bonds are safe and when they are risky. When interest rates are very high (and bond prices are therefore very low), the risk of purchasing bonds is low because if interest rates *do* change, they are expected to fall and to create capital gains. In this situation, Keynes predicted a low overall community L_2: Very few want to hold money because they prefer to hold bonds, from which they expect a capital gain. On the other hand, when interest rates are very low (and bond prices are therefore very high), the risk of holding bonds is high because if interest rates do change, they will tend to rise toward their natural rate; bondholders will experience capital losses.[5] As a consequence, low interest rates induce a desire for a higher L_2 demand for money, and an inverse relationship exists between L_2 and i. This is shown in Figure 20-1.

---

[3]For Keynes, money and bonds are substitutes *only for each other;* neither is a direct substitute for those assets we refer to as real goods and services.

[4]Of course, people have different notions about what the natural rate is. Otherwise, there would be no gambling, which requires a difference of opinion. After all, Keynes was talking about the *speculative* motive.

[5]Sometimes this theory is referred to as the "rubber-band" theory of the demand for money.

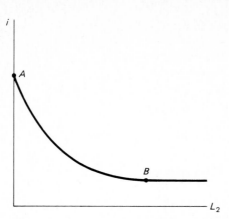

FIGURE 20-1 The Speculative Demand for Money.   This figure shows that L_2 (the demand for money to hold over and above L_1) is inversely related to the interest rate. Only at point A, where $L_2 = 0$ (the L_2 curve becomes perfectly inelastic) do the Keynesian and classical models agree. As the interest rate falls from A, more people become convinced that the interest rate is below the natural rate and that the risk of bondholding rises. It follows that lower interest rates induce people to hold more L_2. At point B, interest rates are at a (subjective) minimum. Here virtually everyone is convinced that interest rates will rise; bonds are extremely risky, and people are prepared to hold limitless money balances. To the right of point B, the curve (the L_2 function) is perfectly elastic; the curve is horizontal in that range, reflecting the fact that at such a low interest rate bonds are so risky that the public is prepared *to hold* limitless amounts of money.

Recall that L_2 is the demand for money over and above L_1 (the transactions and precautionary demands for money). To the classical economists, the L_2 curve would be the same as the vertical axis because as long as interest rates were positive, $L_2 = 0$. Keynes's position is that $L_2 = 0$ only at point A where interest rates are so high that virtually everyone is convinced rates will fall. At point A in Figure 20-1, all money balances will be used for transactions and precautionary motives, and none will be held for speculative motives. With no speculative demand, the classical and Keynesian models become the same model.

As the interest rate falls (causing bond prices to rise), the quantity of L_2 demanded will rise; some people will want to take their capital gains (by selling bonds) and hold money. Lower and lower interest rates convince more and more speculators that the interest rate is below the natural rate; drops in the interest rate induce a greater quantity demanded for money to hold in L_2 as bonds become progressively riskier. Finally, the speculative demand for money curve becomes, at least theoretically, perfectly horizontal (at point B). Virtually everyone is convinced that the market rate is below the natural rate; bonds are so risky that speculators are prepared to hold limitless quantities of money. As will be seen later, this implies that a subjective floor exists on interest rates; interest rates won't fall below the level at point B in Figure 20-1.

Because the curve in Figure 20-1 indicates a preference for money over bonds, the curve is also referred to as a **liquidity preference function.** It is important to realize that as the economy moves from point A to point B in Figure 20-1 the classical k rises (velocity falls). Assume that the level of NNP equals $100B$ and that L_1 equals $20B$ as a result. The ratio of *desired* money balances to NNP, or k, equals 20 percent and the reciprocal of k—velocity—equals 5. Assume that the market rate of interest falls and some people believe that the market rate is now below the natural rate. They perceive that bonds are now relatively risky and they prefer to hold fewer bonds and more money; some people want to substitute money for bonds in their portfolio. Suppose that the community now wants to hold *another* $5B in money in order to meet L_2, the speculative motive. The *desired* ratio of money balances to NNP is $25B/$100B = 25$ percent, and velocity now equals 4. As we move from point A to point B the level of NNP remains constant, but desired money balances rise; as a consequence, the community's desired k rises and velocity falls. In effect, Keynes notes that k and V are functions of the rate of interest and hence not constant. This is a fundamental insight and we will make reference to this point in later chapters.

James Tobin, a Nobel prize-winning Yale University professor of economics, also demonstrated that the liquidity preference function was inversely related to the interest rate. Instead of resorting to a natural rate of interest hypothesis, Tobin theorized that interest is compensation for risk bearing.[6] Most people are **risk avoiders;** they prefer less risk to more risk, other things constant. On the other hand, they are prepared to accept risk if sufficiently compensated. When interest rates are high, the opportunity cost for holding money is high, so people pay a dear price for financial safety (risk avoidance); other things constant, they prefer to hold less money (hold more bonds). When interest rates are low, the opportunity cost for remaining safe (holding money) is also low; hence, there is little inducement to take on additional risk (hold bonds). In short, people want to hold more money at lower interest rates than they want to hold at higher interest rates.

Another Household Decision   In the classical model, households had one key question to answer: How much income should be allocated to consumption and saving? Once a household saved, those funds automatically became a part of the supply of loanable funds because money saved would not be hoarded by rational people. Keynes's and Tobin's analyses, however, indicate that another important question is necessary for households to answer: What form will saving take? That is, households must decide what portion of their wealth (if any) is to be held in bonds and what portion in money. Keynes, who was a successful speculator, noted that at times money was superior to bonds as an asset form. He therefore provided a rational motive for hoarding. The realization that

---

[6]James Tobin, ''Liquidity Preference as a Behavior Toward Risk,'' *Review of Economic Studies,* 1958.

households have this additional decision led Keynes to a radically different theory of the rate of interest. According to the classical theory, the rate of interest resulted from the first decision (the consumption-saving decision). According to Keynes, the interest rate results from the second decision—the money-bonds decision.

KEYNES'S THEORY OF THE RATE OF INTEREST

The classical theory of the rate of interest is that the interest rate is determined at the point of intersection of the saving and net investment curves. Keynes contended that neither saving nor investment was primarily determined by the rate of interest, and he replaced the classical theory of interest with his own theory.

Assume that the money supply, M, is determined by the monetary authorities. Keynes's theory is that (given the level of NNP) the market rate of interest will be determined at the point of intersection of the supply of money and the liquidity preference (L_2, or his demand for money) curves.[7] This can also be viewed alternatively: The equilibrium rate of interest is the one at which the given money supply, minus the amount demanded for L_1, equals the amount demanded for L_2; in Figure 20-2, M_2 is the *net* money supply, or the amount available for L_2.

---

[7]You may recall that for the classical economist, the supply of and demand for money determined the price level.

FIGURE 20-2   In this figure, L_2, the demand for money to hold above L_1 (transactions and precautionary motives), and M_2 (the money supply, M, determined independently by the monetary authorities, minus the amount desired for L_1) determine the equilibrium interest rate, i_e. At any interest rate above i_e, a surplus of liquidity exists and individuals will attempt to rid themselves of excess money balances by purchasing more bonds. This activity will force bond prices up and the interest rate down. At any interest rate below i_e, a shortage of liquidity will lead to bond sales, which reduce bond prices and increase the interest rate.

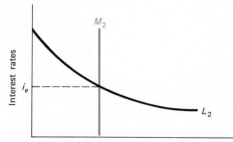

Interest rates

M_2

i_e

L_2

Speculative demand for money and M_2

Consider any interest rate above i_e, the equilibrium rate. By inspection, it can be seen that the quantity of money demanded is greater than the quantity supplied; $L_2 > M_2$. A surplus of liquidity exists. People are holding more money than they wish to hold. Individuals *can* change the amount of money they hold, but *the community cannot.* Individuals can rid themselves of excess money balances by purchasing bonds; bond purchases force bond prices up, and therefore interest rates fall. Complementary analysis indicates that below i_e a shortage of liquidity exists, and this will lead to bond sales which will force bond prices down and interest rates up toward i_e. Note that equilibrium is achieved by changes in bond prices and the resulting change in the interest rate; if the money supply and the money demand are not equated, the bond prices and the interest rate will change until they are. Recall that in the classical model if the supply of and the demand for money are not equated, the price level (nominal national income) adjusts. Thus, in the classical model the supply of and the demand for money determine the price level; in the Keynesian model, the supply of and the demand for money determine the interest rate.

Changes in *M* Lead to Changes in *i* Now let's see how changes in the money supply can lead to changes in the interest rate—the gospel according to Keynes. Consider Figure 20-3, where a picture is worth (nearly) a thousand words. Note how increases in the money supply, a rightward shift from M_2 to M_2', cause interest rates to fall from i_e to i_1. If the Fed buys bonds from the public or from depository institutions, it may be able to affect *directly* the price of bonds and therefore interest rates.[8] At any rate, deposit-expansion multipliers will take effect and the money supply will increase. Increased excess reserves

---

[8]This could be possible if the Fed is a relatively large buyer in the market. Note that the Fed's ability to do so is limited in the horizontal range of the L_2 curve, called the *liquidity trap,* where interest rates are already so low and bond prices so high that bonds are risky to the point that the public is only too willing to sell to the Fed.

FIGURE 20-3 Changes in the money supply, given the speculative demand for money curve, will change the interest rate. Specifically, central-bank open-market purchases of bonds will increase the money supply and cause the interest rate to fall (except in the liquidity trap). Central-bank open-market sales of bonds will decrease the money supply and cause the interest rate to rise.

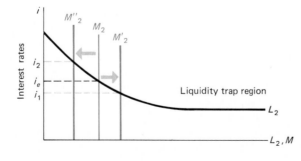

will encourage depository institutions to increase lending, which can be done only at lower interest rates. Complementary reasoning indicates that Fed bond sales will reduce M_2 to M_2'' and raise interest rates to i_2.

KEYNES AND MONETARY POLICY

Consider Figure 20-4. Note that in the **liquidity trap** (horizontal) region of the L_2 curve, changes in the supply of money have no effect on the interest rate. Fed purchases of bonds are welcomed by the public, which considers bonds risky and is prepared to hold an infinite amount of money. Similarly, depository institutions are happy to sell bonds—and hold excess reserves. As a consequence, monetary policy would be ineffective because banks cannot be forced to lend excess reserves.

According to Keynes, expansionary monetary policy is ineffective in periods of recession—and certainly during depressions—because interest rates are already low during such periods. Moreover, the demand for business loans will be quite low anyway, because profit expectations have depressed desired investment expenditures. For monetary policy to be effective, small changes in the money supply should lead to significant changes in the interest rate, which in turn should lead to significant changes in net investment. Thus, $\Delta M_2 \rightarrow \Delta i \rightarrow \Delta Y$. But in a recession, when interest rates are already quite low and the economy is in the flatter ranges of the speculative demand for money curve, changes in the money supply lead to only *very small* changes in the interest rate. Moreover, in a recession investment plans are greatly curtailed and it takes very large reductions in the interest rate to encourage increased investment; the rate of interest must fall greatly to offset the reduction in profit expectations during a recession. For these two reasons—an L_2 curve that is insensitive to changes in the money supply and an investment curve

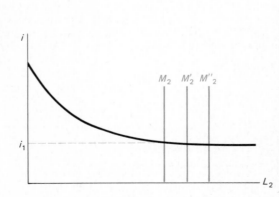

FIGURE 20-4 In the liquidity trap (or horizontal) range of the liquidity preference function, increases in the money supply do not lower the interest rate. At i_1, the interest rate is so low that virtually all speculators believe that it is below the natural rate and will rise, causing the price of bonds to fall. Bonds are so risky that the public is prepared to hold an infinite supply of money and banks are prepared to hold excess reserves. Keynes believed that the Great Depression approached a liquidity trap situation.

that is insensitive to changes in the interest rate—monetary policy is not considered by Keynesians to be effective during a recession.[9]

Keynes maintained that monetary policy is effective only to the extent that it affects the aggregate demand (AD) curve. Since monetary policy was ineffective in a recession or a depression, Keynes favored fiscal policy, which affected the AD curve directly by increases in government expenditures, and indirectly by decreases in taxes that cause consumption to rise.

On the other hand, there is a role for monetary policy in combatting *inflation*. Central-bank bond sales on the open market can decrease the supply of money and cause interest rates to rise. While depository institutions cannot be forced to lend excess reserves, they can be forced to meet reserve requirements.[10]

A TOTAL DEMAND FOR MONEY CURVE

It is now possible to derive a total demand for money curve: $L = L_1 + L_2$. This curve, illustrated in Figure 20-5, indicates the money demanded for all three motives (transactions, precautionary, and speculative) as a function of the rate of interest. The total demand for money (L) function is derived by adding the L_1 and L_2 demands *horizontally*. Note that the L_1 curve is independent of the interest rate; it is primarily determined by the level of Y, as the classical economists maintained and as *we* have *assumed*.[11] Thus, the L_1 curve remains constant as i changes and appears as a line parallel to the vertical axis.

The Derivation of the *LM* Curve   Post-Keynesians have found it convenient to recast the previous analysis in terms of an **LM curve,** the locus of points that indicates equilibrium interest rates and national income levels in the monetary sphere of the economy. This neo-Keynesian curve incorporates the two notions that L_1 depends on NNP (the classical prediction) and that L_2 depends on i (the Keynesian prediction). The *LM* curve is derived by holding the money supply constant; the curve relates real NNP levels to interest rates. It is important to stress that at every point on the *LM* curve, *equilibrium exists in the*

---

[9]This can be shown using the equation of exchange, $\uparrow MV \downarrow = \hat{Y}$ (a "hat" on Y means that it remains constant). Increases in M are offset by decreases in V (k rises as the community merely holds new money), and Y remains constant.

[10]Still, a higher interest rate will reduce L_2; therefore k will fall and V will rise. To some extent, then, decreases in M will be offset by increases in V; $MV = \hat{Y}$; the effect of a change in M on Y is somewhat indeterminate. In short, Keynesians doubt the efficacy of monetary policy because V moves perversely. When M is increased, V falls; when M is decreased, V rises. The effects of fiscal policy seem to be more straightforward to them.

[11]Actually, modern economists believe, and some empirical evidence shows, that the amount that people hold for transactions balances is (somewhat) inversely related to the interest rate. Businesses, especially, economize on transactions balances at relatively high interest rates.

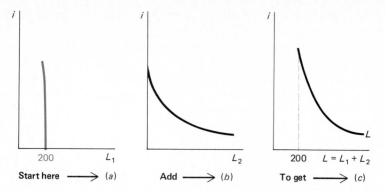

FIGURE 20-5 Deriving the Total Demand for Money Function.   Add panel (a) to panel (b) horizontally to derive panel (c), the total demand for money function. This curve indicates the money demand for all motives as a function of the rate of interest. Note that the *position* of the curve in (a) and (c) depends on the level of NNP; the quantity demanded for L balances, 200, is related to some specific level of NNP. A change in NNP will shift the curve in (c); increases in NNP will shift the L curve to the right; decreases in NNP will shift L to the left. The *shape* of the L curve is determined by the L_2 curve.

money market because the total demand for liquidity (L) and the supply of money (M) are equated—hence, the name LM curve.

Figure 20-6 derives an LM curve. If the money supply is constant, income changes will lead to interest-rate changes. In particular, if the level of net national product rises, there will be an increase in the total demand for money because L_1 increases. Given the fixed supply of money, a shortage will exist because at i_e the quantity of money demanded exceeds the available M, and a scramble for liquidity ensues. As people sell bonds in order to become more liquid, bond prices fall and interest rates rise.

Complementary reasoning indicates that, given M, a reduction in national income to Y_2 will reduce L_1. Therefore, the total demand for money function falls, shifting leftward to $(L_1 + L_2)_2$. Now at i_e, a surplus of liquidity exists because the quantity of money demanded is less than the available supply, M, and money holders will purchase bonds, driving bond prices up and interest rates down. Therefore, given the money supply, increases in national income will cause interest rates to rise; decreases in national income will cause interest rates to fall. Note that in Figure 20-6 the LM curve is upward-sloping, from left to right, and that national income changes lead to interest-rate changes in the same direction, given M. Also, it should be stressed that at each point on the LM curve, $(L_1 + L_2) = M$; the demand for and the supply of money are equated.

A Closer Look at the LM Function

The Classical Range   Figure 20-6 indicates the general shape of the LM function; it will be useful to take a closer look at the shape of this important curve. Consider Figure 20-7. As the economy moves from point C to point A,

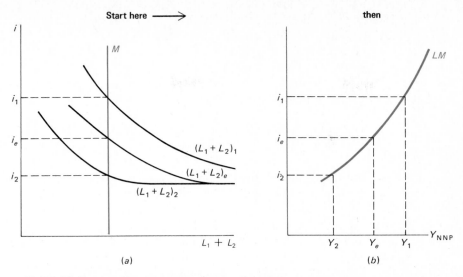

FIGURE 20-6 **Deriving the *LM* Curve.** This figure shows how changes in national income lead to changes in the L_1 demand for money. Given a fixed money supply, a change in the demand for money leads to a change in the rate of interest. As panel (*a*) shows, increases in the level of national income from Y_e to Y_1 cause an increase in the total demand for money from $(L_1 + L_2)_e$ to $(L_1 + L_2)_1$, which causes an increase in the interest rate from i_e to i_1. Complementary reasoning shows how a movement of income from Y_e to Y_2 causes i to fall from i_e to i_2, because $(L_1 + L_2)_e$ falls to $(L_1 + L_2)_2$. Panel (*b*) relates the differing income levels to the changes in interest rates, given the money supply; panel (*b*) shows the *LM* curve.

what is happening? Higher national income levels lead to an increase in L_1, which in turn leads to an increase in the total demand for money function, $(L_1 + L_2)$. Given a constant *M*, this higher income can be transacted only by offering holders of L_2 higher interest rates, to encourage them to part with liquidity. As interest rates rise, the opportunity cost of holding money rises and bonds become less risky; hence, some money moves from L_2 to L_1 and velocity rises.

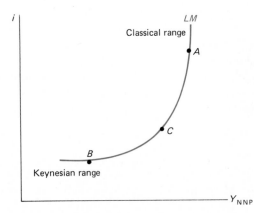

FIGURE 20-7 **A Closer Look at the *LM* Function.** Here are shown the classical and the Keynesian ranges on the *LM* curve. In the classical range, the total *M* is held in the form of L_1 and velocity is at a maximum. In the Keynesian range, reductions in national income create excess balances as L_1 falls, but because interest rates are already low, holders of money are prepared to hold these money balances. As a consequence, velocity is very low in this liquidity trap range.

Eventually, higher and higher national income levels induce interest rates that are sufficiently high to move *all* L_2 balances into L_1 balances. At that point, around point A, $L_2 = 0$ and velocity is at a maximum. Hence, given M, national income is at its maximum point. The vertical region above point A on the LM curve is referred to as the **classical range** because the classical economists maintained that money was only a medium of exchange; they predicted that $L_2 = 0$. The classical range indicates that a maximum NNP level can be reached, given the money supply. Velocity is at a maximum and money becomes a bottleneck to further expansion of net national product.

The Keynesian Range   Now consider what happens in Figure 20-7 as the economy moves from point C to point B. Lower levels of national income lead to a reduction in L_1 and now there are excess cash balances at the prevailing interest rate. With these excess balances resulting from a surplus of liquidity, bond purchases are made which force bond prices up and interest rates down. Eventually, however, very low interest rates make bond purchases so risky that the holders of M are prepared to hold these excess money balances. Thus, in the horizontal region around point B (the liquidity trap), lower income levels reduce the demand for L_1, but these balances are not used to purchase bonds; they are merely *held* in the form of L_2; therefore, *interest rates won't fall*. Since a lower national income no longer leads to a lower interest rate, the LM curve becomes parallel to the horizontal axis. This is referred to as the **Keynesian range,** because it results from Keynes's liquidity trap hypothesis. Note that as the economy moves from point C to point B, velocity continuously falls (k rises) as the community holds more and more cash balances in the form of L_2.[12]

Shifts in the LM Curve

The LM curve was derived for a constant money supply. It follows that a change in the money supply will shift the LM curve. If the money supply were to rise, a surplus of liquidity would *now* exist at any given Y (income level) on the LM curve, and i would fall as people use these excess balances to purchase bonds. The conclusion is that an increase in M will cause the LM curve to shift to the right. Complementary analysis indicates that a reduction in M will cause the LM function to shift to the left. This is shown graphically in Figure 20-8.

A Problem

According to Keynes, the interest rate is a monetary phenomenon; it is determined by the supply of and the demand for money; yet changes in the interest rate can affect aggregate demand (and therefore net national product) through changes in net investment. Also, changes in aggregate demand, by changing L_1 (and, therefore, $L = L_1 + L_2$), change the interest rate. It follows

---

[12]This can be shown through the equation of exchange. Because $V = Y/M$, if Y falls and M is constant, V must rise. Using the Cambridge approach, you should be able to see why k falls.

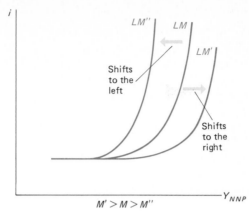

FIGURE 20-8   Changes in _M_ Lead to Changes in _LM_.   This figure indicates that money supply changes lead to shifts in the _LM_ curve. If the money supply were increased, the _LM_ curve would shift rightward from _LM_ to _LM'_; any given interest rate would be associated with a higher level of net national product (except in the Keynesian range). If the money stock were to fall, the _LM_ curve would shift leftward from _LM_ to _LM''_; any given interest rate would be associated with a lower level of net national product.

that the rate of interest is the link between the monetary world and the real world; by changing the money supply, real variables such as employment and output may vary. And when employment, output, and net national product change, the interest rate changes.

But that poses a problem. According to Keynes, the interest rate helps to determine national income, Y. On the other hand, according to the theory of the transactions and precautionary motives for holding money, when Y increases, so does L_1. This means that given a fixed money supply, an increase in income will cause an increase in the rate of interest. This is indicated by an upward-sloping _LM_ curve.

Does the rate of interest help to determine the level of income, or does the level of income help to determine the interest rate? The problem is that the neo-Keynesian model includes a demand for money that is a function of two variables—interest and income. The equilibrium condition is that the supply of and the demand for money must be equated. The model has two variables (net national product and the interest rate) and one equation ($M = L_1 + L_2$); the model is not determinant. Unlike a pure Keynesian model where the supply of and demand for money determine the interest rate, the neo-Keynesian model (which incorporates the classical model assumption that L is a function of Y) yields a situation in which the supply of and demand for money determine _combinations_ of interest and income that satisfy the equation $M = L_1 + L_2$, given M. What is needed is another equation relating i and Y, and that equation is provided by the equilibrium condition in the _product market_ (aggregate demand = aggregate supply). In the next section, combinations of i and Y that satisfy the product market equilibrium are determined. Aggregate equilibrium, the simultaneous equilibrium in both the money and the product markets, is then discussed. In other words, equilibrium Y and i are determined _simultaneously_ by the interaction of the money market and the product market.

DERIVING THE *IS* CURVE

The *LM* curve indicates the locus of equilibrium interest rates and national incomes in the money market. Another curve, the **IS curve,** relates the locus of interest-rate and national-income equilibrium positions in the product market. Before we can derive the *IS* curve, we must first digress slightly and discuss the relationship between interest rates and net investment.

The MEI Curve Keynes agreed with the classical economists that net investment varies inversely with the rate of interest.[13] His method of arriving at that conclusion was somewhat different, however. His complete derivation is beyond the scope of this book; only a very brief and simplified version will be introduced here.

Recall from Chapter 6 that the present value of any income-earning asset is given by the following equation:

$$V_P = R_1/(1 + i) + R_2/(1 + i)^2 + \cdots + R_n/(1 + i)^n$$

If one holds profit expectations constant, the net stream of revenues (R_1, R_2, ... R_n) will also be constant. It follows that an inverse relationship between V_P and interest rates exists; if the interest rate falls, the present value of any income-earning asset will rise. This means that the economic value of each investment good will rise and *now* will be greater than its selling price. Businesses will want to purchase more investment goods, and producers will be willing to produce more because the price of this equipment will be bid up to equal its V_P in the marketplace. This process continues until the increasing marginal cost of each investment good equals the now higher price of capital. In short, a reduction in the rate of interest, given profit expectations, will lead to an increase in net investment.

This relationship, which has come to be called the marginal efficiency of investment (MEI) curve, is shown in Figure 20-9.[14] If profit expectations change, the net stream of revenues (R_1, R_2, and so on) will change and the MEI schedule will shift. More specifically, if profit expectations fall, the net stream of revenues will fall, and the V_P of all investment goods will be lower at *any* interest rate. Economists will therefore predict that net investment will be less at every rate of interest; a fall in profit expectations will shift the MEI curve leftward. An increase in profit expectations, by complementary reasoning, will shift the MEI curve to the right.

---

[13]However, he felt that profit expectations were more important than the interest rate in determining investment. *Given* profit expectations, an inverse relationship exists between *i* and *I*. Such a relationship will be extremely volatile, however. It shifts every time profit expectations change, and Keynes believed that profit expectations changed often and significantly.

[14]Keynes referred to this curve as the marginal efficiency of capital curve.

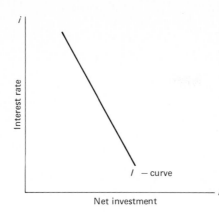

FIGURE 20-9   The MEI Curve.   An inverse relationship exists between the interest rate and net investment, when profit expectations are constant. If the rate of interest rises, given profit expectations, the V_P of all investment goods will fall. That means that the price of investment goods will fall to reflect their economic worth. This eventually leads to a reduction in the demand for capital goods, which is a reduction in net investment.

If profit expectations increase, the MEI curve will shift to the right; more net investment will occur at every rate of interest. If profit expectations fall, the MEI curve will shift to the left.

Deriving the *IS* Curve from the MEI Curve and the Aggregate Demand–Aggregate Supply Framework

Consider Figure 20-10. It shows that a reduction in interest rates causes an increase in the quantity of net investment (a movement along the MEI curve) in panel (*a*). This increase in autonomous net investment causes the aggregate demand curve to shift upward, and national income rises with a multiplier effect from Y_e to Y_1. This is shown in panel (*b*). In panel (*c*), the relationship is summarized: A reduction in the rate of interest leads to a multiple (of the change in investment) increase in the level of national income. By a series of alterations in the interest rate, the *IS* curve is

FIGURE 20-10   Deriving the *IS* Curve.   Here it is shown how a change in the rate of interest leads to a change in the quantity of net investment (because businesses find it profitable to do so) in panel (*a*). This causes a shift in aggregate demand in panel (*b*) and thereby causes the equilibrium level of national income to change. These changes are summarized in panel (*c*), where it is shown how interest rate changes lead to changes in national income. Thus, an inverse relationship between *i* and *Y* exists in the product market. The *IS* curve will shift if the MEI or the consumption function shifts. The next chapter shows that the *IS* curve also shifts through fiscal policy actions.

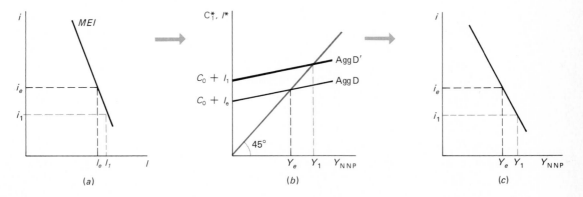

(*a*)   (*b*)   (*c*)

derived. It is depicted in panel (*c*). Note that at every point along the *IS* curve equilibrium exists in the commodity market ($AS_q = AD_q$); therefore at every point, investment (*I*) equals saving (*S*) in a closed, private economy (without international transactions and without government activities); hence, the name *IS* curve.

The *IS* curve will shift if the MEI curve shifts, or if the consumption function shifts. If profit expectations rise, or if the community becomes less thrifty, the *IS* function will shift to the right, i.e., the level of net national product will be higher at any rate of interest because each of these changes will cause aggregate demand to rise and this causes NNP to rise. Also, if we depart temporarily from a closed economy, an increase in government expenditures (other things constant) will increase aggregate demand and therefore national income will be higher at every rate of interest. A decrease in autonomous consumption (increase in autonomous saving), a decrease in profit expectations (which shifts the MEI curve leftward), and a decrease in government expenditures will shift the *IS* curve leftward. We return to a discussion of shifts in the *IS* curve in the next chapter, when we discuss fiscal policy.

AGGREGATE EQUILIBRIUM: PUTTING *LM* AND *IS* TOGETHER

Every point on the *LM* curve represents a combination of equilibrium interest rate and national income in the money market. Every point on the *IS* curve represents this combination in the product market. If both curves are plotted on the same coordinate system, aggregate equilibrium (simultaneous equilibrium in both the money and the product markets) will exist at their point of intersection. Consider Figure 20-11. In this figure, general equilibrium will exist at point *E*, which is the point common to both curves.

To demonstrate that general equilibrium will exist at point *E* let's first consider a nonequilibrium position, such as point *A*. At point *A*, equilibrium exists in the product market because *A* is a point on the *IS* curve. (Remember, all points on the *IS* curve represent equilibrium in the product market.) It is important to note that at point *A*, $Y = Y_A$ and $i = i_1$.

What about the money market? Point *A* cannot be an equilibrium position in the money market because it is not on the *LM* curve. What is the situation in the money market at point *A*? In order to see, consider point *B*, at which *i* is also i_1, but $Y = Y_B$. At point *B*, equilibrium exists in the money market because *B* is on the *LM* curve, and $L_1 + L_2 = M$. (Remember, all points on the *LM* curve represent equilibrium in the money market.)

Now compare *A* (Y_A, i_1) and *B* (Y_B, i_1). At *B* (Y_B, i_1), $L_1 + L_2 = M$, but since $Y_B > Y_A$, L_1 at *B* must be greater than L_1 at *A*. Since both points *A* and *B* are at interest rate *i*, L_2 is the same at both points, because L_2 depends *only* on the interest rate. It follows that at *B*, $L_1 + L_2 > L_1 + L_2$ at *A*. Since at *B*, $L_1 + L_2 = M$ and *M* is constant, we conclude at *A* that $M > L_1 + L_2$; a surplus of money, or liquidity, exists in the money market. Holders of *M* are holding more

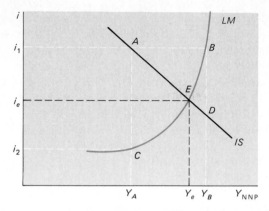

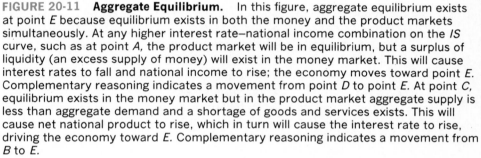

FIGURE 20-11   **Aggregate Equilibrium.**   In this figure, aggregate equilibrium exists at point E because equilibrium exists in both the money and the product markets simultaneously. At any higher interest rate–national income combination on the IS curve, such as at point A, the product market will be in equilibrium, but a surplus of liquidity (an excess supply of money) will exist in the money market. This will cause interest rates to fall and national income to rise; the economy moves toward point E. Complementary reasoning indicates a movement from point D to point E. At point C, equilibrium exists in the money market but in the product market aggregate supply is less than aggregate demand and a shortage of goods and services exists. This will cause net national product to rise, which in turn will cause the interest rate to rise, driving the economy toward E. Complementary reasoning indicates a movement from B to E.

money than they want to hold at A, so individuals will attempt to rid themselves of excess money by purchasing bonds, driving bond prices up and interest rates down. A reduction in interest rates leads to an increase in net investment and causes a multiple expansion in Y. As Y increases and i decreases, L_1 and L_2 increase, until $L_1 + L_2 = M$, and the money market is driven to equilibrium. In short, the economy moves toward point E; interest rates fall from i_1, and national income rises above Y_A.

Complementary analysis indicates that at point D equilibrium exists in the product market but that a shortage of liquidity exists in the money market. This will cause individuals to sell bonds, forcing their prices down and interest rates up. In turn, a higher interest rate will reduce net investment, and therefore national income will fall. As Y falls and i rises, L_1 and L_2 fall until $L_1 + L_2$ = M, and the money market reaches equilibrium.

Consider point C in Figure 20-11. At that point equilibrium exists in the money market but a shortage exists in the product market. Why? Consider point A, which incorporates the same level of NNP but a *higher* interest rate. Because A is on the IS curve, equilibrium exists in the product market by definition. But because the interest rate is higher at A than at C ($i_1 > i_2$), aggregate demand must be higher at point C than at point A. If $AD_q = AS_q$ at point A, then $AD_q > AS_q$ at point C and there must be a shortage of final goods and services at C. Businesses will find it profitable to increase output which, in turn, causes NNP to rise. (Remember, in the Keynesian model increases in AD leave the price level constant because it is a recession-depression analysis and much excess capacity exists in the economy.) The increase in NNP causes an increase in the demand for L_1 balances, so the interest rate will also rise. The level of NNP and the interest rate will rise until point E is reached.

Complementary analysis reveals that a surplus of final goods and services exists at point B; at B, $AS_q > AD_q$. This will cause producers to reduce their output levels, which in turn causes NNP to fall. As a result, L_2 demand falls, causing the interest rate to fall. The level of NNP and the interest rate fall until point E is reached.

At point E, equilibrium exists in both the money and the product markets; hence, aggregate equilibrium exists.

Does Full Employment Exist at Y_e? The *IS-LM* framework will be very useful in the following chapters where monetary and fiscal policies are discussed and where the monetarist Keynesian debate is analyzed. Right now, it is sufficient to note that at point E full employment will not necessarily exist, according to Keynes. Remember, Keynes maintained that capitalism contains no mechanisms that assure full employment and that prices and wages are sticky downward. If Y_e does represent an unemployment situation, nothing assures that the economy will move toward full employment. If Y_e is a full-employment equilibrium, nothing guarantees that the economy will remain there; a shift in the MEI curve would cause *IS* to shift to the right or to the left and thereby cause inflation or recession, respectively. The following current controversy uses the *IS-LM* framework to discuss the possibility of unemployment when prices and wages are free to fall.

CURRENT CONTROVERSY

Can Unemployment Exist with Price-Wage Flexibility?

The classical model assumes price-wage flexibility and predicts that unemployment won't prevail for long, because unemployed laborers will compete for jobs and bid money wages down. Lower money wages will cause the real wage to fall—*if the price level does not fall at the same or at a greater rate.* Lower real wages induce employers to hire more labor and induce suppliers of labor to offer less labor time. This process continues until full employment is established.

Keynes pointed out that price-wage flexibility does not exist in modern economies. In particular, wages and prices are not free to fall when decreases in aggregate demand generate surpluses of final goods and services and surpluses of labor (unemployment). Prices are "sticky downward" because monopolistic businesses have the power to insulate themselves from market forces; businesses choose to reduce output, not prices. Wages are sticky downward because unions resist wage reductions; also minimum wage laws place floors on wage rates. In a welfare state, moreover, laborers can remain idle for longer periods as they collect unemployment compensation and/ or become eligible for welfare. As a consequence, there is less incentive for laborers to offer to work for lower wages when they are unemployed. It follows that unemployment is possible if wages are not free to fall. Even the classical economist would have agreed with Keynes on this point. But Keynes did not rely solely on price-wage rigidity. He showed that unemployment could result even if prices and wages were free to fall according to the dictates of supply and demand.

In order to show how Keynes argued that even price-wage flexibility does not assure full employment of labor, it is necessary for us to relax our assumptions and to modify our *IS-LM* framework. You will recall that our analysis to date has been couched in *real terms* because we have held the price level constant, reflecting Keynes's belief that increases in AD will not cause the price level to rise in periods of recession or unemployment. For this Current Controversy, however, we must couch our *IS-LM* analysis in *nominal* values; i and net national product are nominal values.

Consider Figures 1 and 2, which show simultaneous equilibrium in the money and product markets; i_e and Y_e are determined simultaneously. According to Keynes, an *economywide* reduction in wages will lower the price level at the same rate. Since wages are an important component of marginal cost, general wage reductions will increase the supply of goods and services throughout the economy. Given demand,

FIGURE 1 Equilibrium nominal national net product (Y_e) and interest (i_e) are determined simultaneously in the money (*LM*) and product (*IS*) markets. Unfortunately, the full-employment level of national income exists at Y_f. A depression exists and unemployed laborers offer to work for lower wages. Downward price-wage flexibility causes the *LM* curve to shift to the right, but the economy is caught in the liquidity trap. Lower prices increase the real value of the (constant) money supply, and the *LM* curve shifts rightward (from *LM* to *LM'* to *LM''*). This "Keynes effect" does not help, however, because this increased liquidity is held by the public.

Recession → unemployment → ↓ wages
 → ↓ prices → L_1 ↓→ excess liquidity held in L_2
No change in i, Y, and N (employment).

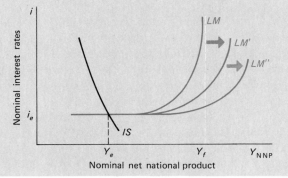

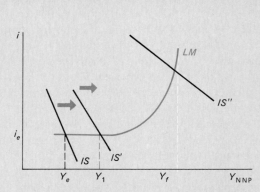

FIGURE 2 In this figure, a lower price level resulting from unemployment increases the wealth of currency holders. This increased wealth causes the consumption function to shift upward, causing the *IS* curve to shift to the right (from *IS* to *IS'* to *IS"*). This process continues until full employment is established at Y_f.

Recession → unemployment → wages ↓ prices ↓→ wealth ↑→consumption shifts upward → *IS* shifts to the right → full employment

general wages and general prices fall (and rise) *together;* there is no reason to believe that wages will fall more rapidly than the price level will fall. It follows that *real* wages will not fall; laborers can affect only nominal wages. Because real wages don't fall, the original unemployment rate remains unaltered and Keynes is able to demonstrate the simultaneous existence of price-wage flexibility and unemployment.

Still, Keynes pointed out, a reduction in the price level could (outside the Keynesian range) have *some* effect on the economy. As the price level falls, so will L_1; less money is required for transactions and precautionary motives. The nominal money supply is held constant but a lower price level creates an excess of liquidity, which *could* lead to increased bond purchases and a lower interest rate which could lead to more investment and a higher level of national income and employment.

In effect the *LM* curve shifts to the right due to what is now called the **Keynes effect.** However, in a depression or serious recession, interest rates are *already* very low and bonds are extremely risky. Consequently, *excess balances that result from a lower price level will merely be held.* Thus, Keynes's liquidity trap prevents the Keynes effect from eliminating unemployment through lower interest rates and higher net investment. This is shown in Figure 1.

However, the classical economists were not to be denied. A. C. Pigou demonstrated that a falling price level *also* increases the wealth of money holders. Consider people who own real estate worth $100, a bond worth $100, and a $100 bill. As prices fall, the present value of the real estate will fall at the same rate as the price level, so real estate owners are not affected. Bondholders will reap capital gains because the present value of a nominally fixed revenue stream increases. On the other hand, bond sellers will experience capital losses; they have fixed nominal obligations which are worth more at a lower price level. Because bondholders benefit only at the expense of bond issuers, no *net* wealth effect is apparent. On the other hand, those people who hold $100 bills (or other currency denominations or coins) are now wealthier; the purchasing power of money rises as the price level falls.

In other words, people's portfolios are not only more liquid—the Keynes effect— but currency holders are wealthier from what is called the **Pigou effect.** An increase in the wealth of some which is not offset by a decrease in the wealth of others will shift the consumption function upward; households will consume more at every income level now that they are wealthier. There is less of a requirement to save and to acquire wealth for retirement or for future consumption. This upward shift in the consumption function causes the *IS* curve to shift to the right; national income will be higher at any given interest rate.

The Pigou effect is indicated in the *IS-LM* framework in Figure 2. Note that as long as unemployment exists, wages and prices will fall at the same rate and the *IS* curve will shift to the right. This process will continue until full employment is established at Y_f. Nothing analogous to a liquidity trap exists in the product market. The conclusion: Price-wage flexibility leads to full employment.

CHAPTER SUMMARY

1   According to the classical economists, people hold money for transactions and precautionary motives; people trade off interest earnings for the convenience and the security that holding money gives. Money held in this form is referred to as L_1 balances. To hold money above L_1 (that is, to hoard) is considered irrational by the classical economists.

2   Keynes provided a rational reasoning for hoarding. He recognized that "bonds" (or assets on which it is possible to receive capital gains or losses) are risky. Because speculators cling to a notion of a natural rate of interest, relatively high or relatively low interest rates increase the expectation of a move toward the natural rate. Bondholders receive capital gains when the interest rate falls; they incur capital losses when the rate of interest rises. It follows that when interest rates are relatively low (i.e., bond prices are relatively high), money becomes an asset form superior to bonds, which are risky. An inverse relationship exists between interest rates and the quantity of money demanded to hold above and beyond L_1; this extra money demanded is called L_2. The relationship between interest rates and L_2 is called the speculative demand function, or the liquidity preference function.

The key question for households, according to the classical economists, is: How much should be saved and consumed out of a given income level? The answer ultimately determines the interest rate, according to the classical economists. Keynes, however, adds another question: How much saving should be held in money and how much allocated to bond purchases? According to Keynes, it is the answer to this second question that determines the rate of interest. The rate of interest is determined by the money supply and the Keynesian demand for money (liquidity preference) curve given any level of income. An increase in the money supply, given the liquidity preference curve, lowers the interest rate; a decrease in the money supply, given the liquidity preference curve, increases the interest rate.

4   The interest rate is the link between the monetary sphere and the real sphere. According to Keynes, a change in the money supply can change the rate of interest, which in turn can change net investment, which in turn shifts the aggregate demand curve, which in turn can change the level of real national income and the employment level. Because Keynes believed that changes in the money supply lead to par-

tially offsetting changes in velocity, however, he doubted the efficacy of monetary policy; he preferred the more direct approach of fiscal policy.

5 Changes in the level of national income cause changes in the quantity of money demanded for L_1 purposes. As a consequence, an increase in the level of national income leads to an increase in the rate of interest, the money supply held constant. An *LM* curve, indicating all combinations of national income levels and equilibrium interest rates (where the supply of and total demand for money are equated), is derived by holding the money supply constant. The *LM* curve indicates a direct relationship between levels of national income and equilibrium interest rates in the money market, holding the money supply constant.

6 Changes in interest rates lead to changes in net investment, which in turn lead to changes in the level of national income. An *IS* curve, which indicates combinations of interest rates and equilibrium levels of national income in the product market, can be derived. The *IS* curve indicates an inverse relationship between interest rates and equilibrium levels of national income.

7 The *LM* curve indicates that changes in the level of national income help to determine the interest rate. The *IS* curve indicates that changes in the interest rate help to determine the level of national income. By analyzing *IS* and *LM* curve interaction, it is apparent that the equilibrium interest rate and the equilibrium level of national income are determined *simultaneously* in the money market and the product market. Aggregate equilibrium exists at the point of intersection of the *IS* curve and the *LM* curve.

8 According to Keynes, and contrary to the classical economists, unemployment can exist even if prices and wages are free to fall without limit. Keynes admitted that a reduction in the price level increases the real value of a money supply; less money is required for L_1 balances and a surplus of liquidity drives interest rates down. In turn, this increases real national income and employment. Eventually, however, these rightward shifts in the *LM* curve are ineffective, as the liquidity trap problem emerges in the Keynesian range; the Keynes effect has its limitations and unemployment persists. On the other hand, A. C. Pigou noted that reductions in the price level increase the wealth of holders of paper currency and coins without lowering the wealth of others. This "Pigou effect" shifts the *IS* curve rightward until full employment is reached. Thus, price-wage flexibility, however unlikely in modern economies, assures full employment.

GLOSSARY

Classical range: The vertical range of an *LM* curve indicating a maximum level of real national income given the money supply, where money is held completely for L_1 and where velocity is therefore at a maximum.

General equilibrium: Simultaneous equilibrium in both the product market and the money market; the point of intersection of the *IS* curve and the *LM* curve.

IS curve: A curve that indicates all the combinations of interest rates and equilibrium levels of national income in the product market.

Keynes effect: A decrease in the price level increases the real value of a constant money supply; a rightward shift of the *LM* curve resulting from a reduction in the price level.

Keynesian range: The horizontal range of an *LM* curve reflecting the liquidity trap, where lower levels of national income reduce L_1 balances but these excess funds are merely held because bonds are too risky.

L_1: The quantity of money demanded that people desire to hold for the transactions motive and the precautionary motive.

Liquidity preference function: An inverse relationship existing between interest rates and L_2; a preference for money over bonds; also the speculative demand function.

Liquidity trap: The horizontal range of the liquidity preference function, where interest rates are at their minimum because all speculators are convinced that interest rates

can't fall any further and can only rise.

LM curve: A curve that shows all the combinations of equilibrium levels of national income and equilibrium interest rates in the monetary sphere of the economy derived by holding the money supply constant.

Natural rate of interest: That rate to which the interest rate usually returns after recessions and inflations have run their course.

Pigou effect: A decrease in the price level increases the real wealth of holders of paper currency and coins without lowering the wealth of others;

a rightward shift in the *IS* curve resulting from a falling price level.

Precautionary motive: The motive which leads people to hold a pool of readily available purchasing power in order to meet unexpected financial obligations.

Risk avoiders: Those who prefer less risk to more risk, other things constant, and who therefore require interest rate compensation before they voluntarily assume risk.

Speculative demand (L_2): The quantity of money *over and above* L_1 that people want to hold because it is a better store of value than bonds.

PROBLEMS

20-1 Consider the graph below.

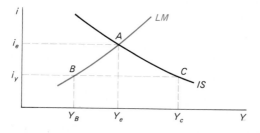

a What point represents general equilibrium?

b Does point C represent equilibrium in the product market? Why or why not?

c Does point C represent equilibrium in the money market? Why or why not?

d What does exist in the money market at point C? Why?

e If the economy is at point C, why will it move to point A?

SELECTED REFERENCES

Ackley, Gardner, *Macroeconomics: Theory and Policy* (New York: Macmillan, 1978).

Hicks, J. R., "Mr. Keynes and the 'Classics': A Suggested Reinterpretation," *Econometrica,* vol. 5, April 1937, pp. 147–159.

Johnson, Harry G., "The General Theory after Twenty-five Years," *American Economic Association Papers and Proceedings,* vol. 51, May 1961, pp. 1–7.

Patinkin, Don, "Price Flexibility and Full Employment," *American Economic Review,* vol. 38, September 1948, pp. 543–564.

Pigou, A. C., "Economic Progress in a Stable Environment," *Economica,* vol. 14, 1947.

Smith, Warren L., "A Graphical Exposition of the Complete Keynesian System," *Southern Economic Journal,* vol. 23, October 1956, pp. 115–125.

Tobin, James, "Liquidity Preference as Behaviour towards Risk," *Review of Economic Studies,* vol. 25, February 1958, pp. 65–86.

Chapter **21**

Inflation

Although the rate of inflation seems to have abated in the United States—at least temporarily—the fear of renewed inflation continues to be a major concern. Indeed, inflation seems to be a worldwide phenomenon and it is a major problem in most countries. This chapter is devoted to an analysis of inflation. In particular we discuss:

1 The modern theory of how the price level is determined
2 The leading theories of inflation, which include the monetary, demand-pull, cost-push, and federal government deficits theories
3 Specific measures of inflation
4 Who is hurt by inflation
5 A constitutional amendment to require a balanced budget.

THE MODERN THEORY OF HOW THE PRICE LEVEL IS DETERMINED

In order to discuss inflation, which is defined as a sustained *increase* in the price level over time, it is important to know how the price level is determined in the first place. You will recall from Chapter 18 that according to the classical economists the price level was determined by the interaction of the supply of and demand for money. This can be shown easily using the equation of exchange:

$$MV = PQ$$

where M = the money supply (narrowly defined as the value of currency plus the value of checking account balances)
V = velocity, or the ratio of nominal net national product to *desired* money balances
P = the price level
Q = real output of final goods and services per year

According to the classical economist, Q is constant at its full-employment level (due to Say's law). As a consequence, P is determined by the value of M—the money supply—and V—a factor that indicates the *demand* for money. From this theory of the price level, the classical theory of inflation is easily demonstrated. Classical economists believed that velocity was constant, so changes in the money supply led to proportional changes in the price level. To them, inflation was a monetary phenomenon: Increases in the money supply led to increases in the price level.

Modern economists believe that the classical theory of how the price level is determined and the classical theory of inflation are too simplistic. We turn now to a widely accepted theory of how the price level is determined. Then we discuss various theories of why the price level *rises*. The leading theories of inflation can be better understood after we understand the modern theory of how the price level is determined.

NEW AGGREGATE DEMAND
AND AGGREGATE SUPPLY CURVES

The *IS-LM* framework developed in Chapter 20 was couched in real terms; the real interest rate and the real level of national income were derived simultaneously through the interaction of the product and the money markets. In the *IS-LM* model, the price level was assumed to be constant (except in the Current Controversy section); hence, changes in nominal and real values were equivalent. The *IS-LM* framework is not suitable for analyzing the determination of the price level. For this reason, an aggregate demand curve and an aggregate supply curve are now derived by varying the price level.[1] The **aggregate demand curve** relates different quantities of national output demanded to various price levels, other things constant; the **aggregate supply curve** relates the nation's aggregate output of goods and services to various price levels, other things constant. This analysis is analogous to the supply of and demand for an individual good or service.

The Aggregate Demand Curve Recall the Current Controversy in Chapter 20, which describes the Keynes effect. The Keynes effect indicates that a falling price level is equivalent to an increase in the money supply because it shifts the LM curve to the right. Even though the money supply remains constant, a lower price level reduces the amount of money required for transactions and precautionary motives (L_1); *real* money balances increase as the price level falls. Figure 21-1 shows how an aggregate demand curve can be constructed. In panel (a), lower price levels cause the *LM* curve to shift to the right due to the Keynes effect. If the *IS* curve remains constant, then excess money balances resulting from a lower L_1 imply a surplus of money in money markets. If there is no liquidity trap, these excess balances are used to purchase bonds, forcing bond prices up and interest rates down. A lower rate of interest causes an increase in net investment, and real national income increases by some multiple of the change in autonomous investment.[2] Thus, a lower price level causes an increase in the equilibrium output quantity demanded by way of a

---

[1]These are not to be confused with the AD and the AS curves, derived holding the price level constant, which were developed in the Keynesian model analyzed in Chapters 19 and 20.

[2]This increased real income causes an increase in the quantity of L_1 demanded; the process continues until the supply of and demand for money are equated and the community voluntarily is holding the existing stock of money.

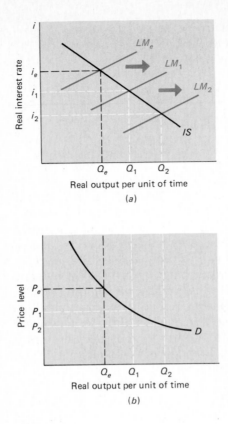

FIGURE 21-1 In panel (*a*) lower price levels shift the *LM* function rightward, which leads to a lower interest rate. Lower interest rates lead to an increase in net investment and a multiple expansion in real output. In panel (*b*) the relationship implied in panel (*a*) is indicated; lower price levels increase the quantity of real output demanded, other things constant.

lower interest rate.[3] Panel (*b*) of Figure 21-1 traces out the equilibrium price level–output combinations resulting from the *IS-LM* framework in panel (*a*). Note that LM_e, LM_1, and LM_2 are associated with progressively lower price levels P_e, P_1, and P_2, respectively.

Shifts in Aggregate Demand What causes this aggregate demand curve to shift? Any non-price-level change that causes either the *IS* or the *LM* curve to shift will lead to a shift in the aggregate demand curve. These include changes in the money supply, shifts in the marginal efficiency of investment

---

[3]Another reason the aggregate quantity of output demanded is inversely related to the price level comes from international trade considerations. If exchange rates for currencies are fixed, then a lower domestic price level will cause a decrease in imports (and therefore an increase in domestic production of import substitutes) and an increase in exports. Thus, a relatively lower domestic price level increases the quantity of domestic output demanded, other things constant. Note further that the Pigou effect can also be used to derive an aggregate demand curve. A lower price level, other things constant, increases the wealth of currency holders without reducing the wealth of others. This net increase in community wealth causes the consumption curve (and therefore the *IS* curve) to shift upward; consumption will be higher at every level of net national product. Thus, a lower price level leads to an increase in the quantity of aggregate output demanded, other things constant.

curve, shifts in the consumption function, and, as you will soon see, changes in government expenditures and taxes.

Fiscal Policy Effects on the Aggregate Demand Curve Consider Figure 21-2. In panel (*a*), the initial equilibrium position is at i_e and Q_e. Then the *IS* curve shifts to the right as a result of expansionary fiscal policy; government expenditures (*G*) increase and/or taxes (*T*) are decreased. The effect is to cause an increase in the level of output at *any* interest rate. However, the supply of money is assumed constant; hence, the *LM* curve does not shift. As a consequence, a higher level of national output and income requires a greater quantity of money demanded for L_1 purposes. A scramble for liquidity ensues and bond sales drive bond prices downward and interest rates upward. Consequently, a higher interest rate "crowds out" further investments. In effect, the levels of national income and output don't expand as much as they otherwise would have if the interest rate had remained constant; the full multiplier effect does not occur. In other words, fiscal policy would have expanded national output and real income to Q_m, but a shortage of liquidity on the money market forced interest rates upward and crowded out private investments. Instead of real income, Q_m, the nation must settle for Q_1. This is also

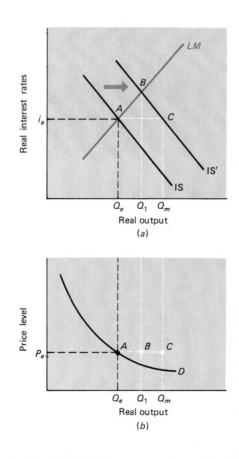

FIGURE 21-2 In panel (*a*) an expansionary fiscal policy shifts the *IS* curve rightward. National income (or real national output) increases but not by the complete multiplier effect because an expansionary fiscal policy simultaneously raises the real interest rate. Consequently, some private investment is crowded out. Panel (*b*) shows that a rightward shift in the *IS* curve leads to an increase in the quantity of national real output demanded at the same price level.

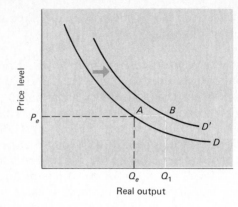

FIGURE 21-3 Figure 21-2 indicated that an increase in the *IS* curve leads to an increase in the quantity of real national output demanded at the *same* price level. This figure indicates the results of increases in the *IS* curve at *all* price levels. Thus, shifts in the *IS* curve lead to an increase in the demand for real national output; national quantity demanded is higher at every price level; an increase in aggregate demand results from an increase in the *IS* curve.

indicated in panel (*b*), which shows an increase in real output at the same price level, P_e, from Q_e to Q_1 and not from Q_e to Q_m. The investment that was crowded out by a higher interest rate reduces Q from Q_m to Q_1.

It is important to realize that point *B*, in panel (*b*), the combination of the new output level Q_1 and the same price level P_e, is one point on a *new* aggregate demand curve. Figure 21-3 shows the results of fiscal policy on the aggregate demand curve at *all* price levels. Figure 21-2 showed the results of an expansionary fiscal policy at only *one* price level, P_e. Figure 21-3 includes the effect of fiscal policy on price level P_e (a movement from *A* to *B*) and on all other price levels as well. In short, expansionary fiscal policy shifts the aggregate demand curve to the right. It is left to you to demonstrate that contractionary fiscal policy shifts the aggregate demand curve to the left.[4]

Monetary Policy Effects on the Aggregate Demand Curve Recall that an increase in the money supply shifts the *LM* curve to the right; a decrease in the money supply shifts the *LM* curve to the left. Consider Figure 21-4, which

---

[4]The aggregate demand curve also shifts if the consumption function or the autonomous net investment function shifts. These shifts would lead to a shift in the *IS* curve, which in turn would cause an increase in the quantity of output demanded at any price level. In an open economy, an increase in net exports (exports minus imports) would also shift aggregate demand.

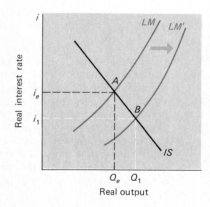

FIGURE 21-4 At point *A*, the supply of and demand for money are equated. An increase in the money supply initially creates an excess supply of money, or excess liquidity. This causes interest rates to fall, which in turn causes an increase in net investment and a multiple expansion in the level of real national output. Such an increase in real national income causes an increase in the demand for L_1 balances. This process continues until the supply of and demand for money are again equated, at point *B*.

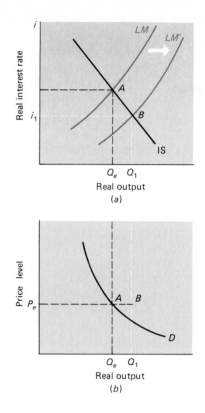

FIGURE 21-5 Panel (*a*) reproduces Figure 21-4. Panel (*b*) indicates that a rightward shift in the *LM* curve leads to an increase in the real national output at the current price level, from Q_e to Q_1 and P_e.

indicates the former case. An increase in the money supply shifts the *LM* curve to the right, from *LM* to *LM'*. The initial equilibrium position is i_e and Q_e (point *A*), at which point equilibrium existed simultaneously in both the product and the money markets. A money supply increase means that now a surplus of liquidity exists at point *A*: $M > L_1 + L_2$. Such an increase can result from an expansionary monetary policy pursued by the Fed (i.e., open-market purchases, a lower discount rate, or a lower reserve requirement). As monetary expansion occurs, interest rates fall. A lower interest rate induces an increase in net investment and a multiple expansion in national income and output.[5] In turn, a higher level of national income increases the quantity of money demanded for L_1 purposes. This process continues until the now higher money supply is held voluntarily by the community. The new equilibrium position is at point *B*, the combination of Q_1 and i_1.

Figure 21-5 indicates how monetary policy affects the aggregate demand

---

[5]Note that the *full* multiplier effect obtains, unlike the fiscal policy result, because no crowding-out effect occurs. There is, however, an effect analogous to the crowding-out effect. A lower interest rate increases the quantity of money demanded for L_2 balances, which reduces the velocity of money. The ultimate increase in net national product, therefore, is less than it would have been had L_2 not been inversely related to the interest rate. More technically, due to the existence of an L_2 demand for money, the *LM* curve is not vertical; a shift in *LM* by a given amount (due to an increase in the money supply) would cause net national product to increase more if the *LM* curve were vertical than if it were positively sloped.

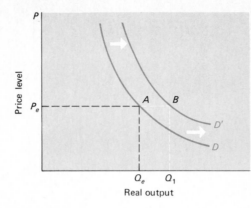

FIGURE 21-6 Panel (*b*) of Figure 21-5 indicated that a rightward shift in the *LM* curve causes an increase in the quantity of real national output demanded at the *current* price level. Figure 21-6 shows that a rightward shift in the *LM* curve leads to an increase in the quantity of real national output demanded at *all* price levels. That is, an increase in the *LM* curve leads to an increase in the aggregate demand curve for real national output.

curve. Panel (*a*) reproduces Figure 21-4, while panel (*b*) indicates that an increase in the money supply leads to an increase in the demand for national output *at the same price level, P_e.*

Figure 21-6 shows how monetary policy shifts the aggregate demand curve. An increase in the money supply causes a rightward shift in the aggregate demand curve, from *D* to *D'*. The quantity of national output demanded is higher at every price level, including P_e.

The Aggregate Supply Curve   It is easy to discern the shape of an individual firm's supply curve. As you will recall from your principles of economics course, the firm's short-run supply curve is upward-sloping from left to right. Before a firm voluntarily produces more output in the short run, price must rise to offset increasing marginal costs. Marginal costs rise because of the law of diminishing returns. A firm increases its output in the short run by using more labor relative to other factors of production; this causes the marginal physical product of labor to fall and, given wage rates, the marginal cost of output rises.

Also, a firm that has the option to produce two goods will increase the output of one relative to the other as their relative prices change. For example, an oil refiner can increase its output of gasoline relative to heating oil. If the relative price of gasoline rises, oil refiners will increase the output of gasoline and reduce the output of heating oil; the supply of gasoline (and heating oil) is directly related to its relative price. Similar statements can be made about farms, and other businesses that can produce more than one good.

The industry supply curve is derived by summing horizontally all the individual firm supply curves. This summation process provides another explanation for the upward-sloping nature of supply curves. At higher relative prices, firms that are inefficient can also produce; at lower relative prices, some firms are too inefficient to operate at all. Therefore, higher relative prices increase the quantity that an industry is willing to supply, because firms that had temporarily shut down will now operate.

You may have noted that quantity supplied responds to *relative* price changes. When the price of one good rises relative to another, its quantity supplied will increase. If so, the *aggregate* supply curve (which relates total output to the price level) need not respond to changes in the price level. If all prices (input as well as output) change at the same rate, relative prices do not change and there is no reason to expect output changes. Similarly, if all prices change at the same rate, households will not change their consumption and laborers will not change the number of hours they work. Hence, the aggregate supply curve is unresponsive to changes in the price level. Of course, prices and wages don't all change at the same rate; some prices will change relative to others and some wages will change relative to others. This will cause some industries to expand and others to contract. Output and employment will increase in those industries that experience relative price increases; output and employment will contract in those industries that experience relative price decreases. Still, the overall effect is that *total* output and *total* employment are unresponsive to changes in the price level. Figure 21-7 shows this. Note how changes in aggregate demand change only the price level. Total output remains constant at Q_f; and, by implication, the employment level remains constant. According to the classical economists, all that occurs in the short run is that the total output level doesn't depart from the full-employment position. Significant changes in the economy lead only to a reallocation of labor and a change in the composition of output.

Keynes, however, pointed out that prices and (especially) wages are sticky downward in modern economies. Increases in aggregate demand lead only to price-level (not output) changes at the full-employment level. Decreases in aggregate demand, however, lead to reductions in output and employment, as well as in prices and wages. This is because monopolistic businesses and powerful unions are prepared to reduce output and employment (of low seniority workers) as well as prices and wages. Minimum wage laws also prevent wages from falling completely. Moreover, a welfare state economy is prepared to "purchase" surplus labor by utilizing unemployment compensation, food stamps, and other welfare plans. As a consequence, wages won't fall (or won't fall as rapidly as prices), and the surplus of labor (unem-

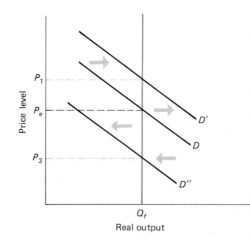

FIGURE 21-7 Because output and employment respond only to changes in relative prices, changes in the overall price level do not affect real national output. That is, aggregate supply is unresponsive to changes in aggregate demand. Even if some relative prices change, some industries will expand while others will contract; the *net* impact on real national output is negligible, hence the aggregate supply curve is vertical.

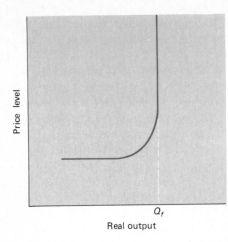

FIGURE 21-8 Because prices and (especially) wages are inflexible downward in modern economies, decreases in aggregate demand lead to reductions in real national output as well as the price level. The result is a J-shaped aggregate supply curve.

ployment) will remain. Decreases in aggregate demand, therefore, lead to decreases in the quantity of output supplied and decreases in the employment level. Figure 21-8 shows an aggregate supply curve along which output increases with the price level up until the full-employment level.

Determination of the Price Level Figure 21-9 shows that the price level is determined at the point of intersection of the aggregate supply and the aggregate demand curves. Note that shifts in aggregate demand affect mainly output levels at high-unemployment situations. Aggregate demand shifts affect *both* output and prices as the full-employment output (Q_f) is approached; at Q_f, further increases in aggregate demand affect *only the price level*. Shifts in aggregate demand can result from increases in the money supply by the Fed. As long as the economy is not in the liquidity trap, money supply increases shift the aggregate demand curve to the right. Note that expansionary monetary policy is effective only at moderately high output levels. At very low output levels, the liquidity trap leaves the aggregate demand insensitive to money supply

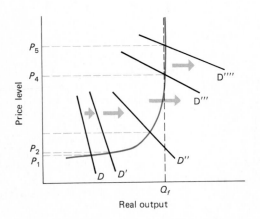

FIGURE 21-9 Increases in aggregate demand, from *D* to *D'* to *D''*, cause both the price level and real national output to increase. The closer the economy is to the full-employment real national output level, Q_f, the more likely it is that increases in aggregate demand will lead mostly to price level increases. Once Q_f is reached, further increases in aggregate demand (above *D'''*) lead only to price level increases.

increases. At full employment, money supply increases shift aggregate demand rightward but the aggregate supply of output is not responsive, and only the price level rises.

GENERAL THEORIES OF INFLATION

Now that we have a theory of how a nation's price level is determined we are in a position to discuss the cause of inflation. Although there are many theories to explain inflation, we will discuss the major three.

Inflation as a Monetary Phenomenon For at least 600 years of recorded economic history, a close connection between inflation and money-supply changes has been observed. The additional gold and silver mined in the new world was brought to the old world at the end of the fourteenth century and caused inflation in the old world. So did gold and silver discoveries wherever they were made. The printing of paper currency in England during the Napoleonic war, in the American colonies during their War of Independence, in the North and the South during the Civil War, and in Germany after World War I contributed to rampant inflation in each case.

An Increase in the Supply of Money Relative to the Demand for Money The relationship between the rate at which the price level is rising and the rate at which the money supply is increasing can be seen by using simple supply and demand analysis. Suppose that there were a major oil discovery and that the supply of oil increased relative to the demand for oil. The price of oil, relative to the price of other goods and services, would fall. For example, if one barrel of oil previously traded for one quart of milk or one gallon of cola, the *relative* price of oil would fall. Due to the major oil discovery, *two* barrels of oil may now be required to purchase one quart of milk or one gallon of cola. Thus, an increase in the supply of oil, relative to its demand, will cause the relative price of oil to rise; it will take *more* units of oil (barrels) to purchase specific quantities of nonoil goods (a quart of milk or a gallon of cola).

By analogy, we can see what happens when the supply of money is increased relative to the demand for money.[6] The relative price of money will fall; it will take more units of money to purchase specific units of nonmoney goods and services. This is what we mean by inflation: *It takes more units of money to purchase the same quantities* (or units) *of other goods and services.*

Do the Relative Prices of Nonmoney Goods and Services Change When the Money Supply Increases? Suppose that the money supply is increased in such a way that the relative prices of nonmoney goods and services do not change. While it takes more units of money to buy one quart of milk and one

---

[6]Or if the demand for money were to fall relative to the supply of money—or if the demand for oil were to fall relative to the supply of oil, for that matter.

gallon of oil, a quart of milk will still exchange for a gallon of cola. Thus, an increase in the supply of money will cause all prices to increase at the same rate; all absolute prices rise, but relative prices remain constant. In this sense, money is *neutral.*

On the other hand, it is possible that the actual process of increasing money itself changes the relative prices of nonmoney goods and services. In that case, when the money supply increases it will take more units of money to purchase a quart of milk and a gallon of cola *and* the relative price of milk and cola will change. For example, it may now take *two* quarts of milk to purchase one gallon of cola; the relative price of milk may fall as a result of an increase in the money supply.[7] Money is then considered nonneutral.

Which is it then? Is money neutral or nonneutral? Honest disagreement exists among economists. While most economists believe that the way in which the money supply is increased in our economy *does* change the relative prices of nonmoney goods and services, an important minority maintains that money is neutral.[8]

In *principle,* this issue can be resolved by observing whether or not relative price changes actually do occur during periods of inflation. In *practice,* it is very difficult to measure the pure effects of increases in the money supply on the price level, because in the real world other things are changing with the money supply. For example, assume for the moment a price-stable economy in which some prices rise while others fall, but the weighted average of all prices doesn't change. In such an environment, a change in tastes in favor of bananas and away from pears will cause the price of bananas to rise and the price of pears to fall in both absolute and relative terms. Similarly, incomes from wages and profits will rise in the banana industry and fall in the pear industry. What is happening will be obvious to one and all—even if some people don't like the situation.

Consider now an economy in which all (output and input) prices are rising at 10 percent per annum. In this situation, a change in tastes in favor of bananas and away from pears will cause the price of bananas to rise by more than 10 percent. The price of pears will rise also, but by less than 10 percent. Similarly, incomes will rise by more than 10 percent for those in the banana industry and by less than 10 percent for those in the pear industry. How will this be interpreted? People in the pear industry will blame their plight on "inflation"; people in the banana industry will complain about how much better their economic situation (their real incomes) would have been if the price level had not been rising at 10 percent! This example points out that changes

---

[7]Note that changes in supply relative to demand could be so great that even the *absolute* price of some goods might fall. For example, a slight increase in the money supply might change the supply of some goods relative to their demand, so that some absolute prices might fall during a period of inflation. Note further that our analogy to an increase in the relative supply of oil breaks down; when the relative price of oil falls, *other* relative prices will change because oil is used to produce other goods. Money, however, is not a factor of production, so other relative prices need not change.

[8]See, for instance, A. A. Alchian and W. R. Allen, *Exchange and Production,* 3d ed. (Los Angeles: Wadsworth, 1983), chap. 19.

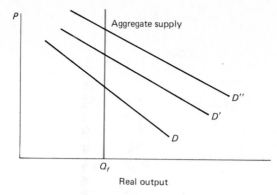

FIGURE 21-10 Increases in the money supply cause the aggregate demand curve to shift rightward, from D to D' to D''. Money is neutral and the net result is that only the price level increases.

in tastes must be considered before computing the results of inflation. Complementary analysis indicates that the effects of technological change, quality variations, and changes in expectations must be eliminated before the pure effects of money supply increases on inflation can actually be measured. We return to a discussion of this issue in a later section of this chapter, when we analyze who is hurt by inflation.

Consider Figure 21-10, which depicts inflation as a monetary phenomenon, using our aggregate demand–aggregate supply approach. Note that the aggregate supply curve is vertical, reflecting the fact that money is neutral; the classical model implies a vertical aggregate supply curve at the full-employment output level. Note that increases in the money supply cause the aggregate demand curve to shift to the right; combined with a vertical aggregate supply curve, the result is that only the price level rises.

Money Supply Increases in a Growing Economy   Modern industrialized societies experience economic growth; the real output of goods and services increases due to increases in the labor force and due to increases in productivity. The proponents of the notion that inflation is a monetary phenomenon maintain that if the supply of money increases relative to the output of final goods and services, inflation will occur. This can be indicated using the equation of exchange: $MV = PQ$.

If M increases relative to V (the money supply increases relative to the demand for money) *and* if M increases relative to Q, P will rise. If an economy tends to grow at a rate of 3 percent per annum (Q rises at 3 percent per annum), then if the money supply increases at a rate faster than 3 percent per year the price level will rise. We return to this point in Chapter 27, where we discuss the feasibility of a monetary policy that is based on the implications of the analysis of this section.

Figure 21-11 shows how inflation results when the money supply increases faster than output.[9] The ratio of the money supply to real (inflation-

---

[9]This graph was reproduced from David I. Meiselman's foreward to R. Schuettinger and E. Butler, *Forty Centuries of Wage and Price Controls* (Washington, D.C.: The Heritage Foundation, 1979), p. 8.

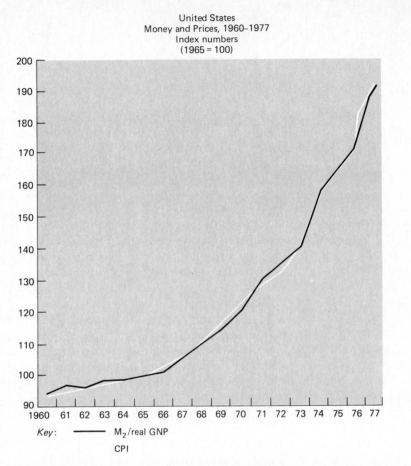

United States
Money and Prices, 1960–1977
Index numbers
(1965 = 100)

Key: ——— M₂/real GNP

CPI

FIGURE 21-11   Inflation Results when Money Increases Faster than Output.   The dark line indicates the ratio of the money supply to real GNP; when it is rising, money increases faster than output. Note that the CPI, measured on the vertical axis, moves in tandem with this ratio. The conclusion is that inflation results when the money supply increases faster than output increases.

adjusted) GNP is indicated by the solid line; when this ratio rises the money supply has increased relative to output. The white line indicates one measure of inflation, the consumer price index (CPI), which we discuss in the next section. Note that the curves are very similar, indicating that there is a very close relationship between the rate at which money increases relative to real output and the rate of inflation.

Demand-Pull Inflation   When the quantity of aggregate demand for goods and services exceeds the economy's ability to supply those goods and services (quantity of aggregate supply), the demand will "pull" price upward. Actually, two demand-pull theories of inflation have already been discussed—the classical and the Keynesian.

According to the classical model, increases in the supply of money, given velocity, lead to an increase in total money expenditures. Because the economy is already at full employment, the increased demand will pull prices higher. Thus, for the classical economist inflation is a monetary phenomenon.

In the Keynesian model, inflation results when the quantity of aggregate demand for final goods and services exceeds the quantity of aggregate supply at a full- (or nearly full-) employment level. For the Keynesian, therefore, inflation is not necessarily a monetary phenomenon.

A simplified representation of Keynesian demand-pull theory is given in Figure 21-12. Output is measured on the horizontal axis; the price level is measured on the vertical axis. Output and employment can increase without any increase in the general price level, as long as the economy is not near the full-employment level of output. Figure 21-12 indicates an aggregate supply curve, S; it becomes vertical at the full-employment rate of output—no more can be supplied. The economy is running at full steam at output rate Q_4. D_1 through D_4 represent possible aggregate demand curves. If aggregate demand increases from D_1 to D_2, then output will increase from Q_1 to Q_2 without any increase in an index of prices. If the aggregate demand curve increases further to D_3, output will increase to Q_3, but there will be some inflation. Finally, if the aggregate demand curve increases to D_4, output will be at Q_4, but there will be considerable inflation. In fact, any increased aggregate demand curve that intersects the aggregate supply curve S along its vertical portion will merely produce inflation, because no increase in output is possible. As long as the economy is not in the flat range of the aggregate supply curve, increases in demand will pull up prices; hence, the term **demand-pull inflation.**

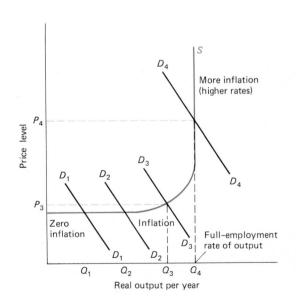

FIGURE 21-12 Demand-Pull Inflation. The aggregate supply curve is given as S. It is horizontal until nearly full employment is reached. When full employment is reached, it becomes vertical. No more output is possible from the economy. If the aggregate demand curve for all goods and services is D_1, output will be at Q_1 per year. Aggregate demand in the economy can increase to D_2 without any increase in the price level. When it increases, however, to D_3, there is some increase in the price level as well as an increase in output to Q_3. After output rate Q_4, however, any increase in demand, such as up to D_4, will merely lead to increases in the price level. Increases in demand pull up prices at any point beyond the flat range of the aggregate supply curve.

Cost-Push Inflation The cost-push inflation theory of price increases has recently emerged as a popular theory. It attempts to explain why prices rise when the economy is *not* at full employment. The theory of **cost-push inflation** attempts to explain the moderate inflation that the United States experienced during its 1969 to 1970 and 1973 to 1975 recessions. There are essentially three causes of cost-push inflation: union monopoly power, big business monopoly power, and increasing raw-materials prices.

Union Monopoly Power—or the "Price-Wage Spiral" Many people feel that unions are responsible for inflation. Their reasoning is as follows. Unions decide to demand a wage hike that is not warranted by increases in their productivity. Because the unions are so powerful, employers must give in to union demands for higher wages. When the employers have to pay these higher wages, their marginal costs are higher. To maximize profits, these businesses raise their prices. This type of cost-push inflation seemingly can occur even when there is no excess demand for goods, and even when the economy is operating below capacity at less than full employment.

The union-power argument rests on the assumption that unions have monopolistic market power in their labor markets. In other words, some unions are so strong that they can impose wage increases on employers even when those wage increases are not matched by increases in the productivity of their labor.

Big-Business Monopoly Power, or the "Price-Wage Spiral" The second variant of the cost-push theory is that inflation is caused when the monopoly power of big business enables it to raise prices. Powerful corporations presumably can raise their prices to increase their profits. Each time the corporations raise prices to increase their profits, the cost of living goes up. Workers then demand higher wages to make up for the decline in their standard of living, and thereby give the corporations an excuse to raise prices again. And so goes a vicious price-wage cycle.

Raw-Materials Cost-Push Inflation Since the 1973 onslaught of higher and higher prices for all forms of energy, a relatively new type of cost-push inflation has been suggested. It is raw-materials cost-push inflation, which results because the cost of raw materials seems to keep rising all the time. Coal is more expensive, as is petroleum, natural gas, and many other basic inputs into production processes.

Whether it be union monopoly power, big-business monopoly power, or higher raw-materials prices, the resultant increased cost of production pushes prices up; hence the term cost-push inflation. One solution offered as a way to stop or at least slow down cost-push inflation is wage and price controls. We will talk about these controls later, and we will see that they have not done much to cure the inflation that still plagues our economy.

Figure 21-13 shows the cost-push theory of inflation in the aggregate supply–aggregate demand framework. Increases in raw-material's costs or wage rates shift the aggregate supply curve leftward from *S* to *S'*; the quantity sup-

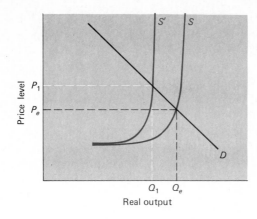

FIGURE 21-13   An increase in union wage rates or an increase in raw materials prices causes the aggregate supply curve to decrease from S to S'. Given aggregate demand, D, the price level rises from P_e to P_1 and the level of real national output falls from Q_e to Q_1. This is an example of cost-push inflation.

plied is less at any price level. Given aggregate demand, D, the result is an increase in the price level from P_e to P_1 and a decrease in the level of national output from Q_e to Q_1.

GOVERNMENT AND INFLATION

As indicated in an earlier chapter, there are three important ways the federal government can obtain purchasing power. It can tax, borrow existing funds, or borrow (or spend directly) newly created money. This chapter has made it clear that money creation leads to an increase in the LM curve and therefore to an increase in aggregate demand, and to inflation. In this section, the impact of federal deficits on the price level is explored. Federal deficits arise when the federal government spends more than it collects in taxes, by borrowing existing funds, or by borrowing newly created money.[10]

Thirty-one states have approved (and more are considering) a petition for a constitutional convention that would require a balanced federal budget on a fiscal-year basis. This ground-swell movement in favor of a balanced federal budget is largely based on the popular belief that federal deficits cause inflation. This section explores the theoretical and empirical justification, or lack thereof, for this position.

Federal Deficits and Inflation in Theory

Deficits and the Supply of Money   Since the 1951 Accord between the Federal Reserve and the U.S. Treasury (discussed in Chapter 26), the Fed no longer is required to purchase any portion of the public debt, nor is the Fed any longer directly responsible for stabilizing government security prices (and, therefore, interest rates). It follows that since 1951 there has been no *direct*

---

[10]Much of what follows in this section is based on S. Hein, "Deficits and Inflation," *Review,* Federal Reserve Bank of St. Louis, vol. 63, no. 3, (March 1981), pp. 3–10.

relationship between federal deficits and Fed open-market operations; increased deficits will not automatically lead to increases in depository-institution reserves or in the money supply.

Still, it is possible that the increased demand for credit by the U.S. Treasury, as it attempts to finance deficits, will cause interest rates to rise. It is alleged that monetary authorities will attempt to prevent this by buying bonds directly, or through open-market operations, and thereby increase depository reserves and the money supply. Therefore, an *indirect* link exists between deficits and inflation, when the Fed "accommodates" the Treasury by monetizing the public debt. While this may be true, it should be stressed that this link is indirect; federal deficits can cause inflation only to the extent that the Fed is willing to pay the price of increased inflation in order to keep interest rates down.[11] Moreover, in the period 1979 to 1982, the Fed had (nearly) abandoned its attempt to stabilize interest rates. In 1983, the Fed again became interested in stabilizing interest rates—at a lower level.

Deficits and the Demand for Money   If inflation is caused by "too much money chasing too few goods," then the increased supply of money (given demand) is only part of the story. A decrease in the demand for money (given supply) can also create a situation of "too much money." Arthur Laffer and others have charged that inflation reduces the demand for money because it imposes a tax on those who hold it. As a consequence, *velocity* rises as people try to spend money as fast as possible in order to convert it to other assets. It is alleged that much recent inflation is caused by such a decreased demand for money. As people reduce cash balances, velocity increases and a *constant* supply of money is consistent with higher price levels. To the extent that large federal deficits are monetized and cause inflation, a further boost to inflation will result as velocity rises with the money supply.

Also, if federal deficits cause interest rates to rise, then (following Keynes's liquidity preference function derived in Chapter 20 and footnote 5 in this chapter), the quantity of money demanded for speculation purposes (L_2) will fall. That is, velocity will rise as the opportunity cost for holding money rises and bonds become less risky.

Federal Deficits and Inflation: The Empirical Evidence   Regarding the size of federal deficits and the *money supply,* the evidence is that from 1955 to 1975 the growth of the federal debt and the growth of the money supply moved in tandem. In 1975, however, a clear break in this relationship occurred. The 1975 to 1980 period was the first sustained period since 1951 during which the money supply grew more slowly than the federal debt grew. During this period, the Fed (reversing a trend) reduced the total proportion of the federal

---

[11]As shall be demonstrated later, some economists feel that such an attempt is self-defeating; debt monetization leads to an increased rate of inflation which causes nominal interest rates to rise as lenders and buyers insist on and permit inflationary premiums.

debt that it held. In short, the link between the federal debt and the money supply was broken (or, at least, loosened). When the federal debt and the money supply increased in tandem, deficits were highly correlated with inflation. From 1975 to 1980, when the federal deficit and the money supply changed independently, the size of the federal debt was no longer as highly correlated with the rate of inflation. As a consequence, a theory which predicts future interest rates based on the size of the federal debt will not perform as well as a theory which directly predicts future inflation rates and interest rates based on money supply increases.

Regarding deficits and the *demand for money,* the evidence is that this effect exists, but its magnitude is not significant. Interest rates would have to increase by 500 percent to induce the same amount of inflation associated with a permanent one percentage point increase in the money supply growth.[12]

Thus, the impact of higher interest rates on the demand for money is very slight; it follows that higher interest rates resulting from higher deficits have little effect on the rate of inflation by a reduced demand for money. Inflation is predicted better by directly observing changes in the money supply.

MEASURES OF INFLATION

Although everyone seems to know what inflation means, in practice its measurement is difficult. There is more than one measure of inflation and two are discussed briefly here.

The Implicit Price Deflator for GNP   Nominal gross national product (GNP) measures the value of output in a given period using the *prices of that period* (alternately referred to as current dollars). For example, 1984 GNP measures the value of all final goods and services produced in 1984, valued at the prices that prevailed in 1984; nominal GNP in 1981 measures the value of all the final goods and services produced in 1981, valued at the prices that prevailed in 1981.

Real GNP measures changes in physical output through time by valuing the goods and services produced in all periods *by using the same prices.* The year 1972 presently is used as the base year; thus real GNP in 1984 is a measure of the value of the output in 1984 using the prices that prevailed in 1972.

The GNP deflator, one measure of inflation, is calculated by dividing nominal GNP by real GNP; it is a measure of the amount of inflation that has occurred from the base year to the current period. The fact that it is referred to as a "deflator" is a sign of the times.[13]

---

[12]Hein, *op. cit.*

[13]If we were living in a period of falling prices, this index would doubtless be called a price *inflator;* dividing it into nominal GNP during such a period would raise nominal GNP to the real GNP figure.

TABLE 21-1

(1) Product	(2) 1972 Price, $	(3) 1972 Quantity	(4) 1972 Value ($P_{1972} \times Q_{1972}$)	(5) 1983 Price, $	(6) 1983 Quantity	(7) 1983 Value ($P_{1983} \times Q_{1983}$)	(8) Value of 1983 Output at 1972 Price ($P_{1972} \times Q_{1983}$)
Hamburger 1		4,100	4,100	2	5,000	10,000	$5,000
T-shirts 2		500	1,000	6	1,000	6,000	2,000
Cola cartons 3		300	900	5	100	500	300
Total			$6,000 1972 nominal GNP			$16,500 1983 nominal GNP	$7,300 1983 real GNP

Table 21-1 provides information sufficient to indicate (roughly) how the GNP implicit price deflator is constructed.[14] Assume a very simple economy in which only hamburgers, T-shirts, and cola are produced. Suppose the market value of all final goods and services produced (nominal GNP) were $6,000 in 1972 and $16,500 in 1983.

A comparison of columns (2) and (5) indicates that the price level increased; hamburger prices doubled, T-shirt prices tripled, and the price of cola cartons rose by 67 percent. On the other hand, the outputs of hamburgers and T-shirts increased, while the quantity of cola cartons produced fell, as columns (3) and (6) indicate. Nominal GNP increased from $6,000 to $16,500, an impressive increase. But are the people in today's economy better off? If so, by how much? All prices have increased, and the output of two goods has increased while the output of one has decreased. The price and output effects must be separated before it is possible to judge the extent to which the community is better off economically.

One way to separate price and output effects is to evaluate the new quantities at the old prices. That is, it is possible to determine the change in the total value of output between 1972 and 1983 if the 1983 outputs are valued at 1972 prices and are then compared to the 1972 values. Column (8) indicates that the sum of the 1983 outputs valued at 1972 prices was $7,300. In other words, that 1983 bundle of goods would have been worth (or would have cost) $7,300 in 1972. Hence, the 1983 *real* GNP was $7,300, using 1972 as a base year for the price level.

After the adjustments for inflation have been made, the 175 percent increase in nominal GNP (from $6,000 to $16,500) is revealed to indicate only

---

[14]Actually, the GNP price deflator is derived by constructing price deflators for individual components of GNP, "in as fine a breakdown as practicable," and weighting the sum of these component deflators based on their relative share to GNP. Thus, the GNP deflator is derived *first* and real GNP is then derived. See the 1979 *Statistical Supplement to the Survey of Current Business* if you are really interested.

a 21.6 percent increase in real GNP (from $6,000 to $7,300). This analysis indicates that real and nominal GNP for 1983 can be calculated directly from price and quantity data; in the process of doing so a measure of inflation has been created implicitly (hence the name implicit price deflator). The **implicit GNP price deflator** can be expressed as the ratio of the current-year output valued at current-year prices (nominal GNP) to the current-year output valued at base-year prices (real GNP); this ratio is then multiplied by 100 for convenience in interpretation. Thus, the formula:

$$\text{Price deflator} = \frac{(P_{1983})(Q_{1983})}{(P_{1972})(Q_{1983})} \times 100 \tag{21-1}$$

yields the implicit GNP deflator for 1983 if 1972 is the base year.[15] Using Table 21-1, the GNP deflator for 1983 is

($16,500/$7,300) × 100 = 226

Thus, a $16,500 nominal GNP in 1983 can be deflated by dividing it by the GNP deflator (226) and multiplying this ratio by 100. That is,

($16,500/226) × 100 = $7,300

which yields the real GNP for 1983 expressed in 1972 dollars. Table 21-2 indicates nominal GNP, the GNP deflator, and real GNP for the United States, for the years 1970 to 1982.[16]

The Consumer Price Index (CPI)   Recall that the GNP price deflator is a measure of the increase of all prices through time. The concern *here,* however, is only with a specific subset of all prices: consumer prices. The **Consumer Price Index (CPI)** is an index of the prices of a fixed market basket of goods and services in eighty-five urban areas. The index is a representation of the prices of goods that are typically purchased by "representative" (urban, working-class) families. Because some goods and services are more important than others, in the sense that they require a higher percentage of the budget outlays of representative people, this index is a weighted average. The CPI includes direct taxes (sales, excise, etc.), but not income or Social Security taxes. In effect, the CPI measures the cost through time of a *given basket of goods and services.*[17] It equals the ratio of a base-year market basket valued

---

[15]Where $P_{1983}Q_{1983}$ equals nominal GNP in 1983, and $P_{1972}Q_{1983}$ represents real GNP in 1983; their ratio is multiplied by 100 to remove the decimal.

[16]Notice that the GNP deflator for 1972, the base year, is 100. Can you demonstrate that this is the case using Equation (21-1) and substituting P_{1972} and Q_{1972} for the P_{1983} and Q_{1983} values?

[17]The base year is assigned the CPI number 100. If the weighted average of prices of the representative bundle rises by 10 percent over the following year, the new index number is 110. A specific bundle that previously cost $100 now costs $110.

TABLE 21-2

Year	Nominal GNP (billions of dollars)	Real GNP (billions of 1972 dollars)	GNP deflator
1970	992.7	1085.6	91.45
1971	1077.6	1122.4	96.01
1972	1185.9	1185.9	100.00
1973	1326.4	1254.3	105.75
1974	1434.2	1246.3	115.08
1975	1549.2	1231.6	125.79
1976	1718.0	1298.2	132.34
1977	1918.3	1369.7	140.05
1978	2163.9	1438.6	150.42
1979	2417.8	1479.4	163.42
1980	2631.7	1475.0	178.42
1981	2954.1	1513.8	195.14
1982	3073.0	1485.4	206.88
1983ᵖ	3309.5	1534.8	215.63

Source: The Economic Report of the President, 1984.
ᵖPreliminary

at current-year prices to the base-year market basket valued at base-year prices—times 100 to remove the decimal.

Of course, the goods purchased in the "representative basket" change through time. For example, for a number of years the CPI representative basket was based on a 1960 to 1961 survey of consumer purchases. More recently, the representative basket has been changed to represent the results of a 1972 to 1973 survey of consumer purchases. The Bureau of Labor Statistics has continued to publish an Index for Urban Wage Earners and Clerical Workers, who comprise approximately 40 percent of the U.S. population. Simultaneously, an Index for All Urban Consumers is published, which reflects the purchasing habits (representative bundle of goods and services) of some 80 percent of the population.

The CPI and the GNP price deflator differ in three important ways:

1 The GNP deflator measures price changes in a much wider basket of goods and services; the CPI basket includes goods consumed by a typical urban consumer, while the GNP deflator basket includes investment goods and publicly provided goods as well.

2 The basket of goods included in the GNP deflator changes annually, whereas the basket of goods included in the CPI is unchanged—except for infrequent, periodic changes.

3 The GNP deflator excludes imported goods because it measures the value of *domestically* produced goods; the CPI includes imported goods in its basket.

WHO IS HURT BY INFLATION?

Can Everyone Be Hurt by Inflation?   It is often stated that *everyone* is hurt by inflation. However, because one person's expenditure is another's receipt, it is hard to imagine how this could be the case. Higher prices paid by buyers must in turn mean higher money receipts for sellers. This is known from the national income accounting identity; the market value of all final goods and services (NNP) is identical to national income.

Perhaps what people mean is that during inflation the price level for the things we buy rises more rapidly than do the wages we are paid for producing them. If this is so, the real wages of labor will fall, and laborers will indeed be hurt by inflation. It must follow, however, that under these conditions nonlabor (or nonwage) incomes (rents, profits, interest receipts) must be rising *more* rapidly than the price level. Nonwage income recipients will be relatively better off economically. The point to understand here is that because some are worse off and others are better off, it can hardly be accepted that everyone's economic position has worsened. Moreover, neither theory nor empirical evidence indicates that wages always rise less rapidly than does the general price level.

Unanticipated Inflation   Recall our earlier discussion of the neutrality of money. In the real world, prices may not all rise at the same rate; and changes in relative prices and in relative incomes will therefore occur. This is especially true when inflation is unanticipated. When buyers and sellers of inputs and of products contract for long periods of time, they implicitly build into their contracts some expected rate of inflation. To the extent that the *actual* rate of inflation is different from the anticipated rate, a redistribution of real income and of wealth will result.

For example, if lenders and borrowers of money agree on a 4 percent interest rate and unanticipated inflation of 5 percent per annum occurs, lenders will be hurt by inflation. On the other hand, borrowers will gain. It can hardly be claimed that both parties have been hurt.

A progressive tax structure during periods of inflation leads to "bracket creep." Even if real incomes remain constant, the increases in nominal income will cause people to suffer a higher tax burden as they climb into higher marginal tax brackets. Even in this situation not everyone is worse off. Some people want the public sector to expand at the expense of the private sector; public sector bureaucrats and those of the liberal persuasion presumably welcome a public sector that is expanding relative to the private sector.

CHAPTER SUMMARY

1   It has long been observed that changes in the supply of money are highly correlated with changes in the price level. Specific evidence exists to indicate that when the money supply grows more rapidly than national output, inflation results.

2 The *IS-LM* framework is couched in terms of real national income and real interest rates. As a consequence, that framework is inadequate to discuss inflation. A new aggregate demand–aggregate supply framework is developed in this chapter.

3 The aggregate demand curve shows an inverse relationship between the quantities of national output demanded at different price levels, other things constant. As the Keynes effect suggests, a lower price level is equivalent to a shift in the *LM* curve, even though the nominal (actual) money supply is constant. A lower price level reduces the quantity of L_1 balances demanded, which in turn leads to a lower rate of interest. This leads to an increase in net investment. The end result is a higher level of national output demanded; a reduction in the price level leads to an increase in the quantity of national output demanded, through a lower interest rate. The aggregate demand curve shifts whenever there is a non-price-level change that causes either the *IS* curve or the *LM* curve to shift.

4 Aggregate supply relates the price level to the quantity of national output supplied. The classical aggregate supply curve is vertical at the full-employment level of output. The Keynesian aggregate supply curve is upward-sloping from left to right and reflects the fact that prices and (especially) wages are sticky downward. Decreases in aggregate demand, therefore, lead to decreases in the quantity of output supplied (and the quantity of labor demanded) as businesses reduce output as well as price.

5 The price level is determined at the point of intersection of the aggregate supply curve and the aggregate demand curve.

6 There are two broad theories of inflation: demand-pull inflation and cost-push inflation. According to the classical model, demand-pull inflation results from an increase in the money supply. The Keynesian model predicts demand-pull inflation when aggregate demand increases relative to aggregate supply at or near full employment. Cost-push inflation is caused by an upward (leftward) shift in the aggregate supply curve relative to the aggregate demand curve. Cost-push inflation occurs if resource prices rise or as a result of some combination of big union–big business economic power struggle.

7 It is widely believed that large federal government deficits cause inflation. Some economists insist that federal deficits can cause inflation only if those deficits are financed or monetized by the Fed. Higher federal deficits can lead to higher interest rates, which in turn can lead to a decreased quantity of money demanded. In turn, this higher velocity of money can contribute to inflation. Evidence indicates that the impact of higher interest rates on the demand for money is very slight; it follows that higher interest rates resulting from deficits have little effect on the rate of inflation, through a reduced demand for money.

8 Inflation is defined as an increase in the general price level over time. Inflation can be measured by constructing a price index, which is a weighted average of the prices of goods and services indicating how prices have changed since a base year. The Consumer Price Index is a price index based on the market bundle of goods and services purchased by a representative urban household. It measures the changes in the cost of a specific bundle of goods and services over time. An implicit price deflator is an index of the weighted average of *all* final goods and services; when divided into nominal GNP, the implicit price deflator provides a measure of the real or constant-dollar GNP. The GNP implicit price deflator is one measure of the change in prices since a base year.

9   It is widely believed that inflation hurts everyone, but that is unlikely because one person's expenditure is another's receipt. Often during an inflationary period, a redistribution of income caused by a change in tastes is blamed on inflation. When such relative price changes occur during inflation, in fact, some will benefit and some will be harmed economically. Unanticipated inflation harms lenders at the expense of borrowers; bracket creep benefits those who prefer an expanded public sector relative to the private sector.

GLOSSARY

Aggregate demand curve: A curve indicating an inverse relationship between the quantities of national output demanded at different price levels, other things constant.

Aggregate supply curve: A curve relating various quantities of national output produced to differing price levels, other things constant.

Consumer Price Index (CPI): A price index based on the market value of a bundle of goods and services purchased by a representative urban household. CPI is the ratio of a base-year market basket valued at current-year prices to the base-year market basket valued at base-year prices.

Cost-push inflation: Inflation caused by an upward shift in the aggregate supply curve relative to the aggregate demand curve; union and/or business power, or increasing raw materials costs shift the aggregate supply curve leftward.

Demand-pull inflation: Inflation caused by an expansion of aggregate demand relative to the productive potential of the economy.

Implicit GNP price deflator: A measure of inflation from the base period to the current period, calculated by dividing nominal GNP by real GNP.

PROBLEMS

21-1   Consider the following table:

Goods and Services	1972 Price	1972 Quantity	1984 Price	1984 Quantity
Pizza	$ 4	10	$ 8	12
Jeans	12	20	36	15
Wine	6	5	10	15
Business equipment	25	10	30	12
GNP		$560		$1,146

a   What is the GNP implicit price deflator for 1984?

b   What is real GNP for 1984?

c   Assuming a base year of 1972, what is the CPI for 1984? (Remember the CPI includes only consumer goods.)

SELECTED REFERENCES

Alchian, A. A., and W. R. Allen, *Exchange and Production,* 3d ed. (Los Angeles: Wadsworth, 1983), chap. 19.

Cagen Phillip, "The Monetary Dynamics of Hyperinflation," in M. Friedman (ed.), *Studies in the Quantity Theory of Money* (Chicago: University of Chicago Press, 1956).

————, *Determinants and Effects of Changes in the Stock of Money, 1875–1960* (New York: National Bureau of Economic Research, 1965).

Hayek, Friedrich A., *Prices and Production,* 2d ed. (London: Routledge, 1935)

Hein, Scott E., "Deficits and Inflation," *Review,* Federal Reserve Bank of St. Louis, March 1981, pp. 3–10.

Laidler, D., and J. M. Parkin, "Inflation: A Survey," *Economic Journal,* vol. 85, December 1975, pp. 741–809.

McCulloch, J. H., *Money and Inflation: A Monetarist Approach,* 2d ed. (New York: Academic Press, 1982).

Schuettinger, R., and E. Butler, *Forty Centuries of Wage and Price Controls* (Washington, D.C.: The Heritage Foundation, 1979).

The Monetarist-Keynesian Debate

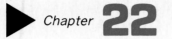
Fiscal Policy

CHAPTER PREVIEW

In Chapter 19 we analyzed fiscal policy in the simple Keynesian model. Now that we have explicitly introduced the role of money in the Keynesian model and have incorporated elements of both the classical and the Keynesian models in the *IS-LM* framework, we are in a position to analyze fiscal policy more realistically. This chapter discusses fiscal policy—in theory and in practice. It begins with the theoretical justification for fiscal policy and moves toward the political reality of the budgetary process. Then the distinction between automatic and discretionary fiscal policy is made. This evolves naturally toward the concept of the full-employment budget. Next a brief history of fiscal policy (covering the period from World War II to the recently proposed amendments to the Reagan tax cut) is presented. The chapter ends with a Current Controversy concerning the feasibility of requiring a balanced federal budget.

FISCAL POLICY IN A THEORETICAL CONTEXT

Fiscal policy is the deliberate changing of levels of federal government expenditures, taxes, and borrowing to achieve such national economic goals as high employment, price stability, economic growth, and a balance-of-payments equilibrium. Fiscal policy is determined jointly by the executive and legislative branches of the federal government.

Recall Chapter 20, which stressed that unless price-wage flexibility exists, aggregate equilibrium is very likely to be achieved at a less than full-employment level of net national product. Consider Figure 22-1, which indicates that the equilibrium level of net national product is Y_e, and the equilibrium interest rate is i_e. According to the Keynesians, nothing assures that Y_e will be a *full-employment* equilibrium level of NNP. Because the Employment Act of 1946 and an amendment to that act, the Full Employment and Balanced Growth Act of 1978, commit the government to achieving the national economic goals listed above, fiscal policy is justified.

A Change in Government Expenditures An increase in government expenditures can stimulate the economy; an increase in real government expenditures *(G)* increases aggregate expenditures directly. If no other types of expenditures,

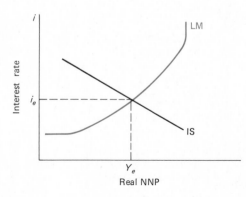

FIGURE 22-1 Aggregate equilibrium will exist at Y_e and i_e. Nothing assures that Y_e will be a full-employment level of real net national product, because price-wage rigidities exist in modern economies. A commitment to national economic goals justifies fiscal policy.

such as consumption (C), investment (I), or net exports (exports minus imports, X−M), are reduced, this net increase in aggregate spending will lead to an expansion of output, real net national product, and employment. In turn, this expansion leads to additional expansion, because of induced increases in consumption. In Chapter 19 we referred to this expansion as the multiplier effect; the ultimate change in real net national product (ΔY) is

$$\Delta Y = \Delta G \left[1/(1 - b)\right]$$

where ΔY = change in real net national product
ΔG = change in real government expenditures
$1/(1 - b)$ = the multiplier, where b = marginal propensity to consume

So far, our discussion is consistent with our analysis in Chapter 19. If we are to analyze the *pure* effects of fiscal policy, however, we must hold the money supply constant—the *LM* curve should not shift due to a change in the money supply. An increase in government expenditures must be *financed;* if the money supply remains constant, an increase in government expenditures requires either an increase in taxes or an increase in Treasury bond sales. The effects of an increase in taxes is analyzed in the next section. Consider now the effects of an increase in government expenditures financed by Treasury bond sales. Suppose the Treasury sells $10 billion in bonds and uses the money received to finance $10 billion in government purchases. Note that the money supply has not changed; $10 billion of the money supply is reduced at the time of the bond sales, but it returns when government purchases are made.

The Treasury competes with others for bond sales; therefore it is possible that the Treasury will have to offer higher than market interest rates in order to obtain the $10 billion of loanable funds. A higher interest rate, in turn, will cause a reduction in business investment expenditures and household consumption expenditures.

Figure 22-2 indicates the effects of an increase in government expenditures in the *IS-LM* framework. An increase in government expenditures shifts the *IS* curve rightward, by the amount $\Delta G \left[1/(1 - b)\right]$. At any interest rate, the level of real net national product will be higher, by the amount of the change in government expenditures times the multiplier.

If the interest rate does not change, real NNP will increase from Y_e to Y_3, where $Y_3 - Y_e = \Delta G \left[1/(1 - b)\right]$, and the full multiplier effect results. In order to finance the government expenditures, however, the Treasury sold bonds which caused interest rates to rise. A change in the product market (a shift in the *IS* curve) led to disequilibrium in the money market. A shortage of liquidity (which would exist at point *C*) caused interest rates to rise, which in turn reduced business investment expenditures and household consumption expenditures. Eventually a new aggregate equilibrium level will be established at point *B*. In comparison with the original equilibrium (position *A*), both net national product and the interest rate are higher at point *B*. Note, however, that the full multiplier effect does not occur; $Y_1 - Y_e < Y_3 - Y_e$. This is true

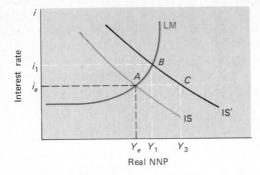

FIGURE 22-2 An increase in government expenditures shifts the *IS* curve rightward, by $\Delta G\,[1/(1-b)]$. If the interest rate does not change, income will increase from Y_e to Y_3; $Y_3 - Y_e = \Delta Y = \Delta G\,[1/(1-b)]$. An increase in net national product, however, increases the amount of money desired for L_1 balances. In turn, this increase in the demand for money relative to the (constant) supply of money causes a shortage of money and liquidity. Bond sales cause interest rates to rise; a higher interest rate causes a reduction in investment and consumption. Eventually aggregate equilibrium moves from point *A* to point *B;* both the real interest rate and real national product rise. The ultimate increase in NNP, however, is not as high as it otherwise would have been; the multiplier effect is lessened; $Y_1 - Y_e < Y_3 - Y_e$.

because the expansionary effect of an increase in government expenditures was partially offset by a decrease in investment and consumption—due to a higher interest rate resulting from the increase in government expenditures. In other words, if we take into account how the government expenditures are *financed,* we see that the multiplier-effect analysis in Chapter 19 was oversimplified.

If government expenditures were to *fall* by $10 billion, a full multiplier effect—in the downward direction—would not result either. The *IS* curve would shift to the left by the full multiplier effect, but a lower interest rate would induce more business investment expenditures and more household consumption expenditures. Some of the contraction in the economy resulting from a reduction in government expenditures would be offset by an increase in net investment and consumption, resulting from a lower interest rate. A lower interest rate would result from a reduction in the government's demand for loanable funds.

A Change in Taxes A decrease in taxes can be expansionary; unlike government expenditures, however, a change in taxes affects aggregate expenditures only *indirectly.* A decrease in real taxes, T (other things constant), increases the amount that households have to spend on consumer goods. A tax decrease, therefore, increases aggregate spending—but not by the amount of the tax cut. Because tax changes affect aggregate demand indirectly through shifts in the consumption function, the AD $= (C_0 + I_0 + G_0) + bY$ curve (see Chapter 19) will shift only by $b\,(\Delta C_0) = b\,(\Delta T)$; if taxes fall by $100, the consumption function will shift upward by $b\,($100)$, where b is the MPC, and not by the full $100. Hence, aggregate demand will only shift upward by $b\,(\Delta T)$; the tax multiplier equals $-b/(1-b)$ [or $-1/(1-b) -1$], where the absolute value of $-b/(1-b)$ is one less than $1/(1-b)$. The tax multiplier is negative because increases in real taxes decrease real net national product, while decreases in real taxes increase real net national product.

Consider Figure 22-3, which shows the effect of a decrease in real taxes. The IS curve shifts to the right, by a distance equal to the value of the decrease in taxes multiplied by the tax multiplier. If the money supply remains constant, the LM curve is unaffected. Note that the new aggregate equilibrium position (C) exists at a higher level of net national product, Y_1, and at a higher interest rate [but not as high as it would have had the interest rate not risen (Y_2)]. The level of net national product has risen because the tax reduction has stimulated aggregate expenditures indirectly because of an upward shift in the consumption curve. The resulting increase in net national product increases the quantity of money demanded for transactions and precautionary purposes (L_1). If the money supply is fixed, a shortage of money or liquidity now exists at the higher level of net national product and i_e (point B). The increased desire for liquidity is met by bond sales which increase the rate of interest; a higher rate of interest induces some to part with their speculative balances (L_2). This process continues until equilibrium is established in both product and money markets—at point C.

Note that an *increase* in taxes will shift the IS curve to the left, by a distance equal to the reduction in taxes multiplied by the tax multiplier. The economy will contract, but not by the full amount of the tax multiplier effect. A lower level of net national product, resulting from a downward shift in the con-

FIGURE 22-3 A decrease in taxes shifts the IS curve to the right, by a distance equal to the reduction in taxes times the tax multiplier. If the interest rate doesn't rise, the new equilibrium position occurs at point B; the full tax multiplier effect results and the change in income is $Y_2 - Y_e$.

A higher level of net national product increases the demand for L_1 balances, however; because the money supply is constant, a shortage of liquidity exists at point B. Increased desire for L_1 balances leads to bond sales and higher interest rates; higher interest rates reduce consumption and investment and real NNP falls below Y_2. Eventually some combination of a higher interest rate and a level of NNP will satisfy equilibrium conditions in both the product market and the money market. In this figure, that combination exists at point C.

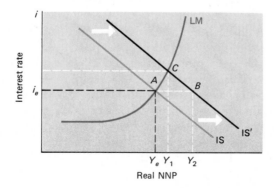

sumption function, will reduce the quantity of money demanded for L_1 purposes, creating a surplus of liquidity at the original interest rate. The interest rate will fall, inducing an increase in consumption and investment expenditures. The result will be that the contraction in the economy due to a tax increase will be offset somewhat by a lower interest rate.

Budget Surpluses and Budget Deficits If the federal government spends an amount that is exactly matched by tax revenues, a balanced federal budget exists. If expenditures exceed tax receipts, a budget deficit exists; if expenditures are less than tax revenues, a budget surplus exists.

Suppose that the government budget is *initially* balanced and that the economy is in a recession. Keynesians suggest that fiscal policy should be expansionary. Real government expenditures should rise. But what about taxes? The previous discussion implies that if increased government expenditures are refinanced by increased taxes, the expansionary potential of the increased G will be *somewhat* offset (not totally offset, because the tax multiplier effect is less than the government expenditure multiplier effect). As a consequence, Keynesians believe that the fiscal policy prescription to fight recession is a budget deficit; some combination of increased G *and* decreased T will shift the IS curve sufficiently to reduce unemployment. Of course, if the government is already in deficit, recessionary fiscal policy requires an even larger deficit.

Similarly, inflation can be countered by a fiscal policy that both reduces G and increases T. If the budget were balanced initially, a budget surplus would be required to fight inflation. If a surplus existed initially, then anti-inflation fiscal policy would call for a larger surplus. If a large budget existed initially, anti-inflation fiscal policy would require a smaller deficit.

AUTOMATIC VERSUS DISCRETIONARY FISCAL POLICY

So far we have been talking about **discretionary fiscal policy,** which is the deliberate and conscious attempt by Congress and the executive branch to create full employment and to stabilize the price level of the economy. Discretionary fiscal policy entails changes in tax *rates* and changes in transfer-payment programs as well as changes in government expenditures for final goods and services. Moreover, all these fiscal policy changes entail specific legislation.

Yet, not all changes in taxes (or changes in tax rates) and in government spending constitute discretionary fiscal policy. Some changes may instead be built-in stabilizers in the economy. These kinds of changes are sometimes called automatic, or nondiscretionary, fiscal policies. There are several types of automatic fiscal policies operating in the economy. When we refer to automatic fiscal policies, we are talking about **automatic,** or built-in, **stabilizers,** which do *not* require new legislation on the part of Congress; Congress does not have to enact such built-in stabilizers into law. Remember, we are examining these in contrast to the discretionary fiscal policy changes that have been discussed up to now.

The main built-in stabilizers are the progressive income tax system, unemployment compensation, the corporate income tax, and other taxes. All these are automatically countercyclical in nature.

The Progressive Income Tax

The 1982 personal income tax schedule indicates that as taxable income goes up, the marginal tax rate also increases—to a maximum of 50 percent. Or, as taxable income decreases, the marginal tax rate goes down. Think about this for the entire economy. If the nation is at full employment, personal income taxes may yield the government, say, $375 bilion per year. But suppose that business activity starts to slow down. When this happens, workers are not allowed to put in as much overtime as before. Some workers are laid off, and some must change to jobs that pay less. Some workers and even some executives might take voluntary pay cuts. What happens to taxes when wages and salaries go down? Taxes are still paid but at a lower rate than before, because the tax schedule is progressive. For example, a single person who makes $30,000 taxable income a year is in the 45 percent marginal tax bracket. If the taxable income drops to only $20,000 a year and puts this person into the 38 percent marginal tax bracket, average taxes paid as a percentage of income will also fall. As a result of these decreased taxes, disposable income—the amount remaining after taxes—falls by a smaller percentage than the fall in pretax income. Taking the progressive nature of our tax schedule into consideration, therefore, the individual feels less of a financial pinch during a recession than would be the case if the tax system were not progressive. The *average* tax rate falls when less is earned.

Conversely, when the economy experiences a boom, people's incomes tend to rise. They can work more overtime and can change to higher-paying jobs. However, *disposable* income does not go up as rapidly as total income, because average tax rates are rising at the same time. Uncle Sam ends up taking a bigger bite. In turn, this means that consumption and aggregate demand do not increase as rapidly. In this way, the progesssive income tax system tends to lessen the impact of abrupt changes in economic activity.

Unemployment Compensation

Unemployment compensation works like the progressive income tax: It lessens the impact of changes in aggregate demand. Throughout the business cycle, automatic changes in unemployment compensation slow down and limit the size of changes in people's disposable incomes. When business activity drops, most laid-off workers automatically become eligible for unemployment compensation from their state governments. Their disposable incomes decline, but at a slower rate than net national product is declining. During boom periods there is less unemployment, and consequently fewer unemployment compensation payments are made to the labor force, other things constant. Less purchasing power is being added to the economy because less unemployment compensation is paid.

The Stabilizing Impact   The key stabilizing impact of these two aspects of our taxing and transfer system is their ability to lessen changes in disposable income, consumption, and the equilibrium level of national income. Previous chapters presented a model in which disposable income (take-home pay) is the main determinant of how much people desire to spend and, therefore, a key activator of general economic activity. Hence, if disposable income is not allowed to fall as much as it would otherwise during a recession, the downturn will be moderated. On the other hand, if disposable income is not allowed to rise as rapidly as it would otherwise during a boom (expansion), the boom will not create inflationary problems. The progressive income tax and unemployment compensation therefore give automatic stabilization to the economy. This argument is shown graphically in Figure 22-4. There government spending is assumed constant. The TT curve incorporates *net* taxes; TT represents taxes *minus* transfers. Also, TT is upward-sloping because taxes are directly related to net national product (the tax structure is progressive) and because transfers are indirectly related to national income.

FIGURE 22-4   Automatic Stabilizers.   Assume that government expenditures for goods and services, *G,* and for various federal transfer programs remain constant no matter what the level of national income; they are fully autonomous and are represented by *GG.* Taxes, on the other hand, vary directly with national income because we assume a constant tax structure. When net national product increases from Y_0 to Y_1, taxes will exceed government expenditures, as shown by the vertical distance between *GG* and the tax line, *TT.* This government budget surplus, which occurs *automatically* during an expansion, could assist in offsetting possible inflationary pressures. Alternatively, when national income falls from Y_0 to Y_2, the resultant automatic budget deficit could help offset or alleviate the recession. Automatic stabilizers are countercyclical by nature.

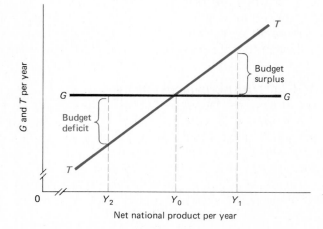

Fiscal Policy and a Full-Employment Budget Assuming no increase in taxes and assuming a balanced budget initially, when the government now spends more it ends up with a budget deficit. If the government has already been running a deficit, it will then have an even larger one. Fiscal policy advocates maintain that an increase in the deficit stimulates the economy, and that a decrease in the deficit has the opposite effect. The government can also run a surplus. That is, it can take in more revenues than it spends. An increase in the government's budget surplus is supposed to have a restraining effect on the economy, just as would a decrease in government expenditures or an increase in taxes. The existence of, or an increase in, the government budget surplus reduces total aggregate demand and depresses economic activity, other things constant.

Economists do not look only at the government's *actual* deficit or surplus. Generally, they do not think it is useful to look at current levels of taxes and expenditures or the current budget deficit or surplus that results. Consider for a moment the following situation. Suppose the economy is at full employment and the government budget is in balance. Then the economy goes into a recession, and incomes fall. The government, however, does nothing. In other words, let's assume that government expenditures on goods and services do not change, nor do expenditures on the various transfer programs such as unemployment compensation, welfare, pensions, and so on. If the tax *rates* are also held constant, government revenues will fall, because tax revenues depend on the level of net national product. A formerly balanced budget goes into deficit, because G is now greater than T. The budget deficit should certainly not be regarded here as an active stimulating policy decision on the part of the government. It is a *result* of the recession and not a conscious counterrecessionary move. Therefore, economists now make calculations to determine whether *at full employment* the government budget *would be* in a deficit or a surplus position. The result is called the **full-employment government budget.** It is defined as what the federal budget deficit or surplus would be if the economy were operating at full employment throughout the entire year. Figure 22-5 shows the results of such calculations for the years 1960 to 1981.

Economists now talk in terms of a *stimulating full-employment deficit* or a *depressing full-employment surplus.* The actual budget deficit in fiscal 1980 may have been $60 billion, but the full-employment deficit was much less. Many economists therefore maintain that this deficit was stimulating but not so stimulating as it would first seem, because at full employment the deficit would have been much smaller. You should be aware that it is very difficult to define "full employment," an issue to which we return in Chapter 25. Because frictional unemployment (occurring when people are temporarily idle because they are between steady jobs) always exists, we are never at "full" employment. Other considerations, such as price-wage rigidities, also make the meaning and measurement of full employment difficult. Through the years the rate of unemployment that has been considered "full" employment has gradually increased. Clearly the amount of unemployment that we consider to represent full employment determines the size of the full-employment deficit or surplus.

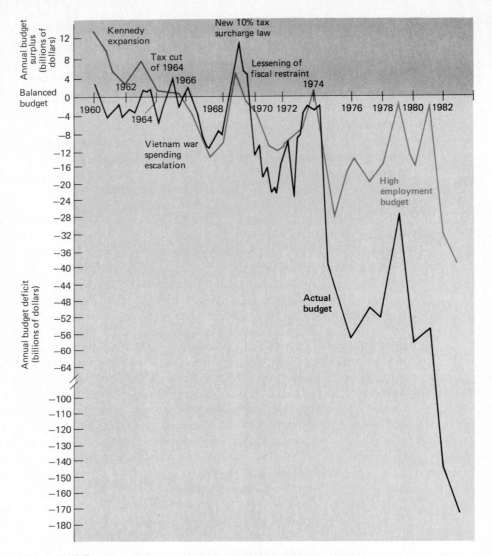

FIGURE 22-5   The Full-Employment Budget and the Actual Budget.   This figure shows the actual budget surpluses and deficits of the U.S. government from 1960 to 1981. It also shows the full-employment budget surpluses and shortages. For the most part, the federal budget has been in deficit for the last two decades. The full-employment budget, however, has not been in deficit for as long a time.
Source: A. M. Okun and Nancy H. Teeters, "The Full-Employment Surplus Revisited," in *Brookings Papers on Economic Activity,* Washington, D.C.: The Brookings Institution, 1970, no. 1; Council of Economic Advisors, *Economic Report of the President,* Washington, D.C.: U.S. Government Printing Office, 1981; and *Survey of Current Business,* April 1982, August 1982, and August 1983.

HIGHLIGHT **A History of the Income Tax***

Proponents of the 1909 income tax amendment to the United States Constitution passed by Congress assured opponents that income tax rates would never rise above 4 to 5 percent, and it was generally agreed that only a very small percentage of the population would pay any taxes at all. As inevitable and as much a part of life as income taxes now seem to be, it is somewhat surprising that Congress passed the first income tax law only as recently as 1913.† That first tax provided for a 1 percent tax on incomes over $3,000 ($4,000 for a married couple) and subjected only 3 percent of the nation's wage earners to tax obligations. A tax of up to 7 percent was levied on the very high annual income groups—from $20,000 to over $500,000.

As might be expected, rates rose during World War I but fell dramatically after the war. During World War II marginal tax rates went as high as 94 percent for a very small percentage of the population. In 1947 some 80 percent of U.S. families had annual incomes of less than $5,000. For them, taxes had doubled between 1939 and 1941, and then doubled again between 1941 and 1947. Still, the average effective tax rate was only 8.4 percent. Marginal tax rates for typical earners were less than 20 percent. In short, until 1947, U.S. marginal tax rates were not very high.

The twin effects of economic growth and inflation have changed the tax situation for U.S. earners. Today, 80 percent of U.S. families have

annual incomes that exceed $11,000; 50 percent earn more than $23,000 per year.

Along with income taxes, one should observe that the Social Security tax has grown even more dramatically. These taxes increased by 7,233 percent between 1947 and 1982—or from $30 per year to $2,170 per year. The result of higher income and higher Social Security tax rates is that over the last few years tax liabilities have increased twice as rapidly as has income for average workers.

Today, average workers face marginal tax rates originally intended for only the very rich. Whether this is fair is a matter of opinion; the possibility that high marginal tax rates create incentive problems is becoming a serious question in the United States.

*Much of what follows was inspired by David Boaz, "A History of the Income Tax: It Jes' Grew," *The Wall Street Journal,* May 14, 1982, op-ed page. Boaz is a vice president of the Cato Institute, Washington, D.C.

†An earlier income tax was passed during the Civil War, but it was later declared unconstitutional; thus the necessity for the 1909 constitutional amendment.

A BRIEF HISTORY OF FISCAL POLICY, 1941 to 1982

Wartime Policy, 1941 to 1946 As was the case in World War I, monetary and fiscal policies were almost completely synchronized during World War II; conflicting goals were made subordinate to the overriding objective of financing the war effort. The plan was to finance the war while keeping interest rates at relatively low levels. It should be stressed that during this period tax changes and government expenditure changes were enacted to finance the war, not to stabilize the economy. As such, they do not qualify as discretionary fiscal policy.

Of course, government expenditures increased tremendously—from $9 billion annually in 1940 to $25 billion in 1941 to approximately $95 billion in 1944. By 1944, annual federal expenditures alone were greater than total GNP in any year during the 1930s.

As was to be expected, taxes also increased rapidly during this period. However, it was deemed desirable to increase tax revenues by considerably less than federal expenditures. Record deficits (for that time) ensued; federal deficits increased from $4.6 billion in 1941 to $53.7 billion in 1943, and they totaled $46 billion and $49.9 billion in 1945 and 1946, respectively. During the war, they averaged more than $40 billion per year.[1]

It follows from these facts that the U.S. Treasury borrowed enormous sums; it tried to do so without changing the money supply significantly. This required spending money obtained by bond sales to the nonbank public; documentaries of that era show campaigns and drives to sell "war bonds," featuring Hollywood stars, athletic superstars, and other national heroes.

1947 to 1961   By the time World War II hostilities had ceased, it was apparent that a tremendous demand existed for durable consumer goods and investment goods. Still, many feared that the decrease in government expenditures (from their near $100-billion-per-annum level) would more than offset this private demand and that the net effect would be a serious recession. As a consequence, price controls were dismantled and an expansionary monetary policy was pursued. Predictably, the recorded price level increased dramatically.

In 1950, the Korean War erupted. Remembering the World War II experience, households and businesses went on a buying spree; by the end of that year, government expenditures for military purchases added to the inflationary fire. Despite an $11 billion decrease in federal expenditures after the Korean War, the 1953 to 1954 recession was short and mild. This was due in part to a $5 billion tax reduction in early 1954; easy monetary policy also began in May 1953.

By the third quarter of 1957, boom turned to recession and unemployment went from 2.5 million in October to above 5.1 million in the last quarter of 1959. It was thought that this recession was due to a decline in business investment expenditures *and* to the federal government's dramatic reduction in military spending in an effort to remain within its budget limits.

By April 1958, the recession had bottomed out and the economy grew until the first quarter of 1960.

1962 to 1968: The Kennedy-Johnson Period   During this period true attempts at discretionary fiscal policy were made; taxes were changed in order to promote full employment and economic growth in the economy. As a reaction to the 1957 to 1958 recession and the return to recession in April 1960, John F.

---

[1]The source of this information is L. V. Chandler, *Inflation in the United States, 1940–1945* (New York: Harper & Row, 1951), p. 62.

Kennedy's political platform promised to "get this country moving again." Once elected, Kennedy tried to deliver on his promise; his administration felt that expansionary fiscal policy would be more efficient than expansionary monetary policy, because changes in fiscal policy would generate less conflict between domestic and international economic goals. Fiscal policy (unlike monetary policy) would not lead to lower interest rates (which in turn might cause people to make financial investments in other countries) as an unwanted by-product. In 1961, Kennedy prodded Congress for tax reductions. In 1962, two steps were taken to induce private investment spending: (1) quicker depreciation write-offs for new investments, and (2) an investment tax credit permitting businesses to deduct 7 percent of the cost of new plant and equipment purchases from their income tax liabilities. In 1962 Kennedy also proposed that personal and corporate income taxes be reduced significantly, but the cumbersome machinery of Congress stalled these reductions.

After President Kennedy was assassinated in 1963, Lyndon Johnson assumed office and continued to prod Congress for a tax cut. Finally, in 1964 Congress approved a reduction of almost $15 billion that was phased in during 1964 to 1965. Unemployment fell from 5.2 percent in 1964 to 4.5 percent in 1965 as spending on consumer and investment goods was stimulated. However, many economists believed that the tax cut would have been even more effective if Congress had not procrastinated for two years. Such may be one of the costs of living in a politically free society. (On the other hand, economists have been known to be wrong.)

By 1965, the escalation of the war in Vietnam had caused national defense expenditures to rise at a relatively rapid rate. From 1965 to 1967, they increased from $50 billion to $70 billion per year; in 1968, they increased by another $10 billion. The unemployment rate remained below 4 percent during the entire 1966 to 1969 period. At the same time, prices started to rise. Soon inflation seemed to be getting out of hand.

In an effort to "cool down" the economy (reduce excessive aggregate expenditures), President Johnson proposed and got a **tax surcharge**—a tax on a tax. Tax liabilities increased by 10 percent as a result of the surcharge.

While policymakers were delighted with the apparent success of the 1964 tax cut in helping the economy to expand, they could not take similar delight in the cooling-off effect of the 1968 surcharge. Inflation did not slow down one bit; in fact, it increased. Many argue that the Johnson surcharge came too late because the economy had started "overheating" in about 1965 or 1966; others argued that demand-pull inflation had become cost-push inflation.

Fiscal Policy in the 1970s In August of 1971, President Nixon set out to solve domestic and international economic problems. He froze domestic prices and wages and allowed the U.S. dollar exchange rate to "float"; that is, the exchange rate was allowed to reflect supply and demand.[2] In addition, foreigners could no

---

[2]Some economists thought it rather contradictory to attempt to solve domestic problems by price controls, while simultaneously trying to solve a balance-of-payments problem by eliminating a controlled price—the fixed exchange rate. As usual, Nixon gave both conservatives and liberals something to lament.

longer convert the dollar into gold; Nixon reneged on the U.S. Bretton Woods Agreement to sell gold to foreign nations at an established price.

Having "solved" the inflation problem by price-wage controls, and having allowed for more flexibility in terms of international transactions (nonconvertibility to gold and a freely floating exchange rate), the Nixon administration then increased aggregate demand through fiscal policy. This was done in order to combat the unemployment rate that had increased during 1970 and 1971. The expansionary fiscal policy included both tax reductions and tax increases in governmental expenditures. Regarding taxes, Nixon's policy called for faster depreciation write-offs for businesses, a restoration of the 7 percent tax credit for business purchases of equipment (which had been repealed by the Tax Reform Act of 1965), an increase in allowable personal exemptions, and an increase in the minimum standard deduction on personal income taxes. Something for everyone.

Simultaneously, federal expenditures exploded. This explosion was the result of an $8 billion increase in Social Security benefits and an $11 billion increase in federal grants-in-aid to state and local governments. In 1972 federal expenditures increased by 11 percent, or $25 billion. Fearing inflationary pressures, Congress instituted fiscal-policy restraints in 1973. From 1973 to 1975, a recession ensued and the unemployment rate rose from 4.8 percent to 8.5 percent; in 1974, President Ford advocated an even more restrictive fiscal policy (a ceiling on federal spending and a 5 percent income tax surcharge on corporations and upper-income families) in the midst of a recession. In 1975 Ford changed policies and wanted to "shift our emphasis from inflation to recession."

In March 1975, a series of tax reductions and rebates was put into effect. A large percentage of the taxpaying population was paid a $100 to $200 rebate on 1974 taxes. A tax credit of $30 per person was instituted, starting in 1975. Additionally, there was an extension of the investment tax credit, which was increased to 10 percent.

In December 1975, the tax-reduction program was extended and modified.

Fiscal Policy Since 1975　The period 1974 to 1975 was considered by many to be the worst recession of the post-World War II era (until the 1981 to 1982 recession). As a consequence, fiscal policy was structured to be highly stimulative for those years. By the spring of 1975 this recession had bottomed out, and President Ford was concerned with making a gradual and long-lasting economic recovery. Moreover, Ford was determined that this recovery be fueled by advances in the private sector and not by expansion of the public sector. As a consequence, his fiscal proposals during 1975 to 1976 stressed:

1　Fiscal stimulus by way of tax cuts, not through governmental expenditure increases

2　Permanent tax cuts

3　Economic initiatives "balanced" between the stimulation of increased consumer spending and the encouragement of increased business investment

The reins of presidential power switched to Jimmy Carter in 1977 and the goals of fiscal policy were altered. The Carter administration shifted its focus toward highly stimulative measures to reduce unemployment. The Tax Reduction and Simplification Act of 1977 called for:

1 Permanent increases in personal standard deductions on income taxes
2 Employment tax credits (for the 1977 to 1978 period) for businesses that hired new employees
3 Extension of the 1975 to 1976 tax reductions through 1978
4 Increased funds for countercyclical revenue sharing from 1977 to 1978
5 Provision of funds for public-service employment, and for other employment and job-training programs.

During 1978 the focus of fiscal policy shifted; unemployment fell faster and inflationary rates increased faster than had been anticipated. As a consequence, fiscal policy moved toward "restraint," defined as continued fiscal stimulus at a gradually reduced *rate* of growth. Thus, the President decided to revise his tax reduction program; he scaled down the amount from $25 billion to $20 billion and then postponed the effective date until January 1979.

By 1979 fiscal policy had again shifted; inflation became the number one concern, and fiscal policy was now aimed at restraining aggregate demand (monetary policy and price-wage guidelines were to help). The federal budget deficit dropped from over $48 billion in 1978 to $27.8 billion in 1979.

Inflation did not abate; the CPI increased by 5.8 percent in 1976, 6.5 percent in 1977, 7.65 percent in 1978, and 11.3 percent in 1979. In 1980 the rate of inflation was 13.5 percent, and the federal budget deficit was almost $60 billion—more than $20 billion higher than anticipated. People were beginning to wonder if the federal budget was getting out of control. President Reagan promised to give new directions to fiscal policy during his tenure in office.

Fiscal Policy in the Early 1980s: Reaganomics   Hailed by the Reagan administration as the largest tax cut in history, the Economic Recovery Tax Act of 1981 called for almost $750 billion in tax cuts over a six-year period. However, some thought that such a program was more an assertion of a free-enterprise ideology than a tool designed specifically for fiscal policy. This act was designed to induce business investment and household saving; virtually everyone was to receive some tax relief under its provisions. It included across-the-board rate reductions for individuals, relief from the so-called marriage penalty tax, and a new, accelerated depreciation system for businesses. Savings incentives for investors and extensive estate and gift tax deductions were also included.

Specifically, the act provided for individual income tax rate reductions equal to 5 percent in 1981, 10 percent in 1982, and 10 percent in 1983. A 20 percent maximum rate on noncorporate capital gains was set. Perhaps the most important aspect of the act was its provision for **indexing.** Since 1984 the tax rate schedules have been revised annually to prevent **bracket creep.** As of 1985 the schedules reflect the percentage by which the CPI has changed over the year (as long as the price level rises).

By mid-1982, however, President Reagan was backing off "the largest tax cut in history." He and the Republicans on the Senate Budget Committee had agreed to a plan that would *raise* taxes by $95 billion over three years. Although this seems "moderate" when compared to calls for $170 billion in new taxes by some Senate Democrats and the "only" $73 billion tax increase suggested by conservative Republicans, one can only wonder "What's going on here?"

Actually, it was estimated that the Economic Recovery Tax Act would reduce taxes by about $471 billion over the fiscal years 1982 to 1985. The 1982 tax increase was expected to raise taxes by approximately $100 billion over that period. Moreover, the combined effects of previously scheduled Social Security tax-rate increases and bracket creep were expected to offset the net tax decrease legislated for 1981 to 1982. This offset has been true of previous tax reductions also. At the time of the publication of this text, it was not at all clear whether the indexing provision of the 1981 Tax Act would be left intact.

THE POLITICAL REALITY OF FISCAL POLICY

While such an analysis seems easy enough, in practice fiscal policy is very difficult business. As will be stressed in a later chapter, current knowledge of the precise economic and mathematical relationships among economic variables is woefully inadequate.[3] Such problems would make discretionary fiscal policy a crude policy instrument even if there were no political problems inherent in using it. Unfortunately, political problems abound.

Although the following brief discussion of the budgetary procedure is accurate, in no way does it indicate how politically difficult fiscal policy is to implement.

It is important to realize that no single governmental body designs and implements fiscal policy.[4] The President, with the aid of the director of the Office of Management and Budget, the secretary of the Treasury, and the Council of Economic Advisors, designs, but only *recommends,* the desired mixture of G and T. It is Congress, with the aid of many committees,[5] that *enacts* fiscal policy. On the other hand, the President has veto power over congressional fiscal policy. An inherent organizational problem exists at the beginning: The power to enact fiscal policy does not rest with one institution. Disagreement as to the proper fiscal policy might (and usually does) emerge

---

[3]Fiscal policy advocates make the implicit value judgment that full employment and price stability are "good" goals whose benefits exceed the costs attendant to their achievement, and they assume that our knowledge of (positive) economics is sufficient to achieve these goals.

[4]Unlike monetary policy, which is the duty solely of the Fed. However, even though the Fed is an independent institution in theory, it too faces (and bends under) political pressure. It is still generally agreed that monetary policy is, at least theoretically, easier to implement.

[5]The House Ways and Means Committee, the Senate Finance Committee, the House and Senate Budget committees, to name a few.

among members of the Congress, or between Congress and the President. While the procedure required for an ultimate solution is clearly spelled out in the U.S. Constitution, in practice it is sometimes a tedious and time-consuming process. During the process, hearings are called and recalled, and scores of expert witnesses testify—and disagree.

Fiscal policy would be difficult even if all the parties involved were sincere, dedicated people who had as a common goal the well-being of the nation. When one considers that special interest groups exist and that politicians often have time horizons that reach no further than the next election, it becomes obvious that there is more to fiscal policy than Figures 22-2 and 22-3 could ever hope to convey. Changing taxes or government expenditures is one thing; working out the specifics is quite another. Whose taxes rise or fall? *Where* are expenditures to be cut or increased? Such questions are political dynamite and not easily resolved. It simply won't do for economists to solve equations and to complain about "political" problems as if they were not entwined with "economic" problems.

A rather dramatic example of the difference between the original intentions and the final results of fiscal policy can be found in President Reagan's economic program. Reagan, during his campaign, and again after he became President, announced that he would:

1 Lower taxes
2 Balance the federal budget by 1984
3 Decrease overall government spending
4 Decrease spending on social welfare programs
5 Increase spending on national defense

In reality, however, once we adjust for inflation and other changes that occurred in the economy (such as increases in Social Security taxes), which may or may not have been due to Reagan's policy, only increased spending on national defense had been accomplished by late 1983.[6] (Note that even though defense spending increased in real terms, it was *not* the most rapidly growing part of federal expenditures. Interest payments on the public debt grew most rapidly during Reagan's tenure.) Contrary to public perception, "transfers to persons" (which include Social Security, welfare, Medicare, unemployment compensation, and so on) *increased* as a percentage of GNP—from 9.4 percent in 1980 to 10.9 percent in 1982.[7] (See Table 22-1.) The budget was far from balanced; the projections (by October 1983) were that there would be nearly a $208 billion federal deficit in 1983 and perhaps again in 1984.

---

[6]See the following *Wall Street Journal* articles: Edwin G. Mills, "The Rise of Federal Spending under Reagan," Feb. 15, 1983; Norman C. Miller, "Reagan's Record, An Economy Spinning out of Control," Feb. 1, 1983; Paul Craig Roberts, "Big Taxes and Big Deficits," Jan. 14, 1983; and Karl Brunner and Alan Meltzer, "Congress and the Administration Pass the Buck," Feb. 7, 1983.

[7]*Ibid.*, Mills.

TABLE 22-1   Federal Spending Categories as Percentages of GNP

Year	Total Spending	Total Less Defense and Interest	Transfers to Persons
1976	22.4	15.8	9.2
1977	22.0	15.6	8.8
1978	21.3	15.0	8.4
1979	21.1	14.7	8.5
1980	22.9	15.9	9.4
1981	23.4	15.7	9.6
1982 I	24.3	16.1	9.9
1982 II	24.2	15.7	10.1
1982 III	24.9	16.1	10.4
1982 IV	26.3	17.4	10.9

Table and note from Edwin G. Mills, "The Rise of Federal Spending under Reagan," *The Wall Street Journal,* Feb. 15, 1983, op. ed. page.
Note: National Income Accounts basis; data seasonally adjusted.
Sources: "Survey of Current Business," "Economic Report of the President," 1983.

In short, either Reagan was unable to do what he wanted, or he was unwilling to pay the political price of carrying out his program.

By 1984 there was widespread agreement that the federal budget was ineffective; Congress seemed unable to control federal spending and the President seemed unable to counter Congress's appropriations for government spending.

Two important issues underlie the debates within Congress and the debate between Congress and the President. First, to what extent should the government sector expand relative to the private sector? Second, should the federal government effect a change in the distribution of income (from high-income to low-income groups) by its taxing and spending (by way of transfers) programs? Conservative Congress members and the President have argued in favor of a shrinking government sector relative to the private sector and against many of the redistribution-of-income programs; liberals have favored the opposite policies. Table 22-1 shows, perhaps surprisingly, that during Reagan's tenure as President the liberals seemed to be having their way.

Why was Reagan unable to do what he was, presumably, elected to do? This is a difficult question to answer, and we certainly don't presume to know the complete answer. A partial answer can be found, however, in economic analysis. Recall from your principles of economics courses that an individual will act *collectively* only if he or she perceives that the benefit in doing so outweighs the cost of joining a group. Mancur Olson has argued that individuals with a common interest will not voluntarily combine and act to further their common interests *unless each individual has an incentive to participate in such collective action.*[8] More collective action will take place in small, homogeneous groups than among large, diverse groups. The existence of many *distributional coalitions* can be explained by this theory. For example, it is likely that special interest groups such as farmers, unions, and people who represent "the poor" will be able and willing to lobby for special privileges. They are small groups that tend to *gain very much individually,* at the expense of many people who lose much collectively, *but lose very little individually* by such special privileges granted to others. Farm subsidies to farmers amount to very much money to *specific farmers,* but cost very little to *specific nonfarmers*—in the form of higher food prices and taxes that must be paid to finance farm subsidies. Farmers have an incentive to organize and lobby for special privileges, and individual nonfarmers have little incentive to organize against farmers.

James Dale Davidson of the National Taxpayer's Union has described the incentive problem in Congress as follows. Select 435 people (the number of congressional representatives) and give them each a credit card with a single, common account number. Further, provide that each person is responsible for 1/435th of the total monthly bill, but that each can keep what he or she buys. Clearly, such a scheme would promote much spending among the 435 people; each person has a tremendous incentive to spend more than 1/435th of the expected increase in total monthly spending. This example may well indicate what each of the 435 members of Congress faces; each member has an incentive to reduce spending that benefits *other* Congress members' constituents, but to increase federal spending that benefits his or her *own* constituents.

Another problem is that the President—even if he *were* of a mind to reduce real government expenditures—usually is unable to use the veto power over legislation. Congress is able to add any amendment to a proposed bill; the amendment need not have anything to do with the originally proposed bill. If the President feels that a specific piece of legislation is really essential, Congress can add special-privilege legislation to the bill. The President, if he wants to exercise the power of the veto, *must veto the whole bill, not just the sections of which he disapproves.*

Thus, a combination of powerful special interest groups that lobby for special privileges, and a congressional system that promotes government spending, have helped to expand the public sector at the expense of the private sector. In 1973, President Nixon indicated that he would impound funds appropriated by Congress that were to be spent on programs he disapproved of; in effect, even though Congress voted funds for specific projects, the President refused to *spend* the funds. Congress retaliated with the Budget Impoundment and Control Act of 1974, which reduced the power of the President to impound funds that are duly authorized by Congress. Since then, def-

---

[8]Mancur Olson, *The Rise and Decline of Nations* (New Haven, Conn.: Yale University Press, 1982).

icits have increased; so has government spending as a percentage of gross national product. (Recall Table 22-1.)

In 1983, several economists, and the editors of *The Wall Street Journal,* called for a constitutional amendment to grant the President the power to reduce or veto individual items in appropriations bills.[9] These people noted that many former Presidents have asked for this power, and that the governors in virtually every state in the union have such power. This proposal implicitly suggests that a *balanced budget* is not the real issue, but that government spending is. We doubt that a presidential line item veto will soon be forthcoming.

We end this chapter with a Current Controversy concerning the requirement of a balanced federal budget.

CURRENT CONTROVERSY

Requiring a Balanced Federal Budget

Thirty-one state legislatures have applied for a constitutional convention to consider a balanced-budget amendment. According to Article V of the U.S. Constitution, Congress must call a constitutional convention when so petitioned by two-thirds of the states. It is not clear that a sufficient number of states (thirty-four) will petition, but even if they do not, a balanced-budget amendment to the Constitution is a possibility if congressional action is taken. Indeed, the U.S. Senate has recently passed one version.*

The following discussion centers around the economic implications of a balanced federal budget. It does not include the political aspects—not because they are unimportant, but because they are beyond the scope of this text. There are at least seven potential problems with an amendment requiring the federal budget to be balanced annually.

1 The automatic stabilizer (nondiscretionary) aspect of fiscal policy would be impaired. In times of recession, tax receipts normally fall. A balanced budget would require that federal expenditures also fall or that tax rates be increased. Such a policy not only ignores the automatic outlays for social welfare (outlays which many people deem desirable), but it runs counter to what Keynesian discretionary policy would require.

2 A greater burden would be placed on monetary policy to stabilize the economy if a balanced budget requirement hampered fiscal policy.

3 Congress could circumvent this requirement by placing more activities in the "off-budget" category; the illusion of solving the problem is worse than realizing that the problem exists.

---

[9]See Henry Hazlitt, "Line-Item Leash on Runaway Spending," *The Wall Street Journal,* Sept. 9, 1983, and an editorial on the same page entitled "Take Your Pick."

4 Federal appropriations are not identical to actual outlays in their timing and effects, and technical problems would doubtless emerge.

5 Complications could arise for long-term projects; multiyear contracts could run into problems under a system of annual budget balancing.

6 Forecasting tax revenues and expenditure outlays is hardly a well-developed art. As a consequence, the budget process would be even more difficult than it already is.

7 Budgets can be balanced in two ways: by cutting expenditures or raising taxes. A balanced-budget requirement might induce Congress to raise taxes, which might well interfere with economic incentives.

*After the 1982 passage, one senator remarked that the Senate vote in favor of the amendment was like the desperate cry of a murderer saying, "Stop me before I kill again."

CHAPTER SUMMARY

1 Fiscal policy is the changing of government expenditures and/or taxes in order to affect national income and output, employment, and the price level.

2 Fiscal policy causes the *IS* curve to shift. An increase in government expenditures, other things constant, causes the *IS* curve to shift rightward, by the amount of the increase in government expenditures times the government expenditure multiplier. An increase in taxes causes the *IS* curve to shift leftward, by the amount of the increase in taxes times the tax multiplier.

3 If changes in taxes or government expenditures leave the money supply unaltered, changes in fiscal policy (*G* or *T*) will not have a full multiplier effect. This is because as fiscal policy changes the level of net national product, the quantity of money desired for L_1 balances will change in the same direction. Thus, increases in *G* or decreases in *T* will drive the interest rate up and crowd out private consumption and investment; the economy won't expand as much as it otherwise would have. Decreases in *G* or increases in *T* will reduce NNP *and* the rate of interest; increased consumption and investment will offset somewhat the contraction of the economy due to decreased *G* and/or increased *T*.

4 Fiscal policy is difficult because information concerning the state of the economy is inadequate and because the precise mathematical relationships among macroeconomic variables is unknown. Moreover, political problems abound.

5 Discretionary fiscal policy refers to the deliberate and conscious attempt by Congress to stabilize the economy. Automatic stabilizers, on the other hand, are those that occur naturally and require no legislative action. Automatic stabilizers are countercyclical in nature and include a progressive tax structure and unemployment compensation.

6 Because a progressive tax structure and the unemployment compensation program are countercyclical, if the government does nothing else to stabilize the economy, a recession automatically generates a budget deficit, and inflation automatically generates a budget surplus. It follows that the mere existence of a bud-

get deficit or budget surplus does not indicate *discretionary* fiscal policy. Therefore, in order to measure what discretionary fiscal policy is, economists calculate what the government budget position would be at a full-employment level of national income.

7 During the World War II years, between 1941 and 1946, monetary and fiscal policy were synchronized to finance the war effort; they were not used as stabilization tools.

8 When World War II ended, it was believed that a recession would result because the expected decrease in government military expenditures was expected to outweigh the expected increase in public spending from pent-up demand. Price-wage controls were lifted and an expansionary monetary policy was initiated; inflation ensued.

9 From 1962 to 1968, during the Kennedy-Johnson period, true attempts at discretionary fiscal policy were made; stabilization policy began in earnest. President Kennedy favored fiscal policy, which he believed had fewer undesirable side effects than did monetary policy.

10 In 1971, President Nixon froze prices and wages domestically, allowed the dollar to float on the foreign exchange market, and initiated an expansionary fiscal policy—lower T and increased G—in order to reduce inflation. Eventually price-wage controls proved unworkable, as shortages permeated the economy; in 1974, price controls were lifted and the price level increased significantly.

11 President Ford initially pursued an anti-inflation policy; it worked but unemployment climbed. So he switched his emphasis toward fighting recession. By 1975, the recession had bottomed out and Ford attempted to fuel the recovery by advances in the private rather than the public sector; his fiscal policies called for reductions in T, not increases in G, and a "balance" stimulation to consumer spending and investment spending.

12 The Carter administration came into office in 1977 and shifted the fiscal focus toward highly stimulative measures to reduce unemployment. Significant reductions in unemployment and significant increases in inflation resulted. As a consequence, the Carter administration attempted fiscal "restraint"—defined as a reduction in the rate of growth of fiscal stimulus.

13 By 1980, both inflation and unemployment had risen dramatically and the Reagan administration set in motion the "largest tax cut in U.S. history." It was expected to reduce taxes by $471 billion from 1982 to 1985; the 1982 tax *increase* was expected to raise taxes by $100 billion over that same period. Moreover, the previously scheduled 1981 to 1982 Social Security tax-rate increase and bracket creep were expected to offset the net tax decrease legislated over that period.

GLOSSARY

Automatic stabilizers: Countercyclical changes in taxes (resulting from a progressive tax structure) and unemployment compensation that occur automatically, without any legislative action by Congress.

Bracket creep: A situation under a progressive tax structure where an increase in nominal (not real) income puts a taxpayer in a higher marginal tax bracket.

Crowding-out effect: When increases in government expenditures or decreases in taxes occur, they cause the interest rate to rise (if the money supply is not altered). In turn, a higher rate of interest reduces the amount of business investment and household consumption in the private sector.

Discretionary fiscal policy: The deliberate and conscious attempt by government to promote full employment and price stability by countercyclical changes in *G* and *T*.
Full-employment government

budget: What the federal budget deficit or surplus would be if the economy were operating at full employment.
Tax surcharge: A tax levied on an already existing tax.

PROBLEMS

22-1   Assume an economy with a marginal propensity to consume of .75 and that government expenditures rise by $10 billion, financed by a $10 billion Treasury bond sale.

a   In what direction will the *IS* curve shift?

b   By how much will the *IS* curve shift?

c   By how much will the money supply change?

d   What will happen to the interest rate, and why?

e   Will the economy expand by the full government-expenditure multiplier effect? Why or why not?

22-2   Assume an economy with a marginal propensity to consume of .75 and a tax reduction of $10 billion. Assume further that the money supply remains constant.

a   In what direction will the *IS* curve shift?

b   By how much will the *IS* curve shift?

c   What will happen to the interest rate, and why?

d   Will the economy expand by the full tax multiplier effect? Why or why not?

SELECTED REFERENCES

Almon, S., "The Distributed Lag between Capital Appropriation and Expenditures," *Econometrica,* vol. 33, January 1965, pp. 178–196.

Blinder, A. S., *Fiscal Policy in Theory and Practice* (Morristown, N.J.: General Learning Press, 1973).

Blinder, A. S., and R. M. Solow, "Does Fiscal Policy Matter?" *Journal of Public Economics,* vol. 2, November 1973, pp. 319–337.

Carlson, K. M., and R. W. Spencer, "Crowding Out and Its Critics," *Review,* Federal Reserve Bank of St. Louis, December 1975, pp. 1–17.

Chandler, Lester V., *Inflation in the United States, 1940–1945* (New York: Harper & Row, 1951).

Hazlett, Henry, "Line Item Leash on Runaway Spending," *The Wall Street Journal,* Sept. 9, 1983.

Miller, Norman C., "Reagan's Record: An Economy Spinning Out of Control," *The Wall Street Journal,* Feb. 1, 1983.

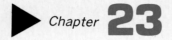
Financial Aspects of Fiscal Policy

Many economics texts treat monetary policy and fiscal policy as if they were separate policies. Suspecting that this cannot be the case, many students think of monetary policy and fiscal policy as if they were inseparable. The truth is somewhere in between; in practice these two policies are interrelated. While *pure* fiscal policy can be conducted without altering the money supply, this chapter examines the financial aspects of fiscal policy; it shows how the various methods of financing federal expenditures affect such monetary variables as the monetary base, financial institution reserves, and the money stock.

Recall from Chapter 18 that there are three basic ways in which the federal government can finance its spending: taxing, borrowing, or "printing" money. This chapter analyzes these methods in greater detail. The impact of each of these three methods on the money supply, on the monetary base, and on bank reserves is described; the different effects of federal borrowing from the public, from depository institutions, and from the Fed are also examined.

We further analyze the different impact on the economy of financing government spending (through taxing, borrowing, or printing money) by examining the budget constraints on both the public and the federal government. The chapter ends with a Current Controversy regarding the (real or imagined) problems of the national debt.

FINANCING FEDERAL GOVERNMENT EXPENDITURES

Taxing One way to finance government expenditures is to tax the public. As taxes are collected, they are deposited in U.S. Treasury accounts at banks throughout the country; these accounts are referred to as **tax and loan accounts.** Taxes are paid when privately owned demand deposits are debited and Treasury accounts are credited by the same amount.

At this stage the money supply has fallen by the amount of the tax revenue because the money supply (by definition) does not include U.S. Treasury deposits. All checks written by the U.S. Treasury are written against its accounts at Federal Reserve banks. As its balances at the Fed are drawn down, the Treasury shifts funds from commercial banks to the Federal Reserve. When the Treasury shifts these funds, total bank reserves and the monetary base fall by the amount of the funds shifted.

When the Treasury spends these tax revenues by writing checks on its accounts at Federal Reserve banks, the public receives these checks. The checks are then deposited in depository institutions which in turn send the checks to the Fed for collection. When this happens the money supply and the monetary base increase, and bank reserves increase by the amount spent.

The eventual *net* effect of these transactions is that neither the money supply nor bank reserves have been altered. Intuitively, if the government taxes people and then spends those tax dollars, the money supply is not altered.

The Impact of Taxation Financing on the Budget Constraints of the Public and the Federal Government

Most students leave their principles of economics course with the notion that individuals and businesses face budget constraints. No individual or business can spend without limit; the spending of both the household and the business sectors is limited by their earnings and by their ability to borrow.

It turns out that even the government has a budget constraint, although it has options not available (legally, at least) to the public: The government can print money and it can tax.

The Public's Budget Constraint   The private, nonbank budget constraint is:

$$\Delta L = Y_d - C - \Delta Z \qquad\qquad (23\text{-}1)$$

where ΔL = change in *desired* money balances

Y_d = disposable income; national income minus taxes plus government transfers

C = desired expenditures by households on goods and services

ΔZ = change in net lending to government (net purchases of government securities by the public)

Equation (23-1) represents the private sector's budget constraint. It implies that (given Y_d) if the public as a whole wants to increase its money balances, it must either spend less (save more) or purchase fewer government securities. Conversely (given Y_d), if the public as a whole wants to decrease its total money balances, it can increase its expenditures or purchase more government securities.

Equation (23-1) can be rewritten as:

$$\Delta L + \Delta Z = Y_d - C = S \qquad\qquad (23\text{-}2)$$

where S represents saving.

Equation (23-2) indicates that the community can save by purchasing government securities or by voluntarily holding more money; annual saving by the public leads to net lending to government *or* to increased cash balances.

The Federal Government's Budget Constraint   The federal government's budget constraint can be written

$$G = \Delta H + T + \Delta B \qquad\qquad (23\text{-}3)$$

where ΔH = change in high-powered money; H consists of printed money and depository institution reserves; H also is called the monetary base

G = government spending for goods and services and for transfer payments

$$T = \text{tax receipts}$$
$$\Delta B = \text{change in net sales of bonds to the private sector by the Treasury } and \text{ the Fed}$$

Note that a government budget constraint *does* exist, however imperfectly, even though H can be increased by the Treasury or by the Fed. That is, eventually increases in G will lead to increases in H (which are inflationary), T, or B that will be deemed intolerable by the public. In turn, the government will be forced to take some action; this forced action is the budget constraint, and it is once again confirmed that "there ain't no such thing as a free lunch." Even for governments.

Equation (23-3) can be rewritten as

$$\Delta H + \Delta B = G - T \tag{23-4}$$

which implies that government deficits must be financed by increases in either H or B. Consequently, Congress and the President decide the size of the deficit through their appropriations and taxation decisions, and the Fed determines how the deficit is financed—by borrowing from the public or by increasing the monetary base.

Budget Constraints and Financing Government Expenditures by Taxing Suppose that the government's budget is balanced and that it finances increased government expenditures of, say, $1 billion by increasing taxes by that amount. Chapter 19 indicated that a balanced budget is slightly expansionary because the *net* effect of equal increases in G and T is an upward shift in the AD curve; national income rises by $1 billion if G and T rise by $1 billion.

Analysis of the probable impact of this balanced-budget effect on the public's and the federal government's budget constraints suggests otherwise. Rewriting Equation (23-4) yields

$$\Delta H = G - T - \Delta B \tag{23-5}$$

A balanced budget implies that $G - T = 0$ and that $\Delta B = 0$; therefore, $\Delta H = 0$; the monetary base (high-powered money) is unaltered. This is consistent with a conclusion that we have already made in this chapter; an increase in government expenditures financed by an equal increase in taxes leaves the money supply unchanged. We relate the money supply to high-powered money in the following Highlight.

Consider now what happens to the public's budget constraint. The increase in income resulting from the net increase in aggregate demand due to a $1 billion increase in G and T means that the *IS* curve will shift to the right by $1 billion; national income will rise by $1 billion if the interest rate doesn't change. This is indicated in Figure 23-1. Because $Y_d - C = 0$ and $\Delta Z = 0$, total L remains constant in Equation (23-2). The level of Y_{NNP} has increased by $1 billion. So L_1 balances rise and the composition of L changes.

HIGHLIGHT: Relating the Money Supply to the Monetary Base

Chapter 8 indicated that a change in depository-institution reserves and in currency leads to a multiple expansion or multiple contraction in the money supply. The money deposit expansion multiplier depends on (1) the form in which the public desires to hold money, and (2) the reserve ratios that depository institutions hold against their transactions deposits and time deposits. We can show how the money supply (M) and high-powered money (H) are related algebraically. Let:

X = time deposits

D = transactions deposits

A = currency

R = depository-institution reserves on transactions deposits and on time deposits

r_d = reserve ratio held against transactions deposits

r_x = reserve ratio held against time deposits

By definition,

$$M = A + D$$

*Because $M = [M/H](H)$

$$H = A + R$$

$$R = r_d D + r_x X, \text{ and}$$

$$M^* = \frac{(A + D)}{(A + R)} \cdot H$$

Substituting for R yields

$$M = \frac{A + D}{A + r_d D + r_x X} H$$

Dividing the numerator and the denominator of the above equation by D gives

$$M = \frac{1 + \dfrac{A}{D}}{\dfrac{A}{D} + \left(r_d + r_x\left(\dfrac{X}{D}\right)\right)} H$$

It follows that changes in H will increase M by the factor

$$\frac{1 + \dfrac{A}{D}}{\dfrac{A}{D} + \left(r_d + r_x\left(\dfrac{X}{D}\right)\right)}$$

which is the money deposit expansion multiplier.

Note, therefore, that changes in high-powered money will increase the money supply by some multiple, depending on (1) the public's tastes for the *form* in which it wants to hold money (A/D and X/D), and (2) depository-institution reserve ratios held against transactions deposits and time deposits (r_d and r_x).

During the depressions of 1907 and 1929 to 1933, the fear that widespread bankruptcy in the banking system would prevent banks from paying off their deposit liabilities led to runs on banks, as people attempted to increase their ratio of *cash* to transactions accounts (and time deposit) balances. The Federal Deposit Insurance Corporation was legislated in 1933 to insure deposits; as a consequence, this source of instability in the money market multiplier has been eliminated. Moreover, the Fed requires that r_d and r_x be higher than depository institutions would prefer them to be, in order to exert monetary control over such institutions. As a consequence, the Fed has control over the monetary base and over the money supply; the Fed can change r_d and r_x (within broad limits) and it can offset (using open-market operations) any changes in the public's taste for the form in which it desires to hold money.

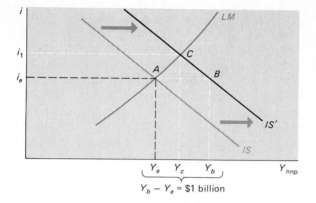

FIGURE 23-1   These curves indicate the net impact on the economy if increased government expenditures are financed by an equal increase in taxes. A $1 billion increase in G and T shifts the IS curve rightward by $1 billion ($B - A$); AD is higher at every rate of interest. Because the money supply is not changed, however, the LM curve does not shift. As a result, the net change is a movement from A to C, and not from A to B; national income rises by less than $1 billion.

Considering the *overall* results, we see that the money supply has remained constant but that the community *wants* to hold more money because of the higher national income level; that is, the desire for L_1 balances increases. This means that at the higher level of net national income and the given rate of interest (point B in Figure 23-1) a shortage of money exists. This will cause interest rates to rise, which in turn causes net investment and consumption to fall. This process continues until some combination of a higher interest rate and a lower level of net national product (point C in Figure 23-1) reduces the quantity demanded for money sufficiently to make the public again want to hold the unchanged money supply. *The public's budget constraint must be consistent with the government's budget constraint;* if a government activity leaves the money supply constant but changes the demand for money, some combination of net national product change and interest-rate change must be forthcoming to restore equilibrium in the money market.

The conclusion is that if a $1 billion increase in government expenditures is financed by a $1 billion increase in taxes, net national product will rise by less than $1 billion because this will cause the interest rate to rise.

Borrowing   Federal government expenditures can also be financed by borrowing from the nonbank public, depository institutions or the Fed. Each is discussed in turn below.

Borrowing from the Public   The U.S. Treasury borrows from the (non-bank) public by selling bonds; the public will buy these bonds voluntarily if the terms (interest rates or bond prices) are attractive. By paying with a check drawn on a depository institution, the public surrenders money for a bond, which is nonmoney. As a result, the money supply, depository-institution reserves, and the monetary base fall by the value of the bond sold. When the government spends these funds, however, and the public deposits its checks in depository institutions, the money supply, bank reserves, and the monetary base again rise. The *net* result (as was true in the previous tax example) is that the money supply, bank reserves, and monetary base are not altered.

Borrowing from the public to finance a deficit: its impact on the budget constraints of the public and the federal government Assume that a $1 billion increase in government expenditures is financed by Treasury borrowings of $1 billion from the public. The preceding analysis indicated that the money supply remains constant. So does Equation (23-3), the federal government's budget constraint. Because $\Delta G = \Delta B$, $\Delta H = \Delta T = 0$; put another way, increased government expenditures are financed totally by increased net sales of bonds to the private sector; therefore, taxes and high-powered money are unaltered.

On the other hand, analysis of Equation (23-1), the public's budget constraint, reveals that the public will desire to hold *more* money balances. As Figure 23-2 shows, assuming a marginal propensity to consume of .75, an increase in government expenditures of $1 billion shifts the *IS* curve rightward by $4 billion; net national product would rise by $4 billion if the interest rate were unaltered. At point *B*, the combination of a higher level of NNP and the same interest rate (i_e), a shortage of liquidity exists because a higher level of NNP increases the amount desired for L_1 balances.

Moreover, before the public voluntarily will increase its Z to accommodate the government's increase in B (note that $\Delta B = \Delta Z$ of necessity), the public must be offered a higher interest rate to part with its L_2 balances. At point *A* the public was in equilibrium; an increase in B requires an increase in Z, so somehow the public must desire to hold less money and more government bonds. Again we conclude that at i_e a shortage of liquidity exists, because at i_e some of the public's demand for money for L_2 balances must be coaxed out by the increased government demand for money.

In short, the interest rate will rise, net investment and consumption will fall, and net national product will fall—below Y_b in Figure 23-2. This process

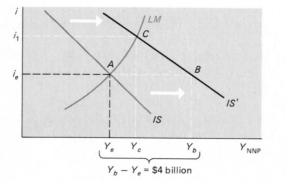

FIGURE 23-2 This figure indicates that an increase in *G* financed by an equal increase in *B* does not cause a full multiplier effect, because of the financial impact of fiscal policy. A $1 billion increase in *G* and *B* (given an MPC of .75) causes national income to rise to Y_c, not Y_b, because some private investment and consumption is crowded out as the interest rate rises from i_e to i_1; national income rises by less than $4 billion.

will continue until some combination of a higher interest rate and a higher level of net national product restores equilibrium in the money market. That combination is indicated at point C in Figure 23-2. The conclusion is that once we take into account the impact on financial markets of financing increased government spending by borrowing from the public, we realize that a full government expenditure multiplier effect will not result. In our example, net national product will rise by *less* than $4 billion.

Borrowing from Depository Institutions The U.S. Treasury can borrow from depository institutions by selling them securities. As with the nonbank public, depository institutions purchase bonds and securities voluntarily if "the price is right."

The ultimate effect of Treasury borrowing from depository institutions depends on whether excess reserves do or do not exist in the banking sector.

Zero excess reserves Consider first the case in which depository institutions have zero excess reserves. In such a situation, these institutions cannot purchase Treasury securities unless they sell other assets.[1] Why not? Because when a depository institution purchases a government security from the Treasury, it creates a comparably valued demand deposit for the Treasury. The depository institution must hold additional reserves against this increased Treasury demand deposit account. Given the assumption of initial zero excess reserves, excess reserves would now be negative. Therefore, depository institutions would have to reduce the public's demand deposits by an equal amount by selling assets, equal in value, to the public. Thus, the money supply (which again includes only the nonbank *public's* demand deposits) initially falls. However, as in the previous example, when the Treasury spends its demand deposits the money supply increases. The net result, again, is that the money supply, depository-institution reserves, and the monetary base are unaltered.

Positive excess reserves Lest you think that the money supply is never altered by fiscal policy, consider the case in which the U.S. Treasury borrows from depository institutions that have excess reserves. Assume in this example that excess reserves exceed the value of Treasury securities sales. That is, some excess reserves still exist after the depository institutions purchase Treasury securities. What happens now? This situation does not require that depository institutions sell assets to reduce the public's total demand deposits. In this case depository institutions will purchase the Treasury securities and create demand deposits for the Treasury; the Treasury will then shift its deposits to the Fed, allowing the Treasury to draw down on its checking account with the Fed in order to permit federal government expenditures.

The net result is that the money supply increases, but only by the amount of the government expenditures financed by bond sales to the depository institutions. Note, however, that total bank reserves and the monetary base are

---

[1] At least they aren't supposed to. On occasion, they do, however; they borrow the needed reserves in the Eurodollar market or from the Fed itself.

not affected. Hence, no multiple deposit expansion in the money supply occurs.

Borrowing from the Fed If the Treasury were to sell securities to the Fed, it would receive demand deposits upon which it could write checks to finance government expenditures. In exchange, the Fed holds interest-earning assets (Treasury securities) that are liabilities to the Treasury. Note, however, that when the Treasury has spent these funds the public has received checks that it would then deposit in depository institutions; the latter would experience an equal increase in total reserves and a somewhat smaller increase in excess reserves. As a result, the money supply could expand by some multiple of the original debt sale. If you think this sounds like the public is getting something for nothing, you may have a point. Still, remember that the public also has increased liabilities because the Treasury's liabilities are the public's liabilities. To the extent that this process is inflationary, moreover, the public also pays for the asset (money) with a "hidden tax."

Printing Money The U.S. Treasury is empowered to print money, but printing money is a rather crude form of financing government expenditures (and reminiscent of the days when kings and queens called in gold and silver coins, melted them down, and either minted coins with higher face values or alloyed them with cheaper metals). Today the government prefers to debase the currency in more subtle ways because the link between open-market operations and borrowing from the Fed is less obvious as a cause of inflation than is the printing of money. In some countries where governments apparently don't have to worry about such subtle distinctions, printing money has often been an inexpensive and politically viable method of financing government expenditures.

If the U.S. Treasury decided to print money to finance government expenditures, the process would simply involve printing the money, depositing the money in its checking account with the Fed, and writing checks on the account. This process is similar to the situation in which the Treasury sells bonds to the Fed: A multiple expansion of the money supply occurs. The only difference is that in the first case the Fed receives an interest-earning security as an asset; but here the Fed receives newly printed (and non-interest-earning) currency. In light of the fact that at year's end the Fed turns over most of its earnings to the Treasury, this distinction is more apparent than real.[2]

We can show how printing money (or Treasury bond sales to the Fed) affects the budget constraints of the federal government and the public, and therefore we can indicate how the economy is affected. Consider the case in which a $1 billion increase in government expenditures is financed by the Treasury's printing $1 billion of new money, or by the Treasury's selling $1 billion worth of bonds to the Fed. High-powered money will rise by $1 billion;

---

[2]For those of you who worry about such things, the Fed's newly acquired assets—paper currency—are the U.S. Treasury's liabilities and therefore are ultimately the *public's* liabilities. Moreover the resulting inflation will assure that the public does not get something for nothing.

$\Delta H = \Delta G = \$1$ billion, because $\Delta T = \Delta B = 0$, according to Equation (23-3). This \$1 billion increase in high-powered money will cause a multiple expansion in the money supply. Other things constant, the public is no longer in equilibrium because the money supply has increased; a surplus of liquidity exists. Equation (23-1) indicates that the public will desire to hold more money balances if $(Y_d - C)$ rises (because $\Delta Z = \Delta B = 0$); therefore, net national product will rise as the community starts spending its excess money balances.

Two forces are at work here. First, total expenditures rise because of the increase in government expenditures and because the increase in the money supply increases private spending. On the other hand, a higher level of net national product will increase the amount of money desired for transactions and precautionary purposes—L_1. While it is safe to predict that net national product will rise, the effect on the interest rate is uncertain because we get our increase in both the supply *and* the demand for money.

This point in the preceding paragraph is demonstrated by the *IS-LM* framework in Figure 23-3. Note that the *LM* curve shifts to the right, reflecting the fact that a \$1 billion increase in high-powered money leads to a multiple increase in the money supply. A \$1 billion increase in government expenditures shifts the *IS* curve rightward by \$4 billion, assuming a marginal propensity to consume of .75.

In Figure 23-3, the *LM* curve is shifted by just enough to leave the interest rate unaltered—at i_e. Consequently, a full government expenditure multiplier effect will obtain. You can demonstrate to yourself that if a \$1 billion increase in high-powered money caused the *LM* curve to shift by less than it did in Fig-

FIGURE 23-3   The *IS* curve shifts from *IS* to *IS'* by \$4 billion if *G* increases by \$1 billion and the marginal propensity to consume is .75. In this example we shifted the *LM* to the right (due to an increase in high-powered money, which leads to a multiple expansion in the money supply) by exactly enough to generate a new equilibrium situation where net national product is \$4 billion higher and the interest rate is unchanged. If the *LM* curve had shifted rightward by *less* than the amount indicated here, the equilibrium interest rate would be higher and the equilibrium level of net national product would be less than Y_b.

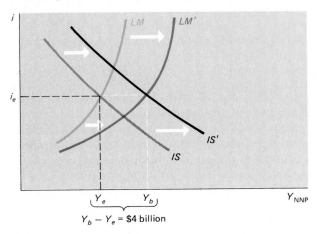

TABLE 23-1 Methods of Financing Government Expenditures

Method of Financing	Monetary Base and Bank Reserves Increased?	Money Supply Increased?
Taxing	No	No
Borrowing from public	No	No
Borrowing from depository institutions with		
Zero excess reserves	No	No
Positive excess reserves	No	Yes, by the amount of borrowing
Borrowing from the Fed	Yes	Multiple expansion
Printing money	Yes	Multiple expansion

ure 23-3 (because of higher reserve requirements or a higher desired ratio of currency to demand deposits, for example), then the equilibrium interest rate would be higher than i_e, and the equilibrium level of net national product would be less than Y_b.

A SUMMARY OF THE MONETARY EFFECTS OF VARIOUS WAYS TO FINANCE FEDERAL GOVERNMENT EXPENDITURES

Table 23-1 summarizes how each method of financing government expenditures affects the money supply, depository-institution reserves, and the monetary base.

CURRENT CONTROVERSY

The Public Debt

Due to Keynes's influence, deficit spending has become an important part of fiscal policy. Since World War II, the U.S. government has been in a budget surplus position in only five fiscal years. As a consequence, the United States has had a growing **public debt;** the cumulative deficit is currently equal to more than $1 trillion. This means that marketable and nonmarketable government securities owned by the public, by government agencies, and by foreigners are equal to this amount.

Much of our public debt was incurred during World War II. Recently, the government has had relatively large deficits and has added to the size of the public debt. Concerned policymakers and laypersons alike sometimes question the advisability of increasing the size of that debt; they are concerned with the *burden* of the public debt. Two myths relating to this question are that the government will go bankrupt or that future generations will have to pay for our current activities.

CAN THE GOVERNMENT GO BANKRUPT?

Opponents of larger public debt point out that if firms always ran in the red—the way the government spends more than it receives—those firms would eventually go out of business; they would go bankrupt. But the analogy between firms and the government is invalid. The government will go bankrupt only when it loses its ability to collect taxes. Interest on the public debt will be paid as long as the government has revenue-raising powers. Moreover, the public debt never has to be paid. It can be, and indeed is, refinanced as it comes due. Every month, some of the debt reaches maturity; it is then "rolled over." If a $1-million Treasury bond comes due tomorrow, the U.S. Treasury may pay it off and at approximately the same time reissue another $1-million bond.

MAKING FUTURE GENERATIONS PAY

Was it possible to have later generations pay for World War II? Not really. The resources used to fight World War II were taken away from that population. There was a trade-off between civilian goods and military goods. During World War II, this nation used a relatively large share of its resources to produce military goods. The people *at that time* had to give up consumption and private investment.

The same argument holds today. If the federal government runs a deficit of $160 billion and finances it by increasing the public debt by the same amount, future generations will not pay for government resources used today. If the government commands, say, $900 billion of current resources, the fact that part of government spending is financed by the issuance of debt does not alter one more crucial fact—$900 billion of resources are being controlled by the government. The production possibilities curve between private goods and government goods will always show a trade-off during any given year.

But What about Interest? Interest must also be paid on increases in the public debt. The government might pay the interest payments by increasing taxes, but that is not in itself a burden. After all, the taxes are paid by some Americans; the interest is received by others. In principle, this is merely a redistribution that cannot properly be called a burden on *all* of society.

Still, in recent years, some economists have revised their thinking somewhat, and the public debt is again under scrutiny. People who are optimistic about the public debt are fond of pointing out that the ratio of the outstanding debt to GNP has fallen since 1945 and even since 1960. But a reversal of that trend seems to have occurred in the late 1970s and early 1980s. High interest rates in recent years have also raised the proportion of GNP required for debt service to levels near those of World War II.

POSSIBLE REAL BURDENS OF THE DEBT

Thus far we have been concerned with the internal public debt. If part of it is held by *foreigners,* then it is no longer true that "we owe it to ourselves." The argument that "we owe the public debt to ourselves" is becoming increasingly untrue. Between 1968 and 1981, the percentage of the U.S. public debt owed to citizens of other countries increased from about 6 percent to about 20 percent. In 1977 nearly all the U.S. deficit was financed by foreign governments; in 1978 (for the first time), our government sold U.S. securities denominated in German marks and Swiss francs. Presumably, future U.S. generations will be "worse off" when this foreign debt comes due. Nonetheless, this still may not constitute a burden on future generations.

Assume that the nation is straining its productive capacity and can get no more output from available resources. However, if it borrows resources abroad by selling public debt to foreigners, it can increase the resources available to it. Future generations must pay the interest that allows for this increased use of resources today. If, however, some of those resources are invested in buildings, dams, and electricity plants, future generations may still be better off. They will be charged higher taxes to pay the interest on this externally owned public debt, but they will also be receiving the greater benefits of more buildings, dams, and electricity plants (income).

And, Finally, Wasteful Government Expenditures   Those opposed to an increased public debt argue that it is more likely that wasteful government expenditures will creep in when deficit spending is readily available. It is further argued that politicians feel they can get away with more spending if current taxes don't have to be raised. Deficit financing—increases in the public debt—gives the illusion of a deferred cost of government expenditures. Also, public borrowing competes with private borrowing. Other things constant, such borrowing may cause higher interest rates and less domestic investment. This "crowding out" could imply that future generations might inherit a smaller capital stock—again, assuming that the government uses its borrowed funds inefficiently.

CHAPTER SUMMARY

1   There are three basic ways in which the federal government can finance its expenditures: taxing, borrowing, and printing money.

2   When taxes are collected, they are deposited in the U.S. Treasury's "tax and loan accounts" at various banks throughout the country. The immediate result is that the money supply falls. The Treasury then shifts these deposits to Federal Reserve bank accounts, at which time total depository-institution reserves, and the monetary base, fall. The Treasury spends these tax revenues, however, by writing checks on its account at the Fed to pay the public for providing goods and services to the government. These checks are then deposited by the public in depository institutions, which in turn send the checks to the Fed for collection. When this happens, the money supply and the monetary base are increased by the amount spent. Ultimately, the *net* impact of all these activities is that neither the money supply nor bank reserves are altered.

3   The federal government's budget constraint also indicates that the net result of an increase in financed government spending and an equal increase in taxes leaves the money supply unaltered. A balanced budget does not change high-powered money (the monetary base). The increase in government expenditures does increase net national product, however, so the public will want to hold more money for transactions and precautionary motives (L_1), as the public's budget constraint implies. Thus, a shortage of liquidity exists at the higher level of NNP and the original interest rate. The interest rate will rise, causing net investment and consumption to fall. As a consequence, the net change in NNP will be less than would have been the case had the interest rate not risen.

4   The federal government can also finance its expenditures by borrowing from (a) the public, (b) depository institutions, and (c) the Fed.

5   The government borrows from the public by offering it a suitable bond price (interest rate). The public pays by writing a check on a depository institution; the public surrenders money for bonds, a nonmoney asset. The money supply, depository-institution reserves, and the monetary base fall. When the government spends these funds and the public deposits the checks in a depository institution, the money supply, depository-institution reserves, and the monetary base rise. The *net* result, again, is that the money supply, depository-institution reserves, and the monetary base are unaltered.

6   The federal government budget constraint indicates that the money supply is unaltered when government expenditures are financed by borrowing from the public. High-powered money is unaltered; therefore the money supply remains constant. The public's budget constraint indicates that the higher level of NNP induced by an increase in government expenditures will increase the public's demand for money. The resulting shortage of money will drive the interest rate upward; so will the fact that in order to coax the public to part with its liquidity (L_2 balances) the government's fiscal agents (the Treasury or the Fed) must offer the public higher yields on bonds. The higher rate of interest will reduce investment, consumption, and net national product below where they would have been had the interest rate not risen.

7   The U.S. Treasury can also borrow from depository institutions by selling them securities at an advantageous price (interest rate). The ultimate effect on the financial system depends on whether or not excess reserves exist initially. If excess reserves are zero, then a depository institution's purchase of a T-bill requires the institution to sell other assets, thereby reducing the public's demand deposits by a comparable amount. The money supply, depository-institution reserves, and the monetary base fall. When the Treasury spends its demand deposits, these three quantities rise; again the *net* effect is zero. If *positive* excess reserves exist in the banking system, then depository institution purchases of T-bills do not necessitate sales of other assets by the institutions. The net result will be that the money supply will increase by the value of government expenditures financed by bond sales to the depository institutions; total bank reserves and the monetary base are unaltered, so no multiple deposit expansion occurs.

8   If the Treasury borrows from the Fed by selling it T-bills, the Treasury receives demand deposits upon which it can write checks to finance government expenditures. When these deposits are spent domestically, the public deposits the checks in depository institutions; total and excess reserves rise and multiple deposit expansion occurs. A hidden (inflationary) tax occurs.

9   The federal government (exclusively) has the option of printing money to finance its expenditures. Only the Treasury is empowered to print money; it can do so and deposit the new money in its checking account with the Fed. The Treasury can then write checks to make expenditures; total and excess reserves rise in the banking system and a multiple deposit expansion occurs.

10 When the federal government finances its expenditures by printing money (or borrowing from the Fed), the federal government budget constraint indicates that high-powered money will rise and lead to a multiple expansion in the money supply. The public's budget constraint indicates that the demand for money balances will also rise because net national product rises due to the increased government spending and due to the spending induced by a larger money supply. Because both the demand for and the supply of money rise, the effect on the interest rate is indeterminate. Net national product, however, will definitely rise.

11 The public debt is equal to the value of marketable and nonmarketable government securities owned by (a) the public, (b) government agencies, and (c) foreigners. In recent years, large federal government deficits have added to the size of the public debt. There is considerable controversy about the *burden* of the public debt.

12 It is unlikely that the U.S. government will go bankrupt. It has the ability to levy taxes to pay its debts. Moreover, the public debt never has to be paid off; it can be refinanced when it comes due.

13 In one sense, it is not possible to have future generations pay for present government expenditures. The opportunity cost of present government expenditures is forgone private goods, which must be forgone now. Taxing some future residents to pay interest to other future residents merely changes the distribution of income in the future; it cannot be said that *all* future residents will be burdened. To the extent that the public debt is owed to foreigners, future domestic residents will be burdened with interest payments to future foreign residents, who will demand goods and services. If, however, the funds borrowed from foreigners are used productively, future domestic residents might be better off.

GLOSSARY

Public debt: The total value of U.S. government debt outstanding.

Tax and loan accounts: United States Treasury accounts at depository institutions throughout the country in which tax receipts are deposited initially.

PROBLEMS

23-1   Using the government budget constraint [Equation (23-4)] and the nonbank public budget constraint [Equation (23-1)], show the implications of an increase in G financed by an increase in T.

23-2   Using the *IS-LM* framework, show the implications of an increase in G financed by an increase in government borrowing.

SELECTED REFERENCES

Brunner, K., and A. H. Meltzer, "Money, Debt, and Economic Activity," *Journal of Political Economy,* vol. 80, September–October 1972, pp. 951–977.

Christ, Carl F., "A Short-Run Aggregate Demand Model of the Interdependence and Effects of Monetary and Fiscal Policies with Keynesian and Classical Interest Elasticities," *American Economic Review,* vol. 57, May 1967, pp. 434–443.

————, "A Simple Macroeconomic Model with a Government Budget Restraint," *Journal of Political Economy,* vol. 76, January–February 1968, pp. 53–67.

Gordon, Robert J., *Macroeconomics,* 3d ed. (Boston: Little, Brown and Co., 1984).

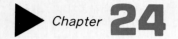
The Monetarists versus the Keynesians

Keynesians and a group of non-Keynesians referred to as monetarists have waged an ongoing debate over the past two decades. Much space within this text has already been devoted to the Keynesian model. Keynesians are the modern followers of John Maynard Keynes and have reformulated Keynes's original model. **Monetarists** maintain that money supply changes play a crucial role in affecting nominal macroeconomic variables; they trace their lineage to classical and neoclassical economists, and from there to Milton Friedman and others.

This chapter discusses the primary issues in the monetarist-Keynesian debate. It points out that the two sides disagree on the effectiveness of fiscal policy and of monetary policy and on whether the types of policies we have utilized are stabilizing or destabilizing. Issues on which the two sides agree are then presented. To clarify the monetarist-Keynesian debate, this chapter relates the monetarist and the Keynesian positions on how the economy reacts to excess money balances, how interest rates are affected by changes in the money supply, and the net effect on the economy of federal borrowing to finance government expenditures. Finally, the Great Depression is analyzed from both the monetarist and the Keynesian points of view.

MONETARISTS AND THE CLASSICAL ECONOMISTS

Modern monetarists, as noted above, trace their roots to the classical economists. Perhaps the most important of these roots is the belief that shocks to the economy are absorbed by changes in relative prices, inputs, outputs, and interest rates, which eventually restore the economy to full-employment equilibrium. An offshoot of this belief is that economic problems can usually be solved by free markets and that government-imposed political solutions are nearly always inferior to market solutions. The monetarists' conclusion, generally, is that governments ought to "do nothing" in order to "solve" economic problems. If left alone, markets will eventually change relative prices in such a way that efficient solutions will emerge.

Another monetarist root that can be traced to the classical economists is the belief that money-supply changes lead to price-level changes. Modern monetarists do not agree, however, with the older quantity theory of money which maintains that money supply changes lead to exactly *proportional* changes in the price level. They reject the older quantity theory of money in favor of the sophisticated quantity theory, which (being less restrictive) assumes a high positive correlation between money-supply changes and changes in nominal national income in both the short run and the long run. These money supply changes lead to changes in the price level and/or changes in national output—that is, to changes in nominal national income, which is the product of the price level and national output. Monetarists accept the classical position that velocity is relatively stable (maintaining that it at least moves in predictable ways), and that money supply increases lead to increases in overall spending.

Milton Friedman. Nobel prize laureate who has been a consistent champion of economic freedom and free markets. *(Courtesy of United Press International.)*

One major disagreement between classical and modern monetarist economists is whether "money really matters." To the classical economist money didn't matter because it was merely a medium of exchange. Changes in the supply of money affected absolute, not relative, prices; money was neutral. Modern monetarists maintain that in the long run changes in the money supply affect only absolute prices, but they stress more strongly than the classical economists (who often ignored short-run effects) that in the *short run* money can affect relative prices. This is an important distinction and its implications will be developed more fully in a later chapter. For now it will suffice to say that if money-supply changes *can* affect relative prices in the short run, they can cause the unemployment rate to deviate from the **natural rate of unemployment.** The natural rate of unemployment, somewhat analogous to Keynes's natural rate of interest, is the rate to which the unemployment level returns after inflation is perfectly anticipated, or after relative prices have been adjusted properly. The natural rate of unemployment is dependent on the degree to which markets are competitive and efficient, among other things; this is explained more fully in Chapter 25. Monetarists are inclined to agree with the classical economists that monetary policy and fiscal policy cannot affect the level of unemployment—in the long run.

It should be apparent now that the monetarist-Keynesian debate *does not* center primarily around the fact that Keynesians favor fiscal policy and monetarists favor monetary policy. Confusion over the nature of the issue is reflected by the fact that the debate was formerly called the monetarist-fiscalist debate.

KEYNESIANS ON MONETARY AND FISCAL POLICY

To be sure, Keynesians do believe that fiscal policy is more effective than monetary policy. Fiscal policy directly affects the AD curve through changes in government expenditures (G) and indirectly through changes in consumption (C) when taxes and transfer payments are altered.

In addition, Keynesians maintain that monetary policy is less reliable and less predictable than fiscal policy and is efficient only if it affects the AD curve. And they feel AD may not be affected very much by a money-supply change. Recall the equation of exchange, $MV = PQ = Y$. According to the Keynesians, increases in the money supply may be offset by decreases in velocity (V). If this is so, then *net* change in MV is unpredictable; and if MV is unpredictable, then changes in $PQ (= Y)$ are also not predictable.

Some Keynesians are prepared to accept a close long-run relationship between changes in the money supply and changes in the price level. Once the full effects of the change in the money supply are eventually worked out, the new equilibrium position will reflect a price level that has changed in the same direction. In the interim period, however, the price level may be affected by nonmoney changes, such as changes in government expenditures. They maintain, therefore, that the *short-run* relationship between changes in the rate of money growth and the rate of inflation is not empirically demonstrated. It follows that there are other determinants of short-run inflation. Aside from increases in the money supply, the Keynesians believe the following to be determinants of the short-term rate of inflation: fiscal policy, changes in autonomous consumption or autonomous investment, inflationary expectations, and shifts in aggregate supply, such as increases in wage rates or raw-materials prices.

According to Keynesians, the *IS* curve in Figure 24-1 is unresponsive to changes in the rate of interest during a recession or depression; net investment is not responsive to lower interest rates at such times. The *IS* curve, therefore, is parallel to the vertical axis, and it intersects the *LM* curve in the liquidity trap, or Keynesian range. Note how an increase in the money supply, which shifts the *LM* curve rightward, has no impact on the real interest rate, i_e (which is at its minimum); therefore it has no impact on real net national product (Y_e). Because $V = (PQ)/M = Y/M$, and because increases in M leave Y unaltered in the liquidity trap, V must fall. In short, an increase in M is offset by a decrease in V, and Y is unaffected by expansionary monetary policy in a depression.

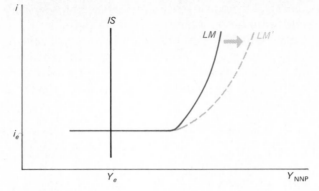

FIGURE 24-1 In a depression or deep recession, a vertical *IS* curve (one which is unresponsive to changes in the interest rate) intersects the *LM* curve in the latter's liquidity trap (Keynesian) range. An increase in the money supply from *LM* to *LM'* has no effect on real net national product (Y_e) or on the real interest rate (i_e). An increase in *M* is offset by a decrease in *V* and therefore the interest rate is unaffected; because the interest rate is unaffected (and because investment is unresponsive to interest rate changes anyway), real net national product is unaffected.

In times of deep recession or depression, interest rates are already low; most speculators feel that the market interest rate is below the natural rate. Therefore, if bonds were to be purchased, capital losses would be higher and money is a superior asset form; the public is prepared to hold more money in L_2 (speculative) balances. Increases in the money supply are merely held by the public, and therefore *V* falls.

This analysis indicates that there are (according to the Keynesians) *two* links in the cause-effect chain between money supply changes and changes in investment. Changes in the money supply must change the interest rate, and changes in the interest rate must affect net investment. *Even if interest rates were to fall due to money supply increases,* net investment must be sensitive to these interest-rate reductions if net national product is to be affected. During periods of recession, this is not apt to occur because profit expectations are low at such times. In other words, just when interest-rate decreases are needed the most, they are not very effective in increasing investment spending.

In summary, effective monetary policy requires that increases in the money supply lead to significant decreases in the interest rate and that lower interest rates lead to significant increases in net investment.

Symbolically, money policy requires that $\Delta M \rightarrow \Delta i \rightarrow \Delta I_n \rightarrow \Delta AD$. However, neither the $\Delta M_s \rightarrow \Delta i$ link nor the $\Delta i \rightarrow \Delta I_n$ link is significant during periods of recession. It follows that the link between ΔM and changes in aggregate demand is very weak, and therefore monetary policy is ineffective during a recession.

Keynesians do feel, however, that a recession can be eliminated by fiscal policy. This is shown in Figure 24-2. Increases in government expenditures shift the *IS* curve to *IS'* and then to *IS"*; national income increases from Y_e to

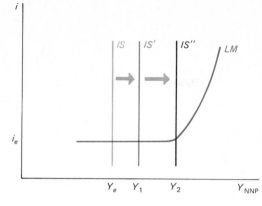

FIGURE 24-2   Increases in government expenditures shift the *IS* curve to *IS′* and *IS″* and real net national product increases from Y_e to Y_1 to Y_2. As long as the economy is in the liquidity trap, increases in government expenditures lead to full multiplier increases in *Y*—because the interest rate does not rise and no crowding out of investment occurs.

Y_1 to Y_2. Because the economy is in the liquidity trap, an increase in *G* leaves the interest rate unchanged; a full government-expenditure multiplier is possible because no crowding out occurs. Thus, the Keynesian solution to the Great Depression was expansionary fiscal policy; this belief is the origin of the monetarist-fiscalist debate that eventually evolved into the monetarist-Keynesian debate.

MONETARISTS ON MONETARY AND FISCAL POLICY

Monetarists, on the other hand, doubt that fiscal policy is very effective. They maintain that changes in government expenditures and/or taxes lead to multiplier effects, other things constant, *but that other things* (such as the interest rate) *are not likely to remain constant.* In order to assess the effects of pure fiscal policy, the money supply must be held constant. Otherwise the effects of money-supply changes may be incorrectly attributed to fiscal policy. If government expenditures rise, while taxes and the money supply remain constant, the increased federal borrowing will cause interest rates to rise and some private investment will be crowded out. This is indicated in Figure 24-3.

Note in Figure 24-3 that an increase in government spending financed by borrowing from the public shifts *IS* to *IS′*. Real net national product rises, but only to Y_1, not Y_m, because at Y_m desired L_1 balances rise; this shortage of liquidity drives up the rate of interest from i_e to i_1. Some private net business investment and household consumption is crowded out by the higher interest rate.

Indeed, Figure 24-3 even indicates that it is possible for an increase in *G*, financed by borrowing from the public, to cause a reduction in investment (and consumption) exactly equal to the increase in *G*. A shift from *IS″* to *IS‴* leaves real national product at Y_p, as a rise in the real rate of interest from i_2 to i_3 crowds out private expenditures by an amount equal to the increase in

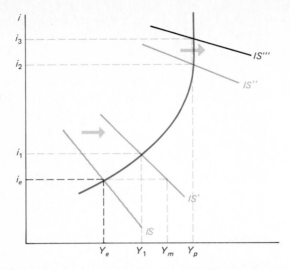

FIGURE 24-3 An increase in government expenditures financed by borrowing from the public shifts *IS* to *IS'*, but real net national product rises only to Y_1 (not Y_m) because a higher level of net national product increases the amount of desired *M* 1 balances, which increases the interest rate from i_e to i_1; thus, *some* private net investment (or consumer spending) is crowded out. Consider the increase in *G* financed by borrowing which shifts *IS''* to *IS'''*. The interest rate rises from i_2 to i_3 and the increase in *G* is *totally* offset by a decrease in I_n (and *C*). Net national product remains at Y_p. Recall that in the vertical range of the *LM* curve, L_2 balances are zero, and money becomes a bottleneck to further expansion. In that range, all of the money supply is used for L_1 balances.

G.[1] This occurs because, in the vertical range of the *LM* curve, all L_2 balances have been coaxed out by the higher interest rates; all money is used for L_1 balances and the lack of money is a bottleneck to further income expansion.

Monetarists point out that the only time a crowding-out effect doesn't occur is in the liquidity trap (the existence of which they deny). For that reason, and because Keynesians assume that the price level doesn't usually rise when AD rises because of much excess capacity for businesses, Keynesian analysis is sometimes referred to as "depression economics."

In their classic work on the monetary history of the United States, Milton Friedman and Anna Jacobson Schwartz concluded that:

Throughout the near century examined in detail we have found that:

1 Changes in the behavior of the money stock have been closely associated with changes in economic activity, money income, and prices.

---

[1]The classical economists also maintained that complete crowding out would occur. If full employment exists, the government sector can expand only at the expense of an equal contraction in the private sector. The crowding-out concept is yet another example of a classical root to the monetarist position.

2 The interrelation between monetary and economic change has been highly stable.

3 Monetary changes have often had an independent origin; they have not been simply a reflection of changes in economic activity.[2]

Monetarists further maintain that changes in nominal national income, employment, and the price level are more closely related to changes in the money supply than to changes in government expenditures or taxes. However, the *time lag* between the onset of money-supply changes and their effects on economic variables is so unpredictable, and political pressures on the Fed so great, that discretionary (deliberate) monetary policy has a *destabilizing* rather than a stabilizing effect on the economy. The monetarists would prefer that the Fed simply follow such a rule as "Increase the money supply at a rate of 3 percent per annum." Because Q, in the equation $MV = PQ$, has increased secularly (but not regularly) at slightly more than 3 percent per annum over the past 100 years, and because V has increased rather slightly over time, a constant money supply would cause the price level to fall (or unemployment to rise, if prices and wages are sticky downward). A 3 percent annual increase in the money supply, therefore, will cause the price level to rise ever so slightly. Monetarists maintain that the specific rate of money increase is not important; what is important is that the Fed follow such a rule and that everyone be aware of the rule.

THE REAL ISSUE IN THE DEBATE

The main issue is not that monetarists prefer monetary policy and Keynesians prefer fiscal policy. The key difference is that Keynesians are in favor of governmental intervention in the economy in order to stabilize it, and monetarists are not. Keynesians believe that fiscal policy is a superior stabilizing tool, but they are prepared to use monetary policy (or anything else) if it works. Monetarists insist that fiscal policy is not very effective in its ability to affect macroeconomic variables. While monetarists present evidence to indicate that monetary policy can affect macroeconomic variables, especially in the short run, their position is that attempts at "fine-tuning" an economy through monetary policy are, for various reasons, destabilizing. *Monetarists, therefore, prefer a* **monetary rule** *to discretionary monetary policy, and they conclude that governmental expenditures and taxes should be changed only to alter the quantity of social goods and services provided by government.* Thus, monetary and fiscal "rules" are the monetarist analogue to the classical prescription of "do nothing."

---

[2]M. Friedman and A. J. Schwartz, *A Monetary History of the U.S.: 1861–1960* (Princeton: Princeton University Press, 1963), p. 676.

THE MONETARIST POSITION

It is now time to be more specific. In this section the logic underlying the monetarist "follow rules" position is presented in greater detail. In the next section the Keynesian counterarguments are presented. Then each position is summarized, and two important points of agreement are noted.[3]

Private Spending Is Relatively Stable, Government Spending Is Not Consumers base their spending on their **permanent income** and not on their current measured income.[4] Permanent income is more closely related to wealth—which includes "nonhuman" wealth in the form of stocks, bonds, real estate, and so on, and human wealth (the present value of a person's lifetime earnings)—than to *current* income. Permanent income indicates an individual's or community's "normal," or usual, income or economic status. Household consumption expenditures (the largest component of private spending, which includes business spending on capital goods), therefore, are based on long-run expectations of future income, and these expectations change very slowly. To the monetarist, it follows that *private expenditure is relatively stable;* at a minimum, it is believed to be more stable than *government expenditure.* Again, monetarists point out that government plays not a stabilizing, but rather a destabilizing role in the economy.

Price-Wage Flexibility To the monetarist, prices are sufficiently flexible upward or downward so that shocks to the economic system (which itself is assumed inherently stable) lead to relative price-wage changes; these changes restore equilibrium to the natural rate of unemployment in the long run. Even if private spending were not stable, this price-wage flexibility would eventually direct the economy back to the natural rate of unemployment. From the natural rate of unemployment, it is a mere half-step to define the natural rate of output as that output rate consistent with the natural rate of unemployment and with the nation's changes in population and productivity. Short-run deviations from the long-run trend of the natural rates of unemployment and the natural rate of output provide the basis for defining recessions and expansionary periods.

Note that price-wage flexibility refers to relative, and not absolute, price changes. It follows that price-wage flexibility can exist during periods of inflation as long as prices and wages change (correctly) at different rates. Unemployment can be reduced in the airline industry, for example, even if wages

---

[3]Much of this discussion can be found in R. J. Gordon, *Macroeconomics,* 2nd ed. (Boston: Little, Brown, 1981), chap. 12.

[4]See Milton Friedman, *A Theory of the Consumption Function* (Princeton: Princeton University Press, 1957).

there are rising—provided that airline wages are rising less rapidly than the price level.[5]

Monetary and Fiscal Policies Are Destabilizing   Even if private spending is unstable and if prices are insufficiently flexible, it is unlikely that monetary and fiscal policies can help to reduce an economy's upswings and downswings. An inherently unstable economy is not fine-tuned easily. There are also theoretical reasons to suspect that monetary and fiscal policies simply make the problems of the private economy worse. Indeed, even Keynesians are not proud of the record of monetary and fiscal policies to date.

Why is fine-tuning so difficult? Changes in policy do not take effect until after an uncertain period of time. Sometimes the period between problem recognition and policy prescription is so long that a new and opposite problem appears. The effects of policy would then be to steer the economy in the wrong direction. The sorry state of forecasting doesn't help. Forecasting models are inadequate at best and it is difficult for economists to convey this message to model users. Political pressures often run counter to economic wisdom; even if economists knew enough to fine-tune an economy (which they don't), fine-tuning may not be politically feasible.

The Long Run   Monetarists insist that even if price-wage flexibility doesn't exist in the short run, it certainly does in the long run. Given adequate time, the economy will generate sufficient relative price changes to move to the natural rate of unemployment; price and wage flexibility increases with time. By pursuing the policy of doing nothing but following rules, the Fed and Congress can remove *the government* as a source of instability, and equilibrium can be restored more quickly.

THE KEYNESIAN POSITION

Private and Government Spending Instability   Keynesians can muster evidence to show that private spending—household spending on consumer durables and business spending on capital goods—is highly unstable. Admittedly, government spending adds to this instability, but government spending is volatile (although it usually rises) because of changing social problems—and not because of discretionary stabilization policy. Governmental instability in spending, however, provides one more reason for monetary and fiscal policies to counteract such instability.

---

[5]If *absolute* prices and wages are sticky downward, inflation can provide the economy with the price flexibility required to restore the economy to its natural unemployment rate. All that is necessary is that some prices and wages rise less rapidly than others. Have we finally found something good to say about inflation?

Price-Wage Flexibility The fact that prices and wages are inflexible downward is central to Keynes's argument, and modern Keynesians believe they can cite empirical evidence to support this argument. To them, price and wage flexibility was not sufficient to reduce unemployment during the Great Depression; extremely high unemployment rates existed for years. In more recent times high unemployment, far from inducing price-wage reductions, has been consistent with inflation.[6]

Monetary and Fiscal Policies as Destabilizing Elements While they are prepared to admit that previous monetary and fiscal policies have not always been helpful, Keynesians maintain that they can learn from the mistakes of those policies. In addition, the necessary fiscal changes suggested by Keynesians have, on occasion, been rejected by politicians. Besides, following fixed rules, when the need for discretionary fiscal policy and monetary policy is *obvious,* would merely commit the economy to longer periods of recession or inflation. How long would it have taken the U.S. economy to climb out of the Great Depression if a monetary rule had been in effect?

The Long Run Granted that the long-run relative price changes resulting from shocks are greater than in the short run, and that the economy will eventually be restored to natural rates of unemployment and output, what is one to do in the meantime? Shall the plights of those suffering from unemployment and/or inflation be ignored? The monetarist rejoinder would probably be that the ill effects of unemployment and inflation are overstated.

Agreement Perhaps surprisingly, monetarists and Keynesians agree on two important issues: (1) In the long run inflation is a monetary phenomenon and (2) in the long run, price-wage adjustments will be sufficient to restore the economy to the natural rate of unemployment and output. However, to the monetarists' constant insistence that in the long run their models work, Keynesians resort to the reply that their teacher gave to the classical economists under somewhat similar circumstances: "In the long run we are all dead."

SOME THEORETICAL ISSUES

To distinguish further between the monetarist and the Keynesian positions, it might be helpful to consider three specific issues. This section discusses how the two opposing groups view

1   What the public does with excess money balances
2   What happens to the interest rate when the money supply changes

---

[6]A monetarist rejoinder would note that only relative, not absolute, price flexibility is required. Today's unemployment rates reflect a good deal of *voluntary* unemployment because our economy provides incentives to people not to work *and* instead to claim that they are engaged in a job search so that they can continue to receive unemployment and other benefits.

3 What happens to national income if deficit spending is financed by Treasury borrowing from the public

Excess Money Balances Presumably at any given moment, the public can be holding more or less money than it wishes to hold. This can come about from money-supply changes by the Fed, from changes in the velocity of money, or from changes in the determinants of the quantity of money demanded, or from all three. The following discussion describes what the public does with excess balances, but complementary reasoning can be used for the insufficient-balances case as well.

According to the Keynesians, excess balances will initially lead to increased purchases of such *financial* assets as stocks and bonds. These increased purchases will increase the prices of such assets and lower their yields (the rate of interest). In turn, lower interest rates increase the quantity of L_2 demanded. This process continues until the money stock and the quantity of money demanded are equal. To the extent that interest rates fall and to the extent that net investment is responsive to lower interest rates, excess money balances can affect AD (aggregate demand) and thereby increase net national product and the demand for L_1 balances.

Monetarists, however, insist that it is also possible that households initially will spend their excess balances directly on *real* assets—autos, videotape recorders, and so on, and that businesses will spend their excess balances on capital goods. This will increase national income, which in turn increases the quantity of money demanded for L_1. This process continues until the money stock equals the quantity of money demanded.

Monetarists suggest that the demand for money is primarily a function of national income, while Keynesians believe that the demand for money is a function of both national income and the rate of interest.

Money-Supply Changes and the Interest Rate Keynesians are quite clear as to what happens when the money supply changes: The interest rate varies inversely with money-supply changes. Consider Figure 24-4. In panel (*a*), the Keynesian position is demonstrated. An increase in the money supply leads to a reduction in the interest rate until the money stock equals the quantity of money demanded. In panel (*b*) the monetarist position is presented. An increase in the money supply from M to M' leads to an eventual increase in the *demand* for money. As the additional money is spent for goods and services, national income rises and a higher national income level causes an increase in the demand for transactions and precautionary balances, L_1. The nominal interest rate will, *in the long run,* rise back to its previous level (i_e)—or maybe even higher; an elaboration on this point is found in the Current Controversy section at the end of this chapter.

Borrowing to Finance Deficits Keynesians maintain that the net effect of an increase in government spending, financed by borrowing from the public, causes an expansion in national income and employment. Increased government borrowing (other things constant) will increase the interest rate, which in turn will

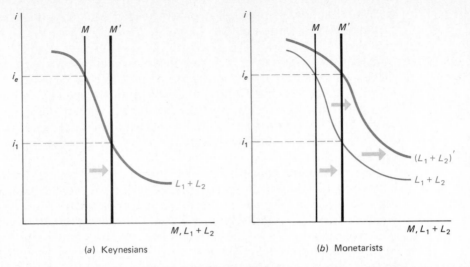

(a) Keynesians   (b) Monetarists

FIGURE 24-4   **Money-Supply Changes and the Interest Rate.**   Panel (a) shows the Keynesian position. An increase in the money supply provides additional liquidity and the interest rate falls. Panel (b) graphs the monetarist position. Here an increase in the money supply from M to M' eventually causes the total demand for money to rise also, from $(L_1 + L_2)$ to $(L_1 + L_2)'$ because nominal income increases. Eventually, therefore, the interest rate rises to its former level, i_e.

reduce the quantity of money demanded for speculative purposes and permit increased spending. In terms of the equation of exchange, a higher interest rate increases the velocity of money, causing net national product to be higher with the same stock of money.

Monetarists argue that higher interest rates crowd out private investment and consumption, and that the net effect of government spending financed by borrowing will be slight. All things considered, the monetarists believe that the case for deficit spending as an expansionary tool is not a theoretically sound one. The following Highlight considers the government expenditure multiplier from a monetarist point of view. Table 24-1 compares the Keynesian and the monetarist positions.

HIGHLIGHT   The Government Expenditure Multiplier

Answer quickly now: If the MPC = $\frac{3}{4}$ and government expenditures rise by $100, by how much will national income rise? As a principles of economics student, you would have answered $400. As a

student of this more advanced course in money and banking, you may not be so sure anymore.

In the first place, you need to know how the increased expenditures are financed. If

they are financed by borrowing from the public, the real rate of interest will rise (outside the liquidity trap) and crowd out some investment and consumption. Private consumption and investment,

TABLE 24-1 Keynesians and Monetarists Compared

Extreme Keynesians	Modern Keynesians	Modern Monetarists	Extreme Monetarists
The money supply doesn't matter: A change in the money supply will not change nominal GNP. An increase, for example, will just mean that individuals will hold more idle cash balances.	The money supply matters somewhat: It is important, but institutional forces can weaken its potency.	Money matters a lot: It is the most powerful determinant of the level of nominal income.	Only money matters.
Interest rates are important, but the money supply isn't. Interest rates affect planned investment and, hence, equilibrium and national output.	Interest rates, along with the money supply, must be watched. The money supply, however, may be affected by changes in AD instead of being a cause of AD changes.	The money supply, not interest rates, should be watched closely; a change in the money-supply changes AD directly, and not only via interest rates.	Watch the money supply closely.
Monetary policy is seldom appropriate.	Monetary policy should not be depended upon. You can't push on a string (make banks lend their excess reserves or make consumers spend additional cash balances); and some sectors are too insensitive to monetary policy to bother with it.	Stabilization should be attempted by stabilizing the growth of the money supply. The Fed should not, however, try to stabilize interest rates.	Use a monetary policy rule for stabilization.
Fiscal policy is a powerful tool, compared to impotent monetary policy.	Stabilize with fiscal policy, for it is a potent stabilizer of AD. The multiplier effect outweighs the "crowding-out" effect.	Fiscal policy is not very effective. The "crowding-out" effect is operating.	Forget about fiscal policy, for it has no effect on nominal aggregate demand. The "crowding-out" effect is 100 percent.

however, *might* rise because the quantity of money demanded falls (velocity rises) as interest rates rise, leaving the public with excess cash balances. The *net* effect is theoretically indeterminate and probably quite small in practice.

Moreover, it is important to ask: On what will the federal expenditures be made? If they are spent on goods or services that would otherwise have been provided by the private sector, increased competition from the public sector will cause the private sector to contract. A federally run post office means reduced private investment in mail-carrier services; more federal parks mean fewer private parks. Do increased government transfers to help the needy mean decreased private and church

contributions? If so, the *net* impact of government activity in these areas may also be negligible.

Consider the permanent-income hypothesis. If government-expenditure (or tax) changes are perceived as being temporary, then people will not spend so much out of their (perceived) temporary income increases. People base their spending decisions on their permanent incomes and not on their temporarily changed incomes. If government-expenditure changes or tax changes are announced as temporary, income recipients will not adjust their expenditures by much, and the multiplier effect will be lessened.

Finally, automatic stabilizers must be considered. Some of

the potential increases in national income resulting from private respending of the government spending will be lessened, as some people move into higher marginal tax brackets and others receive fewer transfers in welfare payments and unemployment compensation. Again, the *net* effect of a change in government spending might be quite small.

Considering all this, is it any wonder that two Keynesians who set out to measure the government-expenditure multiplier concluded that the short-run (one-year) multiplier was only slightly higher than the number 1?* Or that different econometric models assume widely different "multiplier" effects in their predictions?

*L. R. Klein and A. S. Goldberger, *An Econometric Model of the United States, 1929–1952* (Amsterdam: North Holland, 1955). Also see T. M. Brown, "Habit Persistence and Lags in Consumer Behavior," *Econometrica,* July 1952, pp. 355–371.

CURRENT CONTROVERSY

The Great Depression from the Monetarist and Keynesian Points of View

Interestingly enough, both the Keynesians and the monetarists cite the Great Depression as evidence to support their theories. The monetarist view of what happened during the Great Depression is indicated in Figure 1. The money supply has fallen from *LM* to *LM'*. This indicates that the Fed failed to do its job of providing liquidity. Between 1929 and 1933, the Fed allowed over 5,000 banks to go under, thereby causing the money supply to fall by one-third—the greatest contraction of

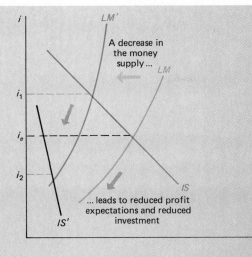

FIGURE 1   **A Monetarist View of the Great Depression.**   First, the money supply fell from LM to LM'; the Fed allowed banks to go under and the money supply fell by about one-third between 1929 and 1933. This caused temporarily high interest rates at i_1. The long-run result of this reduction in the money supply was a leftward shift of the IS curve when the investment curve (MEI) shifted leftward due to a reduction in profit expectations. Interest rates fell below the original rate (i_e) to i_2. Notice that no liquidity trap portion is drawn on the LM curves; the monetarists deny its existence.

the money supply in U.S. history.* Such an event created panic and caused profit expectations to plummet: The net investment curve (MEI) shifted leftward, which in turn shifted the IS curve leftward. That is, the decrease in the money supply from LM to LM' eventually led IS to shift leftward to IS' as a banking panic depressed profit expectations. Nominal interest rates were very low; this reflects the reduced demand for money for transactions and precautionary motives due to the lower level of national income. According to Milton Friedman,† the Fed believed that because interest rates were low, it must have done its job of providing liquidity; *real* interest rates may have been relatively high, however, due to price expectations resulting from a falling price level. (Remember that the real interest rate equals the sum of the normal interest rate and the expected change in the price level.)

Friedman believes that the Fed is still making the same mistake: It looks at interest rates instead of at what is happening to the money supply. Thus, if interest rates are high today, this should be interpreted to mean that monetary policy was expansionary six months to one year ago—and not that money is currently "tight." If the Fed reacts to high current interest rates by increasing the money supply to provide more liquidity, it will cause future interest rates to be even higher. After all, the interest rate is just one price among many, and it, too, will rise in times of inflation. Interest rates rise as lenders add an inflationary premium to them.

Figure 2 presents the Keynesian version of the Great Depression. The IS curve shifted leftward because the MEI curve decreased to nearly zero during the Great Depression. Between 1929 and 1933, private investment fell by nearly 85 percent.

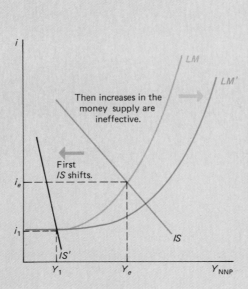

FIGURE 2 **A Keynesian View of the Great Depression.** First, the IS curve shifted from *IS* to *IS'* as a result of a leftward movement of the MEI curve. This caused the interest rate and the level of national income to fall dramatically. The ineffectiveness of monetary policy is then depicted. Since interest rates were already low, the increased money supply from *LM* to *LM'* is held in L_2 balances, because of the high capital loss risk of bond ownership. The banking parallel to this is that banks were prepared to hold excess balances: Bonds were subject to capital losses and loans were subject to a high default risk.

Notice that no classical range exists on the *LM* curve. Keynesians can't imagine a real-world situation in which the demand for money is unresponsive to interset rate changes.

Figure 2 also indicates that increases in the money supply would not have been very helpful because the economy was mired in the liquidity trap. Therefore, increases in the money supply were merely held by the public which feared capital gains losses from risky bonds. At the same time, banks held excess reserves in order to avoid (a) capital losses on bonds and (b) default losses on loans. Increases in the money supply, therefore, shift the *LM* to *LM'*, but the interest rate remains constant at a low level (i_1) and the level of national income remains constant at Y_1.

---

*M. Friedman and A. J. Schwartz, *A Monetary History of the United States* (Princeton: Princeton University Press, 1963), p. 299.

†The monetarist-Keynesian debate also generated some humor. One story is told and retold among economists. In the late 1960s an MIT economist, Robert Solow, noted that "Another difference between Milton Friedman and myself is that everything reminds Milton of the money supply; well everything reminds me of sex, but I try to keep it out of my publications."

CHAPTER SUMMARY

1 A monetarist is a modern non-Keynesian economist with classical roots who believes that (a) changes in the money supply are the predominant influence on the level of aggregate nominal income; (b) the private sector is relatively stable, and disequilibrium-creating shocks to the economy lead to relative price changes that restore the economy to the natural rate of unemployment in the long run; (c) monetary and fiscal policy are inherently destabilizing because of lack of knowledge concerning the precise interrelationships in the macroeconomy and because

of timing problems (lags); (d) changes in the money supply are inversely related to interest-rate changes in the short run but directly related to nominal interest-rate changes in the long run; and (e) excess money balances are spent both on goods and services and on financial assets.

2 Monetarists maintain that in the long run money is neutral: Changes in the money supply alter absolute, not relative, prices. On the other hand, monetarists, unlike many of their classical predecessors, do believe that changes in the money supply can alter relative prices (and therefore real variables) in the short run; unemployment can depart from its natural rate in the short run.

3 Keynesians believe that monetary policy is only one factor among several that determines the level of nominal national income in the short run. Moreover, changes in the money supply lead to opposite changes in velocity, and thereby limit the effectiveness of monetary policy. Moreover, during a recession net investment is unresponsive to interest-rate changes; this is another reason for doubting the effectiveness of monetary policy. Keynesians prefer fiscal policy, which bypasses the effects of the interest rate; fiscal policy affects AD directly through changes in government expenditures and indirectly through changes in taxes which cause changes in the consumption (or investment) function.

4 Monetarists doubt that fiscal policy is effective if the money supply is held constant. If government expenditures are financed by borrowing from the public, interest rates will rise and some private investment and consumption expenditures will be crowded out. In fact, in the vertical portion of the *LM* curve, increases in government expenditures are *completely* offset by reductions in investment and consumption; the government-expenditure multiplier is zero in that special case.

5 Monetarists have produced empirical evidence to indicate that changes in nominal national income, employment, and the price level are more closely related to changes in the money stock than to changes in government expenditures or taxes. However, they believe that time-lag problems and political pressures make discretionary monetary policy *destabilizing*. As a consequence, they prefer a monetary rule that reflects an economy's natural growth rate of output—resulting from increases in population and productivity.

6 The monetarist argues that private spending is more stable than government expenditures. Moreover, monetarists maintain that prices and wages are sufficiently flexible so that shocks to the economic system lead to relative price-wage changes that restore the economy to the natural rate of unemployment.

7 Keynesians muster evidence to show that household spending on consumer durables and business spending on capital goods are highly unstable. Moreover, they say, if government spending is unstable, that just provides one more good reason to rely on monetary and fiscal policies. Furthermore, prices and wages are sticky downward, as depressions and recessions plainly indicate. To the monetarists' complaint that monetary and fiscal policies have been destabilizing in the past, Keynesians reply that they can learn from past mistakes. Following fixed rules in the face of an obvious need for monetary and fiscal policies commits the economy to longer periods of recession and inflation. Keynesians are concerned with the harmful effects of inflation and unemployment during the short run.

8 Monetarists and Keynesians are in agreement on two major points: (a) in the long run inflation is a monetary phenomenon, and (b) in the long run price-wage elasticities will be sufficient to restore the economy to the natural rate of unemployment and output.

9   To Keynesians excess balances lead primarily to increased purchases of financial assets, and this decreases interest rates and induces speculators to increase their L_2 balances; this process continues until the money stock and the quantity of money demanded are equated. Monetarists accept this argument, but they point out that excess balances can also be spent by households on consumer goods and by businesses on capital goods. In turn, these expenditures on nonfinancial assets cause national income to rise and L_1 balances to increase. This process continues until the money stock equals the quantity of money demanded.

10 Keynesians maintain that an increase in the money supply reduces interest rates. Monetarists, in the main, accept this as a short-run analysis. In the long run, however, an increase in the money supply causes inflation and *higher* nominal interest rates (which reflect an inflationary premium).

11 Monetarists maintain that government borrowing to finance deficits generates a crowding-out effect, so that the net impact on net national product is slight. Keynesians suggest that the net impact is positive because a higher interest rate (caused by a high level of net national product that leads to an increase in the demand for L_1 balances) releases L_2 balances that can be used to finance transactions.

GLOSSARY

Monetarists: Modern non-Keynesian economists with classical roots who believe that changes in the money supply are the predominant influence on the level of aggregate nominal income.

Monetary rule: A direction to the Fed indicating that the Fed should pursue a fixed monetary growth rate instead of using its discretion.

Natural rate of unemployment: The rate to which unemployment returns after relative prices have adjusted properly.

Permanent income: Income that reflects an individual's or a community's normal income, or economic status; permanent income reflects wealth (both human and "nonhuman").

PROBLEMS

24-1 List the points of agreement and disagreement between the monetarists and the Keynesians.

24-2 Use the *IS-LM* framework to analyze the Great Depression according to the Keynesians.

SELECTED REFERENCES

Anderson, L. C., and J. L. Jordan, "Monetary and Fiscal Actions: A Test of their Relative Importance in Economic Stabilization," *Review,* Federal Reserve Bank of St. Louis, November 1968.

Ando, A., and F. Modigliani, "Impacts of Fiscal Actions on Aggregate Income and the Monetarist Controversy: Theory and Evidence," in J. L. Stein (ed.), *Monetarism* (New York: American Elsevier, 1976).

Brunner, K., and A. H. Meltzer, "Mr. Hicks and the 'Monetarists,'" *Economica,* vol. 40, February 1973, pp. 44–59.

De Prano, M., and T. Mayer, "Tests of the Relative Importance of Autonomous Expenditures and Money," *American Economics Review,* vol. 55, September 1965, pp. 791–792.

Friedman, M., and Schwartz, A. J., *A Monetary History of the United States, 1867–1960* (Princeton, N.J.: Princeton University Press, 1963).

Friedman, Milton, "Comments on the Critics," *Journal of Political Economy,* vol. 80, September–October 1972, pp. 906–950.

Modigliani, Franco, "The Monetarist Controversy or Should We Forsake Stabilization Policies?" *American Economic Review,* vol. 67, March 1977, pp. 1–19.

Simons, Henry C., "Rules versus Authorities in Monetary Policy," *Journal of Political Economy,* vol. 44, February 1936, pp. 1–30.

Tobin, James, "The Monetary Interpretation of History," *American Economic Review,* vol. 55, June 1965, pp. 464–485.

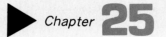

Inflation and Unemployment

In Chapter 20, we developed the *IS-LM* framework in real terms; the equilibrium real interest rate and the equilibrium real level of national income are derived simultaneously through the interaction of the product and the money markets. Because the price level is assumed constant, changes in nominal and real values are equivalent. For that reason a gap existed in Keynes's explanation of the economy: How are the level of net national product and the price level related? In order to fill that gap, Chapter 21 (Inflation) presented a new aggregate supply and aggregate demand model.

Aggregate demand was reformulated as a relationship between different quantities of national output demanded at various price levels, other things constant; aggregate supply was reformulated as a relationship between the nation's aggregate output of final goods and services and various price levels, other things constant. The interaction of aggregate supply and aggregate demand simultaneously determined the equilibrium output level and the equilibrium price level, and a missing link in the Keynesian model was supplied.

A gap in the Keynesian model existed *also* for the relationship between the price level and the employment (or unemployment) level. Because a functional relationship exists in the short run between employment levels and national output levels (nonlabor inputs assumed constant), it follows that the reformulated aggregate supply–aggregate demand approach can eliminate *this* missing link as well. The first section of this chapter does precisely that: It shows how a negatively sloped **Phillips curve** (a relationship between the rate of inflation and the unemployment rate) is implicit in the reformulated aggregate supply–aggregate demand model presented in Chapter 21.

The Phillips curve is important not only because it helps to fill a theoretical gap in the Keynesian model; it is also crucial for stabilization policy. If a stable trade-off between the rate of inflation and the national unemployment rate can be found, then policymakers can be aided immensely. That is, they can select a policy to create the "optimal" combination of inflation-unemployment on the Phillips curve.

As the second section in this chapter indicates, however, the short-run Phillips curve is unstable. Empirical evidence indicates that a Phillips curve trade-off between inflation and unemployment rates exists only in the short run; in the long run, the unemployment rate is independent of the rate of inflation. In the long run the Phillips curve is vertical and its position is determined by the natural rate of unemployment. The difference between the short-run and long-run Phillips curves is resolved by introducing the concept of inflationary expectations; changes in inflationary expectations shift the Phillips curve. Moreover, these shifts do not occur independently of stabilization policy; the Phillips curve shifts as a *direct result* of monetary policy and fiscal policy attempts to move the economy along a given Phillips curve. This section concludes that stabilization policy can work only to the extent that buyers and sellers of labor can be fooled into underestimating the future rate of inflation.

The third section in this chapter expands on the role that expectations play in macroeconomics. It introduces the **rational-expectations hypothesis (REH),** which in this context maintains that stabilization policy can have no systematic effect on the community's expectational errors concerning the inflation rate. Because errors in inflationary expectations are necessary for an effective stabilization policy, it follows that if stabilization policy cannot systematically affect expectational errors for the inflation rate, then stabilization policy cannot *systematically* alter real variables such as employment and output, *even in the short run.*

Finally, because the REH offers such a pessimistic conclusion for the role of stabilization policy, the chapter ends with a Current Controversy on supply-side economics. If stabilization policy cannot solve the problem of **stagflation** (the simultaneous existence of high inflation rates and high employment), perhaps supply-side economics can.

THE PHILLIPS CURVE

The relationship between inflation rates and unemployment rates is referred to today as the "Phillips curve," after A. W. Phillips, whose 1958 article made it clear that the rate of change in money wages was related to the *level* of unemployment.[1] In periods of low unemployment, labor scarcity drives money wages upward, and in times of high unemployment, labor surplus drives money wages downward (or slows down their rates of increase). Phillips indicated that data from the years 1948 to 1957 matched rather closely data from the years 1861 to 1913. He fitted a curve based on 1861 to 1913 data to observations in the 1948 to 1957 period and found that the old curve fit the new data amazingly well. Other economists have cited this as evidence of a stable relationship between money wage-rate changes and the unemployment rate.

The Phillips curve notion changed after 1958. Price-level changes were first linked to money wage rate changes, and the Phillips curve then became the inverse relationship between the rate of inflation and the rate of unemployment. Economists also interpreted the Phillips curve as a trade-off between inflation and unemployment; they observed that a stable relationship would allow policymakers to "choose" a given rate of unemployment (or inflation) and bear the cost of a necessary rate of inflation (or unemployment). In other words, a little *less* inflation had to be purchased at the price of a little *more* unemployment; or, alternatively stated, relatively low unemployment rates would generate relatively high inflation rates.

Figure 25-1 shows a theoretical Phillips curve. Point *A* shows that if policymakers in this hypothetical economy desire only a 4 percent rate of unemployment, they must accept a 12 percent rate of inflation. On the other hand, if policymakers desire a low rate of inflation, such as 2 percent, they must accept a relatively high unemployment rate—10 percent. A curve such as this would help policymakers decide what the "optimal" point on the Phillips curve should be. A nation such as Germany, which has had experience with hyper-

---

[1]A. W. Phillips, "The Relationship between Unemployment and the Rate of Change in Money Wage Rates in the United Kingdom, 1861–1957," *Economica,* New Series 75, November 1958, pp. 283–299.

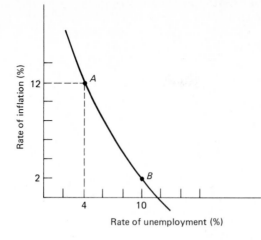

FIGURE 25-1 This theoretical Phillips curve indicates that if society desires a 4 percent rate of unemployment, it must accept a 12 percent rate of inflation. Or, if it desires a 2 percent rate of inflation, it must "pay" for this low rate by suffering a 10 percent rate of unemployment.

inflation, might place a high value on price stability and find that its optimal point is close to *B.* Other countries, such as the United States, might place a higher value on low unemployment (remembering the experience of the Great Depression) and find that *its* optimal point on the Phillips curve is closer to point *A.* Note, therefore, that the optimal inflation-unemployment point is ultimately subjective; it depends on the value judgments of policymakers. Nevertheless, while the usefulness of the Phillips curve is limited, a stable Phillips curve can help to set the framework for the debate among those who weigh the ill effects of inflation and unemployment differently.

Deriving the Phillips Curve from the Reformulated Aggregate Supply–Aggregate Demand Model   Chapter 21 indicated that the equilibrium output level and the equilibrium price level are determined simultaneously by the interaction of the reformulated aggregate demand and aggregate supply curves. Because a functional relationship exists between the level of national output and the level of national employment (assuming nonlabor inputs constant), it is possible to derive a relationship between the price level and the employment level, and from there to related *changes* in the price level (inflation) to the unemployment *rate* (if the full-employment level is known).

Consider Figure 25-2. Panel (*a*) indicates the Chapter 21 aggregate supply–aggregate demand reformulation. As aggregate demand increases from *D* to *D'* to *D''*, the economy moves from points *A* to *B* to *C*; both national output and the price level rise. The aggregate supply curve becomes steeper as the economy approaches the full-employment rate of output, Q_f. This is partially because, as the economy approaches full employment, wage scarcities occur which cause wage rates to rise. The aggregate supply curve also becomes steeper because [as panel (*b*) shows] increases in employment (*N*), other inputs constant, cause national output to increase at a slower rate—which reflects the law of diminishing returns. The graph in panel (*b*) was previously analyzed in Chapter 17. Note that in order to increase the level of national output from Q_e to Q_f, the rate of employment must rise from N_e to N_f. Thus,

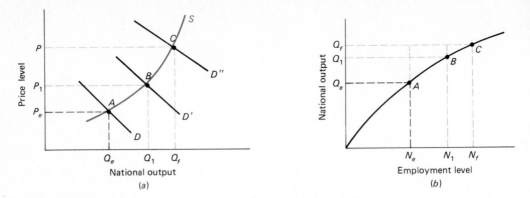

FIGURE 25-2   Panel (*a*) indicates that as aggregate demand increases from *D* to *D'* to *D''*, the output level and the price level both increase; the economy moves from points *A* to *B* to *C*. Panel (*b*) indicates that increases in national output require higher levels of employment. Because a functional relationship exists between national output levels and employment levels as in panel (*b*), a relationship between price levels and output levels, panel (*a*), can be converted into a relationship between price levels and employment levels (see Figure 25-3).

higher price levels are associated with higher levels of national income, and higher levels of national income are associated with higher levels of employment. It follows that higher price levels are associated with higher employment levels. This latter relationship is indicated in Figure 25-3, and it is drawn to be consistent with Figure 25-2.

FIGURE 25-3   Higher price levels are associated with higher output levels, which in turn require higher employment levels in the short run. A movement from point *A* to point *B* implies a rate of inflation of $(P_1 - P_e)/P_e$, and a reduction in the unemployment rate from $(N_f - N_e)/N_f$ to $(N_f - N_1)/N_f$. Thus, an increase in the price level, resulting from an increase in aggregate demand, leads to a lower rate of unemployment. Stated in another way, inflation and the unemployment rate are inversely related.

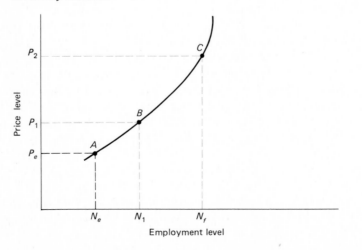

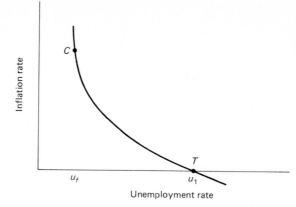

FIGURE 25-4 In the short run, higher rates of inflation are associated with lower unemployment rates. Here a zero rate of inflation is associated with U_1 unemployment, as point T indicates. Note that in the range of point C higher rates of inflation have little impact on the unemployment rate. As the economy moves toward full employment, the rate of inflation increases at a faster rate—the Phillips curve becomes steeper.

To this point, it has been indicated that a positive relationship exists between the price *level* and the employment level. The Phillips curve, however, relates *changes* in the price level (inflation) to the *unemployment rate* (the ratio of unemployment to full employment). Figure 25-3 must, therefore, be adjusted.

Consider the movement from point A to point B on the graph in Figure 25-3. The price level moves from P_e to P_1; therefore, the rate of inflation equals $(P_1 - P_e)/P_e$. Employment moves from N_e to N_1. Assuming that N_f represents full employment, a movement from point A to point B in Figure 25-3 means that the unemployment rate falls from $(N_f - N_e)/N_f$ to $(N_f - N_1)/N_f$. An even greater increase in the price level would lead to a lower rate of unemployment. It follows that higher rates of inflation lead to lower unemployment rates in the short run. Thus, the Phillips curve is derived; it is indicated in Figure 25-4. Note that at point T a zero rate of inflation is associated with a relatively high rate of unemployment. As the economy approaches full employment, or zero unemployment, at U_f (point C) the Phillips curve becomes very steep.[2] Higher rates of inflation are required to reduce unemployment rates by constant amounts.

A Caveat   Note that the Phillips curve shows an inverse relationship between the rate of inflation and the unemployment rate because of the shape of the aggregate supply curve. It is because the aggregate supply curve in Figure 25-2 is upward-sloping that the Phillips curve in Figure 25-4 is downward-sloping. Had the aggregate supply curve not embodied the price-wage downward inflexibility assumption of Chapter 21, the aggregate supply curve would have been vertical. This, of course, was the classical economists' position; because Say's law assured full employment, the national output level was always at or near its maximum. Increases in aggregate demand, therefore, cause only the price level to rise. It follows that for the classical economists aggregate supply is

---

[2]As we will soon show, employment *can* increase beyond N_f—and therefore national output can increase beyond Q_f—temporarily.

vertical—and so is the Phillips curve.[3] That is, no trade-off exists between inflation and unemployment in the short run.

STAGFLATION

Unfortunately for those who wished to base economic policy on the Phillips curve, the relationship between inflation and unemployment rates proved unstable; the Phillips curve varied widely across countries and wasn't even stable within a given country through time. The inflation rate that was originally thought to be consistent with a specific level of unemployment did not remain fixed. After World War II, in those countries that pursued full employment as part of their stabilization policies, unemployment remained relatively high while the inflation rate *increased*. The phenomenon of simultaneous high rates of inflation and high unemployment rates, known as stagflation, became a worldwide problem. In effect the Phillips curve shifted to the right, through

[3]We leave it to you to demonstrate how a redrawing of Figure 25-3 and Figure 25-4, taking into account perfect price-wage flexibility, leads to a vertical Phillips curve.

FIGURE 25-5

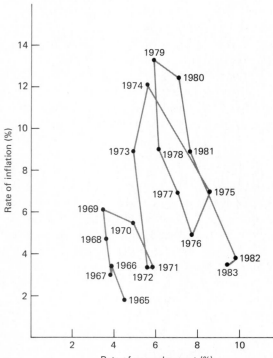

time. Table 25-1 indicates the percentage rate of unemployment and the annual rate of inflation in the United States for the years 1960 to 1983. Note that since 1967 *both* inflation and unemployment have increased (although not continuously). Figure 25-5 plots the data from Table 25-1. There is obviously no simple relationship between the rate of inflation and the rate of unemployment, and note that in some years *both* inflation and unemployment increased.

TABLE 25-1 Inflation and Unemployment in the United States

This table indicates the unemployment rate and the annual inflation rate (December-to-December percentage change in the Consumer Price Index) for the years 1960–1983.

Year	Percentage Rate of Unemployment	Annual Percentage Rate of Inflation
1960	5.4	1.5
1961	6.5	0.7
1962	5.4	1.2
1963	5.5	1.6
1964	5.0	1.2
1965	4.4	1.9
1966	3.7	3.4
1967	3.7	3.0
1968	3.5	4.7
1969	3.4	6.1
1970	4.8	5.5
1971	5.8	3.4
1972	5.5	3.4
1973	4.8	8.8
1974	5.5	12.2
1975	8.3	7.0
1976	7.6	4.8
1977	6.9	6.8
1978	6.0	9.0
1979	5.8	13.3
1980	7.0	12.4
1981	7.5	8.9
1982	9.5	3.9
1983	9.5	3.8

Source: Economic Report of the President, Washington, D.C.: Government Printing Office, 1984, pp. 201 and 225.

THE NATURAL RATE OF UNEMPLOYMENT

Chapter 20 examined the natural rate of *interest*. Keynes borrowed the concept of a natural rate from a neoclassical economist, Knut Wicksell, in order to derive his speculative demand for money function. Milton Friedman and E. S. Phelps have also borrowed the idea of a natural rate to develop the natural rate of unemployment.[4]

The **natural rate of unemployment** is an unemployment rate that consists of two parts: (1) frictional unemployment, and (2) unemployment due to rigidities in the economic system and to interferences with labor mobility or wage-rate changes. **Frictional unemployment** is that unemployment experienced by people who are between steady jobs. In general, they spend a short period of time between jobs when they quit or are laid off from one job and find another. The second component of the natural rate of unemployment results from such rigidities as:

1   Union activity that restricts supply or entrance into jobs
2   Licensing arrangements granted by regulatory agencies
3   Minimum wage laws or laws such as the Bacon-Davis Act that require all workers to be paid union wages on government contracts
4   A welfare system that reduces incentives to work

According to Friedman, stabilization policy can affect only frictional unemployment. Moreover, the effect on frictional unemployment is due only to the fact that workers can be tricked into reducing their average duration of frictional unemployment; workers are tricked into accepting jobs sooner than otherwise. The Phillips curve trade-off between inflation and unemployment is, therefore, due only to a change in the average duration of unemployment for those laborers between jobs. The trade-off results from unanticipated changes in the rate of growth of nominal aggregate demand. This matter is explained in greater detail in the section below.

The Friedman-Phelps Phillips Curve   According to the Friedman-Phelps analysis, nominal wage rate changes can offset the rate of unemployment only in the short run, because only in the short run do laborers and employers confuse nominal wages with real wages. Thus, Friedman and Phelps distinguish between the short-run and the long-run effects of unanticipated changes in nominal aggregate demand.

Consider an economy in which prices have been stable and in which an unanticipated increase in the rate of growth in the money supply causes nominal aggregate demand to rise at a rate that results in a constant rate of infla-

---

[4]Milton Friedman, "The Role of Monetary Policy," *American Economic Review,* vol 58, March 1968, pp. 1–17; and E. S. Phelps, "Money Wage Dynamics and Labor Market Equilibrium," *Journal of Political Economy,* vol. 76, 1968, pp. 678–711.

tion of 5 percent per annum. Individual employers experience a decrease in their inventories and an increase in the prices of the goods they sell. Each firm will interpret the situation (at least in part) as an increase in the demand for its own product. That is, initially each firm is aware only that its selling price has increased and is not aware that *general* inflation is occurring.

In short, each producer incorrectly interprets an increase in the nominal price of its product as an increase in the *relative* price of its product. Individual producers, therefore, are willing to pay slightly higher nominal wages because with their limited information the increase in nominal wages is perceived as a lower *real* wage; what matters to an individual producer is the wage rate relative to *his or her* product's selling price. As a consequence, each employer will attempt to obtain more labor and will voluntarily pay higher nominal wages.

On the other side of the market, frictionally unemployed laborers also have limited information. They are initially aware of only *their* most important price—the wage rate offered to them. As a consequence, laborers view higher nominal wages as higher real wages, because they too are not yet aware that the general price level has begun to rise. They will therefore respond to (perceived) higher real wages by increasing the amount of labor they are willing to offer. Those laborers who are frictionally unemployed will accept work sooner than they would have if the price level had remained stable. Interestingly enough, *unanticipated inflation has led employers to imagine a reduction in the real wage and laborers to imagine an increase in the real wage.* The short-run result will be an increase in both employment (because the average duration of unemployment falls) and the rate of inflation. It appears that inflation has "bought" a reduction in unemployment. However, the Friedman-Phelps analysis maintains that the increase in employment is only a temporary (or short-run) situation. Once employers and laborers realize that the price level (actually) is rising at 5 percent per annum, they will both build this expectation into *new* labor contracts, and the unemployment rate will return to its old level. Laborers who are frictionally unemployed will accept only those jobs that "look good" after taking into account the fact that prices and wages in general are rising at 5 percent per annum.

In the meantime, however, long-term labor contracts made prior to the unanticipated inflation have allowed employers to gain at the expense of laborers—unless these contracts contained a "cost of living clause."[5] The new wage contract will include a 5 percent inflation premium, which laborers demand and employers agree to, because all will now anticipate a 5 percent increase in the price level.

---

[5]The redistribution of income resulting from unanticipated inflation was discussed in Chapter 21. It was noted there that unanticipated inflation helps borrowers at the expense of lenders and aids those who are able to transform their cash holdings into real assets at the expense of those who hold money. Note that in these cases, too, once the inflation is correctly anticipated, these redistributional effects will disappear. Of course, laborers locked into long-term labor contracts might quit instead of waiting for the next contract, or go on a wildcat (unauthorized by the union) strike. If so, the initial trade-off would be reversed.

This analysis can be extended to another case in which the money supply is again unexpectedly increased and causes the level of nominal aggregate demand to rise at a rate that reflects in a 10 percent per annum inflation rate. Long-term wage (and other) contracts were made in the expectation of a 5 percent inflation rate, and again people will be fooled temporarily. Again laborers will increase their labor supplies, and a redistribution of income from laborers to employers will result. Once people fully anticipate the 10 percent annual increase in the price level, the new contracts will reflect this expectation, and the unemployment rate will return to its natural rate. The only way that a permanent or long-run trade-off between unemployment and inflation can exist is if the money supply is continually increased at faster rates—and always unexpectedly. This is an unlikely possibility.

Complementary reasoning indicates that unanticipated reductions in the rate of growth of the money supply lead to unemployment rates temporarily *higher* than the natural rate. It would appear that less inflation is being purchased at the expense of higher employment. But again the trade-off would last only until the new contract time, when everyone would now anticipate the lower inflation rate. Lower-than-anticipated inflation therefore leads to higher unemployment and some redistribution of income only in the short run.

Short-Run versus Long-Run Phillips Curves   By distinguishing between the short-run and the long-run effects of unanticipated inflation, the Friedman-Phelps model can account for (1) the existence of a short-run Phillips curve and (2) a shifting, or unstable, Phillips curve. To see this, consider Figure 25-6, which links the natural rate of unemployment and the measured rate of unemployment to the Phillips curve. The unemployment rate is plotted on the horizontal axis and the *actual* rate of inflation is plotted on the vertical axis. It is assumed that the natural, or long-run, level of unemployment is at U_n, here at 5 percent of the labor force. One Phillips curve is labeled "5 percent," and it indicates the inverse short-run relationship between *actual* inflation and unemployment when employers and employees anticipate an annual inflation rate of 5 percent. Along that curve a temporary trade-off between inflation and the unemployment rate exists; when the actual rate of inflation differs from the anticipated rate of inflation, laborers and employers are fooled. For example, assume that the economy is actually experiencing a 5 percent rate of inflation, and that buyers and sellers of labor correctly anticipate that rate of increase in the price level. The economy will be at point A in Figure 25-6; buyers and sellers of labor correctly anticipate the 5 percent rate of inflation and the unemployment rate is at its natural rate—here assumed to be 5 percent. Suppose that this unemployment rate is considered too high, and some combination of monetary and fiscal policy generates an inflation rate of 10 percent per annum. If this new inflation rate is *unanticipated* by laborers and employers, the economy will move from point A to point B. Some frictionally unemployed laborers will interpret an increase in nominal wages as an increase in real wages and will accept jobs more readily. The average duration of unemployment will fall, and therefore the unemployment rate will fall to 2 percent.

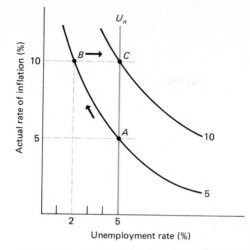

FIGURE 25-6 **The Natural Rate of Unemployment.** Here are two short-run Phillips curves: One is for a 5 percent and the other for a 10 percent anticipated rate of inflation. Each is negatively related to the *actual* rate of inflation. When the actual rate of inflation differs from the anticipated rate, laborers and employers are fooled; a temporary trade-off between inflation and the unemployment rate therefore exists.

In the long run, however, laborers and employers will adjust to a constant inflation rate and unemployment will return to its natural rate of 5 percent (in this figure). As a result, the long-run Phillips curve is vertical and parallel to the vertical axis at the natural rate of unemployment. There is, in short, no long-run trade-off between inflation and unemployment.

It appears that a 5-percentage-point increase in inflation has been traded off for a 3-percentage-point decrease in unemployment. Eventually, however, both employers and laborers will realize that the inflation rate is now 10 percent per annum. New labor contracts will take this into consideration and the frictionally unemployed will again remain unemployed for the "normal" average duration. That is, the unemployment rate returns to 5 percent (the natural rate) and the economy moves from point *B* to point *C*. Note that at point *C* the *actual* rate of inflation is correctly anticipated and that in order to reduce unemployment a still higher unanticipated rate of inflation is required.

Points *A* and *C* are part of the *long-run* Phillips curve, which can be derived by finding the unemployment rate when the inflation rate is correctly perceived. A family of short-run Phillips curves can be drawn, each with a specific anticipated rate of inflation. In the long run, when the specific anticipated rate of inflation is correctly perceived, the unemployment rate will be at the natural rate of unemployment. The long-run Phillips curve will be vertical—in the long run there is no trade-off between inflation and unemployment—and its position is determined by the natural rate of unemployment.

It should be stressed that the previous example points out that the shift in the Phillips curve was *not independent* of stabilization policy. *Attempts to move along a specific short-run Phillips curve caused the curve itself to shift. Stabilization policy can work only in the short run, therefore, because in the long run inflationary expectations will be perceived correctly.*

A Rising Natural Rate of Unemployment For the past two decades the natural rate of unemployment in the United States has been rising. According to Friedman,[6] this is due to two major factors. First of all, women, teenagers, and part-time workers comprise an increasing percentage of the labor force. In general, these groups change jobs more often and experience higher average rates of unemployment. Second, unemployment insurance and other assistance to the unemployed have been made available to more categories of workers; these benefits have also become more generous in duration and amount. Consequently, the unemployed can afford to remain idle for longer periods, as they wait to be recalled to their former jobs—or wait for even better jobs. Therefore, the average duration of unemployment has risen and, other things constant, has led to a higher unemployment rate.

RATIONAL EXPECTATIONS[7]

In the Friedman-Phelps model, monetary policy (or fiscal policy) cannot affect the long-run level of unemployment or, therefore, of output. Unemployment will return to its natural rate and output to its natural rate because in the long run employers and employees will fully and correctly anticipate the inflation rate.[8] Short-run differences in the natural rate of unemployment and the natural rate of output can be achieved by monetary and fiscal policies, because these policies cause people to make errors when they try to anticipate the inflation rate; i.e., monetary and fiscal policies can work in the short run only if people are fooled. Aside from the question of whether short-run stabilization policy is *desirable*,[9] it nevertheless has been accepted that monetary and fiscal policies can affect employment and output in the short run.

---

[6]See Milton Friedman, "Nobel Lecture: Inflation and Unemployment," reprinted in the *Journal of Political Economy*, vol. 85, no. 3, 1977, pp. 451–471.

[7]This section is based on L. Harris, *Monetary Theory* (New York: McGraw-Hill, 1981), chap. 21.

[8]Whether or not employers and employees fully adjust current prices and wages with expected inflation is an empirical question. If they do not fully adjust, then it is possible for the *long-run* Phillips curve to be negatively sloped. The data are mixed; both G. Perry ("Changing Labor Markets and Inflation," *Brookings Papers on Economic Activity*, vol. 3, 1970, pp. 411–441) and R. J. Gordon ("Inflation in Recession and Recovery," *Brookings Papers on Economic Activity*, vol. 2, 1972, pp. 385–421) concluded that people do *not* fully adjust. On the other hand, studies on the 1960s and 1970s (when inflation rates were higher) indicate that people *did* fully adjust. See R. J. Gordon, "Wage-Price Controls and the Shifting Phillips Curve," *Brookings Papers on Economic Activity*, vol. 2, 1972, pp. 385–421.

[9]Fooling people may well leave them economically worse off and may cause a misallocation of resources. If laborers accept jobs sooner or later than they would have otherwise, they will work at jobs that are "inappropriate," in the sense that they would not be maximizing the present value of their lifetime earnings, other things constant.

A recent innovation in economic analysis suggests that monetary and fiscal policies cannot affect output and employment *systematically* even in the short run! This theoretical innovation, first formalized by J. F. Muth in 1961 and applied to the theory of stabilization policy a decade later, is the rational-expectations hypothesis (REH).[10]

The REH leads to the conclusion that short-run stabilization policies[11] have no systematic effects on the errors that people make about the expected inflation rate. But the conclusion of the previous section is that an effective stabilization policy requires that the government generate an inflation rate that is higher than that expected by buyers and sellers of labor. The essence of the REH is that the difference between the community's expected inflation rate and the actual rate is purely random. It follows that *if stabilization policy cannot systematically generate people's expectational errors for the inflation rate, then stabilization policy cannot systematically alter real variables such as employment and output, even in the short run.*

The REH is that people use all available and relevant information when they make their forecasts of inflation (and other economic variables). It is assumed that people take into account past facts and interrelationships among relevant variables, and that they adjust their expectations whenever the facts change. Equally important, people take into account what monetary and fiscal policies probably will be when they forecast the macroeconomic future. If people realize, for example, that an increase in unemployment leads to expansionary monetary and fiscal policies (and to contractionary policies when the unemployment rate is very low), they will build these expectations into their forecasts. A rise in unemployment alerts buyers and sellers of labor that stabilization policy will be such that inflation will soon be on the horizon, and they will build an inflationary premium into their contracts. To the extent that people correctly perceive the implication of policy, actual changes in the money supply are incorporated equally in both actual and anticipated price changes. On average, the frictionally unemployed won't shorten their average duration of unemployment and, on average, employers won't want to hire more labor. Of course, some people will underestimate the actual rate of inflation, and unemployment will fall. On the other hand, others will *overestimate* the actual rate of inflation, and unemployment will rise. The REH concludes that people are just as likely to overestimate the actual rate of inflation as they are to underestimate it. Thus, even in the short run, stabilization policy cannot systematically alter real variables such as employment and output.[12]

---

[10]J. F. Muth, "Rational Expectations and the Theory of Price Movements," *Econometrica,* vol. 29, 1961, pp. 315–335.

[11]A policy can be defined as a sustained pattern of action or reaction. An example is "increase the money supply by 5 percent annually if the measured unemployment rate rises above 6 percent."

[12]See R. E. Lucas, "Expectations and the Neutrality of Money," *Journal of Economic Theory,* vol. 4, 1972, pp. 103–24, and T. J. Sargent and N. Wallace, "Rational Expectations, the Optimal Monetary Instrument, and the Optimal Money Supply Rule," *Journal of Political Economy,* vol. 83, 1975, pp. 241–257.

A Return to the Classical Model The implications of the REH and the Friedman-Phelps model are consistent with the implications of the classical model. The classical model predicted that the economy would tend to produce at a full-employment output. Today it is widely accepted that the economy will produce an output consistent with the natural rate of unemployment. What the classical economists called full employment is now referred to as the natural rate of unemployment.

The classical economists maintained that money was neutral; money-supply changes left real variables unaltered because relative prices would not change. The rational-expectations hypothesis also maintains that monetary policy cannot systematically affect real variables in either the short run or the long run; it can affect only the price level.

The third prediction of the classical model was that money supply changes will lead to proportional changes in the price level. The implication of the REH is that control over the rate of change of the money supply enables monetary authorities to control *only* the rate of inflation. This is equivalent to the long-run version of the classical quantity of money theory, which indicates that the supply of and the demand for money determine only the price level.

Finally, REH and classical economics more or less agree on stabilization policies. The classical prescription was "do nothing" to solve economic problems; the REH implies that government stabilization policies are ineffective at best. While the modern REH conclusions differ somewhat from the classical conclusions, we must give credit to these early economists whose models have not been intellectually refuted. Whether or not the REH and the classical model implications eventually gain widespread acceptance, the theoretical achievements of the classical economists should be recognized. Not many models can stand the test of a century of rigorous debate.

Criticisms of the Rational-Expectations Hypothesis The REH has not gone unchallenged. One criticism is that the government has information superior to the information available to the private sector. It knows better the course of past events and its own policies. If it follows a systematic policy, the government can still generate forecasting "errors" in the private sector. If so, it can affect real variables as well as monetary variables. But it seems unlikely that large corporations and unions have less information than the government concerning past economic events and macroeconomic interrelationships. After all, these groups hire economists and econometricians to gather such information as well as to predict government policy. There are high returns to those corporations (and to those economists) that can predict accurately what government policy will be. The "superior information" argument is not a very strong case against the REH.

Franco Modigliani, a respected economist at the Massachusetts Institute of Technology, has noted that the rational-expectations argument should imply that departures from the natural rate of unemployment and of output should be small, short-lived, and explained completely by random deviations.[13]

---

[13]F. Modigliani, "The Monetarist Controversy or Should We Forsake Stabilization Policies?" *American Economic Review*, vol. 67, 1977, pp. 1–19.

How, then, is one to interpret the Great Depression? Proponents of the REH have rejoined by stating that during the Great Depression the natural rate of unemployment increased greatly,[14] and the official unemployment figures exaggerated unemployment because they included people working on public works projects[15]—which would be equivalent today to including in the ranks of the unemployed people teaching at public schools and universities and people working in the various state, local, and federal agencies.

Another important criticism of an REH conclusion obtained from the Friedman-Phelps model is that the assumption of long-term contracts and commitments is a form of price-wage inflexibility. Consider the following scenario. In 1982, labor and other contracts lasting until 1984 are agreed to by people who have a given set of expectations. Then, in 1983, monetary or fiscal policy is pursued by a government that *now* has more information than the private parties did in 1982. Even though at any given time people in the private sector have the same information the government has, the government can *use* new information while some earlier private contracts are still binding. As a result, governments may be able to affect employment and output in the short run because those who are locked into long-term contracts are unable to use this new information.

Rejoinders to this criticism made by REH proponents are that (1) people in the private sector can gain flexibility by indexing contracts, or by evading the contracts in various legal ways; and (2) monetary and fiscal policymakers are not likely to be any more flexible in their policy timing than are private agencies.

What is startling is that after a half-century both proponents and opponents of governmental intervention to stabilize an economy are still debating the flexibility of prices and wages. The classical-Keynesian debate concerns the degree of flexibility of wage rates and interest rates, while the modern debate centers around the effects of long-term contracts on the flexibility of prices and wages. Modern proponents of a stabilizing role for governments continue to rest their cases largely on an inflexible price structure.

In Chapter 24, it was noted that the theoretical case for predicting what happens to nominal interest rates when the money supply is increased is uncertain. After decades of stabilization policies, this chapter observes, it cannot be demonstrated that these policies can systematically alter real economic variables. These implications, and the fact that economists are still debating the same old issues in new guises, are most troublesome.

---

[14]T. J. Sargent, "A Classical Macroeconomic Model for the United States," *Journal of Political Economy,* vol. 84, 1976, pp. 207–237.

[15]M. R. Darby, "Three and a Half Million U.S. Employees Have Been Mislaid: Or an Explanation of Unemployment, 1934–1941," *Journal of Political Economy,* vol. 84, 1976, pp. 1–16.

Fighting Stagflation by Lowering Marginal Tax Rates

The Keynesians, the monetarists, and that branch of the monetarists known as REH proponents are all concerned with whether government policy can systematically alter real variables by changing nominal aggregate demand. This debate was framed by Keynes, who believed strongly that aggregate demand was the prime determinant of macroeconomic variables.

This section moves in a different direction to ask whether governments can fight stagflation by changing aggregate supply. Consider Figure 1, which shows that a leftward shift in the aggregate supply curve can simultaneously increase the price level and decrease the rate of national output (increase the rate of unemployment). This Controversy will argue that high marginal tax rates—which reduce incentives to workers to work, to households to save, and to businesses to invest in capital goods—have in fact caused such a leftward shift in the aggregate supply curve. If this is true, a reduction in marginal tax rates is the proper antidote to stagflation.

THE STRESS ON TAX RATES

Notice that we stress marginal tax rates. The underlying assumption is that individuals in their capacities as workers, savers, and investors respond to changes on the margin. What is important to the worker contemplating more or less work is the after-tax, or take-home, pay, which is a function of that worker's marginal tax rate. What is important for the saver is the after-tax rate of return on additional saving, which is a function of that saver's marginal tax rate. Finally, what is of interest to

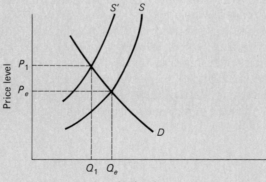

FIGURE 1 A higher marginal tax rate induces workers to work less, households to save less, and businesses to invest in fewer capital goods. This leads to a leftward shift in the aggregate supply curve (from S to S'). As a result, the price level rises *and* the rate of national output falls; simultaneously, this causes a higher rate of inflation and a higher level of unemployment.

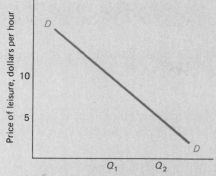

FIGURE 2   The Demand for Leisure.   The demand for leisure (not working) is related to its price. Its price, however, is an individual's after-tax wage rate because when the individual does not work—that is, "buys leisure"—his or her opportunity cost is the after-tax income loss. Assume that with a zero marginal tax rate, the individual makes $10 an hour. The quantity of leisure demanded will be Q_1. If the individual's marginal tax rate increases to 50 percent, then the after-tax wage rate will be $5 an hour (given a pretax wage rate of $10 per hour) and the quantity of leisure demanded will increase to Q_2. It follows that, as the marginal tax rate rises, the quantity of labor supplied falls, because an increase in the quantity of leisure demanded is the counterpart of a decrease in the quantity of labor supplied.

the firm contemplating investment in new plant and equipment is the expected after-tax rate of return. Again, that is a function of the marginal tax rate.

TAX RATES AND THE LABOR-LEISURE CHOICE

From labor's point of view, there is always a choice between more work (and pay) and less leisure, or less work (and pay) and more leisure. The choice at the margin is a function of the after-tax rate of return to working. The greater the marginal tax rate, the lower the after-tax wage and, hence, the lower the opportunity cost of leisure. Figure 2 shows this relationship: The quantity of leisure demanded is greater (the quantity of labor supplied is less), the lower its opportunity cost (i.e., the greater the marginal tax rate).

Ways to Increase Leisure or Reduce Work Effort   There are a multitude of ways in which individuals can respond to higher marginal tax rates. They include

1   Longer vacations
2   Fewer supplemental jobs (less moonlighting)
3   Earlier retirement
4   Greater absenteeism
5   Refusal of higher-paying positions that require more work effort
6   Lower participation rates (the ratio of those in the labor force to the total number in the group) for teenagers and older people.

There has been relatively little empirical work verifying the degree to which Americans respond to higher marginal tax rates. It is agreed that work effort is less, but the crucial question of how much less has not yet been answered.

"MISDIRECTED" WORK
EFFORT AND RESOURCE ALLOCATION

Supply-side economists advocate reductions in marginal tax rates for another reason. They believe that the lower the marginal tax rate the fewer will be the resources that are misdirected. Individuals, in their capacities as workers and investors, put their resources in those economic activities that yield the relatively higher rates of return, but loopholes in the tax laws increase the rate of return on particular activities. For example, individuals may invest in real estate only because of the tax advantages. From a social point of view, society often ends up having "too" many resources in certain sectors because of these special tax loopholes. This is tantamount to an inefficient use of society's resources.

RESOURCES DEVOTED TO AVOIDING TAXES

Another disadvantage of an income tax system with high marginal tax rates is that it encourages the use of resources to find ways to avoid taxes. Millions of dollars worth of lawyers' and accountants' time is used each year in helping high-income-earning individuals legally reduce their tax liabilities. Additionally, a growing amount of resources is devoted to evading tax liabilities illegally.

That part of the economy in which income is not reported is called the cash, underground, or subterranean economy. The subterranean economy is estimated to produce an output between 10 percent and 20 percent of the measured gross national product. Individuals engage in exchanges in cash to avoid records—canceled checks and receipts—that could be used by the Internal Revenue Service to prove that income was earned and not declared for tax purposes. People who deal in resources in large quantities seek out "off-the-book" cash transactions. These exchanges would be made more efficiently (at lower cost) if they were part of the normal economy; according to supply-side economists, they would become part of the normal economy if marginal tax rates were sufficiently reduced. After all, the lower the marginal tax rate, the smaller the benefit from trying to find cash deals by which income taxes are illegally avoided.

PUTTING IT ALL TOGETHER—THE LAFFER CURVE

We are led to conclude that there is a relationship between tax rates and tax revenues. After some "high" marginal tax rate is reached, individuals reduce their work effort, spend more time seeking ways to reduce tax liabilities, and engage in more nonreported (nontaxed) exchanges. The relationship between tax rates and tax revenues has been popularized by Arthur Laffer of the University of Southern California. His now famous (or, as some say, infamous) **Laffer curve** demonstrates a relatively simple proposition: Above some tax rate an increase in tax rates actually

Arthur Laffer. A leader of the supply-side economics movement and originator of the Laffer curve. *(Courtesy of Wide World Photos.)*

reduces tax revenues. Look at Figure 3, which measures tax rates, T, on the vertical axis and tax revenues, R, on the horizontal axis. Tax rate T_1 is the maximum rate that the government can impose before the relationship between tax rates and revenues becomes negative, or inverse. For example, at tax rate T_2, revenues will have dropped from R_{max} to R_2.

A Policy Implication of the Laffer Curve   One policy implication of the Laffer curve is that if the economy is already at tax rate T_2, a reduction in tax rates will actually lead to an increase in tax revenues. This reasoning is the basis for numerous current proposals to cut tax rates.

Criticisms of the Laffer Curve   While one cannot deny the existence of the Laffer curve, one can argue about where an economy is on the Laffer curve. Many economists and policymakers, as well as concerned citizens, believe that a tax cut would stimulate the economy. Some believe that such a tax rate cut would stimulate the economy so much that the government would actually increase its tax revenues. Perhaps the best case that can be made for a tax cut is that even if it doesn't increase tax revenues in the short run, it may do so in the long run by creating a higher rate

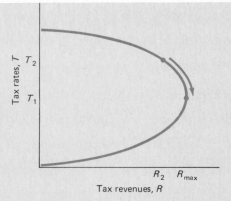

FIGURE 3   The Laffer Curve.   The Laffer curve is a representation of the relationship between tax rates and tax revenues collected. Tax revenues are on the horizontal axis and tax rates are on the vertical axis. The maximum tax revenues collectible, R_{max}, result at the tax rate, T_1. If the government insists on a tax rate of T_2, tax revenues collected fall from R_{max} to R_2. The policy implication of the Laffer curve is that if tax rates were above tax rate T_1, then a reduction from current tax rates of, say, T_2 toward tax rate T_1 would *increase* tax revenues from R_2 to some greater amount. A tax rate reduction leads to an increase in tax revenues. The truth of this proposition rests on the empirical relationship between reductions in tax rates and changes in the amount of work effort, investment, saving, and attempts at tax avoidance and evasion.

of growth in the economy. For example, suppose that all marginal tax rates are cut by 30 percent. In the first two years after that tax reduction, federal government tax revenues may fall. But in the third year, as a result of improved productivity, increased saving, and increased investment, the growth in the economy may increase so much that tax revenues will indeed be greater.

CHAPTER SUMMARY

1   The Keynesian model does not make explicit the relationship between the price level (or the rate of change in the price level) and the employment level (or the unemployment rate). This gap in theory is filled by the Phillips curve, which is the relationship between the rate of inflation and the unemployment rate and which can be derived from the reformulated aggregate supply–aggregate demand model. If prices and wages are assumed inflexible downward and the aggregate supply curve is positively sloped, the Phillips curve is negatively sloped.

2   The optimal point on the Phillips curve depends on a subjective weighting of the costs to society of inflation and unemployment. Even if such an evaluation could be made, however, the Phillips curve is of limited value because it is unstable. In many countries that have lower unemployment rates, stagflation has emerged over time;

and apparently the attempt to move along a Phillips curve has caused the entire curve to shift to the right.

3 An unstable Phillips curve can be explained by an analysis of inflationary expectations. The Friedman-Phelps model states that an expansionary monetary policy can buy less unemployment at the cost of more inflation only if buyers and sellers of labor do not correctly anticipate (or underestimate) the inflation rate.

4 If the Fed pursues an expansionary policy, unknown to buyers and sellers of labor, the price level will rise and unemployment will fall. Eventually, however, buyers and sellers of labor will correctly learn about the new, higher rate of inflation. The unemployment rate will return to its natural rate (which depends on frictional unemployment and institutional market rigidities), and the average duration of unemployment will return to its former length. In the long run, the Phillips curve is vertical at the level of the natural rate of unemployment. Only surprises matter.

5 The rational-expectations hypothesis (REH) maintains that short-run stabilization policies have no systematic effects on errors that people make about the expected inflation rate. Some will underpredict and others will overpredict the true inflation rate; stabilization policy cannot *systematically* bias forecasting errors. It follows that stabilization policy cannot *systematically* affect real variables such as employment and output even in the short run.

6 The implications of the REH model are similar to those of the classical model. The classical model predicts a movement toward full employment; the REH predicts a movement toward the natural rate of unemployment. The classical model maintains that money is neutral; money supply changes leave real variables unaltered because relative prices don't change. The REH predicts that monetary policy cannot systematically affect real variables in either the short or the long run. The classical model predicts that money supply changes lead to proportional changes in the price level; the REH implies that control over the rate of growth of the money stock allows the Fed control only over the rate of inflation. Finally, the classical model prescription for stabilization policy is to do nothing to solve economic problems; the REH contends that governmental stabilization policies are ineffective at best.

7 Critics of the REH maintain that government policymakers have information superior to that available to people in the private sector and that they therefore can induce the community to make systematic forecasting errors. Other critics maintain that even if the private sector always has the same information as policymakers, price-wage flexibility in the form of long-term contracts allows policymakers to influence output and employment.

8 Supply-side economists maintain that discretionary stabilization policy is not necessary to counter stagflation. Their position is that high marginal tax rates have led to low after-tax earnings for laborers, low after-tax interest earnings for savers, and low after-tax profits for business investors. As a consequence of higher marginal tax rates, the supply of labor, saving, and investment has fallen. It follows that a reduction in marginal tax rates will increase the supply of goods and services. Moreover, high marginal tax rates have induced a thriving subterranean economy and have resulted in tax evasion, resource misallocations, and tax avoidance. One supply-side notion is the Laffer curve, which relates tax rates to tax revenues. This curve suggests that if marginal tax rates are very high, a reduction in tax rates can actually lead to an *increase* in tax revenues. Whether or not the United States can increase tax revenues by lowering taxes is an empirical question which has not yet been resolved.

GLOSSARY

Frictional unemployment: The type of unemployment experienced by people who are between steady jobs.

Laffer curve: A curve that relates tax rates to tax revenues.

Natural rate of unemployment: The amount of unemployment due to frictional unemployment and rigidities in the economic system and interferences with la-

bor mobility or wage-rate changes; the rate of unemployment to which the economy returns after stabilization policies are correctly anticipated by the private sector.

Phillips curve: A relationship between the rate of inflation and the rate of unemployment.

Rational-expectations hypothesis (REH): A theory that

states that policymakers are unable to generate systematic forecasting errors in the private sector, and cannot, therefore, systematically alter output and employment levels.

Stagflation: The simultaneous existence of high rates of inflation and of high unemployment.

PROBLEMS

25-1 Consider the following graphs and then answer the questions.

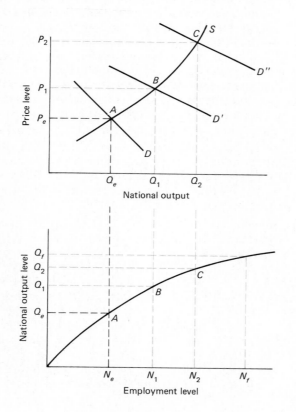

Assume that Q_f represents a full-employment output and that N_f represents a full-employment level of employment.

a What is the level of unemployment at position *A?*

b What is the price level at position *A?*

Assume that aggregate demand increases from *D* to *D′*.

c What will be the inflation rate?

d What is the new unemployment rate?

If aggregate demand had increased from *D* to *D″*:

e What would the rate of inflation have been?

f What would the new unemployment rate be?

g What is the importance of the differing results from a shift from *D* to *D′* versus a shift from *D* to *D″?*

SELECTED REFERENCES

Aaron, Henry S., and Joseph A. Pechman (eds.), *How Taxes Affect Economic Behavior* (Washington, D.C.: The Brookings Institute, 1981).

Alchian, A. A., "Information Costs, Pricing, and Resource Unemployment," *Western Economic Journal,* vol. 7, June 1969, pp. 109–128.

Darby, M. R., "Three and a Half Million U.S. Employees Have Been Mislaid; Or, An Explanation of Unemployment, 1934–1941," *Journal of Political Economy,* vol. 84, February 1976, pp. 1–16.

Feige, E. L., "Expectations and Adjustments in the Monetary Sector," *American Economic Association Papers and Proceedings,* vol. 57, May 1967, pp. 462–473.

Fisher, Stanley, "Long Term Contracts, Rational Expectations, and the Optimal Money Supply Rule," *Journal of Political Economy,* vol. 85, February 1977, pp. 191–205.

Friedman, Milton, "The Role of Monetary Policy," *American Economic Review,* vol. 58, March 1968, pp. 1–17.

————, "Nobel Lecture: Inflation and Unemployment," reprinted in *Journal of Political Economy,* vol. 85, 1977, pp. 451–471.

Gordon, Robert J., "Wage-Price Controls and the Shifting Phillips Curve," *Brookings Papers on Economic Activity,* vol. 2, 1972, pp. 385–421.

————, "Recent Developments in the Theory of Inflation and Unemployment," *Journal of Monetary Economics,* vol. 2, April 1976, pp. 185–219.

Hayek, Friedrich A., *Unemployment and Monetary Policy: Government as Generator of the 'Business Cycle'* (San Francisco, Calif.: The Cato Institute, 1979).

Laffer, A. B., and J. P. Seymour (eds.), *The Economics of the Tax Revolt: A Reader* (New York: Harcourt, Brace, 1979).

Lucas, R. E., "Expectations and the Neutrality of Money," *Journal of Economic Theory,* vol. 4, April 1972, pp. 103–124.

Modigliani, Franco, "The Monetarist Controversy or Should We Forsake Stabilization Policies?" *American Economic Review,* vol. 67, March 1977, pp. 1–19.

Phelps, E. S., "Money Wage Dynamics and Labour Market Equilibrium," *Journal of Political Economy, vol.* 76, 1968, pp. 678–711.

Monetary Policy

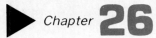
The Targets and Strategies of Monetary Policy

Up to this point we have presented a simplified analysis of monetary policy. It may appear that monetary policy amounts to the determination of the "optimal" quantity of money or (in a dynamic sense) the optimal rate of growth of the money stock. But there is more to monetary policy than the determination of the optimal stock or growth rate of money. For one thing, the "optimal" money stock or growth rate of money is not easy to define because the **ultimate goals** of monetary policy (high employment, price stability, economic growth, balance-of-payments equilibrium) may be in conflict.

For example, suppose that the money supply has been increasing at a rate of 12 percent per annum over a fairly long period and that this policy has led to a rate of inflation of 9 percent, which is deemed "too high." If the Fed then increases the money supply at only 4 percent per annum for several years, the price level will eventually stabilize. However, unwanted by-products might occur (at least in the short run) because this slower growth rate of the money supply could increase the unemployment rate above 6 percent and reduce the annual rate of economic growth of the economy to below 3 percent.

Or, a faster rate of growth of the money supply might reduce unemployment and increase the rate of economic growth, but it might lead to an international-payments imbalance (as will be indicated in Chapter 29) or to an intolerably high rate of inflation. Somehow, an optimal rate of increase in the money supply must take into account the fact that a trade-off exists among these ultimate goals of monetary policy.

Uncertainty about the exact *current* economic conditions and the effects of monetary policy, as well as the lag time between monetary policy and its effects on the economy, also make the notion of an "optimal" quantity of money very difficult to apply in practice. Moreover, recent financial innovations are making it difficult to decide just what money itself is. Just *which* money stock measure—M1, M2, M3, or whatever—should be increasing at an optimal rate?

Another complication in the implementation of monetary policy is that by changing the money supply, the Fed also affects interest rates and credit availability—which themselves have an impact on ultimate goals. This chapter shows that it is not possible for the Fed to control the money supply *and* interest rates (or credit availability) simultaneously. By controlling the money supply, the Fed loses control over interest rates; and to the extent that interest rates themselves have an independent effect on ultimate goals, the Fed may be forced to trade off one ultimate goal for another.

For example, suppose the Fed wants to reduce the rate of inflation and it therefore reduces the rate at which the money supply is rising. This slow-down in the rate of growth of money may cause interest rates to rise, which in turn will discourage home-building and business capital formation. Short-term higher unemployment rates and a lower economic growth rate might ensue.

MONETARY POLICY STRATEGIES[1]

The Fed has at its disposal certain tools: open-market operations, discounting, and reserve requirements. It also has certain ultimate goals, such as price stability, high employment, an international-payments equilibrium, and an acceptable growth rate in real national income. Even if these goals can be defined operationally (defined in a way that they are made quantifiable), it is apparent that they cannot be affected *directly* by the monetary policy tools. Those tools allow the Fed to affect only **monetary instruments**—such as depository reserves, the discount rate, and the monetary base.

A Single-Stage Strategy The overall problem of the Fed is to change the values of its instruments (depository reserves, the discount rate, or the money base) so as to bring about the most feasible paths for reaching ultimate goals.

This single-stage strategy for monetary policy is, simply, to aim the policy instruments directly at the ultimate goals. If the ultimate goals depart from desired paths, the instruments can be altered in desirable directions.

A Two-Stage Strategy An alternative to the single-stage strategy is the two-stage strategy. By using **intermediate targets**—such as the federal funds rate and the growth of one or more of the monetary aggregates, such as M1 or M2—the overall problem is broken down into two separate stages.

In the first stage, the Fed reasons backward from desired growth rates for ultimate goals to determine paths for intermediate targets that are consistent with the ultimate-goal paths. For example, suppose the Fed desires to reduce the rate of inflation from 10 percent per annum to 3 percent per annum over the next two years. The Fed selects some intermediate target, such as a 6 percent growth rate of M1, that is hoped to be consistent with the ultimate-goal path.

In the second stage, the Fed takes the intermediate-target path as given and determines the rate of change in its instruments that is consistent with the intermediate-target path. For example, the Fed might decide that, in order to "hit" the intermediate target of a 6 percent per annum rate of growth of M1, it must increase the monetary base at, say, 2 percent per annum.

Figure 26-1 shows the two-stage, or intermediate-target, approach. You should be aware that the variables listed under the targets and goals are not exhaustive; the lists are merely suggestive.

---

[1]See R. C. Bryant, "Should Money Targets Be the Focus of Monetary Policy?" *The Brookings Review,* Spring 1983, pp. 6–12.

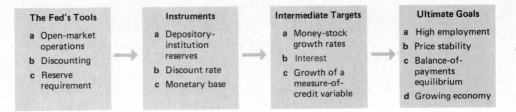

FIGURE 26-1 **Tools, Targets, and Ultimate Goals.** These boxes indicate the chain of monetary policy. The Fed uses the tools at its disposal to reach its ultimate goals. Doing so, however, may require that the Fed set intermediate targets that it *can* affect directly.

CRITERIA FOR SELECTING TARGETS

What criteria are necessary for a variable to be a desirable target for monetary policy? Given that the Fed can choose among several variables to focus on as intermediate targets, how should the Fed go about deciding what variable to affect? In general, there are three criteria for a good target variable: measurability, attainability, and relatedness to higher-level goals.

Measurability   To meet the measurability criterion, accurate and reliable data must be quickly available. The data should also conform to economists' theoretical definitions as closely as possible. Unfortunately, some of the intermediate target variables (money stock and long-term interest rates) rank low on the measurability scale. As noted previously, financial innovation has blurred the meaning of "money stock"; the Fed faces quite a menu of measures of "money stock" (M1, M2, M3, *L*). Moreover (over short periods of time), each one of these measures is subject to measurement errors and revisions, and they are not always highly correlated with each other. This does not necessarily mean, however, that the Fed shouldn't set targets for these target variables—long-term targets are especially feasible.

The measurability of interest rates is also fraught with problems. While "the" interest rate is conceptually a weighted average of all interest rates, *measured* interest rates do not include all rates, or the proper weights. Some of these rates are also difficult to interpret. Published interest rates do not take into account the compensating balances that the lender requires of the borrower or any other restrictions that the lending institution imposes on the borrower. Credit rationing also implies that the posted interest rates are inaccurate. What is the "true" interest rate to those who can't borrow at the going rate (because they have been discriminated against, or "rationed out")? Finally, nominal interest rates don't always allow one to infer readily what the real rate is. Borrowers are motivated by changes in the *real* rate of interest, to which an estimated inflation premium must be added before the nominal rate is determined. Only nominal rates are readily observable, however, because no accurate way of measuring *anticipated* inflation currently exists. The distinction between nominal and real interest rates is especially important during periods of high and variable inflation. For these reasons, among others, "the" interest rate is of limited value as a target.

Attainability The Fed must be able to attain its targeted goal; otherwise, setting the target becomes an exercise in futility. If the Fed could have encouraged conservation of gasoline and fuel oil during the 1970s, it could have helped solve the U.S. balance-of-payments problem. Targets for reduced gasoline and fuel oil use are of little value when the Fed has within its control only changes in the discount rate, reserve requirements, and open-market operations.

Can the Fed in either the short run or the long run attain money stock growth targets? It is important to know if by using its tools the Fed can achieve money growth targets. This crucial topic is discussed in greater detail at the end of this chapter, as a Current Controversy. Alternatively, we want to know if the Fed can achieve any specific interest rate target. Can the tools that affect short-term rates also affect long-term rates?[2] Indeed, can the Fed affect *real* rates or only nominal rates? The key question becomes whether the Fed actually can use its tools to attain intermediate targets. Targets which are unattainable are not very practical.

Relatedness to Higher-Level Goals It is pointless for the Fed to select and attain a target unless the target is related to a higher goal. It is not very useful to attain, say, money stock targets unless they in turn enable the Fed to attain ultimate goals.

To take a different approach, even if the Fed attains its intermediate target, all is in vain if, say, interest rates don't affect employment, the price level, the rate of economic growth, and the payments balance.

A BRIEF HISTORY OF FED TARGETS

This section discusses actual Fed monetary policy objectives from 1941 to the present. It is followed by a Highlight regarding indicators of Fed monetary policy.

1941 to 1951 During this period the Fed's monetary policy consisted of maintaining ceilings on U.S government securities—$\frac{3}{8}$ percent on 90-day bills, $\frac{7}{8}$ percent on 1-year certificates, and 2.5 percent on bonds maturing in 10 years or longer. The Fed pegged these interest rates by purchasing without limitation all government securities offered to it at the chosen levels of interest rates and bond prices; they maintained interest-rate *ceilings* by supporting bond-price *floors*.

---

[2]It is believed that long-term interest rates are more influential in affecting business investment in plant and equipment and housing expenditures than are short-term interest rates.

This meant that the Fed was prepared to monetize all the government securities that banks or the nonbank public were prepared to offer it. From December 1941 to June 1946, the Fed increased its holdings of Treasury obligations from $2.254 billion to $23.390 billion.

In effect, this policy of interest-rate ceilings (bond-price floors) forced the Fed to relinquish control over its volume of bank reserves and over the money supply. The motive for placing a ceiling on government bond yields was a desire to keep the interest costs of the U.S. debt low, and to eliminate the capital loss risks of those who had purchased these securities during the war. After the war the policy to "stabilize" the bond market was continued. In 1947 the interest-rate ceilings on bills and certificates were removed, but they remained on the longer-term bonds until 1951. Supporting bond prices contributed to inflation during the early part of the Korean War (1950 to 1951). The war generated inflation, and in order to stop bond yields from rising the Fed was required to purchase government securities at their supported price floors. In turn, this caused an increase in the money supply and a higher price level. This policy became untenable and in 1951 the Fed announced that it would no longer support bond prices; this announcement has come to be known as the Treasury–Federal Reserve Accord.

1951 to 1973 The Treasury–Fed Accord allowed the Fed thereafter to pursue an independent stabilization policy; the Fed no longer was wedded to a policy of stabilizing Treasury securities prices, which forced it to lose control over the money supply. The principal instrument now became the control of *free reserves.* Recall that free reserves are defined as the value of the excess reserves of member banks minus their borrowings from the Federal Reserve banks. Because it was believed that banks wished to keep their borrowings from the Fed as low as possible, free reserves were considered a good target; banks would want to repay their borrowing from the Fed and use the rest of their reserves to make loans and purchase securities. The Fed concluded, therefore, that it could control deposit creation, bank credit, interest rates, and the money supply by controlling the volume of free reserves.

It is now agreed that such reasoning is flawed. Banks compare the opportunity costs of holding free reserves (foregone interest earnings on Treasury bills and loans) with the benefit of holding these reserves (avoidance of the risk of capital loss on bonds and not needing to borrow from the Fed). At times it is rational to hold excess reserves; this has important implications for Fed policy during a recession. If banks choose to hold excess reserves during such times, the Fed might misinterpret the existence of excess reserves as an indication that it is currently pursuing a "loose" (expansionary) monetary policy. Additional economic stimulation would then seem unnecessary. In effect, the Fed would be pursuing a procyclical policy (one that keeps the economy moving in the same direction; in this case, into a deeper recession). Similarly, a Fed that was wedded to free reserve targets would contribute to inflation. By

1966, after much criticism by monetarists,[3] the Fed abandoned its commitment to target free reserves. It then targeted the federal funds rate.

1973 to 1984   From 1973 to 1975, the Fed zeroed in on *two* targets—the federal funds rate and the growth rate of several monetary aggregates. Both of these targets were set by the Federal Open Market Committee (FOMC) to be consistent with current economic conditions and economic forecasts emanating from its econometric model. For example, early evidence of a business downturn induced the Fed to lower its federal funds rate target and to increase the rate of growth of its money stock targets. This policy required the Fed to purchase securities and led to a lower federal funds rate and an increased money supply. Such a policy would, in principle, be countercyclical (in this example, expansionary).

Also in response to monetarist criticism, in 1975 the U.S. House and Senate passed House Congressional Resolution 133, which instructed the Fed to "maintain long-run growth of the monetary and credit aggregates commensurate with the economy's long-run potential to increase production." The Fed was also required to report quarterly to Congress on its monetary and credit growth-rate targets for the upcoming twelve months. These provisions were incorporated into the Federal Reserve Reform Act of 1977 and the Full Employment and Balanced Growth Act (Humphrey-Hawkins) in 1978.

The restrictions on Fed activity are more apparent than real. The legislation is vague, so the Fed can set a wide range for a target; and, in justifying its past actions, the Fed can choose to emphasize those rates that fell within the target range or that were close to the range. In any case, the monetarists were not pacified; they were still convinced that the Fed was too concerned with the self-defeating policy of stabilizing interest rates, and not concerned sufficiently with money stock targets.

In October 1979, the Fed announced that it would now place more emphasis on monetary aggregates and less emphasis on the federal funds rate. Since then, the Fed has had some difficulty in achieving these money-stock growth targets, and this has weakened the monetarists' case. We return to the issue of attainability of money-stock growth rates at the end of this chapter, in the Current Controversy section.

By February of 1983, disenchantment with monetary growth rate targets prompted the Fed to add to its monetary targets a target for the growth of a credit variable. The Fed targeted total domestic nonfinancial debt, or outstanding debt of domestic governmental units (federal, state, and local), households, and nonfinancial business. Legislation was also introduced in

---

[3]See K. Brunner and A. H. Meltzer, "The Federal Reserve's Attachment to the Free Reserve Concept." Subcommittee Print, U.S. Congress, *House Committee on Banking and Currency, Subcommittee on Domestic Finance,* 88th Cong., 2d Sess., 1964; and William G. Dewald, "Free Reserves, Total Reserves, and Monetary Control," *Journal of Political Economy,* vol. 71, April 1963, pp. 141–153.

1982, by the 97th Congress, to require the Fed to announce target ranges for short-term *real* rates of interest consistent with historical levels.[4]

WHICH VARIABLE SHOULD THE FED TARGET?

By now you are aware that monetarists maintain that the Fed should set monetary-aggregate targets, and not interest-rate targets. In this section each of these targets is assessed. Because each target has its own peculiar problems, there is honest disagreement among economists and the issue is not yet resolved.

It is crucial to understand that, in most circumstances, *both monetary-aggregate and interest-rate targets cannot be pursued simultaneously.* Interest-rate targets force the Fed to abandon control over the money stock; monetary-stock growth targets force the Fed to allow interest rates to fluctuate.[5]

Consider Figure 26-2, which indicates the relationship between the total demand for and the supply of money. Note that in the short run (in the sense nominal national income is fixed), the demand for money is constant; short-run money supply changes leave the demand for money unaltered. In the longer run, however, as the changed money supply causes nominal national

---

[4]The House of Representatives bill H.R. 7218 calls for monthly real interest rate targets, and H.R. 6967 asks for targets for *long-term* interest rates. Senate bill S-2807 calls for annual targets for real interest rates.

[5]This statement is not technically true. Under the (unlikely) conditions of certainty, money-supply targets and interest-rate targets amount to the same thing. The full-employment, price-stable equilibrium level of national income is maintained by increasing the money supply so that the real interest rate remains constant. Also, very *broad* money stock and interest-rate target ranges could be set and met simultaneously, even under uncertainty. For example, the Fed could set a range of targets for M1 growth between 1 percent and 30 percent per annum, and a federal funds rate range of between 1 percent and 35 percent. The Fed can simultaneously attain *both* targets—but to what avail? Such a policy would mean that the targeting process is a fraud.

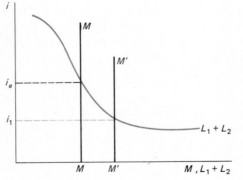

FIGURE 26-2 Choosing a Monetary Policy Target. This figure indicates that the Fed, in the short run, can select an interest rate *or* a money-supply target, but not both. It cannot, for example, choose i_e and M'; if it selects i_e, it must accept M; if it selects M', it must allow the interest rate to fall to i_1. Because these targets present a problem of mutual exclusivity, the Fed must choose one target or the other.

income to change, the demand curve will shift. In the short run, the Fed can choose either a particular interest rate or a particular money supply.

If the Fed wants interest rate i_e, it *must* select money supply M; if the Fed desires a lower (higher) interest rate in the short run, it must increase (decrease) the money supply. Thus, by targeting an interest rate, the Fed must relinquish control of the money supply. Conversely, if the Fed wants to target the money supply at, say, M', it must allow the interest rate to be i_1.

Consider now the case in which the Fed wants to maintain the present level of interest rates. If actual market interest rates in the future rise above the present (desired) rates, the Fed will be continuously forced to increase the money supply. This will only temporarily lower interest rates. The increased money stock will induce inflation, and inflationary premiums will be added to interest rates. To pursue its low-interest-rate policy, the Fed must *again* increase the money stock. Note that in order to maintain an interest-rate target (stable interest rates) the Fed must abandon an independent monetary stock target.

Complementary reasoning indicates that by setting growth-rate targets for monetary aggregates the Fed must allow short-run fluctuations in interest rates when the economy experiences a recession or an expansion.

But which should the Fed target: interest rates or monetary aggregates?[6] It is generally agreed that the answer depends on the *source* of instability in the economy. If the source of instability is variations in the *IS* curve (due to variations in private or public spending), then monetary aggregate targets should be set and pursued. On the other hand, if the source of instability is an unstable demand for (or perhaps supply of) money, then interest-rate targets are preferred. Let's discuss each in turn.

Instability of the *IS* Curve, Stability of the *LM* Curve   Consider Figure 26-3, which indicates a stable *LM* curve and an unstable *IS* curve. This situation could arise because fiscal policy is destabilizing (a high variance in public spending[7]), or because the consumption function or the investment curve varies (a high variance in private spending). If the demand for money curve is relatively stable,[8] then the equilibrium level of income will vary between Y_e and Y_1 if a monetary aggregate rule is followed. Remember that the *LM* curve is derived by assuming a constant money stock and that this is a nondynamic version of a monetary target.

If, however, an interest-rate target is set (keep "the desired" interest rate at i_d), then the *LM* curve becomes horizontal at i_d (specifically, LM_f in Figure 26-3); the money supply must always be adjusted to maintain i_d. Note that

---

[6]And, *which* interest rates or *which* monetary aggregates?

[7]A reason dear to the monetarist's heart.

[8]A monetarist's article of faith. For an opposite view, however, see J. P. Judd and J. L. Scadding, "The Search for a Stable Money Demand Function," *Journal of Economic Literature*, September 1982, pp. 993–1023.

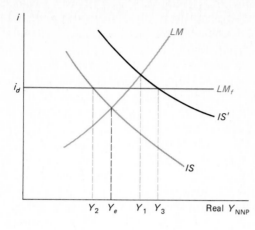

FIGURE 26-3 Stable *LM*, Unstable *IS*.
If the *LM* curve is stable because of a stable demand for money, then an unstable *IS* curve causes the level of national income to fluctuate between Y_e and Y_1 when a money target is followed. On the other hand, with a shifting *IS* curve an interest-rate target set at i_d would cause the level of national income to vary between Y_2 and Y_3. A monetary aggregate target would therefore be more stabilizing than an interest-rate target.

pursuit of the interest-rate target causes the level of national income to fluctuate between Y_2 and Y_3. Since $Y_3 - Y_2 > Y_1 - Y_e$, a money-stock target is more stabilizing than an interest-rate target. The implication is that changes in the money supply to maintain a constant interest rate will be destabilizing or procyclical, when the *IS* curve is unstable. That is, the Fed would be prompted to increase the money supply during an inflation (to keep interest rates down) and to decrease the money supply during a recession (to keep interest rates from falling).

Instability of *LM*, Stability of *IS* Consider Figure 26-4, which shows a stable *IS* curve and an unstable *LM* curve. The *LM* curve is presumed unstable because the demand for money curve is unstable. Under a monetary target policy, the level of national income would fluctuate between Y_1 and Y_2. A constant money supply would cause interest rate and national income fluctuations every time the demand for money changed. On the other hand, a policy of targeting the inter-

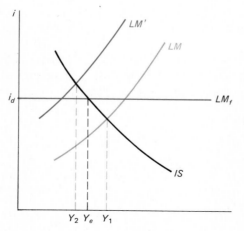

FIGURE 26-4 Stable *IS*, Unstable *LM*.
The *IS* curve is stable, and an unstable demand for money relationship causes the *LM* curve to shift between *LM* and *LM'*. A monetary-aggregate target will leave the money supply unaltered so that the level of national income will vary between Y_1 and Y_2. However, an interest-rate target of i_d will leave the level of national income unaltered at Y_e, and an interest-rate target would be more stabilizing than a money-stock target.

HIGHLIGHT   Fed Watchers

Monetarists have done such an efficient job of convincing people of the importance of money that a whole army of "Fed watchers" has appeared. It includes corporate managers, household investors in money and capital markets, economists, politicians, the media, and almost anyone interested in the economy. Even the Fed itself is a Fed watcher! This is because what is important to the Fed are the *effects* of its policies, not its intentions.

Most Fed watchers are concerned with whether the Fed is pursuing an expansionary or a tight monetary policy. Unfortunately, most people "watch" *interest rates* to see what type of policy the Fed is pursuing. They typically interpret high interest rates as indicating a tight policy, and low interest rates as a sign of an expansionary monetary policy. This kind of interpretation is a risky business. It is risky because of the difference between real and nominal interest rates. A specific high nominal interest rate could be consistent with *tight* money if anticipated inflation is low, and consistent with *loose* money if anticipated inflation is very high.

Fed watchers, therefore, seek alternative **indicators** of Fed policy. They follow changes in monetary aggregates, in bank reserves, or in the monetary base. Interestingly enough, the criteria for a good indicator are similar to those necessary for a good target: measurability, controllability, and relation to the target.

est rate at i_d (a horizontal LM_f curve at i_d) would induce the Fed to increase the money supply when the demand for money increased, and to decrease the money supply when the demand for money fell. An interest rate target would therefore cause the Fed to pursue countercyclical monetary supply changes. In Figure 26-4 an interest-rate target would leave the level of income at (or near) Y_e, the point of intersection of IS and LM_f.

The issue as to which target is "better" turns out to be an empirical one. If IS is more stable than LM, set an interest rate target; if LM is more stable than IS, set a monetary aggregate target.

CURRENT CONTROVERSY

Can the Fed Control the Money Stock?

The question of whether the Fed *can* control the monetary stock is ultimately a question of whether a monetary stock aggregate can meet the attainability criterion discussed earlier in this chapter. That question can be broken into two parts: (1) Can the Fed control the monetary base? and (2) are changes in the monetary base related to predictable changes in the monetary aggregates?

Many economists believe that although excessive long-run monetary growth is the dominant cause of inflation, attempts to control inflation are so difficult that such attempts create more problems than benefits. Since 1973 the Fed has announced monetary growth targets, but it has had little success in meeting those targets. The result has been the same in the United Kingdom and Germany, which also set monetary aggregate targets. Even if one believes that money stock targets have often played second fiddle to interest-rate targets, it must be admitted that the Fed has achieved only slight success in attaining monetary-stock targets since 1979, when it announced its intention to emphasize money-stock targets.

THE FED CAN CONTROL THE MONEY SUPPLY

The issue of the attainability of monetary aggregate targets was examined by Anatal B. Balbach.* He indicates in Table 1 that the Fed can control the monetary base, and in Table 2 he shows that changes in the monetary base lead to predictable changes in M1B (a previous monetary aggregate, defined as currency plus checkable deposits in the hands of the nonbank public; now M1).

Table 1 is a simplified Federal Reserve balance sheet; it shows that the sum of all the accounts over which the Fed has no direct control (gold reserve certificates, float, Treasury deposits, and foreign central bank deposits) varied by $2,076 million per week in 1980. Recall that in Chapter 13 we indicated that changes in those entries on the Fed's balance sheet affect depository-institution reserves. If so, then changes in gold reserve certificates, float, Treasury deposits, and foreign central bank deposits

TABLE 1 Simplified Federal Reserve Balance Sheet

(In millions of dollars)

Assets				Liabilities			
	Level Nov. 5, 1980	Average Weekly Variation in 1980	Net Average Weekly Variation in 1980		Level Nov. 5, 1980	Average Weekly Variation in 1980	Net Average Weekly Variation in 1980
Gold certificates	$ 11,163	$ .28	$ −.21	Monetary base:			
Foreign currencies	3,158	103	50	Deposits of financial institutions	$ 33,177	$3,510	$ −142
Federal Reserve credit:				Federal Reserve notes	119,416	563	207
Security holdings	130,674	3,271	36	Treasury deposits	3,064	746	− 17
Loans to financial institutions	3,371	1,777	− 5	Foreign central bank deposits	236	59	.62
Float	5,217	1,271	− 83	Other liabilities and capital	4,922	257	− 28
Other assets	7,235	267	22				

TABLE 2 Annual Movements in the M1B Multipliers

Year	Average Level of Monthly M1B Multiplier	Year-to-Year Changes of Column 1	Maximum Multiplier in the Year	Minimum Multiplier in the Year	Difference between Maximum and Minimum
1970	2.913		2.950	2.891	.059
1971	2.881	−.032	2.900	2.862	.038
1972	2.875	−.006	2.897	2.862	.035
1973	2.852	−.023	2.891	2.822	.069
1974	2.763	−.089	2.817	2.706	.111
1975	2.685	−.078	2.717	2.649	.068
1976	2.636	−.049	2.675	2.612	.063
1977	2.622	−.014	2.640	2.606	.034
1978	2.596	−.026	2.619	2.583	.035
1979	2.583	−.013	2.599	2.568	.031
1980	2.543	−.040	2.573	2.504	.069
1970–79		Average = −.037			Average = .061

exert an independent effect on the monetary base, over which the Fed has no control. But a $2,076 million weekly variance in those balance sheet entries can easily be offset by Fed open-market operations. In fact, Table 1 also shows that the *net* weekly variation in these accounts (where decreases are subtracted from increases) amount to the much smaller sum of $100 million. This is a trivial change in the Fed's securities portfolio. In short, the Fed can control one portion of its balance sheet (the monetary base) because it can offset the relatively minor changes in its balance sheet that exert an independent effect on the monetary base (by offsetting open-market operations).

Table 2 indicates that the M1B multiplier is relatively constant. The M1B multiplier relates changes in the level of M1B to changes in the monetary base. The equation is $M = mB$, or $m = M/B$. M is the change in the level of M1B, B the change in the monetary base (reserves plus currency), and m the M1B multiplier. Data from 1970 to 1980 indicate that *the M1B multiplier is quite stable*.

Because it seems that, in principle, the Fed *can* attain its monetary aggregate intermediate targets, the search is on to discover why it has not. As we show in the next chapter, the failure of the Fed to attain monetary aggregates has led to charges of Fed incompetence, and to charges that the Fed has not really abandoned its commitment to control interest rates at "appropriate levels."

Laurence R. Roos, president of the Federal Reserve Bank of St. Louis, takes the next step and shows that (1) the monetary base–M1B relationship did not change between 1970 to 1980 and from 1980 to 1981; and (2) the relationship between M1B and GNP is a stable and predictable one,[†] as shown in Table 3. The stability of this last relationship moves the debate from the attainability criterion to the relatedness-to-higher-level-goals criterion discussed earlier in the chapter.

TABLE 3 Changes in the Annual Growth of MIB and GNP		
Period*	MIB	Nominal GNP
1974–1975	0.4%	2.9%
1975–1976	1.1	−0.7
1976–1977	2.0	2.9
1977–1978	0.0	2.0
1978–1979	−0.7	−4.3
1979–1980	−0.2	−0.5
1980–1981	−2.3	−0.1

*Fourth quarter to fourth quarter.
Source: Laurence R. Roos, "The Attack on Monetary Targets," *The Wall Street Journal,* Feb. 3, 1982, op-ed page.

A CONTRARY VIEW

In a more recent study, Ralph C. Bryant, a senior fellow in the Brookings Institution's Economic Studies program, reached a different conclusion concerning the attainability of monetary targets.‡ Consider Figure 1, which indicates specific M1 money **target cones**—a target range for the growth of M1 over a twelve-month period.§ The colored line indicates the *actual* growth of M1. Figure 1 indicates that during much of the period from September 1979 to September 1980, the actual money supply was below or above the target cone; for most of the December 1980 to December 1981 period, the actual money supply was *below* the target cone; for nearly all the December 1981 to December 1982 period, the actual money supply was *above* the target cone. In other words, even though the target ranges for the growth of M1 were relatively large, the Fed was unable to attain its targets most of the time! Bryant also indicates that the variability of weekly averages of daily M1 data are even greater; it is even more difficult to hit M1 targets for periods of less than one month.

Bryant suggests that "variations in nonpolicy factors influencing the money stock cannot be accurately predicted by the Fed and are therefore unexpected disturbances when they occur." He lists such disturbances as follows:

1 Supply of money disturbances
   (a) Bank holding of excess reserves
   (b) Bank borrowings from the Fed

2 Demand for money disturbances in the form of unexpected changes in asset preferences of the nonbank private sector for
   (a) Currency
   (b) Demand deposits
   (c) Savings deposits

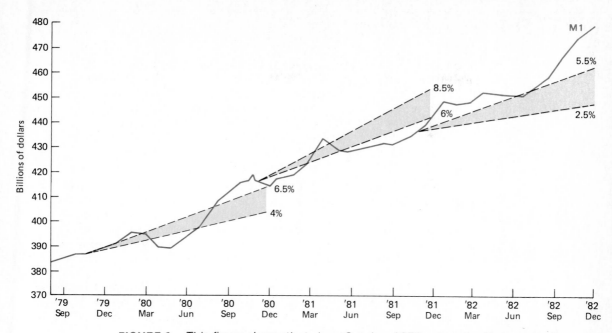

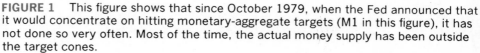

FIGURE 1   This figure shows that since October 1979, when the Fed announced that it would concentrate on hitting monetary-aggregate targets (M1 in this figure), it has not done so very often. Most of the time, the actual money supply has been outside the target cones.

Bryant concludes that, "If close control is defined as continuous prevention of sizable deviations of the actual money stock from a predetermined target path, therefore, close control over the short run [which, according to Bryant, is one to three months] is just not possible." Moreover, Bryant presents evidence that money-stock targets weren't reached because of changes in the nonpolicy factors affecting the money supply, and not because of Fed incompetence, as some of the Fed's critics have charged.

Fed critics have also charged that the Fed did not achieve its money supply targets because it was still wedded to a policy of controlling short-term interest rates. We discuss that issue in the next chapter.

*A. B. Balbach "How Controllable Is Money Growth?" *Review*, Federal Reserve Band of St, Louis, vol. 63, no. 4, 1981, pp. 3–12.

†*The Wall Street Journal,* Feb. 3, 1982, op-ed page.

‡R. C. Bryant, *op. cit.,* pp. 6–7.

§A target cone forms a point in the base month and projects the upper and lower bounds for the money supply target ranges; hitting the target range requires staying *within* the cone.

CHAPTER SUMMARY

1   Monetary policy is not simply a matter of determining the optimal stock of money or the optimal growth rate of the stock of money. It is hard to define the "optimal" money stock because (a) ultimate goals may be in conflict; (b) uncertainty exists about current economic conditions; (c) there are time lags concomitant to monetary policy; and (d) recent financial innovations have obscured the meaning of money itself. Monetary policy is made even more complicated because it *also* entails the control of such nonmonetary stock variables as interest rates and credit availability.

2   The Fed's tools to conduct monetary policy consist of open-market operations, discounting, and changes in reserve requirements. The ultimate goals of monetary policy include an international-payments equilibrium, a stable price level, high employment, and a growing economy. Because its tools cannot *directly* affect its ultimate goals, the Fed uses such instruments as depository-institution reserves, the monetary base, and the discount rate to hit intermediate targets, such as the growth of monetary aggregates (M1, M2, M3) and the growth of a credit variable, and the federal funds rate. By using its instruments to attain intermediate targets, the Fed hopes to be able to attain its ultimate goals more efficiently.

3   There are three criteria for a good intermediate target variable: measurability, attainability, and relatedness to higher-level goals.

4   From 1941 to 1951, the Fed put a ceiling on interest rates by placing a floor on the price of bonds; it agreed to support bond prices by buying from all those who wished to sell at the pegged price. This policy was followed because the Fed wished to keep the interest costs of the U.S. debt low and to eliminate capital gains losses to those who had purchased U.S. government securities during World War II.

5   The Fed's policy of purchasing bonds from all who wished to sell contributed to inflation during the Korean War era, and this support policy became untenable. In 1951 the Fed announced that it would no longer support bond prices; this announcement has come to be known as the Treasury–Federal Reserve Accord. After 1951 the Fed was able to pursue an independent stabilization policy. Originally the Fed targeted free reserves because it believed that banks wished to keep their borrowing from the Fed as low as possible. It is now agreed that such a policy is procyclical.

6   From 1973 to 1975 the Fed targeted two intermediate variables—the federal funds rate and the growth rate of several monetary aggregates. In principle, such a policy can be countercyclical. In 1979, the Fed announced that it would now emphasize monetary-aggregate targets instead of the federal funds rate; but the Fed has had difficulty in achieving these money stock growth targets.

7   Normally, monetary aggregate-growth targets and interest-rate targets cannot be pursued simultaneously; the Fed must choose one or the other. Which of these should be targeted is an empirical question.

8   If the *LM* curve is stable (because the demand for money is stable) and the *IS* curve is unstable (because private and/or public spending is unstable), targeting

a monetary aggregate will be stabilizing. Under such conditions, an interest-rate target will be destabilizing (or procyclical) because the Fed will be prompted to increase the money supply during an inflation (to keep interest rates down) and to decrease the money supply during a recession (to keep interest rates from falling).

9 If the *LM* curve is unstable and the *IS* curve is stable, an interest-rate target is countercyclical, or stabilizing, because the Fed would be led to increase the money supply when the demand for money increased and decrease the money supply when the demand for money decreased. On the other hand, a constant money supply (or constant growth rate in a dynamic economy) would cause interest-rate and national-income fluctuations every time the (unstable) demand for money changed.

10 In recent years, the Fed's ability to control the money supply has been called into question. The issue depends on (a) whether or not the Fed can control the monetary base, and (b) whether or not changes in the monetary base are related to changes in the monetary aggregates. Some evidence indicates that nondiscretionary items on the Fed's balance sheet can be offset by the discretionary powers; as a consequence, the Fed can control the monetary base. Moreover, a stable relationship exists between changes in the monetary base and changes in the monetary aggregates; the money multiplier is empirically stable. Hence, the two conditions necessary to target monetary aggregates are met. Moreover, there seems to be a close relationship between a monetary aggregate (M1B) and GNP. In principle, monetary aggregate intermediate targets *can* be attained. The Fed's inability to hit its monetary targets has led to charges of Fed incompetence, and to the belief that the Fed has not really abandoned its desire to control interest rates.

11 Other evidence indicates that, in fact, the Fed has been unable to attain its monetary stock targets since 1979 because of unpredictable variations in nonpolicy variables—over which the Fed has no control. If so, close control over short-run changes in the money supply aggregates may well prove to be impossible.

GLOSSARY

Indicator: A variable that provides a clue as to whether the Fed is pursuing an expansionary or a contractionary monetary policy.

Intermediate targets: Targets, such as monetary aggregates and the federal funds rate, that link instruments and ultimate goals.

Monetary instruments: Variables (such as depository-institution reserves and the discount rate) that can be controlled by the Fed and that help the Fed to attain its intermediate targets.

Target cones: A target cone forms a point in the base month and projects the upper and lower bounds for the money-supply target ranges; hitting the target range requires staying within the cone.

Ultimate goals: The final objectives of monetary policy, such as price stability, high employment, a balance-of-payments equilibrium, and economic growth.

PROBLEMS

26-1   Analyze the graph below and answer the following questions.

   a   How can LM_f be attained?

   b   If a constant money supply (or a constant money rate of growth) is attained, by how much will national income fluctuate?

   c   If the interest rate i_d is targeted, by how much will national income fluctuate?

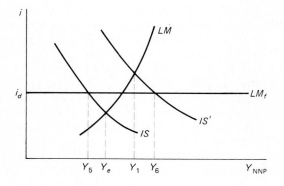

26-2   Analyze the graph below and answer the following questions.

   a   Which is more stable, the *LM* or the *IS* curve?

   b   If interest rate i_d is targeted, by how much will national income fluctuate?

   c   If the money *supply* is held constant (or if a monetary aggregate growth rate is targeted), by how much will national income fluctuate?

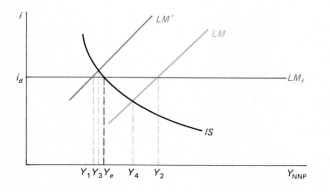

SELECTED REFERENCES

Ando, A., and F. Modigliani, "The Relative Stability of Monetary Velocity and the Investment Multiplier," *American Economic Review,* vol. 55, September 1965, pp. 693–728; and "Rejoinder," vol. 55, September 1965, pp. 786–790.

Balbach, Anatol B., "How Controllable Is Money Growth?" *Review,* Federal Reserve Bank of St. Louis, April 1981, pp. 3–12.

Brunner, K., and A. H. Meltzer, "Predicting Velocity: Implications for Theory and Policy," *Journal of Finance,* vol. 18, May 1963, pp. 319–354.

Bryant, Ralph C., "Should Money Targets Be the Focus of Monetary Policy?" *The Brookings Review,* Spring 1983, pp. 6–12.

Carlson, K. M. and S. E. Hein, "Monetary Aggregates as Monetary Indicators," *Review,* Federal Reserve Bank of St. Louis, November 1980, pp. 12–21.

Friedman, Benjamin, "Using a Credit Aggregate Target to Implement Monetary Policy in the Financial Environment of the Future," in *Monetary Policy Issues in the 1980's,* Federal Reserve Bank of Kansas City, 1982.

Friedman, M., and D. Meiselman, "The Relative Stability of Monetary Velocity and the Investment Multiplier in the United States, 1897–1958," in *Stabilization Policies* (Englewood Cliffs, N.J.: Prentice-Hall, 1963), pp. 165–268.

Judd, J. P., and J. L. Scadding, "The Search for a Stable Money Demand Function," *Journal of Economic Literature,* September 1982, pp. 993–1023.

Meigs, A. J., *Free Reserves and the Money Supply* (Chicago: University of Chicago Press, 1962).

Poole, W., and E. B. F. Kornblith, "The Friedman-Meiselman C.M.C. Paper: New Evidence on an Old Controversy," *American Economic Review,* vol. 63, December 1973, pp. 908–917.

Roos, Lawrence K., "The Attack on Monetary Targets," *The Wall Street Journal,* editorial page, Feb. 3, 1982.

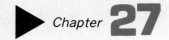

Chapter **27**

A History of Federal Reserve Monetary Policy: 1913–1983

Chapter 11 outlined the history of banking through the creation of the Federal Reserve System. As we indicated there, the banking panic of 1907 created a tremendous interest in monetary reform. That interest resulted in the Aldrich-Vreeland Act of 1908, which called for the appointment of a national monetary commission. The report of that commission was used as the basis of extensive congressional debate. The result was the Federal Reserve Act, passed on December 23, 1913, and the Fed was authorized to begin operating in November of 1914.

FEDERAL RESERVE ACTIONS DURING WORLD WAR I

By August of 1914, World War I had begun, and very soon after the declarations of war a flood of gold started coming into the United States—the gold was payment for munitions and food purchased from the United States by the belligerent nations. Gold also flowed into the United States from neutral countries, as they turned to the United States for manufactured goods that had previously been purchased from the belligerents. From the outbreak of the war in Europe to the U.S. entry into that war on April 6, 1917—an interval of less than three years—the United States had international trade surpluses totaling $5.3 billion. (That is, the value of the goods and services exported to the rest of the world exceeded the value of goods and services imported from the rest of the world.) To finance this international trade imbalance, Europeans borrowed $2.4 billion in the U.S. financial markets, sold almost $2 billion of U.S. financial assets owned by their citizens, and shipped more than $1 billion in gold to the United States. Because the United States, as well as most of the world, was on a modified gold standard (discussed in Chapter 29), this flood of gold into the United States caused the money supply—currency and checking account deposits at commercial banks—to soar 46 percent in the period from June 1914 to March 1917, and this was accompanied by a 65 percent rise in wholesale prices.

The Fed's Inability to Prevent the Money Supply from Growing   One might think that the Federal Reserve System was created just for such a situation. Presumably, it could prevent the gold inflows from Europe from causing a rapid increase in the money supply. To be sure, today the Fed can reduce reserves by selling government securities in the open market. But at that time, the Fed had just been created. It had very few securities to sell in order to combat the increased reserves resulting from gold inflows. At best, the Fed could refrain from acquiring earning assets; this would be about as restrictive a posture as it could take. Unfortunately, such a posture conflicted with the Fed's desire to *acquire* a portfolio of assets that would earn enough income to make the Federal Reserve self-supporting. This overriding objective led the Federal Reserve to acquire $286 million of assets by March 31, 1917.[1] Thus, not only did the Fed *not counteract* the large inflow of gold, it actually added to reserves in the banking system and supplemented the already inflationary pressure of gold inflows that had added to the money supply.

The United States Enters World War I After the entry of the United States into World War I on April 6, 1917, the sources of the growth in reserves in the monetary system changed dramatically. Purchases of war goods by U.S. allies no longer had to be financed by gold shipments; they could now be financed by credit from the U.S. government. After all, the United States was an ally and it wanted to support financially the war effort of its allies. Consequently, gold inflows were no longer the principal source of growth in reserves and, hence, in the money supply.

As the United States assumed responsibility for financing the expenditures of its allies, as well as for financing the expenditures of U.S. forces at home and abroad, the federal government deficit soared. This increase in the deficit occurred in spite of an increase in taxes. From the U.S. entry into the war until June 1919, federal government deficits totaled $23 billion, almost three-fourths of all government expenditures. The Treasury, under Secretary William McAdoo, was determined to finance this borrowing by selling so-called liberty bonds at rates below those prevailing in the open market. In other words, the government attempted to sell U.S. government securities to patriotic individuals and businesses at interest rates below the rates offered in the open market. As a result, the Treasury asked the Federal Reserve to insure the success of the government's borrowing efforts. The Fed was to do this by maintaining a very low discount rate; such a low rate made it easy for member banks to borrow from the Fed. Also, the Fed was supposed to continue to purchase U.S. government securities in the open market, thereby preventing interest rates from rising.

The first "liberty" loan was floated by the U.S. Treasury and carried a 3.5 percent coupon rate. The Federal Reserve set its discount rate at the same level. Member banks were allowed to finance their purchases of U.S. government bonds by borrowing against them at the same rate that the bond yielded. In effect, then, the Fed was monetizing the public debt. (Remember, to *monetize the public debt* means to increase the money supply by the same amount of the increase in debt sold by the U.S. Treasury.) Rather than directly purchase the U.S. government securities sold by the Treasury, the Fed allowed member banks to purchase these securities; the Fed then lent the funds directly to the banks.

The 33 percent increase in reserves from March 17, 1917, through November 18, 1918, was more than accounted for by the increase in Federal Reserve credit. During that same period, the money supply rose 18 percent. The fact that the money supply rose at a slower rate than the increase in reserves was due to a sharp rise in the demand for currency. This probably

---

[1]These assets consisted of bills of exchange, banker's acceptances, U.S. government securities, and municipal securities.

reflected attempts by individuals to conceal their incomes from wartime taxation.

INFLATION OCCURS

Of course, it is difficult to have a rapid increase in reserves and the money supply without some inflation occurring. Between March 1917 and November 1918, wholesale prices rose 23 percent. This increase was roughly proportional to the increase in the money supply—defined as currency plus checking account balances at commercial banks. At the end of the war in late 1918, prices stabilized and then declined briefly. But following a brief recession that resulted from the demobilization, prices started rising at an even more rapid rate than during the war. By the spring of 1919, the economy was experiencing a boom. Expectations of rising prices led to rapid accumulation of inventories as producers tried to buy raw materials before their prices went still higher. As this commodity speculation pushed up the prices of necessities while wages lagged, labor strikes disrupted the economy. Strikes in the railroad, coal mining, and textile industries interrupted production and contributed to further hoarding of raw materials.

FEDERAL RESERVE ACTIONS WITH RESPECT TO THE DISCOUNT RATE

Given the strong demand for credit induced by expectations of rising prices, the Fed's discount rate (which was 4 percent at that time) was decidedly below market rates of interest. The Fed continued to increase credit, mainly by lending to member banks, despite the ending of the war and the need for continual increases in Treasury borrowing. The Fed maintained an expansionary stance after the war ended.

As early as April 1919, several Federal Reserve district banks requested permission to increase the discount rate. The Federal Reserve Board ruled against them, however. The Board supported the view of Secretary of Treasury Carter Glass that the Federal Reserve should prevent the price of liberty bonds from declining. Commercial banks had been encouraged to invest in liberty bonds during the war; they had increased their holdings of government bonds by $4.2 billion. Any increase in the discount rate would increase the cost of continued financing of those bonds. The holders of such bonds would suffer capital losses. Remember from Chapter 6 that there is an inverse relationship between the market value of existing bonds and the market rates of interest. If the Fed allowed and indeed encouraged increases in the rate of interest, such increases would cause the market price, or value, of all government bonds (including liberty bonds) to fall. Actually even though the secretary of the Treasury and many members of Congress felt that it would be unethical for the government to pursue a policy that would cause large capital losses to the holders of liberty bonds, those liberty bondholders were being hurt anyway. After all, a continuing inflation was occurring and, therefore, the real value of the liberty bonds was falling. Consider a liberty bondholder who lent $1,000 to the government in 1917. If prices in general increased by 30 percent three years later, the person redeeming that bond for $1,000 would obtain only $769 in purchasing power.

The Discount Rate Is Finally Raised   Eventually, those in favor of raising the discount rate persuaded the Board to raise it to 3.75 percent on November 3, 1919. In January, the Board further increased the discount rate to 6 percent—the largest increase ever. The prices of existing government securities plunged with this increase in the discount rate and the subsequent increase in all market interest rates. In a three-month period, the $26 billion of government debt outstanding depreciated in market value by $3 billion.

Needless to say, this increase in the discount rate quickly caused member banks to reduce their borrowing from the Fed's discount window. The Fed's restrictive discounting policy, however, came perhaps too late because the stock of reserves in the banking system had already increased by 12 percent from November 1918 to May 1920. This increase in reserves was due mainly to a rapid increase in Federal Reserve lending to member banks through its discount window. The money supply during that same period rose 26 percent. Wholesale prices rose 22 percent. At the peak of the price level in May 1920, prices had more than doubled their 1914 level.

The Fed Overreacts   The rapid increase in prices caused the Fed to overreact. On June 1, 1920, the Federal Reserve Bank of New York raised the discount rate to 7 percent. This increase caused member banks to cut back sharply on any remaining borrowing from the Federal Reserve. Despite large gold inflows at that time, reserves in the banking system fell by 11 percent from September 1920 to July 1921. The money supply declined during that period by 9 percent.[2]

Inflation Disappears   Many prices fell sharply following the increase in the discount rate. By June 1921, wholesale prices had fallen dramatically from the level of May 1920. Additionally, 10 percent of the labor force became unemployed. The Fed was widely criticized because it had increased the discount rate so sharply and had kept the rate high long after it became clear that the economy was in one of the sharpest deflations in U.S. history.

Partly as a result of pressure from the Harding administration, the discount rate was lowered one-half of a percentage point to 6.5 percent in May 1921. Four more reductions in the discount rate brought it down to 4.5 percent by November 1921; recovery began. From July 1921 to May 1923, the narrowly defined money supply—currency plus checking account deposits at commercial banks—increased 14 percent. According to many students of

---

[2]At that time, there was a rise in the currency-to-deposit ratio so that the money multiplier contracted. See Chapter 8.

monetary history, this increase in the money supply caused a vigorous business expansion. Real gross national product rose almost 30 percent from 1921 to 1923 and signaled one of the strongest recoveries in U.S. business history. After falling 23 percent from 1920 to 1922, prices rose slightly in 1923 and then remained stable for the rest of the 1920s.

FEDERAL RESERVE POLICY DURING THE ROARING TWENTIES

During the early 1920s, for the first time in its brief history, the Fed was operating under "normal" peacetime conditions. In May 1922, the Fed established the Committee of Governors on Centralized Execution of Purchases and Sales of Government Securities by Federal Reserve Banks. Its purpose was to unify the monetary policy of the twelve district banks. In April 1923, the committee was abolished and replaced by the Open Market Investment Committee, the forerunner of today's Federal Open Market Committee (FOMC).

Starting in May 1927, the Open Market Investment Committee began to purchase U.S. government securities in order to combat a mild recession. The discount rate was reduced at most of the Federal Reserve district banks. The economy started to recover in late 1927; this recovery was accompanied by a stock market boom. By early 1928, the Fed was concerned about that boom. The bull market in stocks brought the Federal Reserve's objective of promoting economic recovery in conflict with the desire to restrain stock market speculation which might "destablize the stock market." Ultimately, the Fed's concern over stock market speculation caused it to switch to a restrictive monetary policy. The discount rate was raised at the majority of Federal Reserve district banks. In spite of these increases, member bank borrowing from the Fed continued. But stock market speculation did not slow down. Stock prices, which had shown very little change during the four months preceding August 1928, rose 5 percent during the remainder of the year.

As stock prices continued to climb throughout 1929, the Federal Reserve System continued to be concerned about stock market speculation. The Board and the district Federal Reserve banks disagreed, however, about the appropriate action to take. The Federal Reserve Board wanted to use **moral suasion** to get member banks to stop extending credit for stock market speculation. The Board insisted that borrowing from the discount window was a privilege and not a right. In early February 1929, the Board sent a letter to Federal Reserve district banks urging them to deny borrowing privileges to member banks that were lending the money to individuals and businesses that wanted to speculate in the stock market.

The Federal Reserve district banks wanted direct, unmistakable monetary policy restrictions, in the form of increases in the discount rate and open-market sales of U.S. government securities by the Fed. For example, beginning on February 14, 1929, the Federal Reserve Bank of New York requested an increase in the discount rate from 5 to 6 percent. The Board disapproved the request. Throughout March, April, and May, the Board continued to reject a barrage of requests for an increase in the discount rate on the part of the Federal Reserve Bank of New York.

In August, the Board finally approved an increase in the discount rate in New York to 6 percent; simultaneously, however, the Federal Reserve purchased U.S. government securities to ease market rates of interest.

The Bubble Bursts Stock prices continued to rise through August 1929 and reached a level in early September that was 30 percent higher than the level at the beginning of the year. Finally, persistently high interest rates burst the speculative bubble. The stock market reached its peak on September 7, 1929, when the Standard and Poor's composite price index of 90 common stocks hit 254. After falling to 228 on October 4, the stock market rallied to 245 on October 10. Then a selling panic hit the market. On September 24, 1929—Black Thursday—huge blocks of stocks were dumped on the market. Thirteen million shares were traded; this may be compared to a daily average of about 4 million before that time. On October 29, 16.5 million shares were traded; the Standard & Poor's index fell to 162.

The Fear of a Banking Crisis If the effects of the stock market decline could be limited to the stock market, the Fed and member banks would have had no worry. But they had to worry about a full-scale banking crisis. Stockbrokers had borrowed millions to finance purchases of stocks by their clients. Such loans were particularly large in New York City. The reduction in the value of stocks used as collateral for such loans meant that many of those loans could not be easily repaid. To ease the strain on New York City member commercial banks, the Federal Reserve Bank of New York voted to reduce the discount rate from 6 percent to 5.5 percent on October 24. But the Federal Reserve Board unanimously disapproved the request. The New York Fed was worried that a further reduction in stock prices would lead to more serious financial problems; more stock market investors would be unable to repay their loans to brokers, who would, in turn, be unable to repay their loans to commercial banks. Member commercial banks would then find that their current reserves were below their required reserves. In order to add reserves to the banking system in the New York area, the Federal Reserve Bank of New York purchased $50 million of U.S. government securities on October 29 and added another $65 million to its holdings during the next two days. These open-market operations were made on the New York Fed's own initiative; they were far in excess of the amount authorized by the Open Market Investment Committee, which had a standing rule that no more than $25 million could be purchased in any one week by a Federal Reserve district bank.

Several members of the Board were furious when the chairman of the New York Fed, Benjamin Harrison, informed them of his bank's actions, which were taken without prior approval of the Open Market Investment Committee. The Board unanimously passed a resolution calling for the suspension of further purchases of government securities by the Federal Reserve Bank of New

York. The New York Fed did, however, succeed in getting a reduction in the discount rate—down to 5 percent—approved by the Board on October 31.

Discount-Rate Reductions Lag behind Market Interest-Rate Reductions During the period from 1929 to 1933, the Fed allowed the various Federal Reserve district banks to lower their discount rates. Unfortunately, the declines in the discount rate were not as rapid as the declines in market rates of interest, as can be seen in Figure 27-1. The Board was confusing low absolute discount rates with easy money. Only to the extent that the discount rate is below the market rate of interest will member banks be encouraged to borrow more from their Federal Reserve district bank. As Figure 27-1 shows, at no time during this period was the discount rate below market rates of interest; at no time was the Fed's discount policy expansionary. Borrowings from the Federal Reserve declined during the period, and the money supply declined by 2.6 percent from August 1929 to October 1930.

A Banking Panic Ensues The economic situation had become dismal by autumn of 1930. During October, commercial banks started to fail in the midwest and in the south, regions which were particularly hurt by the slump in agricultural prices. This led to widespread attempts to convert checking-account deposits and time deposits into currency. Just as with the banking panics in the late 1800s and early 1900s before the formation of the Federal Reserve System, when the public attempted to convert deposits into currency, numerous banks

FIGURE 27-1 **The Discount Rate and the Market Rate of Interest.** During the period 1929–1933, a crucial period in the Great Depression, the discount rate fell, but it was always above "the" market interest rate (the 3-month T-bill rate). This indicates that the Fed failed to pursue an expansionary monetary policy during that crucial period. (*Source:* Board of Governors of the Federal Reserve Board, *1982 Historical Chart Book,* p. 89.)

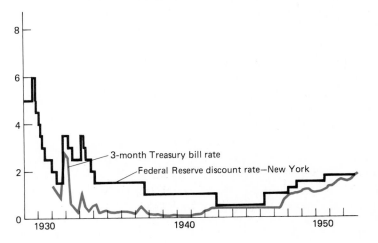

found themselves with inadequate reserves. Such is the nature of a fractional reserve banking system. As banks found they had insufficient reserves, a banking panic started.

By December 1930, the banking panic had spread to New York City. On December 11, the Bank of the United States (a privately owned bank in spite of its name) failed. This bank had 400,000 depositors and was a member of the Federal Reserve System. It was also the largest bank ever to fail in this country up to that time. The failure of the Bank of the United States caused the panic to spread further.

Runs on several other New York City banks occurred and led to huge net withdrawals of currency from the banking system in a short period of time. To alleviate these banking difficulties, the Federal Reserve Bank of New York purchased $45 million of U.S. government securities in the open market; this purchase was for its own account. The Federal Reserve System as a whole, through the New York trading desk, purchased another $80 million of U.S. government securities.

The Open Market Policy Conference (which replaced the Open Market Investment Committee in 1930) approved the New York Fed's actions at its January 1931 meeting. But the Open Market Policy Conference authorized no further open-market purchases; it actually recommended that the Federal Reserve System *sell* some of its government securities. By February 1931, the Fed's holdings of U.S. government securities had fallen by $130 million. This policy of open-market sales was brought to an end by a second wave of bank failures that started in March.

In spite of modest expansionary open-market purchases starting in mid-June, the money supply dropped by 5.25 percent during the five months from March to August 1930—the same drop that had occurred during the previous nineteen months. It was apparent that the Fed was not acting as a "lender of last resort"; the Fed failed to provide liquidity to banks during the banking panic.

THE GREAT DEPRESSION AND THE INTERNATIONAL SCENE

Meanwhile, the contraction of the U.S. money supply was causing international monetary problems. By the beginning of the Great Depression in 1929, most major industrial countries had returned to the gold standard. Because of this linkage of currencies under the gold standard, when one country experiences a decline in income (and therefore decreases the value of its imports relative to its exports), gold would flow to that country from other countries. This is exactly what occurred in the United States vis-à-vis the rest of the world. The decline in the U.S. money supply from 1929 to 1931, and the associated fall in nominal income, reduced the amount Americans spent on foreign goods and services. By 1931, American payments for imports of goods and services had fallen by 47 percent from their 1929 level. The resulting surplus in the U.S. balance of payments (see Chaper 29) produced an inflow of gold to the United States. This inflow was $640 million between September 1929 and September 1931. In principle, these gold inflows should have increased reserves in the U.S. banking system and cushioned the economic downturn. But at that time, the Federal Reserve was *selling* U.S. securities in its open-market operations and restricting member bank borrowings by *increasing* the discount rate.

Financial Crises Occur in Other Countries

The gold inflows into the United States obviously represented gold outflows from other countries which produced a financial crisis that threatened to sweep most of the world off the gold standard. Because a reduction in their gold supply directly reduced their reserves, other nations experienced reductions in their money supplies. Those countries that allowed (did not offset their gold outflows by expansionary monetary policies) such reductions in the money supply ultimately experienced a reduction in prices, thereby making their goods more appealing to Americans. In fact, only France and Italy allowed such a deflation. Other countries were not willing to allow the gold standard mechanism (which caused some countries to inflate, others to deflate, as gold flowed between nations) to operate. They wanted to prevent a reduction in their money supplies due to gold outflows. The Bank of England, for example, largely offset the deflationary effects of its gold outflows by increasing its purchases of securities and its lending to commercial banks. Ultimately, on September 31, 1931, the British government abandoned the gold standard. Other countries followed suit.

The combined effects of deflation in France and the British government's decision to abandon the gold standard led to a fundamental change. The United States started to experience gold outflows. From mid-September to the end of October 1931, the U.S. gold stock fell by 15 percent. Because at that time Federal Reserve notes were required by law to be backed 100 percent by gold and commercial paper that the Fed had (re)discounted, Fed holdings of commercial paper were relatively low, and more gold was required to back Federal Reserve notes.[3] Gold outflows threatened to reduce reserves against these notes below legal requirements. This caused a scare within the Federal Reserve System. In response to the gold outflows, the discount rate was increased sharply. The result was one of the most abrupt reductions in the money supply in U.S. history. In the five months from August 1931 to January 1932, the money supply fell by 12 percent, or at an annual rate of over 31 percent. From January to March 1932, the money supply continued to decline, but at the slower rate of 13 percent per year.

---

[3]In February 1932, the Glass-Steagall Act was passed, which permitted the Fed to use government securities (as well as gold and commercial paper) to back Federal Reserve notes.

THE FED ATTEMPTS TO REVERSE COURSE

Eventually Congress imposed indirect pressure on the Fed to reverse its de facto tight money policy. Congress was considering the passage of a "soldiers' bonus" bill, which would make substantial payments to veterans of World War I. To finance these payments, legislation was introduced in the Senate that would force Federal Reserve district banks to issue Federal Reserve notes. The Treasury was to sell bonds to the Fed in exchange for the Federal Reserve notes that were to be given to the veterans. Fed officials unanimously opposed this legislation as inflationary. They therefore devised a strategy of heading off the legislation by expanding the money supply. For example, the Federal Reserve Bank of New York lowered its discount rate from 3.5 percent to 2.5 percent, and the Open Market Policy Conference approved a dramatic program of U.S. government open-market securities purchases. From February 24 through June 1932, the Fed bought more than $1 billion in open-market operations. This was the largest purchase ever made by the Federal Reserve System up to that time. Unfortunately, even these large open-market purchases had little immediate effect on the money supply because of the outflow of gold.[4] Moreover, soon after Congress adjourned on July 16, the Fed stopped its net purchases of U.S. government securities. After August 10, no net purchases were made until 1933.

Roosevelt Declares a Banking Holiday   In 1930 and again in 1931, there were waves of bank failures. The final wave started in the last quarter of 1932. As the banking panic spread to New York, Governor Harrison of the New York Fed tried to persuade President Hoover to close all the banks for a "banking holiday," in order to stall for time and to calm people who wanted to withdraw their deposits from the banks. This had stopped bank runs in the past. President Hoover refused, but Harrison and the state superintendent of banks did succeed in getting New York Governor Lehman to declare a statewide banking holiday on March 4, 1933—the day Franklin Roosevelt was inaugurated. The day after he assumed office, Roosevelt invoked the questionable authority of the 1917 Trading with the Enemy Act to close all commercial banks and prohibit transactions in gold or foreign exchange. When Congress reconvened in March, it overwhelmingly passed the Emergency Banking Act, which extended the banking holiday and reaffirmed the President's authority to prohibit the export of gold. When the banking holiday ended on March 15, 1933, fewer than 12,000 banks reopened—less than half of the 25,000 banks in operation in mid-1929.

Thus ended the most disastrous monetary collapse in American history. From August 1929 to March 1933 the U.S. money supply declined by 35 percent. Total spending on goods and services had fallen by more than 50 per-

---

[4]The money-supply multiplier had also declined during that period.

cent. Consumer prices had fallen by 25 percent. The seemingly boundless prosperity of 1929 was followed by the bread lines of the 1930s. The official unemployment rate, which was only 3.2 percent in 1929, soared to nearly 25 percent of the labor force during 1933.

Prohibitions on the Ownership of Gold Continue   Following the reopening of the banks, savers' trust in bank deposits was rapidly restored and currency was poured back into the banking system. But the prohibition on dealings in gold and foreign exchange remained in force. On April 5, 1933, Roosevelt made an unprecedented move by nationalizing all gold outside the Federal Reserve district banks. All owners of gold were required to deliver their gold coins, bullion, and gold certificates to Federal Reserve banks before May 1 and to exchange them for currency or deposits at the then-official price of $20.67 per ounce. By calling in all gold, the domestic convertibility of the dollar into gold was ended. That is, individuals could no longer assume that they could exchange dollar bills or dollar deposits for gold. In fact, such an exchange remained illegal from then until December 31, 1974.

On January 31, 1934, President Roosevelt announced that the dollar now would be valued at $35 an ounce for international transactions, 69 percent above the previous official gold price. In effect, the United States returned to a modified gold standard with the restriction that no one in the United States could privately own gold. Gold inflows to the United States during the years 1934 to 1937 amounted to $5.578 billion. These gold inflows added to reserves of the banking system. When the Treasury bought gold, it paid for that gold with a check on its account at one of the Federal Reserve district banks. When the check was cashed, a member commercial bank was credited with additional reserves, which increased reserves in the banking system. The Treasury then printed a gold certificate of a corresponding amount and redeposited it at the Federal Reserve bank. These purchases accounted for most of the increase in reserves from May 1933 to May 1937. During that time the Fed engaged in relatively few net open-market purchases of U.S. government securities. Discount rates at the various Federal Reserve district banks were also set *above* market rates, and this discouraged member bank borrowing.

GROWTH IN THE MONEY SUPPLY PRODUCES SOME RECOVERY

Students of monetary policy maintain that the growth in the money supply during this period produced a substantial recovery from the depressed levels of 1933. Output increased almost 60 percent from 1933 to 1937, but given the depressed level from which it began, it was only 3 percent higher in 1937 then in 1929. Because the population had grown by 6 percent in the interim, per capita income was actually lower than in 1929. The unemployment rate was still a substantial 14 percent in 1937.

The high level of discount rates relative to market interest rates made member commercial banks extremely reluctant to borrow from the Federal Reserve. Member banks, reluctant to lend, accumulated cash reserves in excess of legal requirements as an alternative source of liquidity to meet unanticipated withdrawals (perhaps also because they remembered the 1929 to 1933 banking crisis). In other words, they were holding prudential reserves (reserves above required reserves). By 1936, excess reserves held by member banks totaled $3 billion. Federal Reserve officials felt that these excess reserves were serving no useful purpose and might later serve as the source of an undesired expansion in bank credit. On August 16, 1936, the Fed increased legal reserve requirements by 50 percent in an attempt to immobilize about $1.5 billion of these excess reserves. The Fed, unfortunately, did not understand the circumstances of the time. Banks desired to hold excess reserves as an additional source of liquidity. When the Fed increased legal reserve requirements, banks *further* restricted their loans in an attempt to make up the lost prudential reserves. Consequently, the money supply fell. In the midst of this slowdown in the growth of reserves, the Fed mistakenly increased reserve requirements again in two steps. These increases became effective on March 1 and May 1, absorbing another $1.5 billion in excess reserves. The money supply fell by 6 percent in 1937. The recovery was nipped in the bud.

In the spring of 1937, the economy entered a sharp recession. Many blamed the recession on increased reserve requirements instituted by the Federal Reserve because the money supply contracted so much in response. The decline in industrial production, employment, and income accelerated in August of that year. The recession was short, but it was extremely severe. From May 1937 to June 1939, industrial production and factory employment fell by 25 percent. Real gross national product in 1938 was 5 percent below that in the preceding year. The average unemployment rate jumped from 14.3 percent in 1937 to 19 percent in 1938.

WAR BREAKS OUT IN EUROPE—GOLD INFLOWS OCCUR

War broke out in Europe in September 1939. As occurred at the beginning of World War I, the United States was flooded with gold inflows. The monetary gold stock rose $1.43 billion in the second half of 1939, $3.102 billion in 1939, and $4.272 billion in 1940. No attempt was made by the Fed or by the U.S. Treasury to counteract the gold inflows. Reserves in the banking system therefore increased substantially. These gold inflows financed American exports of food and war materials mainly to France and to Britain. There were also large inflows of money capital, "sheltered" from war-torn Europe.

In the late 1940s, the gold inflows had started to decline. France surrendered to Germany in June of 1940 and could no longer send more gold. Moreover, by early 1941, Great Britain had exhausted almost all its gold reserves.

As the means of financing exports with gold disappeared, Roosevelt asked Congress for the Lend-Lease Act, which provided U.S. government credit that allowed the British to pay for purchases of war materials. A month after the lend-lease program began in March 1941, gold inflows ceased. The gold stock, which had increased by over $4 billion in 1940, rose by less than $1 billion in 1941.

Altogether, the money supply increased 29 percent from August 1939 to November 1941, or at an annual rate of 11 percent. During the same period wholesale prices rose 23 percent, or at an annual rate of 9 percent. Unemployment fell to 9.9 percent.

The Federal Deficit Increases By mid-1941, the expanded defense program initiated in 1940 and the lend-lease program initiated in early 1941 had caused a sharp rise in the federal government deficit. For the calendar year 1941, the deficit was $10 billion, or nearly one-half of total government expenditures. When the United States entered the war, deficits rose to unprecedented (for that time) levels: to nearly $40 billion in calendar year 1941, over $50 billion in 1943, over $45 billion in 1944, and over $35 billion in 1945. For the six years following mid-1940, federal deficits totaled nearly $187 billion.

The Treasury was faced with the necessity of borrowing huge amounts to cover these deficits. The Federal Reserve immediately assumed the subordinate role of helping the U.S. Treasury sell government securities to finance the war effort. The Treasury set the interest rates paid on government securities to range from three-eighths of a percentage point to be paid on Treasury bills, to 2.5 percent on long-term bonds. The Treasury made it clear that this structure would be maintained throughout the war so that investors would have nothing to gain by waiting for later issues.[5]

The Fed Pegs Interest Rates In March 1942, the FOMC pledged to support the Treasury's rate structure by committing itself to buy any amount of securities offered at par value. This *pegging* of government securities prices made such securities perfectly liquid. Because long-term government bonds were perfectly liquid, there was little incentive for the public to buy shorter-term securities that had lower yields. The net result was that the Federal Reserve System ended up holding all the short-term Treasury bills outstanding. The Federal Reserve kept its word. The rate structure remained within the designated pattern throughout the war.

In the process, however, the Fed surrendered its control over the money supply and monetary policy in general. In order to prevent interest rates from rising, the Fed was forced to purchase increasing quantities of government securities in open-market operations. Remember that every purchase of a government security by the Fed constitutes an increase in depository-institu-

---

[5]During World War I, rates on Treasury securities were allowed to rise gradually, inflicting capital losses on those investors who patriotically responded to the Treasury's call for funds early in the war.

tion reserves and results in a potential multiple expansion in the money supply. By the end of 1945, the Federal Reserve banks held more than ten times the amount of government securities that they had held at the time of the bombing of Pearl Harbor. Consequently, during the 4½ years from January 1942 to June 1946, the money supply more than doubled.

Normally such massive increases in the money supply would have led to overt inflation. But inflationary pressure was largely constrained by various direct controls on the economy.[6] Wage and price ceilings were established and many goods were rationed. As a result, wholesale prices rose only 15 percent from the imposition of price controls in May 1942 to the removal of the controls in June 1946. When price controls were suspended in mid-1946, prices soared. Wholesale prices rose 24 percent during the second half of 1946 and this was more than they had risen during the previous 4½ years.

THE FEDERAL RESERVE CONTINUES ITS PEGGING POLICY AFTER THE WAR ENDS

Even after the war ended, the Fed continued to peg the prices and yields on Treasury obligations. Early in 1947, the Fed persuaded the Treasury to accept an unconstrained market interest rate on Treasury bills; the three-eighths of a percentage point paid was terminated. More important, though, the interest rate for long-term government bonds remained at 2.5 percent. The Treasury wanted to maintain the low interest rate policy primarily to minimize the interest cost of the federal debt. Even though the Treasury was not faced with large deficits in the early postwar period, it still had to refinance maturing obligations. It also feared that a decline in bond prices would weaken confidence in those financial institutions with large bond holdings. In addition, the Treasury argued that it would be unfair to inflict losses on the patriotic citizens who had invested heavily to support the war effort.

Despite the interest-rate-pegging policy, the Fed made virtually no purchases of government securities in 1948. A postwar depression was expected; these expectations actually kept market rates of interest below the pegged rates. As a result of zero open-market purchases, the money supply actually fell during 1948 and a recession began in November 1948. By July 1949, the unemployment rate had risen to 6.3 percent, from 3 percent in late 1948. The recession also brought to a halt the postwar inflation. By the end of 1949, inflation (as measured by the rate of change of the consumer price index) had fallen five percentage points from its peak in August 1948.

Inflation Starts Again The 1949 recession provided only a brief respite from inflation, however. The outbreak of the Korean war in mid-1950 drastically altered the public's expectations. Consumers and businesspeople alike, fearing a return of wartime controls and rationing, rushed out to buy goods. This buying spree

---

[6]Of course, repressed inflation resulted, in the form of shortages, black markets, and quality reductions.

and the associated expectation of higher prices pushed up market interest rates to levels which again required the Federal Reserve to buy government securities in order to prevent their prices from falling. The Fed added about $3 billion to its holding of government securities during the last half of 1950; the money supply started to increase rapidly; and the Consumer Price Index rose 8 percent from 1950 to 1951.

An Accord Is Reached between the Fed and the Treasury With the resurgence of inflation, the Federal Reserve felt that it must abandon the interest-rate-pegging program in order to prevent runaway inflation. The Treasury and President Truman, on the other hand, continued to argue that the 2.5 percent long-term bond rate should be maintained. After considerable controversy, this conflict was resolved in early 1951. A joint statement, now known as the Treasury–Federal Reserve Accord, was issued on March 4, 1951. It stated that:

> The Treasury and the Federal Reserve System have reached full accord with respect to debt management and monetary policies to be pursued in furthering their common purpose to assure the successful financing of the government's requirements and at the same time to minimize monetization of the public debt.

Under the terms of the accord, the Treasury exchanged new long-term bonds bearing a 2.75 percent yield on outstanding long-term bonds, and the Fed withdrew its active support from the government securities markets.

The accord was a clear-cut victory for the Federal Reserve. It could return to a monetary policy that was not dictated by interest-rate pegging. However, the abandonment of rigid support prices made government bonds far less liquid than they had been. Because their prices then fluctuated with market rates of interest, long-term government bonds were no longer a close substitute for money balances. After this elimination of a substitute for money balances, the public's demand for money (currency plus demand deposits in commercial banks) increased. Despite a continuing increase in the supply of money, therefore, the increase in the demand for money offset the upward pressure on prices. Inflation ended—at least temporarily.[7]

THE FEDERAL RESERVE UNDER THE EISENHOWER ADMINISTRATION

Under the Eisenhower administration, the Fed regained full freedom. It announced that it would no longer buy or sell long-term government bonds and that it would confine its open-market operations to short-term maturities (especially to Treasury bills). This came to be known as the Bills Only Doctrine. With the Bills Only Doctrine, the Fed gave up the power to engage in **swap**

---

[7]Remember, inflation occurs only if the supply of money increases *relative to the demand for money;* if the supply of money and the demand for money change at the same rate, the price level need not change.

operations (that is, buying some maturities to raise their prices and selling others to lower their prices). By not dealing in securities of various maturities, the Fed left the determination of the term structure of interest rates to the free market. By confining its operation to Treasury bills, which are closest to money, the Fed also reassured those government securities dealers who carried large inventories of long-term bonds that it would not arbitrarily inflict large capital losses on them by selling long-term government bonds.

The Fed Combats a New Recession Early in 1954, the Fed took vigorous action to combat an economic downturn resulting from a combination of a slowdown in the rate of monetary growth (because the Fed feared an outbreak of inflation) and a large cut in government expenditures as the Korean conflict ended. The discount rate was reduced in February, April, and May of 1954, and reserve requirements were lowered in June and July. Large quantities of government securities were purchased by the FOMC. These monetary actions resulted in a substantial acceleration in the rate of monetary growth, to an annual rate of 4 percent from early 1954 to April 1955.

The recovery started at the end of 1954. Industrial production increased by over 5.5 percent from August to December 1954, and rose by another 11 percent during 1955. By the summer of 1955, the unemployment rate had fallen below 4 percent and prices began to rise.

During 1956, the rate of price increase, as measured by changes in the Consumer Price Index, accelerated. From February 1956 to the end of 1956, the CPI rose by nearly 3 percent.

The Fed Runs Hot and Cold The Fed reacted to the increased inflation by raising the discount rate and selling government securities. When unemployment increased in early 1958, the Fed eased its monetary policy by reducing the discount rate and by purchasing modest quantities of U.S. government securities. In that year reserve requirements were lowered; money supply growth increased substantially.

The Concern for Gold The easy money policies of the Fed caused interest rates to fall. Money capital outflows occurred as investors sought higher yields in other countries, and this caused a deficit in the U.S. balance of payments. In turn, this gave the Fed concern for gold outflows, and the Fed therefore abandoned its easy money policy in May 1958 and started raising the discount rate. The Fed also started to sell U.S. government securities. The money supply *declined* at an annual rate of 2 percent from the summer of 1959 to the summer of 1960. The economy entered another recession in the first quarter of 1960.

THE PRESIDENTIAL CAMPAIGN OF 1960

The recession became an important issue in the presidential campaign of 1960. Real output fell at an annual rate of 1.5 percent from the first quarter to the fourth quarter of 1960. The unemployment rate rose from about 5 percent at the beginning of 1960 to over 6 percent by election day. The Democratic candidate, John F. Kennedy, pointed to the recession as evidence of Republican failure in the area of economic policymaking. He pledged to get America "moving again." While it is not clear how many votes were swayed, the economic issue obviously was an important factor in the election of President Kennedy. The Fed responded to the onset of the recession by easing its restrictive monetary policy. Beginning in late March 1960, the Fed started purchasing government securities in open-market operations. It also reduced the discount rate from 4 percent to 3.5 percent in June and to 3 percent in August. Reserve requirements were reduced in September and December 1960. These combined actions brought the decline in the money supply to a halt. The money supply grew at an annual rate of over 2 percent from June 1960 to April 1961. When John F. Kennedy was inaugurated, the economy had already started to recover.

OPERATION TWIST

The recovery was short-lived. The unemployment rate fell from 7 percent in early 1961 to 5.5 percent in 1962 but then started creeping up to the 6 percent level again. Simultaneously, the United States suffered balance-of-payments deficits and gold outflows. The Fed was faced with a dilemma: If it lowered the discount rate and sold securities in open-market operations, market rates of interest would fall. This would stimulate the domestic economy, but it would enlarge the gold outflows resulting from a deficit in the balance of payments. Market rates of interest in other countries would look more attractive to investors, and investment funds (money capital) would leave this country.

The Fed decided to attempt a twist in the term structure of interest rates. The term structure up to that time had been one in which short-term interest rates were lower than long-term interest rates. The Fed now wanted to make short-term interest rates higher than long-term interest rates, because international capital flows respond more to differences in short-term rates. The Fed reasoned that lower long-term rates would stimulate domestic investment spending; simultaneously, higher short-term rates would reduce money-capital outflows to other countries, thereby minimizing the deficit in the balance of payments. To implement this "twist" operation, the Fed abandoned the Bills Only Doctrine in February 1961; it bought long-term bonds and at the same time sold Treasury bills to prevent Federal Reserve credit (and hence reserves and the money supply) from growing too rapidly. Did "operation twist" work? Unfortunately there is little evidence that this strategy had any effect at all.

Kennedy Proposes Stimulative Fiscal Policy Kennedy's economic advisers came up with an alternative solution to the conflict between domestic and international objectives by proposing a stimulative *fiscal* policy. They reasoned that an increase in the profitability of domestic investment and an increase in the federal budget deficit would cause interest rates to rise because there would be an increased demand for loanable funds. This would counteract the tendency for interest rates to fall when the Fed increased the rate of monetary growth.

In 1962 Kennedy took two steps to stimulate private investment. First, he persuaded Congress to accelerate the rate at which firms could depreciate their investments for tax purposes. Second, he convinced Congress to enact an investment tax credit that permitted business firms to deduct from their tax bill an amount equal to 7 percent of the cost of new equipment. These measures had the desired effect and set off an investment boom.

The increased demand for loanable funds to finance this new investment pushed interest rates up in late 1962. As interest rates rose, the Fed's discount rate of 3 percent looked very attractive; member commercial banks borrowed heavily from the Fed. The Fed also purchased government securities in open-market operations. The money supply grew accordingly; after remaining virtually constant from April through September, the money supply accelerated to a 3.5 percent annual rate from September 1962 to March 1964 (despite an increase in the discount rate from 3 percent to 3.5 percent in June 1963).

The economy grew rapidly. From the second quarter of 1963 to the first quarter of 1964, real GNP increased at an annual rate of almost 6 percent. This economic growth did not satisfy President Kennedy, however. In late 1962, he proposed an additional fiscal stimulus; he asked for a reduction in personal and corporate income tax rates, but these were not passed until February 26, 1963. Personal income tax rates were reduced and corporate income tax rates were reduced from 52 percent to 48 percent.

MONETARY POLICY DURING THE VIETNAM WAR

Beginning in June 1965, the United States became heavily involved in the war in Vietnam. Government expenditures for Vietnam war needs increased rapidly along with increased government expenditures for the "Great Society" programs. These increased outlays were not matched by an equal increase in taxes, and the federal government deficit began to soar. An increase in the deficit per se does not necessarily lead to an increase in the rate of monetary growth. Only if the Fed decides to monetize the debt by simultaneously buying U.S. government securities do deficits increase depository-institution reserves and the money supply. The Fed initially did monetize the increased debt. When the Treasury sold its newly issued U.S. government securities to the public, the Fed was unwilling to see interest rates rise because of the ill effects higher interest rates have on the housing and the capital-goods industries. After all, an increased supply of government securities (without increased demand) will lead to a reduction in the price of government securities, which is tantamount to an increase in interest rates. Unwilling to see interest rates rise, the Fed had to purchase large amounts of government securities in open-market operations. The rate of growth of the money supply accelerated. After increasing at an annual rate of 3.9 percent from September 1962 to June 1965, the money-supply growth rate accelerated to 6.5 percent annually from June 1965 to April 1966. At that time the economy was close to full employment; the only thing that could occur with the rapid increase in the rate of growth of the money supply was inflation. The CPI had increased at an annual rate of about one-half percent per year from early 1961 to the summer of 1965. By early 1966 the CPI was growing at a 3.5 percent rate.

The Fed Is in Conflict with President Johnson In December 1965, the Fed became concerned about the acceleration of inflation. It moved toward a more restrictive monetary policy by raising the discount rate from 4 percent to 4.5 percent. This move produced an open conflict between the Fed and the Johnson administration. That administration (like previous wartime ones) wanted to finance the war at below-market interest rates. The Fed bowed to White House pressure and continued to purchase large amounts of government securities in open-market operations. This lasted until April 1966. In May, however, the FOMC moved aggressively toward restraint; the rate of growth of the money supply slowed. In the second half of 1966, the money supply did not increase at all. This period became known as the "credit crunch."

Because the Fed at this time was no longer helping to finance the government deficit by buying bonds in open-market operations, the Treasury borrowed directly from the public by selling bonds. Since the government had to compete with private borrowers for available funds, interest rates rose sharply. High-grade corporate bond rates rose from 4.5 percent in 1965 to over 6 percent in the autumn of 1966.

Rising Interest Rates and Regulation Q Recall from Chapter 10 that Regulation Q imposed maximum interest rates payable on all time deposits. As market interest rates on other types of deposits rose above Regulation Q ceiling rates on time deposits, these types of deposits became extremely attractive and time deposits became unattractive. Although the Board of Governors of the Federal Reserve Board had set interest-rate ceilings on time deposits since the 1930s, such ceiling interest rates never became operational because the Board maintained them above market rates on comparable assets. But in 1966, the interest-rate ceilings under Regulation Q were not raised. In fact, ceilings on some types of time deposits were actually lower. The Fed had become extremely concerned about the ill effects on savings and loan associations of generally rising market interest rates.[8]

Traditionally S&Ls *borrowed* funds on a short-term basis and *invested* primarily in long-term mortgages. As interest rates rose, the cost of borrowing short-term funds increased, but the income earned on S&L portfolios of mortgages increased at a much slower rate. As a result many S&Ls were threatened with insolvency. The Fed felt that any competition from banks offering to pay higher interest rates on time deposits would exacerbate the S&L prob-

---

[8]Actually, at that time the Fed was prepared to make direct loans to S&Ls.

lem. Also, for the first time, the Federal Home Loan Bank Board (FHLBB) set legal limits on interest S&Ls could *pay* on their deposits in an attempt to limit competition within the industry. These measures, however, did not entirely insulate S&Ls from the market. When interest rates rose above ceiling rates, many depositors simply withdrew their deposits and purchased other assets. This process is conventionally known as "disintermediation," a topic discussed in Chapters 1, 4, and 10. The net flow of funds into S&Ls fell to one-fourth the previous year's level. As a result of the higher interest rates and the reduced flow of funds into the mortgage market (in which the S&Ls had previously re-lent), residential construction dropped to its lowest level since the end of World War II.

Restrictive Monetary Policy Ends   By the end of 1966 the economy was showing considerable weakness. Real GNP actually fell during the first quarter of 1967. Concern about the deteriorating economy and fears of further withdrawals from S&Ls caused the Fed to end its restrictive monetary policies. It made an about-face and implemented a highly expansionary policy in early 1967. Aggressively, the Fed began to purchase large amounts of government securities in open-market operations. As a result, the money supply growth rate increased to 7.4 percent from January 1967 to July 1968. Interest rates did fall sharply in 1967 and caused funds to flow back into time deposits and S&Ls. Simultaneously, inflation accelerated; by 1968 the rate of growth of the Consumer Price Index (CPI) was 5 percent.

INFLATION BECOMES A POLITICAL ISSUE

By 1968 inflation had become an important political issue. President Johnson called for a 10 percent surtax and a reduction of $6 billion in federal expenditures in an effort to reduce inflationary pressures. Congress passed the legislation in June. The Fed, however, had different ideas; it continued its expansionary monetary policy and lowered the discount rate from 5.5 percent to 5.25 percent in August 1968. By the end of the year, it had become evident that fiscal restraint alone was not enough to affect substantially the growth of total spending. Thus, the Fed acted to slow the rate of monetary growth. Discount rates were raised from 5.25 percent to 5.75 percent in December 1968 and to 6 percent in April. Reserve requirements against demand deposits at member banks were increased by one-half a percentage point. At the same time, the Fed refrained from open-market purchases of government securities. The rate of monetary growth slowed: After increasing at a 7.6 percent annual rate from January 1967 to January 1969, the rate of monetary growth slowed to 5.1 percent from January 1969 to June 1969. It showed almost no increase during the second half of 1969.

The slowdown in the rate of monetary growth caused interest rates to soar. Three-month Treasury bill rates rose from 5.45 percent in November 1968 to 7.87 percent in January 1970. As during the credit crunch of 1966, the sharp increase in market rates of interest was accompanied by disintermediation and a sharp reduction of funds flowing into the mortgage market. A recession started in the fourth quarter of 1969. The unemployment rate, which had averaged 3.3 percent in the first month of 1969, climbed to over 6 percent by late 1970.

ARTHUR BURNS TAKES OVER THE FED

In January 1970 President Nixon replaced William McChesney Martin, who had been chairperson of the Federal Reserve Board since 1951, with Arthur Burns. Immediately thereafter the Fed actively purchased government securities in open-market operations. When the Penn Central Transportation Company filed for bankruptcy in 1970, the Fed tried to prevent a panic in the commercial paper market by actively encouraging banks to borrow from Federal Reserve district banks at discount rates far below market rates of interest, thereby providing liquidity. In August the Fed also lowered reserve requirements; the discount rate was further reduced in November. As a consequence, the rate of growth of the money supply accelerated to 5.5 percent annually during 1970.

Meanwhile, President Nixon had also taken steps to stimulate the economy. The 10 percent surcharge on income taxes passed in 1968 was terminated and federal expenditures increased. By the summer of 1970, the economy had begun to recover. Although the economy did suffer a temporary setback from a major automobile strike in the fourth quarter, real GNP rose at an annual rate of about 2.5 percent from the second quarter of 1970 to the second quarter of 1971.

A Deteriorating Balance-of-Payments Position Throughout the late 1960s, inflation in the United States caused American goods to lose their competitive advantage in world markets. A U.S. *payments* deficit existed throughout the middle and late 1960s, (despite the fact that it had a *trade* surplus; the value of exports exceeded the value of imports) except for 1969. When short-term interest rates fell dramatically in 1970 and 1971, the U.S. balance-of-payments situation worsened; capital flowed to other countries where interest rates were higher. International investors and speculators feared an imminent **devaluation** of the dollar—a reduction in the price of the dollar in terms of other currencies—and further shifted their assets out of dollars. In 1971, the U.S. suffered one of its largest balance-of-payments deficits ever, and this caused turmoil in foreign exchange markets. Germany and other countries stopped supporting the dollar.

NIXON DROPS A BOMBSHELL

It was against this background of turmoil on the foreign exchange market that President Nixon made a dramatic change in his economic policies. On Sunday evening, August 15, 1971, Nixon announced a radically new policy to deal with the overvalued dollar (the dollar was pegged to other currencies at a rate that caused a U.S. balance-of-payments deficit). The new policy included:

1   A ninety-day freeze on wages and prices
2   A suspension of convertibility of the dollar into gold
3   An import surcharge of 10 percent

In the month that followed, John Connally, Nixon's new secretary of the Treasury, used the leverage of the 10 percent import surcharge to negotiate a new set of exchange rates. This new set of exchange rates effectively reduced the value of the dollar by about 12 percent against the currencies of major industrial countries and raised the official price of gold to $38 per ounce.

The freeze on prices did have a significant effect on the *overt inflation* rate. (Of course, *repressed inflation* resulted.) With the exception of farm prices, which were exempt from controls, the rate of inflation declined sharply. After rising at an annual rate of 4.3 percent from December 1970 to August 1971, nonfarm prices rose at an annual rate of only 1.2 percent during the freeze. Although nonfarm price increases did briefly accelerate to a 3.5 percent annual rate after the freeze, they decelerated again to a 1.5 percent annual rate from February 1972 to December 1972.

With the Nixon wage and price controls in place, the Fed shifted to an extremely expansionary monetary policy in 1972 and increased the money supply at an 8.5 percent annual rate. Both from the monetary and fiscal sides, stimulation occurred and caused a recovery in overall economic activity in 1972. By election day, 1972, the unemployment rate had fallen from 6 percent in late 1971 to only 5.2 percent.

CONTROLS ARE ABANDONED

Nixon gradually phased out wage and price controls and they were finally abolished in April 1974. With the removal of price controls and the sharp increase in oil prices (resulting from the Arab oil embargo and OPEC's subsequent quadrupling of oil prices), inflation increased. The Fed responded in the second half of 1974 by raising the discount rate from 7.5 percent to 8 percent. Open-market operations also became restrictive. The rate of monetary growth fell. In the seven months from June 1974 to January 1975, the money supply grew at an annual rate of only 1.3 percent. Many blamed the recession on the overly restrictive stance of the Federal Reserve. The economy in fact plunged into one of the worst recessions since the 1930s. The unemployment rate climbed from 5 percent in the spring of 1974 to over 9 percent in May 1975.

It wasn't until the second quarter of 1975 that the economy started to recover. This was due at least in part to renewed expansionary monetary policy and increased government spending. The recovery, however, was short-lived. After the first quarter of 1976, the growth rate of real GNP slowed and further progress toward reducing the unemployment rate became more difficult. By election day, 1976, the unemployment rate was still 7.8 percent. Inflation, however, was slowing. After rising at double-digit rates during 1974, the rate of increase in the CPI fell to an annual rate of only 4.2 percent by the last quarter of 1976.

MONETARY POLICY UNDER PRESIDENTS CARTER AND REAGAN

In late 1976, partly in deference to the wishes of the President-elect, Jimmy Carter, the Fed switched to a highly expansionary monetary policy. Throughout 1977, the Fed increased the money supply at rapid rates. Despite this rapid monetary growth, President Carter criticized the Fed publicly for being too restrictive. He replaced Arthur Burns as chairman in early 1978 with G. William Miller. Under Carter's appointee, the money supply continued to grow rapidly. Altogether, from the third quarter of 1976 to the third quarter of 1978, the money supply increased at an annual rate of 8 percent. During this period, the unemployment rate fell from 7.8 percent to only 5.8 percent. By 1978, however, the rate of inflation had accelerated to 9 percent annually.

Because of this high rate of inflation the President had a change of heart. So, too, did the Fed. After permitting the money supply to grow at an 8.2 percent annual rate from the fourth quarter of 1976 to the fourth quarter of 1978, the Fed slowed the rate of growth of the money supply to only 4.7 percent from November 1978 to February 1979. But this monetary restraint did not last long. During the second quarter of 1979, the rate of monetary growth accelerated to an annual rate of 10.5 percent; it continued to grow 10 percent annually in the third quarter. Carter decided to make Fed Chairman G. William Miller the secretary of the Treasury. In his place, Carter appointed Paul Volcker, then president of the New York Fed. Volcker at that time was one of the most outspoken critics of the Fed's inflationary monetary policies. Even after Volcker's appointment, however, the money supply continued to grow at double-digit rates.

On October 6, 1979, the FOMC altered its operating procedures. The Fed announced that in an attempt to control inflation it would now stress attainment of monetary aggregates and become less concerned with targeting the federal funds rate. In separate actions, the Fed raised the discount rate by a full percentage point, to 12 percent, and raised reserve requirements on certain categories of bank liabilities. Following this October policy initiative, the rate of monetary growth did slow to an annual growth rate of less than 5 percent. When in February 1980 the rate of growth of the money supply started to accelerate, the Fed reacted immediately by raising the discount rate to 13 percent.

The year 1980, the first full year under which money growth rates were targeted, was associated with larger variations in interest rates *and* larger variations in the rate of growth of M1 than was anticipated. Also, a short recession appeared, from the first quarter into the third quarter, during that year. In March of 1980, a 3 percent surcharge was added to the 13 percent discount rate for large commercial banks that had borrowed frequently from the Fed. In addition, at the request of the Carter administration, the Fed introduced a credit restraint program that imposed a 50 percent marginal reserve requirement on specific kinds of consumer lending. Following these actions, the money supply *declined* at an annual rate of over 5 percent from February to May.

The year 1981 also saw erratic changes in the rate of growth of the money stock. From January to April, M1 increased at an annual rate of over 13 percent. Then, from May until October, the *rate of growth* of M1 dropped dramatically; during that period, M1 actually *fell* slightly. This monetary restraint contributed to the severe recession that existed from the third quarter of 1981 to the fourth quarter of 1982. During that recession, the velocity of M1 *fell*. In the fourth quarter of 1982, the annual growth rates of nominal GNP, M1, and the velocity of M1 were 1.3 percent, 14.5 percent, and −12.7 percent, respectively. This reduction in velocity stands in sharp contrast to its annual growth rate of 3.2 percent since the post-World War II period. A decrease in the velocity of M1 means an increase in the demand for M1 balances; this volatility in the demand for money represents a strong challenge to the monetarists, who are in favor of targeting monetary aggregates and not interest rates. Remember that Chapter 26 concluded that if the demand for money is volatile, so too will be the *LM* curve, and a monetary policy that targets interest rates will be superior to one that targets monetary aggregates.

By the end of 1981, the Fed switched gears again and started to increase the rate of growth of M1. From November until December, M1 grew at an annual rate of over 12 percent.

From September 1982 to the summer of 1983, M1 increased, at annual rates, by double-digit amounts. This contributed to the strong recovery that existed by the spring of 1983; the recovery was sparked by low interest rates that generated increased household expenditures on durable goods and housing. It should be noted that velocity continued to decline. From the second quarter of 1982 to the second quarter of 1983, the velocity of M1 fell by almost 5 percent. Again, this is in contrast to a steady increase in velocity since World War II.

The inability of the Fed to achieve its monetary-growth targets and the apparent recent volatility in the velocity of money have led to considerable disillusionment with the monetarist approach. It remains to be seen whether velocity will stabilize—after the effects of recent financial innovation and deregulation are fully worked out.

By February 1983, Paul Volcker, chairman of the Fed, believed that the recovery would be long-lasting.[9] He noted, however, the following threats to such progress:

1   The prospect of huge federal deficits increasing real interest rates and thereby reducing investment expenditures.

---

[9]See "Monetary Policy Objectives for 1983," *Summary Report of the Federal Reserve Board,* Feb. 16, 1983, pp. 12–20.

2   The international economic and financial situation, in which a world-wide recession could adversely affect U.S. exports. Nations were becoming increasingly protectionist, and many countries were experiencing huge foreign debts—creating instability in the U.S., and worldwide, financial markets.

3   Attitudes toward pricing and wage behavior. Volcker feared that business and labor—accustomed to the high rates of inflation in the 1970s—would be tempted to test their pricing and bargaining powers more aggressively as the economy surged ahead.

CHAPTER SUMMARY

1   Soon after the Fed was organized, World War I began. Before the United States became actively involved, it sold munitions and food to the belligerent nations and manufactured goods for the neutral nations that had previously purchased from the belligerents. This situation led to massive gold flows to the United States. The consequence of this monetary expansion was, predictably, inflation.

2   After the United States entered the war, in order to finance its *own* war effort, the United States ran relatively large deficits. These deficits were financed by sales of liberty bonds at rates below prevailing market rates. In addition, the Fed purchased U.S. government securities on the open market in order to prevent market rates from rising. Member banks were allowed to finance their purchases of U.S. government securities by borrowing against them at the same rate that the bond yielded. That is, the Fed monetized the public debt.

3   After the war ended, because commercial banks and the public had been encouraged to buy liberty bonds during the war, Congress felt that it would be unethical for the Fed to pursue a policy that would cause capital losses to those who were patriotic. As a consequence, the Fed purchased bonds in order to stabilize their prices. Of course, this led to inflation.

4   Prices on the stock market fell dramatically in 1929 and reduced the value of collateral on which loans were based. The New York Fed wanted to reduce the discount rate so that it could provide liquidity to member banks. The Fed disapproved the request unanimously. In order to add reserves to the banking system in New York, the New York Fed purchased 50 million dollars of U.S. government securities on October 29, 1929, and added another $65 million to its holdings during the next two days. These purchases were far in excess of the amount authorized by the Fed and were made without the Fed's prior approval. The Fed unanimously passed a resolution calling for a suspension of further purchases of government securities by the New York Fed.

5   The Fed allowed discount rates to fall, but market rates of interest fell faster. As a consequence, discount rates were above market rates and member banks had little incentive to borrow. The Fed apparently confused low absolute discount rates with easy money.

6   By autumn of 1930, the economic situation was poor. Commercial banks were failing in the midwest and south, and these failures were spreading to New York City. On December 11, a *privately owned* bank named the Bank of the United States failed; up to that time it was the largest bank ever to fail. Its failure created an even greater panic among depositors everywhere.

7   However, the Open Market Policy Conference authorized no further open-market purchases; it actually recommended that the Fed *sell* securities. The result was a second wave of bank failures.

8   The contraction of the U.S. money supply induced gold inflows to the United States. This would have cushioned its economic downturn, but the Fed sold securities, increased the discount rate, and neutralized these gold inflows. In the meantime, gold outflows from some of the rest of the world induced recessions; other countries abandoned the gold standard. Then the *United States* experienced gold outflows; because Federal Reserve notes were then required by law to be backed 100 percent by gold and commercial paper, the Fed took measures to reduce gold outflows. The Fed *increased* the discount rate sharply. The result was a sharp reduction in the money supply.

9   In 1933, the newly elected President Franklin D. Roosevelt declared a "banking holiday." When the holiday ended eleven days later, fewer than 12,000 banks reopened—less than half of the 25,000 banks in operation in mid-1929.

10 From August 1929 to March 1933, the U.S. money supply declined by 35 percent; total spending on goods and services declined by more than 50 percent; consumer prices fell by about 25 percent; the unemployment rate went from 3.2 percent to about 25 percent.

11 On April 25, 1933, President Roosevelt nationalized all gold outside Fed district banks. All owners of gold coins, bullion, and gold certificates were required to exchange them for currency or deposits at Federal Reserve banks before May 1. The United States returned to a modified gold standard, although private U.S. ownership was prohibited.

12 From 1934 to 1937, gold inflows to the United States amounted to $5.578 billion; this money added to reserves in the banking system, increased the money supply, and induced a modest recovery in the economy. However, the discount rate was still high relative to the market rates, and banks (remembering the recent bank failures) maintained excess reserves. Fearing future unwanted expansion, the Fed acted to eliminate these excess reserves by raising reserve requirements. Banks reacted by restricting loans in order to continue to hold excess reserves, and the money supply fell. The recovery was then halted.

13 World War II broke out in Europe in September 1939. The United States sold arms and nonmilitary goods to belligerents (mostly to England and France); a massive gold inflow to the United States resulted. Large inflows of money capital to the United States also occurred as people moved their liquid wealth to a safer clime. After the United States finally entered the war, federal deficits soared to (then) record levels. In order to help the Treasury finance these record deficits, the Fed surrendered its control over the money supply; the Fed agreed to support Treasury securities prices and thereby put a ceiling on Treasury yields. Massive purchases of Treasury bills by the Fed greatly increased the money supply and overt inflation would have resulted; price-wage controls were instituted, however, to prevent overt inflation.

14 After the war ended, the Fed continued to support Treasury securities prices because (a) the Treasury wanted to minimize the cost of refinancing the Federal debt, and (b) it did not want to impose capital losses on the Americans who had purchased bonds to help the war effort.

15 In 1951, an accord was reached and the Fed was no longer committed to pegging bond yields. As a consequence, Treasury bonds were not as liquid as before, and

the public increased its demand for money. This increase in the demand for money offset the increased supply of money, and inflation (temporarily) abated.

16 Under the Eisenhower administration, the Fed regained its full freedom and announced that it would confine its open-market operations to short-term maturities.

17 Beginning in 1965, the United States became heavily involved in the Vietnam war. In order to pay for the war *and* domestic social welfare programs, federal deficits were financed by Treasury bond sales. The Fed was unwilling to allow interest rates to rise, and it monetized the debt by purchasing bonds on the open market. This increased inflation, and the Fed moved to counteract it by raising the discount rate. This led to a conflict between the Fed and the Johnson administration; eventually a credit crunch ensued. Higher interest rates affected savings and loan associations adversely, however, because they were subject to Regulation Q ceilings on the rates they could pay depositors. As a result, disintermediation occurred.

18 By 1968, inflation became an important political issue; fiscal and monetary policy became restrictive, and by January 1970 interest rates had soared. In August 1971, President Nixon attempted to control U.S. inflation and amend the U.S. balance-of-payments policy by (a) putting a ninety-day freeze on prices and wages; (b) suspending the convertibility of the dollar into gold by foreign governments; and (c) placing a 10 percent surcharge on imports.

19 By April 1974, the price-wage controls had been lifted, and repressed inflation (shortages) was replaced by overt inflation. The Fed responded in the second half of 1974 by raising the discount rate and pursuing restrictive open-market operations. A recession followed, for which the Fed was blamed.

20 On October 6, 1979, the Fed announced that, in an effort to control inflation, it would now place the primary emphasis of monetary policy on the attainment of monetary targets and allow greater volatility in interest rates.

21 Since then, the volatility of both interest rates *and* monetary aggregates has increased. The Fed has apparently been unable to attain its monetary growth targets and the velocity of M1 has reversed its upward trend. This decline in velocity contributed to the severity of the 1982 recession. It also partially offset the rapid increase in the rate of growth of M1 from the fall of 1982 to the spring of 1983.

22 Monetarists feel that the instability in velocity was due to the temporary effects of once-and-for-all adjustments to financial innovations and banking deregulation. Nonmonetarists, of course, disagree.

GLOSSARY

Devaluation: An official act by the government of a country by which the price of its currency is reduced in terms of other countries' currencies.

Monetization of the public debt: The process of increasing the money supply by creating money to finance federal budget deficits; the Fed allows depository institutions to purchase Treasury securities by lending them the funds.

Moral suasion: A monetary tool of the Fed by which the Fed encourages depository institutions to follow voluntarily the Fed's suggestions.

Swap operations: Open-market operations in which the Fed simultaneously buys securities of one maturity in order to lower their yields, and sells securities of a different maturity in order to increase their yields.

PROBLEMS

27-1 List five instances of inappropriate Fed actions during the Great Depression.

SELECTED REFERENCES

Eastburn, David P., *The Federal Reserve on Record: Readings on Current Issues from Statements by Federal Reserve Officials,* Federal Reserve Bank of Philadelphia, 1965.

Ford, William F., "Monetary Policy in 1981–1982: An Insider's View," *Economic Policy Issues,* no. 1, The Conference Board, 1982.

Friedman, M., and A. J. Schwartz, *A Monetary History of the United States, 1867–1960* (Princeton, N.J.: Princeton University Press, 1963).

Hafer, R. W., and S. E. Hein, "The Wayward Money Supply: A Post-Mortem of 1982," *Review,* Federal Reserve Bank of St. Louis, March 1983, pp. 17–25.

Hetzel, Robert L., "The Relationship between Money and Expenditure in 1982," *Economic Review,* Federal Reserve Bank of Richmond, May–June 1983, pp. 11–19.

Laurent, Robert D., "A Critique of the Federal Reserve's New Operating Procedure," *Staff Memoranda Occasional Paper,* Federal Reserve Bank of Chicago.

Meek, Paul, *U.S. Monetary Policy and Financial Markets,* Federal Reserve Bank of New York, 1982.

Monetary Policy Objectives for 1983, Summary Report of the Federal Reserve Board, Feb. 16, 1983.

Selected Papers of Allan Sproul, Federal Reserve Bank of New York, 1980.

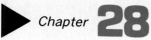

Chapter 28

Problems with Monetary Policy

CHAPTER PREVIEW

1 How can lagged reserve accounting interfere with the Fed's ability to achieve monetary aggregate targets?

2 Did the Fed really abandon control over the interest rate after 1979?

3 How do time lags interfere with the achievement of ultimate goals?

4 Should the Fed follow a monetary policy rule, or should it use its own discretion?

You must be quite aware by now that monetary policy is a tricky business, and that it is more of an art than a science. This chapter presents a more systematic discussion of the problems of monetary policy. Problems mentioned earlier will reappear and new ones will be discussed.

As noted in Chapter 26, there are three criteria for an intermediate target variable: measurability, attainability, and relatedness to ultimate goals. Monetary policy is the Fed's use of the tools at its disposal to achieve its ultimate goals. Three tools at the Fed's disposal are open-market operations, discounting, and changing reserve requirements. Ultimate goals include price stability, high employment, economic growth, and an international-payments equilibrium. But there is a long road between the Fed's tools and its goals. This road is not easy to follow and in many ways the Fed is powerless to achieve some of these goals.

Still, the Fed is committed to do *something,* and it does have tools. What the Fed can do is alter bank reserves and the monetary base. These, then, are potential instruments that can be altered to achieve such intermediate targets as the various monetary aggregates and short-term interest rates. The attainment of these intermediate targets will presumably enable the Fed to reach its ultimate goals.

This chapter divides problems of monetary policy into three major categories: (a) choosing the best intermediate target, (b) attaining the intermediate target, and (c) relating the intermediate target to the intermediate goal. Each is discussed in turn.

CHOOSING THE BEST INTERMEDIATE TARGET

By using its monetary policy tools the Fed can change the total reserves of depository institutions. Changes in reserves, in turn, affect the money stock (one of the monetary aggregates) or short-term interest rates (Treasury bills or the federal funds rates). The first task is to choose between these two targets, because they are mutually exclusive.

At various times the Fed has tried to achieve first one and then the other of these targets. Indeed, at times the Fed has attempted to achieve *both* targets. In October of 1979, the Fed announced a change in its method of conducting monetary policy. The change involves placing greater emphasis in day-to-day operations on the supply of bank reserves and less emphasis on confining short-term fluctuations in the federal funds rate. In other words, the Fed indicated that it would now (primarily) target monetary aggregates and not interest rates.

In recent years, financial innovations have raised questions concerning the usefulness of M1 (or even M2) as an intermediate target. Nationwide NOW accounts, money market mutual funds, federally insured money market deposit and super-NOW accounts have altered the form in which the public holds transactions and savings balances. A greater part of "narrow" money, or M1, now earns interest; eventually, a high percentage of M1 may earn interest at near money market rates. Because part of M1 is clearly a transaction account, but another part is clearly a savings or store-of-value account, the relationship between M1 (or M2) and gross national product has become less certain.[1]

Economists are not yet sure how much time must elapse before the smoke clears and financial innovations level off and people adjust to the new financial accounts. In the meantime, the search continues for the "best" intermediate target. Some have suggested a return to an interest rate intermediate target because, as Chapter 26 pointed out, if the *LM* curve is less stable than the *IS* curve, pursuing an interest-rate target is preferable to pursuing a monetary growth target.

In 1983, Benjamin Friedman, a Harvard economist, suggested that the best intermediate target would be a *combination* of a credit variable target *and* a monetary growth target.[2] The credit aggregate target suggested is total net credit, a broad measure consisting of the aggregate indebtedness of all U.S. borrowers other than financial institutions. According to Benjamin Friedman, total net credit satisfies the criteria for a desirable intermediate target:

1 Data on total net credit are available on a monthly basis and the data are as reliable as the other targets.
2 The Fed can influence total net credit through open-market operations; over a year or so, the Fed should be able to meet a total net credit target.
3 Total net credit bears as close and stable a relationship to financial economic activity as do any of the monetary aggregates. This relationship has persisted in the United States at least since World War I, and the relationship between credit and GNP is also strong in other western industrialized nations.

According to Friedman, the Fed should target both money growth and credit growth, because such a system "would draw on a more diverse and hence more reliable information base for the signals that govern the systematic response of monetary policy to emerging developments."[3]

Under such a scheme, the Fed would pick one monetary aggregate and total net credit, specify growth together for both, and carry out open-market operations aimed at achieving both targets. A deviation in either target from its respective target range would warrant a change in open-market operations that affect financial-institution reserves and the federal funds rate.

Clearly, economists are not yet—if they ever will be—in agreement as to what is the best intermediate target.

---

[1]see Chapters 1 and 3.

[2]Benjamin M. Friedman, "A Two-Target Strategy for Monetary Policy," *The Wall Street Journal,* Jan. 27, 1983, editorial page.

[3]*Ibid.*

TABLE 28-1 Interest Rates Follow Money

Money Turning Point	Date	Interval in Weeks	Annual Rate of Change in M1B	Three-Month Treasury Bills, Weeks Later		
				Three	Four	Five
Peak	Oct. 3, 1979			12.6%	12.1%	12.3%
Trough	Nov. 28, 1979	8	−1.4%	12.1	12.0	12.1
Peak	Feb. 20, 1980	12	+12.1	15.3	14.8	15.6
Trough	April 30, 1980	10	−12.4	8.2	7.7	7.5
Peak	Nov. 26, 1980	30	+15.0	16.2	14.6	14.3
Trough*	Feb. 4, 1981	10	−13.1	14.2	14.4	13.8
Peak	April 22, 1981	11	+23.8	16.8	16.6	15.6
Trough	July 1, 1981	10	−10.6	15.5	15.1	15.4
Peak	Sept. 16, 1981	11	+7.2	13.8	13.4	13.4
Trough	Oct. 28, 1981	6	−5.1	10.3	10.2	10.4
Peak	Jan. 13, 1982	11	+24.6	13.2		

*Corrected roughly for NOW accounts.
Source: Adapted from Milton Friedman, "The Yo-Yo Economy," *Newsweek*, Feb. 15, 1982, p. 72.

ATTAINING THE TARGET

When the Fed shifted its emphasis to the monetary aggregates, wider interest-rate fluctuations had to be accepted. But how well has the Fed succeeded in attaining monetary growth targets since 1979? Has it been able to attain its targets? Has the money supply moved smoothly toward its targets? Unfortunately for the monetarist position (which maintains that the Fed can easily control the money supply), over long periods the Fed has been unable to attain its monetary-aggregate targets. Even when the Fed *was* able to meet its targets, the money supply grew erratically. This unstable growth in the monetary aggregates has led to wide variations in nominal interest rates. There have been wide divergences among the rates of growth in the different measures of money, and at times the different money stock measures have changed in opposite directions. Table 28-1 shows just how unstable money growth (M1B) was from October 1979 to January 1982. Milton Friedman has described this as an "unprecedented volatility in monetary growth" and has noted that the money supply growth from October 1978 to the policy change date of October 1979 was *more* stable than it was *after* the policy change date.[4]

The apparent inability of the Fed to effect a smooth growth in the money supply has caused problems. Erratic monetary growth caused short-term interest rates to hit historic highs in 1979, and over the next two years they varied between 17 percent and 6 percent. This variability is unprecedented in the century for which data exist. Friedman has argued that this erratic growth

---

[4]Milton Friedman, "Monetary Instability," *Newsweek*, Dec. 21, 1981, p. 71.

in the money stock was responsible for the short recession (January to July 1980) and then a too-short expansion (July 1980 to July 1981).

For the discussion at hand, however, a more fundamental problem exists. Do the data since October 1979 mean that the Fed *cannot* attain its monetary growth targets? When we consider that the Fed abandoned interest-rate targets in favor of monetary-aggregate targets because the former proved unattainable, the possible unattainability of the money stock targets is all the more distressing. It may be that neither target is attainable. If neither is attainable, then monetary policy is a "snare and a delusion."

In October 1982 the Fed publicly abandoned M1 targets, and it appeared that the experiment with monetarism had failed. Being a particularly tenacious and resourceful lot, however, the monetarists are not about to concede when they fought so hard to get the Fed to change its target from interest rates to money stocks. The monetarists have blamed the erratic growth of the money stock on the Fed.[5] Because the Fed has not brought about a *smooth* growth of M1, they maintain, there really has been no experiment with monetarism. They argue that one major cause of the problem can be laid at the feet of a rather innocuous Fed operating procedure (discussed in Chapter 14) called lagged reserve accounting (LRA). LRA, you will recall, requires depository institutions to determine the required reserves for the *current* week by adding cash in the vault two weeks ago to the average net reserve deposit balance at the Fed district bank for the current week. The sum of these two figures must equal at a minimum "*x*" percent of average net deposits *two weeks* earlier, where "*x*" represents the required reserve ratio. The LRA procedure, which is a part of Regulation D, was instituted in 1968; it replaced contemporary reserve accounting (CRA). CRA, as you might have guessed, required banks to hold reserves on their current week's total deposits; hence a lag of only one day existed. Fortunately, to understand the differential impact of LRA and CRA, you don't have to be a CPA.

CRA Versus LRA

A depository institution can satisfy reserve requirements by:

1 Reducing its deposit liabilities (making fewer new loans, not renewing old loans when they mature, or selling securities to depositors outright or under repurchase agreements)
2 Selling securities to the Fed
3 Borrowing from the Fed
4 Borrowing on the federal funds market

---

[5]The Fed, in turn, has blamed it on recent financial innovations in the banking industry. Recall from Chapter 26 that recent financial innovations may have called into question the desirability of a money stock target. First, the measurability criterion is affected, because recent financial innovations blur the meaning of "money" and generate redefinitions of the monetary aggregates. Second, financial innovations have made the M1 and M2 monetary targets more difficult to achieve. Third, because M1 includes *savings* as well as transactions balances, the relationship between M1 and GNP is no longer so clear-cut. If you wish to pursue this topic, reread Chapter 26. See also the speech by Anthony M. Solomon, president, the Federal Reserve Bank of New York, entitled "Financial Innovation and Monetary Policy," in the 1981 *Annual Report of the Federal Reserve Bank of New York,* which can be obtained by writing to the New York Fed.

Depository institutions have direct control over option 1, the Fed has direct control over options 2 and 3, and the Fed has indirect control over option 4. If you memorize these options the following analysis will be easier to follow.

Monetary Restraint under CRA versus LRA: Interest-Rate Targets

Before 1979, the Fed targeted the federal funds rate; when it wanted a restrictive monetary policy, it took actions that caused the federal funds rate to rise. The Fed sold securities on the open market to lower bank reserves. Under the LRA system, banks were put on notice that they had two weeks to meet reserve requirements, by obtaining additional reserves. Banks must borrow in the federal funds market, which would cause the federal funds rate to rise. As the higher federal funds rate spread to other short-term interest rates, the public reduced its demand for deposits and increased its demand for interest-earning assets. The result was that deposits eventually fell (or did not expand as rapidly). Any bank movement toward option 3 was immaterial to the Fed because its concern was targeting the interest rate, not the money stock. Under a CRA system, this process is virtually identical to the process under LRA.

Monetary Restraint under CRA versus LRA: Money-Stock Targets

Now consider a restrictive monetary policy under each procedure when the Fed targets the money stock. To reduce the money stock the Fed sells securities on the open market. Under CRA, depository institutions as a whole can influence their current week's required reserves by using option 1 above: They reduce their overall deposits. If it so chooses, the Fed can deny depository institutions the use of options 2 and 3, and it can allow the discount rate to float upward with the federal funds rate. In short, under CRA the Fed provides a fixed quantity of total reserves and forces the banking system to adjust its deposits accordingly—downward in the case of monetary restraint.

What happens, however, when the Fed targets the money stock under a system of LRA? Under LRA the link between current deposits and required reserves is broken. *Because it enters a week with an already-determined reserve requirement, option 1 above (reducing deposits) is not available as a means of meeting the current week's requirement.* Unless the Fed wants to place a specific depository institution in a position where that institution's reserves are deficient, it must provide the quantity of reserves demanded by the banking system. In order to allow the banking system to meet its reserve requirements, the Fed must allow it options 2 and 3 above. This is the fundamental problem: If the Fed *must* provide the banking system with reserves, how can it exercise control over the monetary base *and* achieve its money-stock targets? Under LRA the Fed's supply of reserves must adjust to the banking system's demand; but under the CRA the banking system must adjust its demand for reserves to the Fed's fixed supply (by changing deposits, option 1).

The Fed's reply is that it still has some control over the money stock because it can force depository institutions to borrow from it at the discount window. The Fed doesn't have to buy bonds on the open market in order to provide the system with needed reserves. It can lend the system the reserves it needs. Those institutions, according to the Fed, will feel obligated to *repay* this borrowing quickly; outstanding loans will then be reduced and the money stock will fall. The Fed's position is that banks have been reluctant to borrow from it because (1) the Fed has historically discouraged such borrowing except in emergencies, and (2) the Fed imposes explicit restrictions on the quantity of reserves it will lend to any one bank at a particular time.

It is not surprising that monetarists (and nonmonetarists) suggested that the lagged-reserve-accounting procedure be abolished and that the discount rate be allowed to float with other short-term rates. Perhaps the monetarists, who currently enjoy favor, will have their way on this, too. If so, then maybe the money-supply target can be reached more smoothly. The LRA procedure was replaced by CRA on February 2, 1984. If the money stock targets still prove elusive, then it might be time to find another target.

Did the Fed Really Abandon Its Commitment to Interest Rates?

Some monetarist critics of the Fed have maintained that one important reason the Fed has not been able to attain its monetary-growth rate targets is that it really has not abandoned its commitment to stable interest rates. Because the Fed cannot simultaneously pursue both targets, the Fed has lost some control over the money supply.

This argument has been challenged forcefully by Ralph C. Bryant, a Senior Fellow in the Brookings Institution's Economic Studies Program.[6] Consider Figure 28-1, which shows that the October 1979 decision constituted a major change in the day-to-day conduct of open market operations. Note that before October 1979 the target *ranges* for the federal funds rate were much smaller than they were after October 1979. This indicates that after 1979 the Fed was, *in principle,* more willing to accept variations in the federal funds rate in order to achieve monetary-growth targets. More importantly, Figure 28-1 also shows that, *in practice,* the Fed permitted much higher swings in the federal funds rate after October 1979.

RELATION OF THE TARGET TO ULTIMATE GOALS

Even if the Fed is able to agree on the "proper" intermediate target and is able to attain the intermediate target, fundamental problems still exist. What good would it be to attain interest-rate or monetary-aggregate targets if these targets are unrelated to ultimate Fed goals? This section discusses the problems of time lags and rational expectations, both of which indicate that achieving targets may not lead to attaining ultimate goals.

---

[6]Ralph C. Bryant, "Should Money Targets Be the Focus of Monetary Policy?" *The Brookings Review,* Brookings Institution, Washington, D.C., Spring 1983.

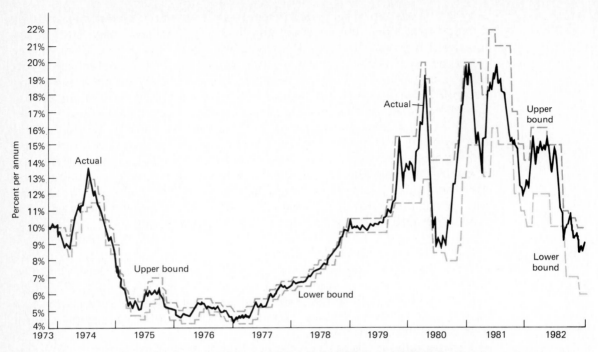

FIGURE 28-1   Federal Funds Rate: Actual Path and FOMC Constraint. This figure shows that a definite change in Fed operations occurred in October 1979. After that date, upper and lower bounds (the broken lines) and actual interest rates (the solid, colored line) fluctuated more than prior to that date.

The Problem with Time Lags

The Fed may be able to attain its intermediate-target objectives, but it may be able to achieve them only after the lapse of a period of time. If time lags are long and variable, meeting a target may worsen the economic problem that the Fed is trying to solve currently.

How does the Fed go about setting a target? Generally, the decision is based on a mixture of data on the current economic scene—the current rate of inflation, the current level of unemployment, the current level of business capital formation, and predictions about future changes in economic activity. The Fed has at its disposal models that give projections of the future values of aggregate economic variables on a quarterly and yearly basis. The numerical values in these models are obtained by feeding past data into a computer that is programmed to reflect whatever the current income and employment determination model indicates is appropriate. The models involved are called econometric models and they give forecasts of future economic activity. Ultimately, however, the theories used in computers are devised by economists. When a particular econometric model doesn't predict well, it is not the fault of the computer.

There are, therefore, difficulties in predicting accurately the future course of economic activity. The ability to predict well depends on using a national income determination model that takes into account all the relationships necessary to make a good forecast.[7] It also depends on the availability of accurate current data. For example, the models that use changes in inventories as a variable often go awry because the data on business inventory changes never seem to be correct the first time they are collected. There are nearly always revisions three or six months later. Weekly data on the money supply are also constantly revised.

The problem of information forms a part of a larger problem called "time lags."

Time Lags for Short-Run Policies

Have you ever taken a shower, turned on the hot water, and had the water come out cold? Then, in an act of frustration, you gave the hot water faucet another turn and got scalded? What happened was that there was a lag between the time you turned on the faucet and the time the hot water actually reached the shower head. Short-run stabilization policymakers face not only a similar time lag but several others as well.

The Recognition Time Lag Before any policy can be made, there must be information on the *current* state of the economy. However, we don't know concurrently what is happening to the rate of capital formation, the unemployment rate, changes in prices, and so on until after each happens, or after a time lag. It is crucial to obtain accurate information as quickly as possible, but sometimes accurate information about the *present* state of the entire economy isn't available for months. In other words, it is possible that we will not *recognize* that we are in a recession until, say, three months after it starts. This is often called the **recognition time lag.**

The Action Time Lag Once it is discovered that the economy is indeed in, say, a recession, a long period may elapse before any policy can be put into effect. This is particularly true of tax cuts and tax increases that are desired for stabilization purposes. A tax cut was first suggested in the Kennedy administration in 1961. It didn't pass until 1964—a lag of three years. Monetary policy does not suffer the same **action time lag** because the Federal Open Market Committee of the Federal Reserve System meets thirteen times a year and can almost instantaneously put into effect any policy upon which it decides. It simply instructs the trading desk at the New York Fed how to proceed. The action lag, then, can be long and variable for fiscal policy but will generally be relatively short for monetary policy.

The Effect Time Lag Even if there were no recognition lag or action lag, there would still be an **effect time lag** because even the most perfect economic policy variable change will not have an immediate impact upon the economy. An increase in government spending, for example, takes time to

---

[7]The ability to forecast also depends on the ability to predict variables such as war, the outcome of political elections, relative price changes, and a myriad of other variables which the model *uses* implicitly but does not explicitly predict.

work itself out; a change in taxes does, too. A change in the rate of growth of the money supply may not have an effect for several months. Economists have spent considerable effort attempting to estimate the effect time lag. Some say that for fiscal policy the lag can extend over several years. The lag in monetary policy, on the other hand, may vary from only a few months to several years.

Taking Lags into Account   Now you can see the problems inherent in trying to stabilize the economy in the short run. Assume you are a policymaker and you have just discovered that the economy is going into a recession. You try to get taxes changed to counter that recession. What kinds of problems will you encounter? First of all, the economy may have already been in a recession for six months to one year before you detected it. Second, it may take another year or two to get Congress to put the tax change package into effect. And third, it may take another year until the major effect of that fiscal policy change is felt in the economy. By that time, the economy may already be on the upswing. Your fiscal policy change will then be inappropriate and will only add fuel to a roaring inflationary fire.

The long and variable lags involved in short-run stabilization policy have prompted some critics of such policies to recommend that no short-run stabilization attempts be made at all. The most outspoken proponent of stable, or nondiscretionary, monetary policy is Milton Friedman, formerly of the University of Chicago. He has been a proponent of the so-called **monetary rule** for many years. A monetary rule would require that the money supply grow at a fixed annual rate that could not be altered by the Federal Open Market Committee (or anyone else, for that matter). That is why such a policy is referred to as nondiscretionary: No one has the discretion to change it. On the fiscal policy side, there are numerous advocates of a long-run commitment to a balanced full-employment budget. There would be no discretionary fiscal policy to change the direction of economic activity in the short run.

Note that the adoption of a monetary rule and a long-run commitment to a balanced full-employment budget would, to a large extent, eliminate short-run stabilization policies.

Coordination   Because stabilization policy can be instituted by using fiscal tools as well as monetary tools, there would seem to be a problem of coordination. What if the fiscal authorities—the President and Congress—decide on one policy, and the monetary authorities—the Fed—decide on another? As a matter of fact, occasionally conflicting policies have been carried out by monetary and fiscal authorities. In 1968, for example, a fiscal policy of restraint was adopted by Congress in the form of a temporary income surtax. Soon after that surtax went into effect, however, the monetary authorities began what would have to be considered an expansionary policy. It seems, therefore, that unless all policymaking is put under one roof, so to speak, the problem of coordination will at times be serious.

When all is said and done, the empirical evidence suggests that monetary policy does have a significant impact on economic activity. Both Keynesians and monetarists agree on this point. The effects of monetary policy seem to be distributed over several years; the immediate effects are strong, but the effects over time are stronger still.

Yet, the variability of the effect lag when combined with the recognition lag implies that timing problems surely exist. The usefulness of monetary pol-

---

HIGHLIGHT   Rules vs. Discretion

Monetary-policy problems that result from the various lags and the rational-expectations hypothesis are considerable. As a consequence, and following a long tradition, some economists favor a rules rather than a discretionary approach to monetary policy. The Fed should be disallowed from using its own discretion in deciding what monetary policy should be. Instead, the Fed should be forced to follow a rule such as: Increase the money supply at 4 percent per annum. This policy is seen to be better than the one in which the Fed changes the money supply in response to recently observed economic events.

This policy of following a clear-cut rule was formalized in 1936 by Henry Simons of the University of Chicago.* Milton Friedman also called for such a rule in 1948,† and has done so in just about every year since then.

Friedman and his allies maintain that the economy is basically stable and that prices and wages are sufficiently flexible to enable it to achieve its natural rates of unemployment and output. By forcing the Fed to follow a monetary rule, a major source of macroeconomic instability (the Fed's policies) will be removed. All that the Fed need do is announce its rule and follow it. Real GNP in the U.S. economy has grown (on average, but with much variability) at about 3.3 percent per annum over the past 100 years. Also, the velocity of M1, in recent decades, has increased slightly. Recall the equation of exchange ($MV = PQ$). If the rule is "increase the money supply at 3 percent per annum"—while Q is increasing at 3.3 percent per annum and V is increasing slightly—P (the price level) will be stable in the long run.

Although a monetary rule has a certain appeal, it is not likely to gain widespread acceptance. For one thing, the ability of the Fed to achieve monetary growth targets has not been demonstrated. There is also the matter of *which* monetary aggregate to target. The effects of a domestic monetary rule should also be considered in a global context. For example, such a rule requires flexible foreign exchange rates. A gold standard or a system of fixed exchange rates eventually would force policymakers to abandon a monetary rule. A monetary rule in addition could prove to be exceedingly difficult in light of the fact that some $3 trillion of Eurodollar deposits exist, and some of these deposits can be used by domestic depository institutions to thwart such a rule. Moreover, it seems foolish to follow a monetary rule when discretionary policy is *obvious* (such as in a depression). Finally, our species has gotten as far as it has because it has an inherent desire to tinker or meddle. Such a desire has been, alternately, a boon and a bane to our welfare.

*H. C. Simons, "Rules versus Authorities in Monetary Policy," *Journal of Political Economy,* vol. 44, 1936, pp. 1–30.

†M. Friedman, "A Monetary and Fiscal Framework For Economic Stability," *American Economic Review,* vol. 38, 1948, pp. 245–264.

icy as a short-run stabilizing agent has therefore been questioned. A boom in April may not be recognized until September, at which time the Fed tries to slow the inflation accompanying it. If, however, the boom peaks in June and the price level stops rising and employment begins to fall, September's monetary restraint will cause an even greater slump.

Rational-Expectations Analysis The rational-expectations hypothesis (examined in Chapter 25) predicts problems for those who would stabilize the economy in the short run by using monetary (or fiscal) policy. The existence of the various lags makes monetary policy difficult and may destabilize rather than stabilize the economy; the rational-expectations hypothesis implies that short-run stabilization is *impossible*. Rational-expectations analysis predicts that monetary (or fiscal) policies cannot *systematically* affect real variables such as output and employment even in the short run. Even short-run departures from the natural rate of unemployment and output cannot be remedied in any systematic way by a change of policy. Rational-expectations analysis also provides a rationale for throwing up one's hands and declaring "Alas, monetary policy is futile."

Accepted economic analysis indicates that *in the long run* neither monetary nor fiscal policy will cause the economy to deviate significantly from its natural rates of unemployment and output. Rational-expectations analysis makes it doubtful that there will even be systematic departures from these rates in the short run. We are led to the tentative conclusion that monetary policy can be used only to achieve the goal of price stability. This conclusion has an appeal for at least two reasons:

1 A *monetary* variable (money supply) is to be used to control a *monetary* phenomenon (inflation).

2 *One* tool (monetary policy) is used to achieve *one* goal (price stability).

CURRENT CONTROVERSY

Monetary Policy and the Subterranean Economy

There is no doubt about it. The public is holding more and more currency. To be sure, higher prices account for an increased transactions demand for currency. Currency holdings adjusted for higher price levels, however, still indicate a 2 percent per annum increase in currency holdings since 1960. At the same time, real demand deposits have remained relatively constant. The result, as Figure 1 indicates, has been a rising ratio of currency to demand deposits since 1968.*

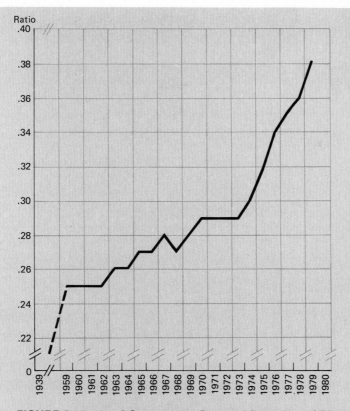

FIGURE 1 **Ratio of Currency to Demand Deposits, 1959–1979.** (*Source: St. Louis Federal Reserve Bulletin,* January 1980, p. 12.)

This is a rather extraordinary increase in the real demand for currency in light of the fact that (1) credit cards and traveler's checks are increasingly popular, (2) higher interest rates have increased the opportunity costs of holding currency, and (3) deposit insurance has greatly decreased the risk of holding deposits.

There is more than a little controversy over the interpretation of this phenomenon. Many believe that the combination of tax bracket creep, business regulation, and income reporting burdens have provided incentives not to report transactions—legal or otherwise—that are financed by currency. Indeed, there is more money outstanding in $100 bills (larger denominations are no longer issued) than in any other currency denomination.

Others have argued that what is really declining is the growth of demand deposits; this lack of demand deposit growth is attributed to such recent financial innovations as NOW accounts, REPOs, money market mutual funds, and automatic transfer systems. All these innovations provide substitutes for demand deposits.

Assuming that a large currency drain is occurring, can monetary policy be hampered? Theoretically, yes. One of the determinants of the amount of money that the banking system can create is the public's desired ratio of currency to demand deposits. A fixed ratio of currency to deposits held by the public would make the deposit multiplier almost totally dependent on required reserve ratios. But if the public holds more currency, as it seems to be doing of late, the increased currency–demand deposit ratio lowers the size of the deposit expansion multiplier. An outflow of cash reduces bank reserves by an equivalent amount.

The Fed, however, receives information on currency drains promptly and can offset them easily by buying securities on the open market. Although a rapidly growing underground economy potentially interferes with the Fed's ability to achieve monetary stock growth targets, the Fed has the tools to offset such occurrences.

*From Norman N. Bowsher, "The Demand for Currency: Is the Underground Economy Undermining Monetary Policy?" *St. Louis Federal Reserve Bulletin,* vol. 62, no. 1, January 1980.

CHAPTER SUMMARY

1   Monetary policy problems can be divided into three major categories: choosing the best intermediate target, attaining the intermediate target, and relating the intermediate target to the ultimate goal.

2   At times, the Fed has targeted interest rates; at other times, the Fed has targeted monetary aggregates. In recent years, some economists have suggested targeting a credit variable.

3   Before 1979, the Fed was primarily concerned with targeting interest rates. This policy resulted in a bias toward increased reserve creation and inflation. In 1979, the Fed announced that it would become concerned more with monetary aggregates than with interest rates. Unfortunately, it has on occasion been unable to attain its monetary aggregate targets. In fact, the growth in the supply of money has been more volatile during the period since the policy change than during the period preceding it. Monetarists have argued that the Fed has the ability to attain monetary aggregate targets, but not the will to do so; some monetarists claim that the Fed has not been able to divorce itself from a concern for interest-rate levels. Evidence exists, however, to indicate that the Fed has permitted wider swings in interest rates since 1979.

4   Monetarists also charge that the lagged reserve requirement (LRA), which replaced the contemporary reserve account requirement (CRA), has interfered with the Fed's ability to attain a monetary-aggregate target. The LRA procedure will be replaced by CRA in 1984. If attainability of monetary-aggregate targets proves to be as difficult as the attainability of interest-rate targets, monetary policy will suffer a serious setback.

5   Even if the Fed is able to agree on the proper target, and is able to attain the target goals, the targets must be related to ultimate goals if monetary policy is to be considered a success. Moreover, the question of *timing* is important.

6   Before any policy can be made, there must be information on the current state of the economy. Information about the current state of the economy won't be forth-

coming until after a time lag. This problem is referred to as the recognition time lag.

7 After the problem is recognized, the policy must be put into effect; therefore, an action time lag exists. This is particularly troublesome for fiscal policy, which requires congressional approval for tax and spending changes. Monetary policy, on the other hand, has a short action time lag.

8 Even perfect policy prescription will have an effect time lag; changes in taxes, government expenditures, and the money supply require time to affect the economy. The effect time lag of fiscal policy has been estimated as dragging out over several years; the effect time lag of monetary policy is highly variable.

9 The ultimate result of all these time lags is that by the time the effects of policy come to pass the current situation may have changed so drastically that policy will be destabilizing rather than stabilizing. Milton Friedman and others have suggested that we forsake discretionary monetary and fiscal policy for a monetary aggregate rule. Such a rule would require the Fed to increase the money supply at a specific annual rate and eliminate the Fed's discretionary powers. The specific rate at which the money stock should grow should be consistent with the economy's normal rate-of-growth trend. By following such a monetary rule, its proponents maintain, an important element of economic instability—stabilization policy itself—can be removed.

10 A monetary rule is not likely to gain widespread acceptance in the near future. The Fed has yet to demonstrate its ability to achieve monetary aggregate targets; the problem of which monetary aggregate to target has not yet been resolved. Moreover, the effects of a domestic monetary rule should be considered in a global context. Moreover, it seems foolish to follow a monetary rule at a time when discretionary policy seems obvious—such as during a depression.

GLOSSARY

Action time lag: The time required between recognizing an economic problem and putting policy into effect. While the action time lag is short for monetary policy, it is quite long for fiscal policy, which requires congressional approval.

Effect time lag: The time that elapses between the onset of policy and the results of that policy.

Monetary aggregate rule: A rule that would eliminate discretionary monetary policy and commit the Fed to increase a monetary aggregate at some specific annual rate.

Recognition time lag: The time required to gather information about the current state of the economy.

SELECTED REFERENCES

Bowsher, Norman N., "The Demand for Currency: Is the Underground Economy Undermining Monetary Policy?" *St. Louis Federal Reserve Bulletin,* vol. 62, no. 1, January 1980.

Brunner, K., "Some Major Problems in Monetary Theory," *American Economic Association Papers and Proceedings,* vol. 51, May 1961, pp. 47–56.

——————, "Has Monetarism Failed?" *The Cato Journal,* vol. 3, Spring 1983, pp. 23–62.

Bryant, Ralph C., "Should Money Targets Be the Focus of Monetary Policy?" *The Brookings Review,* Spring 1983, pp. 6–12.

Fisher, Stanley, "Long Term Contracts, Rational Expectations, and the Optimal Money Supply Rule," *Journal of Political Economy,* vol. 85, February 1977, pp. 191–205.

Friedman, Milton, "Interest Rates and the Demand for Money," *Journal of Law and Economics,* vol. 9, October 1966, pp. 71–85.

Gilbert, R. Alton, "Lagged Reserve Requirements: Implications for Monetary Control and Bank Reserve Management," *Review,* Federal Reserve Bank of St. Louis, May 1980, pp. 7–20.

Meltzer, Allan H., "Monetary Reform in an Uncertain Environment," *The Cato Journal,* vol. 3, Spring 1983, pp. 93–112.

Phelps, E. S., and J. B. Taylor, "Stabilizing Powers of Monetary Policy under Rational Expectations," *Journal of Political Economy,* vol. 85, February 1977, pp. 163–190.

Solomon, Anthony M., "Financial Innovation and Monetary Policy," *Sixty-Seventh Annual Report of the Federal Reserve Bank of New York,* 1981, pp. 3–17.

Tobin, J., and W. C. Brainard, "Financial Intermediaries and the Effectiveness of Monetary Controls," *American Economic Association Papers and Proceedings,* vol. 53, May 1963, pp. 383–400.

International Finance

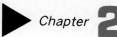

Financing International Transactions

Until now, we have discussed economic transactions and the financial arrangements facilitating these transactions that occur within the confines of a single nation. No complete analysis of financial arrangements, however, can afford to ignore international transactions and the financial institutions that facilitate them. In this chapter, we consider an open economy.

If a family unit is currently spending more than its current income, such a situation necessarily implies that the family unit must be doing one of the following:

1   Drawing down its wealth. The family must reduce its money holdings or it must sell stocks, bonds, or some other asset.
2   Borrowing.
3   Receiving gifts from friends or relatives.
4   Receiving public transfers from a government, which obtained the funds from taxing others.

In effect, we can use the above information to derive an identity; if a family unit is currently spending more than it is earning, it must draw on previously acquired wealth, borrow, or receive either private or public aid. Similarly, an identity exists for a family unit that is currently spending less than it is earning: It must increase its wealth by increasing its money holdings or by lending and acquiring other financial assets; or it must pay taxes or bestow gifts on others.

Additional identities crop up when we consider *all* the household units. For example, given the money supply, the amount by which households are reducing their money holdings must equal the amount by which other households are increasing their money holdings. A moment's reflection indicates that when we consider businesses and governments, each individual unit and each individual group faces its own identities or constraints. (We discussed the government constraint in Chapter 23.) For example, *net* lending by households must equal net borrowing by businesses and governments.

Even though our individual family unit's accounts must "balance"—in the sense that the identity discussed previously must hold—sometimes that item that brings about the balance cannot continue indefinitely. If family expenditures exceed family income and this situation is financed by borrowing, this household may be considered to be in *disequilibrium* because *such a situation cannot continue indefinitely.* Or, if such a family deficit is financed by drawing on previously accumulated assets, the family may also be in disequilibrium because it cannot continue indefinitely to draw on its wealth; eventually, it will become impossible for that family to continue such a lifestyle.[1]

Individual households, businesses, and governments, as well as the entire group of households, businesses, and governments, must eventually reach

---

[1]Of course, if the family members are retired, they may well be in equilibrium by drawing on previously acquired assets to finance current deficits. After all, they do not expect to live forever. This is an important lesson: It is necessary to understand the circumstances fully before pronouncing an economic unit in disequilibrium.

equilibrium. Certain economic adjustment mechanisms have evolved to assure equilibrium. Deficit households must eventually increase incomes or decrease expenditures if they are to reach equilibrium. Businesses, on occasion, must lower costs and/or prices—or go bankrupt—in order to reach equilibrium.

When *nations* transact with each other, certain identities or constraints also must hold. Nations buy goods from people in other nations; they also lend and present gifts to people in other nations. Ultimately, if a nation transacts with others, an accounting identity assures a "balance" (but not an equilibrium); this topic is discussed in the next section.

As is true *within* nations, economic adjustment mechanisms evolve to assure that economic equilibrium eventually exists *between* each nation and the rest of the world. Eventually, interest rates, prices, and income levels change until international equilibrium is restored. The adjustment mechanisms driving the international economy toward equilibrium are discussed in the following section. There we discuss fixed-exchange-rate systems—such as the gold standard and the modified gold standard—and flexible-exchange-rate systems.[2] We then discuss the current international-adjustment-mechanism system. Finally, in a Current Controversy, we consider the issue of whether to "bail out" the U.S. banks that have made loans to less developed nations that now appear to be unable to repay the loans.

INTERNATIONAL ACCOUNTING IDENTITIES

A country, like a person, also must balance its accounts. A country is different from a family unit, however, in that (1) a country's accounts must take into consideration the actions of a central bank, and (2) different countries use different currencies to settle their accounts.

The balance of payments is a record of all the transactions between the households, firms, and government of one country and the rest of the world. Any transaction that leads to a *payment* by a country's residents (or government) is a deficit item—a deficit item will be identified by a negative sign (−) when we use actual numbers. Deficit items include the following transactions: imports of merchandise, gifts to foreigners, use of foreign-owned transportation, tourism expenditures abroad, military spending abroad, interest and dividends paid to foreigners, purchases of foreign assets (such as stocks, bonds, and real estate), deposits made in foreign depository institutions, and purchases of gold and foreign currency.

Any transaction that leads to a *receipt* by a country's residents (or government) is a surplus item and is identified by a plus sign (+) when actual numbers are considered. Surplus items include exports of goods and services, expenditures made by foreigners touring the domestic country, services rendered by the domestic country's transportation facilities, interest and divi-

---

[2]As you will see, a foreign exchange rate is the price of a foreign currency in terms of domestic currency.

dends received from abroad, gifts from abroad, foreign military spending in the domestic country, and loans from foreigners, such as foreign purchases of domestic securities, increases in foreign bank loans to domestic companies, and increases in foreign holdings of the domestic currency. Also included are domestic sales of gold.

The Current Account Balance The current account balance is the amount by which the value of a country's exports of goods and services (including military receipts and income on investments abroad) and transfer payments (private and government) exceeds the value of that country's imports of goods and services (including military payments) and transfer payments (private and government). For ease of exposition, let us refer to the current account balance as the excess of ''exports'' over ''imports.'' As long as you understand that these terms actually include items that are not normally considered exports or imports, no harm is done.

If exports exceed imports, a **current account surplus** is said to exist; if imports exceed exports, a **current account deficit** (a negative number) is said to exist. A current account deficit must be financed by borrowing from abroad (increasing liabilities to the rest of the world) or by selling assets (reducing net claims on the rest of the world). A current account surplus necessarily leads to a purchase of foreign assets (increasing net claims on the rest of the world) or a reduction in net liabilities (repayment of foreign-owned debt).

The Capital Account Balance The capital account balance is the amount by which the value of a country's sales of such assets as stocks, bonds, and lands to foreigners exceeds the value of that country's purchase of such assets from abroad. If the value of such sales is greater than purchases, then a **capital account surplus** (a positive number) exists; if the value of such sales is less than purchases, then a **capital account deficit** (a negative number) exists. A capital account surplus implies a net capital *in*flow; a capital account deficit implies a net capital *out*flow.

The Official Settlements Balance The **official settlements balance** is the sum of the current account balance and the capital account balance. Because of the existence of central banks this sum need not be zero. If both the capital account and the current account are in deficit, the official settlements balance will be negative. That is, the domestic country pays more foreign currency to foreigners than it receives. The official settlements balance must itself be financed by official reserve transactions, such as:

1 Increases in liabilities to foreign official holders
2 Gold sales
3 Use of special drawing rights with the international monetary fund (IMF)
4 Sales of foreign currencies
5 Use of reserves with the IMF

By definition, the official settlements balance must equal the value of the official reserve transactions. In practice, the numbers don't correspond perfectly because of the existence of some private international transactions that are not recorded. Because we know that the sum of the current account balance and the capital account balance must equal the value of the official reserve transaction (a number we can determine with certainty), a term labeled "errors and omissions" (statistical discrepancy) is included to reconcile the differences.

Table 29-1 shows the values of the current account balance, the capital account balance, errors and omissions, and official reserve transactions of the United States for selected years. If there were no central banks, a current account deficit would have to be financed by a capital account surplus: If the residents of the United States spent and gave more than they earned and received in gifts, this deficit would have to be made up by borrowing from the rest of the world. The existence of deficits or surpluses in the official settlements balance of the United States shows that central banks have intervened in the balancing process.

A surplus or deficit in the official settlements balance must be made up by official reserve transactions among the central banks. Table 29-2 shows how the U.S. official settlements surplus or deficit was balanced by official reserve transactions during the years 1975 to 1982. In general, a deficit in the U.S. official settlements balance can be financed by a reduction in U.S. assets claims on foreign central banks or by an increase in borrowing from foreign central banks (an increase in liabilities to foreign central banks). Table 29-2 shows that, for the most part, our official settlements deficits have been made up by borrowing from foreign central banks—the foreign official assets entries

---

TABLE 29-1 The United States Balance-of-Payments Accounts

(In billions of dollars)

	1960	1965	1970	1975	1978	1979	1980	1981	1982
Current account balance	2.8	5.4	2.3	18.1	−15.4	−1.0	0.4	4.6	−11.2
Plus									
Capital account balance	−5.4	−6.3	−12.4	−30.2	−31.5	−10.8	−38.5	−30.2	−28.4
Plus									
Errors and omissions	−1.0	−0.5	−0.2	5.9	12.5	25.4	29.5	24.2	41.4
Equals									
Official settlements balance	−3.6	−1.4	−10.3	−6.2	−34.4	13.6	−8.6	−1.4	1.8
Official reserve transactions	3.6	1.4	9.4	6.2	34.4	−13.7	8.6	1.3	−1.8

Note: Numbers may not add due to rounding. Negative sign denotes deficit.
Sources: Economic Report of the President (various editions) and *Economic Indicators,* September 1983.

TABLE 29-2 Official Reserve Transactions between the Fed and Other Central Banks

(In billions of dollars)

	1975	1976	1977	1978	1979	1980	1981	1982
Official settlements balance	−6.2	−15.1	−36.4	−34.4	13.6	−8.6	−1.4	−1.8
Financed by: U.S. official reserve assets	−0.8	−2.6	−0.4	0.7	−1.1	−8.1	−5.2	−5.0
Plus: Foreign official assets	7.0	17.7	36.8	33.7	−13.7	15.6	-5.4	3.1
Plus: Allocations of special drawing rights	0.0	0.0	0.0	0.0	1.1	1.2	1.1	0.0
Equals:	6.2	15.1	36.4	34.4	−13.7	8.7	1.3	−1.9

Note: Numbers may not add due to rounding.
Source: Economic Indicators, Council of Economic Advisers, September 1983.

are positive in every year except 1979, when a U.S. official settlements surplus existed. In fact, Table 29-2 shows that for most years the U.S. official reserve asset change was *negative*—the United States was increasing its official reserves instead of reducing them. As a consequence, this activity also had to be financed by borrowing from foreign central banks.

THE ADJUSTMENT MECHANISMS

The last section indicated that the United States currently has an international **balance-of-payments disequilibrium**—the United States is in a disequilibrium position with respect to its international transactions. It typically has a deficit in its official settlements balance, and this deficit is financed mostly by borrowing from foreign central banks. If individual family units or businesses have "payments deficits," eventually they must do one of two things: increase earnings or decrease expenditures. In this unit, we discuss the adjustment mechanisms that would—in the absence of central-bank manipulations—move a country toward an overall international balance-of-payments equilibrium. The available adjustment mechanisms are: changes in income, changes in prices, and changes in interest rates. These three economic mechanisms would continue to change until a balance-of-payments equilibrium were restored among nations. There are two basic international monetary systems that would allow these three adjustment mechanisms to work: a **fixed-exchange-rate system** and a **floating-exchange-rate system.** We discuss these two systems now.

Fixed-Exchange-Rate Systems

Since 1821, the world has been on what are referred to as the classical gold standard (1821 to 1914), the gold exchange standard (1925 to 1931), and the Bretton Woods system (1946 to 1971). Each of these fixed-exchange-rate systems will be discussed briefly. First, however, we consider the pure gold standard.

The Pure Gold Standard[3]   Let's consider first a domestic pure gold standard in which we ignore international transactions. In order to establish a pure gold coin system, three things are necessary:

1   Only official gold coins minted by the government are used as money.
2   The government commits itself to purchase gold from the public on demand at a fixed price and to convert the gold into gold coins. For instance, if you discover gold, you can sell it to the government and get a predetermined value of officially stamped gold coins.
3   The government will sell gold to the public at the fixed price. If you are concerned about the value of your gold coins, you can sell them to the government for a predetermined quantity of gold—uncoined, and, therefore, not money.

Under such a system, the supply of gold, in the long run, is determined by the opportunity cost of producing gold. The supply of gold *coins* (money) is determined by the total supply of gold and the amount of gold used for non-monetary purposes (jewelry, etc.). The fraction of the total gold supply devoted to nonmonetary uses depends on the purchasing power of gold in terms of all other commodities. If the price level rises, the purchasing power of gold coins falls; this fall in the relative price of gold coins will induce people to increase the use of gold for nonmonetary purposes. A fall in the price level increases the relative price of gold coins, and a higher proportion of the gold stock will be converted into gold coins—money. In the short run, the stock of gold is limited due to high production costs.[4] The demand for gold *coins* is determined by the community's wealth, tastes, and the opportunity cost of holding money (the interest rate). The supply of and demand for gold coins will determine the price level.

A *pure international gold standard* is established when a number of countries are on a gold coin standard. Under such a system, each government agrees to buy and to sell its particular gold coins (the Americans might call

---

[3]See M. D. Bardo, "The Classical Gold Standard: Some Lessons for Today," *Review,* Federal Reserve Bank of St. Louis, vol. 63, no. 5 (May 1981), for much of what is in the next few sections.

[4]This helped to make gold a good candidate for money. Other desirable attributes of gold are: It is durable, storable, portable, divisible, and easily standardized and recognized.

them "dollars," the British, "pounds sterling"). Of course, the coins can be of different weight, shape, and value. Under a pure international gold standard, exchange rates between countries are necessarily fixed. An **exchange rate** is the price of a foreign currency in terms of domestic currency. Thus, if the United States values its currency at 1 ounce of gold per 20 dollars, and Great Britain sets the price of its currency at 1 ounce of gold per 4 pounds sterling (£), then the exchange rate will be: £1 is equivalent to $5, or, conversely, $1 is equivalent to £$\frac{1}{5}$.

The Adjustment Mechanisms under a Pure International Gold System Suppose that, in our two-economy world, both the United States and England are on a pure gold standard and that there is a balance-of-payments equilibrium. One way for such an equilibrium to exist is for the value of exports to equal the value of imports in each country. Now assume that U.S. residents increase their demand for British goods, other things constant. This action will cause a current account deficit for the United States and (necessarily) a current account surplus for Great Britain. This will cause a flow of gold from the United States to England.[5] Because gold can be converted into money, the British money supply will rise; the U.S. money supply will fall correspondingly. The price level will fall in the United States and will rise in Great Britain. British goods will be relatively dearer and U.S. goods relatively cheaper; as a consequence, the United States will export more and import less, and Great Britain will import more and export less. These actions will help to establish equilibrium.

A decrease in the U.S. money supply will also induce a recession in the United States; an increase in Great Britain's money supply will cause an expansion in Great Britain. As a consequence, real or nominal incomes will fall in the United States and will rise in Great Britain. This relative income change will lead to an increase in British imports (an increase in U.S. exports) and a decrease in U.S. imports (a decrease in British exports). These income effects will also help to restore international-payments equilibrium.

Finally, under a pure gold standard, central banks are supposed to follow the "rules of the game," which leaves very little indeed for central bankers to do. Central banks are supposed to allow their country to fall into a recession when it is in a payments deficit and to allow it to expand or inflate when it is in a payments surplus. A central bank should raise the discount rate (the rate it charges banks to borrow) when the country is experiencing a payments deficit and lower the discount rate when the country is experiencing a payments surplus. In our example, such actions will cause U.S. interest rates to rise relative to British interest rates. This interest rate differential causes short-term capital seeking higher interest earnings to flow to the United States from

---

[5]Technically, the increased U.S. demand for British goods will lower the value of the dollar in terms of the pound sterling. At some lower price of the dollar gold coin (the "gold point"), it will benefit U.S. importers to convert gold dollar coins into gold bullion and to ship the bullion to England—where it can be converted into pound sterling gold coins in order to pay for British goods.

England—thereby lessening the required movement of money from the United States to Great Britain and economizing on the use of gold.

In short, under the pure international gold standard, an international-payments equilibrium is established by relative price-level changes, relative interest-rate changes, and relative income-level changes. Moreover, central banks allow these adjustment mechanisms to work.

The Classical Gold Standard (1821 to 1914) The pure gold standard described in the previous section has never existed. It has problems. For one thing, such a system is extremely costly to operate. Discovering, mining, and minting gold are extremely costly activities. Milton Friedman estimated the cost of maintaining a full gold coin standard for the United States in 1960 to have been more than 2.5 percent of its GNP![6] It is not surprising that nations sought ways to economize on the use of gold for their domestic and international gold standards. The most obvious way to economize on gold was to find substitutes for gold to act as money. As you learned in earlier chapters, these substitutes included government-provided paper money and privately produced bank notes and bank deposits. In practice, therefore, during the period of the classical gold standard, a nation could be on a modified gold standard by maintaining a *fixed ratio of its paper currency to gold* and by requiring its commercial bank to keep a fixed ratio of bank liabilities to gold—or (to save on gold again) a fixed ratio of bank liabilities to government notes and gold.

During the classical gold standard period, gold was economized internationally as well. International trade was financed by credit; by receiving short-term loans, a current account deficit could be financed by a capital account surplus, and the use of gold could be economized. Similarly, long-term loans—investments by developed nations in less developed nations, for instance—also provided a means whereby a nation could finance a current account deficit by a capital account surplus for long periods. In such a case, a prolonged current account deficit is not necessarily a sign of a payments disequilibrium. Nations also economized on gold by using the currency of certain reliable countries as reserves; certain "key currencies" were used as a substitute for gold for international reserves. Thus, payments adjustments didn't actually require gold flow; in many cases, transfers of pound sterling or other key currencies were made in the money markets of the major cities (London, New York, Paris, and Berlin).

In short, the classical gold standard that existed between 1821 and 1914 evolved into a modified gold standard where paper currency and deposits substituted for gold domestically and key currencies substituted for gold internationally. Also, current account deficits were financed temporarily by a short-term capital account surplus and, for long periods, by long-term borrowing that led to capital account surpluses. This financing also economized on gold transfers.

---

[6]Milton Friedman, *A Program for Monetary Stability* (New York: Fordham University Press, 1959).

Another way in which the classical gold standard differed from the pure international gold standard was that nations weren't always prepared to abide by the rules of the game. Some countries simply were not willing to induce a domestic recession or to allow inflation in order to eliminate a payments disequilibrium. Central banks neutralized gold flows by open market operations. For example, a deficit nation could neutralize gold outflows by purchasing government securities on the domestic open market; a surplus nation could neutralize gold inflows by selling government securities on the domestic open market. Such actions, of course, prolonged the payments disequilibrium. Eventually, a policy of neutralizing gold flows became infeasible, and countries would have to either start abiding by the rules *or go off the gold standard completely.*

The Gold Exchange Standard (1925 to 1933)

The classical gold standard broke down during World War I. Only the United States remained on a gold standard, and even then the Fed frequently sterilized gold flows. Other nations did not commit themselves to maintain a fixed price of gold.

From 1925 to 1936, the gold standard was restored internationally, as the major trading countries established a *gold exchange standard.* Under this standard, most countries held gold, dollars, or pound sterling as reserves; the United States and the United Kingdom held only gold reserves. Under this standard, most countries sterilized gold flows in order to insulate their economies from the consequences of adjusting to international-payments disequilibria.

In 1931, Great Britain, facing massive gold and capital flows, went off the gold standard, and the gold exchange standard collapsed.

The Bretton Woods System (1946 to 1971)

In 1944, representatives of the major trading nations met in Bretton Woods, New Hampshire, to create a new international-payments system to replace the gold standard that had been abandoned in the early 1930s. The conference had two main objectives:

1 To create a monetary system that would provide for the relief and reconstruction of the countries that were devastated by World War II.

2 To devise a system of fixed exchange rates and a means of correcting international-payments disequilibria.

A compromise was finally adopted and President Truman signed the Bretton Woods Agreement Act on July 31, 1945. The articles of that agreement created the **international monetary fund (IMF)** to administer the articles and to lend foreign exchange to member countries with balance-of-payments deficits. Each fund member, with the exception of the United States, would establish a par value for its currency in terms of dollars or gold.

Member governments were obligated to intervene to maintain the value of their currencies in foreign exchange markets within 1 percent of the declared par values. The United States, which owned most of the world's already-mined gold stock, was similarly obligated to maintain gold prices within a 1 percent margin of $35 (U.S.) per ounce. Except for a transitional arrangement permitting a one-time adjustment of up to 10 percent in par values, thereafter members could alter par values on exchange rates only with the approval of the IMF. The articles stated that such approval would be given only if the country's balance of payments was in "fundamental disequilibrium." This term, however, was never officially defined.

The Adjustable Peg   The foreign exchange system established at Bretton Woods was based on the concept of the adjustable peg. Par, or pegged, values for each currency were established in 1944 in terms of the U.S. dollar or gold. The term "par value" meant the "appropriate" foreign exchange values that were set at that time. And exchange rates were pegged to those par values. For example, if it were decided that the par value of the French franc would be five francs to one dollar, or 20 cents per French franc, then the foreign exchange rate would be pegged at that level. Exchange rates were, however, allowed to fluctuate under the influence of supply and demand within a narrow band. From 1944 to 1971, the band was 1 percent above and below par value. From 1971 until 1973, the band was 2.25 percent above par to 2.25 below par value.

Under the rules established at Bretton Woods, governments were supposed to intervene to prevent the values of their currencies in foreign exchange markets from falling below the lower limits. When there was an excess quantity supplied of its currency, that is, when the lower limit was reached, the deficit country's government was obligated to buy the surplus up with U.S. dollars in order to support the price of its own currency.

Other Duties of the International Monetary Fund   The IMF could also lend funds to member countries with balance-of-payments deficits. Such loans could come from IMF holdings of gold and currency obtained from the subscriptions of IMF members according to a system of quotas. Each member's quota was set by a formula that took into account its importance in the world economy.

The History of the Bretton Woods System   Immediately after the Bretton Woods system was organized, the rest of the world used about $6 billion of its gold and silver reserves to finance its deficits with the United States. Threatened with a reduction of imports, European countries were faced with a decline in their standards of living, zero economic growth, deflation, and devaluation. The United States solved Europe's balance-of-payments problems by voluntarily lending billions of dollars to Europe under the Marshall Plan (formally called the European Recovery Program). Between mid-1948 and mid-1952, the United States provided $11.6 billion in the form of grants and $1.8 billion in the form of loans to Europe. These voluntary loans averted a "dollar shortage" and allowed European countries for the most part to avoid the problems mentioned above.

The Era of U.S. Deficits   During the 1950s, Europe and Japan built their industrial bases and substantially reduced their balance-of-payments deficits. By 1958, it was the *United States* that had the balance-of-payments deficit. These U.S. deficits, however, played an important role in the new international monetary payments system. Member countries of the IMF had to hold dollar or gold reserves to prevent the foreign exchange value of their currencies from falling during temporary payments imbalances. A major weakness in the Bretton Woods arrangement was that it failed to provide for a *systematic* means by which world reserves of dollars and gold could grow as world trade grew. The IMF subscriptions created a once-and-for-all increase in world monetary reserves; but the IMF could not provide the continuous *growth* in world reserves. The only way the rest of the world could increase its foreign exchange reserves was for the United States to have deficits. In essence, the United States took on the role of a world central bank, and the world was on a key currency standard—the key currency being the U.S. dollar.

During the late 1950s and early 1960s the rest of the world wanted to increase its U.S. dollar reserves. The fact that they did not convert those dollar holdings into gold indicates that they did not want the United States to correct its balance-of-payments deficit by reducing its rate of inflation, which would have allowed U.S. exports to be more competitive in the world market; it would have also induced U.S. citizens to import less. By the mid-1960s, the U.S. deficit was no longer matched by a desire of the rest of the world to increase dollar reserves. Dollar reserves were being *forced* on the rest of the world as a result of accelerating inflation in the United States.

The money supply (M1) in the United States began to accelerate in 1965 to finance the war in Vietnam. The result was an acceleration in the rate of inflation from an annual average rate of 1.7 percent in the 1958 to 1965 period to 5.4 percent in 1969. Under a fixed exchange system, countries that have relatively higher rates of inflation will suffer a deterioration in their trade balances. Starting from a surplus of $6.8 million in 1964, the U.S. merchandise trade balance deteriorated to a deficit of $2.7 billion in 1971. Imports of foreign steel, automobiles, and textiles captured increasing shares of American markets. Soaring quantities of U.S. imports were mirrored by an increase in the supply of dollars on the foreign exchange market. Conversely, as the flow of U.S. exports slowed in 1970 and 1971, the demand for dollars decreased.

If there had not been any government intervention in the foreign exchange market, the excess supply of dollars would have caused the price of the dollar to fall, against the pound and other currencies. However, under the IMF's fixed-exchange-rate system, foreign central banks were required to buy the excess supply of dollars. To prevent the pound from appreciating, for example, the Bank of England had to sell pounds to buy the dollars that were in excess supply.

If the foreign central banks had allowed the purchase of dollars to increase their money supplies, the U.S. inflation would have been exported to other countries. If this adjustment mechanism had been allowed to operate, the U.S. trade deficit would have been less because the rest of the world would have had a rate of inflation similar to that of the United States. But this would have required that other countries allow the Fed to determine their monetary policies. No country would have had an independent monetary policy; a country's inflation rate would have been determined by the U.S. rate of inflation.

Some central banks, notably in Germany, France, and Japan, did not permit their rates of monetary growth to accelerate. Instead, they sterilized the effects of purchasing dollars in the foreign exchange market by selling bonds in domestic open-market operations. Inflation was *not* imported by these countries and, consequently, American trade deficits with these countries continued.

Purchase of U.S. Government Bonds   Since most of the dollars obtained by these countries (to stabilize foreign exchange rates) were used to purchase U.S. government bonds, the foreign governments were in fact borrowing from their own citizens by open-market sales of bonds. This was done so that they could buy the U.S. government bonds that were being issued to finance U.S. budget deficits resulting from the Vietnam war. (In fact, all of the growth in federal debt found its way into the portfolios of monetary authorities from 1966 to 1979. The Federal Reserve absorbed $43 billion and foreign central banks bought $51 billion.) Under the Bretton Woods agreement, though, foreign central banks did have the option of buying gold from the United States at $35 an ounce. Every U.S. secretary of the Treasury during the latter part of this period spent part of his time traveling to Europe to persuade foreign central banks to purchase U.S. bonds rather than gold with their dollars. Most of the European countries and Japan honored the American requests. France did not.

The Demise of the Bretton Woods System   The United States took actions to insulate its gold stock. Although it was illegal for U.S. citizens to own gold, private foreign investors could buy gold at a constant price of $35 an ounce in world gold markets; the United States guaranteed that it would intervene with gold sales in those markets if the price rose above $35 an ounce. This created a potential threat to the U.S. gold stock. Aside from the fact that the gold stock was used to meet obligations to member central banks, private speculators betting on the devaluation of the dollar in terms of gold also had claims on U.S. gold. In March 1968, the United States took the bold step of announcing that it would no longer sell gold to *private* holders of dollars. The gold market was divided into two tiers: gold held by foreign central banks (and treasuries) and gold held privately. The United States continued to honor its commitments to buy and sell gold in transactions with other central banks, but it no longer pegged the price of privately held gold. From 1968 until August 1971, the United States "lost" very little of its gold. The United States continued to sell gold to foreign central banks at $35 an ounce *provided that they did not ask for any!*

To ensure further that the United States would not have to deflate to protect its gold reserves, the United States supported an amendment to the articles of the IMF that permitted the creation of **special drawing rights (SDRs).** It turned the IMF into a world central bank with the potential to create international reserves.

Despite these actions to protect U.S. reserves from being lost to foreign central banks, fixed exchange rates finally collapsed under the stress of accelerating inflation in the United States. During 1970, foreign central banks had to buy $9.8 billion of unwanted dollars. In 1971, they bought a record $29.8 billion. (In addition to the current account deficit of $1.4 billion in 1971, capital outflows caused by investors' fears that the dollar was going to be devalued contributed an estimated $28 billion to the U.S.'s balance-of-payments deficit.) Despite these huge purchases of dollars, foreign central banks were circumspect about using them to purchase gold from the United States. In the first nine months of 1971, even though $21 billion were purchased by foreign central banks, only $4 billion were used to purchase gold. American monetary authorities were, nevertheless, worried. If foreign central banks did demand gold, the United States could not maintain convertibility of the dollar into gold except by reestablishing the par value of the dollar at a price substantially above $35 an ounce.

In addition to threatening the convertibility of the dollar into gold, the "overvalued" dollar also put the American-traded goods industries at an increasingly serious competitive disadvantage. Labor costs were rising, as wages kept up with inflation. While the non-traded-goods industries could pass those higher labor costs on in the form of higher prices, export industries could not. If they raised prices, they would lose sales to foreign producers. Producers of exports and of goods competing with foreign imports put increasing political pressure on the Nixon administration to do something about the loss of sales to foreign producers.

The European and Japanese governments were reluctant to let their currencies appreciate too far against the dollar. European and Japanese export industries enjoyed their competitive advantage in the world market (partially the result of the overvalued dollar), and they used all their influence to resist the revaluation of their currencies. As long as foreign nations refused to let their currencies appreciate, the United States could do little about it. After all, under the IMF articles, responsibility for pegging exchange rates rested with foreign central banks. The United States had the responsibility to peg only the dollar price of gold.

Nixon's Bombshell On Sunday evening, August 15, 1971, President Nixon dropped a bombshell on America's trading partners. Nixon announced a radically new economic program to deal with the overvalued dollar. Included in the program were the following:

1 A 90-day freeze on wages and prices to break inflationary expectations
2 An import surcharge of 10 percent
3 A suspension of the convertibility of dollars into gold

Because the United States no longer honored its IMF obligations to sell gold at $35 an ounce, Nixon put the world officially on a "dollar standard," instead of a gold/dollar standard. In describing these actions, the President acknowledged that "this action will not win us many friends among the international money traders. But our primary concern is with American workers, and with fair competition around the world." The 10 percent surcharge on imports was characterized as a "temporary" action designed to pressure other countries into appreciating their currencies so that "American products will not be at a disadvantage because of unfair exchange rates. When the unfair treatment is ended, the import tax will end as well. . . . The time has come for exchange rates to be set straight and for the major nations to compete as equals. There is no longer any need for the United States to compete with one hand tied behind her back."

The Smithsonian Agreement What finally came out of this new policy was the Smithsonian Agreement of December 18, 1971, which officially devalued the dollar by an average of 12 percent against the currencies of fourteen major industrial nations. Even this devaluation of the dollar, however, was not sufficient to eliminate the excess supply of dollars on the foreign exchange market. The U.S. balance-of-payments deficit was still a substantial $10.4 billion during 1972. In early 1973, partly in reaction to the rapid expansion of the money supply in the United States during 1972, private speculators sold large amounts of dollars in the foreign exchange market. Foreign central banks purchased about $10 billion in the first three months of the year alone—compared to a deficit of $10.4 billion for the whole year of 1972—in an attempt to support the dollar. When this massive intervention failed to stabilize the dollar (even after an additional devaluation of the dollar in February), fixed exchange rates were abandoned.

The Floating-Exchange-Rate System

On March 16, 1973, the finance ministers of the European economic community (EEC), the common market, announced that they would let their currencies float against the dollar. (Japan had let the yen float against the dollar on February 12.) The communiqué argued that official interventions in exchange markets might be useful at appropriate times in order to facilitate the maintenance of "orderly" conditions. Each nation in the EEC stated that it "will be prepared to intervene at its initiative in its own market, when necessary and desirable, acting in a flexible manner in the light of market conditions and in close consultation with the authorities of the nation whose currency may be bought or sold." In other words, the international monetary system was now on a managed float or, as it is sometimes called, a **dirty float.**

A System of Pure Floating Exchange Rates

Establishing the Equilibrium Exchange Rate Unlike a fixed-exchange-rate system, a system of pure floating exchange rates allows exchange rates to be set by supply and demand. In order to see how, let's consider the

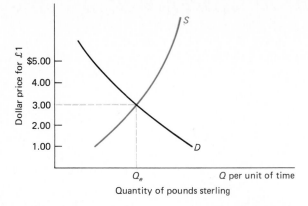

FIGURE 29-1   Given these curves, the equilibrium exchange rate will be established at $3; one British pound sterling will be equivalent to three U.S. dollars. At a high price, a surplus of pounds exists; at a price higher than $3 per pound, the British will have a payments deficit and the United States will have a payments surplus. A surplus of pounds will cause the dollar price of the pound to fall toward $3. At any dollar price per pound below $3, a shortage of pounds exists; the United States will have a payments deficit and Great Britain will have a payments surplus. This shortage of pounds will drive the dollar price of the pound upward, toward $3 per pound.

exchange rate of dollars for British pound sterling. We will show how the dollar price of one pound sterling is determined. Consider Figure 29-1, which indicates the dollar price of one pound sterling on the price (vertical) axis and the quantity of British pound sterling on the quantity (horizontal) axis.

An inverse relationship exists between the dollar price of one pound and the quantity of pounds demanded because, as the dollar price of a pound falls, U.S. citizens will experience substitution and income effects. As the dollar price of pounds falls—it takes fewer dollars to purchase one pound of British sterling—British goods are now relatively cheaper (other things constant). United States citizens will substitute British-made goods for American-made goods; that is, Americans will import more British-made goods. Also, as the dollar price of one pound falls (other things constant), U.S. residents experience an increase in their real income: *Their same money income will allow them to purchase more goods than before if they purchase British-made goods.* Such an increase in their real income will induce Americans to import more British-made goods. Normally, both the substitution effect and the real-income effect will induce U.S. residents to purchase more British goods (increase their imports) as the dollar price of one pound falls.[7] In turn, this

---

[7] A lower dollar price per pound might encourage U.S. residents to be more generous to British relatives or to travel in England. The United States government might also be induced to give more military aid to Great Britain. Similarly, U.S. businesses might be more inclined to purchase British-made parts and assemble them locally, or to make outright investments in England. All of these activities will increase the quantity demanded of pounds.

increase in the quantity of British goods demanded increases the quantity of British pounds demanded.[8]

A direct relationship exists between the dollar price of one pound and the quantity of pounds supplied, because a higher dollar price for pounds induces British residents to purchase more American-made goods, and British residents therefore offer more pounds on foreign exchange markets. At higher dollar prices per pound, the British can get more dollars—and therefore more American goods—for their money. At higher dollar prices per pound, therefore, American goods are cheaper and the British experience substitution and real-income effects that induce them to want to import more U.S. goods.[9] Of course, larger imports of American goods will require British residents to make greater quantities of pounds available to American sellers.

As Figure 29-1 shows, the equilibrium exchange rate will be established at $3 per pound—where the supply and demand curves intersect. At any price above $3 per pound, the quantity of pounds supplied by the British exceeds the quantity of pounds demanded by Americans; a surplus of pounds exists. The British would experience a payments deficit, and the Americans would experience a payments surplus (assuming they are the only two countries). Because a surplus of pounds exists, the price of pounds will fall, which increases the quantity of pounds demanded by Americans and decreases the quantity of pounds supplied by the British. This process will continue until equilibrium is restored at $3 per pound.

At any price below $3 per pound, a shortage of pounds exists; the American quantity of pounds demanded exceeds the British quantity of pounds supplied. The Americans would experience a payments deficit, and the British would experience a payments surplus. In the absence of any government intervention (remember, this is a *pure* floating-exchange-rate system), a shortage of pounds will drive up the dollar price per pound; this will lead to a decrease in the American quantity of pounds demanded and an increase in the British quantity of pounds supplied.

At $3 per pound, the equilibrium exchange rate is established. Note, furthermore, that an international-payments equilibrium is also established.

Changes in the Equilibrium Exchange Rate   Consider Figure 29-2, which shows a decrease in the demand (from *D* to *D'*) for pounds. A decrease in the demand for pounds can come about if:

1   The price level in Great Britain rises more rapidly than the U.S. level rises. If the British rate of inflation exceeds the American rate of inflation, for example, Americans will want to reduce the quantity of British-made goods they purchase at *any* dollar price for pounds. As a consequence, Americans

---

[8]After all, British sellers (or gift recipients) want to be paid in their own currency so they can spend it locally.

[9]Or give gifts to their relatives in the United States. See footnote 7.

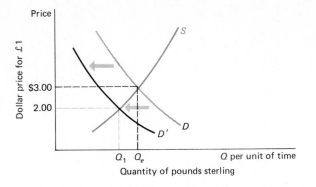

FIGURE 29-2 A decrease in the American demand for pounds, from D to D', could come about if (1) Great Britain experiences a higher rate of inflation, (2) interest rates are relatively higher in the United States, or (3) real incomes fall in the United States, other things constant. Such a decrease in the demand for pounds causes a surplus of pounds at the old exchange rate. The dollar price of pounds will fall—the pound will depreciate and the dollar will appreciate—until a new equilibrium exchange rate is established at two U.S. dollars for one British pound. At the new equilibrium exchange rate, an international-payments equilibrium is restored.

will reduce the quantity of pounds they want at every dollar price per pound.

2 Interest rates are higher in the United States relative to Great Britain. In such a situation, American citizens will want to purchase fewer British securities at *any* dollar price per pound; the quantity of pounds demanded falls at every dollar price per pound.

3 Real income falls in the United States, other things constant. If real incomes fall in the United States, its residents will want to import fewer goods at *any* exchange rate; the quantity of pounds demanded by Americans will fall at every dollar price per pound.

Figure 29-2 shows that the new equilibrium exchange rate will be established at two U.S. dollars for one British pound. A decrease in the demand for pounds from D to D' causes a surplus of pounds at the old exchange rate; the quantity of pounds supplied by the British now exceeds the quantity of pounds demanded by Americans at the previous exchange rate. This will cause the dollar price of pounds to fall—the dollar will appreciate relative to the pound because it takes fewer dollars to purchase one pound (this is called **currency appreciation**). Simultaneously (and of necessity), the pound will depreciate—the pound can buy fewer dollars (this is called **currency depreciation**). Eventually, the new exchange rate will be established where the quantity of pounds supplied by the British equals the quantity of pounds demanded by the Americans. At that equilibrium exchange rate (two dollars can purchase one pound), an international-payments equilibrium will also be restored.

FIGURE 29-3 **The Dollar Afloat.** This graph shows the real value of the dollar relative to an index of a weighted average of ten foreign currencies. Note that since early 1980 the dollar has appreciated dramatically.

The Floating U.S. Dollar Figure 29-3 shows how the dollar has fared relative to a weighted (by the extent of trade) average of ten other currencies.[10] Note that immediately following the March 1973 decision to float the dollar, the dollar depreciated relative to the other ten currencies, confirming the belief that the dollar was overvalued. From mid-1975 to early 1977, the dollar appreciated, and then it plunged rapidly during 1978. Note that since late 1980, the dollar has appreciated quite rapidly. Although the reason for this appreciation is not totally clear, it is generally agreed that the recent dollar appreciation has occurred, at least partly, because real interest rates are relatively high in the United States and because political and economic instability have increased in much of the rest of the world—especially in Europe, Latin America, and the Middle East. The second explanation implies that the United States is still considered a safe haven for investors and has become a financial refuge in troubled times. If this is true, this can account for the fact that, during 1982 and 1983, the United States enjoyed (1) a large current account deficit that was financed mostly by a capital account surplus (if we include errors and omissions), and (2) an appreciating dollar on the foreign exchange markets. In effect, U.S. citizens are benefiting from a current account deficit because they are living in a country that is relatively stable politically and economically.

---

[10]The ten countries whose currencies are included in the weighted average are: Belgium, Canada, France, Germany, Italy, Japan, The Netherlands, Sweden, Switzerland, and the United Kingdom.

WHICH IS BETTER—FIXED OR FLOATING EXCHANGE RATES?

Under a fixed-exchange-rate international-payments system, disequilibrating changes (such as gold discoveries or changes in tastes or technology) require that resources be reallocated until a new equilibrium is restored. Such disequilibrating changes also require that resources be reallocated under a floating-exchange-rate system. Under both systems, the basic economic mechanisms that bring about resource allocation and restore equilibrium in international payments are essentially the same: price effects, income effects, and interest-rate changes.

What is different about the two systems is the *process* by which equilibrium is restored. Under a gold or modified gold fixed-exchange-rate system, gold must flow from the deficit nation to the surplus nation; under a Bretton Woods–type system, ultimately the deficit country must experience a reduction in the money supply and the surplus country must experience an increase in the money supply. Under any fixed-exchange-rate system, then, surplus countries must inflate and deficit countries must experience recession; these are the rules of the game under a fixed-exchange-rate structure. In periods of a payments disequilibrium, under a fixed-rate standard, monetary and fiscal policies must be geared to achieve a payments equilibrium—other ultimate goals, such as less unemployment and price stability, must become of secondary importance. Even if an international-payments equilibrium currently exists, monetary and fiscal policy actions to attain other goals must be carried out with an eye toward how these actions will affect the balance of payments. For example, if an international-payments equilibrium currently exists but unemployment is high, an expansionary monetary policy may well lead to an international-payments deficit. Under a fixed-exchange-rate standard, therefore, monetary and fiscal policy are carried out in order to achieve one goal—an international-payments equilibrium. Policymakers, therefore, are not very free to pursue *other* goals. Moreover, the rules of the game require that individual trading partners are not free to carry out monetary and fiscal policies that are independent of the other trading partners. Under a fixed-exchange-rate system, a nation that is determined to pursue inflation domestically will "export" inflation to other nations; a nation in the throes of a recession will export its recession to other countries.

In short, a fixed-exchange-rate system requires that each nation's other ultimate goals become secondary to one ultimate goal—an international-payments balance. If nations are not willing to play by the rules of the game—if they sterilize gold flows by refusing to inflate or deflate their money—a fixed-exchange-rate system will not work smoothly. Such a system will be characterized by prolonged and chronic payments disequilibria and occasional (and sometimes not-so-occasional) official exchange-rate (or gold price) adjustments.

When a disequilibrating change occurs *under a floating-exchange-rate system, an international-payments equilibrium will be restored automatically, without any governmental or central bank intervention.* Deficit nations will find that their currency depreciates; surplus nations experience currency appreciation. Note that *only one price* has to change—the exchange rate—and not the *price level* of each country. Moreover, because a payments imbalance will eventually disappear under a *pure float system,* nations can pursue other ultimate goals. And nations can do so independently of each other.

While a floating-exchange-rate system seems superior "on paper," in practice it has problems. Under a floating-exchange-rate system there are "rules of the game" too. A nation must *allow* its currency to inflate or deflate. Nations are not always willing to allow their currency to float because there are costs to doing so.

A deficit nation will experience a currency depreciation; it will take more units of the local currency to import the same quantity of goods and services. But this means that the price of imports will rise and, other things constant, the standard of living will fall in the deficit country. This reduction in living standards also occurs because a currency depreciation means that local producers have an incentive to export more, further reducing the local availability of goods and services. There will be a strong temptation for policymakers to cushion (or offset) such reduction in living standards by intervening in the exchange market; policymakers may put pressure on the central bank to support the deficit nation's currency by purchasing it with foreign exchange reserves (gold or foreign currency reserves).

The surplus nation, on the other hand, will experience a currency appreciation. The nation will increase its imports and decrease its exports and the surplus will eventually be eliminated. Such events, however, may well be interpreted as putting local producers at a competitive disadvantage in international markets for goods and services. Local producers (and their unions) may well put pressure on policymakers to make their goods more competitive on national markets by selling their currency on international exchange markets, thereby forestalling currency appreciation.

In short, there are strong political pressures for central banks to intervene in the foreign exchange markets under a floating-exchange-rate system.

When everything is said and done, fixed exchange rates become somewhat flexible, and flexible exchange rates become somewhat fixed, because political pressures exist to resist the resource reallocations that are necessary to adjust to shocks that cause disequilibrium in the international balance of payments. In that respect, *if nations are not willing to "pay the price" to adjust to change, it doesn't make any difference whether the world is on a fixed-exchange-rate system or a floating-exchange-rate system.*

The real issues are:

1   Do floating exchange rates cause *unnecessary* changes in exchange rates (and, therefore, unnecessary changes in resource allocation, which gen-

erate changes in exports and imports) because speculation is greater under flexible exchange rates than under fixed exchange rates?

2 Are interferences with free trade such as tariffs, import quotas, and currency restrictions more likely under a fixed-exchange-rate system (when governments wish to insulate their economies from world changes that cause disequilibria in international payments) than under a floating-exchange-rate system, where currency depreciation is an option (but causes other problems)?

Ultimately, these are empirical questions that only time will answer. If policymakers refuse to play by the rules of the game under either payments system, we may never know the answer to the first question. The second question really asks: Which payments system presents the greatest temptation to policymakers to resist the winds of change?

CURRENT CONTROVERSY

Can the IMF Solve the World-Debt Crisis?

In November 1983, the United States increased its IMF quota by $8.4 billion. Other developed nations have also agreed to increase their quotas; the total increase in IMF reserves will be $42 billion. It is expected that this money will be lent to less developed countries (LDCs) to help them meet short-term payments on their enormous foreign debts. How did the current world debt crisis arise? Is this "IMF solution" the best way to deal with the crisis? We turn to these issues now.

A SHORT HISTORY OF THE LDC FOREIGN-DEBT CRISIS

In 1973, on the eve of the first oil price shock, the total foreign debt—public and private—owed by the LDCs was slightly less than $100 billion. The private international banking system held 36 percent of this foreign debt. In 1979, another increase in OPEC oil prices shocked the world, and private banks (mostly in the United States) received a fortune in deposits because the OPEC nations were unwilling (some say unable) to spend all their oil earnings. By depositing their wealth in safe western banks, the OPEC nations were able to earn a fairly high rate of return. The private banks recycled these "petrodollars" largely by making loans to LDC *governments*. Such loans were considered safe because "governments don't default on loans."* In fairness to private banks, it should be pointed out that these loans were encouraged by the United States government and other governments.

Borrowers and lenders were both counting on continued inflation in the United States (and in other developed countries), which would have reduced the *real* value of such nominal-dollar-denominated debt. Unfortunately for these borrowers and

TABLE 1 Foreign Debt of Selected Countries, 1983

(In billions of dollars)

Country	World Debt
Brazil	$90
Argentina	$40
Venezuela	$35
Israel	$21.5
Chile	$21
Philippines	$18

Source: Charles Hanley "'Debt Bomb' Setting off World Political Explosions," Bowling Green, Ky., *Daily News,* Oct. 26, 1983, p. 1-C.

lenders, the United States curtailed its inflation, and the world entered its largest recession since the 1930s. The real value of the debt did not fall, and developed nations reduced their imports as they became more trade-protectionist. Higher interest rates also led to higher costs for debt restructuring and for new loans that were sought to help pay old loans. By the end of 1981, the total foreign debt of non-OPEC LDCs had grown to $470 billion, and 53 percent of this debt was owned by private international banks.

It is estimated that by the end of 1983 the total foreign debt of the non-OPEC LDCs (including the Eastern communist bloc) was nearly $700 billion, most of which was owned by private banks. Table 1 shows the total foreign debt of selected countries, as of October 1983.

WORLD-DEBT CRISIS: SHORT-TERM ILLIQUIDITY OR LONG-TERM INSOLVENCY?

A vigorous debate has emerged concerning how this foreign debt problem can best be resolved. Not surprisingly, the proper solution to the problem depends on how one interprets the root of the problem. Debaters are split as to whether the world foreign debt problem is basically a short-term liquidity problem or a long-term solvency problem.

Those who see the problem as a short-term liquidity problem believe that when the world recession is over, and after four or five years of world economic growth has increased LDC exports, the LDCs can pay off their loans.† Therefore, they believe that the IMF solution is proper.

Critics of the IMF solution are many and varied.‡ They see the problem as a long-run solvency problem; they all believe that most of the LDCs cannot possibly repay their debts. Table 2 seems to support their contention. Note that the ratio of annual

TABLE 2 Selected Countries and Their Total Foreign Debt and Their Yearly Debt Service to Exports Ratio*

Country	Total Debt**	Annual Debt Service to Annual Exports Ratio (%)†
Brazil	$86.3	129
Mexico	84.6	122
Argentina	38.8	179
South Korea	37.2	53
Venezuela	33.2	95
Philippines	20.7	91
Chile	17.2	116
Peru	11.2	90
Colombia	10.2	94

*End of 1982.
**Billions of dollars.
†The ratio of interest plus principal payments to the value of exports.
Source: Morgan Guarantee Letter and data provided by Frederick Heldring, deputy chairperson, CoreStates Financial Corporation and Philadelphia National Bank, in a lecture on Aug. 12, 1983, to the University of Wisconsin Prochnow Banking Seminar for College Faculty Participants.

debt service (interest payments plus principal) to annual exports (the source of payment out of *current* earnings) is extremely high for all these nations. Note that current *imports* are also paid out of exports; the fact that these nations also run deficits on their current accounts makes the inability of repayment seem very likely indeed.

The critics also agree that the IMF is the wrong institution to solve the problem; they basically agree that the essence of the problem is that *the LDCs have not used the loans productively.* The IMF prefers to extend loans to *governments,*§ and LDC governments have used the funds to:

1 Invest in very expensive and prestigious "mega projects" (chemical plants, hydroelectric dams) whose end products could have been imported more cheaply

2 Subsidize inefficient state-operated or nationalized industries

3 Support their own currencies to prevent currency depreciation on the foreign exchange markets

4 Purchase armaments for national defense

However, the critics differ on the solution to the long-range solvency problem. Some maintain that the banks and their stockholders (and the owners of those deposits over $100,000) should pay the price for making bad loans in order to discourage the practice. Their solution is to require banks to value the loans at their true value and to set aside greater reserves for bad loans. Both of these measures would reduce current profits, so banks are fighting this solution.

Another solution suggests that the U.S. government *itself* (not the IMF, over which the United States has less control) bail out the banks and the LDCs. The price, however, would be increased bank disclosure of foreign lending, and the LDCs would have to support U.S. foreign policy. Taxpayers and borrowers (who would pay higher interest rates if the U.S. government borrows the money to bail out the banks and the LDCs) would foot the bill.

Another solution offered is that the private banks accept payment of the LDCs' assets (resources, equity in businesses) for the debt. Although this is a common solution to insolvency, the LDCs themselves might be "somewhat" reluctant to do this; they might find, however, that this solution is preferable to default and to loss of access to foreign funds in the future.

If the critics are correct, the IMF bailout will solve the world-debt crisis only temporarily. Over a longer period, the result of throwing good money after bad will be an even more severe foreign debt crisis.

---

*They apparently forgot that more than twenty nations had defaulted on their World War I debts to the United States. Only Finland paid; Britain, France, Germany (which borrowed to meet its war reparations payments to Britain and France), and Italy did not. Austria, Hungary, Nicaragua, the USSR (on Czarist-initiated loans) Imperial China and several U.S. states in the 19th century also defaulted on loans.

†This position is held by W. S. Ogden (vice chairperson of Chase Manhattan Bank), "A Banker's View of the Foreign Debt Issue," *The Wall Street Journal* (hereafter *WSJ*), Nov. 8, 1982; and Donald T. Regan (U.S. Secretary of the Treasury), "The United States and the World's Debt Problem," *WSJ*, Feb. 8, 1983; and (understandably) by many private U.S. bankers and officials of the borrowing countries.

‡See W. E. Simon (former U.S. secretary of the Treasury), "Cut Off the International Loan Lushes," *WSJ*, Apr. 6, 1983; Paul Craig Roberts (former assistant Treasury secretary), "The High Cost of Funding a Growing IMF," *WSJ*, Feb. 3, 1983, and "The Bank's Friends Have Put Them over a Barrel," *WSJ;* Marshall Wright (Exxon Corporation vice president), "On the Trail of a Lending Binge," *WSJ*, Sept. 7, 1983; George Champion (chairperson of Chase Manhattan Bank, 1961–1969), "Foreign Debts: A Proposal for U.S. Banks," *WSJ*, Jan. 1, 1983; Gustav Rains (Yale University), "For Latin American Economies, Lessons in Asia," *WSJ*, Oct. 12, 1983; and Manual F. Ayau (president of Universidad Francesco Marroquin in Guatemala City), "Lending Institutions Stall Latin American Progress," *WSJ*, Nov. 18, 1983.

§Indeed, some critics maintain that it was the belief that the IMF or a similar international agency would bail out banks that encouraged private banks to lend to governments in the first place. See G. E. Nunn (San Jose State University), "How the Banks Got Drawn into Ponzi-style Foreign Lending," Letters to the Editors, *WSJ*, June 29, 1983.

CHAPTER SUMMARY

1   If a nation is spending more (on imports or gifts) than it is currently receiving (in exports or gifts), then it must finance this activity by borrowing or selling assets.

2   When a nation is in a position in which it cannot continue its current transactions with other nations (due to borrowing constraints or due to dwindling, limited assets), it is said to be in an international-payments disequilibrium. An international-payments equilibrium is one of the Fed's ultimate goals.

3   The economic mechanisms that drive a nation into a payments equilibrium are: interest rates, price changes, and income changes.

4   The international-payments systems that have been developed to assure a balance-of-payments equilibrium are: fixed-exchange-rate systems and floating-exchange-rate systems. An exchange rate is the price of foreign currency in terms of a unit of domestic currency.

5   An international gold standard is one form of fixed-exchange-rate system. Each nation on a gold standard (a) imposes a fixed ratio between gold held by the government and currency in circulation (the ratio is 1 to 1 on a pure gold standard), and (b) agrees to buy and sell gold in unlimited quantities at "official" rates in terms of currency. Because each nation fixes the price of its currency to a given quantity of gold, in effect each country's currency has a fixed value relative to other countries.

6   If a nation has an international-payments deficit under a gold standard, gold will flow out of that country and into those countries that are (of necessity) experiencing international-payments surpluses. As a consequence, deficit nations experience a reduction in their price levels and income levels and an increase in their interest rates. Surplus nations experience an increase in their price levels and their income levels and a decrease in their interest rates. These actions create an international-payments equilibrium.

7   The rules of the game under the gold standard require that deficit and surplus nations do not offset gold flows by sterilizing gold movements.

8   The Bretton Woods system (1946–1971) was another fixed-exchange-rate system. It established an IMF to help nations adjust to *short-term* disequilibrium in their international payments. The IMF lent reserves to countries that suffered from short-term illiquidity, in order to induce that country to keep its exchange rate fixed in terms of other countries. When a "fundamental disequilibrium" (never defined precisely by the IMF) existed, a nation was allowed to change its official exchange rate significantly.

9   The basic reserve under the Bretton Woods system was the U.S. dollar; all countries except the United States were allowed to use the dollar as a reserve and as a means of settling international payments. Such a system required that the United States continually run a deficit on its payments. While this system worked for a while, eventually nations accumulated more dollars than they wanted to and everyone became concerned about "financing U.S. deficits." Some nations attempted to exchange their acquired dollars for gold owned by the United States.

10 Not wanting to sell its gold at the official price—which was artificially low in terms of dollars—the United States abandoned the Bretton Woods system in 1973 and allowed the U.S. dollar to float with respect to other currencies.

11 Since 1973, the world has been on a floating-exchange-rate system. Exchange rates fluctuate to reflect the supply of and the demand for the currencies of individual countries.

12 Most nations are not willing to allow their currency to appreciate or depreciate very much in the short run. Therefore, they intervene in the international-exchange-rate market to support their currency; they buy it with reserves when it is depreciating or sell it when it is appreciating. Such government intervention generates a "dirty float" payments system and causes a payments disequilibrium.

13 The foreign debt of LDCs reached $700 billion by 1984. Most of the developed nations increased their reserves to the IMF in order to help finance these debts

until the world economy recovers sufficiently for LDC governments to earn enough foreign exchange to meet their payments. Some believe that the world debt crisis is not one of short-term liquidity, however. These people criticize the "IMF solution" and maintain that the borrowed money has not been used wisely. Further loans to LDCs, they maintain, will result in throwing good money after bad money.

GLOSSARY

Balance-of-payments disequilibrium: A circumstance in which a nation cannot continue its current international transactions indefinitely.

Capital account deficit: A situation in which the value of a country's sales of such assets as stocks, bonds, and land to foreigners is less than the value of that country's purchase of such assets from the rest of the world; a net borrowing situation.

Capital account surplus: A situation in which the value of a country's sales of such assets as stocks, bonds, and land to foreigners exceeds the value of that country's purchase of such assets from the rest of the world; a net lending situation.

Currency appreciation: A situation in which it now takes more foreign currency to purchase a unit of domestic currency.

Currency depreciation: A situation in which it now takes less foreign currency to purchase a unit of domestic currency.

Current account deficit: A situation in which the value of a nation's exports of goods and services (and public and private transfers to the rest of the world) is less than the value of its imports of goods and services (and public and private transfers from the rest of the world).

Current account surplus: A situation in which the value of a nation's exports of goods and services (and public and private transfers to the rest of the world) exceeds the value of its imports of goods and services (and public and private transfers from the rest of the world).

Dirty float: When governments intervene in a floating-exchange-rate system in order to keep their own currencies from appreciating or depreciating.

Exchange rate: The price of foreign currency in terms of a unit of domestic currency.

Fixed-exchange-rate systems: An international-payments system in which exchange rates are pegged at some official level and only minor fluctuations are permitted.

Floating-exchange-rate system: An international-payments system under which exchange rates are allowed to rise or to fall as supply and demand conditions dictate.

International monetary fund (IMF): An international agency, created by the Bretton Woods Agreement, to help nations that have temporary liquidity problems.

Official settlements balance: The sum of the current account balance and the capital account balance, plus errors and omissions.

Special drawing rights (SDRs): A reserve asset created by the IMF which countries can use to settle international payments.

PROBLEMS

29-1 Suppose that the United States, England, and Germany adopted a gold standard and defined the value of their currencies as follows: 1 ounce of gold is equivalent to $35, £10, or 100 marks. What is the exchange rate between:

    a The dollar and the pound?

    b The dollar and the mark?

    c The mark and the pound?

29-2 The diagram below shows the supply of, and the demand for, British pounds, as a function of the exchange rate—expressed in U.S. dollars per pound. Assume they are the only two countries in the world.

  a How might the shift from D to D′ be accounted for?

  b If the exchange rate were pegged at $2.60 per pound, what would now exist?

  c What would cause the supply curve to shift rightward (increase)?

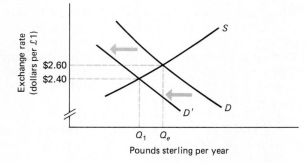

29-3 Assume that the United States and England are the only two countries in the world. If the exchange rate between the pound and the dollar is $3 per £1, and the United States experiences severe inflation (relative to England), what would happen under

  a A flexible-exchange-rate system?

  b A gold standard?

SELECTED REFERENCES

Bordo, Michael D., "The Classical Gold Standard: Some Lessons for Today," *Review,* Federal Reserve Bank of St. Louis, May 1981, pp. 2–17.

Boyd, J. H., D. S. Dahl, and C. D. Line, "A Primer on the International Monetary Fund," *Quarterly Review,* Federal Reserve Bank of Minneapolis, Summer 1983, pp. 6–15.

Friedman, Milton, *A Program for Monetary Stability* (New York: Fordham University Press, 1959).

Mundell, Robert A., "International Monetary Options," *The Cato Journal,* Spring 1983, pp. 189–210.

Salerno, Joseph T., "Gold Standards: True or False," *The Cato Journal,* Spring 1983, pp. 239–267.

Yeager, Leland B., "Stable Money and Free Market Currencies," *The Cato Journal,* Spring 1983, pp. 305–326.

Answers to Problems

Chapter 1: (No Problems)

Chapter 2:

2-1   45; $[N(N - 1)]/2 = \dfrac{10(9)}{2} = \dfrac{90}{2} = 45$

2-2   Yes, if the paper can be converted into full-bodied money, or if it can be converted into anything of a higher value, such as consumer goods.

2-3   Yes. Coins can be used to purchase anything; stamps must be converted into coins first. As a consequence, the less liquid stamps are inferior to cash and will drive out coins from the poker game. That is, at every opportunity, everyone used stamps (instead of money) to ante or bet—including the sociologist.

Chapter 3:

3-1   At first, money included various metals; stamping procedures changed the form of money to stamped coins. Warehouse receipts (paper) then became money; the form changed from coin to paper. Demand deposit accounts became acceptable, so paper currency was not even necessary. Now credit cards and electronic banking help to dispense with demand deposits; the form of money is still changing.

3-2   M1 consists of the values of currency plus demand deposits at commercial banks, other checkable deposits, and traveler's checks issued by nonbanks.

3-3   M2 consists of the values of M1 plus overnight REPOs, plus overnight Eurodollars, plus money market mutual funds, plus savings deposits, plus small-denomination time deposits.

Chapter 4:

4-1   You probably would examine closely the records of deposits and withdrawals you were already keeping. Then you would be aware of those instances in which withdrawals exceeded (or nearly exceeded) deposits. You would also attempt to calculate the probability that loans won't be repaid. After a long period, it would be apparent what a "prudent" reserve ratio was. Depending on whether you were conservative or daring, you would then decide what the reserve ratio *above* the prudent ratio should be. Of course, a trade-off exists; higher reserve ratios are safe but they have an opportunity cost in forgone earnings. If a central bank were around to bail you out during bank runs, you would be inclined to maintain a very low reserve ratio.

Chapter 5:

5-1 Money market: a, b, e, g
Capital market: c, d, f

Chapter 6:

6-1 **a** $2,000
b $1,000
c $500

6-2 8%

6-3 $P = \dfrac{\$70}{(1.1)} + \dfrac{\$70}{(1.1)^2} + \dfrac{\$70}{(1.1)^3} + \dfrac{\$1,070}{(1.1)^4} = \$904.90$

Chapter 7:

7-1 $i_B = \left(\dfrac{F - P}{F}\right) \times \dfrac{360}{n}$

$i_B = \left(\dfrac{\$10,000 - \$9,700}{\$10,000}\right) \times \left(\dfrac{360}{91}\right) = 11.868\%$

7-2 $i_y = \left(\dfrac{F - P}{P}\right) \times \dfrac{365}{n}$

$i_y = \left(\dfrac{\$10,000 - \$9,700}{\$9,700}\right) \times \dfrac{365}{91} = 12.405\%$

7-3 $i_y = \left(\dfrac{F - P}{P}\right) \times \left(\dfrac{365}{n}\right)$

$i_y = \left(\dfrac{\$10,000 - \$9,700}{\$9,700}\right) \times \left(\dfrac{365}{79}\right)$

$i_y = 14.289\%$

7-4a $P = \dfrac{F}{\left(i_y \times \dfrac{n}{365}\right) + 1}$

$P = \dfrac{\$10,000}{\left(.10 \times \dfrac{91}{365}\right) + 1}$

$P = \$9,756.75$

b $P = \dfrac{F}{\left(i_y \times \dfrac{n}{365}\right) + 1}$

$P = \dfrac{\$10,000}{\left(.25 \times \dfrac{81}{365}\right) + 1}$

$P = \$9,474.37$

Chapter 8:

8-1a 20
b $20 million

8-2

The Fed		Bank 1	
Assets	**Liabilities**	**Assets**	**Liabilities**
+$1,000,000 U.S. gov. securities	+$1,000,000 depository-institution reserves	+$1,000,000 reserves	+$1,000,000 demand deposits owned by Mr. Mondrone

8-3a

Bank 1			
Assets		**Liabilities**	
Total reserves Required reserves +($50,000) Excess reserves +($950,000)	+$1,000,000	Demand deposits	+$1,000,000
Total	+$1,000,000	Total	+$1,000,000

b $950,000

Chapter 9:

9-1a They both have a yield of 9% per year.
  b Y is riskier because the expected rate of return is more variable.

9-2 The fund would have Atlanta pay $10 million to Dallas and $30 million to St. Louis and have Richmond pay $100 million to San Francisco.

Chapter 10:

10-1 Income levels and expected changes in income levels, population and expected population changes, expectations of new businesses coming into the area, present ratio of population to banks in the area, and how successful present banks are.

10-2 If a bank opens and it fails, then it wasn't needed; if a bank opens and it stays open, then it was needed.

Chapter 11:

11-1a $2 in greenbacks is equivalent to $1 redeemable paper money.
  b $40 in greenbacks buys 1 ounce of gold.

11-2a $40 in redeemable paper currency buys 1 ounce of gold.
  b $4 in greenbacks is equivalent to $1 redeemable paper money.
  c $160 in greenbacks to buy 1 ounce of gold.

Chapter 12:

12-1 $10,000/$90,000 = 11.11%

12-2 $5,000/95,000 = 5.26%

Chapter 13:

13-1 $j = (a + b + c + d + e + f + t + h) - (r + k + l + n + o)$

13-2 Assets: U.S. government securities and federal agency obligations, cash items in process of collection, gold certificates, float.

Liabilities: Federal Reserve notes, deferred availability cash items, foreign central banks and IMF deposits with the Fed.

Chapter 14:

14-1 $10,000,000 (.12) − $10,000 = $1,190,000

14-2a 12 percent
  b 8.33

14-3a Nothing.
  b $8,000

    c Increase its lending or purchase more securities.
    d 12.5

Chapter 15:

15-1a They rise by $1,000, in the form of demand deposits owed to borrowers.
    b Nothing.
    c They rise by $120.
    d There is a reserve deficit of $120.

15-2a Nothing.
    b They change only in composition; securities fall by $120, and reserves with its Federal Reserve bank rise by $120.

Chapter 16:

16-1a The public's asset composition is changed: less money in demand deposits, more in T-bills.
    b The Fed's assets (T-bills) and liabilities (reserves owned by the depository institution) fall by an equal amount.
    c The depository institution loses an equal amount in liabilities (demand deposits owed to the public) and assets (reserves with the Fed.).

16-2a The Fed realizes an increase in its assets (the value of the T-bills) and an equal increase in its liabilities (in the form of reserves owed to the selling depository institution).
    b The depository institution changes its asset composition; fewer T-bills, more reserve deposits at the Fed.
    c It will increase by some multiple of the value of the T-bills purchased by the Fed.

Chapter 17:

17-1 He will still save 10 percent of his income because his real income has remained constant and the real interest rate has not changed.

17-2 He will still work 38 hours per week; the marginal utility for the 38th hour hasn't changed, nor has his real wage.

17-3 If nominal interest rates more than doubled, he would save a higher percentage of his income; if his money wage more than doubled, he would voluntarily offer more than 38 hours per week.

Chapter 18:

18-1 $V = Y/M$; $V = \$3T/\$500B = 6$

18-2a $k = L_1/Y = \$4,000/\$20,000 = 0.2$
    b She will now hold $9,000 for transactions and $3,000 for precautionary motives, on average.
    c $k = L_1/Y = \$12,000/\$60,000 = 0.2$

Chapter 19:

19-1a 160
   b 140; 4
   c 140; in both parts **b** and **c**, AD shifted downward by 5; therefore the new equilibrium level is 140 in both problems.

19-2a 3
   b 4; if $\Delta G = 4$ and $\Delta T = 4$, then $\Delta Y = 4$; this is referred to as a balanced budget multiplier, and it equals one.

19-3a .4
   b 4, if $\Delta G = 4$ and $\Delta T = 4$, then $\Delta Y = 4$ *regardless of the MPC;* the balanced budget multiplier equals the number 1

Chapter 20:

20-1a Point A
   b Yes, because C is on the *IS* curve.
   c No, because C is not on the *LM* curve.
   d A shortage of liquidity exists at point C. Because at point B the interest rate is the same and therefore L_2 is the same. On the other hand, point B is associated with a lower level of Y and therefore L_1 must be higher at C than at B. If $M = L_1 + L_2$ at B, then $L_1 + L_2 > M$ at point C; a shortage of liquidity exists at C.
   e If a shortage of liquidity exists at C, people will sell bonds to gain liquidity. This action causes bond prices to fall and interest rates to rise; higher interest rates reduce net investment; therefore Y falls. A combination of higher interest rates and lower levels of Y reduces the shortage of liquidity; this process continues until point A is reached.

Chapter 21:

21-1a $\dfrac{(P_{1984})(Q_{1984})}{(P_{1972})(Q_{1984})} \times 100 = \dfrac{\$1,146}{\$618} \times 100 = 185.44$

   b $\dfrac{\text{GNP}_{1984}}{185.44} \times 100 = \dfrac{\$1,146}{185.44} \times 100 = \$618$

   c $[(P_{1984})(Q_{1972})/(P_{1972})(Q_{1972})] \times 100 = [850/310] \times 100 = 274.19$

Chapter 22:

22-1a Rightward.
   b $\Delta G[1/(1 - b)] = \$10$ billion $(4) = \$40$ billion
   c Zero.
   d Rises, because a higher level of NNP increases the quantity of money demanded for L_1; at the previous equilibrium interest rate, there will be a shortage of liquidity.

e No, because a higher interest rate will reduce private expenditures on investment and consumption thereby somewhat offsetting the increase in government expenditures.

22-2a Rightward.

b $\Delta T[-b/(1-b)] = -\$10$ billion $(-3) = \$30$ billion

c Rises. See part **d** in the previous question.

d No. A higher interest rate crowds out some private consumption and investment spending, thereby somewhat offsetting the expansionary effects of the decrease in taxes.

Chapter 23:

23-1 $G = T = \Delta H = \Delta B$; because $G = T$, $\Delta B = \Delta H = O$, and the money *supply* remains constant. However, an increase in G shifts the IS curve by $\Delta G = \Delta T$, causing Y to rise. But the money supply doesn't rise; therefore the interest rate will rise and Y will fall. The ultimate increase in Y will be less than the increase in G and T.

23-2

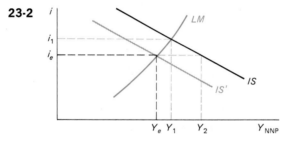

An increase in G causes a shift from IS to IS'. Because this increase in G is financed by an increase in borrowing by the Treasury, the money supply remains constant and LM does not shift. A higher level of national income increases L_1; given M, a shortage of liquidity exists at i_e and Y_2. Therefore, i rises to i_1 and some crowding out occurs. The level of national income rises from Y_e to Y_1, and not from Y_e to Y_2, because the interest rate rises to Y_1.

Chapter 24:

24-1 *Agree:*

a In the long run, inflation is a monetary phenomenon.

b In the long run, prices and wages are sufficiently flexible to restore the economy to its natural rate of unemployment and output.

Disagree:

a Money is the most important determinant of aggregate nominal income in the short run.

b Fiscal policy is effective.

c Monetary and fiscal policies can be stabilizing.

d The private sector is relatively stable.

e Excess money balances are spent only on financial assets.

f Increases in the money supply lower the interest rate.

g Government spending financed by borrowing has a positive net effect on the economy.

24-2

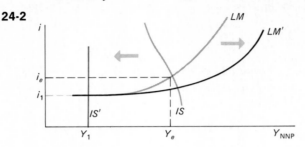

The *IS* curve shifts to the left, resulting from a reduction in profit expectations and wealth, into the liquidity trap; income falls from Y_e to Y_1 and interest rates fall from i_e to i_1. Interest rates are low and increases in the money supply are ineffective; an increase in *LM* to *LM'* leaves i and Y unaffected, as the community holds more money and banks hold excess reserves.

Chapter 25:

25-1a $(N_f - N_e)/N_f$
  b P_e
  c $(P_1 - P_e)/P_e$
  d $(N_f - N_1)/N_f$
  e $(P_2 - P_e)/P_e$
  f $(N_f - N_2)/N_f$
  g Higher rates of inflation induce lower rates of unemployment.

Chapter 26:

26-1a By increasing the money supply when interest rates are falling, and decreasing the money supply when they are rising—according to the Keynesians
  b Between Y_1 and Y_e
  c Between Y_6 and Y_5

26-2a The *IS* curve is more stable here.
  b It will remain at Y_e.
  c Between Y_3 and Y_4.

Chapter 27:

27-1a Disapproved the New York Fed's request for a lower discount rate on October 24, 1929.
  b Passed a resolution calling for the suspension of further purchases of government securities by the New York Fed in that same month.
  c Allowed market interest rates to fall faster than the discount rates.
  d Authorized, in January 1931, no further open-market purchases and even began to *sell* government securities; by February its holdings of U.S. government securities fell by $130 million. This created a second wave of bank failures.

e Neutralized gold inflows from September 1929 to September 1931 by selling U.S. government securities.

f Raised the discount rate when gold started to flow out of the United States in October 1931, thus causing a sharp decrease in the U.S. money supply.

g Allowed the U.S. money supply to fall by 35 percent over the period August 1929 to March 1933.

h Increased reserve requirements in 1936, thereby halting the economic recovery.

i Failed to act as a lender of last resort during the banking panic.

Chapter 28: (No Problems)

Chapter 29:

29-1a One pound costs $3.50; $1 costs £0.2857.

b One mark costs 35¢; $1 costs 2.857 marks.

c One mark costs £0.1; £1 costs 10 marks.

29-2a The U.S. price level falls relative to England's; U.S. interest rates rise relative to England's; U.S. incomes fall relative to England's; a U.S. change in tastes away from England's goods.

b A surplus of British pounds.

c An increase in the demand for U.S. goods by England; England's price level (or income level) rises relative to that of the United States; U.S. interest rates rise relative to England's.

29-3a The United States would incur a payments deficit and England a payments surplus as U.S. exports fell and imports rose; England's exports would rise and its imports would fall. Interest rates would rise in England (in the short run) relative to those in the United States. These actions would lead to a depreciation of the dollar and an appreciation of the pound. Eventually, it would cost more than $3 to purchase £1.

b Gold would flow from the United States to England for the same reasons as in part **a**. This would reduce the money supply in the United States and increase the money supply in England. Eventually, the price level in the United States would fall relative to England's price level.

Name Index

Subject Index